NECESSARY EVIL

The Life of
Jane Welsh Carlyle

JANE BAILLIE WELSH
from a miniature by Kenneth Macleary, July 1826

MRS GRACE BAILLIE WELSH
from a miniature

DR JOHN WELSH
from a miniature

NECESSARY EVIL

The Life of

Jane Welsh Carlyle

by

LAWRENCE AND ELISABETH HANSON

" . . . *a brave woman, and, on the whole, a 'Necessary Evil' to a man.*"

Thomas Carlyle to his wife
on her forty-third birthday.

THE MACMILLAN COMPANY: NEW YORK

1952

TO
J. M. McWILLIAM AND JOHN MACKAY
IN MEMORY
OF THE EVENING RIDE
TO HIGH PINGARIE

Contents

Contents

List of Illustrations

The portraits of Dr Welsh, John Sterling, Geraldine Jewsbury, Erasmus Darwin, Lady Harriet Baring, Thomas Carlyle and Jane Welsh Carlyle are reproduced by courtesy of the National Trust (*frontispiece and facing pages* 114, 220, 344, 440, 498); of Jane Welsh, Jane Welsh Carlyle, Edward Irving and Francis Jeffrey by courtesy of the Board of Trustees of the National Galleries of Scotland (*facing pages* 114, 498); of John Forster by courtesy of the Director of the Victoria and Albert Museum (*facing page* 220); of Mrs Welsh and Jane Welsh Carlyle by courtesy of Miss M. R. Chrystal (*frontispiece and facing page* 282); of Lord and Lady Ashburton and Lady Harriet Baring by courtesy of the Marquess of Northampton (*facing page* 344); of Thomas Carlyle by courtesy of Miss Smart (*facing page* 498); of Godefroi Cavaignac by courtesy of the Musées de Versailles (*facing page* 282); of George Rennie by courtesy of the Governor of the Falkland Islands (*facing page* 440); and of Giuseppe Mazzini by courtesy of the British Council (*facing page* 282).

Preface

———————

Three years ago we decided to attempt to collect and edit all the letters of Jane Welsh Carlyle. These letters seemed to us too good to be, as they then were, either out of print or unpublished. Eventually we found that such a plan was, for the moment at least, impracticable. By that time we had examined the manuscripts of thousands of letters by and to the Carlyles. This mass of material, much of it unknown and even more unused, seemed to us to warrant if not positively to demand new biographies of Thomas Carlyle and of his wife. We chose to write the latter.

This is a biography of Jane Welsh Carlyle, but inevitably it is also more than that. It is the story of a marriage between two remarkable people. And as Jane Carlyle cannot in any adequate sense be considered apart from her husband, this book is also a study of Thomas Carlyle in so far as he and his work affected her.

Both Carlyles were prolific letter writers, and both told their own version of their story almost day by day. Their accounts often vary a great deal, and, if a reasonably accurate picture is to be obtained, these accounts must be considered together, and their many friends and relations should also be allowed their say. Such a synthesis we have attempted here. As far as we are concerned, the controversy of the past is dead and we have no wish to revive it. We have one aim only in this book—to discover and to present as far as possible the truth about the Carlyles as people and as man and wife.

In this we have been helped greatly by the material at our disposal. Many letters are known to have been destroyed, others are still missing, but with these reservations it may be said that we have seen all Carlyle manuscript letters of consequence in public and private hands in this country, and many outside it.

We owe our greatest debt to the magnificent collection of Carlyle material in the National Library of Scotland—a collection which must be the foundation of any Carlyle study—and we are grateful to the Librarian for permission to use this material. We should like to express our thanks to the Keeper of Manuscripts, Mr W. Park, and to his staff for their helpfulness. We are also much indebted to the Librarian of the University of Edinburgh for permission to use Carlyle material in his Library, and we have much appreciated the kindness of the Keeper of Manuscripts, Mr C. P. Finlayson.

Of private collections, the most valuable to us has been the Ashburton Papers in the possession of the Marquess of Northampton. Lord Northampton's generous agreement that we should make what use we thought necessary of this material has been of considerable help, for it has enabled us to put into right proportion for the first time one of the most vexed questions in the married life of the Carlyles. We have also to thank Lord Northampton for his kind hospitality, for his permission to reproduce here the Landseer portraits of Lord and Lady Ashburton and the portrait of Lady Harriet Baring, and for his trouble in reading through and approving the part of this book dealing with the Carlyles and the Ashburtons. We should also like to thank Mr H. V. Phelps for his helpfulness and kindness. We are most grateful to Miss Elizabeth J. Carlyle for her help, and we must thank her and her sister, Mrs Harland, for permission to use letters from Thomas Carlyle and his wife.

For permission to use manuscript material we have also to thank the Director of the British Museum, the Director of the Victoria and Albert Museum, the Librarians of the Alexander Turnbull Library and the John Rylands Library, and the private owners listed on another page. We are specially indebted to Mrs G. E. Bayley, Mrs H. H. Horsburgh, Mrs E. E. Morgan, and Mr H. D. Drysdale. We are indebted to Professor Waldo H. Dunn and to Miss Antonia White for kindly sending transcripts of letters. Mr Peter Irving most helpfully sent us material which he has collected for a biography of his great-grandfather, Edward Irving; Mrs E. W. Bell generously handed us all the Carlyle material collected by her for very many years; and Mr James Jamieson has favoured us with his exceptional knowledge of Haddington and its people.

In Haddington, we gladly thank for their interest, helpfulness and hospitality: The Rev. and Mrs J. R. Thompson, Mr and

Mrs H. D. Drysdale, Mr Thomas Todrick, Miss C. B. Young, the Editor of the *Haddington Courier*, and Mr C. Stodart of Leaston. In Edinburgh: Lady MacLeod of 22 George Square, Miss M. Tait, Mrs M. J. Drysdale, Mrs Mary Rose. In Fife: Dr Thomas Howden of St Andrews, Miss L. D. White of Auchtertool House, Mr J. Dewar of Kirkcaldy. In Dumfriesshire: Mr W. Chapman of Tower of Lettrick and Nether Craigenputtock, Mr Mitchell of Craigenputtock, Mr John Gladstone of Capenoch, Mrs Ralston of Holm Hill, Mrs Brown of Templand, Mr Spiers of Penfillan, the Rev. and Mrs D. Syme, Mr S. D. Cook and Mr M. S. Hunter of Thornhill, the Rev. J. Campbell of Durisdeer, Miss Smart of Carronbridge, and the ministers of Moniaive, Closeburn and Dunscore. Our thanks must also go to Mrs Strong of Carlyle House, Mr M. D. Anderson, Mr George Whalley, Mr J. G. B. Walker, Mr J. R. B. Walker, Miss B. Carpenter, the Librarian of the Manchester Public Libraries, Miss Lillian W. Kelley, Mr William Watt and Mr A. E. Haswell Miller for their helpful interest. The writing of this book has been made much easier because of the kindness and hospitality of Dr and Mrs J. M. Dawson, Mr and Mrs E. M. Dawson, Mr and Mrs W. A. Anderson, and Miss E. C. Marshall.

For permission to reproduce illustrations, we thank the Directors of the National Portrait Gallery, of the National Portrait Gallery of Scotland, and of the Victoria and Albert Museum; the National Trust; the British Council; the Musées de Versailles; Sir Miles Clifford, and the Presbyterian Historical Society of England. For permission to quote from copyright material we have to thank The Bodley Head Ltd, Sir John Murray, George Allen & Unwin Ltd, and Kegan Paul & Co Ltd.

As rather more than ninety-five per cent of this book is taken from manuscript sources, and as paper is so scarce, we have omitted general notes and have restricted references to the quotations.

Jane Welsh Carlyle has not always been fortunate in the way her letters have been presented. There have been omissions, some of them necessary at the time, but also suppressions, misreadings, and even deliberate alterations of the text in order to present a desired picture of the writer and of her husband. And with only one exception a formal punctuation has been imposed upon her letters, on the grounds, it appears, that these letters were written hurriedly and without regard to punctuation. In fact, as the manuscripts make clear when Jane Welsh Carlyle does not state it for herself, only a small percentage of these letters was written hastily. The original punctuation and methods of emphasis in the letters are not only characteristic of the writer, but often make her meaning clearer than pedantic punctuation. Certainly, it is not always consistent; but then she was not a consistent woman; and to show her letters otherwise than as written is to obscure the writer. We have therefore restored all omissions and suppressions, together with the original punctuation—with one exception, that we have made uniform all quotation marks within the letters (in the originals they are sometimes single, sometimes double) because there is a real risk of confusion if this is not done. Apart from this, the letters now appear as written. It may therefore be said that, of the many hundreds of letters and quotations from letters included in the text, not only are a great number printed for the first time, but that the greater part of the remainder are printed for the first time as written.

The title of this book is one of the most frequently used and, in our view, the most apt of the many nicknames given by Thomas Carlyle to his wife. It should be read as Carlyle intended and his wife understood it.

Edinburgh, January 1950   L.H. – E.M.H.

I

JANE WELSH
1801 - 1817

The moorland estate of Craigenputtock lies on the border of Dumfriesshire and Galloway, in south-western Scotland. It was farmed for centuries by the Welshes of Collieston, kinsmen of the famous minister of Ayr who defied his King and married a daughter of John Knox. Later the Welsh family divided, one son remaining at Collieston, the other farming Craigenputtock, until then a part of the larger estate. Eventually the Collieston branch of the family died out, but John Welsh followed John Welsh as small laird of Craigenputtock. They wrested a living out of their bleak land, respected and sometimes feared by the men of Dumfries when they came down to market with their flocks of sheep, for there were blackguards among them but no blockheads.

This claim was made by the John Welsh who was born at Craigenputtock in 1757. But though neither blackguard nor blockhead, he lacked the stamina which had kept the Welshes in their unproductive spot for centuries—or perhaps he learned sufficient wisdom to leave it. He was an only son, and his mother, widowed early, first broke with tradition when she sent him down to school at Tynron in Nithsdale—a soft green valley, the antithesis of Craigenputtock. No Welsh had ever before left his home to seek education, and the effect of this revolutionary step was quickly seen. John lived with Thomas Hunter and his family at the farm of Pingarie in Tynron, and fell in love with the eldest girl, Elizabeth. Neither family approved the match, but the pair took matters into their own hands and were secretly married. Elizabeth was then barely nineteen, John Welsh a year younger. He was so far true to tradition as to bring his wife back to Craigenputtock, where she bore him two children, the eldest, John, in 1776. But she had no wish to stay in this desolate place and see her children run wild; and he seems to have had no strong feeling for his birthplace.

The matter was settled by his failure on the farm, which had deteriorated during his long absence. His farming experience in fertile Nithsdale was of no use to him on the moors of Craigenputtock. He fell into debt, and in 1779, three years after returning there, he sold the 400 acres of Nether Craigenputtock so as to pay his three elder sisters their portions, let off the remaining 800 acres with the main house, and moved down to the farm of Milton in Tynron, where three children were born in the next four years. In 1785 he made his final move, to the beautiful farm of Penfillan, looking down sloping fields to the Nith. There he began to prosper, and by 1793 he had repaid his debts, including loans from Tynron Kirk Session.

With Craigenputtock in strange hands for the first time for centuries, there was a further and even more drastic break in the Welsh tradition when the younger John, instead of following his father on the land, was sent to Edinburgh University to study medicine. This bold move prospered. The boy was an excellent scholar and while still in his teens was noticed by one of the outstanding surgeons of the day, who took him as apprentice and later recommended him for a commission in the Perthshire Fencibles. He was then twenty. He stayed nearly three years with this famous Scottish regiment, until he had saved money enough to take a practice. Then he bought a junior partnership in Haddington, eighteen miles east of Edinburgh.

John Welsh had chosen well. His partner was old, the practice was a good one, and he soon made it even better. He was an excellent doctor, hard-working, sound but advanced, and his practice spread rapidly. He had grown into a handsome man, tall, black-haired, with bright hazel eyes; and his agreeable manner, impressive appearance, and independent and conscientious character soon made him a figure of note in the town, feared at times (for he spoke his mind) but always respected.

He spent his holidays, as he had spent his army leave, at Penfillan where, since the removal there in 1785, nine more children had been born to his father and mother. He never lost an opportunity during these visits to ride up to Craigenputtock. Although he had been taken away from the farm when an infant, his family pride was strong, and he made up his mind that, before long, a Welsh should again live there.

There was another family of Welshes in Nithsdale who had no connexion with the family at Penfillan—the Welshes of Morton Mains near Thornhill. Although this family was in decline, it had in its day been as well known and respected locally as the Welshes of Craigenputtock. One member of the family still flourished—Walter Welsh, a prosperous stock farmer by Moffat Water, some miles to the east of Nithsdale. A son, John, was in business in Liverpool; two daughters, Jeannie and Grace Baillie Welsh, lived with their father. Robert Hunter, a cousin of John Welsh the doctor, also farmed near Moffat, and provided a link between the two Welsh families. Grace could and did cap John's tales of his John Knox connexion with a claim to be descended through her mother's family, the Baillies, from William Wallace. She also boasted of a strong gypsy strain, and talked with pride of Matthew Baillie "the last of the gypsies" who was hanged at Lanark after a career of some notoriety. He, it was said, "could steal a horse from under the owner if he liked, but always left the saddle and bridle; a thorough gentleman in his way, and six feet four in stature". But there was nothing of the gypsy about Grace; she was a beauty—tall, fair-complexioned, with fine eyes and a manner that was not less charming for its capriciousness. She and John Welsh made a handsome pair, and no-one was surprised when, in 1800, they decided to marry. After the marriage Walter Welsh and his daughter Jeannie moved to the farm of Castlehill a few miles outside Thornhill, while the young couple settled down in the doctor's house at Haddington. There, on July 14, 1801, was born their only child, Jane Baillie Welsh.

Haddington, one of the oldest Royal Burghs in the country, was then at the height of its importance. It was the county town of East Lothian (or Haddingtonshire as it was often called) and the centre, then as now, of one of the richest agricultural and seed-producing districts in Scotland. The main road from Edinburgh to London ran through it, and it was a famous posting stage for the great coaches of the day. The early years of the nineteenth century were known in Haddington as "the time of the barracks". Invasion by the French was considered imminent, and landings were expected at the sandy bays of nearby Aberlady and Gullane. A volunteer force was formed, regulars were brought in, barracks were hurriedly built on all sides and camps thrown up, and the troops with their horses and artillery crowded the already busy streets.

Young Mrs Welsh entered with zest into the social life of this thriving little town; and when her husband's partner retired, leaving him as the senior doctor, she readily filled her place as one of Haddington's first ladies. Her charm and beauty were famed throughout the town; and, to a lesser degree, her mental gifts, for she was quick in understanding. But she was excessively temperamental; her father-in-law claimed that he had seen her in fifteen different humours in a single evening, and all who met her commented on her waywardness. John Welsh was precise, punctual, decisive, a disciplinarian, dominant inside his home as well as outside it; and he was worshipped by both his wife and his daughter. To Jane he was perfection—a standard by which every other man was to be measured; his tall figure and stern, strong face, the height of romance; his discourse (for his was a typically Scottish blend of taciturnity and eloquence), the gift of genius. Only his restrictions on her freedom were to be guilefully overcome.

Jane was difficult to resist. She had not the good looks of her parents, but her small, sallow, gypsy face and lively manner fascinated everyone. She was, said her devoted maid and companion Betty, "a fleein', dancin', lightheartit thing that naething would hae dauntit," and people's hearts warmed to see her scampering down the road to school of a morning, a little beaverskin cap perched on her head, satchel in hand, big dark eyes bright with mischief, her hair streaming behind like a long black silken scarf—"the prettiest little Jenny Spinner that was dancing on the summer rays in her time". She was to be seen everywhere about the town; watching the Haddington 'Fly' 'The Good Intent' set off for Edinburgh from the Blue Bell a few doors down the High Street from her home; seeing the steaming horses changed for the London four-in-hand, the Yellow and Blue Mail, at the George, at the far end of the street; sampling the gingerbreads and cookies from the stalls set up in the street on market day; admiring the gorgeous scarlet uniforms of the Haddington volunteers, with their round hats, tufted and cockaded; listening to the military band playing in

the Vetch Park east of the town; lingering about the door of
Paterson the turner at work in his shop in Hardgate, and doing
her utmost to persuade him to fashion her yet another spinning-
top—or peerie as it was called; hanging over the parapet of the
ancient Nungate Bridge to see the fish leap; watching the
townsmen, when the day's work was done, enjoying themselves
solemnly on the Bowling Green and Ball Alley to each side of
the bridge; plaiting daisy necklaces and dandelion chains on
the Bleaching green, or wandering by her favourite Haughs,
the green meadows sloping down to the river, and through the
"butts", the walled passages that intersect the beautiful old
town. From the lofty windows of her father's surgery, she could
survey the crowded High Street or, passing through the great
drawingroom at the back of the house, she could step into the
glass garden room, and so down to her own quiet, high-walled
garden, with its flowers and lawn and tall pear tree, whose
branches brushed the warm stone of the house. There were tea
parties for her friends in the drawingroom, with many queer
rooms and passages for games afterwards; and one party in
particular at which the chief guest—Mrs Welsh evidently had a
taste for the unusual—was one of Haddington's oddities, Mysie
Hamilton or "Meal-Mysie", who spoke like a man. She was an
hermaphrodite, one of the boys whispered to Jane, but her awe
was not lessened nor her knowledge increased by the information. To all she did, the peace and mellow charm of Haddington
formed a background, unheeded then, but never to be forgotten.

She was spoilt and precocious, indulged by her mother,
praised by her father and made much of by the townspeople,
who admired her vivaciousness and were astonished by her gift
of repartee—she was rarely at a loss for a word. Nevertheless,
there were limits to her freedom. Her mother, whose moods
were incalculable, might at any moment pull her up short; and
her father's strong sense of discipline, though beguiled for a
time, invariably asserted itself. He, though proud of her pretty,
feminine ways, was anxious that she should take, as far as
possible, the place of the son he had so much desired. He took
her on his horse, perched in front of him, when he rode to
patients outside the town, and encouraged her to develop her
gifts so that she might rightfully take her place as a member of
an ancient family with its seat once more in Craigenputtock,

which he intended should one day be hers. To all this the little Jane listened earnestly, adoring this tall, strong, all-wise man who rested so much hope on her; and she made many a vow to grow up the wise and learned woman he wished for.

He wanted her education to be thorough—a boy's rather than a girl's. Before she was five, she was put to school; and when she begged him to let her "learn Latin like a boy" he was minded to allow it. Mrs Welsh, anxious to have her as a companion rather than a boyish scholar, protested; she wanted her daughter to learn subjects more in keeping with the usual pursuits of her sex. Father and mother discussed the matter interminably; they could not agree; and eventually the question was settled by Jane herself. She found a Latin grammar in the house, and selecting from her admirers (of whom she already had several) a boy famed for his knowledge of the language, she began secretly taking lessons with him. She could do nothing by halves; in her passion for learning she sat up studying late into the night, and, before she at last went to sleep, tied a weight to one of her ankles so that she should wake in good time. This being discovered, her father forbade her to rise before five in the morning, but she studied on.

Soon she had learned sufficient for her purpose. One evening when she was supposed to be in bed, the doctor and his wife sat over their after-dinner coffee. Suddenly a voice was heard from under the table triumphantly chanting "*Penna*, a pen; *pennae*, of a pen . . ." and so on through the declension. Having demonstrated her knowledge, she came out of her hiding place and ran to her father, crying "I want to learn Latin; please let me be a boy!" This seemed irresistible, to Dr Welsh at least, and Jane had her way.

When she began going to school, there were two schools in the town, side by side in Church Street, a few hundred yards from the doctor's house—the Grammar School under William Graham, and the English School under Richard Hay. These schools in some degree complemented each other, and Jane, like other children, attended classes in each. She learned reading, writing, and (when she had won her battle) Latin in the Grammar School, and English and mathematics in the English School.

She quickly distinguished herself. One lad nearly twice her age, attending the Grammar School before and after his work, years later remembered sitting on the same bench with her, reading Ovid together. She more than held her own in every sense, for she had courage as well as quick wits. One day the master, coming back unexpectedly to the classroom, found one of the bigger boys with a bleeding nose and a blackening eye, and threatened that he would keep everyone in school unless the culprit owned up. He directed his warning at the other senior boys; and when Jane called out in her small voice that she had hit the boy because he had taunted her, he burst out laughing, and everyone escaped punishment.

Outside the school, Jane was no less determined to match the boys in all they did. At first they seized every opportunity to make fun of her. On the way to school she had to pass a turkey-cock who sensed her fear, and ran at her, gobbling and swelling alarmingly. This happened every morning, and the boys soon discovered how she dreaded to pass the place. They gathered by the side of the road with some labourers, jeering at her as the turkey made its usual attack. But the child, afraid as she was, hated still more to show her fear in such company. She darted at the threatening bird, seized him by the throat, and swung him round. The men clapped their hands and shouted "Well done, little Jeannie Welsh!" and the boys slunk away. The turkey never molested her again, nor did the boys. This test overcome, she made it her business to rival the boys in all their feats. Chief among these was the crossing of the high, arched Nungate Bridge. The more daring of the boys walked along the parapet overhanging the river far below. For a time Jane watched them; then, one morning, she left her house earlier than usual, went to the bridge, lay face down on the parapet, and crawled to the other side. Before long, she was running across. When this became wearisome, she set herself harder tasks—leaping the mill dam further down the river with such assurance that one old woman who had paused to watch her said "Providence had stickit a fine callant". The boys could not long resist this combination of bravado and charm, and most of them, in school and out of it, soon became her willing slaves. Jane accepted this homage with composure; she liked the company of boys and made no secret of it, but she also put their admiration to good use—as witness the early enlistment of the Latin scholar in her service.

Her father was pleased but not satisfied with her success at school; and when she was ten years old he looked about for a tutor, and asked the advice of his old mathematics professor at Edinburgh, Sir John Leslie. Sir John recommended Edward Irving. This choice entranced Jane, for Irving was no stranger to her. She had seen and admired him from a distance many times since he had come to Haddington the previous year—in the summer of 1810—as master of the school recently built alongside the others, and intended mainly for the teaching of higher mathematics. She was not alone in her admiration. The whole town was impressed by the appearance and attainments of this lad of eighteen, standing well over six feet, with broad shoulders, ruddy cheeks, and a shock of thick black hair—a cheerful, kindly lad, whose only fault appeared to be an excessive turn for argument, a not uncommon weakness in Scottish students. And although a cast in one eye might seem to mar his good looks, in fact it was accepted, by Jane and the rest of the town, as something of a distinction. Irving taught enthusiastically and well, and out of school he spent most of his time playing and walking about the neighbourhood with his boys (a particularly spectacular jump across the mill dam was known for years as "Irving's Leap"), and passing on to them his own enthusiasms, particularly in astronomy and metaphysics. To crown his popularity, the town was soon buzzing with the story of his visit to Edinburgh with his bigger pupils to hear the celebrated divine, Dr Chalmers, preach at St. George's; of the man who barred entrance to the one empty pew with his arm; and of Irving, finding persuasion useless, suddenly thundering in his powerful voice, "Remove your arm, or I will shatter it in pieces!"—so that the man, awed and astonished, slunk away, and the Haddington party was comfortably seated.

He and Jane got on famously. She was always ready to admire a striking or handsome man, particularly when he showed earnestness of purpose that reminded her of her beloved father. To Irving, this quickwitted, dainty but daring little thing, with the expressive black eyes—alternately mocking and appealing—was a perpetual delight. He leaped at the chance of forming the mind of such a rare child, mapped out a strenuous programme of education, and was soon spending almost every spare moment with his new pupil. They worked together, played

together, and were often to be seen walking up the Plantations
—a beautiful tree-bordered walk leading to the Garleton Hills
that stand between Haddington and the sea—the small girl
dancing up and down the road as she walked, ever and again
taking the arm of her tall companion, who would be pointing
out the beauties of nature, going over a Latin verb, or often
enough himself running and leaping like a child. But these were
informal moments. Dr Welsh believed in making the most of
every day, and Irving was therefore engaged in October 1811 as
tutor for two hours before school—from six to eight every
morning—and again after school until his pupil's bedtime. He
was no ordinary tutor, and his first act when he arrived in the
dark autumn mornings was to take Jane in his arms, carry her
to the door or window, and tell her the names of the stars and
planets still shining far above their heads. And when the evening
lessons were over, he would often set her on the table at which
they had been working, and teach her the rudiments of logic—
for he considered this essential for a full education.

Before long, Irving was much at home in the Welsh house.
The doctor, who enjoyed sharpening his wits in discussions with
the young tutor; Mrs Welsh, gracious, beautiful, hospitable;
and the solid, roomy, soundly furnished house: it was all a new
world to him.

He was, however, already showing traces of the fanaticism
that was to destroy him; and at the supper parties then so
popular in Haddington he began to speak fervently of the high
destinies of the human race in heaven, where the saints were to
rule and judge angels. But this sort of language seems not to
have disturbed the Welsh household, and it certainly did
nothing to impair Jane's devotion. She worked desperately hard
for a child of ten, yet not always hard enough to satisfy either
Irving or her father. Irving had to make a daily report on her
progress. If his report was not good, she was punished by Dr
Welsh. One day the culprit, tempted for once to play a game
instead of attending to her homework, sat on the table, small,
downcast, conscious of failure. Irving, pen in hand, looked at
her compassionately, reluctant to write the word that would
bring trouble on her. He lingered so for a long time, hesitating
between justice and mercy, while Jane, silent for once, awaited
her fate. At last he cried, despairingly: "Jane, my heart is broken,

9

but I *must* tell the truth!" And he wrote the fatal word, *pessime*.

This decision seems to have done him little harm with his pupil, in whose eyes he, like her father, could do no wrong. She made quick, if irregular, strides in the classics, and was soon modelling her entire life on the ancient Romans. This manner of thought had begun in her earliest years, when her father told her many a story of Roman and Greek, so that, after she had dealt with the turkey-cock, she considered not so much that she had earned the half-crown given to her by her proud parents for bravery, but that she had "deserved well of the Republic, and aspired to a civic crown."

When Irving read Virgil with her, the Roman virtues took even firmer hold of her mind.

> "Would I prevent myself from doing a selfish or cowardly thing, I didn't say to myself, 'You mustn't, or if you do you will go to hell hereafter.' Nor yet, 'If you do, you will be whipt here;' but I said to myself, simply and grandly, 'A Roman would not have done it'."

This resulted in the tragi-comic fate of Jane's doll, an incident in which either Irving or, more probably, Dr Welsh plays a singularly humourless part. Jane at this time was no more than ten or eleven. "It had been intimated to me by one whose wishes were law," she wrote years later, "that a young lady in Virgil should for consistency's sake drop her doll." She decided that the doll must emulate Dido: and so she put it, with all its dresses and lying on its four-poster bed, on a pyre, repeated over it the last words of Dido, assisted it to stab itself with a penknife, and set fire to the pyre.

> "Then, however, in the moment of seeing my poor doll blaze up . . . my affection for her blazed up also, and I shrieked and would have saved her and could not, and went on shrieking till everybody within hearing flew to me, and bore me off in a plunge of tears."

The companionship between Jane and her youthful tutor, with its hard work, long hours, its fun and confidences and growing affection on both sides, lasted less than a year. Irving had been recommended to the Academy just being formed at Kirkcaldy, on the far side of the Forth. He did not wish to leave Haddington, and tried but failed to get his salary increased to the amount offered him at Kirkcaldy. In August 1812 he left to take up his new post.

Irving, who, like so many others who met her, seems to have been bewitched by Jane—"a paragon of gifted young girls" was his description—used his influence with her after he had gone away. He was at heart a desperately earnest young man and he urged her, in letters which grew increasingly sententious, to cultivate her mind and pursue her studies as if he were beside her, to spurn the temptations of flattery and avoid the futilities of feminine society. He commended her to his friend, James Brown, who had taken his place at the Mathematical School.

Jane did continue with James Brown, who also took Irving's place as her tutor, but the change gave her mother the opportunity of again raising the question of her general education. Mrs Welsh feared that Jane would become hoydenish and vulgar if she mixed so much with the boys at school and she wanted her brought up in a manner more in keeping with her social position. She was still opposed by Dr Welsh, delighted with Jane's aptitude for learning, and perhaps less afraid than his wife that she would lose any of her charm—the adulation of the boys suggested quite the opposite. This time the parents reached a compromise. A Mrs Hemming had recently set up a school for girls in the town; and Jane boarded there, learning the more ladylike accomplishments, and continuing to take additional lessons from Brown.

A month or two after Irving had left the town, Jane wrote to an aunt telling her that she had gone to Mrs Hemming's to "draw and play with her", and enclosing a specimen of her drawing. The letter, the first of Jane's to be preserved, in no way foreshadows the brilliance to come.

Mrs Hemming, formerly governess to the family of the Chief of Coll, in the Western Isles, brought with her as pupil Sibella Maclean of Arnabost. Sibella was fourteen at the time, but she and Jane became good friends in spite of the difference in their ages. Jane, says her friend, was full of fun and high spirits, generous and kind, and remarkable for the ease with which she could master any subject. Sibella does not mention the hardships, even to shortage of food, that Carlyle later says the girls had to endure, and about which Jane said nothing at home until her parents discovered it and at once took her away. This was at the end of 1813. In the last few days of the year she returned to James Brown's Public School—for he had now been appointed headmaster of the joint Mathematics and English Schools. Her advance under him was spectacular, to the consternation of some of the pupils—consternation, but not resentment, such was her charm. Tom Dods, brother of William the Latin scholar, once complained to the master that it was impossible to learn the whole of the task set to the class—"he hadn't *time* for so much". "Then" said James Brown, "make time, sir! Miss Welsh can always make time for as much as I like to give her!"

This was no exaggeration. Jane, encouraged by Irving and exhorted by her father, worked with furious zeal to justify their flattering faith in her. She was often at school long before classes began; and she remembered years later how Brown, coming in at seven one morning, found her asleep "betwixt the leaves of the Great Atlas, like a kept lesson!" She had been working there since five, and had dropped off, tired out, just before the master walked in.

Two of her best friends at school were Janet and Agnes Burns, daughters of Gilbert Burns, brother of the poet. Burns was factor to Lord Blantyre at Lennoxlove, and on Saturdays Jane often walked to her friends' house at Grant's Braes, a mile out of the town, where Mrs Burns gave them all (she had twelve children) dinners of rice and milk with a few currants that tasted like nectar to the hungry Jane. In another direction, at East Linton, Jane visited her friends Grace and George Rennie at the grand farmhouse of Phantassie with its lovely garden. George was a clever boy and already showed signs of following his uncle John, the famous engineer and builder of Waterloo Bridge. But for the moment he, like many another—John Ferme, for example, Hamilton Veitch and William Dods—was content to be a worshipper at the shrine of Jane. Some she despised, such as George Cunningham, "the boy who never got into trouble and never helped others out of it—a slow, bullet-headed boy, who said his lessons like an eight-day clock, and never looked young." But none—despised or accepted—succeeded in claiming more than a fraction of her attention so long as there were soldiers in the town. Her first love, at the age of nine, was a Master Scholey, the Artillery Boy, and her passion for him was so great that she could never bring herself even to come into his presence. She conducted her courting through the medium of his mother, and her dearest aim was, not Master

Scholey himself, but merely his portrait. For this, she gave away her most precious possession, a gold filigree needle-case, but without making clear that she expected something in return; and when the next day she plucked up courage to go back for the portrait, his regiment had moved on.

Heartbroken only for the time, she began sending proposals of marriage (for with true canniness she provided for at least one rejection) by indifferently written letters into the officers' quarters; but instead of a husband or two, she received by return only a couple of half-crowns and some barley sugar. She loved them still, however, fiercely and without favour; was overcome with pride and joy and excitement when, in 1816, the Black Watch marched through the town to celebrate the victory at Waterloo; and the sound of the bugles morning and evening from Bothwell Castle in Hardgate often brought tears to her eyes. One such occasion, typical of many, she recalled more than once in later years. She was in a field by the river with George Rennie, his sister and a distant cousin who lived in Edinburgh, Eliza Stodart. It was summer, calm and hot. The four children played in the field, then, sitting with their backs against a hay-stack, they fell quiet. The bugles sounded out, and Jane suddenly felt very happy "the sky was so bright, the air so balmy, the whole universe so beautiful." She was easily moved to tears; weeping bitterly and impartially over the graves of a young army officer, Sutherland, shot in a duel, and of little Ann Cameron who had been burned to death.

Equally typical of the young Jane is the small figure, like a round black bundle bespattered with white flakes, who hurled snowball after snowball at the boys in High Street; and who, stealing out of the house in the darkness of a winter morning, would trot down the road surreptitiously, accompanied by James Robertson, the groom, with stable lantern and besom, to the frozen Tyne for a solitary skate and slide before breakfast. It was her pride to arrive first, but once she found one of the town boys, John Wilkie, there before her. When the ice had been swept it was as slippery as glass, and a man standing by advised her to hang on to the boy's coat tails to steady herself. She did; and the two of them flashed off along the ice in the near-darkness. All went well for a time, but at the critical moment—the shooting of the falls that slant across the river below Nungate

Bridge—John Wilkie began to lose his balance or his nerve or both, and tore his coat tails out of Jane's hands. She "clashed" down on one side like a ninepin, went home with a black eye, and would not speak to him for weeks afterwards.

Every summer Dr Welsh took his family to Nithsdale, where both Jane's grandfathers lived within a few miles of each other. She much preferred her maternal grandfather, Walter Welsh, a fine looking shaggy-faced man with great bushy eyebrows and beard and an abundance of grey hair, and who made a great fuss of his little Pen, as he called her, after Penfillan and to distinguish her from his daughter Jeannie. In the past few years his farming had not prospered, and he had moved across the river from Castlehill to the farm of Strathmilligan, a few miles beyond Tynron. His reverses had made him pensive and irritable—flashing into hot temper if crossed—but Jane could always raise a chuckle or a flute-like laugh. He had a keen sense of the ridiculous—in himself as well as in others—a sense which his grand-daughter inherited abundantly. He often took Jane on a pony up the lanes towards Sanquhar, and was punctilious in returning by a different route—this, Jane explained to the family, "to va-ary the schane Miss"; mimicking him to such perfection that all, himself included, roared with laughter. Fair-haired Aunt Jeannie in her own quiet way made her niece welcome. She had an unhappy history—her former fiancé had robbed and almost ruined his partner, her brother John at Liverpool—but it had not soured her. She humoured her father, kept his house in perfect order, and was kindness itself to her sister and brother-in-law and their irrepressible daughter. Strathmilligan was within reach of Thornhill, a straggling village extending along both sides of the main road from Dumfries to Glasgow; and here, as child, girl and young woman, Jane was royally treated, stepping from shop to shop with her orders like a young princess.

At Penfillan, life was decidedly sterner. The large house abounded with uncles and aunts, many of them only a few years older than Jane—one actually a month younger—but all ready to claim authority over her. She did not care for her grandmother, a pious, strict woman, and although she could not help loving her grandfather for his likeness to her father—to the day of his death he had the same tall upright figure, the same black hair and bright eyes—his manner was severe, his kindness was without love. He had many oddities which his sharp little grand-daughter was quick to pounce upon. Of these, perhaps the most remarkable was his belief that the worth of a man was to be estimated strictly by his inches; before consenting to begin an acquaintance, he would often insist that the man or woman should stand before him and be measured.

Intercourse between the two Welsh families was slight; their chief bond being Dr Welsh, when he could leave his thriving practice in Haddington. His wife and daughter spent most of their holidays at Strathmilligan but often drove down to Penfillan—Jane protesting violently, or fallen sullen, her face dark with discontent when her mother was taking her to Penfillan, but all brightness and charm when the gig was pointed the other way. In the summers after she had reached her teens, her father would take her on the long uphill road to Craigenputtock —no longer alien. Dr Welsh had already made good his promise to himself; he had prospered, had bought Craigenputtock, and had willed the estate to Jane—for he had little faith in the business abilities of his wife. Nor was this all; he was not content simply with the possession of Craigenputtock; the farm had been neglected for many years, and he was determined to put it right. So he put George, one of his many brothers, into the farm to carry out extensive improvements. Dr Welsh was, indeed, an absolute godsend to his father's family. His favourite brother, Douglas, was cared for in his house after a shooting accident in which he had lost an eye; he helped Benjamin, the youngest, to get his medical training, and eventually brought him to Haddington as his assistant; another brother, William, who had spinal trouble, spent five years in his house; yet another, Robert, was helped by Dr Welsh to set up as a lawyer in Edinburgh; in fact, all the Penfillan children were to be found at some time or another in the Haddington house for rest or recreation.

Dr Welsh, then, was a contented man, and he had reason to be; Craigenputtock was his; he had bought his house in Haddington, had extended it, and had installed in the front portion a junior partner, Thomas Howden; he had a beautiful and devoted wife; and his daughter was a constant and ever-growing delight to him. He did not often express his pride in words, but Jane was quick to sense and to rejoice in it. She too was happy in Haddington, and was glad to return there from her summer visits to Nithsdale. Her much petted dog Shandy was always at her heels as she walked about the town—usually making her favourite circle along The Haughs by the river, up the path by Dods' Gardens, and back by the long, walled Babbie's Butts to Sidegate and so into the High Street. But her progress was rather more sedate now, as her appeal to the young men began to assume a more serious nature. She had exchanged the school for a governess who, it seems, was neither strict nor efficient. And there was a new servant, Betty, little older than herself, who quickly became a cross between nurse, confidante and devoted friend.

The only discordant note in her life at this time was the uncertain relationship between herself and her mother. Mrs Welsh's variable humour had not mellowed with the years; she was ever ready to fly into a mood for the slightest and most inadequate reason. She must have endured much from the visitations of the Penfillan family; and not the least of her trials was her own daughter who, when Dr Welsh was absent, proved uncontrollable, and in sharpness of tongue and quickness of wit, more than a match for her mother. Mrs Welsh, like Jane, had been thoroughly spoiled; her beauty had accustomed her to flatteries which her good sense and humour were not always strong enough to counteract. She grew imperious, demanding immediate assent to her plans and sudden notions, even when these were transparently unwise; and, to be contented, she needed either unquestioning obedience or a firm hand. The firm hand she obtained from her husband. For the rest, Mrs Welsh "was not easy to live with for one wiser than herself, though very easy for one more foolish." But Jane was no fool and could not endure foolishness in others. She was in no mind to pander to her mother's whims; she had whims of her own. To make matters worse, both she and her mother were far from strong. A serious illness had left Mrs Welsh delicate. Jane was already constantly ailing, the result no doubt of the years of excessive study which her father and Irving, with more pride than good sense, did everything in their power to encourage, and also perhaps of her premature birth (she was a seven months' child). So there were headaches, "vapours", temperaments, tears, reproaches in the drawingroom and bedrooms of the Welsh house.

This apart, Jane enjoyed her life immensely in her early and middle teens. She had not forgotten Irving's advice—or at least, she often recalled it. At thirteen she wrote her first and only novel, read it aloud, and was generally admired. Her father called her his dear clever child—praise that she was never to forget. A year later she wrote a 5-act Tragedy *The Rival Brothers* which was praised by C. H. Terrot, then minister of Haddington church. It was so "very wild and bloody" that by the end of the last act none of the *dramatis personae* was left alive to speak the epilogue. From time to time she read and studied in bursts of enthusiasm or penitence, after hearing from Irving or having a heart to heart talk with her father. At other times, she made verses to express the feelings of the moment, and played and sang the sentimental songs of the day. She even, with heroic self-discipline, sat down occasionally to her needle-work. But she was more often to be found skating on the frozen Tyne (making her first acquaintance with the minister after a violent collision), or revelling in the dances at the Assembly Room just across the way from her house. And she was beginning to enjoy the occasional visits with her mother to Edinburgh —to her Uncle Robert in Northumberland Street, or to the George Square house of Eliza Stodart's uncle, John Bradfute the bookseller, where she had long and intimate talks with Eliza, and in the evening the rare excitement of the theatre, to see Mrs Jordan, or some great actor or singer of the day.

She was beginning to feel her power over the opposite sex. Though without any pretensions to beauty, she was growing more and more attractive, with her "very lovely but too *thoughtful* eyes, and that *half-obstinate*, half-capricious lip, which does not agree very well either with them or with itself". Her eyes, even then, seemed irresistible, luring men to speech which her tongue made them regret. Occasionally, for short spells, she lost her heart, though never her head, to a particularly romantic-looking youth, but for the most part she took pleasure in observing and commenting on the antics of those who strove to win her favours.

Her mother and father regarded their daughter's popularity with mixed feelings. Dr Welsh had faith in Jane's good sense, but Mrs Welsh was afraid that she would commit some indiscretion—she already had visions of a brilliant marriage for the brilliant girl. For this, however, it was necessary for her to acquire more polish than Haddington society could provide; and Mrs Welsh persuaded her husband to send Jane to a finishing school. In 1817, when she was sixteen, Jane left Haddington for Miss Hall's school, off Leith Walk, in Edinburgh.

II

THOMAS CARLYLE
1795-1819

A little more than four years after Irving had moved to Kirkcaldy, another school—in some sense a rival establishment—was formed there, and as master came Thomas Carlyle. The two men knew each other slightly, for both came from Annandale. Carlyle was born on December 4, 1795, three years after Irving, at Ecclefechan, a village six miles from Irving's birthplace, Annan. Irving as a boy had walked to Ecclefechan and back of a Sunday to sit under John Johnston in the little meeting house attended by the Carlyles; and it was this John Johnston who gave the young Thomas his first Latin lessons. Carlyle, like Irving, and following the accepted pattern of Scottish life, had been sent from school at Annan to the University at Edinburgh as a divinity student. He, too, had become a teacher after leaving Edinburgh—recommended by the same Professor—and had specialised in mathematics; but whereas Irving had gone to Haddington, Carlyle had returned to his old school at Annan as mathematics master. Now, backed as Irving had been by the classics and mathematics professors at Edinburgh, he took the post at Kirkcaldy.

Thus the careers of the two Annandale youths had followed similar lines. But the resemblance was more superficial than real. Irving had made something of a mark at school and even more at the University; his family was of consequence in Annan; he was open-hearted, cheerful, and was popular wherever he went; and he had never doubted that the church was his destiny. In all these things, Carlyle differed from him.

Carlyle was the eldest son of his father's second marriage. The family, which came originally from the English town of Carlisle, had a long and at times distinguished history, but many

generations before the birth of Thomas their fortunes had fallen.
His father, James Carlyle, had been brought up as a peasant, in
poverty and indiscipline. He was a rough, hard hitting, passionate man who made a life for himself by sheer force of character.
He had learned the trade of stonemason, worked hard and well,
and in a simple way had prospered until, by the time Thomas
was born, he was living in a cottage he had built, respected by
all his neighbours. The main element in this steady progress
was a deep, unshakable religious conviction which had sustained
him throughout his hard life, and in which he now brought up
his family. The wildness of his early years and the struggles of
the later ones had made him a stern man who would have no
truck with what he considered to be ungodliness—a long list,
in which poetry and fiction were included. Apart from his
narrow faith, but subordinate to it, his chief characteristics
were a violent and at times ungovernable temper, a ready but
restricted sense of humour and a painful inarticulateness.
Although in spite of his lack of book-learning he could talk
pithily and forcefully on moral questions, which he regarded
with the utmost simplicity, he could neither express nor explain
his feelings. His passionate nature had no normal outlet, and
after a period of suppression would break loose in an outburst
the more fearful for his customary self-control—as when, during
an illness of his wife, he suddenly collapsed in "a torrent of
grief; cried piteously, and threw himself on to the floor, and lay
moaning" whilst his children stared amazed and uneasy. As a
result: "We *durst not* freely love him. His heart seemed as if
walled in." Even his wife confessed that she did not understand
him. She was some fifteen or sixteen years younger, and
illiterate—she could not write when she married. Perhaps
because of this imperfect understanding between husband and
wife—their relationship in many ways was more like father and
daughter than husband and wife—her deepest feeling was given
to her first born. She watched over him with all the love of her
tender, pious nature. Yet she too was inarticulate, and could
not have conveyed to him, had she dared, what she felt.

In this frugal, taciturn household, where a growing family
(there were eight children of the second marriage) lived in two
or three rooms, eating the plainest of food, Thomas, like the
rest of the children, was brought up to work hard, to disregard

his own inclinations, and to fix his eyes on things eternal. A strict Calvinistic spirit brooded over his childhood. Laughter was sometimes heard in the Carlyle house, but gaiety was unknown, pleasure a sin, and happiness a state to be shunned. The family circle was for the most part a silent one, devoted to work and to righteousness.

Father and mother were united by a wish—characteristic of their time and situation—that their eldest son should in a special way be given to God, and Thomas, from the moment of his birth, was marked out for the ministry. Up to a point he was eminently suited to the future his parents worked and prayed for; he was highly intelligent, hard working, and he had the conviction of the truly religious that his life was a consecrated one. But his upbringing—for he was as passionate and as strong willed as his father—made him grow into a morose, bitter child, and his dissatisfaction with his life showed itself, as so often with clever children, in sarcasm and self-pity. He was by no means inarticulate—he early showed an exceptional gift for disputation—but silence was thrust upon him outside his home by excessive consciousness of his shortcomings and his lack of social graces.

His school life at Annan, where he was sent at the age of ten, was disastrous. His mother had made him promise not to lift a hand against his school-fellows, and when the town boys mocked and bullied the uncouth, unfriendly villager, his only consolation, until he broke his promise, was to tell himself that all were against him because they were the jealous, the inferior and the ungodly. Nor was his position bettered when he began to fight. The physical torment stopped but the unhappiness remained; he then despised as well as hated those forced to respect him. He had never learned to smile, to laugh freely, to open his mind, to display his many good qualities. He made no friends, and began to take a savage pleasure in his isolation. He was set apart—had not his parents told him so a thousand times?—and his sufferings were but another sign that he was one of God's elect.

After four years of misery, he set out for the University at Edinburgh, embittered, resentful, misanthropic. His belief in himself was high, but his confidence in his ability to communicate that belief to others was almost destroyed. At University, therefore, he was also unhappy and unsuccessful; unfortunate in his tutors, and without Irving's way of bringing himself to their notice. He learned little, either of letters or of manners, from his fellow students, who were repelled by his armour of sarcasm and obstinacy.

Then he began to question the reason for his leaving home. His mind was too enquiring and his nature too proud to accept meekly and uncritically the doctrines by which his parents lived. He began to move away from his mother's earnestly repeated prayers that he should study the Bible; preferring to read largely in other directions that still further unsettled his mind. He found himself in a dilemma shared on the surface by many divinity students—the dilemma of the man who discovers that the faith in which he has been raised is based on grounds which will not always bear examination. But the likeness was no more than skin-deep, for Carlyle could not relapse into materialism; the incompatibility of Puritanism and modern thought did not free him from religion but merely extended its range, the forms only became inadequate, the spirit remained. It was all but plain to him by the time he left University that he could not enter the Church, but he was reluctant to grieve his parents—his mother, who rested her hopes on him, his father who had sacrificed so much to let him go to Annan and Edinburgh. To postpone a decision, he applied for a school post, and arranged to attend Divinity Hall in Edinburgh for a few days each year so that he might, if he wished, become a minister later—a procedure that Irving, for a different reason, had adopted three years earlier. He then went back to Annan as teacher in mathematics. He had another good reason for seeking the post; the salary of £70 a year would help to free him from dependence on his father, and enable him to save against a return to it. But he had no wish to teach and little aptitude for it, and his time out of school was almost as wretched as the time spent in it. Resentful still of his treatment there as a schoolboy, and still conscious of his gaucherie, Carlyle kept himself to himself; and, feeling lonely and out of place, was too shy, proud, and full of hatred to make the effort to join in the society of the little town. He was thus rated conceited and unsociable; and his knowledge of this further aggravated his self-consciousness. But however unpleasing he might seem, he was conscious in himself of unusual powers; and he read steadily and thought deeply, in the belief that some day, somehow, he would know how to apply those powers.

During one of his visits to Edinburgh he again met Irving, and they had an unsatisfactory exchange of words; Carlyle, as usual, on the defensive against possible slights, and Irving, whose sense of humour must have been tickled, determined to give him some cause for his suspicions. When, a year later, Carlyle was offered the school in Kirkcaldy, and arranged to go there on a trial visit, he expected opposition or at least coldness from Irving, particularly as he knew that complaints of Irving's harshness with his pupils had been one reason for the setting up of the new school. Nor were his doubts removed when Irving, meeting him by chance in Annan, said: "You are coming to Kirkcaldy to look about you in a month or two: you know I am there; my house and all I can do for you is yours—two Annandale people must not be strangers in Fife!" The doubting Thomas, as Carlyle styles himself at this time, thought merely, "Well, it would be pretty!" He found the utmost difficulty in believing good of any man without the clearest of proofs; but when, soon afterwards, he went to Kirkcaldy, Irving carried out his offer in a manner that shook Carlyle's doubts. He made him a guest in his house until he had settled down, he invited him to make free use of his library and he introduced him to his friends.

Irving's welcome was sincere. He had met no-one in Kirkcaldy of his own age or interests, he was looked at askance by many of his pupils' parents as unorthodox, and, as a gregarious, intelligent man, he needed a companion almost as much as the closed-in Carlyle. He soon perceived beneath Carlyle's unattractive exterior a sensitive and honest man, and a man of great talent. In time, his friendliness, his faith in the younger man's abilities, and his refusal to be put out by surliness or sarcasm completely won over the sceptical Carlyle, who found, for the first time in his life, a man to like and to trust. Irving's friendship, he said, made his life at Kirkcaldy a comparatively genial and useful one—a momentous admission. The two men walked and talked together on Kirkcaldy sands; they went for long walking tours, during which Carlyle met other men who, he discovered, were also good companions, and they visited houses (to Carlyle's "rustic eyes, of a superior, richly furnished stratum of society"), but with Irving always "the natural King among us". In Irving's house, or in his company, he came to know most of the interesting people in Kirkcaldy, whom he found a great deal more likeable than the inhabitants of Annan —an amiable delusion, since he and not they had changed. Apart from Irving's house, he was most at home in the Manse, despite the "cackling" of the boys and girls there (Carlyle was nineteen years old at the time) and the "feeble intellectuality" of the talk. He did not approve of the understanding that had grown between Irving and a former pupil, Isabella Martin, the eldest daughter in the Manse; she "was of bouncing, frank, gay manners and talk, studious to be amiable, but never quite satisfactory on the side of *genuineness*. Something of affected you feared always in these fine spirits and smiling discourses, to which however you answered with smiles. She was very ill-looking withal; a skin always under blotches and discolourment; muddy grey eyes, which for their part never laughed with the other features; pock-marked, ill-shapen triangular kind of face, with hollow cheeks and long chin; decidedly unbeautiful as a young woman."

Far different was his opinion of another former pupil of Irving—Margaret Gordon, a fair, serious girl, an Aberdeen-shire Gordon, but born in Canada, and with a speech and outlook that suggested a stranger. In women, Carlyle needed the elegance and good birth which he himself lacked, and a lively intelligence which he was able to match. Irving had shown signs of an interest in Margaret, but his undefined attachment to Isabella forbade a development of his inclinations, and his friend was left alone in the field. Alone, but the affair did not prosper; for the girl's aunt, poor but well-born, with whom she lived, looked with disfavour on the awkward country youth who had little to recommend him but his brains. Margaret liked Carlyle well enough; she could see that intellectually he was beyond the common run of men, and she prophesied a brilliant future for him; but her heart was not free; and Carlyle himself was uncertain of his feelings, knowing only that she attracted him. Thus he found at Kirkcaldy his first and best friend and his first romantic attachment, and for the first time in his life he experienced a fair amount of light-hearted-ness. But satisfied he was not; "I continue to teach" he said, "(that I may subsist thereby) with about as much satisfaction as I should beat hemp".

Irving was of a like mind. So at the end of 1818, a short time after Irving had introduced Carlyle to Margaret, they decided to throw up their jobs and go to Edinburgh, which they had often visited during their walking tours. Carlyle tells a friend at the beginning of November:

> "In a fortnight I shall quit my present situation. . . . The desire which, in common with all men, I feel for conversation and social intercourse, is, I find, enveloped in a dense repulsive atmosphere—not of vulgar *mauvaise honte*, tho' such it is generally esteemed—but of deeper feelings, which I partly inherit from Nature, and which are mostly due to the undefined station I have hitherto occupied in society. If I continue a schoolmaster, I fear there is little reason to doubt that these feelings will increase, and at last drive me entirely from the kindly sympathies of life."

Carlyle and Irving both disliked teaching, but there the likeness ended. Irving had never swerved from his intention to go into the ministry. He had by now been licensed to preach; and Carlyle was impressed by his fine delivery, his honesty, and his command of his subject. But he had no wish to follow Irving's example, and had already made up his mind not to apply for a licence. So, in Edinburgh, his plight was no better than before; he merely exchanged work that was distasteful for a life of uncertainty. The one certain thing was his determination not to enter the ministry—nor, if he could avoid it, another school. He thought of farming, of tutoring, of engineering, of emigrating to America. For a time he attended law classes, but he thought little of the lectures or the lecturer. Indeed he thought poorly of most things; partly because outward pessimism had become almost second nature to him; partly because he was beginning to suffer considerable pain from indigestion. He had never eaten well or wisely; at home, while he was a child, the family diet had consisted of porridge, potatoes and milk; and after he left home, lack of money, and anxiety to save what he had to preserve his precious independence, had made him save it in the easiest possible way, by eating little and rarely. He was a heavy and confirmed smoker; he had smoked openly since he was eleven. And he worried; he was for ever worrying, about his state and his future. This dyspepsia threw gloom over almost all his pursuits. He had friends in Edinburgh; he and Irving, on their visits from Kirkcaldy, had mixed with a set of more or less like-minded University men, and now found company ready for them if they wished. Irving, a gregarious man, did wish; but Carlyle was troubled by doubts, serious doubts, about them, himself, the world, and could enjoy neither their company nor his own.

> "The time was when I would have stood a tiptoe at the name of Edin^r
> —but all that is altered now. The men with whom I meet are mostly preachers and students in divinity. These persons desire, not to understand Newton's philosophy but to obtain a well 'plenished manse . . . I doubt my career 'in the above line' has come to a close."

Although miserably conscious that his small savings were draining away, he was helped from more than one quarter. Dr Brewster gave him work for his Edinburgh Encyclopaedia. Tait, the bookseller, offered him odd writing jobs. But this hackwork, he felt, was not fulfilling his destiny. He sensed the stirrings of great powers within himself, he saw the world at odds, and he believed, cloudily but with fervour, that the one should be used to mend the other. He was a prophet who knew not how or where or even what to prophesy.

Not until he had been a year in Edinburgh did light appear; and then dubiously. Irving was again his good angel. He had been offered a post as assistant to the famous Dr Chalmers in Glasgow, and was now fairly launched on his chosen career; but before leaving Edinburgh he advised Carlyle to write for *Blackwood's* and the *Edinburgh Review*. Carlyle protested violently when the suggestion was made—the *Edinburgh Review*, he said, was no magazine for his work to appear in. But he bore the advice in mind and, eventually, followed it and so began the career which was to bring him fame and, what was more to his mind, which enabled him to do that which he felt called to do.

III

EDWARD IRVING

1819-1821

Irving had been open and generous with Carlyle in all things but one. His advice, his company, his friends were all at Carlyle's disposal. But one person who was more than a friend he did not introduce. This was Jane Welsh who, until she left her finishing school in Edinburgh early in 1819, used the Bradfute house as her home, coming there on Saturdays with her gloves and stockings to be mended. Eliza Stodart, the elder by a year or two, was a good friend to her, and the two girls spent many a happy and amusing hour with their confidences over the bedroom fire. These confidences mostly concerned Jane's admirers; for she was not long in Edinburgh before the drawingroom of 22 George Square became a happy hunting ground for young men.

When Irving heard that Jane was in Edinburgh he made haste to call on her. Jane received him kindly; so kindly that the susceptible young man fell instantly in love with her. The delightful creature now before him was, he told himself, largely his own creation; and he was perhaps credulous enough to believe that Jane had not looked so at another man. Those large black eyes of hers were quite capable of inducing such delusions. "Every man," said a relative of Jane's, with pardonable exaggeration, "who spoke to her for five minutes felt bound to propose". Irving did not propose in so many words—he was, after all, pledged in a fashion to Isabella Martin—but he haunted Jane like a great shadow, wrote her a most indifferent sonnet on a lock of hair she had given him, and besieged her with letters —one of which intimated plainly that he was trying to break the tie at Kirkcaldy. But the tie was not to be broken, not, at least, with honour; Isabella's father refused to release Irving.

27

All this took time. Irving at first hastened to bring along many of his Edinburgh friends, only to find that Jane was by no means disposed to give him all her attention. At last he flew into a passion, demanding how she could treat him so. She left the room; and he, at once penitent, followed her and begged her to return. "The truth is" he explained "I was piqued. I have always been accustomed to fancy that *I* stood highest in your good opinion, and I was jealous to hear you praise another man." He was forgiven, but he had learned his lesson and did not introduce Carlyle. At Kirkcaldy, before he had met the grown up Jane, Irving had boasted of his remarkable girl pupil and her beautiful mother and distinguished father; in Edinburgh, he said nothing. Carlyle was not interested just then in any other woman but Margaret Gordon. He noticed during the winter of 1818–19 that Irving, usually so boisterously cheerful, was often gloomy, but without suspecting the cause.

Jane was a practical girl, and after she had been "finished", and had returned to Haddington, she did not waste time in repining. The local men lacked the sparkle, the brains, and above all the address of the visitors to George Square; she knew them all only too well, from their schooldays onwards. This did not make for romance, but she gallantly did her best; admiration is admiration, from whatever quarter it comes; and in that commodity, at least, the Haddington men were as good as any. Besides, there was an undeniable pleasure in practising the airs of Edinburgh and in observing their effect; and her progress along High Street and up Sidegate to church on a Sunday had to be seen to be believed. Dances at the Assembly Hall, parties at the Fermes, the Howdens, the Donaldsons, the Rennies, the Rougheads, the Dods, the Veitches (the number of family friends seemed endless) games, escorted walks by the river— her life throughout the spring and summer of 1819 was filled with colour, with herself the acknowledged queen. There were differences with her mother from time to time, when the doctor's house was thrown into an hysterical uproar; there were blinding headaches, with prolonged sickness and prostrating pain; but these things were soon forgotten in the pleasures that followed. At the back of her mind, enriching every experience, was her father, "almost her divinity", saying little but looking at her with pride—still, in her eyes, the handsomest, the most romantic, and the wisest man in the world. With him she felt secure, confident that through his faith in her she would do great things.

One day in September, Dr Welsh had to drive some way out of the town, to visit his country patients, and he asked Jane to go with him. He had noticed, or his wife had again emphasised, his daughter's freedom with the men of the town. He did not reproach her for this directly, but spoke with regret of her fondness for the pleasures of "visiting and seeing sights". He warned her that good looks and charm could not by themselves make her what he knew she could be and ought to be—for that, she would have to work hard, and use her will and her wisdom. Above all, she must choose wisely when she came to take a husband. He did not think she had yet met anyone who would be a worthy life-partner. He spoke seriously and with unusual emphasis, and at first Jane, thinking him severe, was annoyed. Seeing this, he took her hand, and told her that she would one day thank him for restraining her idle inclinations. "You will not always be at home with me" he said. Jane, quick to respond, drove home in a fervour of renunciation, and determined to be all that he desired.

She never spoke to him again. One of his patients that day had typhus fever; he caught the infection.

Jane said afterwards:

> "I was forced away from him—but I sat by the door of his room, and heard his voice—and when it was opened I saw his face—and sometimes I stood an instant by his bed in spite of their efforts to remove me—and then he looked so anxious, and said to my Mother 'Will you not send her away?' Oh my God! the recollection of that short awful period of my life will darken my being to the grave."

The rest may be told by the servant Betty:

> " . . . the next day he was waur, an' on the Sabbath morning he was sae bad they put a laddie on a horse to ride to Edinburgh for the doctor, but before the laddie was weel awa', the breath gaed clean oot o' him! There was deid silence in the hoose for aboot half an oor, an' the first that brak it was Miss Jean. She was sitting on the stair, when up she got wi' a scream, an' cried, 'I maun see my father!' an' rushed to the locked door o' his room; but before she could open it, Dr Howden gat her in his airms, an' she fainted clean awa'. He carried her through the drawingroom, ye ken, to the little bedroom aff it, an' laid her on the bed beside her puir mother that was lying there in a deid swoon; an' there they were, like twa deid corpses! Eh, but it was waefu'!"

Her father died on September 19, 1819 and for a time she was inconsolable. She had good friends; the three Donaldson girls, daughters of the former Town Clerk, invited her up to Sunny Bank, the big new house beyond Hardgate which they shared with their brother Sandy, the Welshes' lawyer; the Rennies welcomed her at Phantassie, the Burns at Grant's Braes; wherever she went she found sympathy, but she was not to be consoled. For a week neither she nor her mother left the house; a house not of mourning only, but of bitterness—for Jane believed that Benjamin, who was then training with his brother, had been the cause of his death. Benjamin, confident that he could deal with the case himself, had not consulted Dr Howden, the regular partner, until a full day had passed.

In church, Jane tried to comfort herself with the thought that all three of them were again under one roof (her father was buried in the ruined choir of the building), and she promised herself that one day—"perhaps that day may not be far off"—she would lie in the same grave. The phrase "all three" was significant. All differences with her mother were now forgotten, she watched over her tenderly, and declared "I have no wish to live except for two purposes—to be a comfort to my poor Mother, and to make myself worthy of being reunited to my adored Father." For some time she and her mother were inseparable. Samuel Smiles, then a small boy living a few doors from the doctor's house, later remembered watching the two women in black, walking slowly arm in arm up the High Street. "Mrs Welsh" he said "was a beautiful woman: tall . . . and commanding. Jeanie was less lovely; her face was too angular for beauty. Nevertheless, she had many admirers."

But this was no time for admirers; and when Eliza Stodart came to stay, Jane's conversation was all of her father's virtues. She and her mother were to spend some weeks in Nithsdale, but she had no wish to go. "I feel that I never can leave this place". To her devout grandmother at Penfillan, for the first and last time not entirely alien to her, she wrote in the language that she could appreciate. "We must kiss the rod" she said "even while we writhe under the tortures which it inflicts".

In Nithsdale there was the inevitable discussion at Strath-milligan and Penfillan about the future of mother and daughter. Mrs Welsh was determined not to leave Haddington. Jane's immediate future was also soon settled. She was still under the influence of that final day with her father. What could be simpler and nobler than for her to pass on her knowledge to others? She had no sooner come to this decision, than one pupil was hers with embarrassing rapidity. Her aunt Elizabeth (a month younger than herself) was, said Jane, "seized with wondrous passion to grow clever". A month or two later, Jane had three pupils at home; her aunt Elizabeth, Ellen, one of the thirteen Howden children, and Ellen's recently orphaned cousin to whom Jane was teaching "everything". She was conscious of virtue:

> "It gave me a melancholy pleasure to think that the care and anxiety which my adored father spent on my education might be of use to one like me left destitute of this first blessing. . . . I never allow myself to be one moment unoccupied—I read the books he wished me to understand —I have engaged in the plan of study he wished me to pursue—and to the last moment of my life it shall be my endeavour to act in all things exactly as he would have desired."

But there are signs, even at this early hour, that the old Eve is raising her head. George Bell and his son Benjamin—"one of the most frank, unaffected young men I have seen"—had called, and she tells Eliza: "By the bye, Benjamin had a party some time ago of young Drs from Edinburgh—amongst whom was my old Barkly Museum friend Mowbray Thompson—who does not seem to have forgot me. He is immensely improved". These memories brought Jane down to earth for a moment: "I dare say you are a little curious to know the state of my *affairs* at present". But she pulls herself together: "My *sentiments* and *views* are very much changed and I believe in time I shall be *really sensible*—tell Mr Aitken that I can read two pages of Italian at a time . . ."

She had not become "really sensible" by the summer and autumn of the next year, 1820, when she and her mother were again in Nithsdale. The country without her father seemed sad, dull and cut off from life, but she discovered two pleasures, both of them male. The first was her uncle Robert, the Edinburgh lawyer, who stayed two days at Strathmilligan. Jane had long thought he looked "divine"; now she goes so far as to say that *"had it been possible* for the loss of such a father to be supplied, it would have been supplied by his brother". Her other pleasure was somewhat younger—Robert MacTurk, the good-looking eldest son of the landlord of Strathmilligan. He not only drove them to Dumfries in his gig when they left for Liverpool, but, quite unable to tear himself away, abandoned the gig and accompanied them in the coach as far as Penrith.

At Liverpool, Jane fell foul of her Aunt Mary. "Between ourselves", she told Eliza, "I don't like her. She is certainly a well-principled woman; but good principles cannot in my opinion make up for a *total* want of all feminine graces of mind". The full truth of the matter then appears: "She cannot bear to be contradicted in anything".

By early Spring of the next year, 1821, Jane was openly back where she had begun. She had stayed again with Eliza in George Square, and exclaimed on her return:

> "Well! my beloved Cousin, here I am once more at the bottom of the pit of dulness, hemmed in all round, straining my eye-balls and stretching my neck to no purpose. Was ever Starling in a more desperate plight? but I *will* 'get out'—by the wife of Job, I *will*! Here is no sojourn for me. I must dwell in the open world, live amid life; but *here* is no life, no motion, no variety. It is the dimmest, deadest spot (I verily believe) in the Creator's universe . . . everything is *the same*, everything is stupid; the very air one breathes is impregnated with stupidity. Alas my native place! the Goddess of dulness has strewed it all with her poppies!"

No more is heard of the determination to devote herself to a life of learning, of her attentions to her mother, of her wish to die. Her father, indeed, she had not forgotten—was never to forget; but to mention him at this time would have been to invite self-criticism. She discusses her admirers with unconcealed enjoyment. She tells Eliza at length about the antics of her "quondam lover", the "goosish man", who

> "presumed to flatter himself, in the expansion of the folly of his heart, that *I might possibly change my mind*. Ass! I change my mind indeed! And for him! Upon my word, to be an imbecile as he is, he has a monstrous stock of modest assurance! However I very speedily relieved him of any doubts which he might have upon the matter."

She spoke too, but briefly, of another admirer, Dr Fyffe, a choleric, dapper, bearded little man, who had come in as apprentice when Benjamin took his brother's place as partner of Thomas Howden. He was wasting her time, she declared, and his "*fuffs* and explosions" were bad for her nerves. She asks after her cousin, William Dunlop, renowned in Edinburgh for his wit. Is he coming to Haddington soon? "A visit from any man with brains in his head would really be an act of mercy to us here."

.   .   .   .

In Edinburgh, in the Spring of 1820, one year earlier than this letter of Jane's, Carlyle finally abandoned the law school, and set off for Kirkcaldy on a surprise visit to Margaret Gordon. The visit was short, and, as the aunt did not leave the room, it was unprofitable. Carlyle moved on soberly to Glasgow, where Irving welcomed him. A few days later he left for home—now at Mainhill, a small and dreary farm a mile or two above Ecclefechan, which his father had taken to keep his family about him. Irving walked with him for the first ten miles; and Carlyle, softened by his friend's affection, told him of his unsatisfactory visit to Kirkcaldy, and confessed his lack of orthodox religious belief. Irving received both these communications equably, and like the good friend he was, wrote to Margaret Gordon, telling her of Carlyle's disappointment. Some weeks later Carlyle, in deepest gloom about his future and worried by dyspepsia in consequence, was overjoyed to hear from her.

> "Your coming to see me in Fife, appeared not only a proof of the noble triumph you had obtained over your weakness (forgive the expression) but seemed to be an intimation that I still was thought worthy of that esteem with which you formerly honoured me. . . . Permit me to entreat you not to desert the path Nature has so evidently marked you should walk in. It is true, it is full of rugged obstacles . . . yet these present a struggle which is fitted only for minds such as *yours* to overcome."

Carlyle read into the friendly letter a great deal more than was there, replied ardently and at once, and was almost as quickly thrown back into gloom:

> "What a risk did you run in sending your Letter! . . . You ask me to write you often, this, I must repeat would not be doing justice to you— think me not vain—I have adopted the title of Sister, and you must permit me to usurp the privileges of one. You promise never to indulge

those 'vain imaginations' which have made us both so unhappy. Yet tell me, do they not still require steady restraint? And would not I by acceding to your request, encourage that '*weakness*' it has been my object to remove? . . .

One advice, and as a parting one, consider, value it: *cultivate the milder dispositions of your heart, subdue the more extravagant visions of the brain*. . . . *Genius* will render you *great*. May *virtue* render you *beloved*! Remove the awful distance between you and ordinary men, by kind and gentle manners; deal mildly with their inferiority, and be convinced they will respect you as much and like you more. Why conceal the real goodness that flows in your heart?"

Irving tried to persuade Margaret to relent, but succeeded only in extracting the admission "What a noble character is Mr Carlyle!" Carlyle spent much of the summer deploring her loss, but made no attempt to carry out her parting advice. Only when he began "living riotously with Schiller, Goethe and the rest" did he recover spirit. "They are the greatest men at present with me." When he walked over to see Irving at Annan, he was full of the marvels of Goethe's *Faust*. Irving did him good; he was unfailingly cheerful and confident. "One day", he said, "we two will shake hands across the brook, you as first in Literature, I as first in Divinity; and people will say—'both these fellows are from Annandale: where is Annandale?' "

By early autumn, Carlyle, who was proving an apt pupil of his German masters, was rhapsodising sentimentally:

"I hear not of Margaret, and know not if I ever shall. Such beings are shadows, radiant shadows, that cross our path in this dark voyage; we gaze on them with rapture for a moment; and pass away—borne onward by the tide of Fate, never to behold them more, never more."

He was, in other words, cured; and a month later, in October, he was off to England for the first time. But not for long. An acquaintance, Matthew Allen, had passed on an offer of a travelling tutorship to a Yorkshire merchant's son. After Carlyle had assured himself that the post did not call for "constant attendance and sympathy", that there was "no snobbery among the Yorkshiremen" and that the young man's father would "forget the distinctions of rank" and would not "trespass", he agreed to meet his prospective pupil in York. But he liked neither the young man "a dotard, a semi-vegetable", nor the place "the Boeotia of Britain; its inhabitants enjoy all sensual pleasures in perfection; they have not even the idea of any other."

In Edinburgh, he continued for the rest of the year and the early months of 1821 "scratching a livelihood" from occasional translations, articles, reviews and a pupil or two. He told a friend;

> "About twenty plans have failed; I have about twenty more to try; and if it does but please the Director of all things to continue the moderate share of health now restored to me, I will make the doors of human society fly open before me yet."

This was written on one of his more optimistic days. He was often bilious and depressed, but Irving, who still kept a kindly eye on him, encouraged him to persevere: "I am beginning to see the dawn of that day when you shall be plucked by the literary world from my solitary, and therefore more dear, admiration . . . But I shall always have the pleasant superiority that I was your friend and admirer". Three months later, Irving, in Edinburgh for the General Assembly of the church, found his friend again struggling with dyspepsia, unable to sleep or eat. He had arranged to preach on the last Sunday of the month at Haddington—the first time he had visited the town as preacher—and he invited the sickly Carlyle to accompany him "and see the world for a day or two". Carlyle agreed —"the man could not have been kinder to me, had he been a brother"—and on Saturday, May 26, the two young men (Irving was then twenty-eight, Carlyle twenty-five) set out from Edinburgh.

IV

JANE WELSH and THOMAS CARLYLE
1821–1822

Irving always brought out the best in his friend, and Carlyle was "as happy as a lark" as they climbed out of Musselburgh. The Forth lay wide and shining on their left beyond the battle-field of Prestonpans, with the hills of Fife looming up on the far side of the Firth, and the bare triangle of the Bass Rock rising sharply out of the water ahead of them. They loitered, argued, laughed their argument away—Carlyle had a loud and jolly laugh contrasting oddly with his speech and appearance—and walked on, until the Garleton Hills, leftward, and the Lammer-moors, to their right, grew higher, and the sun was hot above their heads. Between the two ranges of hills ran the sheltered valley of the Tyne, about which Haddington was built; but Carlyle could see nothing of the town except the hollow in which it lay. Irving, however, had no thought of walking straight down into Haddington; he was all for showing his friend Athelstaneford, where John Home had written his *Douglas*; so they struck off the road, climbed the hills, dropped down the other side to the church and leaped over the wall of the churchyard. Only then did they make for Haddington, retracing the walk by the plantations so often taken years earlier by Irving and Jane.

One of Irving's main ideas in bringing Carlyle to Haddington was to introduce him to Jane and her mother. He was now resigned to his engagement, and was trying to alter his feeling for Jane into one more suitable for a friend and spiritual adviser. At this moment he appeared to have succeeded; Carlyle thought him composed when they met Jane. But they did not go at once to the Welshes; they called at the Manse. The minister's daughter Augusta (called Miss *Dis*gusta by Jane) was there. Carlyle found her "tall, shapely, airy, giggly, but a consummate fool".

The sun was going down when they were shown into the diningroom on the ground floor of the doctor's house. Jane was sitting by the side of a young man about Carlyle's age who, he soon discovered, was her uncle Benjamin. Mrs Welsh soon left the room—her severe costume and air repelled Carlyle, and her beauty and elegance made him ill at ease—and Irving lost no time in communicating his pride in Jane: "From Wallace and from Knox" he said, waving his hand towards her, "there's a Scottish pedigree for you!" Benjamin, though "bad-colding", as he called it, was sprightly, but Carlyle did not take to him. He was aware of a bright pair of eyes watching him while he said his first conventionalities to her mother, but neither he nor Jane had much to say. But he had heard and seen enough to make him anxious to return. Back in their room at the George, Irving asked him playfully: "What would you give to marry Miss Augusta, now?" Carlyle replied: "Not for an entire and perfect chrysolite the size of this terraqueous globe". Evidently the young men were easily amused, for at this sally Irving roared with laughter. When he had recovered, he asked slyly: "And what would you take to marry Miss Jeannie, think you?" "Hah," said Carlyle, "I should not be so hard to deal with there I should imagine". There was more laughter from Irving, and there the matter rested.

Jane had heard of Carlyle; from James Brown, who had walked with him and Irving on one of their long excursions from Kirkcaldy; and from Brown's friend, Robert Storey, at whose manse at Roseneath the party had stayed during their walk. Storey—also an admirer of Jane—told her that Carlyle had plenty of talent and a fine vein of satire. Irving too had praised his friend. But none had described Carlyle adequately, and his appearance made an immediate and powerful impression. Although some inches less than the giant Irving, he was tall, thin, angular, and had extraordinary eyes—bright blue, deeply set, and, when he was interested, full of fire and feeling. Many people were to be fascinated by these eyes and Jane was no exception. She had seen, too, that he had a fine head and forehead, with a mop of brown hair in sufficient disarray to complete his resemblance to her idea of genius. His

37

overlong, too prominent jaw might, indeed, be considered a
fault, but at a pinch it could be taken as emphasising the firmness of his character. Jane it seems took the pinch. This serious
young man, with the romantic appearance and the voice of a
prophet, could also laugh—not perhaps at himself, but that
would come. The next evening he and Irving were back again
at the doctor's house. This time, they were shown into the
drawingroom. Both women, and Jane in particular, were "very
humane" to Carlyle; but for some time he was quite overcome
by the grandeur and beauty of the room, solidly and richly
furnished, with its fine stone fireplace, its great windows looking
down into the walled garden and over to the church and hills
and trees beyond. Carlyle was ever conscious of differences in
station; and perhaps never more so than now. "The drawingroom," he said, "seemed to me the finest apartment I had ever
sat or stood in . . . I felt as one walking transiently in upper
spheres, where I had little right even to make transit". What
with Jane and the room she was in, his critical spirit was near
collapse; he felt able to make only one small mental reservation,
about the "superfluity of elegant whimwhams" on the tables.

This night, too, he said little; but the next evening, when he
and Irving came again, he began to talk in earnest. They were
in the little parlour next to the diningroom, and they stayed
long. Irving began to bring out his friend, leading the conversation where he knew Carlyle would follow; and, perhaps
because of the more intimate room, perhaps because he was
becoming used to the presence of the elegant women, something
of Carlyle's emphatic and often witty talk began to appear,
"the two ladies benevolently listening with not much of speech,
but the younger with lively apprehension of all meanings and
shades of meanings". Carlyle was beginning to subscribe to the
view of Jane held by many, that "as a listener she was miraculous, so that her big, black eyes seemed to be flashing with
comprehension and sympathy, and men felt compelled to talk
to her without reserve". Jane was herself carried away. Only
from one other man had she heard talk of this kind. Carlyle
might almost be her father, with his strong, individual arguments his power of thought and wide-ranging mind. He was
not her father however, but a young unattached man of highly
original appearance. Such a phenomenon in a Haddington

sittingroom was enough to keep even Jane Welsh silent. Before the young men had left Haddington the day following, however, she had spoken to some purpose.

> "The beautiful bright and earnest young lady was intent on literature as the highest aim in life, and felt imprisoned in the dull element which yielded her no commerce in that kind, and would not even yield her books to read. I obtained permission to send at least books from Edinburgh."

So Carlyle. But when he and Irving had gone back to Edinburgh, Jane began to have doubts. Carlyle might be an embryo genius—there was every sign of it—but was he not too much of a rough diamond? A little unconventionality was all very well, but this latest admirer was positively uncouth. He had no manners, had no idea where to put his hands and feet, did not know how to eat or drink, and talked broad Annandale.

Then there was George Rennie. Of all the men who had made love to her, Rennie, after Irving, had won most favour. He was young, handsome, intelligent, he came of a good family and had fine prospects. At one time, she considered herself practically engaged to him; and she still thought warmly of him.

Carlyle saved her from serious thought about the matter. Soon after he returned to Edinburgh, "so full of joy, that I have nothing done since but dream of it", he sent books with a letter advising her at length how to read them. He could not resist some sentimental passages.

> "It seems as if we had known each other from infancy. . . . Positively, I must see you soon or I shall get into a very absurd state. . . . And then if I should come to visit Jane herself *professedly, what* would Jane say to it? What would Jane's friends say?"

Jane read the books, and returned them with her compliments to "Mr Carslile". Carlyle protested against this mishandling of his name, but for the moment he was silenced, and he merely sent more books. These too were returned to "Mr Carslile"; but the pill was sweetened by the news that she had dismissed her German master in Haddington; she would now learn by herself, and with Carlyle's help. This brought a renewal of his suggestion—temperately phrased this time—that he should visit Haddington, to supervise the German. The offer was declined, but some hope was held out:

> "Sir . . . I . . . will gladly avail myself of your advice respecting my studies if you can make it convenient to call on me in Edinburgh at 22 George Square, where I intend being for the evening of Saturday next until Monday forenoon."

Irving had duly written his thanks. He too seemed a little preoccupied with his friend's unfamiliarity with drawingrooms. "I wish both of us were of that rank and consideration in the world, which could make our acquaintance as creditable before the world as we have found without any of these vulgar recommendations it was welcome in your eyes". He also begged Jane

> "not to put religion away from you . . . study it with half the intensity you have studied Literature, practise it with half the diligence, and if there flow not in upon your spirit a gust of new nature, and come not forth an efflorescence of new fruitfulness, then do I consent that you shall give it up for ever."

This strain in Irving was not to Jane's liking, and she delayed her reply. But he had already turned to Carlyle:

> "Between ourselves, there is too much of that sort of furniture ['all sorts of extracts in Poetry, of a sentimental and erotic cast'] about the elegant drawingroom of Jane Welsh, our Friend. I could like to see her surrounded by a more sober set of companions than Rousseau your friend and Byron and such like . . . I don't think it will much mend the matter when you get her introduced to Von Schiller and Von Goethe, and your other nobles of the German Literature. And I fear Jane has already dipped too deep into that spring."

Writing again to Jane a month later, Irving still pressed his point. Jane, as a practical answer to his appeals, had sent him an English composition. He praises it, but adds

> "To me it were positively a greater treat to find the tenderness of Christian sentiment and the workings of Christian affection than to see the refinement of Collier or the depth of Staël. My soul is divorcing itself from the world and its tastes, and longing to be wedded to purity and wisdom and effulgence of love which are in God, and which are revealed in Christ . . . This is my wish, my dear pupil, for myself and for those whom I love."

To this letter Jane did not reply at all. Rousseau and Byron remained on the tables in Haddington; and when, after some delay, she came to Edinburgh in the late summer, Carlyle called on her by request "immediately after breakfast" in George Square, and promptly introduced her to Schiller and

Goethe. Before she went back to Haddington that day, she had agreed to try her hand at translation, and he had promised to send her the poetry he was trying to write. Early the next month she was writing to him with more freedom.

"Dear Sir, Goethe will not come to me! I have tried again and again, but cannot master the spirit of the original in my translation. Here are my first lines . . . Now as I have kept my promise to give you my verse translations, and tame enough they are in all conscience, to go by the carrier—I trust you fulfil yours to let me have all your own poetry. All!"

To Irving, Carlyle wrote "I saw the fair pupil in Edinburgh. She is certainly the most fit to read German of any creature I have met with." He tried to reassure his friend: "Take no fear of these people, I tell you. They are good men—some are even excellent. Schiller for example, you most certainly would like."

To Jane, he wrote many pages, a most correct letter, with the warmth only of a master for his pupil, or at most, of one student for another. He warned her not to study too hard and outlined in detail his plans for their future work, which seemed to defeat his own warning—for she was, in addition to German, to study history, to read Robertson, Hume, Watson, Russell, Voltaire, Tasso and De Staël. In Edinburgh he had pressed her to see him again, and Jane had spoken vaguely of a possible late autumn visit. "I still entertain a *firm trust* that you are to read Schiller and Goethe with me in October. I never yet met any to relish their beauties; and sympathy is the very soul of life".

But he had taken too literally Mrs Welsh's habitual gracious-ness, and her conventional hopes of a return visit. His long letters to Jane were beginning to disturb her. He was no gentle-man, he had no money, no future, no friends of moment, not even any certainty about what he wished to do. She liked what she had seen of him, boorishness notwithstanding, for he had an appealing manner, and she wished him well; but not for nothing had her daughter won the name of "the Flower of Haddington."

Jane, therefore, had to pick her way delicately; all the more so, because she had by no means made up her own mind about this man who was so difficult to classify. So she replied to Carlyle—now at Mainhill for the summer:

"Dear Sir, I cannot write to you. It is not my spirit's subjection to the prejudices of weak minds, nor blind reverence towards the dull cere-monial of life that hinders me. But I hate to deceive anyone—and I fear to deceive my Mother. Rest assured that my friendship will *never* fail you, as long as you merit it. As you value the continuance of our intercourse do not write to me again. I know nothing of my Mother's plans, but I rather think October will not be *the* Month. Burn this forthwith and forget that I have written it."

This hint of a league against oppression pleased Carlyle as it has always pleased every man. In November, Jane was once again at George Square, where she and Carlyle began to read Schiller and Goethe. She unbent a good deal during her stay. They walked out together, and a fragment of their conversation in Princes Street has been preserved. They were looking in the shop windows as they strolled along, and Carlyle said "How many things are here which I do not want". "How many things are here which I cannot get" said Jane. Carlyle was much impressed by her answer; and it is true that the remarks characterised the outlook of each. He told her that he was working hard, translating and tutoring, writing more articles for Dr Brewster; that he had been invited to write again for the *New Edinburgh Review* and had chosen Goethe's *Faust* as his subject; and above all that he had thoughts of a book, encouraged by a reading of *Wilhelm Meister*. The idea of a book particularly struck Jane's imagination, which ran with little encouragement on the discovery and development of genius. She urged him to the work, to develop his talents, to win fame, and promised to reply to his letters when she returned to Haddington. She did in fact write once.

> "Oh Mr Carlyle if you wish me to admire—to love you (admiration and love is with me the same feeling) use as you ought your precious time and the noble powers that God has given you, and waste no hours or thoughts on *me*. And do not laugh at fame. It is indeed a name—perhaps an empty name—but yet it is the object of no low ambition, and ambition is the crime of no low soul. I will not write again. Do not urge me lest you wear out my patience and with it my esteem. . . . When you have finished your review of Faustus send it to me with a letter such as my Mother may read without anger—and when you have written four-and-twenty pages of your book bring them. I have nothing more to say and you will not be satisfied with this—but I cannot help it—I dare write no longer. I am as nervous as if I were committing a murder and my ideas, like my pen, are dancing about at such a rate I cannot stay them. God bless you. Do your duty—let me do mine—and leave the rest to destiny."

She adds a postscript: "I know not how I shall get this to the

Post-Office as I never go out my going today voluntarily would excite surprise. What a purgatory you have placed me in!"

The proprietorial note in this letter did not escape Carlyle; he lost his head and invited himself to Haddington forthwith;

"When I compare the aspect of the world to me now with what it was twelve months ago, I am far from desponding or complaining. I seem to have a motive and a rallying-word in the fight of life: when the battle is waxing fierce without, I shall remember it and do bravely. *Alles für Ruhm und IHR!*"

Jane was displeased:

"I have read the Tragedies—I thank you for them. They are Byron's. Need I praise them. I have also read your eloquent history of Faust. For it too I thank you. It has fewer faults and greater merits than its Author led me to expect. I have moreover read your Letter—for *it* I do *not* thank you . . . there is about it an air of levity . . . ill-timed in treating of a subject, to you the most important of all subjects—your own *destiny*. . . . Besides this there is about your letter a *mystery* which I detest. It is so full of *meaning* words underlined—*meaning* sentences half-finished—*meaning* *blanks* with notes of admiration—and *meaning* quotations from foreign languages that really in this abundance of *meaning* it seems to indicate I am somewhat at a loss to discover what you would be at. . . . Now Sir, once for all, I beg you to understand that *I dislike* as much as my Mother *disapproves* your somewhat too ardent expressions of Friendship towards me; and that if you cannot write to me as to a Man who feels a deep interest in your welfare—who admires your talents—respects your virtues, and for the sake of these has often—perhaps too often—over-looked your faults—if you cannot write to me as if—as if you were married you need never waste ink or paper on me more. 'Alles für Ruhm und Ihr'! On my word, most gay and gallantly said. One would almost believe the man fancies I have fallen in love with him, and entertain the splendid project of rewarding his literary labours with myself. Really Sir I do not design for you a recompense so worthless. If you render yourself an honoured member of society . . . I will be to you a true, a constant, a devoted *friend*—but not a Mistress—a Sister—but not a Wife. *Falling in love* and marrying like other Misses is quite out of the question—I have too *little* romance in my disposition ever to be in love with you or any other man; and too *much* ever to marry without love. . . . You propose coming here. . . . As you neither study *my* inclinations nor consider *my* comfort, it is in vain to say how much I am averse to your intended visit, and to how many impertinent conjectures it will at present subject me, in this tattling, ill-natured place. I leave it then to yourself to accomplish it, or not, as you please—with this warning that if you come, you will repent it. . . . If you think me more *prudent*—or rather more *rational* than formerly, resolve the difficulty thus. *Now* I am *using* the language of my own heart. *Then* I was *learning* that of *yours*. Here I am Jane Welsh—in Edinburgh I was Mr Carlyle's *Pupil*."

She was now reading *La Nouvelle Héloïse* and wrote in an ecstasy and with a hint of the future letter-writer, to Eliza Stodart:

> "I never felt my mind more prepared to brave temptation of every sort than when I closed the second volume of this strange book. I believe if the Devil himself had waited upon me in the shape of Lord Byron I would have desired Betty to show him out. . . . This Book this fatal Book has given me an idea of a love so *pure* (Yes you may laugh! but I repeat it), so pure, so constant, so disinterested, so exalted—that no love the men of this world can offer me will ever fill up the picture my imagination has drawn with the help of Rousseau. No lover will Jane Welsh ever find like St Preux—no Husband like Wolmar—(I don't mean to insinuate that *I should like both*)—and to no man will she ever give her heart and pretty hand who bears to these no resemblance. George Rennie! James Aitken! Robert MacTurk! James Baird!!! Robby Angus!—O Lord O Lord! where is the St Preux? Where is the Wolmar? Bess I am in earnest—I shall never marry."

But she had not yet considered all her admirers. Of one she writes:

> "He threatens me with a visit in a week or two. It will surely come to a crisis—what do you think of it? He is about the age of Wolmar—but Wolmar had not a bald head—nor a lame leg—neither did Wolmar make puns or pay compliments. . . . I have just had a letter from Thomas Carlyle he too speaks of coming. He is something liker to St Preux than George Craig is to Wolmar. He has *his* talents—*his* vast and cultivated mind—*his* vivid imagination—*his* independence of soul—and *his* high-souled principles of honour. But then—Ah these *buts*!—St Preux never kicked the fire-irons—nor made puddings in his teacup."

Although she had only mentioned George Rennie briefly, he was still much in her mind:

> "When Friday comes I always think how neatly I used to be dressed—and sometimes I give my hair an additional brush and put on a clean frill just from habit—Oh the devil take him—he has wasted all the affections of my poor heart—and now there is not the vestige of a flirt about me—but I will vex that renegade heart of his yet."

Within a week or two she is writing:

> "George Rennie—read—wonder—but be silent—George Rennie is on the sea! and will soon be in Italy! What does he seek there? you will ask. His friends answer 'improvement in the art of sculpture'—I answer—— 'ruin'. . . . I resolved to return him his letters, lest I might *never* have another opportunity, and I seemed to keep them like a sword over his head. I sealed them, and scarcely had finished when I heard a rap. I

knew it at once. . . . He half advanced to shake hands with me; I made him a cold bow. He placed a chair for me and went on conversing with my Mother. He looked well—handsome—quite in high health and seemingly in high spirits. I scarcely heard a word he said, my own heart beat so loud. . . . I summoned forth my fortitude, and enquired for Margaret. 'She is very unwell,' said he, 'and wearying exceedingly to see you. *We* have been expecting you at "Phantassie" for a long time. *I* wish you would go today. The carriage is up. I brought it for a Miss Wilson who has come from Edinburgh; so you had best just go with us'. Oh the Devil incarnate! . . . At length he rose. He took leave of my mother; then looked at me as if uncertain what to do. I held out my hand; he took it, and said 'Goodbye'. I answered him 'Farewell'. He left the house —the very room where—no matter—as if he had never been in it in his life before—unfeeling wretch! . . . I am done with him *for ever.*"

She had, of course, done nothing of the kind. At this unpropitious moment, in February 1822, Carlyle arrived on his forbidden visit.

"Mr Carlyle was with us two days during the greater part of which I read German with him. It is a noble language!—I am getting on famously. He scratched the fender dreadfully—I must have a pair of carpet-shoes and handcuffs prepared for him the next time. His tongue only should be left at liberty—his other members are most fantastically awkward."

So Jane told Eliza Stodart cheerfully enough. In fact, Carlyle, an uninvited guest, was made to feel so. He returned to Edinburgh thoroughly wretched until a letter from Irving to Jane, sent to him for forwarding, gave him an excuse to appeal to her: "You bid me write to you as a *friend*. Vain injunction! I must exhibit the true state of my feelings when I write, or else write like a shallow fool: and I never felt *friendship* of this sort towards anyone." He was, he declared, "a perfect wreck".

Jane mocked his sentimentality and extravagance. She was hard put to it to consider him at all at this time, when so much of her thought was for the absent Rennie. She told Eliza:

"One night when it was very stormy I lay awake till four o'clock in the morning, thinking on the perils of such a night at sea. . . . The very elements seem to have leagued with *that Wretch* against me; for it is impossible to hear such winds and not to *think* of him. God grant he may not be drowned!"

But Carlyle, knowing nothing of Rennie, soon recovered his spirits and wrote again, repeating his fault:

"Oh for a friend—a bosom-friend—the treasure which many seek and few successfully—to be our own and ours alone, to have but one soul and spirit with us, to reflect back our every feeling, to love us and be loved without measure!"

Jane, exasperated, fell on him:

"Is it possible, Mr Carlyle? Can a Man of your genius and learning find nothing with which to entertain a young woman of an inquisitive spirit besides these weary, weary professions of regard, and apologies for making them? Admire me—by all means admire me, since it be your pleasure so to do—but—for mercy's sake—let it, henceforth, be in *silence*. And tell me no more of the '*helpless agitations' into which my displeasure throws you*—if you would not have me to repeat the experiment, for my amusement—for really, Mr Carlyle in a state of *helpless* agitation at a girl's frown, is, to me, a far more ludicrous spectacle than the Elephant dancing waltzes to the beat of a little drum. But *I must not take notice of your absurd expressions*—Oh! No—*that is very unkind*—'It is cruel and unjust to be angry at what you say for you mean well'? What an unfortunate being I am! From my childhood I have been in the habit of looking for people's *meaning* in their words and actions only—and now, at the age of twenty, I discover that, (would I avoid judging cruelly and unjustly) *these* are the very things to which I must not on any account attend. The *sentiments* you entertain towards my unhappy self seem to be now *most thoroughly anatomized*—the subject had, therefore, best be dismissed for ever, before your letters degenerate into absolute nonsense. You are not my *Friend*—you are not my *Lover*. In the name of wonder, Sir what *are* you? Oh! I had forgot—'A wreck!'—'a perfect wreck!!!' For Heaven's sake Mr Carlyle be, *if you can*, a *Man*—if not try at least to *seem* one."

This letter silenced Carlyle for some weeks, but Irving filled the gap. Three months earlier—at the end of December—he had preached a trial sermon in the Caledonian Church, Hatton Garden. The sermon caused a sensation, and he was appointed minister from the following summer. As soon as he returned to Glasgow, where he was still assistant to Dr Chalmers, he told Jane his news, and incidentally made clear his self-imposed philosophy of compensation. His head, he says, is almost turned with "the approbation I received". But he believes that, with God's help, he will "rise toweringly aloft into the regions of a very noble and sublime character." And so, he adds, "would my highly gifted pupil, to retain whose friendship shall be a consolation to my life: to have her fellowship in divine ambitions would make her my dear companion through eternity." He is coming to Edinburgh, and will visit Jane and her mother in Haddington.

Jane's comment on this letter is short and to the point: "Mr Irving is making a *horrible* noise in London, where he has got a church. He tells me, in his last, that his head is quite turned with the admiration he has received—and really I believe him." When Irving called, however, he was received graciously by Mrs Welsh and rather more than graciously by her daughter. Not for nothing was it said of Jane that she seemed born "for the destruction of mankind", and that "if *flirting* were a capital crime, she would have been in danger of being hanged many times over." Carlyle was temporarily in disgrace, Rennie had fled, the little Dr Fyffe was a bore, and the rest were out of town or grown dull through familiarity. Irving, it is true, was now fairly pledged to Isabella Martin, and his religious fervour was growing increasingly uncomfortable; but somewhere still was the bold and dashing young man, the protective, affectionate tutor, the ardent if forbidden lover; and there was no task more to Jane's liking than to uncover such a desirable past. Irving went away with *La Nouvelle Héloïse* under his arm and his head in a whirl, trying to muster all his resolutions. He succeeded, but could not resist announcing his success in a letter which must have given Jane much pleasure:

> "My well-beloved friend and pupil, when I think of you my mind is overspread with the most affectionate and tender regard which I neither know how to name nor how to describe. One thing I know, it would long ago have taken the form of the most devoted attachment, but for one intervening circumstance, and have shewed itself and pleaded itself before your heart by a thousand actions from which I must now restrain myself. Heaven grant me its grace to restrain myself and, forgetting my own enjoyment, may I be enabled to combine unto your single self all that duty and plighted faith leave at my disposal. When I am in your company my whole soul would rush out to serve you, and my tongue trembles to speak my heart's fulness—but I am enabled to forbear, and have to find other avenues than the natural ones for the overflowing of an affection which would hardly have been able to confine itself within the avenues of nature if they had all been opened. But I feel within me the power to prevail and at once to satisfy duty to another and affection to you. I stand, truly, upon ground which seems to shake and give way beneath me, but my help is in heaven."

He returned Rousseau "little comforted" by the book. Carlyle, he reported, was not so much aggrieved as he would have expected. "Such a parting from you would have gone far to kill me".

In London, even amidst the exhilaration of his success, Irving had found time to visit Margaret Gordon, but, he told Carlyle, "she has not Jane Welsh's heart". He had also remembered Carlyle in a more practical way. His preaching had attracted a Mrs Strachey, wife of a well-known official in the India office. She invited him to her house, and introduced him to her sister and brother-in-law, Mr and Mrs Buller, a wealthy couple recently back from India, who were seeking a good tutor for two of their sons while they were at Edinburgh University. Irving promptly recommended Carlyle, to whom the Bullers offered £200 a year and board. After consulting Jane, he accepted, and by the Spring of 1822 he was giving Charles and Arthur Buller several hours' tuition every day. They liked him and he them. "They are *great Boys, singularly great*" wrote Jane to Eliza, mimicking him.

In April, Carlyle tried again. "My dear Madam" he wrote, "I happened to fall in with these books lately; and thinking they might perhaps amuse you for a little, I have made bold to send them. You will pardon me for doing so, if it be offensive to you". He also offered to send some "subjects of literary composition".

Several days later, towards the end of April, Jane replied: "From a sheet of paper pretending to be a letter, that came to me some days ago, I learned to my great surprise and satisfaction, that the wrecked Mr Carlyle has been restored in mind and body to his lamenting friends." She accepted his offer, and signed herself "Yours with humility, Jane Baillie Penelope Welsh". Carlyle replied at once. Why did she not write a Tragedy? Her particular talents, he feels, contain "the very essence of dramatic genius". He suggested two subjects. But if he were blinded by fondness, she was not.

> "I have neither genius taste nor common-sense—I have no courage no industry no perseverance—and how in the name of wonder can I write a tragedy! I am not at all the sort of person you and I took me for—I begin to think that I was actually meant by nature to be a fine Lady . . . even my ambition is expiring very fast—I am as proud of striking the shuttle-cock two hundred times as if I had written two hundred admirable verses."

He protested, but was ready with another suggestion. Why should they not both write a poem every fortnight on subjects to be chosen alternately? He longed for a talk with her, even for half an hour. "It is a year about this very hour since I saw you for the first time! How many years will it be before I can totally forget all that!" Between his posting of this letter and her receiving it, she had been three days in Edinburgh. Mrs Welsh had decided at the last moment to go during the General Assembly, when many notables were to be seen and heard; but she had kept close watch on her daughter's movements. Not even half an hour could be given to Carlyle "although *I really wished it*".

Jane complained:

> "My mind is still in an evil way. I came home full of wise resolution. . . . I opened 'Mary Stuart' after breakfast but Dr Fyffe interrupted me, and teased me to play at shuttlecock till I consented. When we had finished, I observed the Piano open and Lord Byron's 'fare thee well' (my favourite song) staring me in the face. I sat down and played and sang badly till dinner time. The evening I spent as I spend too many, at an odious tea-party."

So went every day. Perhaps the "practical project" would turn her mind to better things. "Do let us set about it forthwith." They set about it; and she reported in the next month, June, that her faculties were in "*full force*"—German and Italian lessons, several hours of reading every day, an hour of Beethoven, and of course the poems. She sends him two. One, *The Wish*, began:

> Oh for a valley far away!
> Where human foot has never been,
> Where sunbeams ever brightly play,
> And all is young, and fresh, and green.

And so on, for seven exemplary stanzas, including the inevitable

> There could I spend my peaceful days,
> With only *one* my lot to share
> One in whose soul-depths I might gaze
> And see my thoughts reflected there.

But her sense of humour would not allow her to send off the poem in this form. She sprinkled the title and all the more extravagant lines with exclamation marks—and, in one case, an "Oh Lord!"—and added an extra stanza:

> Is this the destiny that I desire?
> Oh no! I'm infinitely better here;
> I verily believe I should expire,
> If doomed to solitude a single year.

A prophetic utterance, this; but for the moment she merely dismissed the poem as "a silly little thing", and her writing generally as "trash". Carlyle, his critical sense submerged, would not hear of it. The verses were proof "at once of your genius and diligence". He saw "a niche in the Temple of Fame . . . which I imagine your powers will yet enable you . . . to occupy".

Jane was undoubtedly reading a great many books, but they seem to have been on the light side. The histories she treated somewhat scurvily, but she wept "two whole hours" at the end of *Corinne*. It was not that her respect for learning had lessened. Her father had laid a strong foundation, and Carlyle was finishing the work. She had never swerved from her first impression, that Carlyle was a genius and would, properly encouraged, become famous. She urged him repeatedly to apply himself to some great work, reproached him when she thought him hesitant and uncertain—as he often was—and encouraged every sign that he was studying or writing or taking what she considered a practical step towards greatness. But in Haddington she was hopelessly spoiled, with one admiration and one diversion after another. When stirred by Carlyle or by the memory of her father, she studied feverishly, but the nearer and more obvious attractions usually proved fatal.

Her relapses were more or less faithfully reported to Carlyle, although the reason behind such frankness is at times suspect. Thus she tells him now of her bald admirer who had at last come to the point of proposal. He was pestering her with "ridiculous" letters; she feared to put an end to the matter because "there is a deep mill pond within a few minutes walk of his house". She was "nearly killed" by falling from the top of a very high wall "in trying to prevent Dr Fyffe seeing my ankles (which you may perhaps know *are no* great things)". She does not say what she was doing on the wall. But what are these to Byron?—"sinner as he is, there is nobody like him". She has a new portrait of him and "can scarcely help crying when I look at it and think I may chance to go out of the world without seeing its original". In church, she was lost in thought of him, "and when the people rose to pray I continued sitting." She did not forget Irving. His silence was unaccountable; he had not written to her for six weeks.

Irving was then on his way to Haddington to make his farewells before going to London. In the evening, he retraced with Jane one of the walks they used to take in earlier years, but this walk was not wholly pleasant. He made over to Carlyle, he said, the duty of forwarding her in literature, reserving to himself her "religious and moral improvement." This proposal met with some resistance from Jane. He was not to "preach" to her in his letters, she said. He agreed, but half-heartedly. He was oppressed by the parting and by fears for the future.

Irving gone, she turned her attention again to Carlyle. He had again offended. He had finished his long-drawn-out translation of Legendre; he was for the moment free from the Buller boys, and had grown on excellent terms with their parents; above all, he was progressing well with Jane, who was now signing herself "yours affectionately." But there were many moments—and this was one—when even such a tale of successes could not move him from depression, when they seemed as nothing to the long struggle between his natural piety and his lack of a settled faith, and availed nothing against his self-contempt:

> "Some comfort it would have been, could I, like Faust, have fancied myself tempted and tormented of the Devil . . . but in our age of Down-pulling and Disbelief, the very Devil has been pulled down. . . . To me the Universe was all void of Life, of Purpose, of Volition; even of Hostility: it was one huge, dead, immeasurable Steam-engine, rolling on, in its dead indifference, to grind me limb from limb."

This, to himself. To Jane, he was more circumspect and practical—she had no part, now or later, in this secret place of his heart—yet despondent enough.

> "Something must be done if I would not sink into a mere driveller. For the last three years I have lived as under an accursed spell—how wretchedly, how vainly so, I need not say. If nothing even now is to come of it, then I had better have been anything than what I am. But talking is superfluous: I only beg for a little respite, before you mark me down forever, as an unhappy dunce, distinguished from other dunces only by the height of my aims and the clamour of my pretensions. Will you not write to me soon? It were a kind act."

Jane wrote, but not as he hoped. She could see, or she chose to see, only one side of his appeal. This kind of talk from the man she had distinguished and was encouraging as a genius and, in the far future, as a possible suitor, was not to be tolerated. She reproached him in a "sharp Note." There may have been more than one reason for the sharpness of the note. George IV spent the second half of August in the capital, which was *en fête*, and Jane and her mother duly came in from Haddington to enjoy the processions and admire royalty. But Carlyle was no longer there. A week or two earlier he was on his way down Leith Walk to bathe one sultry day, desponding still,

> "when, all at once, there rose a Thought in me, and I asked myself: 'What *art* thou afraid of? . . . what is the sum-total of the worst that lies before thee? Death? Well, Death; and say the pangs of Tophet too, and all that the Devil and Man may, will or can do against thee! Hast thou not a heart; canst thou not suffer whatsoever it be; and, as a Child of freedom, though outcast, trample Tophet itself under thy feet, while it consumes thee? Let it come, then; I will meet it and defy it!" And as I so thought, there rushed like a stream of fire over my whole soul; and I shook base Fear away from me forever. I was strong, of unknown strength; a spirit, almost a god. Ever from that time the temper of my misery was changed: not Fear or whining Sorrow was it, but Indignation and grim fire-eyed Defiance."

In such a mood Edinburgh became intolerable. He longed for the quiet of the country where he could think into this miracle—for it seemed no less. Then came the crowning outrage; the city was placarded with exhortations "that on His Majesty's Advent it was expected that everybody would be carefully well dressed, black coat and white duck trousers if possible." Carlyle flew into a passion at this "effloresence of flunkeyisms" and made haste to take himself away before the King arrived.

From a man supposedly panting for her presence, this seemed strange behaviour to Jane—inexplicable, indeed, since Carlyle had wisely kept his vision to himself. She relieved some of her feelings in her note, which reached Carlyle the day before he decamped, but even so the Edinburgh visit had lost much of its savour. Matters were not improved by a temporary falling out with Eliza—doubtless because Jane was in bad humour—and it was with relief that she went north with her mother after the celebrations, to a cousin at Fort Augustus.

Carlyle came back from Annandale early in September, began work with the Buller boys, and wrote to Jane who was still in the Highlands. He was at once restored to favour. "Never did letter meet a warmer welcome . . . Not a word of hogs, cheviots, Falkirk Fair, or the Caledonian canal!" But for all her complaints, she did not lack company in the intervals between studying the classics she had brought with her; there was the garrison of the nearby fort; and whatever she might think privately of the officers and their wives, she quickly adjusted herself to meet their wishes, playing the part of "a lively, dashing, goodhumoured, thoughtless blockhead of a girl." This character "*took*" she assured Carlyle, "it won the hearts of the women and turned the heads of all the men in the place." This may be; but a woman who was there at the same time said it was common talk at Fort Augustus that the pretty widow would get two more husbands before her daughter got one. To Carlyle, Jane pooh-poohed her easy and misleading popularity; it was nothing, she said; what was really important was that she had made a new friend. She went into some detail—he was six feet two, slender, very graceful, an artist, with elegant manners, a quick sense of humour, well-read but ill-directed, clever, enterprising, ambitious—"that expression of yours, '*all in good time*' is never heard from *his* lips. I recommended to him to study German one Saturday, he commenced it under a Master on Monday, and by the Monday following he had read half of one of Schiller's plays". They had ridden together twice. He had no "genius", she feared, but "I think he is affectionate". Carlyle showed commendable patience with this recital; possibly because the artist, Benjamin Bell, had gone abroad; possibly because Jane appealed to him, when she returned home:

> "These last two months of idleness have done me a deal of mischief. I cannot study seriously for an hour. I have even forgot the way to rhyme. I shall die in a few years without having written anything—die—and be forgotten. Do . . . tell me what to do."

He did not escape admonition.

> "Write me a long letter as soon as you like and let me know all your designs. It is with a feeling of regret, you would scarcely give me credit for, that I see your days fleeting away unmarked by one struggle for immortality. Oh if I had your talents what a different use I would make of them!"

Carlyle wrote the long letter, two full sheets of it, sitting up till past midnight over the weekend. He had no difficulty with the first part of it—the advice to Jane. "Your object is simple—the attainment of intellectual eminence". The means to achieve the object were also plain; she should familiarise herself "with whatever great or noble thing men have done or conceived since the commencement of civilisation", rigidly setting aside some hours every day for study. She should begin with history. Four hours each day would be sufficient—"reserving the other twelve for your Mother and your friends and those accomplishments and amusements which befit your sex and rank."

So much for Jane "a person ,rich in solid knowledge, and habituated to the use of strong and brilliant faculties". But he! "what an ass! I sit and spin out long plans which it would require a lifetime to complete; I feel astonished at my own temerity when I approach the commencement of them; I falter, I hesitate, and at length give them up in despair". He had been considering a novel of "a noble mind struggling against an ignoble fate"—what of a joint effort in this kind? The "fat bookseller" Boyd had offered £150 for a life of Milton with critical notes. "Tell me, if you can, to what hand I ought to turn me".

Before he had read Jane's answer, Carlyle had been advised by an old University acquaintance, Galloway, to put in for the Professorship of Mathematics at the Royal Military College. It was worth £200 a year, with a free house and long vacations. Carlyle, asking for more details, explained that: "when the College classes are once fairly begun, and my pupils settled in them . . . *then*—to read—to write—to—in short to do wonders!" But he seemed more interested in the appearance of *The Liberal*, which the Edinburgh booksellers refused to sell.

Jane too he told about the magazine. "Hunt is the only serious man in it, since Shelley died: he has a wish to preach about politics and bishops and pleasure and paintings and nature, honest man; Byron wants only to write squibs against Southey and the like".

"Ah poor poor Byron. I—even I must give him up" replied Jane. But this was just a little froth at the end of a letter which began seriously enough, in the Rousseau vein. She had been touched by Carlyle's efforts to mould her mind. She abandoned the My dear Sir.

"My dear *Friend*. . . . Our meeting forms a memorable epoch in my history; for my acquaintance with you has from its very commencement powerfully influenced my character and life. When you saw me for the first time, I was wretched beyond description—grief at the loss of the only being I ever loved with my whole soul had weakened my body and mind —distraction of various kinds had relaxed my habits of industry—I had no counsellor that could direct me, no friend that understood me—the pole-star of my life was lost, and the world looked a dreary blank. Without plan, hope, or aim, I had lived two years when my Good Angel sent you hither. I had never heard the language of talent and genius but from my Father's lips—I had thought that I should never hear it more. You spoke like him; your eloquence awoke in my soul the slumbering admirations and ambitions that *His* first kindled there. I wept to think, the mind he had cultivated with such anxious, unremitting pains was running to desolation; and I returned with renewed strength and ardour to the life that he had destined me to lead. But in my studies I have neither the same pleasures, or the same motives as formerly—I am *alone*, and no one loves me better for my industry—this solitude together with distrust of my own talents, despair of ennobling my character, and the discouragement I meet with in devoting myself to a literary life would, I believe, have, oftener than once, thrown me into a state of helpless despondency; had not your friendship restored me to myself, by supplying (in as much as they can ever be supplied) the counsels and incitements I have lost."

In this mood she could not work hard enough or long enough. Hume, Clarendon, Rollin; she tried them all; toiled through a part of Tacitus; read some Schiller, and Alfieri's *Rosamunda* (he "must have written it with a live coal in his Stomach") and, with something of a fall, *The Curse of Kelama*—its author "must either be the craziest or the most conceited mortal that ever invented rhymes". But what of her Italian and "dear dear German"? Carlyle had said nothing of these. Very well: "I mean to devote four hours more, equally '*constantly, faithfully, and inflexibly*' to the study of languages". But her greatest enthusiasm was given to Carlyle's latest idea.

"I should like above all things 'to make a hero and heroine such as the world never saw'—do let us set about it!—the creatures of our joint imaginations will be a most singular mixture of genius and imbecility."

She grows more serious—"Would to God the alacrity of your execution was equal to the boldness of your projects!"—and she asks what has happened about the proposal of the fat Bookseller. Write soon, she says, and signs herself "Your very sincere friend."

Carlyle, his assurance leaping, advised her in unmistakably proprietorial tones to limit her study: "the only thing you want . . . is the humble but indispensable quality of *regularity* . . . Six hours are all that I can possibly grant you; four are all that I require; and I answer for the result".

His own affairs were still uncertain. The fat Bookseller "is laid upon the shelf"; he is considering the Sandhurst professorship; but for all the uncertainty and self-condemnation, his letter is the letter of a happy man. "I do not see the Bullers till two o'clock, and have done with them before tea; I am at liberty all the morning, in better health than I have been for two years". And he and Jane were to write a novel: "to come forth *together*—to mingle our ideas—to be as one in that matter! —the very thought is delightful." This was bold language, but it met no reproof. Their relationship was far from definition, but both were content for the moment to leave it so. They were enjoying their intimacy immensely, in their different ways; and when Carlyle refers to the fortunes of Irving, it is as though he speaks of someone dear but detached, and forever outside the magic circle.

V

THE COMMONWEALTH
1822 – 1823

"Brother Jack"—John Carlyle, now studying medicine at Edinburgh with his brother's help—in his "zeal against waste-paper" promptly burned a newspaper cutting lying about Carlyle's lodgings in Moray Street. The cutting was from the *True Briton*; it was destined for Jane; and it conveyed news of Irving, "who is making an immense figure in London". Carlyle did not exaggerate. When Irving began as minister in 1822, the congregation of the Caledonian Church, which would hold 600 people, had fallen to fifty. A few months later, fifteen hundred people were struggling to get into the little church every Sunday. Irving's sermons—which commonly lasted an hour and a quarter—had become the talk of the town. The Duke of York and other members of the Royal Family came to hear him. Society flocked to Hatton Garden, and the political leaders were seen there: "The preacher was every whit as much the rage as ever Kemble or Kean."

Dr Chalmers hoped only that Irving "would not hurt his usefulness by any kind of eccentricity or imprudence". Irving had no doubts.

> "At sight of Canning, Brougham, Lady Jersey and Co. crowding round him, and listening week after week, as if to the message of Salvation, the noblest and joyfullest thought . . . had taken possession of his noble, too sanguine, and too trustful mind: 'That Christian Religion was to be a truth again, not a paltry form, and to rule the world,—he, unworthy, even he the chosen instrument!' "

So Carlyle. Jane, reporting as usual to Eliza, took a different view: "What think you of the '*great* centre of attraction', the '*Spanish Adonis*', the renowned Edward Irving? did I not tell you how it would be? Oh I *do* share in his triumph! but I fear—I

57

greatly fear he has not a head for these London flatteries!" Her
forecast was true enough, but for the moment, flattered and
fêted though he was, Irving still had thought for his friend. He
urged Carlyle to join him—"Remember London is your
destination . . . Scotland breeds men, but England rears them"
—and he persuaded Taylor of the *London Magazine* to commission an article on Schiller.

Jane's foresight owed something to pique; Irving's first letter
from London had been a disappointment: "I could wish . . .
that your mind were less anxious for the distinction of being
enrolled amidst those whom the world hath crowned with their
admiration, than among those whom God hath crowned with
his approval". He went so far as to warn her against "the cruel
treatment of another, and the deification of oneself." In return,
she made sharp fun of his Christmas letter:

> "The most grotesque performance (I dare swear) that was ever penned
> beyond the precincts of a lunatic Asylum. It begins with 'It is past
> midnight!' after stating that he is suddenly and irresistibly impelled to
> write 'by one of those strong movements coming from whence he knows
> not but to him like the motions of a higher spirit' he proceeds to an
> elaborate description of his *two* candles, one of which he has extinguished
> that he may have light to finish his letter. . . . From the candles he flies off
> to a pack of fiddlers under his window '*breathing* the most melting and
> most melancholy music'. The said fiddlers parade Gloucester Street till
> (if I may judge by the fatigue I endured in following them) they must
> have been ready to fall down. After playing 'Erin go brah'—'Auld
> lang syne'—'Lochaber no more', &c, &c, &c, they take their departure
> (I hoped forever); '*but again it comes!' a strain more sweet from distance, and
> endeared by the tender associations of friendship. It is—'Caller Herring!'*—
> Here his soul is '*entirely overwhelmed*' and he winds up the article of the
> fiddlers by declaring 'he is laid prostrate on the sofa' (a most inconvenient
> writing posture, one would imagine!!) 'given up to the silence of his own
> thoughts!' The candles, sofa, and soul-subduing fiddlers are followed by
> God, a London bookseller, his fair pupil (that's me), the vision of judg-
> ment, and the Caledonian chapel—all jostling each other in most
> disrespectful manner. Just when the confusion is at the thickest—his
> candle goes out and leaves him in the dark, which event he relates in
> characters formed with scrupulous nicety. Was there ever any thing so
> absurd?"

She then quotes a typical Irving pulpit extravagance to
despatch him " 'Is it not a shame, yea a black and a burning
shame' to enslave his gigantic powers to such paltry worse than
womanish affectations?"

Carlyle was mildly upset. "What a wicked creature you are to make me laugh so at poor Irving! Do I not know him for one of the best men breathing, and that he loves us both as if he were our brother? . . . He has merit to . . . make him still one of the worthiest persons we shall ever meet with. Let us like him the better, the more freely we laugh." He could afford to be generous. The Schiller commission had made him feel for the first time that his work bore some relation to his inclination and talent; Boyd, the bookseller, was talking about a translation of *Wilhelm Meister*; and his relationship with Jane seemed to be growing firmer with every letter they exchanged. They had established what Carlyle called their Commonwealth—an association ostensibly of letters, which had come into being with the proposed collaboration in a novel, with Jane as "task mistress", but which Carlyle at least reckoned to extend into other fields. When he says of her most recent letter "it puts me in such a humour as you cannot conceive: I read it over till I can almost say it by heart; then sit brooding in a delicious idleness, or go wandering about in solitary places, dreaming over things—which never can be more than dreams"—when he describes her as a "shining jewel" and speaks of her "native loveliness", her comment is a model of good sense:

> "I see you do not know how to manage us women: no wonder!—You ought above all things to beware of seeming grateful for any favour we may please to confer on you. . . . Would you continue to enjoy the sunshine of my smiles you must also abstain from flattery (at least of the *common sort*). I have been stuffed with adulation ever since I left the Boarding-school (at that time I was as ugly a little bundle of a thing as ever you set your eyes on); and adulation like sweetmeats palls the appetite when presented at all hours of the day. I value one compliment to my judgment above twenty to my person (for the latter, my glass declares to me every morning, is totally unmerited, whereas I may be tempted to believe the former has some foundation)."

Carlyle again took his life in his hands when he sent her the first part of the proposed novel, in which the heroine appeared unblushingly as Jane, somewhat idealised:

> "Think of a slender delicate creature—formed in the very mould of beauty—elegant and airy in her movements as a fawn; black hair and eyes—jet black; her face meanwhile as pure and fair as lilies—and then for its expression—how shall I describe it? Nothing so changeful, nothing so lovely in all its changes: one moment it was sprightly gaiety, quick arch

humour, sharp wrath, the most contemptuous indifference—then all at once there would spread over it a celestial gleam of warm affection, deep enthusiasm—every feature beamed with tenderness and love, her eyes and looks would have melted a heart of stone; but ere you had time to fall down and worship them—poh! she was off into some other hemisphere—laughing at you—teasing you—again seeming to flit round the whole universe of human feeling, and to sport with every part of it. Oh! never was there such another beautiful, cruel, affectionate, wicked, adorable, capricious little gypsy sent into this world for the delight and vexation of mortal man."

This, too, passed muster; Jane regretting only that she had not his gifts. She had read the story so many times that she would soon be able to say it by heart. Emboldened, he pressed for details of her life, so that he might imagine her at every hour of the day. She obliged, and the decidedly unremarkable account was received with raptures.

Carlyle was for ever pressing her to come to Edinburgh again, and in the new year, 1823, was given February as a possible month. He "longed vehemently" for the time to come, when he proposes to talk to her for "about half a century". The visit fell through, but early in February Jane wrote:

"I have news for you that I hope will please you as much as it did me—my Mother wonders you do not think of coming out!!!—Now do you not see the fruit of my restrictions? Had you come sooner on your *own* invitation or mine—you would have found nothing but cold looks and I should have been kept on thorns until you left me—and now I am formally desired to invite you here, '*in case it may be that you are standing on ceremony*'—and come when you like dear you are sure of a hearty welcome."

This invitation, and the form of it—never had Jane been so forthcoming—overjoyed Carlyle so much that he burned two of his replies, fearing them too ardent; sending finally a most temperate note, admitting that their Commonwealth was better guided by her than by him. He proposed Friday, February 14.

"I have told my Mother that you are coming" replied Jane, "and she seems in perfect good humour. What generalship it has required to bring matters to this point! My Mother took it into her head when you was last here to dislike you with all her heart—as my regard for you increased hers seemed to diminish in an inverse ratio. . . . The storm that threatened '*the Commonwealth*' was truly terrible—but, you may thank your stars, I have brought it into a safe port."

Benjamin had died, and Jane was having some trouble with

Dr Fyffe who, now Dr Howden's partner, and a favourite of her mother, was given the run of the house; and who, as long as he behaved himself, was too useful as playfellow and handy man to be dispensed with. For the moment she kept her difficulty to herself; telling Carlyle merely that out of pity she took Fyffe's arm when walking.

The weekend visit passed off pleasantly. There was no more talk of the Annandale accent, though it was as broad as ever, no more sarcasm about Carlyle's clumsy hands and feet, though these were as clumsy as ever. Mrs Welsh was charming, and kept her reservations (of which she had many) to herself. Carlyle revelled again in the lovely house, and could not praise sufficiently Jane's "noble devotion" to her literary tasks, and her improvement "as a woman," with affections more catholic, tastes more simple, nature more kindly and affectionate, and "every way amiable"—a judgment which must have made Jane smile. He was allowed to take away her Tragedy, which gave him "more real enjoyment than any regular tragedy has given me of late . . . it was as if I had been surveying on the mountain tops the sources of some clear and shining stream along whose banks I had often lingered with delight". Her "Child-chair" sent him into rhapsodies: "when I saw the poor little thing standing so quietly beside the hearth . . . I could have rhymed like a Lake-poet over it". He also got on good terms with Shandy; a feat which was probably worth more to him than all the cleverness and grace he could muster. Before he left, there was some talk of the postponed visit to Edinburgh being made in the following month.

To Eliza, her only other correspondent in these early months of 1823, Jane makes clearer why she was growing so well-disposed towards Carlyle. Against his extravagant praise she was proof—she had too much commonsense, and her sense of humour was too strong—but outside events helped him. Haddington had been showing its worst side of late. First, there was the New Year visit of Robert Welsh and his wife. Jane's view of Robert had changed since he had married a young wife: "my precious Uncle, sneezing, snarling, and sometimes snoring—*the Lady* dressing, yawning, and practising postures." Any hope the aunt may have had of getting into the good graces of her niece was wrecked when, reported the contemptuous

Jane, she called "a certain, witty, dashing, accomplished friend of mine '*a heavy-looking LAD*.' Oh the indiscriminating Ass!" She also told Carlyle of the insult to Benjamin Bell—for he it was. But, added she, a true east Scotswoman for all her ancestry, "what could one expect from Port Glasgow?"

When they had gone, there was George Rennie to tantalise and vex: "we are to have no war after all; our travellers on the Continent will be exposed to no inconveniences; and so—well! no matter!" She pulls herself together:

> "I am going to forget him immediately. I could have done so long ago, but for one little action, that has made a strange impression on my senses. My spur required to be shifted from my left foot to my right; and you cannot think with what inimitable grace this small manoeuvre was accomplished. Whenever his idea occurs to me, I fancy him with one knee on the earth—his horse's bridle flung across his arm—his hands employed in fastening the spur—and his eloquent eyes fixed assuredly *not* on what he was doing. . . . However I *will* forget him."

By the time she reached the postscript, her newly made resolutions had collapsed: "There is some chance of George Rennie paying a visit to Phantassie during the spring or summer." Then comes a brief, bored account of her day, and a final remark which shows how dependent she has become on Carlyle:

> "Often at the end of the week my spirits and my industry begin to flag—but then comes one of Mr Carlyle's brilliant letters that inspires me with new resolution—and brightens all my hopes and prospects with the golden hues of his own imagination. He is a very Phoenix of a Friend!"

The "grand visit" to Edinburgh was delayed, to Jane's disgust for more than one reason. "I have got a fine head of hair lately—altogether I am looking rather more captivating than usual—I pray Venus it may last till I get to town." March passed, and April, and still there was no move. Carlyle was in despair. The Bullers had taken a house near Dunkeld in Perthshire where he was soon to join them. He hoped first to see his family in Annandale, but could not bring himself to leave Edinburgh while there was a hope of Jane. In the middle of April, Fyffe arrived at his lodgings, bearing a long letter from Haddington, whose contents, had he guessed them, would certainly have driven him to one of his "explosions". Jane hoped to be in Edinburgh the next Saturday—Mrs Welsh was bound

for Nithsdale, but she was to remain at George Square. Carlyle
was overjoyed, and Fyffe suddenly became "one of the prettiest
dapper little gentlemen I have ever set my eyes on" with his
"little farthing-face". He begged her to arrange at least one
meeting every day. But Saturday came and went and there was
no Jane; not until the last day of the month did he hear from
her, in a note from George Square.

> "I am sorry you made so sure of us on Saturday. We do not always ride
> when we put on our spurs. We only got here last night. Come tomorrow
> in the early part of the day or after tea—we might miss you in the fore-
> noon—be very *reasonable* for a little while—when my Mother goes to D^{shire}
> I will see you as often as you please."

Carlyle called, but Mrs Welsh, who had not been blind to
Jane's eagerness to go to Edinburgh, took good care that the
two should not be left alone. Jane was furious: "We might as
well be in the antipodes as here under such constraint. It is
insufferably provoking." They met four times and spent one
hour alone. Worse was to follow; for when Carlyle arrived at
George Square for the fifth time, mother and daughter had
flown. Mrs Welsh had decided that both should go to Nithsdale,
and, after arguing for two days, Jane had been overborne. They
had left at a moment's notice for their Highland cousin's house
beyond Corstorphine, some miles outside Edinburgh. From
there, Jane wrote despondently at the prospect of Nithsdale—
none of her relations liked her, she declared, and she despised
the Penfillan family for so quickly forgetting her father.

Carlyle took the disappointment well. The Bullers had given
him an extra week in Edinburgh, and he had calculated "on
spending some sixteen hours per day of it beside you". He was
now going to Mainhill instead, but would try to look in at
Corstorphine before he left. He urged Jane to remember that
Mrs Welsh had her interests at heart, and bade her regard
herself in Nithsdale as "an eaglet condemned to mix with
creatures of a lower wing . . . but only for a time". He plied her
with tasks to keep her mind busy—Goethe and Gibbon chief
among them. Another letter the next day told her that he could
not call after all—his coach left earlier than he had thought.
Jane sank into self pity;

> "You would pity me if you could witness my situation. Except a Bible,
> a book of psalms and a volume of Blair's Sermons, I can find nothing to

read in the whole house. It has rained almost incessantly since we left Edinburgh so that I cannot get across the threshold, and as the characters within doors are plain and simple, requiring no study, sewing God help me! is my only resource."

She is very much the spoiled young lady. Nor did her situation improve when she and Mrs Welsh reached Nithsdale. They went to a house new to them, for Walter Welsh had moved back across the river from Strathmilligan to the farm of Templand— a long low house standing high above the Nith. Jane's grandfathers now faced each other across the valley; from Templand she could catch glimpses of Penfillan amidst its trees, halfway up the opposite green slope; and when at Penfillan she could plainly see the southern corner of Templand less than three miles away over the river, where Walter Welsh sat and sauntered and dreamed away his last years. But she had no wish to be at either place; she felt oppressed, bored, angry and contemptuous by turns—but chiefly bored. The best she could say of the company at Templand was that

"I am better treated than past experience gave me leave to hope, and if my Grandfather would compliment my Mother without eternally wondering how she came to have a daughter 'so very short, so very sallow, and altogether so very unlike herself' I believe I should have nothing to complain of."

For the Penfillan family, and for her grandfather in particular, she had not even the semblance of a good word:

"When I saw it again I forgot my former visits there had ended in vexation. It was *his* father, *his* mother and sisters I was about to see. . . . My Grandfather was coming along the avenue—he is the very image of my Father and never did the likeness seem more striking. Had he received me as *he* would have done I should have worshipped him. Fool that I was to hope it for a moment! He gave me his hand with a cold cruel smile 'Miss Welsh I'm glad to see you. How are you Miss Welsh? I hope your friends are all well. I am going to the village on business, *ladies*—but please step in to the house—I will be with you by and by.' My God! I thought my heart would burst!"

Her feelings were reflected in her attitude towards Carlyle, now at Kinnaird House with the Bullers. She writes more warmly than ever before:

"every day and every hour of the day I think of you. Forget you by the month of August? What an idea! My best friend, be assured you can never be forgotten while I recollect *myself*. Your existence is so identified with all my projects and pursuits that it can only be effaced when I have ceased to feel, or when my being has undergone a change even worse than annihilation. Oh, no! We shall never forget each other, our friendship is no paltry intimacy, contrived by interest or idleness. I am persuaded it was planned by Mother Nature before we saw the light and founded on a surer basis than fortune or caprice. There is no doubt of it, we shall be friends *for ever*."

She also unburdens herself with unusual freedom about a protracted love affair. A year earlier, she tells Carlyle, a man (she does not give his name) proposed, was gently refused, and appeared to accept his fate. Recently, he announced that he had decided to leave the country. He watched her as he spoke, and suddenly burst out—"in *such* a tone"—"You do not care whether I go away". He began to sob and storm round the room, and she, afraid that this outcry would bring the household about them, threw her arms round his neck and besought him to be quiet. At this, naturally enough, he was quiet; and came the next day to say that his mind had changed; he intended to remain where he was. She made as if to leave the room, and he said "Take care, take care Jane what you do! . . . The hour that brings me another letter such as your last, will be the last of your existence."

Such was Jane's account. What shall she do? she asks Carlyle; and what will he think of her now? Will he ever again call her "my noble Jane"? She begs him to write very soon.

There was reason for this belated revelation. Carlyle, going back to the Bullers, had met Fyffe:

"he took his place beside me on the roof, and we journeyed together. 'Miss Welsh, Sir' said he, 'arrived at her Grandfather's the night before last.' This joyful intelligence was given with an air of knowingness and self-sufficiency which I relished very little. The topic of 'Miss Welsh' I studied to avoid for the rest of the day."

Carlyle nevertheless went on to praise Fyffe—"a jewel of a man"—sufficiently to make Jane thoughtful, for Fyffe was the importunate suitor.

Her position did not become less difficult when Carlyle advised her to tell the man that there was no hope. This, she said, she had done, and perhaps she had; but if so, Fyffe took little notice. He was in a strong position. His wealthy uncle in Moffat had known Mrs Welsh for years. He had another claim to distinction in the eyes of both women; a Baron in Vienna—

also wealthy—as a second uncle. He was firmly planted in the Welsh house. And, as Carlyle himself had said, he was a very pleasant little man, always ready to admire, to play games, to run errands. A month or so later he is conveying from Templand to Edinburgh two pairs of shoes, two books for Sam Aitken (Bradfute's partner), and a despairing letter from Jane to Eliza:

> "If ever my excellent Mother gets me wheedled here again! three weeks indeed! I conjectured how it would be from the very first. Oh my beloved German, my precious, precious time! . . . We have got my Uncle from Liverpool, his wife, the most horrid woman on the face of the earth, and five such children! in addition to our *family-party*—and what with the Mother's scolding and the children's squalling, and my Uncle's fighting and my Grandfather's fidgetting, I am half-demented."

She had just come back from a week with her uncle George and family, now at a farm appropriately named Boreland:

> "and such a week! There was no amusement within doors, and the weather precluded the possibility of finding any without. The only book in the house 'Coelebs in Search of a Wife' was monopolised by a young Lady who, I strongly suspect, had come there on Coelebs' errand—and the rest of us had no sort of weapon whatever to combat time with. For four whole days I had nothing for it but to count the drops of rain that fell from the ceiling into a bason beneath."

The one bright spot in her ocean of ennui was an encounter, if it can be so called, with her artist friend, Benjamin Bell, on her twenty-second birthday. She had believed him to be still "inhaling the air of Goethe". Then she saw him—on the opposite bank of the Nith.

> "Let any human being conceive a more tantalizing situation! saw him —and durst not make any effort to attract his notice—tho', had my will alone been consulted in the matter, to have met him '*eyes to eyes and soul to soul*' I would have swam—ay swam across, at the risk of being dosed with water-gruel for a month to come. Oh this everlasting etiquette! how many, and how ungrateful are the sacrifices it requires!" "Providence" she declares, "has surely some curious design respecting this youth and me."

All this, except the last sentence, she faithfully repeats to Carlyle. She has heard of yet another impending marriage among her friends, and adds, after giving Eliza the news, "I declare I cannot hear of these marryings and givings in marriage without some feelings of irritation—but *espérance!* it is my motto."

Benjamin Bell's return helped to stiffen her attitude to Carlyle, who had not pleased recently. Writing of Fyffe (though he did not know it) he said she could "admire him, praise him, be his sister, anything but his Mistress"—an irritatingly proprietorial remark. Nor did she like his attitude towards the Bullers. They were paying him handsomely, allowing him free time to continue his *Schiller* and his translation of *Wilhelm Meister*, and were generally as charming as people could be, but he was for ever complaining of them, although his lot, by Jane's reckoning, was brighter by far than hers, marooned in country she disliked, with people she despised, and her movements dependent entirely on the whims of her mother.

Carlyle, too, realised well enough from time to time that he was an unreasonable—one might fairly say impossible—man in a home other than his own; but always he relapsed, and railed and threatened. He nearly frightened his mother out of her wits by ominous remarks which gave the impression that he was dying of dyspepsia. But his dyspepsia was an effect and not a cause—a symptom of his wounded egotism. Dependence on other men was anathema to him and, of all forms of subservience, tutoring appeared one of the most menial. He had taken the post because to refuse such a good salary, with Irving expecting and Jane pressing him to take it, was scarcely possible. At first, in Edinburgh, the admiration of the Buller boys and the friendliness of their parents had softened his vanity sufficiently to make the position bearable, but after the move to Perthshire he was no longer able to delude himself or others that he was master of his own fate. He had to go off as a servant to a place that he at once made up his mind to dislike because it had not been his choice. The generosity of the Bullers—he was treated more as an honoured guest than as a tutor—aggravated his sense of injury unbearably. He saw himself, the regenerator of "the entire terraqueous globe", in a cushioned prison, which prevented him from developing his genius, and delayed the moment when he could ask Jane to marry him. He could not reasonably complain about his situation, and when he did complain he was shamed into a retraction. This was yet a further cause for bitterness; the very kindness of these people robbed him of an outlet for his bile. But of the bile itself, he could and did complain almost incessantly. He did not go so far with Jane as with his mother, but he grumbled a good deal. Jane sympathised with him, but she must have wondered how, if he suffered so much, he managed to keep out of bed, and even to appear the picture of vigorous health, walking and riding tirelessly. She could scarcely avoid comparison with her own devastating headaches, which were bringing her to her bed for hours, sometimes for days.

Yet it was none of these things, but Carlyle's increasingly intimate tone that Jane, ostensibly at least, took exception to. His hopes of meeting her had certainly been poorly recompensed during the past months. The weekend at Haddington, the four heavily chaperoned calls at George Square—these were the sum total of his success. He was longing to expound his plans for the future of both, and he also wanted simply to see and be near her. Frustrated in this hope time and again, his letters grew more and more ardent. They were love letters pure and simple, and none but the most obtuse could have failed to read them as such. Jane was far from obtuse, yet she made no protest; indeed she replied in warm fashion for the friend she protested herself to be; and the letter written by her which finally brought about the explosion appears every whit as ardent as Carlyle's own. She wrote, it is true, from "Hell" as Templand had now become, and that may account for some of her strong language:

> "Oh you have no notion how great a blessing our correspondence is to me! When I am vexed I write my grievances to you; and the assurance I have that your next letter will bring me consolation, already consoles me—and then, when your letter comes, when it repeats to me that *One* in the world loves me—will love me ever, ever; and tells me more boldly than Hope, that my future *may* yet be glorious and happy; there is no obstacle I do not feel prepared to meet and conquer. I owe you much! feelings and sentiments that ennoble my character, that give dignity interest and enjoyment to my life—in return, I can only love you, and that I do, from the bottom of my heart."

Carlyle's reply took the expected form:

> "Jane loves me! she loves me! and I swear by the immortal powers that she shall yet be mine, as I am hers, thro' life and death and all the dark vicissitudes that await us here or hereafter."

He thought himself unworthy and his future uncertain:

> "The only thing I know is that you are the most delightful, enthusiastic, contemptuous, affectionate, sarcastic, capricious, warm-hearted, lofty-minded, half-devil, half-angel of a woman that ever ruled over the heart

of a man; that I will love you, must love you, whatever may betide, till the last moment of my existence; and that if we both act rightly our lot *may* be the happiest of a thousand mortal lots."

His letter did not reach Jane until the middle of September, when she had at last escaped to Haddington. She was dismayed:

"Is it not true that you believe me, like the bulk of my silly sex, incapable of entertaining a strong affection for a man of my own age without having for its ultimate object our union for life? . . . In my treatment of you I have indeed disregarded all maxims of womanly prudence, have shaken myself free from the shackles of etiquette—I have loved and admired you for your noble qualities, and for the extraordinary affection you have shown me—and I have told you so without reserve or disguise—but *not* till our repeated quarrels had produced an explanation betwixt us which I foolishly believed would guarantee my future conduct from all possibility of misconstruction. . . . My Friend I love you—I repeat it tho' I find the expression a rash one—all the best feelings of my nature are concerned in loving you. But were you my Brother I would love you the same, were I married to another I would love you the same. . . . Your Friend I will be, your truest most devoted Friend, while I breathe the breath of life; but your Wife! never never! Not though you were as rich as Croesus, as honoured and renowned as you yet shall be."

Carlyle at once reassured her; he had no wish to wed any more than she; they were friends, no more. But having said as much, he continued to write exactly as before: "I will love you with all my heart and all my soul, while the blood continues warm within me." He also lets fall a gentle threat. When she marries, he will stop writing to her, though he will remember her always.

Jane's experience began to fail her. Nothing, it seemed, would shake him either into a withdrawal and proper friendship, or into a definite proposal. She had at last met her match. Rennie, the only other stubborn suitor, had been forced to run away. This man stayed where he was, took, in effect, no notice of her reproaches, but wrote and wrote and made himself indispensable.

Carlyle's little threat produced an effect that must have surprised him. If he intended to stop writing to her when she married, then, Jane declared, she would never marry.

"You are incessantly in my thoughts . . . and were the memory of you torn away from me, my whole existence would be laid waste. Oh I do love you my own brother! I even wish that Fate had designed me for your Wife, for I feel that such a destiny is happier than mine is like to be."

Being still a devotee of Rousseau, Jane found no difficulty, in her more romantic moments, in mingling love and friendship as the acme of human relationships. She had also just been in bed for a week with violent headache, her grandfather John Welsh had just died suddenly, and she had by no means regained her self-control. She was so disturbed by the mere thought of losing Carlyle that she remembered only at the last moment to tell him that Irving was coming to Haddington.

VI

INVITATION TO LONDON
1823–1824

Jane had heard from Irving in February, 1823, apologising
for his neglect, and saying

> "I have such a treat every day I pass a window in which there is a
> beautiful head of Miss Kelly, the exquisite performer of *Juliet*; it has
> the very cast of your eye in one of its most piercing moods, which I can
> never stand to meet, and the roundness of your forehead, and somewhat
> of the archness of one of your smiles. I must positively have it bought."

Then there was a long silence, and at intervals throughout the
summer she complained caustically of his neglect. "What is
become of our gigantic Friend . . . he has not a head for these
London flatteries. . . . It is all over with him if he forgets his
earliest and best friends." And again, "our illustrious Friend"
had promised to send her a copy of his book—"these helps of
our devotions"—"but possibly he may not feel the same interest
in our 'devotions' now that he has so many other people's to
attend to."

Carlyle defended Irving: "if he does not write to his friends,
the reason is, not that he has ceased to love them, but that his
mind is full of tangible interests continually before his face." He
passed on the news that Irving was coming North that autumn
to marry Isabella Martin. Jane heard it without pleasure. But
when she returned to Haddington her vanity was soothed;
awaiting her was a copy of Irving's book, and a letter to say that
he would like to be with them, and to preach in Haddington,
before his marriage. His coming, early in October, caused
something of a sensation in the town, to say nothing of the
feeling aroused in Kirkcaldy, but to Jane all real and imagined
slights were forgiven by this impressive compliment. "He loves
us still—better than many hundreds of his other friends. . . . I

71

have got the Orator's portrait—so like him, and so handsome!"

But this was nothing to the delight caused by a suggestion he made—a suggestion that sent Jane hurrying to tell the news to her "Dearest Friend"—for this is what it had now come to.

"I am almost out of my wits with joy. . . . You and I are going to London! You and I! We are to live a whole summer beside each other, and beside the One whom next to each other we love most. We are to see such magnificence of Art as we have never seen, and to get acquaint with such excellence of Man and Woman as we have never known—in short, we are to lead, for three months, the happiest, happiest life that my imagination hath ever conceived. In the same house for months, together in our occupations, together in our amusements, always together! No duties to interfere with the duty of loving each other; no pitiful restraints to vex our happy intercourse. Delightful prospect! Oh that it may not fade from us ere we reach it! Surely the Almighty's self hath put this plan into the heart of our Friend—surely it is not designed that it shall miscarry. Our Friend is determined that you shall come, and my Mother is willing that I should go."

The prospect shattered the remnants of caution:

"I know the noblest heart in Britain loves me. How comes it that I have such a Friend as you? that I deceive you without seeking to deceive you? I am so different from my idea in your mind! stript of the veil of poetry which your imagination spreads around me I am so undeserving of your love! But I *shall* deserve it—*shall* be a noble woman, if efforts of mine can make me so. This summer in London will make a new creature of me—I shall set myself, with my whole soul, to perfect my life and character through the counsel and example of my two friends."

Irving had spoken to some purpose during his final walks about Haddington, picturing the pleasures in store and the chances of advancement for Carlyle to be found in the circle of his famous patron, Mrs Basil Montagu, whose daughter was engaged to B. W. Procter (Barry Cornwall). Carlyle had said that he might go with the Bullers to Cornwall. "Cornwall!" cries Jane, "will you go to Cornwall? . . . is it not more for your advantage to go to London? Barry Cornwall made a thousand pounds the first year he was there—and you have ten times the genius of Barry Cornwall."

Irving left for his marriage at Kirkcaldy. He had arranged to meet Carlyle on his honeymoon. "If you can bear with '*The Lord*' and Mrs Montagu, you will have great delight in his visit" said Jane. She asked about Irving's wife-to-be; what kind of woman was she? "Tell me how he gets on with a wife—it

must be very laughable". Carlyle travelled a day or two with
the married couple. Irving was in high spirits, and the two men
at least had an excellent time. Carlyle gave an indifferent
account of Mrs Irving; she was not beautiful, "has no enthusiasm, and few ideas that are not prosaic or conceited", but had
many household virtues. He was little more enthusiastic about the
London visit. Irving had pooh-poohed Carlyle's objections. "All
seemed possible to him; all was joyful and running upon wheels".
Not so Carlyle; he was sleeping badly, was tired of the Buller
household, tired of the *Schiller* and the *Wilhelm Meister*, which
seemed poor, unworthy, useless, and was in no mood to believe
good of anything. Irving's honeyed words fell on stony ground.

> "He figured out purposes of unspeakable profit to me, which when
> strictly examined all melted into empty air. He seemed to think that if
> set down on London streets some strange development of genius would
> take place in me, that by conversing with Coleridge and the Opium-eater,
> I should find out new channels for speculation, and soon learn to speak
> with tongues. There is but a very small degree of truth in all this."

He had his doubts of "this seraphic Mrs Montagu, for the whole
of which I would not give three straws". Not even the promised
presence of Jane could stir him to more than a sigh at what
might have been. They must creep before they could walk, he
insisted; and he adjured her to keep her eye firmly on the
Musaüs she was supposed to be translating.

Much of this was sheer dyspepsia, but it was undeniably not
lover-like; and Jane, temporarily crushed, replied mournfully
that she could see that London was not to be their fate. Haddington seemed unendurable:

> "Surely there is not such an uninteresting place on the face of God's
> earth. . . . About a dozen magpies of girls, as many old women acid as
> vinegar, three gentlemen, one a puppy, another an idiot and the third
> Dr Fyffe are all the society I have from year's end to year's end."

In her disappointment, she turned on Irving. He had not
written to her. Did he love her at all? she wondered. Nor was
that all: "Do you know they are giving out that I am dreadfully
disappointed at his marriage!!! and that he has used me very
ill—*me* ill! was there ever anything so insufferable?"

She had caught a "furious cold" after a tea-party: "poor
little Dr Fyffe! his hand shook so when he felt my pulse!" But
even this satisfaction could not cheer her beyond the mention

of it. The house was again filled with guests, and she had done
little or nothing to her intended translation; she was good for
nothing but marrying and making puddings.

Carlyle was shocked: "To think that *you* should be oppressed
by bodily disease, that the pure sanctuary of your being should
be darkened and deformed by the continual intrusion of
material pain". He brushed aside the puddings: "You shall
make immortal food for the souls of generous men in lands and
ages that you have never seen and never can see." He himself
was utterly miserable. "Poor Devil! I wonder what is to become
of me". He is tempted "to cut these Bullers. The place does
nothing earthly for me but bring in two hundred pounds a
year. . . . Woe is me that I cannot live on air!" Could he not see
her again? He was to be in Edinburgh later that month to
consult a doctor about his dyspepsia. Jane was still convalescent;
at Dr Fyffe's recommendation "I am half drowning myself in
cold water every morning, eating beef, beef and nothing but
beef—I feel certain I have eat a cow within the last fortnight".
She had not yet spoken to her mother about the proposed visit.
Mrs Welsh was no more reconciled to the friendship than she
had been a year earlier; she had no mind to see her daughter
throw herself away on this irresolute, ailing young man who,
within a few days of his twenty-eighth birthday, had done
nothing, for all his fine talk. There had been altogether too
many geniuses about the place, if her daughter were to be
believed. The two women were getting on each other's nerves.
Mrs Welsh was difficult, no doubt; and apart from her temperamental nature, she had cause to be difficult. She had been
widowed at forty, still beautiful, still passionate, and it was no
easy matter to resign herself to the role of hostess to her daughter's young men. She had Jane's impulsiveness, but neither her
commonsense nor her ability to harden her heart; though she
had some happy touches (as when, for instance, she thanks
Carlyle for the loan of *Delphine*, but declares that she will never
again undertake six volumes of love). She suffered a good deal
at her daughter's tongue, but she had her moments, for at Jane's
age she had been married and a mother, and when tempers rose
Jane was not allowed to forget it.

Jane eventually made "the dreaded communication" in
November. She read out parts of Carlyle's last letter

"and asked her awkwardly enough if you might come. '*May he come!*' she said after me, with a portentous smile, 'if *you* can answer that question, I suppose it is quite unnecessary that *I* should be consulted.' What was her meaning think you? I declare, like God's power, she passeth 'all understanding.' However it is understood that you are to come."

Carlyle's week-end was a sober one, partly because he had now been forbidden by the doctor to smoke, partly because he became convinced, with Jane's help, that her present milieu was fatal to her happiness—"encircled with drivelling and folly . . . companionless"—and prevented her from improving her mind. He had also noticed that Fyffe "presumed to feel more than friendship" for Jane. He returned dismally to the Bullers. The lack of tobacco, or the doctor's medicine, or both, had left him worse than ever; and his first letter showed what Jane called "the blue-devils". Fyffe too had now seen plainly in what direction the wind blew, and he attempted to ridicule his rival. There was a stand-up fight between Jane and the little doctor. Then, early the next year, 1824, she was whirled off to George Square for her health.

Carlyle arrived back in Edinburgh in mid-February, and despite her "frigid cousin's drawingroom" at George Square, she managed to see a good deal of him. Carlyle had good news. The Bullers had decided for London instead of Cornwall, and he was to join them there in May. He had finished his *Schiller*, though he had still work to do on his *Wilhelm Meister*, and he was feeling better. Jane too was more friendly; she apologised humbly for a fit of temper—"tirevee" she calls it—and promised as recompense "a whole dozen of voluntary kisses". At times they read together, mostly in Goethe, and she took back to Haddington with her at the beginning of March the printed sheets of the first part of the translated *Wilhelm Meister*—or she would have done so, had not Carlyle forgotten to bring them to the coach. "Well my beloved genius, did I not tell you that you would not be back at the coach office in time?" she asks in high spirits. She is once more filled with good intentions; to set about her translations, and to read *Wilhelm Meister* as it is sent to her. She has read some of it, but wishes that it was not so "queer".

Mrs Welsh had grown slightly more tolerant of the friendship since the Edinburgh visit. She saw that her daughter was in better health and spirits; that Carlyle was well received by

John Bradfute; and she heard much of the Bullers and their good connexions. Jane seized this moment to begin showing Carlyle's letters to her mother, having previously arranged with him that German, Italian and French should be used for intimate passages. Carlyle at first forgot himself occasionally—"remember! no *darlings* or any thing *of that nature in English*"—but Mrs Welsh was "highly pleased" with the confidence as well as the letters. She sends her best regards, talks of Carlyle in friendly manner and is soon, according to Jane, "in rapture with you and your letters". She appeared well disposed towards a visit from him in May.

Jane was still working intermittently at her translations and reading *Wilhelm Meister*—"the unaccountable propensity to kissing which runs thro' all your *dramatis personae* perplexes me sadly"—but she was hindered, as usual, by tea parties (which according to Haddington etiquette lasted three hours) morning rides, and evening parties; and once again, by visitors. This time, the chief visitor was her young Aunt Grace, and Jane writes about her in much the same terms to Carlyle and to Eliza. "At the first" she tells the latter, "she was quite intolerable with her fine-Lady airs, and '*toploftical*' notions. . . . *Here* no one shall play *the* Miss Welsh but *me*. She decamps tomorrow—Praise be to God in the highest! for I am '*sick of imitating Job*' for this bout."

In spite of the "Dearly Beloved" and "devotedly yours" at which she had now arrived, there is no sign that Jane regarded herself as promised to Carlyle. She is still the pupil of Rousseau; she has not entirely forgotten the Commonwealth, and occasionally, when she remembers the desirability of it, she throws in a "Brother" or two; and she continues to take a lively interest in other men. Dr Fyffe, though still in disgrace, is dealt with at some length. "I have run against the little gunpowder man of medicine, in the entry, several times" she told Eliza. " . . . He is now trying to dazzle my wits with a white hat, silver headed Jockey whip and bits of *leggings* of so bright a yellow that it does me ill to look at them: but *c'est assez!*" She longs for Carlyle to come to Haddington "providing Dr Thumb does not shoot you dead". She still cherished a romantic picture of Benjamin Bell, and she has not forgotten Rennie. He "is to be home on a visit in the beginning of June" Eliza is informed. She adds archly, "that is nothing either to you or me".

But she was becoming more and more dependent on Carlyle for what she believed were her worthy pleasures, her aims beyond Haddington, and she had grown more fond of him than she bargained for. When he, absorbed in his *Wilhelm Meister* at Mainhill, did not write to her until he had finished it, she abandoned all pride and reserve. "In the name of heaven why don't you write to me. . . . You cannot conceive what anxiety I am in about you." And when his letter came: "Devil! That I had you here to beat you with a stick! Such a fright you have given me!"

In this letter, Carlyle gave news of Irving. Jane, waiting impatiently to hear more about her summer visit to London, had complained: "Not a word from the Orator! So, my magnificent Chateau en Espagne is completely demolished! I will not go now, not a foot length, though he was to write to me on his knees (which there is no great probability of his doing)." Carlyle sympathised with her "passion at the Orator", but insisted again that Irving loved her well. "The fumes of this sweet wine, which he has been drinking by the barrel, have flown to his head." He had just had a letter with a message for Jane. Irving had not written direct, he told his friend, because he was unable to fulfil his invitation. His house was fit for a man —he looked forward to having Carlyle there—but not for a lady.

This was a little ingenuous of Irving, but the poor fellow had woven himself into a tangle. He had always been a sanguine and impetuous man, but never quite so thoroughly as on that day in Haddington when he had invited Jane to London. Swept from the last vestige of sense by a desire to see more of her; anxious too, in the goodness of his heart, to bring together her and Carlyle, the only other man he considered worthy of her; he had overlooked the feelings of his wife-to-be and of himself in cooler moments. Isabella Martin had heard enough and to spare of Jane Welsh during the eleven long years she had waited for Irving to marry her. Married, the last thing in the world she wanted was to have this abominable flirt in her house for three dangerous months. She put her foot down; and Irving realised that he could not wholly trust himself as yet. The visit must be put off. How to do it, and save the friendship he so much valued? After breaking the news through Carlyle he explained the matter to Jane.

"I have no money, and my house will be furnished piecemeal, and will hardly be ready for the habitation of a lady till the end of Summer . . . on every account it will be more convenient and pleasant for us to have your company next Spring."

This of itself would hardly satisfy Jane, so he added:

"One thing more, my dear Jane, into your own ear. My dear Isabella has succeeded in healing the wounds of my heart by her unexampled affection and tenderness; but I am hardly yet in a condition to expose them. My former calmness and piety are returning. I feel growing in grace and in holiness; and before another year I shall be worthy in the eye of my own conscience to receive you into my house and under my care, which till then I should hardly be."

"Stupendous Ass" burst out the infuriated Jane, "What an idiot I was once to think that man so estimable! But I am done with his Preachership now and forever". She was alarmed too; Irving has been

"telling me such nonsensical things; and among the rest, that he is full of joy because Thomas Carlyle is to be with him this month! Can he mean you? This month! and twenty days of it already past and gone! The man must have been delirious when he wrote such an impossible story. You can never, never mean to be in London this month! You promised to be here before you went, in words that it would be impiety to doubt. I have looked forward to your coming for weeks. You cannot dream of disappointing me!"

Carlyle did not disappoint her; he came—the London by May had now become June—and did his best to console her. Not only was she barred from London, but she had lost her romantic idol. "Byron is dead!" she wrote before Carlyle arrived,

"I was told it all at once in a roomful of people. My God if they had said that the sun or the moon had gone out of the heavens it could not have struck me with the idea of a more awful and dreary blank in the creation than the words Byron is dead."

They mourned together, walked out to Paradise, a pretty little place just beyond the town, sat talking in the sunny garden of the doctor's house and on the bleaching green, strolled along the river bank, through the ruined choir of the church where they tended her father's grave, past the mill, and so by the tree-lined path that brought them out at the far end of the town. She wore a gimp bonnet and he a hat that she had had sent out from Edinburgh—for "my intended husband" she told Eliza when ordering it, but the confidence was not repeated to Carlyle.

He stayed almost a week. For the first time there seemed, to him at least, some kind of unspoken understanding between them. He sailed soon afterwards in a fishing smack from Leith. All the first day he had the Bass Rock in sight, and he thought of Jane a few miles inland beyond it. In the second week of June he was in London.

VII

CARLYLE IN LONDON
1824 – 1825

Jane did not see Carlyle again for ten months. His purpose in going to London—to rejoin the Bullers as tutor—fell through in a few weeks. He took exception to their change of plans, advised them to send Charles, the eldest boy, to Cambridge, and withdrew from his post. He left the family on good terms, although he spoke unjustly of the kind-hearted Mrs Buller, calling her "light, giddy, vain and heartless" which meant only that she was not as serious-minded as he would have wished. When, on his taking his leave, she invited him to a rout—"a grand, fashionable affair"—he refused scornfully. "I did not go a foot length," he boasts to his mother. "I want to have no further trade with her or hers, at least except in the way of cold civility." This was a far cry from his description of her two years earlier as "one of the most fascinating women" he had ever met; but he was still a touchy young man, too ready to imagine slights and brood about inequalities. He did not return at once to Scotland. He was offered £90 for making a book out of his Schiller articles, and he decided to stay on in London to do this work, and to look about him to see whether a literary career there were possible.

On his arrival, he had gone to the Irvings in Islington, where he was made as much at home as was possible in a house perpetually filled with admirers—some of them good friends, but most of them religious fanatics. The doors of the little Caledonian Church were still crowded long before they opened (plans were already afoot to build a bigger church in Regent Square) and it was still necessary to get a ticket to obtain a seat or even standing room, "but the first sublime rush of what once seemed more than popularity . . . was now quite over; and there remained only a popularity of 'the people' . . . which was a sad change to the sanguine man."

Irving was credulous, and could not always resist an appeal to his vanity; but Carlyle admired him because "he had endless patience with the mean people crowding about him, and jostling his life to pieces; hoped always they were not so mean; took everything, wife, servants, guests, world, by the favourablest handle." And when, later, his first child was born he "went dandling about with it in his giant arms, tick-ticking to it, laughing and playing to it."

All this was faithfully reported to Jane in Haddington. She shuddered at the thought of the baby—"kiss '*Him*' for me—I would not do it myself for five guineas. Young children are such nasty little beasts"—and was not particularly concerned with Irving, whom she judged almost entirely by his behaviour towards herself. What she wanted to know was, how was Carlyle acquitting himself in the literary world of London? What famous people had he met, and what were they like?

He was discouraging:

> "As a Town London is not worth looking at for above a week; and I know scarcely one or two of Irving's friends whom you are likely to take pleasure in, or draw advantage from. There is no truly intellectual person in his list; scarcely, indeed, in London."

Jane replied sharply. Where were all the distinguished people that he and Irving had told her about? "Discontented mortal that you are! If like me you had lived all your days in a little provincial town, you would know better how to appreciate such good company."

Carlyle bestirs himself to tell her more. Irving had introduced him to his "Noble Lady," the third wife of Basil Montagu. Their home at 25 Bedford Square was not only a literary centre, but a social "menagerie"—for there were children by all three marriages, and Mrs Montagu had brought with her a daughter from a previous marriage. She was the moving spirit of that miscellaneous establishment. It was a desperately difficult house to rule—"she is like one in command of a mutinous ship, which is ready to take fire" said Irving—but she was equal to it. Carlyle visited her every week, and enjoyed himself, though to bolster his wavering self-confidence he affected a cynicism he did not always feel.

> "You may draw on her for any quantity of *flattery* you like, and of any

degree of fineness. Irving she treats with it by the hogshead; me by the dram-glass, in a stolen way, having almost turned my stomach with excessive doses of it at first. If there is an eccentric virtuoso, a crack-brained philosopher in London, you will hear of him at that house; a man of true sense is a *specie* whom I have scarcely ever met with there. Yet they are kind and good, and as the world goes very superior people: I talk with them in a careless, far-off, superficial way, for an hour or two with great ease and enjoyment of its kind."

He by no means received a general welcome. The Montagu boys all disliked his clothes, his manners, and his dialect, but Mrs Montagu herself was kind. She saw promise in this rough diamond, introduced him to people who might help him, and took him with Irving to Highgate to see Coleridge, one of Irving's gods. Carlyle thought him "sunk inextricably in the depths of putrescent indolence".

Carlyle often saw Procter at Bedford Square: "essentially a Small" but "a decidedly rather pretty little fellow"; Allan Cunningham was "my dear, modest, kind, good-natured Allan"; but Thomas Campbell has "no living well of thought and feeling in him; his head is a shop not a manufactory; and for his heart, it is as dry as a Greenock kipper."

"Whom have we left?" asked Carlyle. De Quincey "carries a laudanum bottle in his pocket; and the venom of a wasp in his heart." Maginn "has been frying him to cinders on the gridiron of *John Bull*." Hazlitt "is *writing* his way thro' France and Italy: the ginshops and pawnbrokers bewail his absence." Leigh Hunt "writes 'wishing caps' for the Examiner, and lives on the lightest of diets at Pisa." As for the other "spotted fry" . . .

"Good Heavens! I often inwardly exclaim, and is *this* the Literary World? This rascal rout this dirty rabble, destitute not only of high feeling or knowledge or intellect, but even of common honesty? The very best of them are ill-natured weaklings: they are not red-blooded *men* at all; they are only *things* for writing 'articles'."

He had nothing but good to say of Henry Crabb Robinson, the most widely read Englishman of his time in German literature. They met at Lamb's, of whom Carlyle thought poorly, and spent what Crabb Robinson described rather surprisingly as an agreeable evening. Soon, Carlyle was telling his brother Alick that Crabb Robinson "gives me coffee and Sally Lunns (a sort of buttered roll) and German books, and talks by the gallon in a minute."

This life in London, with its unusual excitements, late hours and strange food, brought many attacks of indigestion. A young manufacturing chemist, John Badams, whom he had met at Bedford Square, persuaded Carlyle to stay for some weeks at his home in Birmingham, where he put him through a home-made cure. Carlyle returned little better than he had set out, but he liked Badams, his housekeeper, Mrs Barnet, and her daughter Bessy.

His most enjoyable friendships, which even dyspepsia failed to sour, were made with Mrs Strachey and her cousin, Kitty Kirkpatrick. As soon as he arrived in London he was shown a room in Irving's house which she and her cousin had furnished luxuriously; the two women soon dashed up to the house in "a brave carriage"; and not long afterwards he was writing glowing descriptions to Jane of "this singular pearl of a woman." This, replied Jane, a little bewildered, is "the only woman to whom I ever heard you give praise without some mixture of sarcasm". He had more to say as he came to know Mrs Strachey. "I think I have made one *friend* here, and that is almost like an epoch in my life. . . . She loves and reverences nobleness of mind in others, and follows it more honestly, than any creature I have ever seen—with *one* exception". The compliment could not save him. "What a precious creature this Mrs Strachey must be!" replied Jane. "I am sure I shall like her; since she has the grace to be fond of you. How old is she?"

She might have spared her anxiety, but Mrs Strachey's plans for Carlyle were another matter. He, his new friend observed, was taken with Kitty Kirkpatrick of the "soft brown eyes and floods of *bronze*-red hair" and "merry curl of her upper lip, *right side* of it only". She had money, he had brains, they looked well together. It was at least a possible match. Mrs Strachey had Carlyle out often to her fine house in Fitzroy Square, and to her country place at Shooter's Hill. In early autumn she invited him and the Irvings to Dover; they arrived first and stayed with Kitty, who had taken a house there, until the Stracheys appeared. From Dover, Mrs Strachey soon afterwards sent Carlyle off to Paris with her husband and Kitty for twelve days which were certainly not the least enjoyable in his life; his letters from that place are positively sunny. His difficulty was, how to explain the fascinating Kitty in terms that would not disturb

Jane? By the time he was a guest in her house and on the point
of going with her to Paris, some reference became imperative:

> "This Kitty is a singular and very pleasing creature; a little black-eyed,
> auburn-haired brunette, full of kindliness and humour, and who never I
> believe was angry at any creature for a moment in her life. Tho' twenty-
> one, and not unbeautiful, the sole Mistress of herself and twenty thousand
> pounds, she is meek and modest as a Quakeress. . . . Good Kitty! it is like
> pitchy darkness between long-fingered morn and tallow candle-light,
> when I stroll with her, the daughter of Asiatic pomp and dreamy
> indolence, and the Fife Isabella, skilful in Presbyterian philosophy and
> the structure of dumplings and worsted hose. Would you or I were half
> as happy as this girl! But her Mother was a Hindoo Princess (whom her
> Father fought for and scaled walls for); it lies in the blood; and philosophy
> can do little to help us."

As for Paris, he had been "as it were half-forced to accompany
them."

Jane was humorously acid:

> "I congratulate you on your present situation. With such a picture of
> domestic felicity before your eyes, and this 'singular and very pleasing
> creature' to charm away the blue devils, you can hardly fail to be as
> happy as the day is long. Miss Kitty Kirkpatrick—Lord what an ugly
> name! 'Good Kitty'! Oh! pretty dear delightful Kitty! I am not a bit
> jealous of her—not I indeed—Hindoo Princess tho' she be! Only you
> may as well never let me hear you mention her name again."

This and her next letter, written after Carlyle had broken the
news of the Paris visit, were milder than might have been
expected, because she had herself been anything but lonely.
"My Evil Genius has been at work again" she tells Carlyle.
There was, first, the exciting affair of Dugald Gilchrist, a love-
sick young man who "haunted" her, and was invited to
Haddington with his sister: "he has fair silky locks, the sweetest
eyes in nature, a voice like music, and a heart so warm and true
and so wholly, wholly mine!" At last she "did not scruple . . . *to
say that I was engaged*"; and though she followed the blow with
half a dozen consolatory kisses—on his forehead—he "cried all
the rest of the day; my Mother sat and cried beside him; and
his Sister and I cried in another apartment."

His state grew worse. "He lay for three days and nights without sleep and almost without sustenance, tossing on his bed and
crying his lovely eyes out." Then came a letter from Carlyle.
Jane turned pale—"I always do when I get a letter I have been

looking for"—then, seeing Dugald watching her, she blushed. He fainted, and the fall "was followed by spasms which lasted near an hour." Carlyle is asked to imagine Jane's feelings. "You will have some idea of them when I tell you, it entered my mind for *one instant* to promise that I would be his wife!" But Dugald recovered without the sacrifice, and was soon out of favour. "I find him" says Jane "a fool, whom one cannot see too seldom. Only think after he left Haddington he insisted . . . that I had *flaxen* hair!" She had "a faint hope that Dr Fyffe may knock Mr Gilchrist's brains out, and be hanged himself for the murder." For Fyffe, overcome by jealousy, had exploded once more. He wrote to Jane "imploring that I would *meet him—curse him*—and *part with him forever.*" Jane declined, and "what do you think the little Viper did? He packed up all the scraps of my handwriting which he had in his possession, with a great quantity of other relics equally precious and sent them to me with the worst-bred letter I ever read in my life."

"Is this his last explosion, think you?" she asked. She could afford to be cheerful, for even with Carlyle in London, with Dugald and Fyffe dismissed, she had still two strings to her bow. Benjamin Bell was back in Edinburgh and "has not forgotten me! This much I know and no more." Best of all, perhaps,

> "the handsomest and most fashionable man in Britain is to dine here—he is one of the Life-guard, and a Cousin of my Mother's—he wears mustachios and four huge rings, and chains and the Lord knows what and he is six feet two inches high and only eight and twenty!"

This Captain James Baillie proved as good as his description, and he joined the mother and daughter at Templand that autumn. Nithsdale, in spite of its many relatives, began to take on a most agreeable air. Even the fiasco of the long-awaited meeting with Benjamin Bell could not shake Jane's equanimity.

> "Oh Jupiter!" she tells Eliza, "that broad-brimmed hat and calico great-coat! . . . Do you know, the vulgar cast of his countenance and the volley of nonsense he overwhelmed me with, gave a shock to my nervous system, which it did not recover for four and twenty hours."

Her nervous system was helped by the arrival of Baillie; and by the time she wrote to Eliza she was playing chess and cards with him at Templand, wearing a lock of his hair in her ring, paying morning calls escorted by him, strolling through the

woods and fields with him, sitting on a green bank and talking
sentiment with him.

> " 'You were sure that he was not a person at all to *my* taste'—*Lord help
> your simplicity!* how you mistook the matter! He is my very *beau idéal* in all
> respects but one: his nature is the most affectionate I ever knew, his spirit
> the most magnificent; he has a clear, quick intellect, a lively fancy: with
> beauty, brilliance, sensibility, native gracefulness, and courtly polish, he
> wants but *genius* to be—the destiny of my life."

There was, in fact, another hindrance, for Captain Baillie was
to marry "one of the loveliest and most accomplished women in
England." To be married or not, however, Baillie had invited
her south—an offer renewed later in a letter "of *fifteen* pages."
The news—though not the fifteen pages—is passed on to
Carlyle.

> "I am to visit him either in London or at his place near Brighton. And
> then I shall be introduced into the *Great world,* and its novelty will
> doubtless charm me for a time; tho' I am pretty sure it will have no
> abiding attraction for me. Here is another fine Chateau en Espagne! God
> grant it may not share the fate of the last!"

She hoped for much pleasure from the visit, provided that
Baillie's wife did not prove another "dear Isabella".

A month or two later, in a letter sprinkled with Baillie's
favourite expression, Jane was asking Eliza

> "is not this a 'd—d odd' affair of our handsome Cousin's? . . . he wishes
> me to come and keep house with *him* and Phoebe in Sussexshire, that I
> may be present at his marriage, if it *does* take place, or comfort him if it
> does *not*. *Comfort* the most bewitching man 'in all England'! there *would*
> be an office!—if I were foolhardy enough to try it."

She did not go to Sussex, but she succeeded in drawing from
Carlyle the first breath of criticism since their meeting more
than two years earlier. He welcomed Baillie's invitation, "in
spite of all the artificial barriers with which you will be girt
about among your fashionable friends," but he was pained by
her attitude towards Irving. Since his return from Paris, when
he settled in rooms in London, he had persuaded Irving to give
Jane a formal invitation, and urged her to accept it. She
declined:

> "my cousin says I shall do no such thing—that after having lived with
> Mr Irving I will be blue and evangelical past redemption, and that he

does not want me to be instituting family worship in his house and reforming his whole ménage."

This made Carlyle uneasy:

"Nor in spite of your gay Cousin's objections must you cut the poor Orator: he confidently expects you, he loves you, and his fellowship will do you good. His affectations cannot infect your clear and active spirit for an instant; and there is a fund of sincerity in his life and character, which in these heartless aimless days, is doubly precious. The cant of religion, conscious or unconscious, is a pitiable thing, but not the most pitiable; it often rests upon a groundwork of genuine earnest feeling; and is, I think, in all except its very worst phases, preferable to that poor arid spirit of contemptuous *persiflage*, which forms the staple of fashionable accomplishment, so far as I can discern it, and spreads like a narcotic drench over all the better faculties of the soul in those that entertain it. No, my dearest, that will not do for you! Nature meant you for more serious things, and in spite of all your wanderings, you will yet attain them. O that I had power to form you, and form your destiny, according to my image of what you should be!"

Jane would give him no satisfaction. "The Orator has only *one* voice in the matter" she said. And when he pressed her further:

"his Wife, unless she is a very different woman from what I take her to be, will hardly forgive me for the good I have done her: the recovering of a faithless Lover, I should think, is a benefit for which one woman is not likely to be very grateful to another."

Carlyle did not relish this kind of talk.

"Do not mock and laugh, however gracefully, when you can help it! But for your own sake, I had almost rather see you sad. It is the earnest, affectionate, warm-hearted, enthusiastic Jane that I *love*; the acute, sarcastic, clear-sighted, derisive Jane I can at best *admire*. Is it not a pity you had such a turn that way?"

This was plain speaking but it was also romantic speaking. Carlyle refused to recognise that the qualities which he deplored were a part, and a very important part, of her nature. She was a more faulty and more interesting woman than he would admit, but he preferred to contemplate an idealised woman occasionally marred by regrettable faults. This time he had no doubt that Baillie's influence could be traced in this fault and in her uncalled-for

"you will not speak Annandale, surely, after having *travelled*. It would be so delightful to find you about a hundredth-part as 'elegant' as my amiable cousin! I am quite sure I should fall in love with you if you were."

He was unable to reassure her. He remained in speech as much a product of Annandale as she was of Haddington. Nevertheless, the dialect was, to her, symptomatic of his laggardliness, and she was for ever dinning into him the necessity of developing his talents in such a favourable atmosphere and so, implicitly, of winning her the sooner.

Carlyle would have none of it. He was not going into society, he was not going into the literary market. He began even to doubt whether literature was not a mirage, leading him from the first duty of man. He talked of turning farmer. Early in the New Year, 1825, Jane wrote sarcastically of his latest letter: " 'If you had land of your own you would improve it'! Suppose you improve mine? It is to let at present, and I know none that has more need of improvement."

Carlyle took her seriously. If she says the word he will rent Craigenputtock.

> "I proceed to it, the moment I am freed from my engagements here; I labour in arranging it, and fitting everything for your reception; and the instant it is ready, I take you home to my hearth and my bosom, never more to part from me whatever fate betide us!"

He explained:

> "Depend on it, Jane, this literature, which both of us are so bent on pursuing, will *not* constitute the sole nourishment of any true human spirit. . . . Literature is the *wine* of life; it will not, cannot, be its *food*."

It rests with her whether he is to be "a *right* man, or only a hard bitter Stoic."

Jane scoffed at him

> "You and I keeping house at Craigenputtock! I would just as soon think of building myself a nest on the Bass Rock. Nothing but your ignorance of the place saves you from the imputation of insanity for admitting such a thought. Depend upon it you could not *exist* there a twelvemonth. For my part, I would not spend a month on it with an Angel."

As for marrying him, "I love you—I have told you so a hundred times; and I should be the most ungrateful and injudicious of mortals if I did not—but I am not *in love* with you."

> "Have you" she asks, "any *certain* livelihood to maintain me in the manner I have been used to live in? Any fixed place in the rank of society I have been born and bred in? No! You have projects for attaining both— capabilities for attaining both—and much more! but as yet you have *not*

attained them. Use the noble gifts which God has given you! You have prudence (tho' by the way this last proceeding is no great proof of it)— devise then how you may gain yourself a moderate but *settled* income; think of some more promising plan, than farming the most barren spot in the county of Dumfriesshire . . . apply your industry to carry it into effect, your talents to gild over the inequality of our births and then— we will talk of marrying. . . . At all events I will marry no one else."

Carlyle protested, but Jane, annoyed at this backward step from his rightful future, was adamant. The most she would concede was:

"Not many months ago, I would have said it was *impossible* that I should ever be your Wife: at present, I consider this the most *probable* destiny for me. And in a year or so perhaps, I shall consider it the only one."

She dismissed Craigenputtock, which Carlyle still hankered after. "Will you be done with this wild scheme of yours? I tell you it will *not answer*—and you must positively play Cincinnatus somewhere else."

Carlyle abandoned Craigenputtock, though he did not forget it, but still held to his intention of going back to the land. He would go to Mainhill and look about him. He praised Jane's sincerity, and gave her a piece of his mind:

"Shall I confess it, dear as you are to my heart, I feel that I do not love you with a tithe of that affection which you might merit and obtain from me. It seems as if I *dared* not love you! . . . As yet, it seems to me, I am but in contact with you on some small corners of my being: but you shall yet see me and know me altogether. I hope you will not hate me; ultimately, I know you will not; but at any rate you shall not be deceived."

And he followed this with the wish:

"O my own darling, *were* you but the being which your endowments indicate, with what entireness could I give up my whole soul to you, and love and reverence you as the fairest work of God, and *be* one heart and mind and life with you to the latest moment of my existence!"

He proposed, when he came to Haddington from Mainhill, "to spend a whole fortnight, if your Mother will allow me, in lecturing you and being lectured!"

Subdued for a while by this candour, Jane accepted the retreat from London: "tho' self-willed as a Mule with others, I am tractable and submissive towards *you*; I hearken to your voice as to the dictates of a second conscience." But she re-

covered sufficiently to threaten to "ring such a peal in your
ears" if her copy of the promised *Life of Schiller*, just published,
did not soon reach her. Did he not believe her? Then let him
ask Dugald's sister, who had been her pupil for months ("I
cannot think how this *bur* of a girl is to be got rid of") "how
long she has heard me rail at a time, and she will tell you what
will make your hair stand on end."

But this was no more than a flourish. She was often ailing and
in bed through the winter, and felt melancholy and guilty. Her
literary work was practically at a standstill, and she had no
confidence in it. Carlyle's words were still echoing in her
conscience. She longed for him to come. They must be open
and sincere with one another when they met.

> "Would to Heaven all doubts and uncertainties were ended! and that
> we loved *each other* as both of us *might* love! How happy, how unspeakably
> happy should we be! And what hinders it? Nothing but the miserable
> perversion of my own sentiments! It is this which raises up a barrier of
> separation betwixt us; but for this my whole soul would rush to meet
> yours, and be one with it for ever. Surely I must be the weakest of
> creatures! I know where the evil lies, and do nothing to mend it, my
> existence is a sort of waking nightmare, I see the *right* way straight before
> my eyes—the *only* way of escape from the disquietudes which pursue me,
> and I have not power to follow it. Yet do not despise me, or altogether
> despair of me. I hope that, ultimately, I shall be everything—anything—
> you wish."

Carlyle left London in March, 1825, when his *Schiller* was
done; and left after all, "with regrets", though he had changed
his mind about Jane's proposed visit. Irving was good but could
not speak or act one hour without cant. His wife thought him
near a God, would not say him nay. "Rejoice that *you* came not
near him! It would have shook the whole establishment!"

In Annandale, he found that his father had already arranged
a year's lease of Hoddam Hill, a pleasant farmhouse some five
miles from the family at Mainhill. Alick was to run the farm,
and his mother with one or two of her younger daughters was
to look after the house. The lease did not begin until the end of
May, and after a week or two at home, Carlyle left for Edinburgh. From there, early in April, he went to Haddington.

VIII

ENGAGEMENT AND MARRIAGE
1825 – 1826

Carlyle stayed at Haddington for the better part of a month, visiting Edinburgh every now and again to settle what work he should take with him to Hoddam Hill. When he left Haddington early in May, he and Jane had come to an understanding; they had agreed that Mrs Welsh should no longer read their letters; and Jane had promised, when at Templand in the summer, to visit Carlyle's mother at Hoddam Hill. The understanding and the arrangements were made without the knowledge of Mrs Welsh.

Mrs Welsh, according to her daughter, had again been difficult in Carlyle's absence. For six weeks, Jane claimed, she was never in the same humour for two hours at a time. She had thrust Dugald's sister on her for the winter. She was often unkind about Carlyle's letters:

> "My Mother came in with a letter—I ventured to enquire if it was for me? 'You may be sure of that', then handing it to me, with a glance at the address, and a smile that boded evil 'I suppose *that* will cure your head'. I replied very boldly 'I have no doubt but it will help' and broke the seal with a horrible thumping at my heart. But before I had deciphered the first three lines, I was requested to *finish my tea. Tod und der Teufel!* (I mustn't swear in English!) *my* tea indeed! I gulped it down like as much senna."

Her mother's jealousy, said Jane, "is so intolerable that I am actually frightened when anyone shows me kindness." In her eyes, her life had been "a continual sacrificing of my inclinations and opinions, for peace's sake; and there is no peace after all!"

That there was much embroidery here is certain; Jane was no sinecure to live with when she did not get her own way, and she was no martyr. Dissension there was, however—which Jane's ownership of Craigenputtock and the Haddington house did nothing to modify—and Mrs Welsh may well have felt in exasperated moments that even Carlyle as son-in-law would be preferable to a dissatisfied, shrewish daughter. She had been pressed hard by Jane to approve the match, but had agreed to recognise an engagement only when Carlyle had shown himself worthy of her daughter and able to keep her in the manner she was accustomed to. She still considered Carlyle unsuitable in temperament for Jane as well as deficient in breeding and prospects, and when he was actually in the house her objections strengthened.

Again they walked by the river, sat in the arbour at their favourite Paradise, lingering on the way there and back at sunny resting-places. They planted seeds in the garden, talked of Goethe, who had replied warmly to an enthusiastic letter from Carlyle; and of Byron, a fragment of whose handwriting sent her into adolescent ecstasies.

> "This, then, was *his* handwriting, *his* whose image had haunted my imagination for years and years; whose wild, glorious Spirit had tinctured all the poetry of my Being! *he*, then, had seen and touched this very paper—I could almost fancy that his look and touch were visible on it!"

They also, following out their policy of sincerity, spoke more or less freely of former lovers—"love me very dearly—more dearly than you ever loved Margaret Gordon" begs Jane after Carlyle had left. But some things were still left unsaid, and Jane was reticent about Irving. Of her present admirers she made free; and she exercised her gift for comedy to some effect when one of them actually invaded the doctor's house while Carlyle was there. "Who do you think is living at the George Inn, and here every day?" she asks Eliza in the middle of April.

> "*Himself!* Mr Benjamin Bell! . . . He was come, he said, to reside among us for some time, to recruit his strength, he had been ill—confined to bed for three months—it was necessary that he should leave town, and his acquaintance with us and Dr Fyffe had induced him to fix on Haddington as the place of his retreat. How d—d odd! This curious annunciation was addressed to my Mother—I kept talking to Mr Carlyle all the while about the Peak of Teneriffe—meanwhile the tea-kettle commenced a song '*most musical, most melancholy*' which quite distracted my Mother's attention. She would not believe such sounds could be produced by a mere tea-kettle. Mr Carlyle lifted it to convince her of the fact; he replaced it again. He tried it in various positions, but the kettle would

not be prevailed upon. 'It was chagrined,' he said—and so was Mr Bell. He talked for two hours, however, with a miraculous command of absurdity, and then departed, after promising to be exceedingly troublesome to us. I behaved to him then and every time I have seen him since, in the most *pococurante* manner imaginable. I suspect he will soon be convalescent enough to return to the city. What a winding up of our Romance.''

Jane and Carlyle agreed that she should make over the rent of Craigenputtock to her mother for life, as well as the Haddington house and furniture, to ensure to her an independence when they married, and to relieve Carlyle's scruples. Both believed that they were marrying out of their class, and Carlyle was reluctant to add to his consciousness of this the burden of marrying "an heiress". Jane carried out this arrangement, and at the same time, without Carlyle's knowledge, willed Craigenputtock to him in the event of her death.

Much of their talk during this month was a discussion of ways and means. Carlyle lived frugally, and had saved £200 from his salary with the Bullers and his earnings from *Schiller* and *Wilhelm Meister*. He could have had pupils again at Edinburgh, but he yearned for the country, where he could be rid of "drenching myself with castor oil and other abominations". He had told his mother "*I will recover my health*, though all the books in the universe should go to smoke in the process " But when he saw Jane, this drastic resolution weakened; some books must be written if they were ever to be married. Tait, the Edinburgh bookseller, eased his problem; he wanted to publish three or four volumes of German Romances in translation, and offered the work to Carlyle who accepted, believing that it could be done with sufficient ease to allow him plenty of time out of doors. But this would do no more than keep him profitably occupied for his year at Hoddam Hill. It did not offer a settled income, and it did not appear to help him to a settled mind about his future.

Thus the talk at Haddington was often mournful and sometimes angry. Jane grew impatient to see a man of such talents unsettled and obscure. She suspected that Carlyle's pride had prevented him from making the most of his time in London. Nor she was always satisfied that he was showing the requisite ardour to be married. He protested a good deal, but the plain

fact remained that this year in the country, for which he was
eager, seemed neither to make possible nor even to advance
their marriage. She reproached him, he said "harsh" things,
and they spent miserable hours. Before he came, Carlyle had
made light of Jane's threat to nag him. He rejoiced, he said, to
hear of her gifts "in the scolding line. What heavenly music we
shall make! What a melodious concord of treble and bass!" The
reality was less pleasant, Jane's power of invective proving quite
shocking; and when he left, the manner of their parting seemed
ominous to both. They were not alone, he felt dreary and
constrained, and they could not even kiss.

Jane was now writing her autobiography, which was to end,
she told Carlyle, with the words

> "On the —th day of July, my beloved *Mr Sansterre* was waiting for me
> in the lower district of Annandale; he had the audacity to clasp me in
> his arms, and kiss me, and here my *Life came to a close!*"

But before the end came she had grown discouraged:

> "My *Life* is drawing to a close: there are already from forty to fifty
> pages of it—quite enough truly on so worthless a subject. . . . Love I find
> is a far more inspiring thing than ambition—but still I have no Genius—
> no particle of Genius; I write neither easily nor well; and my little
> narrative is so *ennuyeuse*, that it will be an affliction for you to read to the
> end of it. As Nature has made a sheep of me, and not an eagle, I cannot
> with all the straining in the world raise myself off the ground. Oh
> Heaven! if I were not a sheep!"

Even the seeds they had sown were not prospering:

> "The Beans are taller than this paper. I examine *yours* every day; but
> cannot discover the smallest appearance of a house on it. How many
> fathoms deep did you sow the other seeds? None of them have come up
> except three Lupins, two peas, and a few carrots in the place of *mignonette*.
> . . . I am sorry to say the omens to be drawn from our row-family are
> anything but favourable. You and I and Hope are quite dead."

Jane gave Mrs Welsh the deed conveying to her the life rent
of Craigenputtock, and the Haddington house. With the deed
she enclosed a letter asking her mother not to mention the
subject—she did not want either thanks or protests. She also
said, of the house:

> "In the event of my marriage, which may *possibly* happen some time
> within the next six years, you might find it more advisable to sell than

let it (for of course we will never part); but that is a far-away consideration."

Far away it seemed indeed; too much so for her patience. Carlyle sounded altogether too contented. Not long before, he had told her "the period of romance and extravagance should now be past with us; it is only clear judgment guided by prudence and integrity that can carry us through in safety." She protested, showing herself, in her expectation of an ardent love from Carlyle, as unrealistic as he in his wish for an ever sweet-natured Jane:

> "Dearest, will you please to recollect that two hundred a year is not to be gained by hoeing cabbages; that it would scarcely be advisable to set up house-keeping on less; and that—I am heartily sick of my existence in this miserable Haddington. What a cold Lover you are that need to be reminded of this!"

She urged him to keep in touch with his London friends. "Their affection for you is worth cherishing." She had read a letter from Mrs Montagu, liked it, and asked to take part in the correspondence. Carlyle duly made the suggestion. He praised Mrs Montagu's faith in human nature, which had enabled her to believe, as he put it, "that under the vinegar surface of an atrabilious character, there might lurk some touch of principle and affection, notwithstanding my repulsive aspect." He went on:

> "Miss Welsh of Haddington . . . is a person you will love and tend as a daughter when you meet; an ardent, generous, gifted being, banished to the pettiness of a country town; loving, adoring the excellent in all its phases, but without models, advisers or sympathy. Six years ago she lost her father, the only person who had ever understood her; she never alludes to him yet without an agony of tears. It was Mr Irving's wish, and mine, and most of all her own, to have you for her friend, that she should live beside you till she understood you, that she might have at least one model to study, one woman with a mind as warm and rich to show her by living example how the most complex destiny could be wisely managed. Separated by space, could you draw near to one another by the imperfect medium of letters?"

The appeal brought forth more than either of them anticipated. Carlyle had made clear to Mrs Montagu his hopes of marrying Jane, and had given the impression that Jane was favourably inclined towards him. But Irving had told her a different story. He had passionately loved Jane, and she him; and but for the call of duty, they would probably have been man and wife. Mrs Montagu was a determined woman and she disliked ambiguities. She had divined the force and talent beneath Carlyle's uncouthness; she liked him, and thought of him as her discovery. She was not willing that his future should be clouded by an unsatisfactory marriage. She was also kind-hearted, and knew by her own experience what misery an ill-suited couple could inflict on each other. She decided to intervene before it was too late; and Jane was startled to receive from her, not the pleasantries and London literary gossip she expected, but an appeal to make up her mind between the two men. If she decided firmly for Carlyle, said her new friend, her "whole will must be *thrown into fusion*, and cast according to another mould."

Jane laughed this off as best she could: "I had *two* sheets from Mrs Montagu, the other day, trying to prove that I knew nothing at all of my own heart! Mercy! how romantic she is!" So she told Carlyle. But she was alarmed to learn that Mrs Montagu had written to him at the same time, and in the same sense.

> "In writing to Miss Welsh" Mrs Montagu told Carlyle, "I have had a task of considerable difficulty. 'Her heart is in England, her heart is not there' and I feared to be the means of stirring an old flame. . . . If Miss Welsh were to pass one week with me, she might be satisfied that to be Mr Irving's wife would (to a spirit of her tone) be entire and unmixed misery: they are not the least fitted to each other."

Carlyle dismissed this—"she labours under some delusion, I believe, about your secret history"—but Jane felt uneasy. "I have heard from the 'noble lady' again, and written again," she told Carlyle as lightly as she was able. "She will surely be satisfied *now* that there is no worm of disappointment preying on my damask cheek; for I have told her in luminous English that my heart is *not* in England, but in Annandale!"

Mrs Montagu was not satisfied. When Jane and her mother reached Templand towards the end of July, another letter was waiting.

> "There is now before me on my table" it began "a beautiful green Mandarin Bason, a Greek Tazza could not exceed its elegant proportions, and its scarcity only seems to increase every person's opinion of its value. —It is to me *valueless*; . . . for notwithstanding its elegance and beauty, *it has a flaw in it*. . . . Shall such a flaw be found in my dear Jane Welsh?

Shall she stop half-way in nobleness and sincerity? Shall she be allowed to 'keek with critical dissection' into another heart laid at her feet, and shall she shut up the inner recesses of her own from one whom she professes to love and live for? No, my dear young Lady, the past as well as the present must be laid open; there must be no Bluebeard's closet in which the skeleton may one day be discovered. You have received a new and a dear guest to occupy your heart, not as tenant at will, but as tenant for life; and if, with a noble show of friendship, you have still only a show of it, what conclusion will that 'soul of fire' arrive at?"

Jane chose to regard this letter as a threat—a well-meaning one but a threat nevertheless. She decided to make the best of a not very bad job. Carlyle must be told, that was plain, but told what? That she had had a little-girl passion for his friend, and had afterwards flirted with him even though she knew him to be engaged? Her dramatic sense and her practical sense rejected the unpalatable truth. This was not what Irving had told Mrs Montagu; it was not what Mrs Montagu—unless she were forestalled—would tell Carlyle; it was not what she must, and immediately, tell Carlyle. If a confession had to be made, it should be worthy of one who had brought man after man to her feet; it should also, if possible, stir Carlyle from his apathy. "It is many a weary year since I have been so idle or so happy"— this was the kind of thing he was writing to her from Hoddam Hill. Who would dream that he was her affianced? Where were the protestations, the feverish efforts to earn sufficient to marry her? Of the true cause of his contentment she knew nothing. He had

"conquered all my scepticisms, agonising doubtings, fearful wrestlings with the foul and vile and soul-murdering Mud-gods of my Epoch. . . . In a fine and veritable sense, I, poor, obscure, without outlook, almost without worldly hope, have become independent of the world. . . . I had, in effect, gained an immense victory; and, for a number of years, had, in spite of nerves and chagrins, a constant inward happiness that was quite royal and supreme; in which all temporal evil was transient and insignificant."

This was the heart of his happiness at Hoddam Hill, but he kept it to himself; wisely, for Jane would scarcely have understood what he meant, nor could she have approved wholly if she had understood.

So she, fuming in solitude at Templand, could see only a man in no haste to be married. He needed a shock. She sent Mrs

Montagu's letter on to him with a covering letter in her best Rousseau style:

"I thought to write to you from this place with joy; I write with shame and tears. The enclosed Letter, which I found lying for me, has distracted my thoughts from the prospect of our meeting, the brightest in my mind for many months, and forced them on a part of my own conduct which makes me unworthy ever to see you again, or to be clasped to your true heart again. I cannot come to you, cannot be at peace with myself, till I have made the confession which Mrs Montagu so impressively shows me the need of. Let me tell it then at once. I have deceived you—*I* whose truth and frankness you have so often praised, have deceived my bosom friend! I told you that I did not care for Edward Irving; took pains to make you believe this. It was false; I loved him—must I say it—*once* passionately loved him. Would to Heaven that this were all! it might not perhaps lower me much in your opinion; for he is no unworthy man. And if I showed weakness in loving one whom I knew to be engaged to another, I made amends in persuading him to marry that other and preserve his honour from reproach. But I have concealed and disguised the truth; and for this I have no excuse. . . . Write, I beseech you, instantly, and let me know my fate. This suspense is worse to endure than any certainty. Say, if you *can*, that I may come to you, that you will take me to your heart after all as your own, your trusted Jane, and I will arrange it as soon as ever I am able; say no, that you no longer wish to see me, that my image is defaced in your soul, and I will think you *not unjust*. Oh that I had your answer! Never were you so dear as at this moment when I am in danger of losing your affection or what is still more precious to me, your respect."

By some mischance, the letters did not reach Carlyle for nearly a week. Jane, now seriously worried, scribbled a frantic note which, as the handwriting and the form of the letter make plain, bears none of the marks of careful composition.

"Mr Carlyle do you mean to kill me? Is it just of you to keep me so long in doubt? Your displeasure I have merited, perhaps your scorn, but surely not this terrible silence. Write then for Heaven's sake! and kindly, if you can, for I am wretched beyond all expression. Had I but strength, I would come to you this very day, and when I held you in my arms and you saw my tears you would forget everything but the love I bear you. Oh I do love you my own Friend—above the whole earth—no human being was ever half so dear to me—none none—and will you break my heart? Alas I thought when we parted that some evil destiny was hanging over us, but the loss of your affection was the very last thing I feared and have I indeed lost it? Speak tell me. It is inhuman to leave me in this suspense. Be your answer what it may I will love and venerate you to the last. You may be no longer mine but I will be yours in life in death through all Eternity."

Before this arrived at Hoddam Hill, she had read Carlyle's reply to her earlier letter. She discovered for the first but not the last time that he was good on great occasions.

"Your letter reached me but a few hours ago; I was doubly shocked on reading it a second time to find it dated *Sunday*. What a week you must have had! It were inhuman to keep you another moment in uncertainty. You exaggerate this matter greatly; it is an evil, but it may be borne; we must bear it *together*; what else can we do? . . . There was a want of firmness in withholding an avowal which you thought might give me pain, there must have been much suffering in the concealments and reservations it imposed on you: but there is a heroism in your present frankness, a fund of truth and probity, which ought to cancel all that went before."

But this was not all that Carlyle had to say. Jane's confession —and still more her hysterical thanks—reproached his conscience. He felt himself the greater sinner.

"Alas, alas! I deserve no gratitude. What have I done? Assured you that my affection is still yours, that you are even dearer to me for this painful circumstance. But do you know the worth of that affection? Have you ever seen *me* and my condition in the naked eye of your reason? You have not: you do not know me; the affection you rejoice in is worse than worthless; it is hurtful, it may be your ruin. What is my love of you or of anyone? A wild peal through the desolate chambers of my soul, forcing perhaps a bitter tear into my eyes, and then giving place to silence and death! You know me not; no living mortal knows me—seems to know me. I can no longer love. My heart has been steeped in solitary bitterness, till the life of it is gone; the heaven of two confiding souls that live but for each other encircled with glad affection, enlightened by the sun of worldly blessings and suitable activity, is a thing that I contemplate from a far distance, without the hope, sometimes even without the wish, of reaching it. Am I not poor and sick and helpless and estranged from all men? I lie upon the thorny couch of pain, my pillow is the iron pillow of despair: I can rest on them in silence, but that is all that I can do. Think of it, Jane! I can never make you happy. Leave me, then! Why should I destroy you? It is but one bold step and it is done."

Jane had never felt more alone, or more committed, than at this moment—estranged once more from her mother, and conscious of disapproval on all sides—and Carlyle had never seemed so desirable. She proceeded, with some thoroughness, to settle her destiny.

"Leave you! Obey the voice of reason! You know not what you say! 'Entreat me not to leave thee—for whither thou goeth I will go—and where thou lodgest I will lodge—thy people shall be my people and thy

God my God—where thou diest I shall die, and there will I be buried.' This is my decision which altereth not! It is too late to think of parting dearest—when my fate—my being are interwoven with yours. It is too late of obliging reason when I love. . . . You can no longer love, you say. I hear but believe not. This is a mere delusion, my darling—you *can* love, will, shall love—not Jane Welsh perhaps but your wife you will love. Your heart is *not* dead. . . . You will yet be happy! We both shall be happy! And suppose we should not, what then. Assuredly we cannot fail to be miserable, and if we *must* suffer, it is better, surely, that we should do so *together* than alone."

Carlyle acquiesced. "Who knows, too, but we may still be happy?"

The next and most imperative step was to see him. This was not easy.

"My Mother, as usual, has got new impressions of things—she now sighs and looks terribly cross at the least allusion to you—even my projected visit which at first found such ready approval is all but openly opposed. I will come however, notwithstanding. Her *opinion* it is my duty to respect, but not her caprices. . . . What a life I lead! What a profitless, pleasureless life! If I thought it would continue to the end, the end should not be far off."

But Jane was not made to suffer deeply for long. So she tells Eliza in the middle of August,

"One day, I am ill, and in bed; the next, in full puff at an entertainment. . . . What pains me most is that between headaches and visiting my *education* is completely at a stand . . . but . . . it is in vain to think of toiling up the steep of knowledge with a burden of sickness on one's shoulders; and hardly less difficult for a young person with *my attractions* to lead the life of a recluse."

She adds, "I purpose going to Dumfries in a week or two, on a visit to my Grandmother, and afterwards into—the lower district of Annandale—to see—the country." A fortnight later she did go to her grandmother, who had moved from Penfillan to Dumfries with her daughters Elizabeth, Anne and Grace; and from that uncomfortable position, with all four women disapproving of her and of her visit to Hoddam Hill, she wrote her first letter to Carlyle's mother.

"You must not receive me as a stranger, remember; for I do not come with a stranger's feelings. Mr Carlyle has made me already acquainted with every member of his family: and no one *he* loves can be indifferent to me, who have a Sister's interest in all that concerns him. Moreover you must prepare yourself to like me, if you possibly can, or your Son, I assure you, will be terribly disappointed."

Carlyle had no cause for disappointment. He had warned Jane again and again of the "Hibernian aspect of things" at Hoddam Hill; but these warnings were needless, as he at last came to see. "I might insult your love of me, and awaken doubts about what is not doubtful, if I made any more apologies." In fact, her visit was satisfactory to all. The Carlyles were a united and, in their taciturn way, a loving family, and their efforts to welcome a dear friend of Thomas endeared them to her. She surprised and pleased them by quickly making herself at home, and she soon had in young Jean an ardent worshipper. A horse had been found for her, and she and Carlyle rode about the countryside. They agreed that they would marry when Carlyle had finished his translations and had been paid for them—that is, some time in the next year. How they were to live, or where, still remained undecided. He rode back with her to Dumfries after she had stayed at Hoddam Hill nearly three weeks, and they parted sadly at the gate of her grandmother's house, where, she wrote that night, "my Grandmother and Aunts have been lecturing me . . . " but "I found a Letter (very kind) from my Mother awaiting me."

Jane successfully arranged for Carlyle to visit Templand, where she sought allies. "My Aunt bids me repeat to you, in her name . . . 'that every one who loved her adored Jane Welsh, is sure of having a friend in *her*'." Mrs Welsh too would be glad to see him "that is, if she happens to be in the same humour then as now." He had to postpone the visit. He was "drowned in drugs" and very melancholy, unfit for human society. "What am I to do or to attempt?" he cried. "How am I again to mingle in the coarse turmoil of men, and gather from their selfishness and harsh contradiction the means of happiness?" He had burned his boats gladly enough when Jane handed him the torch and charmed him on; but Jane gone, and her charm with her, his promise rose up against him; the need to earn the living that marriage demanded had a bleak and unlovely look. He tried to warn her, knowing himself an indifferent companion under compulsion. He would like to think that their life together would be as happy as their time at Hoddam Hill "but that were an error". When he came, in October, he brought a suggestion from Irving, whom he had seen in Annan. A University was to be formed in London; why did not he apply for a Professorship? Jane urged him to this. "I hope in Heaven you may go to London, I like the idea of it more than any scheme you have proposed to me."

The sight of Carlyle living in the house beside Jane renewed all Mrs Welsh's worst fears, and the day after he went home she made a last effort to stop the disaster, as she felt it to be.

> "Oh mercy! what cruel, unreasonable things she said! But nothing distressed me so much as her bitter reflections against you, whom she accused of having 'bewitched and poisoned my mind'. She was unjust, I told her; my connexion with so wise and honourable a man could be attended with no ill consequence. . . . She sulked for four and twenty hours, and then wrote me a long epistle. . . . 'She *had*, indeed, given her consent to our union,' (she said) 'when you should have made yourself *a name and a situation in life*; but only because I asked it, with tears, *upon my bended knees*, at a time too, *when my life-seemed precarious*' (to the best of my recollection I was enjoying tolerable health). 'Afterwards, however, when you came to Haddington, and she watched your temper and perceived its *effect* upon me, it was then her soul was torn,' &c, &c."

Jane dismissed the appeal:

> "A pack of damned nonsense, the whole of it! 'Temper'! 'Effect'! Truly, she has seen her own temper have a hundred times worse effects upon me than ever yours had, without being troubled with such tender solicitude. No! my own Darling! we shall not be parted on this account."

Carlyle, though he denied being an ill-natured man, "nor even, all things considered, very ill-tempered," replied that Mrs Welsh's "views of me and my connexion with you I cannot greatly blame; they coincide too nearly with my own," but to this Jane, of course, would not listen.

Mrs Welsh also protested against the intimacy with Mrs Montagu—a woman whom Jane had never seen, knew little about, but for whom she professed unbounded love and admiration. Jane declared that she would go on writing "as long as I have ink and paper; and no man, woman or child shall prevent me from loving and admiring her as ardently as I please."

The storm was stilled, for the moment, by the arrival of Captain Baillie, still unmarried, at Templand, "if possible, more Adonis-like, witty and elegant than ever. Such an air! such a voice! such a profusion of little dogs!" But Jane was no longer amused:

"I wish, in my heart, he were returned to the place whence he came; for I will confess to you, dear friend, that—you have not the slightest cause to be jealous—jealous! Oh mercy! when I compare this fine-gentleman with the *man* I love; what is he after all? A mere painted butterfly, fluttering over the flowery surface of the Earth—the creature of a sunshiny day! while he—my own—is like to the royal Eagle, who soars aloft thro' the regions of ether, and feasts his eyes on the glories of the Sun."

Jane had written to Mrs Carlyle before she and her mother left Templand in November, that she would always remember and love her friends in Annandale. This was not mere politeness; she liked this kind, shrewd, devout woman who doted so on her Thomas, and who laughed admiringly at Jane's witticisms. Jane showed every sign of intending to be a good family woman. She was flattered by the devotion of her little namesake, and reminded her of her promise to be a dutiful child and loving sister. Early in the new year, 1826, she helped to persuade Haddington notables to appoint James Johnston to the newly formed Parish School—this, at the particular request of Carlyle, who wished to help the son of the old Ecclefechan preacher. And when old James Carlyle quarrelled with his landlord, and both Hoddam Hill and Mainhill had to be given up, she was asked twice by Carlyle to try to use her influence to get them another farm. Jane brushed his apology aside. "Of whom, in all the world but me, would Thomas Carlyle have asked a favour *twice*?" She acted promptly. "Your letter found me in bed, at the extremities of fate—but oh miracle of love! I rose up an hour after as well as ever I was in my life, and wrote to *the* major himself on the subject of your solicitude." This farm finally went to another man, and the Carlyles arranged to move to Scotsbrig, near Hoddam Hill.

Baillie had followed Jane to Haddington but he still failed to charm: "They are gone, my Dearest! fairly gone!" she writes early in December.

". . . I am still alive, and blessing God for all his mercies—most of all for the great temporal blessing which I enjoy in thee. Indeed, so long as that is continued to me, not all the Dogs and Dandies betwixt here and Bond Street could drive me to utter despair; for strange as you may think it, young man, I have an affection for thee which it is not in the power of language to express."

But Jane fared little better in the emptied house. Mrs Welsh was still not reconciled to an early marriage—"unless my

Mother alters the line of conduct which she is at present pursuing with me I cannot suffer you to come here"—and in January, when Carlyle came to Edinburgh to see his publisher, they did not meet. He was cast down. "O why did you join yourself with *me*? I declare I could sometimes weep for you." He was finding his lodgings insupportable, the night noises were preventing him from sleeping, and he thought of renting a cottage near the city. He would bring two of his sisters to keep house for him. "Or would you—?—But no! You shall not: I love you, and will not make you miserable." This method of courtship had its effect: "take up house, *with Mary and Jane* . . . " exclaimed Jane. "Indeed you will do no such thing."

But could she live contentedly, or at all, "with a sick ill-natured man in poverty"? He had no sooner asked the question than his conscience smote him. He would try to help her make the best of her bad bargain. Brewster had spoken to him about the editorship of a proposed literary newspaper. He thought of it.

Jane let him off with no more than an **und**erlining—the literary newspaper "is perhaps better than *farming* after all." She was preoccupied by the question of a house. His sisters "would make but sorry housekeepers in a situation so new and strange". Then, after Carlyle had gone back to Hoddam Hill, Mrs Welsh began to relax her opposition. Where did Jane wish to live? she asked. That, said Jane, depended on Carlyle and on her—for she did not expect ever to leave her. "At this she burst into tears and exclaimed throwing her arms about my neck, 'Why have you never said as much before?' " Mrs Welsh, returning generosity for generosity, pressed Jane to take back money, houses, furniture, and marry Carlyle. She would go to Templand. Jane would not hear of it. She and Carlyle would marry when he could afford it. The two women, friendly again —"now I am actually basking in the April-sunshine of her smiles"—put their heads together. The result was a suggestion that Carlyle should rent his cottage outside Edinburgh, and she and her mother would take another nearby "so that we may all live together like one family until such time as we are married, and after." How did he like this "magnificent project"? "Should you not like to have such agreeable neighbours? We would walk together every day and you would come and take tea with us at nights. To *me* it seems as if the kingdom of Heaven were at hand."

Carlyle was discouraging. "It is impossible for two households to live as if they were one." He did not believe Mrs Welsh would ever like him, he could get no pleasure from Jane unless they were alone, and the number of parties and formal visitors would be as great in Edinburgh as in Haddington. "The moment I am master of a house, the first use I turn it to will be to slam the door of it in the face of nauseous intrusions of all sorts." He insisted: "the Country is my place in Summer."

Jane's patience began to give way. What did he want to do? where to live? One moment it was the country, then Edinburgh, then the country again. Would he prefer, after all, to marry Kitty Kirkpatrick, who had fifty thousand a year? He need not worry about her; there was always Captain Baillie, or a Doctor-cousin, or an interesting young widower with three small children—all eager to have her. "But what am I talking about?" she added "as if we were not already married—alas, married past redemption."

"We are *not* married already" he replied bluntly. If she knew any man whose wife "*all* things considered" she would rather be than his, "then *I* call upon you . . . to accept that man and leave me to my destiny." She seemed in her secret soul to think him whimsical and unstable, idle and with a diseased imagination. "I thought we were *one*, and I find that we are still *two*; that far from sympathising with me . . . in my great enterprise . . . you scarcely approve of it, you do not even seem to know with any accuracy what it is . . . Alas! Jane you do not know me: it is not the poor, unknown, rejected Thomas Carlyle that you know, but the prospective rich, known and admired."

This lecture was received by Jane with hurt dignity. She was pledged to him, and considered herself as married. "If you love me, cease, I beseech you, to make me offers of freedom; for this is an outrage which I find it not easy to forgive." He apologised. He did better; proposing that they should marry within six months. "Dare you wed a wild man of the woods and come and live with him in his cavern, in hope of better days?" Fit proposal, indeed, to a pupil of Rousseau. But Jane was rapidly becoming practical as marriage approached, and she may have been relieved to find the cavern no worse than the farmhouse of

Scotsbrig. But even Scotsbrig was a far cry from civilisation as she knew it, and from the sources of Carlyle's advancement. She agreed to marry him when he suggested, but still stood out about her mother. Mrs Welsh could scarcely be expected to live at Scotsbrig, and "I may not put my Mother away from me even for *your* sake." Why should they not all live together?

In many words, Carlyle declined.

> "*The Man should bear rule in the house and not the Woman.* This is an eternal axiom, the Law of Nature . . . which no mortal departs from unpunished. . . . I must not and I cannot live in a house of which I am not head. I should be miserable myself, and make all about me miserable. Think not, Darling, that this comes of an imperious temper; that I shall be a harsh and tyrannical husband to thee. God forbid! But it is the nature of a man that if he be controlled by anything but his own reason, he feels himself degraded; and incited, be it justly or not, to rebellion and discord. It is the nature of a woman again (for she is essentially *passive* not *active*) to cling to the man for support and direction; to comply with his humours, and feel pleasure in doing so, simply because they are his; to reverence while she loves him, to conquer him not by her force but her weakness, and perhaps (the cunning gypsy!) after all to command him by obeying him."

His plan, he repeated, was to marry her as soon as the translations were done, and to live at Scotsbrig, at least until the winter. Then, perhaps, if his health had mended, they might try for a furnished cottage in Edinburgh. He would have £200—"and many an honest couple has begun with less." He reminds Jane that the Scriptures bid a woman leave Father and Mother, and cleave unto her Husband.

This plain speaking cleared the air. Both women gave way. Jane no longer insisted that her mother should live with them; Mrs Welsh said that she would live at Templand. She wrote a postscript to the letter announcing these withdrawals.

> "My Dear Sir—Jane has read to me what she has communicated to you respecting our future *destinations:* which I trust will meet with your approval. This long perplexing emigration of ours now draws to a close. May God grant that it may draw us *all* together in the bonds of love and happiness."

In a further postscript Jane asked him "Are you happy? You must be the most ungrateful of mortals if you are not, in the near prospect of having such a Wife! Oh mein Gott *such* a Wife!" Carlyle was pleased, and sounded triumphant as well as excited when he told John Carlyle, still studying medicine at Edinburgh. "I really do believe she and I are going to be married this very summer!" He also showed some perplexity. "God knows, my good Jack, I look forward . . . to this affair with very *queer* feelings." All now seemed settled until Carlyle's parents asked who was to be mistress at Scotsbrig. He had not thought of this. Nor had he thought of the strain on his family of living up to Jane; nor of the effort called for from Jane to accept the Carlyle way of life. And his parents would not consider visits from Mrs Welsh. The plan collapsed.

Carlyle's next idea was that Mrs Welsh should go to Templand as planned, while he and Jane lived in the Haddington house. This tactless suggestion was rejected outright. He overlooked the embarrassment to Jane, who would be considered in Haddington as marrying beneath her. He did not consider the impossibility of avoiding the social life he detested; nor Jane's often professed dislike of the place; nor the position of Fyffe, living in part of the same house as his successful rival.

Jane retaliated with an offer by her mother to rent a furnished house for them in Edinburgh. Again he objected: "I have never yet recovered, the people here say, from my last three weeks residence there." He must live where he was able to sleep:

> "Will you believe it, this humble requisite is fully nine-tenths of the comfort I anticipate and have enjoyed from owning a house. In *all* other points, my taste is of the most catholic description, and my toleration absolutely boundless. But with nocturnal noises I would turn my back on the Tuileries itself."

He tried to anticipate Jane's scorn:

> "This seems remarkably ridiculous, but it is no less true than it is ridiculous; and laughing from others throws no light on it any more than mourning or execration from myself. If you meditate it well you will find this slender fact a key to many peculiarities in my conduct."

In any case, he added, a furnished house could not be found, and, if it were, he could not afford to maintain it. He still feared that Jane did not appreciate his poverty; and he made clear that he would do no uncongenial work to keep up a position in Edinburgh.

> "Have you figured yourself planted here, in the midst of splendour and scarcity, your sick Husband, whom your caresses melted into weakness but could not soothe into peace, forced to *hawk* the laborious products of

an aching head and heart for a piece of money, and become the drudge of gross thick-sided booksellers that he and his might be saved from ruin? By God's blessing, I will live in a dog-hutch, on the produce of the brook and the furrow, before this shall even threaten me."

The most sensible plan, he repeated, was to live in Haddington for the time being.

Jane replied with some sharpness. She was neither ignorant of poverty nor afraid of it. The great thing was for him to make up his mind. She would be happy enough in the country but she feared that a life of solitude would soon weary him. "Will you" she demanded "tell me plainly what on all this earth we are to do are we to be married or no: and if we are, where *are* we to take up house—in Annandale, in Edinburgh or where?"

In Haddington, answered Carlyle. He could see no good reason why he and Jane should not occupy the Doctor's house. All he wanted was a postponement of its sale for a year at least, and a loan of the house for that time. What was unreasonable about that? Visitors? He would deal with them.

Jane spared him the truth, but again refused. The stalemate was broken by Mrs Welsh who, fearful that Jane might give way and alarmed at the prospect of them in Haddington, took her to Edinburgh without a word to Carlyle and rented a house at 21 Comley Bank, a small terrace about fifteen minutes' walk north of Princes Street.

The long struggle about a home had taken them almost to midsummer, but once a house had been rented matters moved quickly. Dr Fyffe bought the Haddington house for a handsome sum, and by the beginning of August Mrs Welsh and her daughter were at Comley Bank, putting the place to rights. Much of the furniture from Haddington was used to furnish the new house; the rest was sent to Templand. Carlyle offered to help the settling-in, but Jane told him to stay where he was until she was safe in Nithsdale. She was now in a better humour, free of Haddington, and within sight of a home of her own.

"It is no love-dream from which we must wake the first year of our marriage. . . . It is now five years since we first met—five blessed years! During all that period my opinion of you has never *wavered*, but gone on deliberately rising to a higher and higher degree of regard; and . . . in the seventeen months that I have held myself your affianced Wife, I have never for a single instant doubted the wisdom of my choice. . . . Oh, without doubt, we shall be as happy as the day's long."

Carlyle, though more canny, was emphatic enough:

> "I swear it will break my heart if I make thee unhappy. And yet I am a
> perverse mortal to deal with, and the best resolutions make shipwreck in
> the sea of practice: but thou must be a *very* good Wife, and I will be a
> very good Husband."

On the last day of August the work was done, and she wrote
to him from Templand "escaped alive from horrors as of the
Bottomless Pit", and invited him there. "Mercy! to think we
have not seen each other for a whole year; and once no more than
sixteen British miles betwixt us! O glorious instance of patience
and long suffering!"

He came the next week. His translations were nearly at an
end; there seemed nothing to hinder the marriage later in the
month. He returned to Scotsbrig and worked hard to finish the
last volume; but this effort and the anxieties of the future
showed themselves in a fierce bout of dyspepsia.

> "I have been a very wicked man of late weeks . . . so splenetic, so sick,
> so sleepless, so void of hope, faith, charity; in short so altogether bad and
> worthless. I trust in Heaven I shall be better soon; a certain incident
> otherwise will wear a quite original aspect."

"For heaven's sake" replied Jane sharply "get into a more
benignant humour; or *the* incident will not only wear a very
original aspect, but likewise a very heartbreaking one."

Carlyle, recovered and repentant, apologised:

> "Believe me Jane, it is not I but the Devil speaking out of me which could
> utter one harsh word to a heart that so little deserves it. O, I were blind and
> wretched, if I could make thee unhappy! But it will not and shall not be;
> for I am not naturally a villain, and at bottom I do love you well."

They were at peace again, but Jane was conscious of disappointment in her friends and family. Mrs Welsh was resigned
but no more, Aunt Jeannie would give her namesake anything
she wanted, and Walter Welsh thought well enough of his
grand-daughter's choice except that he would smoke tobacco
and he would not drink whisky—a scale of values that seemed
to the old man close to madness. But this said, and all was said
in Carlyle's favour. Even Eliza Stodart thought Jane unwise to
marry him. "Your views of men and things 'have little sympathy with mine'" said Jane. For her, the coming marriage
was "the greenest, sunniest spot in all my being".

She was even more emphatic to a comparatively recent member of the Welsh clan, the wife of her uncle George at Boreland.

> "They would tell you, I should suppose, first and foremost, that my intended is *poor* . . . and, in the next place, most likely indulge in some criticisms scarce flattering, on his birth (the more likely if their own birth happened to be mean or doubtful) and, if they happened to be vulgar-fine people with disputed pretensions to good looks, they would to a certainty set him down as unpolished and ill-looking. But a hundred chances to one, they would not tell you he is among the cleverest men of his day; and not the cleverest only but the most enlightened! that he possesses all the qualities I deem essential in *my* Husband—a warm true heart to love me, a towering intellect to command me, and a spirit of fire to be the quickening starlight of my life. . . . Such then is this future Husband of mine—not a *great* man according to the most common sense of the word, but truly great in its natural, proper sense—a scholar, a poet, a philosopher, a wise and noble man, one who holds his patent of nobility from Almighty God, and whose high stature of manhood is not to be measured by the inch-rule of Lilliput!—Will you like him? no matter whether you do or not—since *I* like him in the deepest part of my soul."

This is well said, but it did not alter the fact that in this view of the marriage Jane stood almost alone. But she had made up her mind. If she had needed assurance beyond her own convictions, she could have obtained it from a letter Mrs Montagu had written to her rather more than a month earlier. "If Mr Carlyle is near you," wrote this lady, "tell him that a lady, and a handsome one too, declared to Mr Montagu and myself her 'firm belief that the author of the Life of Schiller might have chosen a wife, without the smallest chance of refusal, from any unengaged lady in England.' Is not this true fame?" Jane agreed that this was fame of a kind, although not so desirable as the other fame she kept steadfastly in mind for Carlyle. But Mrs Montagu's words were timely. In the more than five years since they had met, Jane first, and Carlyle of late had expressed many doubts, but she at least worried no more than convention demanded in the last few weeks: "I am resolved in spirit and even joyful." She intends to be a very meek-tempered wife. Indeed she has already begun. "My Aunt tells me she could live forever with *me* without quarrelling—I am so reasonable and equal in my humour." Even Walter Welsh had looked across the table at her when she was eating her porridge one evening, and said, "She was really a douce peaceable body that *Pen*."

So Carlyle was reassured—if he needed reassurance—and Jane coupled this with a last appeal.

> "Oh my dearest friend! be always *so* good to me and I shall make the best and happiest Wife! When I read in your looks and words that you love me—feel it in the deepest part of my soul, then I care not one straw for the universe beside; but when you fly from my caresses to—smoke tobacco, or speak of me as a new *circumstance* of your lot, then indeed my heart is 'troubled about many things' ".

Carlyle replied as expected. "I swear I will love thee with *my* whole heart, and think my life well spent if it can make thine happy."

Eight days after this letter, on October 17, 1826, they were married at Templand by Charles Anderson, the minister of Closeburn. Mrs Welsh, Aunt Jeannie, Walter Welsh and John Carlyle were the only people present. Later the same morning, Jane and her husband left by chaise for Edinburgh.

IX

COMLEY BANK
1826 – 1828

Jane Carlyle of Comley Bank was a very different person from Jane Welsh of Haddington. Her idleness and selfishness seemed to have dropped away with her maiden name. Like most women, she took tremendous pleasure and pride in the first home of her own and in the man she had married. She respected the marriage state and had a strong sense of what was due to the other partner; and she resolved to think less of herself and more of her husband.

Her resolutions were at once put to the test. The excitement of the preparations for the wedding, and the ceremony itself, quiet though it was, had proved altogether too much for Carlyle's nerves and digestion. Even more difficult was the change from single to married life. He was a solitary, and had a half-virginal, half-hypochondriacal horror, which he was never to lose, of living with other people. To Jane eventually he became accustomed, but the transitional period was long and painful, and during it he was extremely difficult to live with. But Jane took it all in her stride; was kind and meek, her thoughts only for him.

They arrived at Comley Bank late on the evening of October 17, to find that Alison Grieve, the maid Mrs Welsh had brought for them from Haddington, had lighted a large fire and laid a meal ready for them. Carlyle was "very sullen . . . sick with sleeplessness, quite nervous, bilious, splenetic and all the rest of it", but he was aware of his good fortune:

> "The house is a perfect model of a house, furnished with every accom-
> modation that heart could desire; and for my wife I may say in my heart
> that she is far better than any other wife, and loves me with a devotedness,
> which it is a mystery to me how I have ever deserved. She is gay and

happy as a lark, and looks with such soft cheerfulness into my gloomy countenance, that new hope passes over into me every time I meet her eye."

This, to his mother; to John a few days later he was more wary: "To this hour I dare not let myself out about my matrimonial views; for I am yet all in a maze, scarce knowing the right hand from the left in the path I have to walk." But he sends a message to his mother:

"I do believe I shall get *hefted* to my new situation, and then be one of the happiest men alive. . . . On the whole this wife of mine surpasses my hopes: she is so tolerant, so kind, so cheerful, so devoted to me! O that I were worthy of her!"

To John, he continues:

"Why am I not happy then? Alas, Jack, *I am billus*: I have to swallow salts and oil; the physic leaves me pensive yet quiet in heart and on the whole happy enough; but next day comes a burning stomach, and a heart full of bitterness and gloom."

At the end of the first month his feelings were unchanged.

"I have not yet learned to exist here without drugs" he tells his mother, but "my good little wife is the best of all wives: I declare I am astonished at the affection she bears me, and the patience with which she listens to my doleful forebodings and turns them all into gay hopes. In *every* thing great and little she gives me entirely my own way."

Jane added a postscript to "My dear new Mother":

"I wished to send you glad tidings of great joy; that your Son was well and happy beside me, and that we had got all the burble of this life unravelled and adjusted. But alas! Man proposeth, God disposeth, and we are still, some of us, in the Slough of Despond. Nevertheless you must not let your kind heart be troubled, for with all its drawbacks, our lot is far from unhappy. We love each other, have done ill to no one, and one of us at least is full of hope."

Carlyle's biliousness was the effect of the demands being made upon him, of time, tenderness, understanding, intimacy, that he found the utmost difficulty in fulfilling; his need was as much for a companion as for a wife—an admiring, unquestioning companion on whose bosom he could rest when tired, sick and dispirited. Also, he had no work to do: and, though not worried immediately by lack of money, he was no man for idleness. Still, he was content enough in his reluctant, guarded way, although some entries in his journal show him strangely preoccupied by thoughts of life as a continual nightmare, of an awakening in hell, of a wife who bore devils.

Jane was happy without conditions. She had her own house, her own man, she had made her bed and was determined to lie comfortably on it if at all possible.

> "We are really very happy; and when he falls upon some work we shall be still happier. Indeed I should be very stupid or very thankless, if I did not congratulate myself every hour of the day, on the lot which it has pleased Providence to assign me: my Husband is so kind! so, in all respects, after my own heart! I was sick one day, and he nursed me as well as my own Mother could have done, and he never says a hard word to me—unless I richly deserve it. We see great numbers of people here, but are always most content alone. My Husband reads then, and I read or work, or just sit and look at him, which I really find as profitable an employment as any other."

In a Christmas letter Carlyle tells Mrs Montagu, "I am wedded to the best of wives, and with all the elements of enjoyment richly ministered to me, and health—rather worse than ever it was wont to be. Sad contradiction!" Still, "in spite of ill-health, I reckon myself moderately happy here, much happier than men usually are, or than such a fool as I deserves to be."

The calls of visitors—a sore point with Carlyle—were finally regulated by the institution of a Wednesday evening at home at which Jane or her maid dispensed tea, coffee and refreshments. These Wednesday evenings became well known to the Edinburgh *literati*, and were soon considered one of the events of the week. Carlyle's talk was worth going miles to hear; a great impassioned stream of words, challenging most of the accepted figures and doctrines of the day in exaggerated but memorable language. Jane, when given the chance, could be pithy and satirical as well as listen irresistibly; she was fast learning the art of the literary hostess, and found favour with Carlyle's friends and acquaintances.

Of these visitors the most important by far to the future of the Carlyles was Francis Jeffrey, editor of the *Edinburgh Review*. Carlyle met Jeffrey at a critical moment. In January 1827, he had begun to write, ostensibly with Jane's help, the "didactic novel" that they had talked about so often years earlier. In fact, Jane's part in it was no more than advisory, and that only for a

JOHN STERLING

from an engraving pasted on the screen at 5 Cheyne Row

EDWARD IRVING

from a painting about 1826

FRANCIS JEFFREY

from a painting by Colvin Smith

short time. She was no writer of books—her talent lay elsewhere —and she knew it well. Carlyle, too, soon abandoned all efforts to develop her as a writer. The writing of this book, *Wotton Reinfred*, did little more than improve his temper by keeping him . active; he was not ready for it, but, fortunately for himself and those about him, before he fully realised this he had met Jeffrey. *German Romance*, published at last in January, was read and admired by Procter. He sent Carlyle a letter of introduction to Jeffrey, who was crying out for "some clever young man who would write for us."

In his University days, Carlyle had admired Jeffrey in the Courts, one of the best advocates of his time; "a delicate, attractive, dainty little figure . . . perhaps hardly five feet in height." Later, when first urged by Irving to write, he left an article at Jeffrey's house, but without success. Now, one evening in February, Jeffrey read Procter's letter and offered "to give him a lift". He saw that his visitor was clever, sincere, original, and might be useful for the *Review*; and his own manner was so free and easy that the prickly young man was charmed into appreciation. Carlyle's independence remained, and he insisted that Jeffrey should read his *German Romance* to satisfy himself that a commission was deserved, and was no charity.

At this time his book still promised well; but, though it stiffened his pride outside his home, it made him more approachable within it, as Jane in her own way tells his mother.

> "The new book is going on at a regular rate, and I would fain persuade myself that *his* health and spirits are at the same regular rate improving: more contented he certainly is since he applied himself to this task; for he was not born to be any thing but miserable in idleness."

Their lot was pleasant, she said, many pleasant people came to see them, and "*alone* we never weary." They had plenty of books. "There is a Piano too, for '*soothing the savage breast*' when one cares for its charms, but I am sorry to observe neither my playing nor singing seem to give Mr Carlyle much delight." With an excess of modesty she adds,

> "It is my Husband's worst fault to me that I will not, or rather *cannot* speak; often when he has talked for an hour without answer, he will beg for some sign of life on my part; and the only sign I can give is a little kiss. Well! that is better than nothing—don't you think?"

A few weeks after the meeting with Jeffrey, Mrs Welsh came up from Templand. She told them that the tenant at Craigenputtock was neglecting the farm and was not paying his rent. This news coincided with a suggestion to Carlyle from a London publisher that he should translate Goethe's autobiography; and with a renewal of his stomach trouble—caused mainly by the presence of Mrs Welsh in the house. He had not forgotten his Craigenputtock proposal three years earlier. He now made it again. His plan was that he and Jane should move there, that Alick, who was still unsettled, should farm the place, and that John, now a fully-fledged doctor, should take a practice in Dumfries. All the members of both families would once more be close together, he would regain his health in the country, and the money from his new book would keep him and Jane in comfort for some time.

Mrs Welsh received the suggestion enthusiastically. She could not bear to think of Craigenputtock falling again into the state from which her husband had rescued it; nor did she wish to lose the rent. But the attraction of having Jane near her was the deciding factor.

These reasons weighed with Jane too, and perhaps even more strongly, for her father remained her idol. Her conscience troubled her for leaving her mother, whom he might be said to have left in her charge; and the six months' separation since her marriage soon brought back all her natural affection. So she also supported the plan, but unselfishly, for she was well content with her life and home in Edinburgh. London would have been even more satisfactory, but Edinburgh was at least alive, she met and talked with interesting people, dispensed hospitality, was in her small way tasting the joys of reigning over a circle, and a growing circle, of intellectuals and oddities, for both of whom she had a fancy. It was difficult not to think of Craigenputtock as a backward step, but she was newly-wed, the habit of obedience was still strong in her, and Carlyle said they could not afford to live in Edinburgh much longer. She had decided she would be guided entirely by him in financial matters—a decision from which she never swerved. "She is a *true* wife," he told Alick, "and would murmur at no scene or fortune which she shared along with me."

His excited letters showed plainly how great a part the

reunion with his family had played in his plan. He longed now, as he was to long again and again, to be back where, to his father's obvious pride, he defeated all opponents in argument; where his brothers and sisters looked up to him as to a great man; and where his mother frankly worshipped him. In the midst of his family he had the unqualified assurance of potential greatness, he was uncritically received, his foibles too familiar to attract attention; he was free to come and go, to be silent, talkative, cheerful, irritable just as he felt inclined; he was at ease. With his family he had always the triumphant sense (perhaps the most satisfying in the world) of the difficult child who has made good. Jane, dutiful though she was trying to be, could not yet offer him what his family offered. She had faith in him, but not endless patience; her mind was sharper and clearer than his, and her tongue could wound.

So it was settled; and Carlyle set off in April to visit Craigen-puttock with Alick. He found the land neglected, but had less trouble than he expected in ending the tenant's lease. He was back at Comley Bank early in the next month, after settling that Alick and his sister Mary should take over the Craigenputtock farm at Whitsun. No date had been fixed for his own removal. From Jane's letter—a deeply affectionate letter—to him while he was away, it seems clear that the move, as far as she was concerned, was still in the air; but in his reply Carlyle writes lyrically.

> "O Jeannie! How happy shall we be in this Craig o' Putto! . . . my little wife will be there forever beside me, and I shall be well and blessed, and the latter end of that man will be better than the beginning. Surely I shall learn at length to prize the pearl of great price which God has given to me unworthy; surely I already know that to me the richest treasure of this sublunary life has been warded, the heart of my own noble Jane! Shame on me for complaining, sick and wretched though I be!"

Thanking Mrs Welsh for her help, he declared "It shall go *very* hard with me, if you have ever reason to repent of what you did."

Perhaps these resolutions were not to take effect until the move was made; for by the next month he was speaking caustically of Mrs Welsh, and had not a great deal to say for himself: "I fight with dulness and bile in the forenoons as of old; I still walk forth diligently; talk *de omnia scribili*, when I can find

fit or unfit audience." Only Jane was "as well and good as
ever" which meant, patient with him. The truth was, his plans
were going astray. The translation of Goethe had fallen
through; *Wotton Reinfred* was at a standstill, about to be abandoned, and plainly no money maker; John was talking of going
to Munich to study medicine there; and Alick, of getting
married. Carlyle would need more money than he had reckoned
on—for John was now firmly set in the habit of looking to him
to pay the cost of his studies, Alick's marriage would mean
structural alterations at Craigenputtock, and the two expected
sources of money had collapsed. Mrs Welsh offered to pay for
additions to Craigenputtock, but this still left Carlyle with
John, himself and Jane to support. He had to pocket his pride,
and ask Jeffrey for work. Jeffrey commissioned an article on
Richter for the *Edinburgh Review*. It was soon done, was printed
in the July number, and earned Carlyle twenty guineas.

At the end of June he and Jane spent a day in Haddington
with the Welshes' lawyer, Alexander Donaldson, to discuss how
to raise money to pay for the Craigenputtock improvements;
and on the first day of July they went off to Templand and
Scotsbrig for the summer. From there they visited Craigenputtock, where Alick was trying to get the farm into some sort
of order. Alick presented a problem to Jane, difficult to deal
with tactfully. He was, unlike Carlyle and John, without culture
or any pretence of refinement; and Carlyle put the matter
gently indeed when he said "the difficulty of settling Alick's
manner of existing in the house had not a little perplexed her."
They decided that Alick must have a room or rooms of his own;
and that the house itself—a single-storeyed building—needed
another storey if they were to be at all comfortable in it. Carlyle
gave the work to his uncle John, who still kept on the family
trade of mason.

The last part of Jane's stay at Templand was darkened by her
discovery that her beloved Aunt Jeannie—"the helpfullest and
most gentle-hearted creature that ever God made"—was ill.
After a struggle, she made her aunt confess that she had suffered
from a tumour for the past twelve years, but had said nothing of
it for fear of worrying her father and sister. Dr Russell from
Thornhill decided she must be operated on; and soon after
Carlyle and Jane had returned to Edinburgh, they took a

furnished house a few doors away for Mrs Welsh and her sister. That autumn, Aunt Jeannie had the operation—a successful one, the doctors claimed.

When the Carlyles came back to Comley Bank, Jeffrey at once called on them, and if he had had any doubts about employing Carlyle, they no longer existed after he met Jane. He and she soon discovered, in the Scottish manner, a dim but definite cousinship between the Jeffreys and the Baillies; but it may be suspected that on Jeffrey's part at least this was merely an excuse for intimacy. Women of Jane's intelligence, charm and sense of humour were rare in Edinburgh, and Jeffrey "became, in a sort, her would-be openly declared friend and quasi-lover; as was his way in such cases." Carlyle explains:

> "He had much the habit of flirting about with women, especially pretty women, much more the both pretty and clever; all in a weakish, mostly dramatic, and wholly theoretic way (his age now fifty gone); would daintily kiss their hands in bidding good morning, offer his due *homage*, as he phrased it; trip about, half like a lap-dog, half like a human adorer, with speeches pretty and witty, always of trifling import. . . . My little woman perfectly understood all that sort of thing, the methods and the rules of it; and could lead her clever little gentleman a very pretty minuet, as far as she saw good."

Jane took a less restricted view of these activities—a little civilised flirtation came pleasantly after the bleak rigours of Carlyle's devotion. She grew fond of the man with

> "the little short grey head and round brow, the arching of his eyebrows, the settling of his chin into his neckcloth, the jerking movements, the neither Scotch nor English speech."

From this time the Carlyles saw a good deal of Jeffrey—at Comley Bank, at his fine new house in Moray Place, and at Craigcrook, his lovely estate outside Edinburgh—and would doubtless have seen more had not Jane and Mrs Jeffrey, understandably, been something less than friendly. This was Carlyle's first substantial acquaintance, on terms of equality, with a man of intellect, refinement, and influence in the world of letters; their arguments sharpened his still cloudy mind, and their intimacy gave an indispensable fillip to his self esteem. They disagreed, but Jeffrey commissioned more articles, provided that Carlyle "did not treat the whole earth not yet Germanized as a 'parcel of blockheads' "; and this brought requests for work from other journals. The first two articles caused something of a stir in the city; Carlyle was denounced on more than one side as leader of "the Mystic school"—an attack which did him nothing but good, since his main need at the time was to become known.

Jane, to whom all this activity, friendship and publicity was so much nectar, made great fun of this, and for a long time afterwards, with the penchant for *coterie* speech which was to become so marked in her, she was for ever joking about the Mystic school which she declared consisted of a single individual, Carlyle, or at most two, including herself as pupil. Jeffrey entered into the fun, insisting that Jane was "the Master Mystic". Anyone further removed from the mystical than Jane would be hard to find, but she accepted the compliment gaily. Carlyle considered that the cap fitted, and was by no means averse to wearing it. He had nothing but praise for Jeffrey, thanked Procter for giving him "one of the kindest and most pleasant friends", and told John that Jeffrey was "by much the most lovable of all the literary men I have seen."

To Jane, the notice that Carlyle was attracting profoundly affected the Craigenputtock plan. Was it not absurd to hide themselves in a desert when he was just beginning to make a name? She was determined on London, sooner or later, as the one place where he was likely to be appreciated fully; and she was strongly supported by all their friends, and in particular by Jeffrey. Carlyle began to waver. He had heard more rumours of a professorship at the newly formed University in London. Jane, anxious to stir him to some definite attempt for the post, asked Aunt Jeannie, whom he liked without reservation, to put in her word. She did so from her sick bed at Comley Bank. He wrote a diplomatic note to Crabb Robinson and asked Jeffrey to intercede personally with Brougham, the power behind the University appointments. Jeffrey agreed, though he expressed doubts

> "whether the patrons of the new University either *will* or *ought* to appoint such a person to such a charge. . . . As a man of virtue, temper, genius and learning, I shall most readily and warmly recommend you—but I know you would not wish me to disguise those singularities of opinion on which (though I think erroneously) I believe you most value yourself."

Despite these discouraging words, Jeffrey made great efforts to secure Carlyle's appointment. Charles Buller, just beginning to make a name for himself, was brought into the struggle, and even Brougham's friend James Mill took a hand. In his application, Carlyle told Procter, he had said:

> "I have a message to my fellow men on this very subject of Moral Philosophy; can I be allowed to deliver it from your pulpit? . . . there seemed to be a *Truth* in me, which there or elsewhere I must and would deliver. 'Elsewhere' Mr Brougham seemed to think would be better."

There was, in fact, no possibility that he would be accepted. The Benthamites, he said, did not love him and would not give him a hearing; but this was scarcely a matter for wonder, since he lost no opportunity of criticising them.

Before a decision was reached, the year was far gone and the Carlyles were still in Edinburgh. Whatever he might think of some of his visitors and she might say of them, they both—and Jane particularly—gained pleasure and a sense of importance from the people that came about them, hung on his words or talked spiritedly under the light of her dark eyes. Many came to hear Carlyle, and returned to see his wife. Such was De Quincey.

> "A bright, ready, and melodious talker, but in the end an inconclusive and long-winded. One of the smallest man figures I ever saw; shaped like a pair of tongs, and hardly above five feet in all. When he sate, you would have taken him, by candlelight, for the beautifullest little child; blue-eyed, sparkling face, had there not been a something, too, which said '*Eccovi*—this child has been in hell.' "

Jane, too, pitied him, and thought more of his conversation than Carlyle did. "What wouldn't one give to have him in a box, and take him out to talk!" she said. That winter, she heard that he was ill alone in his lodgings, had him brought to Comley Bank and nursed him back to health. Ever after this, De Quincey could not say enough of the "most angelic woman I ever met upon this God's earth"—a pardonable exaggeration.

Irving came to see them in May 1828, when the Church Assembly was being held. No church in Edinburgh would hold the people who wished to hear him. "The town" said Henry Inglis, one of the first of Carlyle's disciples "was quite divided about him, one party thinking that he was quite mad, another that he was an entire humbug." But whatever people might think, all were curious to hear him; and the church was packed to the doors by six o'clock every morning. His followers arranged a great dinner in his honour; and it was on the day of this dinner that he called at Comley Bank. He greeted them with his now customary salutation "The Lord bless you"; and for all Jane's efforts his conversation remained stilted, self-conscious, and full of religious mannerisms. He stayed only half an hour, and on rising to go he asked to pray with them, despite their obvious embarrassment. The praying done: "Farewell. I must go, then—and suffer persecution, as my fathers have done!" He strode off to his dinner, leaving Jane annoyed and Carlyle depressed. "I do not think he will go altogether mad," said Carlyle, "yet what else he will do I cannot so well conjecture."

A few months earlier, another university post—the chair of Moral Philosophy at St Andrew's—fell vacant. Carlyle decided to apply, and to his astonishment was strongly supported—by his old professor Leslie Brewster; John Wilson; Procter; Buller; Edward Irving—"*five* heroical pages on my merits"; Jeffrey—"The dear little 'Duke' (Jane says, she could *kiss* him) has written me a paper, which might of itself bring me any Professorship in the Island"; and even by Goethe. Well might Carlyle say "I am recommended and witnessed for as few men can be". The post, like the London appointment, hung in the wind for months, and then was given to another man; but the incident had shown in what esteem Carlyle was held in and outside Edinburgh.

The outcry against the proposed move to Craigenputtock was redoubled. "Do not run away to Dumfriesshire," urged Jeffrey,

" . . . You can be as quiet here as there, when the reading or the studious fit is on you, and you surely may divert yourself as well, and certainly give more pleasure, when you condescend to be social."

And again:

"I think it has been your misfortune not to have mixed sufficiently with intelligent men of various opinions, and open and intrepid minds. . . . Think better of this scheme . . . and ask Jane if she does not in her heart think my plan a wiser and safer one than yours."

Jane kept her views to herself, although there was no doubt what they were, even had she not later made her feelings clear. Carlyle was undecided, doubtful of the wisdom of moving. His plans were ever changing. He even talked of taking Jane to Germany "for the study of music and painting" and to sit at the feet of Goethe at Weimar—stirred by John's enthusiastic letters from Munich, and by the correspondence with Goethe.

"How we are to be disposed of for next year is still as uncertain as ever," he writes to John towards the end of March.

"The plasterers have not done at Craigenputtock . . . and the road is lying as we left it. For this year there will be many drawbacks at the Craig, and only one furtherance, the cheapness of living. Heaven direct us how to do!"

A few days later, the whole matter was thrust aside by a message from Templand. The operation on Aunt Jeannie had proved a failure, and she was unlikely to live much longer. Jane at once left for Templand; and Carlyle took the opportunity of looking again at Craigenputtock, while Jane stayed on to help her mother to nurse the dying woman—one of the few people whom she loved with complete unselfishness, and about whom she never wrote an unkind word. Soon after she arrived, her mother collapsed, worn out with nursing, and she had two sick people to attend to. Her Uncle John came down from Liverpool; but although she was glad of his kind commonsense, he too had to be provided for, as well as her silently grieving old grandfather. The time of strain was short; Aunt Jeannie died at the beginning of April. Carlyle came over from Scotsbrig for the funeral; and he, with Dr Russell, John Welsh and his two sons, Walter and Alick, attended the funeral at the Welsh burying place in the small churchyard of Crawford.

The unfinished state of the alterations at Craigenputtock had given Carlyle a considerable shock; he had "many doubts and misgivings about removing thither for the present", and had all but decided to take on the Comley Bank house for another year. But he had done nothing about renewing the lease before the sudden rush to Templand, and by the time that he and Jane were able to get home later in the month, they found that the house had been let over their heads; "so that" Carlyle argued, "no rational alternative remains for us." He did not convince any of his friends that such a move was necessary, since Edinburgh possessed plenty of small houses to let, and the removal to one of them would have caused less trouble and expense than

the cumbersome move to Craigenputtock. However, he was
something of a fatalist; and the letting of the house appeared as
a sign. John might take that practice in Dumfries after all, he
persuaded himself, "and then, as we contemplated, we are all
in sight of one another! So it has been ordered, and surely it
is best so."

He made no pretence that the move was for the benefit of
anyone but himself and his family. Silence, peace, economy—
that was what he sought at Craigenputtock; where also

> "I may find more health, and what I reckon weightier, more scope to
> improve and worthily employ myself, which either here or there I reckon
> to be the great end of existence, and the only happiness one has any right
> to look for or even to wish."

He no doubt hoped that Jane's headaches and the digestive
troubles which had begun to afflict her too would disappear,
and that she also would be the better, physically, for the move.
But he was aware of all that she was giving up.

> "Her modest days in Edinburgh" he said, "which never demanded
> much to make them happy, were beginning to have many little joys and
> amusements of their own in that bright scene, and she would have to
> change it for one of the loneliest, mooriest, and dullest in nature. To her
> it was a great sacrifice, if to me it was the reverse; but at no moment,
> even by a look, did she ever say so. Indeed I think she never felt so at all.
> She would have gone to Nova Zembla with me, and found *it* the right
> place had benefit to me or set purpose of mine lain there."

Jane, it seems, did not complain; but Jeffrey was not so
obliging. He never minced his words, and he did not do so now.
When, towards the end of May, having seen off their six cartloads of furniture to Craigenputtock, the Carlyles stayed their
last two days in Edinburgh with Jeffrey at Moray Place, he told
Carlyle exactly what he thought; that it was stupid of him to
bury himself in a desert, and unkind to sentence Jane to such a
fate. Carlyle brushed it all aside; his arguments "availed
nothing . . . the step had been well meditated, saw itself to be
founded on irrefragable considerations, of health, *finance*, &c,
&c, unknown to bystanders; and could not be forborne or
altered."

"I will come and see you at any rate," said Jeffrey; and on
that understanding the Carlyles set out for Craigenputtock.

X

CRAIGENPUTTOCK
1828 – 1831

Jane could have had few pleasant thoughts when they began the long climb up to Craigenputtock from the nearest town, Dumfries, sixteen miles away. Much of this journey, up Glenesslin, is picturesquely wooded, with farms and cottages within hail of the road. But when the trees fall away and the river dwindles to a marshy stream, the eye of faith is needed to avert depression. The moors swell out on all sides, they fill the horizon, stony and shapeless. Houses have long since been left behind, there is no sign of man, or of life, except for birds high in the vast sky, and an occasional sheep feeding. When the watershed is reached, the moors expose the distant hills of Galloway; but this relief is snatched away as the cart track turns aside to Craigenputtock; from the slight hollow in which the house stands nothing is to be seen but the surrounding trees, stripped and beaten by the gales, and, beyond them, mile upon mile of bleak solitude.

Well might Jane remember on her journey that, of the three wives who had preceded her at Craigenputtock, two had gone mad, and the third had taken to drink. There had been something more than laughter in her mind when she said of young Jean Carlyle, sent there a few months earlier to keep house for Alick, "I hope they took her garters from her, and everything in the shape of hemp or steel". She would not live at Craigenputtock with an Angel, she had said; now she was to live there with Thomas Carlyle. She was a month or two short of twenty-seven. The best years of her life were immediately before her. She had just tasted the pleasures of building up and presiding over a small but lively intellectual circle. She was married to a man who had dominated this circle as she believed he would

125

dominate all. Now their circle had dwindled to Alick and a maid, Carlyle seemed further than ever from the future she had dreamed for him, and she had to face the scorn of all who had predicted that by marrying beneath her she would herself degenerate. When she reached Craigenputtock her gloomiest forebodings seemed inadequate; the place was in chaos, the plaster still wet, the painters and carpenters still at work, the fireplaces not yet in, the chimneys filling the house with smoke, and every room reeking with damp. But this "bewildering *heap*", as Carlyle called it, was for the time Jane's salvation. Although her mother had not allowed her to do housework, she was a practical woman, and accepted the disorder as a challenge. Craigenputtock was her father's birthplace and her ancestral home, left to her as a trust. They were not yet pinched for want of money, and she and Carlyle rode often down to the shops at Dumfries. This activity, which went on for months, with the workmen still in the house, gave the illusion of Craigenputtock as a populous place—an illusion fostered by the time of year when the country was at its nearest approach to geniality, and communications were free.

Of the two, Carlyle was the less reconciled to the move. He could settle to nothing, feared that he would never be well, and (applying the philosophy he had taken over from his father) began to praise sickness as a form of discipline. Jane, busier than ever in her life, and gradually restoring order, was in good health and spirits, and "in love with *us both*" as Carlyle tactfully told Mrs Montagu. Before going down to her mother at Templand for a day or two, while the good weather lasted, she set out her sensible philosophy in a letter to Eliza:

> "The solitude is not so irksome as one might think—if we are cut off from good society, we are also delivered from bad; the roads are less pleasant to walk on than the pavement of Princes Street but we have horses to ride; and instead of shopping and making calls, I have bread to bake and chickens to hatch. I read, and work, and talk with my Husband and never weary."

She had leaped her first hurdle with surprising ease. She was not only busy, but thinking of others instead of herself—a state which at least helps to withstand regrets—anxious to make the house quiet and orderly so that Carlyle could do himself justice in his work, and showing some thought for her mother whose life at Templand, where Walter Welsh was ageing quickly, had become difficult. She had an excellent companion and helper in Grace Macdonald, whom she had brought with her from Edinburgh, and whose only fault as far as she could see (and she had exceptionally sharp eyes) was the assumption at times of "second table" airs. She might have been almost completely happy at this time, had it not been for Alick. He was a small round-faced man of rough and ready manners and inclined to moroseness. He lived in a small room behind the drawingroom; but such conditions—a door connected his room with the drawingroom—invited embarrassment, and she pressed Carlyle to build his brother a cottage. Carlyle laughed indulgently at Alick's roughness but agreed. The cottage was built immediately behind the house; and by November Alick and his sister Mary were established in it. Family union was preserved by the meeting of all four in the diningroom for tea every Sunday. The workmen had all gone, and Jane at last had the house—and Carlyle—to herself: Alick's room was turned into a comfortable study, and up the narrow stairs, driven through the thick stone wall of the original single-storeyed house, were the two new front bedrooms linked by a dressingroom, and, over the study, a small guest room—favoured with Craigenputtock's only open view. Downstairs again, leading from the small hall, was a passage (off which were a bedroom for Grace, and a storeroom) leading to the big stoneflagged kitchen, the pleasantest room in the house, looking into the yard. The view from all the front rooms was as depressing as could be—a steep green slope cut off much light and all outlook—but Jane did her best to enliven a hopeless prospect by planting roses in front of the house and on the new porch, and shrubberies and strawberry beds on the slope.

    Carlyle was worried about the drain on his money. Craigenputtock had cost him more than he had anticipated—in helping Alick to set up the farm, and in building the cottage—and John, after his year in Munich, had now "found that he could neither have peace in his lifetime, nor sleep quiet in his grave, had he missed studying six months in Vienna." Carlyle and Jane appealed to him mildly: "Gird up thy loins, man!" wrote Jane in the flush of victory over her first Craigenputtock suet dumpling (a special favourite of John's) "and come home to us! and another dumpling shall not be wanting—a dumpling as big as the moon to celebrate the wanderer's return. God bless thee Jack—and cure this rage for travelling, which is the only thing which prevents your being 'an ornament to society in every direction'."

But John stayed on, and Carlyle paid up again after a slight moan: "O Jack! thou art beside thyself; much learning doth make thee mad." The savings on which he had reckoned to live for a year or two at Craigenputtock were almost exhausted soon after he had settled in, and he set grimly to work to replace them.

He wrote articles with difficulty—"none can say how bilious I am and am like to be"—he became more and more particular about his food (the bread from Dumfries soured on his stomach, he complained) and he spent almost all his day alone in the study, which he had christened the Devil's Den. After breakfast, he wrote until the late dinner. Between dinner and tea, he and Jane read a chapter of *Don Quixote*—they were learning Spanish, as at Edinburgh they had learned Italian. After tea, he went back to his study, and ended the day by smoking a final pipe in the new cottage with Alick and Mary. So passed each day. If he could not write, he read, walked in the woods with an axe or climbed the hill that sloped up almost from their windows—the Craig, about which he would often see hovering the puttocks (hawks) that gave the house its name. He was not to be disturbed—that was understood. Jane had to make the most of the break for Cervantes. But she was busy herself, she had a piano, and a pony for the thirty-mile ride to Dumfries and back, and the slightly shorter journey to Templand. She was still young enough to treat Craigenputtock as an adventure. And when she felt bored or neglected she could always write a letter. Her art was still in embryo, but little touches in even the most purposeless letters indicated what pleasure she was to give herself and her correspondents in later years. She now tells Eliza

"Could you but see how it stands with me just at present, you would not be too much elated by this favour. For I am sitting here companionless 'like owl in desert'; with nothing pressing to do, having learnt my daily task of Spanish, and also finished a shirt—let me speak truth—a nightshirt I was making for my Husband; and it is come into my head as a resource from ennui that I should write somebody a letter: and thus, Dear, all you have to be proud of is, that my choice of an object has fallen on *you*. I tell you this out of my natural love of plain dealing. You would know what I am doing in these moors? Well! I am feeding poultry (at long intervals, and merely for form's sake), and I am galloping over the country on a bay horse, and baking bread, and improving my mind, and eating, and sleeping, and making, and mending, and in short, wringing whatever good I can, from the ungrateful soil of the world. On the whole, I was never more contented in my life: one enjoys such freedom and quietude here; nor have we purchased this at the expense of other accommodations; for we have a good house to live in, with all the necessaries of life, and even some touch of the superfluities."

In the late summer and autumn, she had many visitors, eager to see how the Carlyles were settling in—and for other reasons. Her uncle Robert came down from Edinburgh with his sister Anne, to see what hopes there were of grouse shooting. Her uncle George and his wife drove up from Boreland. Henry Inglis stayed two or three days, to sit at the feet of his master, but found himself some of the time holding a hank of wool for his hostess to wind, tying up her ramblers in the front garden, watching her sewing and baking, and much of the rest telling her all his hopes and fears for the future. As a final honour, he christened Jane's pony Harry, breaking one of Carlyle's cigars over his nose.

Mrs Welsh came over occasionally, but would not stay the night. Jean Carlyle shuttled proudly back and forth from Scotsbrig while the weather held, and James Carlyle, now grown old and subdued, stayed for a week. He spent most of the day with Alick, but he was tremulously proud of Thomas, and perhaps even more of Jane, who made him, like the rest of the Scotsbrig people, so much at home.

The most welcome visitor was Jeffrey, who came as promised with his wife, child, and maid, to see how his protégés were faring in the wilds. The party arrived in the first week of October, and had to fight their way across the moors in the teeth of a gale. The track to Craigenputtock was a river of mud, and Jeffrey, obliged to open one gate after another to let the carriage through, was in a sorry state when he arrived. The drive up to the front door, and the new porch of which Carlyle was particularly proud, were not yet finished, and the Jeffreys had to follow the track, as it is again today, into the farmyard at the back, where, having no coach house, the Carlyles covered the coach with a glazed sheet. To dash at a task and do it well was Jane's particular forte. She now had a chance to show her gifts as frugal housewife and as hostess before the admiring

Jeffrey and his critical American wife; and, the short stay not taxing her patience, she triumphed in both capacities. Fires blazed in every room, the solid furniture from Haddington was polished till it shone, the house was scoured from top to bottom, the table was daintily laid, the food was varied and tempting. Carlyle was struck with amazement and pride at her "consummate art", and Jeffrey was surprised, and not a little shocked, to find that some cooking he had praised was her own.

Jeffrey was in great form, quizzing his daughter "Sharlie", dazzling an unexpected guest with his fun, mimicry, and nimbleness of mind, and outstaying even the tongue of Carlyle. "And how on earth did Mr Jeffrey get himself amused at Craigenputtock?" says Jane. "Why, in the simplest manner: he talked—talked from morning till night, nay till morning again —I never assisted at such a talking since I came into the world; either in respect of quantity or quality." One evening he began to mimic public speakers: "The little man strutted about, full of electric fire, with attitudes, with gesticulations, still more with winged words, oftener *broken*-winged, amid our admiring laughter." One night he lost his temper with Carlyle for some particularly "monstrous exaggeration"; but for this he apologised later, as also for dragging Jane out for "rough walks".

When the Jeffreys left for Edinburgh three days later, Carlyle, closing the door of their carriage, said that it "carried off our little temporary paradise". At this Jeffrey, not surprisingly, gave a sniff, and the carriage "rolled prosperously away."

Jeffrey was as shrewd as he was witty, and from Edinburgh he wrote:

> "I cannot bring myself to think that either you or Mrs Carlyle are naturally placed at Craigenputtock. . . . Take care of the fair creature who has trusted herself so entirely to you. . . . think seriously of taking shelter in Moray Place for a month or two, and in the meantime be gay and playful and foolish with her, at least as often as you require her to be wise and heroic with you. . . . You have no *mission* upon earth, whatever you may fancy, half so important as to be innocently happy, and all that is good for you of poetic feeling and sympathy with majestic nature, will come of its own accord, without your straining after it."

To this sane advice Carlyle turned a deaf ear, as he did also to Jeffrey's further complaint that

> "you mystics will not be contented with kindness of heart and reasonable

notions in anybody—but you must have gifts and tasks and duties—and relations with the universe, and strugglings to utter forth the truth—God help you and your vain-glorious jargon."

He told his brother that Jeffrey "chatters unprofitably about *Mysticism* and so forth." He added, "I am very much alone in this world".

By the middle of November, the last visitor had gone. The one event of the week, and the one link with civilisation, was the visit of the carrier who, when the track was not impassable, called on Wednesdays. "You cannot figure the stillness of these moors in a November drizzle" Carlyle told John, but "I sit here in my little library, and laugh at the howling tempests"; and "the Goodwife too is happy, and contented with me, and her solitude, which I believe is not to be equalled out of Sahara itself". He was right; she was contented; more so than he. She did not complain of his absence day after day in his study—he must work and work hard, she knew—and she was grateful for the hours he did give her. The solitude was too new to affect her nerves; the sense of adventure was still strong; and there was a prospect of Edinburgh later on: the Jeffreys had pressed for a visit, and Carlyle had agreed, if he finished three commissioned articles in time.

He did not finish them in time, but "sat for many weeks at my desk, writing duller and duller *Articles*" until he became bilious and could write nothing. "I shall never be well", he cried, "while I inhabit this carcass". The Edinburgh journey was postponed until Spring, and there were frayed tempers in the house. All are quite well here, Jane told Jean at Scotsbrig, "but exceedingly cold and illnatured . . . I hear you are very diligent and very good. I on the other hand am very idle and bad. I have done no one useful thing for a week except making *thee* two *daidlies*." She ends a chatty letter by sending a kiss to old James Carlyle—"if any of you dare give it him."

There was a moment of excitement in the quiet house a few days before Christmas. Jane asks Eliza to get her "a brown earthenware coffee-pot, such as they sell in china shops for three and sixpence or four shillings" and explains:

"some mornings ago there came a letter to Grace Macdonald from some absent lover with '*hast*' on the outside, and Heaven knows what within— but things of moment, evidently, from the consequences—as she all at once bolted up from her peaceful occupation of toasting bread for breakfast, and dashed the poor old coffee-pot with its precious contents on the kitchen floor."

Soon afterwards, just before the end of the year, Jane rode off to Templand where her cheerfulness was so welcome that she could not get away until after the New Year, 1829, without offending Mrs Welsh deeply. She told Carlyle why she was delayed, in a loving letter beginning "Goody, Goody, dear Goody"—her pet name for him—"you said you would weary; and I do hope in my heart you are wearying." No doubt he was, for she was audience, companion, cook, confidante, cheerer and comforter all in one; but though he welcomed her back, he was busy, for Craigenputtock had "a wide throat for money". An article on Burns was finished and cut by Jeffrey after much protesting. Carlyle had written another on Novalis, and was now at work on an essay on Voltaire. He was also to write on *The Signs of the Times*. The trip to Edinburgh was again postponed; he had too much to do, and money was too badly needed. John was still an expense; he had moved nearer home, to Paris, from Vienna, but he was strongly resisting Carlyle's hints of a practice at Dumfries; nothing less than London would content him. So Carlyle wrote on, and Jane cooked and sewed and read and wrote her letters and rode about on Harry whenever she could. For three months Carlyle—surveying all comings and goings from his study window—saw no one, not even a beggar; and the household had to make the best they could of one another.

Not until June was there a break in the long seclusion. John, home at last, was at Craigenputtock for a week or two when news came that Irving was to walk through Dumfriesshire on his way to Glasgow and the Assembly in Edinburgh. He intended to preach his way through Scotland, proclaiming the true faith: "I will do it though they should carry me bound hand and foot to prison." But his martyrdom was not yet; his progress across the county was one long triumph. He preached throughout in the open. At Annan, where he began, thirteen thousand gathered to hear him—several times the population of the little town. At Dumfries, an even greater number was massed, but, he said, "my voice easily reached over them all." He preached for three hours. Later that day—

Sunday—he preached for four hours to a crowd of six thousand. The next day he rode up to the Manse at Dunscore, the parish church of Craigenputtock, to meet neighbouring ministers at dinner. The Carlyles, though they had attended church once only since their arrival more than a year past, received a special invitation. After the dinner Irving rode back with them and stayed two days. Much of the old, unspoilt, attractive Irving reappeared during this short visit.

The next evening Irving was to preach at Dunscore. Carlyle went with him "with most of our people" but Jane stayed behind, cooking the dinner—or, as Carlyle romantically phrased it, " 'field-marshalling', the noble little soul!" Irving preached in the churchyard—for even in that sparsely populated district more people had come than the church would hold—and afterwards he and Carlyle rode homewards pleasantly in the dusk to eat Jane's dinner. He left the next morning.

One result of the visit was again to turn Carlyle's thoughts Londonwards, for Irving insisted that his friend's true place was there. He did no more than think about it when a sense of the incongruity of his surroundings overcame him—as it did frequently—and when the demands or corrections of editors forced him to admit his dependence on the articles they commissioned, which he dismissed, with less than justice to himself, as journalism. Jane encouraged the plan when he discussed it, but did not broach the subject herself—Carlyle was not a man to be driven. But the thought was in his mind, and remained there, growing a little more tempting every time they talked of it.

Irving's triumphant march from one Dumfriesshire parish to another seems to have struck Jane's imagination, and she told a divinity student: "Now, William, don't be going about seeking for a church, like the rest of them, but go out to the highways and hedges, and preach away like a house on fire." This William Corson, brother of their nearest neighbour at Nether Craigenputtock three miles across the moors, found his way to Craigenputtock more often than Carlyle wished—he was "very stupid, used to come and bore me"—but this may be because the young man came to see Jane. He thought her very pretty, and compared her to Mary, Queen of Scots. She always called Carlyle by his surname, Corson noticed. She, he said, was much respected in the neighbourhood and called "the lady", but

Carlyle was looked down upon, as it was thought that he had married for money. She had a generous way with her that the country people appreciated; and once, after Corson and others had helped her to clear snow from the door she gave them all a dram of whisky, although spirits were not usually seen in the house. She was aware of her responsibility as her father's daughter, though she joked about it, and took pleasure in regarding herself as the grand lady of the district. Old Esther of Carstamin, the daughter of a neighbouring laird, who had come down in the world, was fed and clothed by Jane, and Esther, not to be outdone, hobbled up to Craigenputtock one day with her only remaining treasures, two old plates "as *a memorandum*" of her "when I am gone"; though, as Jane told Eliza ruefully, "so long as she is on foot, I shall not want for a living memorandum." But Esther was not long on foot; she fell ill and could not leave her hovel; and Jane walked across the moors to her night and morning to make her last days easy.

Early in July the Jeffreys passed through Dumfries, and Carlyle and Jane rode down to spend a night with them. Jeffrey had been elected Dean of the Advocates, had resigned his editorship of the *Edinburgh Review*, and was on his way to London to take up his appointment. They all put up at the 'King's Arms'. Carlyle stayed up talking with Jeffrey till two, then joined Jane for a disturbed night in a bed "opulent in *bugs*", and breakfasted at nine the next morning "all bug-bitten and short of sleep". Jeffrey made fun of the waiter and quizzed his daughter as usual. This 'Sharlie' was no favourite with Carlyle. She had a slight physical deformity which both fascinated and appalled him. He suspected that she was jealous of her father's attentions to Jane. If so, her jealousy must have increased when, after breakfast, Jeffrey gaily carried off Jane to visit "an old flame of his", Mrs Richardson, a novelist living in the town. Carlyle was content to be left with Mrs Jeffrey, "a sincere and hearty kind of woman, with a great deal of clear natural insight, often sarcastically turned. . . . She liked my sincerity and I hers". She endeared herself to him on this occasion by belabouring Brougham. As for the visit to Mrs Richardson: " 'These old loves don't do!' said Mrs Jeffrey."

At Mrs Richardson's, Jeffrey and his hostess were gratifying "some good though melancholy feelings", but according to Jane the meeting did not pass without embarrassment. Then, after arranging that the Carlyles would visit them in Edinburgh in the autumn, the Jeffreys drove off, and Jane took Carlyle to call on Mrs Richardson, who was anxious to see him. He described her to John, off already to London to try his hand at journalism, as

"among *all* manner of Elgin Magazines, and L.E.L.'s Poems, and Dundee Couriers, and Literary Gazettes, and Poetasterism and *Kleinstadterei* of every colour and degree. She is really a good worthy woman; well bred and well intentioned; but dwells in a habitation as of Bristol card, not of brick and mortar."

Jane's view was more pithy: "Mrs Richardson is getting out a new edition of that weary book, and fitting out her daughter Willie for India; neither ware, I am afraid, will find a ready market." A few days later, Jane was given a pleasant surprise; for both her mother and Eliza came to Craigenputtock for her twenty-eighth birthday.

In October, as Carlyle was now up-to-date with his articles, they paid the promised visit to the Jeffreys at Craigcrook. They stayed a fortnight. Jane enjoyed the comfortable house, the civilised talk, the people, and the dinners, and Carlyle did not entirely disenjoy himself, though he said later that they had stayed a week too long. But this was as much a matter of principle as anything else; enjoyment through any means but work was growing abhorrent to him. His dislike of living in any house but his own or his parents' interfered with his sleep and digestion. And his conscience reproached him for his brusqueness to Jeffrey during their "stormy sittings"—as Mrs Jeffrey called them—after the wives had gone to bed. Jeffrey tried once more to make him less misanthropic, extravagant in thought and speech, and above all, less Germanic in outlook; but it was a hopeless task and towards the end of Carlyle's stay he began to tire. "You are so dreadfully in earnest!" he said, looking at the stubborn mouth, and the fanatical blue eyes staring back at him defiantly.

Before returning home they stayed for a few days with the Donaldsons at Haddington, and were presented, to their embarrassment, with a portrait of Sandy Donaldson to hang at Craigenputtock. A few more days were spent at George Square with "fat, comfortable" Bradfute and Eliza, now quite reconciled to Carlyle, and when they left Jane was in tears.

Carlyle never forgot "the gloom of our arrival" towards the end of October. The evening was

"miserable, wet, windy . . . with the yellow leaves all flying about; and the sound of Brother Alick's stithy (who sometimes amused himself with smithwork, to small purpose) clink-clinking solitary through the blustering element. I said nothing, far was she from ever, in the like case, saying anything!"

Jane kept a good heart, even though the rain continued to pour down—had not stopped when she wrote to Eliza a fortnight later:

"I liked Edin^r last time, as well as I did at sixteen (you know how well that was) and I cried as much at leaving it; yet, returned to our desert, it affrighted me only the first day. The next day it became tolerable, and next again positively pleasant. On the whole, the mere outward figure of one's place of abode seems to be a matter of moonshine in the long run: you learn (if you are not an entire goose) to pronounce it, once for all, '*particular neat*,' or, as it may happen, particular *un*neat; and then naturally betake yourself into some other train of speculation. The only thing which makes one place more attractive to me than another is the quantity of *heart* I find in it."

As for Sandy Donaldson, he had been hung

"over the mantlepiece in my own room, whence he looks down upon me with the most bewitching simper night and morning. The first time I had occasion to dress in his presence I found myself unconsciously stepping behind the curtains."

One good reason for the serenity of her philosophy was Carlyle's own satisfaction. He had just been asked to write an *Historical View of German Literature* for a proposed 'Cabinet Library'; and he was borrowing German books—from, among others, Eliza's fiancé David Aitken, minister of Minto—and reading hard. Jane felt, with him, that books rather than occasional articles were the only satisfactory means of making him known—would, in fact, bring them both to London, where his genius must surely assert itself. No more was heard of readings in Spanish—Carlyle's time had become too precious— but this too Jane took in good part.

Carlyle found time during November to write to Mrs Montagu. Could she help John to a doctor's post? he asked. He was worried about this roaming brother who lacked, it seemed, the will to work. Another letter that he ought to have written—

to Jeffrey—remained undone, and Jeffrey rapped him over the knuckles. Carlyle's contemptuous handling of established literary figures when they talked together at Craigcrook still rankled. He would do better to admire more and criticise less, Jeffrey tells him. "There are so few high intellects in the world that it is pitiful to see them grudging and carping at each other." ¡He made fun of Carlyle's preference for solitude, tobacco, and freedom from the "idle socialities you hold in such contempt, and the audacious contradictions which wear out your spirit still more." And he warned him, yet again, against surrender to his intolerant and unsocial disposition. Carlyle was unmoved; he was more concerned about the snow which had followed the rain, and isolated Craigenputtock.

Just before the snow first began to fall, the Carlyles had gone down to Scotsbrig—it was Carlyle's habit to visit his parents, alone or with Jane, after he had finished an article or had been from home—and had brought Jean back with them for a few days. But the days drew out to weeks, and Jean was growing restless; "having," as Jane told Mrs Carlyle, "a firm conviction that Scotsbrig cannot stand, should she stay another week." Then Jane caught a chill which developed into a sore throat, diphtheria was suspected and the household was thrown into uproar. Jean nursed her until Mrs Welsh forced her way over from Templand; Alick's handyman on the farm sat for two days, in Carlyle's words, "booted and spurred, in readiness to ride for a Doctor, to Dumfries"; and a family gathering on New Year's Day, 1830, for which a goose had been killed, had to be abandoned. Mrs Welsh left "by constraint" soon after Jean, and Carlyle took over the remnants of nursing. But Jane was soon up, and writing to Eliza:

> "There is nothing like a good bit of pain for taking the conceit out of one. Had I been newly returned from Edinburgh, my thoughts still wandering on the mountain tops of vanity, it is probable I should have found life here in this grimmest of weather almost intolerable; but being newly recovered from a sore throat I am quite content beside a good fire, with a book or work, and the invaluable capacity of swallowing."

If there were any doubt about her recovery, her last few lines would have settled the matter. "I am still wearing signals of distress, a nightcap and shawl—that, partly, I confess, from a secret persuasion that these equipments render my appearance more interesting." A month later, she had fully recovered, but the weather had not: "Oh for a sight of the green fields again," she cries to Eliza "or even the black peat-moss—anything rather than this wide waste of blinding snow!" All was quiet; too quiet for her: "I saw in one of your letters to my Mother that you were living very quietly; yet gentlemen bring you nice nosegays. We, I imagine, are yet quieter; a gentleman either with or without a nosegay is a thing we never dream of."

Men were scarce indeed at Craigenputtock. Carlyle did not want company; he was becoming more and more attached to the idea of silence and long-suffering, writing in his journal "Does it seem hard to thee that thou shouldst toil in darkness, sickness, isolation? Whose lot is not even thus? Toil then, and *tais-toi*". Jane complained to his mother that "Carlyle never asks me to go with *him*, never even looks as though he desired my company." She could not look to him for distraction, and she did not seriously expect it. She admired him increasingly for the signs of genius he showed—his speech, his writings, his very attitude towards his work. She was grateful to him for his care of Craigenputtock; the trees he had planted, the dykes he had rebuilt, the barn, the house, the drive—they were so many wreaths on the altar of her father's memory. "*He* would have done that", she would say in approval. Pride, gratitude, trustfulness—all these feelings he satisfied in her. But there was much that he could not give her. Open appreciation of her and her efforts had no more place in his philosophy than courtship after marriage—for him the soul speaking to soul, silently, the woman diligently serving, the man ever striving, each with pride in their hearts for the other, with love even, but little talk of it unless parted. Then, he was voluble enough on paper, but, together again, he had few words of affection, and fewer actions. With the small change of life he had no patience, of liveliness not much more than an inkling; it had been rated next to a sin in his experience, and he had in this sense been old from his birth. He could and did laugh heartily, but there was little lightheartedness in him. Of the social and domestic amenities he was, and remained, ignorant and scornful. He was misanthropic, she was gregarious. Love him as she might, the longing for company, for gaiety, for lightness, for compliments persisted. In these matters he could be no help to her. "Be gay

and playful and foolish with her . . . be innocently happy"—
these recommendations of Jeffrey sounded like madness to him.

So she had to look elsewhere. Little relief was to be found at
Scotsbrig or at Templand, her only refuges from Craigenputtock. She had spent three weeks in Edinburgh during the
last two years; it was not to be thought of as anything but a rare
diversion. Besides, she was a sensible woman who wanted to
count her blessings in her own home. There, her amusements
had to be found. The material was not promising—consisting
only of Alick and the general man of all work, Elliott—but the
starving do not pick and choose, and she did her best. Elliott
was soon at her beck and call, digging the garden, mowing a
lawn for her and laying down another one, gravelling the
garden paths, with Jane keeping a close but friendly eye on him,
until it seemed that his business was to beautify Craigenputtock
rather than to help on the farm.

Alick, as a member of the family, presented a difficult
problem. Jane's feelings towards him had changed a good deal
since his removal into the cottage. What close at hand had
seemed repulsive, at a distance showed itself as mere rusticity
All her maternal instincts came into play; there was good stuff
in Alick—he had, she discovered, an excellent sense of humour,
but it needed to be brought out. She began, practically enough,
by cutting his hair, and introducing order and comfort into his
cottage. But his melancholy persisted, and she decided that he
was pining for a wife. His own attempts to find one had been
unsuccessful, so she took the matter in hand. When next at
Scotsbrig, she asked that Jenny Clow and her family should be
invited to tea. Jenny was much admired for her fine figure, but
in other ways too Jane judged her suitable for Alick, and it was
not long before Alick thought likewise.

Alick's melancholy was also due to the fact that he was not
making the farm pay. He had difficulty in meeting the rent; and
once, when half a year's rent was overdue, Jane had to gallop to
the Bank at Dumfries and then on to Templand with the money
for Mrs Welsh—she could not endure the thought of money
owed by a Carlyle to her mother, though the gesture practically
beggared them. In spite of Alick's desperate state, he and
Carlyle managed during the summer to raise ten pounds for a
gig: "a fine, stout, substantial, old-fashioned, bottle-green

vehicle, as ugly, as light and as sure, as Philosopher could desire it." For the first time, it was possible to drive from Craigenputtock in bad weather without getting soaked to the skin, and in hot weather without being smothered in dust. They could fetch and return visitors who had no horse; and they were at last relieved from complete dependence on the once-weekly carrier from Dumfries.

Carlyle perhaps bought the gig as a challenge to fate. Never had his money fallen so low. The plan for publication of his *History*, over which he had laboured for months, was suddenly cancelled; and although he had long since become dissatisfied with this "compilation" as he called it, the loss of time was serious. He tried to sell the *History* elsewhere, or to break it up into articles, but was unsuccessful; things Germanic, he was told, were at present unsaleable.

He had to write more articles; and when Jeffrey, back in Edinburgh for the summer, appealed to him to "wander down from your Blasted Paradise, hand in hand with your Blooming Eve, to seek a peaceful shelter in our lower world" he refused— he was too busy. He did not add, short of money; but Jeffrey realised that this was part of his trouble. He had already offered him an annuity of £100, but his offer was refused "at once, in my handsomest, gratefullest, but brief and conclusive way". He could not accept it, Carlyle said, without feeling himself in a position of inferiority. Twice afterwards Jeffrey repeated his offer. The first time Carlyle refused it again, even more shortly. The second time, he at once changed the subject. This, he claimed, was no mere pride, but sober calculation; and he complained that the offers were made "less of godlike pity for a fine fellow and his struggles, than of human determination to do a fine action of one's own".

Towards the end of June, Carlyle's sister Margaret, the eldest of the girls, died of consumption. This loss, though not un-expected, cast an added gloom over the year. The weather throughout the summer and autumn was wet and dreary, keeping Carlyle indoors, and making him cry out in his journal "Rain! rain! rain! The crops all lying tattered, scattered, and unripe; the winter's bread still under the soaking clouds!" As they would not come to Edinburgh, Jeffrey decided to come to them, and his visit brightened the middle of September. The party had been expected for a month or more, but arrived, eventually, at less than a day's notice. Carlyle was at Scotsbrig, (some thirty miles away) when the message came, and Jane was unprepared for visitors, and with less money than ever before. She sent an urgent note to Carlyle, and galloped down to Dumfries and back, bringing with her the essentials for a party of four. By the time Carlyle reached home, the three Jeffreys and their servant were already there, comfortable, fed, and being entertained. Jane had everybody well trained. Bretton—who had replaced Elliott on the farm—waited at table "like the Steward of some Royal Hotel", and a new woman in the kitchen "cooked to a very hair's-breadth". Jeffrey, said Carlyle, "was more than usually friendly and interesting", there were fewer arguments, and "he left us, and we were left, with real regret". He insisted on carrying off Carlyle's ill-fated *History* to see if he could find a publisher for it. The only hint that the stay of four days held anything but pleasure is Carlyle's remark that Jeffrey might come to Craigenputtock without his womenfolk the next year, "which will be a much more commodious method."

While Jeffrey was at Craigenputtock a letter came to him from London. "Dear Sir, I am dying! can you send me £100, and so consummate your many kindnesses to me? W. Hazlitt". Jeffrey, whose kindness did not end with the Carlyles, sent £50 the moment he reached Edinburgh, and asked for a report from the doctor. John Carlyle also made enquiries for him. But it was too late; before the money could reach him, Hazlitt was dead. Carlyle spoke pityingly of Hazlitt, in whom "there lay some tone of the 'Eternal Melodies', which he could not fashion into terrestrial music, but which uttered itself only in harsh jarrings, and inarticulate cries of pain."

Soon afterwards, Carlyle and Jane went to Dumfries in the gig, and when returning in the dark Carlyle suggested that they turn aside to Templand—a shorter drive, and where Jane was in any case soon expected. It was on this visit, one morning, that Carlyle later remembered having the first thoughts of what was to become *Sartor Resartus*; but the germ of it appeared a little earlier, when he noted in his journal

"what is a man if you look at him with the mere logical sense, with the understanding? A pitiful hungry biped that wears breeches. Often when

I read of pompous ceremonials, drawing-room levées, and coronations, on a sudden the *clothes* fly off the whole party in my fancy, and they stand there straddling in a half ludicrous, half horrid condition!"

He began to write

"the strangest of all things. . . . A very singular piece, I assure you! It glances from Heaven to Earth and back again in a strange satirical frenzy, whether *fine* or not remains to be seen."

By the end of October *Teufelsdreck*, as he first called it, was sent off, as an article, to Fraser in London.

This was satisfactory; but his spirits were still overcast by "this almost ghastly solitude," and London appeared even more desirable. He tells John: "I think it not impossible that I may see you this winter in London! I mean to come whenever I can spare the money; that I may look about me again among men for a little."

Craigenputtock was beginning to get on his nerves. He was no longer sure that he could do his best work there, although there is still no hint in his letters or journal that he had fears, or even thought, for Jane's feelings. She as his wife would naturally follow him gladly—his mind in this matter was still as simple as that. By the end of December he was describing the past year as one of the most worthless he had spent for a long time.

"I care not for poverty, little even for disgrace, nothing at all for want of renown. But the horrible feeling is when I cease my own struggle, lose the consciousness of my own strength, and become positively quite worldly and wicked."

He felt himself lonely, and cried out for Irving, with whom John was then living in London. "Oh were I but joined to such a man! that we might fight together for God's *true* cause even to the death! With one such man I feel as if I could defy the earth."

Of all this, Jane heard a great deal. In spite of Carlyle's exhortations to silence in his journal, he was the last man on earth who could keep silent. Attempts at suppression would leave him more and more irritable, his hot temper would flare up over trifles, and then it would all come out—his doubt about living on at Craigenputtock, the possibility of a move to London, the all-absorbing question of *Sartor*. He was still commenting on Jane's silence: "she sits beside me here where I write, and reads or sews, and never utters *mum*." But if she were silent then, she had plenty to say when given the chance. At last, in sheer desperation it may have been, she fell into the habit of sitting by Carlyle while he shaved of a morning—the one time of the day when his creed of silence was practically enforced—and giving him her news and views. She too was tired of Craigenputtock, and dreaded its air of stagnation. She longed for company, for a chance to talk and laugh. The one benefit that the country had promised—to her health—had proved an illusion. Her headaches were now worse than ever, and more frequent. They decided that they would not spend another winter at Craigenputtock; but where it should be spent remained uncertain. Fraser was still holding the manuscript of *Sartor*, and Jane, anxious that Carlyle should make it into a book that would display his genius and focus attention on him, had little difficulty in persuading him to withdraw it.

This was in January, 1831, and from that moment the outlook at Craigenputtock steadily brightened. Carlyle wrote hard and hopefully; this at last was his own work, no compilation or article but an idea conceived and worked out by himself alone. "Hang them! I have a book in me that will cause ears to tingle." He owed much to others in the development of his theme, but the matter was his own, and the manner too. Their plan now was that, when *Sartor* was finished, they should take it to London and try to sell it; and that Carlyle should see whether he could not find enough work there to support a home. "I would desire nothing better could I fly away with the whole premises, and set them down somewhere about Highgate or Pimlico; and there find work".

He worked more cheerfully when this was settled, and Jane's spirits rose with a bound. She could not escape her headaches, but she faced calmly enough the inevitable snowstorms and isolation in the early months of the year, and the moment the road was clear and she had a visitor or two to discuss, her letters sparkled again.

"O Eliza Eliza! We were sitting at breakfast yesterday morning suspecting nor evil nor good—sipping a highly nutritive beverage of tea and whipt egg—and talking pleasantly enough on some transcendental subject—when suddenly, an unusual sound of carriage wheels, louder and louder, nearer and nearer, interrupted the whole operation. I thought it could be no one else but Miss Anderson of Sanquhar, and ran to receive her 'in my choicest mood!' but Lord have mercy! what was I come out for to see? Seated in an open gig—muffled curiously in Indian shawls, my astonished eyes rested on the large muscular figure of —Miss Scot! yes Mary Scot, of Haddington. 'Hee, hee, hee!—Mrs Caarlile!—Hee, hee, hee!' But it was no hee-heeing to me! the intensity of my astonishment quite paralysed me—and it was minutes before I could express the joy which I really always feel at recognising a Haddington face—belong to whom it may. She was obliged to be off the same evening. But we made the best use of our time—I took nothing in hand the whole day but *milking* news from her (a rather rural metaphor), which she with unabating copiousness supplied."

Jeffrey wrote often to her from London, telling her of brilliant functions at Court and of Paliamentary debates, but Jane had no use for this kind of gossip—her *métier*, as she knew well, was as hostess of small artistic and intellectual groups—and she felt and said that Jeffrey was spending his time poorly—a riposte, perhaps, to his criticisms of Carlyle: "Well, well, my wrangling little, earnest, kind child", replied Jeffrey, "you need not rail any longer at Parliament and court people, for I am done for the present, with both—my committee have unseated me." He was much more concerned about the obvious signs that Jane was giving, in her defence of Carlyle, of becoming a mere mouthpiece for him.

> "You really are but a better kind of great baby after all—a smart intelligent child certainly, with sweet dispositions, and a good and a *great* heart, but a little spoiled, and not quite so deeply seen in the mysteries of human nature as you fancy yourself, but if you were a little less scornful and more indulgent, I should care less about your false judgments."

They wrangled on, but he meant so well and was so kind that Jane could do no less than forgive him. When he was last at Craigenputtock she had told him how worried Carlyle was about John, who sat stubbornly in London, insisting on trying to earn a living by his pen, and talking of abandoning medicine altogether. He had one or two articles accepted, and promptly sent Carlyle most of the money he received for them—for he was determined to pay back all that had been spent on him. But he was soon obliged to borrow the money back again; and it seemed plain to the anxious brother at Craigenputtock that he was simply wasting his time. He wrote again and again, telling him to abandon journalism, to make up his mind what he really wanted to do, or to come back to Craigenputtock.

When it became clear that John would neither leave London nor, unaided, make any decision, Carlyle, swallowing his pride, appealed to Jeffrey, who was on the spot. Jeffrey saw John, discovered that he most wanted a post as travelling physician with some rich family, and promised to recommend him.

Jeffrey still hammered away at Carlyle for being "scornful and intolerant", for his "filthy pride and foolish straining after ideal unsocial elevation". He begged him to stop dreaming of

"the Cynic's tub, and that unseemly romance of encountering the primitive lot of man, with your habits of mind and body, and a young and delicate wife, whose great heart and willing martyrdom would only make the sacrifice more agonising to you in the end."

Alick had duly married Jenny Clow and, reported Carlyle, was much more cheerful in consequence. But his farming went from bad to worse; at Whitsun he gave up the farm; and a new tenant, unknown to the Carlyles, moved into his cottage. Jenny left without regret—she had avoided the house when Jane was there—but Alick could not find a farm to suit him, and he and the unwilling Jenny soon returned, were lodged in the peat store, and did odd jobs about the place.

While Alick was away, and strangers were in the cottage, the Carlyles' longing to leave Craigenputtock grew even stronger: "within fifteen miles not one creature that we can so much as speak to." Then Carlyle's horse died and Jane's pony fell ill, leaving no horse to ride or to draw the gig. Summer though it was, the solitude of Craigenputtock seemed overwhelming, for now that their presence there had lost its piquancy, visitors were few. Carlyle began to feel desperate to be off, and before *Sartor* was finished he was writing to Jeffrey of his readiness to work at any honest job in London. He had set £50 as the least sum with which he could venture to London; but when *Sartor* was done, by the end of July, he had nothing like that amount of money—he and Alick at one time could muster only a dozen pence between them. He hesitated no more, he again pocketed his pride, and asked and obtained a loan from Jeffrey. But the loan determined Carlyle to go alone; he would not borrow more than was absolutely necessary. His plan was to get *Sartor* published (it was a work of genius, Jane assured him) and to spy out the land so that both might go to London later. He reckoned to be back in a month.

He left Craigenputtock at the beginning of August. The packing on the night before he went was a dreary business for Jane. When it was finished, she was not far from tears. This was the first long separation since their marriage five years before, and her fears began to rise. Who knew what might happen to Carlyle in London, or when they would meet again? She spoke jokingly, as was her way, but could not disguise her uneasiness. Carlyle, in high spirits, tried to comfort her, but she was out of sorts and would not be comforted.

At two o'clock the next morning, Alick drove Carlyle away.

XI

OWL IN DESERT
1831

After a day or two alone, Jane began to adjust herself to the new solitude. "Today" she told Carlyle "I am in my usual middle state—and have been going about 'siding things' as they say in Liverpool—in East Lothian dialect 'redding up'—or in your brief and energetic dialect 'making an earthquake'." Alick's wife watched the upheaval sceptically: "Jenny said when she found me today sitting amidst a litter of books papers and needlework—"You are not without *a sort* o wark here I think, but you never seem to get *settled* to'." But even the jealous Jenny appeared preferable to no company at all: "A *betterish* dinner having been prepared. . . . I thoughtlessly—*madly* I should say—invited Alick and Jenny. Alick indeed took off . . . as soon as the repasts were ended; but she sat *on—on* . . . toning forth an occasional 'ee-a' and 'dooth'." Then Alick went off with Jean, who had been on a visit, to Scotsbrig for a few days, and "the Colony dwindled into an unintelligible whinner: there are just Jenny, old Mary, and I left, but there is a gun amongst us besides gig whips—and I am quite delivered now from the foolish tremors I used to have about thieves."

Mrs Welsh took a less philosophical view of her daughter's position and insisted that she come to Templand for a week or two. Jane, half reluctant, half relieved, agreed. She was wild for news of Carlyle, and had no sooner arrived at Templand than she tore off along the road to the post office in Thornhill in the blazing heat, despite her mother's protests; but the postmistress handed her a letter, not from Carlyle, but from Mrs Montagu "entreating me to come to *her* and give you an agreeable surprise . . . offering me funds—and pressing the offer on my acceptance with much—rhetoric." Jane's pride was roused:

"She knows me little if she dreams I should entertain such an idea for one instant."

At Templand also were Isabella MacTurk, sister of the Robert who had long ago lost his heart to Jane; and a young man, Robert Barker, who followed Jane about like a shadow: he was, she told Carlyle, madly in love with her. But to such an extent was the old Jane overlaid by the wife anxious for her absent husband, that she could take little pleasure in her new admirer. Indeed, she might not have mentioned him at all had not Carlyle assured her that he had "still taken up with no other women". She had heard from him at last, and all was well, or at any rate he was alive and in London. He had stayed on the way with John Welsh at Liverpool, and had met there a Dr Carson, at one time an admirer of Jane: "one of the veriest *Hashes* I ever set eyes on; civil enough, but to me almost frightful and a *hideux reptile* when I fancied him as your Lover." Carlyle seems to have enjoyed the journey, preaching mysticism for six hours on end to a friend of Alick's he met in the boat; but in "the village of Birmingham" he threw away half a crown on a "cup of hot sugar-and-water." He missed John, who was waiting at the Angel while he was put out at Piccadilly, but they were soon settled in John's new lodgings in the house of George Irving (Edward's brother).

He visited Jeffrey in Jermyn Street; his wife was "as kind as ever", Charlotte "came simpering in", and Jeffrey handed round a portrait of Jane, which so affected Carlyle that "for little I could have *grat* over it." Jeffrey advised Carlyle to take *Sartor* to John Murray, and wrote a letter to the publisher, recommending Carlyle as "a genius". Carlyle had seen his Birmingham friend, Badams, now in London, but he "is in no good way", drinking brandy heavily. At Bedford Square John was in disgrace, and Mrs Montagu seemed "embittered and exasperated". The news from Shooter's Hill was also depressing. Mrs Strachey looked "like a flower frozen among ice" and he did not care for the company she was keeping. One friend, a "fat button of a creature" annoyed him so much that he was provoked "to run tilt, and I fear transfix her." Nor was his first sight of William Godwin more satisfactory; the philosopher played whist instead of philosophising, and Carlyle took himself off in disgust.

Irving was now dealing in miracles—'the Gift of Tongues'. "Yet I love the man and can trustfully take counsel of him". Even his wife seemed to have improved, though she remained "*very* straitlaced, and living in the *suds* element." Irving again urged Carlyle to settle in London, and he talked vaguely of taking a house outside London, perhaps in Enfield (where Badams was living), but did not see how he could afford it. So he wrote on, almost every other day, and always as a lover—"I love my own woman," he said, "beyond the whole sisterhood, and am positively far fonder of her than when I wrote from London of old, and was not her Husband but only her Lover."

Jane's letters were as loving, as frequent and as long. She had less to say but the greater art in saying it, and began to show her genius for making letters "out of my own inside".

Alick came over to Templand during her stay, bringing with him the youngest Carlyle brother, Jamie. Alick was evidently determined to live up to the company in which he found himself—Jane had taught him too well—and she now thought he must be going out of his wits.

> "I was playing to them and he broke out in such a strain of lyrical recognition as set us all in astonishment. 'It was heavenly' he said 'it transported him out of this earth into a new world of *celestial delight—these strings were like so many little winged spirits speaking to him out of the skies*'!"

After a week at Templand, Jane began to miss her independence—and did not scruple to show it. Robert Barker was puzzled:

> " 'At Craigenputtock she is the brightest most delightful creature in the world—and here always sullen and miserable looking!' 'It is a pity it should be so' said my Mother with much emphasis and tossing. 'Fortunate rather' I coolly replied 'it is surely fortunate that I produce the pleasantest impression in the place where I oftenest am and where it is my duty to be'."

When she went home towards the end of the month Isabella decided to keep her company for a few days, and Alick, who was to fetch them, again distinguished himself.

> "We waited dinner for him till half after four, when he at length arrived—and how think you—*mortal drunk*. . . . I could have cried with shame and vexation, but I tried to laugh it off, as the rest were trying—most unsuccessfully. Knowing his style of driving in such cases, nothing would have persuaded me to risk myself and another in the gig with him

except my impatience to get him away from a place where he was making such a deplorable figure—where of all places I had wished him to appear to advantage, at least to be himself. Isabella was willing to take her chance—and off we came about seven having vainly waited to see if he would sober—and of course drove like Jehu up hill and down dale over stick and stone, making such hair-breadth turns! O mercy."

Once safely home, Jane's spirits soared. " 'My foot is on my native heath, and my name's Macgregor!' I can breathe again, and think and feel, and write." She and Isabella solemnly danced quadrilles to the accompaniment of their own singing and broke a bottle of wine with their dinner. But when Isabella went to bed, the silence of the house, the empty study, the contrast between London as she imagined it and Craigenputtock as she knew it, were too much for Jane's good spirits. "I have danced and drank and wined and yet *my* heart is na light". But, she added, "It is some comfort to think that you do not take up with other women."

Her anxiety to hear from Carlyle—particularly now that he had hinted of a change in his plans—banished sleep by night and rest by day. She was for ever looking out for the carrier or for any moving speck on the moors which might be a farmer bearing a letter for her. Finally, desperate because the carrier had not called, she walked the three moorland miles to Nether Craigenputtock where the carrier sometimes left letters. She walked so fast that Isabella, worn out, sat on a stone and would go no further. Jane arrived breathless, only to hear Miss Corson "simper forth" that there was no letter for her. A thousand fears rushed through her; Carlyle was ill, was dead, was faithless. She was all for galloping down to Dumfries at once, but Alick said Harry was not well enough to carry her. Two days more she waited, in a fever, unable to settle to anything. Her last resource—her own letter-writing—failed her; she could not write a line until she had discovered why Carlyle had not written.

On the evening of the second day, idle and restless, she wandered across with Isabella to the little house in the yard in which Alick was still spending most of his time. An unamiable and outstanding characteristic of Jane was her possessive manner with other women's husbands; and if she could make their wives jealous, so much the better. Seeing Alick with

Jenny—who, she tells Carlyle gravely, "has been quite insufferable of late with *jealousy* of her husband—whether with Isabella or me or both I cannot say"—Jane decided that Alick's hair was too long; it needed cutting, and she would do it that instant. So she cut Alick's hair, and Isabella sat looking on, while Jenny, who was far advanced in pregnancy, "was nearly beside herself—cried till bed time and broke out on me with a burst of impertinence that filled me with weender and amazement." Her comment was: "poor Alick! I am wae for him."

At dawn, the last remnant of Jane's self-control gave way, and despite heavy rain, despite Alick's warning about Harry, she was off to Dumfries at breakneck speed by six in the morning. So fast did she drive that she reached the post office before the London mails had arrived. But when they did come, she was rewarded by two letters which, as she told Carlyle in a scribbled note from the town, made her "as happy as one can be in Dumfries amidst a plash of rain—and the prospect of retching all the way home."

The letters contained good news. Jeffrey had introduced John to the Lady Clare, a rich young Irishwoman who needed a travelling physician—a post which carried a salary of some £300. If he got the post, John would be able almost at once to begin repaying the money that Carlyle had spent on him, and Jane could come down to London, provided she felt able to make the journey alone. They could then both live there at least through the winter.

Jane returned to Craigenputtock with a high heart. She had no doubts about making the journey, she told Carlyle, "but I must consider calmly on all sides as well as the pleasant one." This admirable attitude collapsed the next day, when the carrier at last arrived, bringing two more letters from London. John had been given the post, she could come to London for the winter—that was the gist of the favourable news. For the rest, London was empty, uninteresting, Mrs Montagu no true friend, Badams "at Death's door", *Sartor* still unplaced, and Jeffrey unable to find Carlyle a Government clerkship. Jane was so excited that she tried to read both letters at once, failed, stumbled through one after the other, and "felt a strong disposition to rush out into infinite space—and tell the dead craigs and running brooks—that my Husband was well and took up with no other women!" Sleep was out of the question. She roamed about the silent house in an ecstasy; found a stub of one of Carlyle's cigars in his study and smoked "half an inch" for the sheer pleasure of identifying herself with him.

> "And so between vague apprehensions and anxious listening on the one hand, and thoughts of your love and goodness on the other—of my probable journey to London—my meeting with my own—John's good fortune—Mrs Montagu's desertion to the Dragons—Badams' misfortunes and all the interesting things you tell me—I tumbled on till seven."

When she considered Carlyle's adverse news more soberly, he seemed to be making much fuss about little. " 'The town is empty.' O mercy—it will be full enough any day of the year for one who has been so long used to a desert." He scorned Mrs Montagu's suggestion of " 'giving *you* money' to come hither. *Jane Welsh Carlyle* a taker of money in this era of the gigmen!" He found: "She goes upon words—words. . . . On the whole, my original impression of the 'noble Lady' was the true one." He preferred Sarah Austin—"a true Germanised spiritual screamikin"—whom he had met once or twice. Jane was—not too seriously—dismayed by this change of front. "I have written a note to the Noble Lady. Oh how sadly you have defaced her fair image in my soul; but I must still *try* to love her—there are so few women in the world to be loved!" She added: "This Mrs Austin indeed!"

The literary men of London were dismissed comprehensively as "the Devil's own vermin"; and he was disturbed by what he called the 'gigmania' all about him. "Yes, Jeannie," he wrote "though I have brought you into rough, rugged conditions, I feel that I have saved you: as Gigmaness you could not have lived; as woman and wife you need but to see your duties in order to do them." This tirade against Bohemianism on the one hand and gentility on the other left Jane unmoved. She was excited and too much preoccupied by the work before her to pay much attention. The settling up could not be hurried, though she did her best. Carlyle was little help. He wrote despondently. Nothing was going right. All hope of publishing *Sartor* had, for the present at least, disappeared. There were bugs in his lodgings. He could not sleep. He never wanted to see Craigen-puttock again, but London seemed little better. Jane replied soothingly:

"At Craigenputtock we have always had a secret suspicion that we were quite wrong—removed out of the sphere of human activity fully as much thro' cowardice as superior wisdom . . . and thus all our doings are without heart and our sufferings without dignity. With a goal before me I feel I could leap six-bar-gates—but how dispiriting tethered on a barren heath—running round and round. Yet let it not be forgotten that at Craigenputtock you have written Teufelsdreck—yes the candle sometimes burns its way *thro'* the bushel—but what a waste of light!"

But although she wrote sensibly and managed the disposal of the animals at Craigenputtock advantageously, she was feeling neither sensible nor well. Her alternations of depression and exhilaration, her lack of sleep, her fearful dreams when she did sleep, and, brooding over all, the frightening solitude around her—for Alick and Jenny had left soon after the scene in the cottage—had played havoc with her nerves and digestion. She was prostrated with headaches, was often sick. At last she appealed to Scotsbrig for company: "A thousand thanks my dear kind mother" she told Mrs Carlyle "for sending Jean and Alick to my rescue. If some such mercy had not been vouchsafed me I think I must soon have worked myself into a fever or other violent disorder."

Mrs Carlyle was upset by the London plan. John's restlessness worried her, but the absence of the beloved Thomas was a far worse blow. Jane tried to reassure her:

"Don't grieve that he is not returning so soon—it is for all our goods. *Here* he was getting more and more unhappy—more and more dissatisfied with the world and himself—I *durst* not have counselled such a step—but whenever he proposed it himself, I cordially approved it."

She hoped to follow Carlyle in a few days, towards the end of September. She was about to leave for Templand, having settled up at Craigenputtock, and was taking Jean "as a sort of protection against my Mother's agitations".

The next day, at Templand, she began with her mother's help to get together the kind of wardrobe she felt London demanded. Carlyle was writing repentantly: "Why should I dwell in the element of contempt and indignation, not rather in that of patience and love." He had been reading Luther, and felt ashamed of himself. He would take Irving's advice, and pray, if he knew how. Then—a flash of the old Carlyle—"The *best* worship, however, is stout working." He was particularly ashamed of himself for thinking "crabbedly" of Jeffrey. He was not of them, but he was kind. "Frivolous gigmanity *cannot* unite itself to our stern destiny. . . . But oh, my dear Jeannie, do help me to be a little softer, to be a little merciful to *all* men, even gigmen." He thinks she will like John Stuart Mill, five years younger than herself, whom he has just met. "A slender, rather tall and elegant youth, with small clear Roman-nosed face, two small earnestly-smiling eyes; modest, remarkably gifted with precision of utterance, enthusiastic, yet lucid, calm." Mill "seemed to profess, almost as plainly as modesty would allow, that he had been converted by the head of the Mystic School." Mill spoke warmly to his friend John Sterling of Carlyle, who "means to employ his stay here in improving his knowledge of what is going on in the world." Mill helped him practically by introducing him to Fonblanque, editor of the *Examiner*.

By this time, Jane had begun to doubt whether she would like Mill, London, or anything else ever again. The arrival of Alick and Jean at Craigenputtock had merely saved her from a complete breakdown; and at Templand, Mrs Welsh, though anxious to please, was the last person to deal with her daughter in such a state. Jane needed calm, and, above all, the certainty that everything was being done to get her ready quickly for London. Instead, she was given a fortnight of her mother's agitations, hurried inefficiencies, fears, flurries, and insistence on farewell parties—all of which increased the harm done by the six solitary weeks at Craigenputtock. "I can see, by your last two letters especially," says Carlyle, "that it is not well with you; your heart is, as it were, choked up, if not depressed. You are agitated and provoked." This was putting the matter mildly. When at last, on September 22, Jane set out on her first visit to London, she was little better than a nervous wreck.

XII

LONDON INTERLUDE
1831 - 1832

Jane took the boat from Annan to Liverpool, and was sick during the entire twenty-four hour passage. Her cousin Alick Welsh drove her to her Uncle John's house in Maryland Street. She had always tolerated her uncle, an unpretentious, worthy man, though she much resented his overbearing wife. Helen, the eldest daughter, was prim but kindhearted. But the merry Jeannie—Babbie to Jane—was her particular favourite. She saw little of the elder sons: Walter was a minister, Alick in his father's sugar business. Johnnie and Mary were still children. She found the household restful to the point of boredom, and was thankful to get into the coach which, after a day and a night, landed her at the Angel.

Carlyle and John were waiting for her. They had prepared a dinner of chops and rice pudding, and in the evening Irving walked up to see her. She was by this time in a state of collapse, and one of her blinding sick headaches forced her to bed for two days. The third day she walked to Bedford Square with Carlyle. She found Mrs Montagu kind and helpful but a shade too gracious. She took Jane out to Epping to see the lunatic asylum run by Carlyle's old University acquaintance, Matthew Allen— "a place to which any sane person might be delighted to get admission"—and Jane called once or twice at Bedford Square as a matter of form, but in general their intercourse

"seems to be dying an easy natural death. Now that we *know* each other the 'fine en-thu-si-asm' cannot be kept alive without more hypocrisy than one of us at least can bring to bear on it. Mrs Montagu is an Actress—I admire her to a certain extent but friendship for such a person is out of the question."

Procter had been seeing a good deal of Carlyle, and Jane took to his wife who became for a time "my most intimate acquaintance here." But of all the women she met, Jane was impressed most by Sarah Austin. She was, Carlyle had told her,

> "an exceedingly vivid person, not without insight, but enthusiastic, as it were astonished, rapt to ecstasy with the German Apocalypse . . . with a pair of clearest, warm blue eyes (almost hectically intense), considerable mouth, and moustache on the upper lip, compared with which thine cannot name itself (mole and all) in the same week: an eagerness, a warmth in her whole manner and look, which has in it something feverish."

Perhaps Jane, when she at last met Sarah Austin, was reassured by that moustache. The hectic intensity was to prove too much for her Scottish common sense, but for the moment she declared that "If I *'swear everlasting friendship'* with any woman here it will be with her."

But before Jane could receive anybody, something had to be done about the lodgings. The house was noisy and infested with bugs. As soon as she felt better she set out with Carlyle to find a new home. She settled the matter in a day; and they moved to rooms in Ampton Street, off Gray's Inn Road. Jane liked the people who let the rooms, and satisfied herself that the whole house was clean—the only clean one, she told her mother-in-law, that she had seen since she left Scotland. The day they moved in, John left "to join his Countess at Dover". They were bound for Italy, and he went off in good spirits.

Jane soon endeared herself to the family at Ampton Street, and in particular to the daughter, Eliza Miles, a quiet religious girl, a follower of Irving, who could not do enough for the lodger from Scotland. This was as well, for Jane needed more attention than she could get from Carlyle, who had to be out most of the day and evening, meeting the younger literary men, as well as one or two of the more famous, improving his acquaintance with the editors of the literary and political magazines, and again trying to get *Sartor* printed. When at home, and there were no visitors, or none that he must see, he was often busy writing articles; first, his *Characteristics*—"it indicates decisively enough that Society (in my view) is utterly condemned to destruction, and even now beginning its long travail-throes of Newbirth"— then a paper on Dr Johnson. "Any other woman" he told Alick "might have gone mad beside me."

Jane did not go mad, but she took long to recover; her head-aches persisted, her digestion revolted—"at present" she tells John in December, "life is all sicklied over with the pale cast of stomach"; and she caught chills and colds in the unfamiliar climate—"one day a ferocious frost, the next a fog, so thick that you might put it in your pocket; a dead sea of green coloured filth under foot; and above an atmosphere like one of my Uncle's sugar-boilers." In his Christmas letter to Jean, Carlyle is still writing "My good Wifie has not been so well as I could wish . . . she does not lie in bed, is not even dispirited; but always in a sickly sort of way." Not until the new year, 1832, could he report that Jane

"is now growing decidedly better. She walks out every day, all wrapped in furs, cloaks and what not, lifted out of the mud-sea on 'French clogs'; is quite resolute in her own way, and quietly perseverant, and indeed she begins to bloom up again, and look like her former self."

Jane's outings, apart from her walks, were therefore much restricted. She went once with Carlyle to the theatre in Drury Lane to see "the silliest piece in the world rather indifferently performed", but she was much impressed by the theatre itself "especially the beautiful lustre in the centre of it." She paid a disastrous visit to the Irvings' house, which she thought a far worse Bedlam than Dr Allen's asylum, and where

"people are to be found at all hours *'speaking with tongues'* that is to say shrieking and howling in no tongue. I happened to be there one night just when a lady was under the inspiration of 'the spirit'; and the horrible sounds she made almost threw me who am not of a hysterical tempera-ment into a fit. I could not help crying all the way home."

Carlyle, too, was appalled: "Nothing so shocking and altogether unspeakably deplorable was it ever my lot to hear. Poor Jane was on the verge of fainting, and did not recover the whole night."

Once they went up to Enfield to see Badams and his wife—"very pretty and lively and clever." They stayed a few days, but not happily. Carlyle thought the marriage ill-made, but whatever the reason Badams was clearly past hope; and the visit would have been intolerable but for Jane's determined brightness. It was here that they met Charles and Mary Lamb, who walked over at least once a day from their nearby cottage.

Neither Jane nor Carlyle could make anything of them; "a very sorry pair of phenomena" said Carlyle.

> "Insuperable proclivity to *gin*, in poor old Lamb. His talk contemptibly small, indicating wondrous ignorance and shallowness, even when it was serious and good-mannered, which it seldom was; usually *ill*-mannered (to a degree), screwed into frosty artificialities, ghastly make-believe of wit;—in fact more like 'diluted insanity' (as I defined it) than anything of real jocosity, 'humour', or geniality. He was the *leanest* of mankind, tiny black breeches buttoned to the knee-cap and no farther, surmounting spindle-legs also in black, face and head fineish, black, bony, lean, and of a Jew type rather; in the eyes a kind of *smoky* brightness or confused sharpness; spoke with a stutter; in walking tottered and shuffled. . . . He was infinitely astonished at my Wife; and her quiet encounter of his too ghastly London wit by cheerful native ditto."

Jane's view was even more uncompromising.

> "I have seen most of the Literary people here, and, as Edward Irving said after his first interview with Wordsworth 'I think not of them so highly as I was wont'. . . . Some of them indeed (Charles Lamb for instance) would not be tolerated in any society out of England."

Lamb's idea of humour was certainly not theirs, but the incident which finally turned Jane against him occurred one evening at supper. He was highly amused at the Carlyles' habit of eating porridge. "Let us taste the stuff anyhow," he cried, when Jane's porridge had just been placed before her at table. He forthwith dipped his spoon into her bowl and put it in his mouth. Jane at once asked the servant to remove her bowl. To Lamb she said "Your astonishment at my porridge cannot exceed my surprise at your manners"—which was not the way to deal with Lamb.

Her remarks on literary men applied strictly to those who had "arrived". Her interest had been always, and was to remain, in the struggling man, the unacknowledged genius, the representative of lost or hopeless causes. These satisfied her strong sense of the romantic. Carlyle himself had first appealed to her as just such a one; and, had this tendency of hers needed encouragement, he would have supplied it, with his resolute opposition to the established in men and things. In fact she needed no encouragement; but the benefit to her of his way of thought was seen when there came to Ampton Street the type of man she most admired, drawn in the first place by his

increasing reputation as a destroyer of the humbug, preten-
tiousness, and self-satisfaction on which in his view the age had
grown fat and unhealthy.

The most regular caller was, indeed, not of this class. "The
little Dear"—Jeffrey—had been ill when Jane first arrived, but
he now came "skipping" over to Ampton Street twice a week,
and had to be conducted back almost to the very door; he had
no sense of direction and when Carlyle left him at the western
end of Long Acre, and he had only to cross Leicester Square, he
still managed to lose his way. Though in no sense romantic,
Jeffrey was charmingly and indefatigably helpful, always "as
gay as a lark", and now that he had abandoned the practice of
taking his womenfolk with him, Jane found him enlivening even
when his playfulness and habit of talking down to her offended
her dignity. He was always ready to talk about the Reform Bill,
the fate of which was still hanging in the balance; but Carlyle
would have no truck with such talk, which he claimed was
making the publishers shy of considering his *Sartor*; and Jane
was frankly bored. "Everyone" she told Helen Welsh "is tired
of thinking about the Reform Bill".

Jeffrey's visits were usually made in daylight. With darkness
came what Carlyle called "these poor Disciplekins", those
better described as fellow labourers, and a number who came
into no category but their own: "Scarce a night passes that
some acquaintance new or old does not drop in at tea, and then
follow such bouts of talking." When Jane first arrived, people
had "the impudence or the ignorance to congratulate me on
the change of climate I have made," and she "perhaps not
without a touch of national prejudice" and unwell into the
bargain, promptly found London "detestable" and the women
notable for their "universal ugliness". But when Carlyle's
visitors began to fill the room in Ampton Street her first impressions faded. "Nowhere have I found more worth, more
talent or more kindness". There was Allan Cunningham "a
most sufficient *poet* as I have ever met with . . . looking in all
respects merely what he is—a cultivated Scottish Mason."
There were the Procters—that is, until Carlyle, prompted by
Jane, discovered that Procter was mostly "a worn out dud,"
that Procter regarded him (he chose to think) as "a proud
mystic" and that his wife was shallow. There was Henry Taylor

from the Colonial Office—"a solid, sound-headed, faithful, but not a well-read or wide-minded man"—an admirer of the Lake poets, and a literary dilettante. James Hogg, the Ettrick Shepherd, appeared in "a gray Scotch plaid, the like of which was never seen here before." Charles Buller, devoted to Carlyle, charming and intelligent, brought a host of friends about them. Charles himself—"grown a great tower of a fellow, six feet three in height, a yard in breadth"—first called in November and was followed after he had been talking for an hour with the Carlyles by John Mill. The two of them sat on more or less indefinitely, making, as Jane put it, "a pleasant forenoon call of seven hours and a half".

This pleasantry barely covered Jane's delight. She could have listened to Mill, in particular, for many hours; and to observe his devotion to Carlyle was one of her first pleasures at this time.

> "Among all the literary people that come about us the one I like best is Mr Mill (son of Mill the Utilitarian) but *he* is no Utilitarian—he belongs rather to the class to which my Husband belongs and which for want of a fitter name has been called 'the Mystic school' ".

Anyone less mystical, unless it were Jane herself, would be difficult to imagine; but at that time all, himself perhaps most of all, thought of him as Carlyle's most promising and, in his reasonable way, most ardent follower.

Late in their stay, Leigh Hunt was added to the growing company. The men found much to like in each other—each was a rebel in his way, greatly though they differed in nature and outlook; and Hunt was immediately charmed by Jane and she by him—for he filled many of her requirements as a romantic figure, in spite of being very much married, and burdened with a quite unmanageable family.

So the men came in by ones and twos and threes to talk, to listen, to look. One evening, Carlyle noted, there were six of them, talking hard. He was usually the greatest talker of the lot, and his great laugh could be heard far down the street. He talked one night, he said, enough to fill a novel; and many nights were the same. But there were times when, anxious to write, he would go into the bedroom, leaving Jane to manage the visitors. This she did with success. She was a charming novelty to these London literary men, with her satirical stabs uttered in a soft Scottish voice, her side-splitting stories told with such provoking coolness, and her creative silent attention.

The disciples gave pleasure, but a certain visitor, calling unexpectedly, caused real excitement. "You may fancy how my heart leapt," she told Jean, "when a card bearing the name of *Gustave d'Eichthal* was sent up the other day when I happened to be alone." She had admired this leader of the Saint-Simon brotherhood ever since, two years earlier, he had written appreciatively to Carlyle after reading *Signs of the Times*. In person, he exceeded her wildest hopes: "He is a creature to love at first sight—so gentle and trustful and earnest looking—ready to do and suffer all for his faith." They talked together until Carlyle came in. Jane's instinct was all for putting men at their ease, and she was at her best when faced with what appeared to her as a saintly version of Byron. He spoke English very well, she thought, but he had the slight accent which gave the crowning touch to his romantic air and figure. He came again, bringing with him an even more remarkable companion: "at first sight ugly all pitted with small pox but by and by you wonder at your first impression his countenance is so pre-possessing and so commanding."

Carlyle again met Crabb Robinson, who was shown verses from Goethe to Carlyle and Jane. Crabb Robinson thought Carlyle behaved like a religious zealot, with Goethe as his god, and Cobbett and Napoleon as minor deities, and his peculiar notions and exclusiveness in taste made him, he found, an uncomfortable companion. But he knew, even so early, that Carlyle was not a man to be ignored. Editors had a similar belief, and asked him to write for them; and James Fraser brought along Daniel Maclise one day to draw Carlyle for his magazine—a difficult task made easier by Jane.

Although Carlyle had to give up a project of lecturing in public ("none but quacks have ever been known to worship here" he said after he and Jane had heard Robert Owen) and although *Sartor* still could find no publisher, he had other satisfactions. "I find myself," he tells Alick,

"respected by all whose judgment I respect; feared and wondered at by a much greater number; despised, at least openly, by no one. With incessant long-continued exertion, there is *much* possible for me; I may become a Preacher of the Truth, and so deliver my message in this Earth, the highest that can be entrusted to man."

This did not consort with the writing of commissioned articles:

> "I pride myself that I have never gone half a foot out of my road in search of what are called 'prospects'. . . . Thank Heaven I know my trade; it is to *write truth* while I can be kept alive by so doing, and to die writing it when I can no longer be kept alive."

In this mood, even London could do little for him. Yet he had other moments, many of them, in which London appeared not only desirable but necessary. His health there had been almost uniformly good, for he was so fully occupied that he had no time to think about himself. And of what use, after all, was the prophet crying aloud in the wilderness? And such a wilderness! "Castle of many chagrins; peatbog Castle, where the Devil never slumbers nor sleeps!" He argued the matter out with himself in a letter to his mother:

> "You are ill-lodged, in brick houses, thin as shells, with the floors all twisted, and every article indicating its showiness and its weakness. You are ill-fed, unless you can live upon beef; your milk is of the bluest, your water of the muddiest; your eggs rotten, your potatoes watery, and exactly about ten times the price they are in Annandale, namely one penny per pound! You are ill-bedded and ill-clothed unless you prefer show to substance; all these things are against you. Nevertheless there is a great charm in being here; at the fountain-head and centre of British activity, in the busiest and quickest-moving spot that this whole Earth contains. I find myself greatly enriched with thoughts since I came hither; and by no means disposed to repent of my journey. Nor am I without encouragements, such as I need, for holding on my way: in all open minds, I find ready access; and sometimes even grateful invitation.'

As for Jane, she

> "considers herself, on the whole, and indeed evidently is, in an improving way, 'decidedly better than she was'. She has had but a sickly time of it here, yet has not been unhappy, 'there is such excellent company'. She has seen no 'sights' hardly; and cares little or nothing about such. Good talk is what she delights in, and I too; and here, amid the mass of Stupidity and Falsehood, there *is* actually some reasonable conversation to be come at. She has met with some valuable people; and I believe has improved herself in more ways than one."

All then was well, whatever he should decide. He had always spoken of a return to Craigenputtock for the summer at least; he needed only a definite incentive to return. One such was the cholera epidemic in London that winter and spring. Neither Jane nor Carlyle was afraid of it, he said, but if it grew too bad, they would "run for Craigenputtock".

The major incentive came, without warning, in the new year. Jane, in common with most women of her time, would allow no smoking in her house, and, there being no garden in Ampton Street, Carlyle was to be seen every day on the cistern at the back of the house "perched aloft 'on that bad eminence' with the long pipe in his mouth, for all the world like the emblem over a tobacconist's door." One morning towards the end of January, Carlyle was on his cistern smoking when he heard the postman's knock. He thought there might be a letter from home, and hurried upstairs. There, he found Jane in tears with an opened letter in her hand. The letter was from Scotsbrig. His father had died suddenly. James Carlyle was 73, and had been failing gradually for some time, so that the shock of his death was doubly softened for Carlyle. Yet he grieved bitterly, and leaned heavily on Jane:

> "oh, how good and tender she was, and consolatory by every kind art, in those black days! I remember our walk along Holborn forward into the City, and the *bleeding* mood I was in, she wrapping me like the softest of bandages:—in the City somewhere, two Boys fighting, with a ring of grinning Blackguards round them; I rushed passionately through, tore the fighters asunder, with some passionate rebuke ("in this world full of death"), she on my arm; and everybody silently complied."

Jane was at her best at such moments, and she had such a vivid memory of her sufferings on the death of her own father, that she could console and sympathise with her whole heart.

Carlyle wished to go home to bury his father, but the honour of chief mourner fell to his step-brother, John of Cockermouth, as he called him—and as he had work promised and unfinished, he stayed on. The call of London was still strong, but his inclinations to be with his mother were stronger. He waited two months, until he had finished his article on Dr Johnson, and then left.

Two painful partings had to be made. One, with Badams, was clearly final. He "burst into tears: 'Pressed down like *putty* under feet,' we heard him murmuring, 'and no strength more in me to rise!' " He was invited to spend some of the summer at Craigenputtock but he merely said, "No, alas," knowing his fate. Of the Irvings, the Carlyles had seen little. Jane was not to be tempted to their house again, except for a farewell call, nor was Carlyle anxious to go. He deplored Mrs Irving's encouragement of every fanatical step taken by her husband, and Jane, of course, had no good word to say for her. At the one formal visit, Jane was disgusted by what Carlyle called "Mrs Irving's hypocritical final *kiss*."

By this time Irving had fallen entirely into the hands of fanatics. One of the last intelligent members of his congregation described a sermon:

> "This maudlin composition, every word of which he read, was delivered in high false tragic tones, accompanied by extravagant action, at once ungraceful and uncalled-for, more like the results of galvanic excitement, than of pure passion, while the face and raven hair of the preacher gave him no little resemblance to a wild, savage, shaggy portuguese shepherd."

Irving's language was typified by the phrase "You will be watered with the sweat of the blood of your Saviour", and he was ending his letters with exhortations such as "Oh my Brother, our occupation ought to be in sighing and crying for the Lord's appearance."

All this was anathema to Carlyle; and he became even more grieved and angered when Eliza Miles once or twice came running home in tears after a scene in Irving's church, when some had exercised their "Gift of Tongues", and others called for order. Carlyle would not go near the church, but he peremptorily instructed his family in Annandale that there was to be no gossip and no criticism of Irving. The two men still walked out occasionally, Carlyle once noticing curious looks at his tall companion with the wide black hat, brown skin, and flowing black hair, by many who mistook him for the sensational Paganini: but though the affection between them was still strong, there was no longer any true intimacy. When Irving called at Ampton Street to say goodbye, Carlyle spoke to him seriously. He thought that the 13th chapter of *Corinthians*, to which Irving always appealed, was too narrow a basis for so high a tower as he was building on it. He urged him to abandon the fanatics. He spoke for twenty minutes, Irving sitting on the floor between him and Jane with head bent down, looking pained but making no sound. After Carlyle had finished, he defended himself in a low mild voice, then left them.

During all this Jane said next to nothing. Her feelings were made clear later, when she said "There would have been no tongues had Irving married me."

Soon after this visit, on March 25, saying *au revoir* rather than farewell, and carrying with him the manuscript of *Sartor*, Carlyle took Jane by coach to Liverpool on the way back to Craigenputtock.

XIII

RETURN TO CRAIGENPUTTOCK
1832–1834

The retirement to Craigenputtock was a misfortune for Jane, and scarcely less so for Carlyle. There was little pretence by either that it was anything but a retreat. Carlyle had spoken of spending only the winter in London; he had expressed doubts about obtaining work enough to stay there; but it is clear that to stay was his hope. He had good excuses for the return—the need for silence and seclusion in which to think and write, for instance; but in his letters, and even more in his journal, the sense of failure is unmistakable.

To Jane, all the sacrifices of the past years appeared to have been thrown away, her careful encouragement of Carlyle and suppression of her own wishes and individuality gone for nothing. And was it necessary to retreat? She had seen Carlyle listened to, admired, by some of the foremost literary men in London. She had heard his work praised, his future eulogised. A Carlyle was needed in London—she was told so on all sides and she believed it. She had assured herself that the genius she had perceived, encouraged and defended for ten years, and in which she had placed all her faith, was at last coming into its own. For herself, she had tasted paradise only to have it snatched from her. Ailing though she often was, London had proved all that she expected; she had experienced enough of the exhilaration of sophisticated, intellectual company to know it to be essential to both of them. In London she could use her gifts to help Carlyle, enjoy herself, and feel herself extended, useful, admired. At Craigenputtock Carlyle at least had his writing, whatever his private feelings might be, but there was no relief for her from a sickening sense of disappointment.

And so the return to Craigenputtock began inauspiciously;

Carlyle was irritable with himself, Jane and the world, and Jane (after a short time) was nervy and almost always unwell. There soon arose at Craigenputtock what was to become the familiar background music of the later life in London—a duet of hypochondriacs. Hitherto Jane had tried, often with success, to subordinate her own sufferings to Carlyle's well-being. She gave sympathy and did not expect a great deal in return. But now she was not always so careful to disguise the effects of a sleepless night, of sickness, headaches, and all the minor ills that came on her. Complaints were heard on both sides of the breakfast table—and few could be more cruel than Jane when her tongue was roused by anger, wounded pride, or a sense of injustice.

The journey home was none of the best. "Wild" and "unpleasantly chaotic" was Carlyle's description of the coach ride to Liverpool, but from Jane, he noted, there was nothing but patient goodness. To save money, they returned as they had come, by the boat to Annan. "Sick, sick my poor woman must have been" cries Carlyle in recollection "but she retired out of sight, and would suffer with her best grace in silence". The sight of Alick and other Carlyles at Annan renewed Carlyle's grief at the loss of his father. Jane wept for him, and for herself too. At Dumfries, they heard that Goethe was dead. Carlyle felt that he had lost a second father and was wild to begin some tribute to him. He worked hard on a *Funeral Oration*. They stayed for a time at Templand and Scotsbrig and got back to Craigenputtock towards the end of April. Carlyle had a bad first week: "exceedingly out of my element, inclined to be wretched and sulky: no work would prosper with me." Jane he thought better, now that she had set to work. And so she was for a time, in the fine spring weather, with Carlyle busy but not absorbedly:

"My Husband" she tells Eliza Miles "is as good company as reasonable mortal could desire. Every fair morning we ride on horse-back for an hour before breakfast. . . . Then we eat such a surprising breakfast of home-baked bread, and eggs, &c, &c, as might incite anyone that had breakfasted so long in London to write a pastoral. Then Carlyle takes to his writing while I, like Eve, 'studious of household good', inspect my house, my garden, my live stock, gather flowers for my drawingroom, and lapfuls of eggs; and finally betake myself also to writing, or reading or making or mending, or whatever work seems fittest. After dinner, and only then, I lie on the sofa and (to my shame be it spoken) sometimes *sleep*, but oftenest dream waking. In the evening I walk on the moor (how different from Holborn and the Strand!) and read anything that does not exact much attention. Such is my life,—agreeable as yet from its novelty, if for nothing else."

For a time there is much to be said for clear skies and fresh air; and always for a house of one's own. But Jane herself, even in this moment of complaisance, was clear enough that it could not survive the summer. She tries to persuade Eliza Miles to come to Craigenputtock:

"I never forget my gentle Ariel in Ampton St,—it were positive sin to forget her, so helpful she was, so beautiful, so kind and good! Besides this is the place of all others for thinking of absent friends, where one has so seldom any present to think of. It is the stillest, solitariest place that it ever entered upon your imagination to conceive—where one has the strangest shadowy existence, nothing actual in it but the food we eat, the bed one sleeps on, and (praised be Heaven!) the fine air one breathes; the rest is all a dream of the absent and distant, of things past and to come."

But Eliza could not come, and Carlyle was now back in his study most of the day: "My sole comfort and remedy is Work! Work!" But he was conscious of his blessings: "a kind, true-hearted wife . . . fresh air, food and raiment;" he had opened a heartening correspondence with John Mill, which kept him in touch with London; and he had still good hopes of enough work to keep them alive at Craigenputtock. He wrote, first, on Ebenezer Elliot's *Corn Law Rhymes*—an article that was noticed by Emerson in Boston, who felt curious to know the writer. Of greater importance, as it was eventually to prove, was a commission for an article on Diderot. With the money earned, he hoped to arrange for *Sartor* to be published at his own expense. For visitors they had only John Welsh for a day's fishing, until, on August 12, Robert Welsh and a crowd of young followers descended on Craigenputtock for the grouse. Carlyle fled the house in disgust, and soon afterwards let the shooting so that he should be interrupted no more. In the late summer, to prepare himself for the *Diderot*, he began reading, for as many as eleven hours a day, books on the French Revolution. "There is *no* other course for me in this lone Desert" he told Alick, "where if a man did not work, he might so easily run mad." He sought advice and the loan of books from Mill, and urged him to write on the Revolution itself. Jane saw less and less of him. He was not unaware of her loneliness, but his consolation rested in renunciation of personal pleasures—the Calvinistic gospel of his childhood.

> "Her life beside me constantly writing here is but a dull one; however, she seems to desire no other; has, in many things, pronounced the word *Entsagen*, and looks with a brave if with no joyful heart into the present and the future. She manages all things—poultry, flowers, bread-loaves; keeps a house still like a band-box, then reads, or works (as at present) on some translation from Goethe. I tell her many times there is *much* for her to do if she were trained to it: her whole sex to deliver from the bondage of frivolity, dollhood and imbecility, into the freedom of valour and womanhood."

The lesson was dinned into her on all sides. Sarah Austin says of a translation: "How I wish Mr Carlyle may like—in any degree—what I have done. And then you, like a loyal wife as you are, will like it too." John Carlyle was nearer the mark when he told her that some occupation to fill her whole day would do more for her than all the medicines in existence. But her trouble was almost total lack of company. She was never intended to be solitary and silent and serious. Carlyle commented on her lack of conversation; but it is difficult to talk with a man who is more of a lecturer than a conversationalist, and usually "so dreadfully in earnest". What he meant was, that her contributions to his own subjects were inadequate. No doubt they were; she was no Carlyle, no Mill, no Goethe; but she was no fool, she had plenty to say in her own right, and a genius for extracting good things from a select company. But company there was none; and a man with a message is a poor listener on any subject but his own, and often enough on that too. So Jane was driven to listen or to talk about the affairs of the house, which interested her, but not to the exclusion of everything else. Her health began to fail; she was for ever bilious, headachy, or complaining of indigestion.

Carlyle was himself discontented. He longed for a library; he began to wonder, again, whether life so cut off from men was tolerable, even possible, for a writer. He spoke about his "imprisonment", and early in the autumn he writes in his journal "I must to Edinburgh in winter; the solitude here, generally very irksome, is threatening to get injurious, to get intolerable". Jane put the matter succinctly; "Carlyle is going mad for speech—and proposes making a descent on the Capital about the beginning of Winter and filling it with a whole deluge of articulate sound." And to Eliza Stodart: "The grim prospect of another winter in this solitude is too frightful for my Husband, who finds that it is absolutely essential for carrying on, not only his craft, but his existence, to hear from time to time a little human speech." She was writing to ask Eliza to look about for a small furnished house, for Carlyle, herself and a maid. Eliza had not written for eighteen months to Jane who says:

> "In prolonged bad health and worse spirits I judged there could be small call upon me to be sending letters out as it were, into infinite space—no sounds of them ever more heard. Still vainer seemed it to apply for sympathy to one who was apparently nowise concerning herself whether I remained behind in a nice flower-potted London churchyard, or returned in a state of total wreck to my own country. A few days before I left London a certain Dr Allen said to Carlyle in a complimentary tone as I left the room, 'Mrs Carlyle has the remains of a fine woman'! Think of that now! at thirty to pass for a remains!"

She asks:

> "Does your Uncle ever make the *smallest* mention of me? ever inquire if the mischievous creature who broke his folder is still working devilry on this planet? Alas no! she is sober enough now—a long succession of bad days and sleepless nights have effectually tamed her. O Bess for one good laugh with you, for the sake of old times! I do not remember the time when I laughed."

Even with Edinburgh in view, Carlyle's dissatisfaction persisted:

> "I sit here (in the library) . . . having dulness only to struggle with. . . . Jane is sitting in the dining-room. . . . She is not quite so brisk as she was. . . . Recreation we have none; a walk, a ride, on some occasions a combined *drive* for health's sake alone. Miss Whigham (of Allanton) called here the other day, and this is simply our only call since we came from London! Poor William Corson, indeed, bounces up about once in the month to tea; but he is nigh distracted and one cannot count on him. I tried the schoolmaster, but he is a poor raw-boned Grampus. . . . I have tried some of the peasants, but them also without fruit. In short, mortal communion is not to be had for us here."

By the middle of October he had finished the *Diderot*, and waited only for payment to go to Edinburgh. He and Jane went over to Templand where Mrs Welsh was "bilious and terrified" of the cholera, then they drove on to Lockerbie, where Alick

was not very happily established in a new farm. He had named
his daughter, born early in the year, Jane Welsh Carlyle, but
that was his only satisfaction, and he was talking of emigrating to
America. Jane was twice more called to Templand within the
month, to nurse her mother: "Indeed I am harassed on all
sides at present".

Carlyle had been able, a month earlier, to repay Jeffrey the
£60 he had borrowed, and also, thanks to John's prosperity, the
loan that his brother had accepted more than a year before.
Jeffrey had been astonished and pained by the retreat to
Craigenputtock, and was not pleased by what he heard from
Jane of her life there, and particularly by the efforts she was
still making to accommodate herself to Carlyle's manner of
thought. To Eliza Miles, she had jeered at the fate of any "fine
lady" set down to live at Craigenputtock; and a little later
Carlyle was reporting that "Anti-gigmanism is the fixed un-
alterable Athanasian Creed of this house: Jane is almost
stronger in it (and in Anti-fine-ladyism) than myself." Jane had
written to Jeffrey in this sense. He did not perceive how much
of this was self-protection, and reproached her:

> "I like to think of your gallopings, but not of your musings at home.
> You must allow me to regret that you are not more cheerful and more
> social. . . . O my dear Friend, be happy; and believe that all opinions
> *must* be false which tend to depress an innocent spirit."

He had called on Mrs Austin, who was surely imaginative and
mystical enough for Jane: "Yet she wears her mind open to the
enjoyments and even the *vanities* of the world you despise."

The appeal was, in fact, unnecessary. Jane could never do
more than pay lip-service to Carlyle's glorification of *Entsagen*;
her nature and inclinations were all opposed to it; had not this
putting aside of pleasure for duty seemed sanctified by her
father's teaching, and had it not seemed necessary to adopt such
an attitude if Craigenputtock were to be endurable, it would
have been given short shrift. Unaware of this, Jeffrey feared
that Carlyle was dragging Jane down with him into misanthropy. Come to Craigcrook, he said; and, when he heard
that they intended to winter in Edinburgh, he repeated the
invitation.

The Edinburgh visit, timed for the beginning of December,
was postponed at the last moment because Walter Welsh was

dying, and Mrs Welsh, who had nursed him devotedly for years, was again ill. Jane went down at once. Carlyle immediately began to miss her, wrote lovingly, and urged her to return as soon as possible. But it was he who came to her; Walter Welsh died soon afterwards, and Carlyle made the journey from Templand to Crawford to represent Jane at the funeral. They spent some time helping Mrs Welsh to decide her future movements. She wished to stay at Templand, but to get rid of the farm, and this was duly done. In the first week of December they were home again but Jane returned once more to Templand when her mother wrote to her unhappily. While there, she had a letter from Eliza Stodart. She had discovered a house, not far from Comley Bank. Should she take it? Yes, replied Jane. She had no wish to come specially to Edinburgh: "and really the notion of going ten miles, without my Husband, is frightful to me, I am so very *feckless* grown."

She was identifying herself more closely than ever before with Carlyle, through sheer weakness. She was now all but a chronic invalid, with strength only to struggle through each day—none at all to assert herself. In any case, she dared not oppose Carlyle in more than minor details; apart from his appearance and manner, which gave an almost irresistible sense of conviction to all he said, she felt the necessity of believing him in the right; otherwise, her miseries and his, the life at Craigenputtock, everything, would have been in vain, and she was not strong enough to face such a thought.

Edinburgh, which they reached early in the new year, 1833, was doomed for Jane, because Carlyle was, if anything, more unhappy, more restless and uncertain there than he had been at Craigenputtock. The stay began disastrously. The house pleased them both: it was at Stockbridge, near the Water of Leith, and had beautiful views. Then they discovered that the floor above their own was rented by a prostitute, whose parties went on into the early hours. Carlyle, short of sleep, became almost intolerable, and Jane wrote despairingly to John. She feels sick and heartless:

"every one gets the start of poor me! Indeed for the last year I have not made one inch of way but sat whimpering on a mile stone lamenting over the roughness of the road. If you would come home and get my interior to rights it would wonderfully facilitate the problem of living for me."

She added, in her best Carlyle fashion, "but perhaps it is best for me that it should *not* be made easier."

While Jeffrey was at Craigcrook, he cheered them both; he played shuttle-cock with Jane, bantered her affectionately in the old manner, and was his usual chaffing self with Carlyle, "talking like a pen-gun (of very *light* calibre), always brisk and in good humour." But he had to go to London a few weeks later and Carlyle could find no one to replace him. The only person he could talk to with patience was Sir William Hamilton; and even that mild man innocently offended—he "does not attain earnestness", and he had given a supper that "has done me mischief". "All is Whiggery here" he lamented; he heard nothing but "hollow jargon"; his ears were bewildered by "inane chatter"—"one's heart is for hours and days overcast by the sad feeling: 'There is none then, not one, that will believe in me' ". The unhonoured prophet was forced to console himself with the reflection: "continue to believe in *thyself*. Let the chattering of innumerable gigmen pass by thee as what it is. . . . Neither fear thou that this thy great message of the Natural *being* the Supernatural will wholly perish unuttered."

This was poor comfort to Jane, who was in bed, ill; but, though the doctor who was called in confessed that he could do little for her, she managed to conceal much of her depression from Carlyle, as appears from his report to his brother. "She bears up with fixed resolution, appears even to enjoy many things in Edinburgh, yet has grown no stronger of late." Her sense of humour was still with her. One day she fainted from the pain in her head. "It will not be permanent," Carlyle assured her. "As if" she commented "I could fancy it would be permanent without instantly cutting my throat."

In March, Jane told Eliza: "Our charming young friend upstairs has been creating such an infernal disturbance of late, that we were resolved, should any resource present itself, to leave her the house to herself." The resource appeared unexpectedly. An old school friend of Jane offered them a floor of a furnished house in Great King Street. The owner of the Stockbridge house made no objection:

" 'She was quite aware of the night-noises—had left the house in consequence of having such disagreeable and disreputable neighbours!' So you and I know what to do, dear, when we happen to have a house we can no longer occupy ourselves—just swear it is all right and tight, and let it to some innocent third party."

Jane's one clear gain from this Edinburgh stay was the meeting with Susan Hunter. One of Susan's sisters had been Francis Jeffrey's first wife, another had married Jeffrey's only brother, John; both had died young. John Jeffrey lived on alone in Edinburgh, and Susan and her remaining sister, sometimes with their brother John Hunter, used often to stay with him. The Carlyles met them all at Craigcrook before Francis Jeffrey left for London, and Jane and Susan quickly took to each other. Susan, says Carlyle, "was a tall, lean, cleanly trim and wise-looking, though by no means beautiful woman, except that her face and manners expressed nothing that was not truthful, simple, rational, modest though decided." Jane liked her because she was kind, and "several things that women rarely are—straight-forward and clear-sighted among the rest," and came to long for her brisk and cheerful voice and person, to "wind me up . . . when I was quite run down; so that from being a mere senseless piece of lumber, I began to tick and tell people what o'clock it was." Even in the midst of her headaches, Susan was welcome. Soon after they had met, Jane was writing

"I do not know how I should like you as an adversary, but bringing, as you do, so much vehemence and clearsightedness to the *right* side of most questions (that is to say to *my* side) I feel thoroughly disposed, in true German style, to 'swear everlasting friendship' with you."

Mrs Welsh, who had come to stay with them, was anxious to meet John Jeffrey "whom I have engaged that *she* will like better than the Advocate. For *me*, of course it would be a shame did I not remain true to my *first* love." Jane might have added that John Jeffrey had fallen in her favour for a remark, passed on to her, that she had been "distinguished as a flirt".

This friendship, and the bright letters it produced, showed that, given company to her liking, Jane could be as well as she was ever likely to be. She had come to Edinburgh, as she had gone to London the previous winter, with health and spirits worn low by many months of solitude at Craigenputtock. In London she recovered because Carlyle was well and (for him) contented and because she met many interesting and stimulating people. In Edinburgh the recovery did not come; Carlyle was neither well nor contented, and she met few people.

Carlyle indeed draws so unattractive a picture of himself that it was no wonder Jane lacked company. "The talent of conversation", he says, " . . . has . . . quite forsaken me. . . . I appear like a wild monstrous Orson amongst the people, and (especially if bilious) smash everything to pieces. The very sound of my voice has got something savage-prophetic." In Edinburgh, such behaviour was considered merely bad manners and egotism run mad, and his originality went for nothing. At first he had found Edinburgh people "beautiful to look upon after mere black-faced sheep"; but although, after a month or two, his views of the people had changed greatly for the worse, he was still reluctant to return to the sheep: "one thing I have as good as ascertained: that Craigenputtock cannot for ever be my place of abode; that it is at present, and actually, one of the worst abodes for me in the whole wide world . . . of solitude I have really had enough." Where should he go? Edinburgh was "one of the dullest and poorest, and, on the whole, paltriest of places". The longer he stayed, the more severe his judgments grew. In contrast to London's "boiling uproar", Edinburgh seemed "almost stagnant" and the people "all of *one sort*: meet twenty of them in a day, they are all most probably talking of the same subject; and that mostly an insignificant one, and handled in an insignificant way." By the end of March he was recalling that in London "amid its huge deafening hubbub of a Death-song, are to be heard tones of a Birth-song; while here all is putrid, scandalous, decadent, hypocritical, and sounds through your soul like lugubrious universal *Noenia*, chaunted by foul midnight hags." And just before he left, in May, he told Leigh Hunt: "Such a dreary morass of Dulness, Halfness, Unbelief, embarrassment, poverty spiritual and economical, it seems to me I never dwelt in: the truth is, Ruin, here as elsewhere, is advancing with quite notable rapidity." Mill in London was urging, "there is surely no place so good as this."

To complete his discomfiture, he had bad news of Irving. Since the Carlyles had left London the previous spring, he had been dismissed from his church. In the middle of March he was summoned before the Presbytery at Annan, where he had been ordained, and was deposed from the Scottish church. He at once began to preach throughout the countryside. Carlyle felt "a mixture of admiration and deep pain . . . he must go from wild to wilder. This is the issue of what once appeared the highest blessing for him—Popularity!"

The Edinburgh visit was destined to breed wretchedness to the very last day—and beyond. The story was told to Eliza when Jane at last reached Craigenputtock: "we were in Edinburgh *two days* after you and all our acquaintance supposed us gone!" They had missed the coach.

> "Let us drop a veil over the disgraceful home-march! Enough to say that I was forthwith deposited in bed with the dreadfullest headache, and remained there most of the time we had to wait; glad my existence was unknown, that so I might be left in quiet. It was now too apparent to me that I had got Influenza, I only hoped that I might brave it out, and keep up till I was landed at *home*. But I could get no further than Templand, after suffering by the way such misery as I shall not soon forget. There I had to keep my bed for a week. My Mother too was laid up with it for three days, so I had the additional vexation of being looked on as a pestilence."

Jane was not usually backward in making the most of her troubles—her letters owe much of their charm to the seasoning of exaggeration she adds to small misfortunes—but she did not overstate her condition in the coach. She was so ill by the time they reached Thornhill that she could not bear the final drive to Templand, less than a mile away, and she staggered along the road, hanging on Carlyle's arm. At Templand she collapsed into one of her headaches, the like of which Carlyle had never seen in his life: "agony of retching . . . and of spasmodic writhing, that would last from twenty-four to sixty hours."

Before leaving Edinburgh, Jane had gone by herself to Haddington and had sat by the side of her father's grave. Now, driving up to Craigenputtock she had a painful shock; one of the plantations, to the left of the house, was a mass of blackened stumps; it had caught fire through the tenant-farmer's carelessness:

> "O Eliza, I could cry yet to think of this—to think of my Father taking such a world of pains to plant these woods—to think they have had rain and sunshine vouchsafed them for more than twenty years, to be finally consumed in one night thro' the carelessness of a lout like Macadam!"

During the summer her health and spirits began to improve. Soon after her thirty-second birthday she told Eliza that she felt better than she had done for two years.

"It has even seemed as if my beauty would emerge from its premature eclipse; at least it has occasionally struck me that my glass reflected something more than 'the remains of a fine woman', the animated presence of an average sort of woman. Nothing indeed *that* to found conceit upon; but like *the penny roll* it may be '*made to do*'."

The main reason for the improvement was a feeling that the time at Craigenputtock was limited. There was talk of a visit to France—a result of Carlyle's growing interest in the Revolution —and even when this fell through, they were both agreed that a move to London must be made at the earliest possible moment. This was cheering; so, in lesser degree, was the presence of John Carlyle who spent two months of his summer holiday at Craigenputtock. John was not Jane's ideal of a man; he was small, spare, spruce, with the broad round face typical of most of his family, and was described by her as "one of the people who seem to have been born in creaking shoes." Nevertheless, he was a man, travelled, cultured, and with time to spare. He was company. His view of Jane was far from favourable; he thought her idle, fanciful, and not a particularly good wife for his brother; he understood no better than his sister-in-law Jenny, Jane's way of working by fits and starts; but though brusque, pedestrian, and exceedingly dogmatic, he was kind, he prescribed for her ailments, and, finding her good company, he read Italian with her, told her of his travels, and would listen in return to her. This was, by Craigenputtock standards, bliss; and Jane accepted philosophically the news of successive visitors who failed to arrive. Thornton, eldest son of Leigh Hunt, actually got as far as Edinburgh on his way to them, but could not face the rest of the journey. Henry Inglis could not get away, and Mill elected finally to visit Paris. Both mothers stayed for a while, and there were flying visits by Walter and Helen from Liverpool, and the Donaldsons from Haddington. But when all further hope for the summer was abandoned, a new face appeared at Craigenputtock for a single day. Mill had written doubtfully of a Ralph Waldo Emerson, introduced by Gustave d'Eichthal, who was anxious to meet Carlyle. Mill gave him a note, but, he said, "I do not think him a very hopeful subject."

Mill was mistaken—for the time at least. Carlyle found Emerson "the most amiable creature in the world." Jane was less enthusiastic, but "thankful to Providence for the windfall of a stray American, 'come out for to see' whatsoever things were wise, and of good report, from one end of Europe to the other. With such accuracy of investigation did he prosecute this object, that he arrived, by paths unknown, at the door of Craigenputtock, which was, of course, opened to him with all the pleasure in life. To find the Christian charities inside, and even the Graces seemed to occasion him the most agreeable surprise. Carlyle had been represented to his Transatlantic Imagination, quite *Teufelsdrockish,*—a man severe—living in complete isolation, and partial barbarism: the Individual before his bodily eyes was shaven and shorn, overflowing with the milk of human kindness, *und mid Weib im Hause*; a blessing which the amiable American estimated highly—himself having *lost it* after an *exceedingly brief* trial. He went 'on—on'—and we saw him no more."

Emerson admired Carlyle's "extraordinary powers of conversation". Carlyle "expressed some impatience of his total solitude". He was surprised to hear how well his work was being received in America; but not so Jane: "That is always the way", she said "whatever he has writ that he thinks has fallen dead, he hears of two or three years afterwards." After staying a night, Emerson was off in the morning to visit Wordsworth—he was making a quick tour of notabilities. Mill was taken aback. "I should have thought *he* was about the last person who would have interested you."

On his return to Craigenputtock, Carlyle had arranged to publish *Sartor*. It was received, according to Fraser, with "the most unqualified disapproval". This had an immediate effect on editorial demands. No further request for articles was made. Carlyle's future at once seemed uncertain, the French trip was abandoned for fear of wasting the money he had been slowly saving, and the home in London receded into the indefinite. Carlyle doggedly read on in the French Revolution, but Jane, her hopes of London dashed and her company gone, began to show signs of a return of the previous winter's ill health. Early in September, Mrs Welsh, her fears easily roused, carried her off with Helen Welsh to take the waters at Moffat. Carlyle wrote penitently, and with much affection, to his "little Janekin":

"Take a little amusement, dear Goody, if thou canst get it. God knows little comes to thee with me, and thou art right patient under it. But, courage, dearest! I swear better days are coming, *shall* come. The accursed, baleful cloud that has hung over my existence *must* (I feel it) dissipate, and let in the sun which shines on all. It *must*, I say. What is it but a cloud, properly a shadow, a chimaera? Oh, Jeannie! But enough.

If I am happy, art not thou, also, happy in my happiness? Hope *all* things, dearest, and be true to me still, as thou art."

She was glad enough to be back from "detestable Moffat," and returned in time to entertain

"a broken-down Barrister who is now literally lying among the pots,— having made his last stand against the world, on a not too solid basis of whisky and water. He with a pretty pettish wife of the fine Lady sort, but also taking into whisky exhibited to us for one mortal week a specimen of that sort of company which is worse than none; which at Craigenputtock of all places one is tempted to deny the possibility of. But they also passed on, and again all was silent and continues silent to this hour. Yet here in the midst of this almost fearful silence we are fixed for the winter—resolute to assert the superiority of mind over matter, by neither going out of our wits nor attempting our lives thro' the dismalities of the ensuing season."

The "dismalities" were kept at bay fairly successfully through the later part of autumn. The piano had been tuned, and Jane was playing, sewing, writing as usual to Eliza Stodart.

"It is so pleasant to talk with you about old times, whether by the fireside or on paper, with the profoundest disregard of all sense or ceremony. But so it is. 'Man' as Carlyle was saying last night, 'is a mass of contradictions'. What a quantity of wisdom, new and old, falls from his lips in the course of one solar day! . . . On the crumbs that fall from *his* table I might positively set up a respectable little bread shop of my own, if I were not too indolent to gather them up into a whole. . . . This indeed would be, not '*lighting the candle at both ends*,' as we see some improvident couples do, but a notable invention for *burning the candle twice over*".

There were changes in the Carlyle family; Jean married her cousin, James Aitken, and went to live in Dumfries; and Jamie also wished to marry. As this latter marriage might affect the position of old Mrs Carlyle—for Jamie intended to live at Scotsbrig with his wife—Carlyle appealed to him to delay the wedding.

"I understand what wonderful felicities young men like you expect from marriage; I know too (for it is a truth as old as the world) that such expectations hold out but for a little while. I shall rejoice much (such is my experience of the world) if in your new situation you feel *as* happy as in the old; say nothing of happier."

Jeffrey again besought Jane to winter in Edinburgh: 'It is not good for either of you to be so much alone." She was still defending Carlyle, but Jeffrey still refused to take seriously her "magnanimous purpose of fighting for your pet fancies—or convictions as you call them." He also reaffirmed his affection and admiration for Carlyle, and a sincere desire for his happiness—"or if that word offends you—your wellbeing—rightmindedness—strong workingness—or whatever else is your favourite synonym for a desirable condition of being."

Carlyle had no difficulty in resisting such teasing; he was unable to grasp the fact that flippancy could cover seriousness and wisdom, and he recoiled from it instinctively. It is less easy to understand how Jane resisted a manner so much after her own heart. But she was still conscientiously identifying herself with Carlyle, and resist it she did. Both—Carlyle particularly—shrank from Edinburgh, and as he was reluctant to venture on London when all editors seemed shy of printing him, they decided to stay and brave out Craigenputtock and swallow their declaration of never wintering there again. In the first month of the new year, 1834, Carlyle tells Sarah Austin, "I do not think you ever in your life saw such a solitude as this." He read most of the day, "*smoked* most of all". Jane, determined to keep away the illness of the previous year, went to the drastic length of taking a cold shower every morning—a course she was only partially successful in persuading Carlyle to follow. Carlyle had now as many books to read as he chose—the library of Barjarg nearby had been made free to him—and a subject was fixing itself in his imagination. There were, then, no parties or dinners at Craigcrook, but Carlyle did, for the last time, seek Jeffrey's help. In gloomy moments he once again began to think of giving up writing. He even talked of emigrating to America, influenced by Alick and by the reports of Emerson. These wild ideas, if not quite obliterated by Jane, who had other plans for him, were put aside by the news that an Observer was needed for the new Observatory in Edinburgh. Carlyle asked Jeffrey about it, but did not fully explain his qualifications which were considerable. Jeffrey replied at once that the post would not suit him. But, he added, even had it suited him, he still would not have recommended him. A teacher, said Jeffrey, must teach what is thought worth learning, in a way that is thought agreeable, "and I am afraid you have not fulfilled either of these conditions. No man ever did more to obstruct the success of his doctrines, by the tone in which he promulgated them. It is arrogant, vituperative, obscure, anti-national, and inconclusive."

This letter, though not differing in essence from many that Jeffrey had written, caused much indignation at Craigenputtock. Carlyle called it "a polite fish-woman shriek" and his mother, who was on a visit, declared "He canna hinder thee of God's providence". Carlyle did his best to remain philosophical —it was "very wholesome to have my vanity humbled from time to time"—and he replied lightly.

This exchange took place in the early days of the new year. A few weeks ter Jeffrey wrote again. He was about to leave for London, and, realising that Carlyle was looking for an academic post, warned him again that he would not be appointed to one while he held to his present views. The chair of Rhetoric in Edinburgh was likely to fall vacant, and Jeffrey wished to save Carlyle the mortification of application and refusal. He ended with an apology for his "vivacities" with Jane, adding "but who would not be provoked to see Titania in love with Bottom?"

Carlyle was hurt by this rebuff. Yet never was a word spoken in better season; for Jeffrey's last letter coincided with an offer from Mill of work on a new review, the *London Review*, in which he was interested. Mill, back from Paris, had whetted Carlyle's interest in the old Revolution by descriptions of the leaders of the Revolution of 1830; particularly of Godefroi Cavaignac, "a man of irresistible power and indomitable will" who, in an interview with Louis Philippe, had demanded that a Republic should be set up.

Thus poised between expectation and disappointment, only the slightest push was needed to send the Carlyles flying. The push came from Grace Macdonald, who told Jane in the middle of February that she had decided to leave in the summer. Jane lost patience at this new blow, for Grace was a companion as well as a servant. She declared that she would tolerate Craigenputtock no longer. "Let us burn our ships" she cried. And so "the cup that had long been filling ran over with that smallest of drops," Carlyle explained to Jean. They put the house up to rent, decided to leave at Whitsun, wrote to their London friends to look about for a house, and engaged as maid Bessy Barnet, daughter of Badams' former housekeeper at Birmingham.

Carlyle was more expansive with John: "our heads and hearts have been full of this great enterprise, the greatest (small as it is) that I ever *knowingly* engaged in. . . . A strange shiver runs through every nerve of me when I think of taking that plunge; yet also a kind of sacred faith."

In her postscript to the same letter, Jane spoke in similar terms, but in her own way. She complained of her usual fate in having to write in the margins and in between lines—"he leaves me nothing but dregs"—but she made fair use of her dregs:

> "Here is a new prospect opened up to us with a vengeance! Am I frightened? Not a bit. I almost wish that I felt more anxiety about our future; for this composure is not *courage*, but *diseased indifference*. There is a sort of incrustation about the inward me which renders it alike insensible to fear and to hope. I suppose I am in what Glen calls the *chrysalis state* or the *state of incubation*. Let us trust that like all other states which have a beginning it will also have an end, and that the poor Psyche shall at last get freed. In the meantime I do what I see to be my duty as well as I can and wish that I could do it better. It seems as if the problem of living would be immensely simplified to me if I had health. It does require such an effort to keep oneself from growing quite wicked, while that weary weaver's shuttle is plying between my temples."

She has a canary, Chico, which sings all day long "like—like anything". He also was to take part in the great adventure.

The next month or two were filled with preparations, and more expressions of doubt and wonder. The dare-devil attitude adopted by both Jane and Carlyle seems barely warranted by the facts. Both, for all their language, were full of Scots caution. They had been careful with their money, and Carlyle was able to take more than £200 to London. Although most of the Welsh furniture was going to London, some was to be stored at Craigenputtock. And if for any reason they failed in London, there would always be a home waiting for them at Templand or Scotsbrig, or at Craigenputtock, for that matter, as soon as Mrs Welsh could dispose of the next tenant.

Carlyle eventually grew impatient with the upheaval—he hated confusion in a house—and, fearing that the Scottish habit of letting houses at Whitsun also obtained in London, he rushed off in May. Leigh Hunt had several houses for him to look at; one only a few yards from his own house in Upper Cheyne Row, Chelsea. Carlyle lodged again with the Miles family at Ampton Street, began to inspect the houses, and wrote long, loving letters to Jane at Craigenputtock and gave her minute directions how to prepare and send the furniture—"tie all bedposts together". He was looking up his friends and acquaintances—Jeffrey, Buller, Irving, Cunningham, and Hunt, but avoiding "all Huntesses and Huntlets". Eliza Miles was very good to him, and longing to see Jane.

Jane replied no less lovingly, and described her actions no less minutely. She had sold an old carpet for 25s., the drawing-room chairs for 7s. 6d. each, and the dining table for £3—it had a broken leg, she reminds Carlyle. She stayed on at Craigenputtock until all was settled, towards the end of May. On her last day there: "O Good what I would give for a long long sleep in your arms. . . . 'Was I wae' to leave the Puttock? To be sure I was! but I made little greeting—just a little in our own room all alone immediately before starting."

Carlyle's one grief at leaving Craigenputtock had been the parting with his mother: "it is a kind of *forsaking*." Jane had less feeling for her mother, dreading her emotional outbursts. She had forbidden her to come to Annan to see her off: "one has enough to do at present without *scenes*."

The choice of houses had narrowed to one at Brompton, suggested by Mrs Austin, and the one at Chelsea suggested by Hunt. Carlyle had not for long escaped "Huntlets": "Nondescript! unutterable! Mrs Hunt asleep on cushions, four or five beautiful, strange, gipsy-looking children running about in undress, whom the lady ordered to get us tea." One boy, "a sallow, black-haired youth of sixteen, with a kind of dark cotton nightgown on, went whirling about like a familiar, providing everything: an indescribable dreamlike household." But the house they recommended struck him favourably.

"The street runs down upon the river, which I suppose you might see by stretching out your head from the front window, at a distance of fifty yards on the left. We are called 'Cheyne Row' proper (pronounced *Chainie* Row), and are a 'genteel neighbourhood'; two old ladies on one side, unknown character on the other, but with 'pianos'. The street is flag pathed, sunk storied, iron railed, all old fashioned and tightly done up; looks out on a rank of sturdy old *pollarded* (that is, beheaded) lime trees standing there like giants in *tawtie* wigs (for the new boughs are still young); beyond this is a high brick wall; backwards a garden, the size of our back one at Comley Bank, with trees, &c, in bad culture; beyond this green hayfields and tree avenues, once a bishop's pleasure grounds, an unpicturesque yet rather cheerful outlook. The house itself is eminent, antique, wainscoted to the very ceiling, and has been all new painted and repaired; broadish stair with massive balustrade (in the old style), corniced and as thick as one's thigh; floors thick as a rock, wood of them here and there worm-eaten, yet capable of cleanness, and still with thrice the strength of a modern floor. And then as to rooms, Goody! Three stories beside the sunk storey, in every one of them three apartments, in depth something like forty feet in all—a front dining-room (marble chimney piece, &c), then a back dining-room or breakfast-room, a little narrower by reason of the kitchen stairs; then out of this, and narrower still (to allow a back window, you consider) a china-room or pantry, or I know not what, all shelved and fit to hold crockery for the whole street. Such is the ground area, which of course continues to the top, and furnishes every bedroom with a dressing-room or second bedroom; on the whole a most massive roomy sufficient old house with places, for example, to hang, say, three dozen hats or cloaks on, and as many crevices and queer old presses and shelved closets (all tight and new painted in their way) as would gratify the most covetous Goody—rent, thirty-five pounds! I confess I am strongly tempted. . . . Our row, which for the last three doors or so is a street, and none of the noblest, runs out upon a 'Parade' (perhaps they call it) running along the shore of the river, a broad highway with huge shady trees, boats lying moored, and a smell of shipping and tan. Battersea Bridge (of wood) a few yards off; the broad river with white-trowsered, white-shirted Cockneys dashing by like arrows in thin long canoes of boats; beyond, the green beautiful knolls of Surrey with their villages—on the whole, a most artificial, green-painted, yet lively, fresh, almost opera-looking business, such as you can fancy. Finally, Chelsea abounds more than any place in omnibi, and they take you to Coventry Street for sixpence."

Jane told him not to settle on either house until she had seen them. But, she went on,

"I have a great liking to that massive old concern with the broad staircase and abundant accommodation for *crokery*! And dressingrooms to one's bedrooms is charming! I should not quarrel with the quantity of room even tho' (like my china assiettes) it might be asked 'what we had to put in it'."

But was it not too near the river—damp—unwholesome? And "another idea presents itself along with that wainscote—if bugs have ever been in the house! must they not have found there as well as the inmates 'room without end.'" She was excited, and changed her mind almost from line to line. Let Carlyle decide. She will approve whatever he does. The situation is not of great importance, he has good legs to take him anywhere: "and for me my chief enjoyment I imagine will always be in the society of my own heart's darling and within my own four walls as heretofore." Then back to her mother, who "is in the most gracious *bountiful* mood—giving me gowns &c, &c, has even bought a superior silk handkerchief for Alick! and a gown for little Sister Jenny whom she never saw! What a mercy for you Dearest that I have not *her* turn for managing the finance department!—we should soon sit rent free in the King's bench."

A few days later she left for Liverpool—seen off from Annan by old Mrs Carlyle—and on June 5 she and Chico arrived in London.

XIV

CHEYNE ROW
1834

Jane at first voted against the house at 5 Cheyne Row, then changed her mind, fell in love with it, and finally thought it nearly twice as good a bargain as any other they had seen. They settled on it; and on June 10, Carlyle told John:

> "a Hackney Coach, loaded to the roof and beyond it with luggage and live-passengers, tumbled us all down here about eleven in the morning. By 'all' I mean my Dame and myself; Bessy Barnet, who had come the night before; and—little *Chico*. . . . At two o'clock the Pickfords did arrive; and *then* began the hurly-burly; which even yet has but grown quieter, will not grow quiet, for a fortnight to come. However, two rooms and two bedrooms are now in a partially civilised state; the broken Furniture is mostly mended; I have my old writing-table again (here) *firm* as Atlas; a large wainscoted drawing-room (which is to be my study) with the 'red carpet' tightly spread on it; my Books all safe in Presses."

Jane was no less enthusiastic to Mrs Carlyle:

> "I could not have made myself a better house if I had had money at command—and for my servant—I expect she will be sister to me as well as servant. No fear but that we shall get a living and my Husband will be healthier and happier than he has been for long years."

Eliza Miles had come to help them settle in, and the house was taking shape at a great rate. But the change, the excitement and the work—for Jane, when she worked, did so until she was exhausted—made her more cautious a month later:

> "When I look round on my floors once more laid with carpets, my chairs all in a row etc I flatter myself the tumult is subsided—but when I look within! Alas I find my wits by no means in a row; but still engaged at an uproarious game of 'change seats the Ring's coming.' "

But she was clear enough about the benefit of the change; and the truth about her feelings at Craigenputtock began to appear:

186

"At all rates we are well out of Puttock—everywhere is suffering in store for one, but nowhere did I ever find or do I ever expect to find suffering of so base a sort as we had there."

Carlyle remained optimistic:

"We . . . have air and quiet hardly inferior to Craigenputtock, an outlook from the back-windows into mere leafy regions. . . . Yet in *half an hour* (for it is under two miles to Piccadilly) we can be, with a pair of stout legs, in the most crowded part of the whole habitable Earth."

He bought a new set of garden-tools and talked of turning gardener. "It is of admirable comfort to me, in the *smoking* way: I can wander about in dressing-gown and straw hat in it, as of old, and take my pipe in peace."

He too thought well of Bessy who, like Grace Macdonald before her, was more a companion than a servant. And for the moment he was satisfied in himself. He was feeling well, and he had begun to prepare for a book on the French Revolution, which Fraser had agreed to print, and for which Mill (who had withdrawn from the undertaking) was sending him "a whole barrowful" of books. He reckoned that his money would last for at least a year, but an editor was needed for the new *London Review*, and he had expectations of the post. He again thought of lecturing—a project never far from his mind. But perhaps his greatest satisfaction came from the welcome he received from the people who sympathised with his views, or who were attracted by his strong personality.

Of these, John Mill was one of the most regular callers at Cheyne Row; he was there one or two evenings a week, and he came every Sunday afternoon for a walk with Carlyle. Allan Cunningham looked in for a chat from time to time, as did Charles Buller and his mother. The Hunts were at hand, and although Leigh Hunt always waited for an invitation, he received one often enough (sometimes three or four times a week), for both Jane and Carlyle grew fond of him.

"Hunt is always ready to go and walk with me to all lengths if I want him. . . . He is a man of thoroughly London make, such as you could not find elsewhere, and I think about the *best* possible to be made of his sort: an airy, crotchety, most copious clever talker, with an honest under-current of reason too, but unfortunately not the deepest, not the most practical—or rather it is the most *un*practical ever man dealt in. His hair is grizzled, eyes black-hazel, complexion of the clearest dusky brown; a thin glimmer of a smile plays over a face of cast-iron gravity. He never laughs—can only titter, which I think indicates his worst deficiency."

For all his titter, Hunt had a pretty sense of humour, which endeared him to both. He talked well and musically. His voice fascinated Jane, who soon christened him "The Talking Nightingale". Notes were often passing from one house to the other, such as this typical one from Jane:

"My dear Sir, My Husband is just gone out leaving orders with me to write you a note inviting you to come to tea—I said it was of no use, you were predetermined *not* to come, especially if *I* asked you. He answered I could try at least, and tell you he had finished his day's work, and was really very desirous you would come. So behold I try! and what can I do more?—I cannot annihilate your laziness, or dislike, or pet, or caprice or whatever it is that makes you so obstinately stay away—I cannot make you as happy to come to us, as we are to have you come. I can but (as Edward Irving recommends in all such emergencies) '*pray to the Lord*' and assure you, that in *your* solitary instance at least, I break thro' my established principles of liking, in throwing away a very large quantity of affection on you which you seem totally insensible of and of course ungrateful for. Mrs Hunt also takes but a Motherless charge of me. Bless you all nevertheless."

Of the evenings with Hunt, Carlyle has left a record:

"He enjoyed much, and with a kind of chivalrous silence and respect, her Scotch tunes on the piano, most of which he knew already, and their Burns or other accompaniment; this was commonly enough the wind-up of our evening; 'supper' being ordered (uniformly 'porridge' of Scotch oatmeal), most likely the piano, on some hint, would be opened, and continue till the 'porridge' came—a tiny basin of which Hunt always took, and ate with a teaspoon, to sugar, and many praises of the excellent frugal and noble article. It seems to me, in our long, dim-lighted, perfectly neat and quaint room, these 'evening parties' of three were altogether human and beautiful; perhaps the best I anywhere had before or since!"

Jane had a soft place in her heart for this handsome man who was so courteous to her. He appreciated the stories she was beginning to tell with assurance and wit. He praised her playing and singing and enjoyed the bright clean home she kept—so different from his own. How much Jane agreed with his conversation is another question; but admiration she always welcomed, provided only that it was expressed in the right way. Carlyle had kept her on short commons—more and more she had to wait for his letters whenever she needed reassurance of her hold on his affections and of her charms as a woman. Mill, whose manner and talk were naturally "wintry (or *sawdust*-ish, as old Sterling once called it)" was too much preoccupied to be more than kind and polite. Hunt's graceful attentions therefore came at a good moment.

Jane's affection for Hunt did not extend to his family or his home, and she was soon complaining of Mrs Hunt, who had none of her husband's scruples.

> "She is every other day reduced to borrow my tumblers, my teacups, even a cupful of porridge, a few spoonfuls of tea are begged of me because 'Missus has got company, and happens to be out of the article'—in plain unadorned English because 'missus is the most wretched of managers, and is often at the point of having not a copper in her purse.' "

A month or two later:

> "Mrs Hunt I shall soon be quite terminated with I foresee. She torments my life out with borrowing. She actually borrowed one of the brass fenders the other day and I had difficulty in getting it out of her hands—irons, glasses, tea-cups, silver spoons, are in constant requisition —and when one sends for them the whole number can never be found. Is it not a shame to manage so with *eight guineas* a week to keep house on!"

There were other visitors outside the circle, increasing the pleasant sense of busyness and importance: "Mrs Austin sends me occasional '*three-pennies*' overflowing with '*dearests*' and all that, asks me to her *soirées* now and then, and even flashes down here in wheeled vehicles at rare intervals." John Mill had introduced the Carlyles to the Harriet Taylor whose name was now so often on his lips, and whom, Jane told John Carlyle "I could really love; if it were safe and she were willing—but she is a dangerous looking woman and engrossed with a dangerous passion and no useful relation can spring up between us." She wishes that he would come back from Rome and meet Mrs Taylor, and "tell me whether to fall desperately in love with or no." Carlyle was at first interested in this "living romance heroine, of the clearest insight, of the royalest volition, very interesting, of questionable destiny, not above twenty-five." But after a dinner—always a testing time for him—at her husband's house, he began to change his mind. Mill was there, and Mrs Taylor's spiritual adviser, W. J. Fox the Unitarian, who had "a tendency to pot-belly and *snuffiness*". The husband he found "an obtuse, most joyous-natured man, the pink of social hospitality." The Carlyles walked home from Regent's Park discussing the evening. She was still fascinated by this dark-eyed beauty, but he was doubtful. Mrs Platonica Taylor, as he began to call her, had, he thought, affected "a kind of sultana noble-mindedness, a certain girlish petulance, and felt that it did not wholly prosper." A few weeks later, knowing Jane better than she knew herself, he observed that, although Mill's "dearest friend" seemed for the present "all that is noble", "we shall see how that wears."

They renewed acquaintance with Henry Taylor, now coming into prominence through his verse drama *Philip von Artevelde*. Jane thought him "a goodish man but no Poet." She revelled in her new position. "Where is the stillness, the eternal sameness, of the last six years?" she triumphantly asks Eliza Stodart. "Echo answers at Craigenputtock! There let them 'dwell with Melancholy' and old Nancy Macqueen, for this stirring life is more to my mind."

She gives Eliza a list of her

> "*circle* of acquaintances. One of these who lives in prodigious *shine* with wife and family, you may happen to recollect something about—a grave handsome man who has been here repeatedly, and treats me with infinite respect, and takes immensely to my Husband—a sort of person with whom one talks about 'the condition of art' in this country, and such-like topics of general interest, and studies to support the reputation of a rather intellectual and excessively reasonable woman. Can you divine who I mean? Impossible. George Rennie! How has it happened? quite simply ... I heard he was there, I wondered what he was like; I sent him my address. He came instantaneously with his Sister Margaret. Bess did I feel awkward? to be sure I did, and looked awkward, for I was within an ace of fainting and he looked like one of his own marbles. But neither of us I believe entertained a particle of tenderness for the other. Nevertheless— it was mere queeziness from the intense sensation of the flight of time, which such a meeting occasioned one—fifteen years! only think! He is much improved by age, in appearance, manner, and also I think, in character—but he lives in the wretchedest atmosphere of '*gigmanity*'— his wife is a perfect fool—the whole kin of them are fools—and poor George . . . is still self-willed and vain enough to show me as often as I see him that I made an escape."

Carlyle, too, was busy at work that he liked, and appeared to be a changed man:

> "He is rapidly mending of his Craigenputtock gloom and acerbity" Jane told his mother. "He is really at times a tolerably social character,

and seems to be regarded with a feeling of mingled terror and love in all companies."

In the morning, on Carlyle's good days, as they breakfasted together in the back part of the ground floor room, he would speak of his growing hopes for *The French Revolution* and would seek her advice or criticism; and she was always ready, when he was in good humour, to delight him with her witty tales of Chico, who had taken a wife, of her bargains at the shops, of the oddities of their maid and their visitors. But after the first month or two it became clear that his humour varied as much as ever.

Jane had over-estimated the effect of change. For her it did wonders. People were life to her, even when they did no more than serve as subjects for her wit. But Carlyle, though kinder, warmer-hearted than his wife, loved man rather than men. The move to London was good for him; it brought him into the notice he needed, rubbed off the roughest of his corners, encouraged his sense of humour, expanded his sympathies, broadened his mind. But he remained a solitary. He had warned Jane years earlier, before they married, that he had a devil. She with excusable vanity, had promised herself and him that her love and faith would exorcise the devil. She took too much on herself. Carlyle's devil was beyond the power of love, beyond any power. It tormented him when he was idle and would not let him be when he was at work. The creative, prophetic spirit in him was a sullen master, filling him with doubts and despair, rending unwilling words from him. Jane could, and did, help him, soothing, ministering, sympathising, but her power grew less as her methods of consolation grew familiar. She could not write his books, resolve his doubts, remove his burden. Thus Carlyle is found writing in his journal less than two months after the settlement at Cheyne Row that his state is "almost frightful to *speak of*". He had "no practical friend, no confidant, properly no companion. For five days together I sit without so much as speaking to anyone except my wife. Mood tragical, gloomy, as of one forsaken, who had nothing left him *but to get through his task and die.*" He often thought of death. "Can friends do much for one?" he asks; and answers "almost nothing." Hunt is "limited, even bigoted"; Mrs Austin "a Niagara of gossip;" even Mill "speculative merely."

What is the meaning of all this? Carlyle explains. He has written nothing for a month. *The French Revolution* seethes in his mind "vague, boundless, without form and void". He fears "coming to absolute beggary . . . no man will give me money for my work". He is dyspeptic through sitting at his desk day after day, brooding, the words not coming. He is "weary, dispirited, sick, forsaken, every way heavy laden". He adds "what I suffer is, as much as may be, locked up within myself."

But these things, even if unspoken, are not to be hidden. The breakfasts, when the book was at a standstill, were ominous introductions to the day, heavy with irritation, sarcasm, complaints, despair, from which Carlyle was not often to be coaxed or roused.

Such breakfasts, such days, were not new to Jane. But of Craigenputtock little good was to be expected; of London, much. She told herself that Carlyle was a genius, and was behaving like one; but this consolation is a limited one to a proud and loving woman. London had this advantage over Craigenputtock, that friends broke into the moods and scattered them. But only for a time; Carlyle was capable of despairing with even greater violence because his brooding (out of which something great might at any moment appear) had been interrupted. And she saw less of him than ever before. He was up in his study for week after week without sign of an end. But Jane kept cheerful. London was too new to her, her visitors too interesting, her own powers too obviously expanding, to admit of more than temporary depression. Her health remained good, and she took vast pride in her house, which she was constantly improving, in her strip of garden, and in her management of the household money. Her one grief was the loss of Bessy Barnet, who had to go back to her family; but the girl who replaced her seemed, at first, adequate.

Carlyle suffered a rebuff when the editorship of the *London Review* was given to Mrs Taylor's protégé, W. J. Fox, who had abandoned his pulpit. But the darkest shade on his spirits at this time—apart from his travail over *The French Revolution*—was caused by Irving. Soon after his arrival in London, he had met Irving by accident in Kensington Gardens. He was shocked by the change in his friend, who looked ill and old. Irving admitted that he was not well, but would not discuss his health, and when

Carlyle, trying to cheer him, succeeded in raising "a small bit of Annandale laugh" the laugh was worse than all that had gone before, coming as if from the lips of a dying man. For some weeks afterwards Carlyle sought him in vain; he could not get into his house, and suspected that Mrs Irving was keeping him out. When, after three months, he did get in, Irving "lay there on a sofa, begged my pardon for not rising. . . . He complains of biliousness, of pain at his right short rib; has a short, thick cough, which comes on at the smallest irritation."

Carlyle told Irving that he ought to go south, to the sunshine, but Irving was hopelessly in the grip of the fanatical "elders" of his Newman Street "church". In September, when they ordered him "to do a great work in his native land" he obeyed, asking only that he might be allowed to go "by degrees to Scotland, with the hope of gaining strength, as well as doing the Lord's work, by the way". He called at Cheyne Row to say farewell. He rode up in the late afternoon and stayed an hour. He seemed to have lost some of his faith in the Gift of Tongues, and was perhaps already regretting, as he later said, that he had not "kept Thomas Carlyle closer to me: his counsel, blame or praise, was always faithful; and few have such eyes!" He was glad to hear that Carlyle was writing history. He promised to look after his own health.

Carlyle never forgot Irving's "fine chivalrous demeanour" to Jane, his look of admiration as he gazed around the room, and his smiling compliment, breaking through suppressed sadness: "You are like an Eve, and make a little Paradise wherever you are." He said goodbye quietly and lovingly, then Carlyle held the bridle of his horse while he mounted, and watched him ride slowly up the street. Three months later, Fraser called to tell Carlyle that Irving lay dead in Glasgow.

XV

THE STERLINGS
1835

Early in the next year, 1835, a disaster came on the Carlyles. *The French Revolution*, which appeared their one obvious hope of surviving in London, had at last got under way; it had grown into a three volume work, of which, by January, after working as if "possessed", Carlyle had finished the first. He hoped to have all three ready by May—the end of his first year in London. He and Jane were becoming known, he had been approached to write articles, a future seemed at last to be opening before him. Mill, who had worked assiduously for him as he wrote, took home in February the finished first part of the book, to make notes on it. A few weeks later, early in March, Carlyle was sitting at tea with Jane after working "all day like a nigger" on the second part, when they heard Mill's "short rap" at the front door. This was followed by a hurried step, and Mill burst into the room looking as white as a ghost and "the very picture of despair". He gasped out to Jane to go down to Mrs Taylor, who was waiting in a carriage outside. They at once thought that Mill had come to tell them that he and Mrs Taylor were running away together. But when Mill's distress would allow him to speak, the news he had to tell was very different. The manuscript that he had borrowed had been accidentally burned by a maid. Nothing remained but four or five sheets. He had left it lying on a table the previous evening he said (though in fact it seems to have been Mrs Taylor who had done so) and the girl mistook it for waste paper and lit the fire with it.

The blow was severe, for the finished draft was gone in every sense—Carlyle had kept none of his notes, and the mood in which he wrote it had long since disappeared—but he took the shock well. Indeed, he was so distressed by Mill's misery, that he and, less willingly, Jane (who had come back after a word or two with Mrs Taylor) were consolers rather than consoled. Mill, whose tact had been utterly drowned in the disaster, stayed no less than three hours, with nothing but protestations to add to his first announcement. By the time he finally left, Jane (whose liking for him had declined as his intimacy with Mrs Taylor increased) was furious with him, and in a passion of sympathy for Carlyle. He, his true kindliness coming out, said "Mill, poor fellow, is very miserable; we must try to keep from him how serious the loss is to us." She threw her arms round his neck, lamented his loss, comforted and encouraged him. They sat together late into the night, discussing what should be done. Mill had insisted that he should pay for the loss of Carlyle's time, and Carlyle decided to take £100, which he reckoned he had spent since the book was begun. His grief was deeper than Jane's, for he had lost something of himself. But she was angry for him, concerned for them both; she had placed great hopes on this first considerable work he had attempted. Her business that night was to see that he wrote on, and she did not leave him until he was sufficiently heartened to promise her "it *shall* be written again".

A misfortune of this kind drew them together, and brought out the best in both. Nevertheless a change was taking place in their relationship; one that Jane made clear during the year and was to emphasise with every year that passed. This change was shown by her attitude towards Mrs Montagu. From the moment she reached London, she avoided the "Noble Lady" and resolutely rebuffed all advances. Such an advance was made in the beginning of the new year, after the death of Irving, when Jane received what she called a "sentimental effusion" from Mrs Montagu, "threatening as heretofore to come and see me but has not been yet—nor will not: the only pity is that she will not let the matter lie quite dormant, it is not worth telling so many lies about." Four months later, she was writing: "The Noble Lady has *taken up the thread of our old relation* but it remains held only at one end."

Mrs Montagu was kind and she meant well. But she was no longer dealing with Miss Welsh of Haddington, to whom a grand London lady was an object of awe. Nor was she dealing with the country wife of Craigenputtock who did her utmost to identify herself with her husband. To the Jane of Cheyne Row, Mrs Montagu's advances appeared patronising, and made not so much to Jane Carlyle as to the wife of the promising Thomas Carlyle. This was doubly insufferable. Jane's Scottish pride resented patronage; still more, she was no longer contented with reflected glory, as she told a new addition to her circle—John Sterling.

Carlyle had heard of Sterling before he met him in Mill's office at the India House one day in February:

> "A loose, careless-looking, thin figure, in careless dim costume, sat, in a lounging posture, carelessly and copiously talking. I was struck with the kindly but restless swift-glancing eyes, which looked as if the spirits were all out coursing like a pack of merry eager beagles, beating every bush. . . . His address, I perceived, was abrupt, unceremonious; probably not at all disinclined to logic, and capable of dashing in upon you like a charge of cossacks, on occasion: but it was also eminently ingenious, social, guileless."

He and Sterling left together and

> "walked westward in company . . . arguing copiously, but *except* in opinion not disagreeing. . . . We parted with the mutual wish to meet again; which accordingly, at his Father's house and at mine, we soon repeatedly did."

Sterling was five years younger than Jane. He had been joint founder of the Cambridge "Apostles" with F. D. Maurice; had later edited the *Athenaeum* for some months, again with Maurice; had studied philosophy in Germany; and was now curate to his former tutor, J. C. Hare, at Hurstmonceaux. He at once became a favourite with both Carlyles; he fought Carlyle and sparred with Jane, and all were pleased. Jane quickly discerned a fine romantic spirit hidden lightly under Sterling's black cloth; an English version of D'Eichthal, but with a lively sense of humour; handsome in his careless, hawk-like fashion, earnest, good, but above all, romantic. She heard of his efforts to help the Spanish revolutionary movement five years earlier, of how he raised money and helped to fit out the brig that was to carry the exiles back to start an insurrection against the monarchy, and of how, when the plot was discovered at the last moment, he escaped from the ship to warn his friends, defying the armed police who threatened to fire on him. This was Byronic in the best sense of the word, and Jane's sympathies were immediately aroused for the many exiles then in England. As for Sterling, he was no less than "an angel of Heaven!" she told Eliza, "*ostensibly* a Clergyman of the Church of England, and Author of *Arthur Coningsby*, a highly original novel."

He was the first of a long trail of men younger than Jane who came to sit at Carlyle's feet, and spent much of their time sitting in her drawing-room. He was not only an entertaining companion and a worthy opponent, but a good correspondent; and he was soon bringing from her some excellent letters. How quickly they had taken each other's measure is to be seen from her first letter to him, written a fortnight after they had first met, in which she stakes her claim to attention.

> "You did kindly to send the little separate note: the least bit '*all to myself*', (as the children say) was sure to give me a livelier pleasure, than any number of sheets in which I had but a secondary interest. For in spite of the honestest efforts to annihilate my *I-ety*, or merge it in what the world doubtless considers my better half; I still find myself a self-subsisting, and alas! self-seeking *me*. Little Felix, in the *Wanderjahre*, when, in the midst of an animated scene between Wilhelm and Theresa, he pulls Theresa's gown, and calls out, '*Mama Theresa I too am here!*' only speaks out, with the charming trustfulness of a child, what I am per-perpetually feeling, tho' too sophisticated to pull people's skirts, or exclaim in so many words: Mr Sterling '*I* too am here.' "

She wrote lightly, but she was serious. Her invariable and unusual form of signature, Jane Welsh Carlyle, remained as a silent pledge to it. The "Welsh" stood there defiantly between Christian and married names for the rest of her life, asserting pride in family, pride in self. Her "I-ety" had always been strong in her, and, until she married Carlyle, had been fostered by all, even by her father, except in his bleakest moods. For more than eight years, doing violence to her nature, she had kept down her longing for attention, for the last word, her lively sense that she should by right stand in the centre of the picture. At first, she had tried to make of herself what the conventions of the time expected of a wife. And before this phase could exhaust itself she was carried off to Craigenputtock for six years, virtually alone with Carlyle. There, her potential brilliance of speech was dimmed to meal-table anecdotes or to conversations with the maid, Alick or Jenny; her instinct to dominate had to be satisfied with the choice of a meal, and the ordering of those whom it was no compliment to triumph over.

But no sooner was she settled in Cheyne Row, with interesting men and women coming to see Carlyle, than her "I-ety" began to assert itself, her wits were sharpened, and her tongue was loosened. She was incapable merely of doing her duty by Carlyle—to feed his friends, to keep the conversation going if he were absent or engaged, to be the gracious, ministering figure in the background. At the sight and sound of these rich fields ready for harvesting, all the Haddington self-confidence returned, reinforced with the knowledge and the wisdom that eight years with Carlyle had taught her. These people should respect her for herself, not as Carlyle's wife; they should be her friends in her own right if she so wished. This was the challenge she made to Sterling—her modest declaration of independence. To this extent she threw down the gauntlet to the conventions, but only to this extent. It was her pleasure and pride to feed Carlyle, to keep house for him, to listen to him, appreciate him, encourage him. When he was present, she remained, and was content for many years to remain, a secondary figure. But she was not content to be his shadow.

Carlyle agreed. He was proud of Jane, and took great pleasure in hearing praise of her, and in her witty remarks as long as she did not actually interrupt him. Besides, her popularity with his friends proved most convenient; he could go off to write whenever he pleased, leaving them to her; and, as was often to happen, he could let her take over the management of friendships in which he had lost interest. All he asked was, simply, that his wishes should come first, his comfort be put before all else, the household so arranged that his sleepings, wakings, walks, hours of work or of reverie should be when, how and as he wanted them. This he was given without more than an occasional sarcasm from Jane. She thought even more of him when she saw him shine out in the debates now so frequent at Cheyne Row—and she was more than ever convinced of his greatness as a writer. She tells his mother

"I have just had a call from an old rejected lover who has been in India these ten years—tho' he has come home with more thousands of pounds than we are ever likely to have hundreds or even scores the sight of him did not make me doubt the wisdom of my preference. Indeed, I continue quite content with my bargain—I could wish him a little *less yellow*, and a little *more peaceable*; but that is all!"

Although she resisted his irritations and rebellions and sometimes complained of them lightly to others she gave him full credit for his attack on the sickening task of re-writing. She read as he wrote, encouraging him:

> "The book is going to be a good book" she told John Carlyle "in spite of bad fortune—and what is lost is by no means to be looked upon as wasted—what he faithful *did* in it and also what he magnanimously *endured* remains."

Sterling's note to Jane had accompanied a thirteen-page letter to Carlyle about *Sartor*. This had now run its course in *Fraser's Magazine*, and Carlyle had bound up the parts and sent them to a number of friends, including Emerson. Sterling's criticism expressed "amazement, admiration, horror," but admiration was the ruling emotion; and this, together with his and his family's liking for Jane, soon determined him to live in London. For a short time there seemed a danger that his move would come too late. Carlyle was having a dire struggle, and when Emerson invited him to give a lecture tour in America, where *Sartor* was being praised, he was tempted to throw up the task and go where he was appreciated and could earn money easily. This move (which was encouraged by the likelihood of Alick emigrating) hung in the wind for some years, until Carlyle thought himself financially safe, and it gave Jane some anxious moments. When she wrote to Sterling in the middle of the year, Carlyle had been more than usually insistent that London life was intolerable and that they should cut adrift and make for America. If Sterling does not hurry back, Jane tells him, he may not see them before "our good or evil star actually shoots over the Atlantic". She had been looking at a house in Cheyne Walk which might suit him, and:

> "If a Fairy would grant me three wishes this evening, my first would be that we might remain where we are, my second that you might be settled in Cheyne Walk, and the third like a thrifty Scotchwoman I would beg leave to lay by in reserve for future need."

Sterling came to London, though not for some months and not to the Chelsea house. The American scare passed over, Carlyle subsiding amidst his customary growls to the ordeal of

The French Revolution. Sterling brought with him to Cheyne Row "a whole retinue of curious persons". Of these, the most important to Jane for the next few years were his parents. "His father is Irish; the redoubtable Sterling of the *Times* Newspaper, really a notable man; who flies greatly about this place—for the time." So Carlyle, who also reported that Sterling's mother and Jane were "swearing an eternal friendship". To Jane this plumping out of her circle was almost all pleasure. Mill had seen less of them since the loss of the manuscript, leaving only Hunt as a regular caller; but the Sterlings more than made up for the loss. The elder Sterlings, who had no daughter, made a great fuss of her. Edward Sterling, "The Thunderer of the *Times*" was much like his leading articles—pompous, hearty, domineering, longwinded—but these characteristics Jane kept in check with only occasional outbursts of impatience. She played chess with him, flirted with him, and generally had him, in Carlyle's words, "at her apron string, and brought many a comical pirouette out of him from time to time." He, she claimed, "would go through fire and water for me; and if there were a third worse element, would go through that also." She bore with him the more readily because of his wife, to whom she felt, she told Carlyle's mother, "as to a third Mother. Whenever I have blue devils I need but put on my bonnet and run off to her and the smile in her eyes restores me to instant good humour." Between them, Jane was given a royal time, reminiscent of her Haddington days. She summed up to Jean Aitken: the Sterlings

> "from the master of the house down to the footman, are devoted to me body and soul . . . I have only to say 'I should like to see such a thing', or 'to be at such a place', and next day a carriage is at the door, or a boat is on the river to take me if I please to the ends of the earth."

From other quarters came other friends—less intimate than the Sterlings, but varied, helpful and interesting. Henry Taylor remained outside Jane's circle, but Carlyle liked him well enough—perhaps because Taylor's laugh reminded him of Irving. He and Jane dined with him occasionally. The dinners, there and elsewhere, were not always to their taste—they both had exceptionally touchy digestions—and Jane did not spare her hosts or fellow guests: "at Mrs Manderson's (George Rennie's Sister's) there was huge venison to be eaten and new service of plate to be displayed; and Mrs G. Rennie talked about the 'aars' (arts) and the great Sir John favoured us with 'ideas' on the Peel administration." At one of the Taylor dinners they met Thomas Wilson and his sister Henrietta, an affluent pair with literary inclinations. The Wilsons were devout church people, and rather staid, but they took to the Carlyles and helped them whenever Carlyle pride made help possible. Miss Wilson was particularly captivated by Jane, and she used often to drive down to Chelsea for an hour or two. Jane thought she and her brother were "about the best people we know here; the lady, verging on old-maidenism, is distinctly the cleverest woman I know." The Wilsons this summer sent the Carlyles a hamper of Madeira—ready, said Jane, for the celebrations when Carlyle had finished his re-writing. The new version, now nearly finished, was, she thought, perhaps less vivacious than the original, but better thought out and constructed.

At the other extreme from the respectable Wilsons were what Carlyle called "Sprinklings of Foreigners" who, hearing of him as an opponent of the established order, had begun to call at Cheyne Row. With one or two exceptions these people—mostly political exiles—did not appeal to Carlyle. He thought of them as ineffectual idealists, fanatics, dreamers and drifters. To Jane they appealed by their romantic aura, by their chivalrous manner, their homelessness, and, when the romance wore thin, by the opportunity they gave her for anecdote and laughter. Carlyle, willing enough to humour her as long as his work was not disturbed, made no serious attempt to discourage them; by occupying so much of Jane's time they enabled him to work with a quieter conscience. One of the first of the"Sprinklings" was the big, bull-like, black-eyed Garnier, with the scars of deep sabre slashes across his face—a rhinoceros, Carlyle called him— a true soldier of fortune, waiting impatiently for another war to begin. Garnier, for all his roughness, was frank, good-humoured, and had a manner with her that Jane could not find inside England, or Scotland for that matter; she listened to his tales of wars in Germany and elsewhere, and she helped him whenever she was able—with a meal, a coat, or a recommendation for work.

Then there was Countess Clementina Degli Antoni: "the woman to make my Husband faithless if such a one exist."

"I am learning from her to speak Italian—and she finds she says, that I have a divine talent (*'divino talento'*)."

Another Italian exile, Comte de Pepoli—"one of the first poets of Italy, the handsomest and best mannered of men"— came every Wednesday, and sometimes more often, to talk Italian to Jane, and "makes my thoughts melodious for the rest of the day".

To Jane, Craigenputtock began to seem like a nightmare. She had found a foster mother and father in the Sterlings, admirers of the safer sort in young Sterling and Leigh Hunt, stout friends in the Bullers, good respectable pillars in the Wilsons, and romance in her growing little colony of exiles. Carlyle asked her why she did not put an advertisement in the window—"House of refuge for stray dogs and cats"—and have done with it. But he was proud of her.

> "The waste wilderness of London" he says "was becoming a peopled garden to us, in some measure, especially to *her*, who had a frank welcome to every sort of worth and even kindly-singularity in her fellow-creatures, such as I could at no time rival."

This was true; but to Jane his presence in the house if not in the company put the seal on her pleasure; it was a satisfaction and a pride to know that her husband, in brilliance and weight of speech, was a match for any man, and that he would dominate the company in his way as completely as she dominated it in hers. When he was not there, when he was writing in his room or walking through Hyde Park considering his book, she had the comfortable feeling that he was making that which would demonstrate to the world what she had never doubted—his greatness.

XVI

GODEFROI CAVAIGNAC
1835 – 1836

On the last day of August 1835, Mrs Welsh came down to stay. Jane had refused all invitations to Templand: at first because she had no wish to leave the "exciting talk" of Chelsea; later, because she was not well enough to travel. Carlyle was still in the throes of re-writing—often, in despair, throwing the work aside, then desperately taking it up again. He wrote and talked and acted like a haunted man. Friends, dinners, parties were no protection against his savage gloom. Jane's nerves were on edge. She had lost her second servant, recommended by Mrs Austin. She had sent the third back to her home after six months as "hopelessly incompetent" (though Carlyle might have seen hope of a kind in this girl who had been found in the kitchen one morning, sitting by the half-cleaned, unlighted range reading *Wilhelm Meister*); and she had summarily dismissed her fourth, a "half distracted Irishwoman". Now her fifth, "a mutinous Irish savage" and, added Carlyle, "an ugly woman too, with the face of a Polar Bear", was clearly destined to follow her predecessor at any moment. Sometimes the servants' oddities gave Jane a chance to make Carlyle laugh over his meals, but as the weeks wore on he was more difficult to rouse and she felt less able to make the effort. In the heat of the summer, she became irritable and depressed. Her sense of humour left her. There were scenes. For six weeks, she wrote in September, she had had continual illness: "One day taking the form of intolerable headache, another day of equally intolerable colic, and many days together animating me with a noble disposition to hang or drown myself."

The arrival of Mrs Welsh not only allowed her daughter to go to bed, but spurred Carlyle on to have done with "the unutterable manuscript". He finished it in a burst of writing, by the middle of September. "The little Dame will do well enough now" he declared. "Especially, she says, as the Manuscript is over too!" But he, though relieved, was a bundle of nerves. At tea, soon afterwards, he, Jane and Eliza Miles (who often looked in to help Jane) were sitting at supper when the maid clattered down the plates before Carlyle. He "exploded", told her in the name of God and the Devil to leave the house; which she did at once, leaving Jane and her mother to manage alone. Carlyle bewailed the changing relations between "Master and Servant" and spoke gloomily of "Society . . . rapidly rushing towards unknown changes and consummations". He insisted that, rather than be "bedevilled with *such* a set of unfortunates", he would get "some small apartment, and sweep it out and arrange it for myself with my own hands". This desperate resolve was not necessary, however, for the women did the housework, helped—or hindered—by a small local girl, Sarah Heather, promptly christened by Jane (who had her pet name for all) Sereetha the Peesweep—Sereetha being the way the little girl pronounced her name. But Carlyle had by this time decided "to run for Annandale", and at the beginning of October he left by boat, with strict instructions from Jane to bring back a Scottish servant. He was seen off ceremoniously at the docks by Garnier.

Once away from each other, Jane and Carlyle began to reproach themselves.

"Try all that ever you can" she wrote "to be patient and good-natured with your *povera piccola Gooda*, and then she loves you, and is ready to do anything on earth that you wish; to fly over the moon, if you bade her. But when the *signor della casa* has neither kind look nor word for me, what can I do but grow desperate, fret myself to fiddlestrings, and be a torment to society in every direction?"

Reading hastily, he agreed: "Alas! the state of wreckage I was in, fretted, as thou sayest, to fiddlestrings, was enormous". His health had improved, but he was still bilious, even at Scotsbrig, and took a sober view of the future:

"And thou, my poor Goody, depending on cheerful looks of *mine* for thy cheerfulness! For God's sake do not, or do so as little as possible. How I love thee, what I think of thee, it is not probable that thou or any mortal will know. But cheerful looks, when the heart feels slowly dying

in floods of confusion and obstruction, are not the thing I have to give . . .
My poor Goody! it seems as if she could so easily be happy; and the easy
means are so seldom there."

Mrs Welsh liked neither London nor the people in it, and she
and Jane spent much of their day quarrelling. Jane was glad
enough to have her mother about when she was ill, but the
moment she recovered—as she did soon after Carlyle's departure
—these attentions turned in her eyes to unwarrantable fussiness.
Every letter to Carlyle contained a complaint—usually in
Italian or German—about her mother's ill humour, and was
answered with appeals, in German, for patience.

But complaints from Jane were no sign that she was not
enjoying herself, nor even that she was on bad terms with the
person about whom she complained. Her tongue and her pen
both ran away with her. She found the sport much to her liking,
and promptly forgot her grievance the moment she had uttered
it. So she and her mother, loving and fighting by turns, lunched
with Sandy Donaldson and his family, down from Haddington
for a visit, went to the British Museum, inspected a prison,
bought a secondhand sofa, and were just in time to see the King
and Queen at Chelsea Hospital.

> "My Mother's enthusiasm of loyalty on the occasion was a sight for
> sore eyes! 'Poor Queen *after all!*' She looked so frost-bitten and anxious!
> curtsied with such a *cowering* hurriedness to the veriest rabble that ever
> was seen. I was wae to look at her—wae to think of her when I heard
> that the very same night they hissed her at one of the theatres!—Poor
> thing!"

There were also plenty of visitors. "I had some private misgiving that your men would not mind me when you were not
here . . . but it is quite the reverse." There was no longer any
doubt about Jane's standing in the Cheyne Row circle. Garnier
came twice in the first fortnight; a friend of Mill's twice; Pepoli
twice, and was already "gliding into a flirtation with—*mia
madre!* who presented him, in a manner molto graziosa, with
her tartan scarf." He was, said Jane, "my Mother's chief indeed
I think only favourite here . . . which was curious as they had no
medium of communication but their eyes!" Only Mill showed
signs of falling away. He called once and "tried evidently to
yawn as little as possible". John Sterling was a regular visitor
until later in the month, when he too came less; because,

explained Jane disgustedly: "he is so occupied in *waiting upon* his wife." His father, now nicknamed the Stimabile (a result of Jane's Italian lessons), was away part of the time "so that he has not been deadly." Later, he came "only once or twice a week" because he fell foul of Mrs Welsh, who thought his attitude to Jane too proprietorial, and because of some heated political arguments with Jane. "All the men take fright sooner or later at my *violence* tant mieux!"

Another visitor, who was to be a persistent member of Jane's circle, had been introduced by Susan Hunter, in London for the summer. He was G. L. Craik: "a solid fellow" said Carlyle . . . "with an honest oxlike strength and steadiness". Jane called him "a good hearted pleasant man"—but this was to Susan. Privately she found him boring. He wrote assiduously for the Society for the Diffusion of Useful Knowledge—which brought him the nickname at Chelsea of "Useful Knowledge Craik". He was three years older than Jane, a Scotsman shy, solemn, statistical, and soon a confirmed worshipper. He was unhappily married, and she sometimes pitied him, but at other times he irritated her by his awkward devotion as he sat mute or worse than mute in the Cheyne Row drawing-room. Her name for him was Creek, and he repaid her handsomely for moments of boredom by providing rich material for her wit. One book of his, *The Pursuit of Knowledge under Difficulties*, gave her and Carlyle and other favoured people immense fun.

But Craik this summer was only just beginning to take his bearings at Chelsea. Susan it was who provided an unexpected sensation. When Carlyle was about to go to Annandale, Jane invited her "to keep my Mother and me from wearying". Susan came for two days. She was curious to see Leigh Hunt, and Jane asked him over for the evening:

> "he actually came—found Pepoli as well as Miss Hunter, was amazingly lively, and very lasting, for he stayed till near twelve. Between ourselves it gave me a poorish opinion of him to see how uplifted to the third Heaven he seemed by Susan's compliments and sympathising talk."

Susan could not take her eyes from Hunt; and Hunt, not unwilling to be admired, asked them all to come to tea a few days later. Susan came back for the purpose and slept another night in Cheyne Row, but she did so in disgrace. Jane, in a thoroughly bad temper, made short work of Mrs Hunt at the tea; she "behaved smoothly and looked devilish and was drunkish." But this was nothing to the inconstant Hunt, who

> "sang, talked like a pen-gun, ever to Susan, who drank it all in like nectar; while my Mother looked cross enough—and I had to listen to the whispered confidences of Mrs Hunt. But for me, who was declared to be grown *'quite prim and elderly'* I believe they would have communicated their mutual experiences in a retired window-seat till morning. 'God bless you Miss Hunter' was repeated by Hunt three several times in tones of ever-increasing pathos and tenderness as he handed her downstairs behind me. Susan for once in her life seemed past speech. At the bottom of the stairs a demur took place—I saw nothing but I heard with my wonted glegness—what think you?—a couple of handsome *smacks!* and then an almost inaudibly soft 'God bless you Miss Hunter!' "

"Now just remember" she complained to Carlyle "what sort of looking woman is Susan Hunter; and figure this transaction! If he had kissed me, it would have been intelligible, but Susan Hunter, of all people!" Susan went back to Scotland without receiving another invitation, and months passed before Jane wrote to her again. Hunt was treated more leniently.

Carlyle and Jane wrote to each other every day or two—he was given all her news, and was rarely out of her thoughts: "The house looks very empty without you, and my mind feels empty too". And when there was no time for a letter, they adopted the habit of the Carlyle family of sending newspapers on which the sender placed a mark or a few words to indicate an arrival, a departure, or merely good health.

Carlyle found a servant, one Anne Cook. He considered her satisfactory except for what in Annandale was called "a misfortune", who could, he thought, be left in charge of the grandmother. Jane made light of the "misfortune". If she had had to lead the life of an Annandale girl, she would by this time have had several. Bring her, she said, and "oh, for goodness sake procure a dozen of bacon hams! There is no bottom to my appetite for them." She was anxious to have him home again— strong and cheerful if possible, but, if not possible, "I wish you were come anyhow". Her Italian was improving rapidly; she had not only written Carlyle a letter in Italian but had translated four songs, had written "a long excessively spirituosa letter to 'mia adorabile Clementina' and many graziose cartucie besides. In truth, I have a divino ingegno!"

She was in high spirits, a very different woman from the one
Carlyle had left a month earlier, and prepared for all good
things to have come of his holiday. It was as well she was
stronger, for he returned in a sorry state. He had brought Anne
Cook (who had spent the entire time in a sort of stupor) with
him on a practically non-stop journey of two days, and got
down from the coach at Holborn "half dead". After an "endless" drive in a cab, surrounded by luggage, he arrived at
Cheyne Row "more like mad than sane". His month in the
country had nevertheless done him good, and after Mrs Welsh
had gone Jane could report to his mother that he "conducts
himself pretty peaceably at present; writing only in the forenoons". John Sterling, who had given up his curacy and now
lived in London, was often in the house: "by far" said Carlyle
"the lovablest man I have met for many a year." There was
another attraction in him for Carlyle: "He and Taylor often •
seem to me very strangely like the two *halves* of Edward Irving,
living apart". Sterling was taking the place of Mill as chief
disciple, and had brought with him others, less welcome, though
interesting—his friend Maurice, then Chaplain at Guy's
Hospital; James Spedding, who was editing the works of Bacon;
and Spedding's brother Tom. Of James Spedding, Jane could
say no more than that he was "sensible"—the Speddings
remained Carlyle's friends rather than hers. Maurice, who
developed an admiration for Carlyle, neither she nor her
husband could accept as an intimate:

> "I am never in his company" she says "without being attacked with a
> sort of paroxysm of mental cramp! he keeps one always with his wire-
> drawings and paradoxes as if one were dancing on the points of one's
> toes (spiritually speaking). And then he *will* help the kettle and never
> fails to pour it all over the milk pot and sugar bason!"

Both Jane and Carlyle were pleased with Anne Cook:

> "hardy as a Highlander" said Carlyle, "full of assiduity, good-nature,
> and wild Annandale savagery, which causes the Cockney mind here to
> pause astonished. Broader Scotch was never spoken or thought by any
> mortal in this metropolitan city."

Jane at once began to get fun from her odd sayings, and her

> "perfect incomprehension of everything like ceremony. I was helping her
> to wring a sheet one day, while she had the cut finger, and she told me

flatly it was *'clean aboon my fit'*. 'I should get at it by practice,' said I; 'for weaker people than I have wrung sheets.' *'May be sae,'* returned she very coolly; *'but I kenna where yeel find ony weaker, for a weaklier like cretur I never saw in a' my life.'* Another time, when Carlyle had been off his sleep for a night or two, she came to me at bedtime to ask—'if Mr Carlyle bees ony uneasy thro' the nicht, and's gaan *staiveren* aboot the hoose, wull ye bid him gee us a cry at five i' the morning?' "

Anne's views of some of the visitors—particularly the Sprinkling of Foreigners—were plainspoken. Jane's "handsome Italian Count"—Pepoli—Anne at first called *"a fleysome body"*. Then Jane noticed that whenever Anne knew that Pepoli was coming "she puts on a certain net cap with a most peculiar knot of ribbons", and she confided to Jane that she thought him "a real fine man, and nane that comes can ever be named in ae day with him." She was rewarded, when she let him out of the door, with *"I weesh you gooday"*.

Carlyle, though now rich in friends, comfortably housed and well cared for, was soon bemoaning his lot. He took stock, in his journal—always the repository of his more sombre thoughts—of the outlook on his fortieth birthday, in December, and found that "Providence again is leading me through dark, burning, hideous ways towards new heights and developments". As to the conditions in which he lived—to write of those he thought impossible and unprofitable. He adjured himself "Be silent, be calm, be not mad." He could obey only the final injunction. He was again worried about his work. The book was progressing, but much more slowly than he had hoped. The vast subject was still growing under his hand.

He looked around once more for other ways of earning a living. In the first month of the new year, 1836, Basil Montagu hinted that he might be able to help. Carlyle went to see him, and came away raging with wounded pride:

"A clerkship under him at the rate of £200 a year, whereby a man lecturing also in mechanics' institutes in the evening, and doing etceteras, might live. I listened with grave fixed eyes to the sovereign of quacks, as he mewed out all the fine sentimentalities he had stuffed into his beggarly account of empty boxes—for which too I had been sent trotting many miles of pavement, though I knew from the beginning it could be only moonshine ... the *faith* of Montagu wishing *me* for his clerk; thinking the polar bear, reduced to a state of dyspeptic dejection, might safely be trusted tending rabbits."

Less than a month later, Jane was horrified to hear that Fonblanque, through Hunt, had offered Carlyle a post as editor of the Radical newspaper at Lichfield, and that he was considering it.

"O mercy no!" she cried to John Carlyle "not to a little English provincial town! Not to anywhere, if I might have my wish. 'A rolling stone gathers no moss'—we have rolled and rolled till we hardly know which end of us is uppermost; and I desire of all things now, to stand still and gather moss. Where could one be better than here? To be sure one is threatened with starvation; but for the rest '*tout va bien!*' "

Carlyle refused the post.

Then Mill, who had amalgamated his *London Review* with the *Westminster*, asked for articles from Carlyle. His anxieties slightly allayed, he wrote on, now well into the second volume of *The French Revolution*, with only occasional ominous mutters in his journal:

"our money runs fast away daily. It will be about *done* at the time this book is done; and then—my destiny, as it were, ends. . . . Some vague outlook, which I half know to be inane, opens in my imagination to America, or some western woods and solitude. . . . Why not quit literature —with a vengeance to it—and turn, were it even to sheep herding, where one can be well?"

These asides notwithstanding, he finished the second volume towards the end of April 1836. He had breakfasted with Samuel Rogers, banker, poet and literary oracle:

"a half-frozen sardonic Whig-Gentleman! no hair at all, but one of the whitest bare scalps, blue eyes, shrewd, sad and cruel; toothless horseshoe mouth drawn up to the very nose; slow-croaking, sarcastic insight, perfect breeding."

To be acknowledged by Rogers was sign enough that, although Carlyle had published nothing since the move to London nearly two years earlier, he was becoming widely known.

Jane had no doubts at all of the benefits of London:

"I have set myself very seriously to the business of loving since I came here" she had told Eliza Stodart towards the end of February "conscious that my long sojourn in the wilderness had developed certain misanthropical tendencies in me that were leading me rather devilward; into the region of hatred and all uncharitableness! With a good deal of effort I have got up a sentiment for several men and women, which has a good right to go by the name of friendship in these days. I have even

executed two or three *innocent flirtations* with good effect, and on the whole
live in great amity with my fellow creatures. They call me *'sweet'*, and
'gentle'; and some of the men go the length of calling me 'ENDEARING'
and I laugh in my sleeve, and think Oh Lord! if you but knew what a
brimstone of a creature I am behind all this beautiful amiability! . . . And
so I sit here in No. 5, Cheyne Row and make grave pantomime, and
grave speech in acknowledgment of all the wisdom I hear uttered by the
celebrated men and women of the age; thinking my own thought all the
while which is often this or something like this—'Was not sitting under a
haystack in a summer's day with Bess and George Rennie . . . worth a
whole eternity of this idle speculation and barren logic?' "

But this, Jane explains, is no criticism of her London friends,
who are good people and have been "incomprehensibly kind"
to her.

"The Sterlings still *'all adore me'*! . . . load me with kindnesses, and
treat me as if I were a sort of necessary to their existence: the very footman and Lady's-maid 'have been quite anxious' if I have staid away
half a week. Mrs Sterling's portrait in oils hangs over my mantlepiece—
—and the whole thing is in the most flourishing condition—if it do
but last."

She now speaks Italian "like a nightingale," the Countess is one
of her "special friends; it is so delightful to be called *'carissima
amica!'* etc etc, that it is worth while to keep up an Italian
friendship or two for the purpose." And always, to complete
her pleasure, was Carlyle—"on the whole the cleverest man I
meet with still and the truest."

How well this lively, intelligent atmosphere agreed with her,
and how much she enjoyed recreating it for her friends, is shown
in her bright letters. She saw herself as the moving spirit of an
ever-widening circle, stimulating and satisfying, from Carlyle
wrestling upstairs with the book that was to bring him fame,
to the red-haired, bespectacled Craik sitting for hours on the
edge of the sofa. The unpredictable Hunts slipped in and out of
the picture. Both she and Carlyle were now sitting to Thornton
Hunt; Carlyle "is getting himself depicted as one of the sulkiest
commonplace men in the Island"; she was "if possible even
more odious, with a frightful mechanical smile covering over
the most vulgar devilishness." New faces were to be seen at
Cheyne Row almost every month. For the newest, and, in Jane's
opinion, the most remarkable, she had to thank the "fascinating
half angelical half demoniacal Mrs Taylor." This lady was now

regarded with coolness by both Carlyles as a bad influence on John Mill. In Jane's absence one day, she had come to Cheyne Row, dined with Carlyle, "drank tea with him, and stayed with him till '*the night was getting on*' but failed to excite in his strong heart all the warmth of gratitude which so remarkable a benefaction deserved." But the man she introduced to Jane, and whom Jane brought home to Carlyle as soon as might be, was a benefaction indeed.

> "We have another foreigner" she told Susan Hunter "that beats all the rest to sticks. A freed republican of the right thoro'-going sort, an '*accusé d'Avril*' who has had the glory of meriting to be imprisoned and nearly losing his head; a man with that sort of dark, half-savage beauty with what one would paint a fallen angel; who fears neither Heaven nor Earth for aught one can see; who *fights* and *writes* with the same passionate intrepidity; who is ready to dare or to suffer, to live or to die without disturbing himself much about the matter; who *defies* all men and *honours* all women—and whose name is Cavaignac!"

Godefroi Cavaignac, who had just escaped from prison and fled into exile, appealed to both the Carlyles. To Carlyle, long predisposed towards him by Mill's reports from Paris in Craigenputtock days, Cavaignac appeared as

> "a fine Bayard soul (with figure to correspond), a man full of seriousness and of genial gaiety withal; of really fine faculties, and of a politeness (especially towards women) which was curiously elaborated into punctiliousness, yet sprang everywhere from frank nature."

To Jane, this tall, dark, serious, passionate Frenchman of her own age was the essence of romance—man of action and man of thought in one. He came often to the house, patiently discussing the Revolution with Carlyle, and talking long over a cup of tea or coffee with Jane—telling her of his struggles to set up a republic in the 1830 revolution, of his brother who still kept up the fight in France, and of his much loved mother and sister. He was brusque but charming, and had an excellent sense of humour. Soon he was saying, to Jane's infinite contentment, "Vous n'êtes pas Ecossaise, Madame; désormais vous serez Française!"

But a Cavaignac about the house was heady work for a highly-strung woman with a moody genius to feed and soothe and listen to, and a house more than ever full of people, to say nothing of dinners, theatres, excursions, parties elsewhere—for she was a general favourite. She was enjoying life too well, living on her nerves, yet she could not resist stimulation. Often, she admitted, she was too exhausted to sleep. The history of Haddington was repeating itself; but whereas in Haddington she had her mother to nurse her when necessary, and bring her out of her headaches after too much excitement, in London she had to rely on the maid or on Carlyle. Neither was an adequate substitute. Carlyle was too busy writing his book and worrying about his health, his lack of money, his spiritual state, to have much time to spare for a woman's vagaries. In his view it was he who needed calm, encouragement, protection from everything that hindered his work.

John Carlyle had spent a month in Cheyne Row, but soon after midsummer he went up to Annandale for the rest of his leave. While this favourite brother was about, Carlyle could talk away his troubles, or forget them in listening to John's tales of travel. Alone, his fears came thick about him again. He could not bear the thought of falling into debt. The third volume of *The French Revolution* was still to be written, but he dared not give his time to it; it would take months to finish, and might prove a failure when published. He accepted Mill's offer, and wrote two articles. He also persuaded Fraser to print a story he had written at Craigenputtock, *The Diamond Necklace*. All this meant a precious hundred pounds, and another six months' breathing space. But the writing of articles was a painful business when his heart was in his book. "My dispiritment, my sorrow and pain are great, but I strive to keep silent". He strove in vain. He was self-tortured and over-worked, and Jane was over-excited and worn from headaches and loss of sleep. They quarrelled about the most ridiculous things—even about Carlyle's hats. He had long since run to excess in hats. He liked the brims rather wider than possible, and had boasted in the days of Craigenputtock about the vast span—"two feet and one half-inch"—of his latest hat. Now, to combat the London summer heat, he went out one day and re-appeared in a perfect giant of a hat—and pure white into the bargain. Exaggerated though they were, these wide brimmed hats suited Carlyle's picturesque face, as Jane knew well enough. But at sight of the latest monster, she shrieked and all but cried. He promised not to wear it when she was with him, but would not give it up. For days they were scarcely on speaking terms, until finally she gave way, and allowed that he looked well in it.

This difference about next to nothing was typical of their state. Mill and John Sterling were both going abroad for their health. "Mill's malady," Jane explains to Susan "is of the *nerves*, and Mrs Taylor I imagine has a good deal to do with it." But they were seriously worried about Sterling, who had trouble with his lungs—"and I fear that he will never recover". The tension grew intolerable. London stewed in heat. There was no relief to be found in the little garden with its rose cuttings from Craigenputtock and strawberry plants from Templand. Jane's nerve snapped.

> "A sudden thought struck me; that if I did not get out of London I should surely die! And you know how everything must submit and arrange itself, when once 'a sudden thought' strikes some women. In the present instance it was no sooner thought than done; I did what was comparable to taking up my bed and walking; I rose from my sofa and got into a mail coach."

She arrived at Templand in the middle of July, "shattered with agitation". On the way she stopped at Manchester, where Carlyle's youngest sister Jenny, recently married to a small tradesman, Robert Hanning, was now living. They were kind, but

> "the bed is as hard as a deal board . . . there is moreover a species of bug in it which raises lumps 'the size of a hazel-nut'—and to crown all you are next door to a '*Jerry shop*', where drunk people issue into the street all night long, trying who to rage loudest."

From Manchester to Liverpool she made her first journey by train

> "after a flight (for it can be called nothing else) of thirty-four miles within an hour and a quarter. I was dreadfully frightened before the train started; in the nervous weak state I was in it seemed to me certain that I should faint, and the impossibility of getting the horrid thing stopt!"

At Liverpool her trunk was piled up with many others—a hundred, Jane said for good measure. "You must take your turn Mam, you must take your turn" said the man as Jane passed through the crowd of passengers. But that was about the last thing in the world that Jane was ever prepared to do. "Stand out of the road, will you" she demanded "there is the trunk before my eyes and I will lift it away myself without troubling anyone." Whereupon the clerk cried out in a rage "for Godsake give that Lady her trunk and let us be rid of her." So Jane drove off victoriously in her omnibus, and completed her triumph by persuading the driver to go out of his way and put her down at the very door of 20 Maryland Street. There, after the astonishment was over, they were "as kind as ever; and as inconsiderate about sleep". And there were more bugs. "I thought the bugs of Manchester had left nothing for the Liverpool ones to do; but I was mistaken; I had twenty new bites on my neck and arms the first night."

Then to Dumfries by coach (her uncle paying the fare to save her the sea crossing by Annan) and the meeting with Mrs Welsh in the lobby of the Commercial Inn. "Such an embracing and such a crying! The very Boots was affected with it, and spoke in a plaintive voice all morning after." This reception was almost enough to make Jane wish she had never left home; and her longing to be away from London heat and bickering and to be cared for by her mother had all but disappeared by the time they reached Templand. However, she had made her gesture, had spent some of their precious money, and had to make the best of it. This she was incapable of doing most of the time. She wrote sarcastic, unhappy letters to Carlyle, complaining of her mother—"she will give you every thing on earth except the thing you *want*—will do anything for you except what you *ask* her to do"; complaining of her young cousins from Liverpool who had come up to visit her—"in perpetual movement, seeking whom they may devour"; complaining of her early awakenings, of the incessant rain, of everything. She was chagrined to meet a former schoolboy lover from Haddington, now married to "a beautiful wife, much fitter for him than I—young as himself, and silly as himself, and happy-hearted as himself". She mourned over the "sad gaiety" of a long letter from John Sterling—"I do not think we shall ever see him again". The idea of accompanying Mill and Mrs Taylor (who had asked her to go with them on Mill's health trip) made her ready to shriek.

Nothing could go rightly with her in such a mood. Every man's hand was against her, and nature itself snatched the very fruits of the earth from her lips: "You need not be envying me the gooseberries—there are plenty; but the '*mountain thrushes*'

pick them all." She lost no chance of mocking Carlyle's often
expressed longing for Annandale:

> "the thought you are apt to dwell on too exclusively: that 'God made
> the country and Man the town' is to be taken with large reservations,
> is indeed to be '*strongly doubted*'. You may depend upon it Sir, Man and
> even the Devil have had a very considerable hand in making the
> country also."

She discovered that a maid she had dismissed some months
earlier thought of her still with "the greatest love and respect
than one human being could bear to another", and was quick
to point the moral:

> "It is highly consolatory to be loved and respected by a person whom
> you have scolded for six months, without intermission; as it proves there
> must be an *inexpressible something* in you which triumphs over all con-
> tingencies. If Jane Ireland loves and respects me there is no reason in the
> world why *you* should not do the same; you have never had quite so bad
> a time with me as she had, poor girl!"

Carlyle deplored her bitterness. "Oh! that Edinburgh style of
mockery! . . . I flung it off, and am alive. Oh that my poor
much-suffering Jane had done so too!" He begged her to be
patient with her mother. "They are *her* ways, though very
tormenting." But he was a little worried about her abrupt
departure—"Oh my poor lassie, what a life thou hast led!"—
and he promised better things.

> "I wish to heaven I were better, cheerfuller; but I take heaven to
> witness I will be as cheerful as I can. . . . In any case, what refuge is
> there but here? Here is the place for my poor Goody; let us sink or swim
> together."

Jane was just as anxious to come back as he was to have her
at home again, and at the end of August she returned as
abruptly as she had left. Carlyle missed her at the coach stop,
as her coach was early, so she got into a Chelsea omnibus.

> "By and by, however, the omnibus stopt, and amid cries of '*No room
> Sir*'—'*Can't get in*'—Carlyle's face beautifully set off by a broad-brimmed
> white hat gazed in at the door, like the Peri who '*at the Gate of heaven stood
> disconsolate.*' "

Walking along the Strand, he had recognised Jane's trunk on
top of the omnibus. "This" said Jane "seems to me one of the
most indubitable proofs of *genius* which he ever manifested."

At home again, she felt like a new woman.

"It is a strange praise to bestow on the Metropolis of the World, but I find it so delightfully *still* here! not so much as a cock crowing in the mornings to startle nervous subjects out of their sleep! and during the day no inevitable Mrs this or Miss that, brim-full of all the gossip for twenty miles round interrupting your serious pursuits (whatever they may be) with *calls* of a duration happily unknown in cities! The feeling of calm, of safety, of liberty which came over me on re-entering my own house was really the most blessed I had felt for a great while."

She looked round her with pride:

"*The piano* which refused any longer to do the service of one, is exchanged for a horizontal grand one of age *very advanced indeed*, but retaining much of its original sweetness. Then, on one of the tables stands that really very admirable bust of Shelley, which you may have read in the newspapers has lately been executed by Mrs Hunt. And over it hangs a splendid print of Albert Dürer's, which poor John Sterling sent as a parting gift, when he set out for Bordeaux. Another little print hangs over my bookcase, no other than the Count Pepoli—presenting as *the Examiner* has it—'*an earnest, melancholy, gallant* countenance' to the public, but with a little too much of the whites of his eyes seen according to *my* judgment".

She was, in short, delighted with everything, having thrown off her nervous depression as quickly as she had succumbed to it two months earlier.

XVII

ERASMUS DARWIN AND RICHARD MILNES
1836–1837

Carlyle had done with his articles, and was struggling through the last volume of *The French Revolution*. He was still describing himself in his journal as "sick, forlorn . . . empty as I am in purse and in hope." But he was more mindful of Jane than hitherto. "My chief pity in general, in these circumstances of mine, is for Jane" he told John Carlyle. "She hoped much of me; had great faith in me; and has endured much beside me, not murmuring at it."

Jane was, in any event, determined to make the best of her life—and no one was more whole-hearted than she so long as a mood lasted. The weeks at Templand had taught her a salutary lesson—that it was useless to look elsewhere for contentment, that rest in itself was valueless, and that, however much she might at times feel unsatisfied in her London life with Carlyle, there was no other life for her. She did not always remember this lesson, but whenever she forgot it, or challenged it, the truth was sooner or later brought home to her. Now, in the last months of 1836, she made the house a bright place, bearing with Carlyle when he could not control himself, keeping a rein on her own bitter tongue, and commenting helpfully and optimistically on the manuscript, which she read in rapid bursts as it was written.

She got a good deal of fun out of a new portrait of Carlyle, painted this time by a man whom Carlyle had met in Dumfries, and who was anxious to make his way in London. Carlyle protested; he and his work were both worthless: "What steads the oil shadow of me . . . ? Rather let such a man be altogether suppressed." But Jane insisted that he should have a good portrait taken "before you grow quite old." So he gave way, and, as it happened, enjoyed the sittings, for the painter was an amusing man. The picture was finished and was "glaringly recognisable". Carlyle at forty-one had not changed greatly from the Carlyle of his marriage ten years earlier; his hair had grown a shade darker, perhaps, but there was as much of it as ever, his blue eyes still glowed emphatically. He wore a dressing gown most of the day and his long thin body appeared even more angular as he walked up and down, talking, but his face was more handsome, more striking than ever as it had refined, and Jane when in good humour, as now, could never tire of looking at him.

She, at thirty-five, showed the passing of the years more plainly. She had adopted the customary hair style, banded smoothly over each ear, and this gave her face a subdued look. But if this hair style was deliberately fostered to emphasise the subjugation of woman and the abandonment of female vanity after marriage, it succeeded with Jane only when her face was at rest. Then she looked pensive, sad, and often, after bad nights, downright ill, with heavy shadows under her eyes. But the moment these eyes lighted up, and her wide mouth creased in a smile, she was no longer a member of a depressed sisterhood, but an independent, difficult, remarkably attractive woman. She was helped in cheerfulness by her friends, and particularly by Cavaignac. As the year drew on, he came more and more; his sister had died after following him into exile, and there was no one who could show—and feel, for the moment—greater compassion than Jane. He amply repaid her patience and sympathy by his gallantry, on which Jane flourished like a young girl. At the beginning of the new year, 1837, he gave her a small but elegant gift to mark the "*jour de l'an*"—a pledge of his affection which was repeated every year of his life.

John Sterling provided pleasure of another kind; she could keep herself and her circle alive to him by means of the letters "all about nothing" that she was now writing frequently— letters filled with wit, malice, kindliness, commonsense—a fascinating medley. And there were other satisfactions. If Sterling's father came too often for her patience, his wife was still anxious to mother her, Hunt could be sent for on a dull evening, Craik sat on patiently for as long as he was tolerated, and the Wilsons' carriage was occasionally at her service.

In November, the Wilsons brought with them a friend who had just returned from a tour of America—a ruddy, strong-looking, plain-spoken woman carrying an ear-trumpet, who, although a year younger than Jane, looked her senior. She was well known to the Carlyles by name. Ever since, a few years earlier, Harriet Martineau had published her *Illustrations of Political Economy* and *Illustrations of Taxation* her work had had something of a vogue, and she was much sought after in London. Perhaps the titles of these books had prepared Jane for a blue-stocking; certainly an unfavourable description by Jeffrey and a recent caricature had prepared her for ugliness. So far from the truth did she find this that, in a month or two, she is writing that of all visitors

> "the one I take most delight in is Harriet Martineau! The horrid picture in Fraser with the Cat looking over its shoulder was not a bit like, and the Artist deserved to have been hanged and quartered for so vile a calumny. Neither does the idea generally formed of the woman merely from her reputation as a *Political Economist* do her more justice than that picture! They may call her what they please, but 'it is plain to me and to everybody of sense' (as my Uncle Robert said) that she is distinctly good-looking—warm-hearted even to a pitch of romance, witty as well as wise, very entertaining and entertainable in spite of the deadening and killing appendage of an ear-trumpet, and finally, as 'our Mother' used to finish off a good character, '*very fond of ME.* ".

Carlyle liked her well enough to "mean to cultivate the acquaintance a little". But she was too fond of her own way, and her intellect was too limited to please him long. He thought she would have been better suited as Matron of an Institution, or head of a big dress shop. She was a queer blend of the skittish, the enthusiastic, the managing and the freakish—but sufficiently different from other women to interest Jane. Harriet Martineau admired Carlyle, but tended to undervalue and pity Jane. At that time, she said, Carlyle was

> "as variable as possible in mood. When my friend and I entered the little parlour our host was usually miserable. Till he got his coffee, he asked a lot of questions, without waiting for answers, and looked as if he was on the rack. After tea, he brightened and softened, and sent us home full of admiration and friendship, and sometimes with a hope that he would some day be happy."

She used to come down to Cheyne Row on impulse, demand dinner, and praise the meal Jane whipped up. For a time this

GERALDINE JEWSBURY

from a photograph

JOHN FORSTER

*from a drawing by Maclise,
May 22, 1840*

ERASMUS ALVEY DARWIN

from a photograph, 1868

kind of unconventionality pleased them—pleased Carlyle at any rate, who had not to prepare the meal. "There is Harriet Martineau presents him with her ear-trumpet with a pretty blushing air of coquetry, which would almost convince me out of belief in her identity" said Jane. They returned the visits, going to the crowded soirées in her small house in Westminster, mainly to see the notable people there. Of this they tired quickly enough; Jane in particular, who always preferred to be the hostess. Long years afterwards, Carlyle remembered one walk there on a wet muddy night; how, on the way from the omnibus stop in Regent Street, one of Jane's goloshes came off; and how, in one of the fits of impatient irritation that used to come over him, he complained of his muddied fingers as he replaced it.

In some quarters Harriet Martineau was no favourite—one of these being the Darwin family. Dr Darwin had "a horror" of her, and talk of a fictitious romance between her and his eldest son, Erasmus Alvey, became a staple family joke. Erasmus, so called after his famous grandfather, had begun to call at Cheyne Row—not, however, to meet Harriet Martineau—and contributed greatly to Jane's comfort by offering the use of his carriage. Jane was often taken in the Sterlings' carriage, but she had to pay for the pleasure in listening to old Sterling, and in going where he wanted to go. Darwin would drive her where she pleased. He was a tall, courteous young man, three years her junior, something of a dilettante because of poor health (an immediate bond between him and the Carlyles) and with a spare, sardonic sense of humour that endeared him to Jane. He admired Carlyle—had heard of him during his travels in Germany—and this too gave him favour in Jane's eyes. He soon grew into the habit of attending at the door with his carriage when she had to shop—saving her, as perhaps he knew, not only the inconvenience of omnibuses but the cost of the fares, all of which, in these early London days, had to be considered with care. She would gaily issue her orders for the day, and off they would roll, with Darwin politely handing her in and out, carrying her parcels, attending to all her wants.

From Erasmus Darwin to their last new acquisition of 1836 was to step from satire to broad comedy. Richard Monckton Milnes, younger even than Darwin, appeared already to be making a name in Parliament, but his sympathies were veering unsteadily between politics and literature. Charles Buller, who was also coming to the fore in the House, brought Milnes to Cheyne Row. His friend was an easy man to like; the very look of his chubby face and wrinkling smile was disarming. He was soon Dicky Milnes to both Carlyles—he was the most obvious Dicky—and added them to his ever-widening circle. He was an incorrigible host, and an inveterate collector of under dogs and champion of lost causes; and had Carlyle possessed no other recommendation than his apparent determination to defy convention in everything, he would have been sure of an honoured place at a Milnes's breakfast. But he had other recommendations; and when Milnes had heard him talk, and had come to know something of Jane, the Carlyles were ranked among his outstanding social captures. He was the first to see the potentialities of Carlyle as a literary lion, the first to produce him as a unique character in London society.

In the early days of January 1837, Carlyle finished *The French Revolution*. He wrote the last word upstairs in his writing room. Jane was there. Carlyle's valediction was in character. "They have not had, for a two hundred years, any Book that came more truly from a man's very heart; and so let them trample it under foot and hoof as *they* see best!" This was familiar language to Jane. "Pooh, pooh; they can't trample that!" she declared; and sent him off on his usual morning walk.

She was right; but many difficult months had to pass before her faith was justified. The correcting of the proofs caused an uproar—"*Quelle vie!*" she cried to John Sterling, who was still wintering at Bordeaux. "Let no woman who values peace of soul ever dream of marrying an author! That is to say, if he is an honest one, who makes a conscience of doing the thing he pretends to do." Then she fell ill; the Sterlings' doctor came, looked grave, talked of her lungs, and Carlyle, with John Sterling in mind, hastily summoned her mother from Templand. But by the time Mrs Welsh arrived, the illness had shown itself as influenza, and Jane was about again.

She rose from her bed to encounter immediate trouble. They were again running short of money. Carlyle once more began to talk of lecturing in America. Jane, alarmed, for she thought she had laid that ghost, spoke to Henrietta Wilson. Harriet Martineau was called in. The women put their heads together.

Why should not Carlyle lecture in London if he was so set on it? If he could reproduce, in a lecture hall, the kind of talk that kept his friends spellbound at Cheyne Row, he might become famous overnight. At worst, he should earn enough to remove to a distance, until the fate of *The French Revolution* was known, his chronic fears of beggary and debt.

The plan was put to him. In spite of his repeated talk of lecturing, he recoiled. He had no wish to play-act, as he called it. He prophesied total failure. No one would listen to him. The hall would be half empty. But Jane persisted, and at last wrung a reluctant agreement from him. Henry Taylor was brought in, and Thomas Wilson and one or two others. They all, Henrietta Wilson in particular, canvassed indefatigably among their friends, obtained two hundred subscriptions of a guinea for six lectures, hired Willis's Rooms, printed tickets and circulated prospectuses. The subject was to be German Literature, for which Carlyle at last made use of his abortive History written long since at Craigenputtock.

Jane had sad work with him before the lectures began on the first of May, but she joked her way through it—to others if not to herself:

> "One of his Lady-admirers" she wrote to her Uncle John "(by the way he is getting a vast number of Lady-admirers) was saying the other day that the grand danger to be feared for him was, that he should commence with '*Gentlemen and Ladies*' instead of '*Ladies and Gentlemen*', a transmutation which would ruin him at the very outset. He vows however that he will say neither the one thing nor the other; and I believe him very secure on that side. Indeed, I should as soon look to see gold pieces or penny loaves drop out of his mouth, as to hear from it any such humdrum unrepublican-like commonplace. If he finds it necessary to address his audience by any particular designation, it will be thus; '*Men and Women*'! or perhaps in my Penfillan Grandfather's style, '*Fool-creatures come here for diversion!*' "

Carlyle did not want her in the room for the first lectures, but she drove with him "to our place of execution", as he put it, and gave him a drop of brandy before she left him. Then she sat at home, waiting. But the vigil was not long and the result was a happy one. A few were repelled by his unconventional delivery, but more were fascinated by his appearance, and by the originality of his language. The rest were simply bludgeoned into attention by "the wild Annandale which occasionally grew high and earnest"—Carlyle's own mild description. After two lectures, he allowed Jane to hear the remainder, which she did with mixed feelings, for Carlyle looked so ghastly before he began speaking, his usual ruddy colour drained away, and was in such a state of nerves when he began that she felt ill herself until Henrietta Wilson whispered to her, "Never mind him, my Dear, people like it; the more of that, the better does the lecture prove." And at the end of three weeks, when the lectures were finished, he found himself £135 in pocket, and with sufficient reputation to be sure, if he wished, of attracting an audience for a further series.

But there was no talk of more lecturing. He could not bear to hear the word. He was tired—of himself, the book, London, everything. He could think of nothing but escape from the "horrid misery". Early in June, soon after his book was published, he fled to Annandale, where for three months he "lay like one buried alive."

John Carlyle, who was coming back again on leave, had suggested that Jane, Mrs Welsh, Carlyle, and himself might spend the summer in Scotland together, but neither Carlyle nor Jane wished it. Jane was nervy and still weak but "I expect to grow strong, now that he has nothing more to worry him." She was also too close to her last Scottish holiday to think without a shudder of repeating it. So she wrote to Eliza Stodart, now married to David Aitken and living in the manse at Minto:

"I do not think of accompanying him, having almost a cat-like attachment to my own house, as well as a constitutional incapacity for travelling, to say nothing of the preference I give to London before all other places. It is in fact a jewel of a place; for this reason, that if you want to be solitary you may have your humour out as completely as if you were at Craigenputtock, and if you are socially disposed you may have society to all lengths and of every possible *cut*. . . . Never has it happened to me to hear in London that phrase which in small towns and even in Edinͬ one is constantly hearing; such and such people 'are not in *my* way'. People are content here with simply *having* ways, without trying to persuade their neighbours that they are the only ones that lead to salvation! They have ascertained that from the centre to the circumference there are many more radii than one, and they are only moved to astonishment and disapprobation when a fellow-creature flies *over the circumference*."

Carlyle's reason for going alone—apart from the fact that he wanted to—was:

"Quiet observation forces on me the conclusion that Jane and her mother *cannot* live together . . . and I am further bound to say that the chief blame does verily not lie at our side of the house . . . poor Mrs Welsh, with literally the best intentions, is a person you cannot live with peaceably on any other terms I could ever discover than those of disregarding altogether the whims, emotions, caprices, and conclusions she takes up chameleonlike by the thousand daily. She and I do very well together on these terms: at least I do. But Jane and she cannot live so."

The differences between Jane and her mother did not send Mrs Welsh away, although they may have had something to do with Carlyle's hasty retreat. Mrs Welsh declared from time to time that she must go back to Templand, but she could not bring herself to leave before Jane's birthday, which she tried always to mark in some way. And when the birthday—Jane's thirty-sixth—had passed, she still could not tear herself away, for she loved her daughter dearly. The women, fortunately, were not often left alone together. Elizabeth Fergus, sister of an old Kirkcaldy friend of Carlyle, called frequently—not, as Jane soon discovered, entirely on their account, for she was interested in Pepoli. Cavaignac told Jane that his mother—"ma mère" to her—thought Elizabeth "not entirely destitute of sense"; a judgment in which Jane heard a familiar ring. "Surely" she told Carlyle " *'ma mere'* and *you* have learned to praise in the same school!"

Jane was diverted by a concert got up on Pepoli's behalf. She, her mother and Elizabeth were all there, attended by Darwin. The audience, she said, was "a most deplorably *gratis* looking house". Pepoli's verses were read by "a charming old man" and were followed by a speech by Pepoli himself. "My Mother and Elizabeth wept—I tore my program into a hundred pieces. . . . Mr Darwin said with provoking quietness 'poor dear Pepoli'!"

Jane rarely tired of thinking and talking and writing about the lectures. "Nothing that he has ever tried seems to me to have carried such conviction to the public heart that he is a real man of genius, and worth being kept alive at a moderate rate." She wondered whether he would not do better to lecture rather than write books. £135 for six lectures, finished in three weeks— this seemed an easy way of earning money, and, if she could believe what she heard, of making oneself known. Then came news of *The French Revolution*. It was being well received. *The*

Times printed a favourable review by Thackeray—"a half-monstrous Cornish giant" Carlyle explained to his brother John, "kind of painter, Cambridge man, and Paris newspaper correspondent, who is now writing for his life in London. I have seen him at the Bullers and at Sterling's".

One of those who brought the good reports to Jane at Cheyne Row was a newcomer in person, though not by repute. This was Anthony Sterling, John's elder brother, an army man just back from India. Anthony was an angular, stern and rather rigid man, preoccupied by a detestation of his father. He cut a pleasantly martial figure in the Chelsea drawingroom—"the most wonderful compound of Cavaignac and—Mr Bradfute"—and after Jane had taken him in hand he became quite civilized. "Your brother" she wrote to John "is a great favourite with Carlyle, and with me also, only one dare not fly into his arms as one does into yours." Perhaps not, for Anthony was unmarried; but he escorted her to the opera, theatres, parties.

In the first week of August, the elder Sterlings took her on a tour of the west country, "doing" Oxford, the Wye valley, Worcester, Clifton, and Malvern. She began indifferently in Oxford:

"What disgusted me was to observe in every bed room, *laid before the looking glass*, a *bible* and *book of prayers* with a small hassock underneath (and this preparation I was told was universal thro' all the Inns at Oxford) *my* hassock (of green cloth) had a drawing printed on it, which I was at the pains to examine—it represented a sportsman (for consistency's sake let us hope *a parson*) in the midst of a stubble field taking aim at three birds which he could not fail to hit, the tips of their wings being touching the muzzle of his gun! Moreover the waiters, all large elderly men, had a sort of 'mazed abstractedness and sad gravity of look which gave one a notion they must have some time or other been unsuccessful graduates: while the maids *my-ladied* us at such a rate, and made their reverences so profoundly that the free Briton-blood rushed to my face in very shame for them. From all which I inferred that Oxford was a place much under the domination of Cant—Cant in its two most killing shapes, of *Religion* that *keeps its hassock* and *Respectability* that *keeps its gig.*"

As the tour went on she sickened more and more of it:

"genuine, unsophisticated Nature I grant you, is all very amiable and harmless—but beautiful Nature which man has *exploited*, as a Reviewer does a work of Genius—making it a peg to hang his own conceits upon ... which you look out upon from pea-green arbours—which you dawdle about in on the backs of donkeys—and where you are haunted with an everlasting smell of roast meat—all that I do declare to be the greatest of bores—and I would rather spend my days amidst downright acknowledged brick houses and paved streets than any such fools' paradises."

Her companions did not escape:

"I now perceive the use my company is of to them both, better than I did when we set out: I furnish, as it were, the sugar and ginger, which makes the alkali of the one and the tartaric acid of the other effervesce into a somewhat more agreeable draught."

Even the motherly Mrs Sterling had a "querulous, qualifying, about it and about it way." And Jane had little mercy on old Sterling, nicknamed for the moment "his Whirlwindship". He annoyed her by his "preternatural effervescence of raptures". He and she rode up Malvern Hill on donkeys, attended by a Welsh boy. The donkeys took their time.

" 'The Devil confound your donkeys!' exclaimed my vivacious companion (who might really, I think, 'but for the honour of the thing', and perhaps some small diminution of the danger of bursting his lungs, have as well walked!) 'they are so stupidly stubborn that you might as well beat on a stick.' 'And isn't it a good thing they be stubborn, Sir?' said the lad, 'as being, you see, that they have no sense; if they wasn't stubborn they might be for taking down the steep, and we wants no accidents, Sir.' 'Now,' said I, 'for the first time in my life I perceive why Conservatives are so stupidly stubborn; stubbornness, it seems, is a succedaneum for *sense*.' A flash of indignation—then in a soft tone, 'Do you know Mrs Carlyle you would be a vast deal more amiable, if you were not so *damnably* clever!' "

She longed to be back in Cheyne Row again, and begged Carlyle to say when he intended to return. "O my Darling, we will surely be better, both of us, *there* again; effervescing even:—don't you think so?"

Carlyle evidently did not think so, for he made no move to come home. Her letters had disturbed him. He enjoyed "so lively a pen" and so did his mother, to whom Jane's letters were a joy. Yet he felt that all was not well. Why these headaches, these depressions, why this feverish gaiety?

"I do not at all like the state she is in" he told John Carlyle "but I cannot alter it. I try always to hope it will alter. She writes in great spirits; but there is no fund of real cheerfulness. There is not even a serious melancholy visible. My poor Jane!"

What Carlyle, and old Sterling before him, deplored was a result of the conflict in Jane between her aspirations and her inclinations—a conflict which allowed her no genuine peace of mind. As long as she kept herself occupied all was well, but the moment she was idle and alone and free to consider her life she became dissatisfied. Her father, Irving and Carlyle were all responsible for some part of this dissatisfaction, but Jane, like all clever and facile people, remained her own worst enemy. She was too intelligent to be completely contented with the life she was most fitted for, and insufficiently thoughtful or deeply-feeling to find the serious work she believed herself called to do. She could not resolve this dilemma, she could only escape from it. The admiration she was now receiving on all hands provided a substitute for a true sense of her own importance—but it left her, as Carlyle observed, with no "real cheerfulness". Her pleasure was drawn from excitement, and so led always to depression and a sense of futility. Carlyle could do nothing for her. He was for ever agonising about his own idleness, and for ever preaching that work was man's duty and his reward—a gospel to which Jane, though her conscience was touched, was unable to respond.

However, this did not alter the fact that she wanted him home; she preferred strife, frustration, indifferent health and a good deal of happiness with him to a peaceful stagnancy without him. And when he came back, in the middle of September— "in a kind of dead-alive state" as he put it—she sent a paean of thankfulness to his mother.

> "You know the saying 'it is not lost what a friend gets' and in the present case it must comfort you for losing him. Moreover you have others behind—and I have only him—only him in the whole wide world to love me and take care of me—poor little wretch that I am. Not but what numbers of people love me after their fashion far better than I deserve—but then *his* fashion is so different from all these and seems alone to suit the sort of crotchety creature that I am. Thank you then for having in the first place been kind enough to produce him into this world and for having in the second place made him scholar enough to recognise my various excellencies and for having in the last place sent him back to me again to stand by me in this cruel east wind."

XVIII

KIRKCALDY HELEN
1837 – 1838

Carlyle needed much persuasion before he would believe that *The French Revolution* had been anything but a failure. Solitude and silence in Annandale seemed at first to have done him little good. He was "sick and sad", and all Jane's attempts to cheer him were beaten down by his pessimism. She was waiting for him behind the door, and sprang out to give him a surprise, pouring out her good news about the book before he had taken off his hat. "It has been a great success, Dear!" she said; and when he was settled comfortably before the fire in the parlour she told him of all she had read and heard about the excellent reception of his book. She tried for a long time to rouse him, but he was apathetic. "The fate of that thing is *fixed!* I *have* written it; that is all my result"—this was the burden of his replies. At last she lost patience, and went off in a huff to get him his tea. "Ah, you are an unbelieving creature!" she cried.

He remained unbelieving for some time. He was reluctant to think that he was coming more and more to be accepted, to receive praise instead of abuse. Even the abuse had often enough been magnified in his imagination—he had been noticed from the very first moment that his writings were published. He took a perverse but, in the light of his childhood, understandable pleasure in the thought that every man's hand was against him. Whether he liked it or not, however, Carlyle was now becoming a power in the literary world, and beyond it, and was honoured, early in 1838, with an invitation to dinner with the Chancellor of the Exchequer. Jane was adamant that he should go, and he got more pleasure from it than he expected. If he had doubts about his increasing reputation, Jane had none. She was triumphant, and her sense of virtue rewarded carried her through the winter reasonably enough.

One general criticism of *The French Revolution* was its style, but there came to Cheyne Row one glowing exception in the form of a letter from Phoebe Chorley, whose brother was slightly known to Carlyle. Jane, sending a copy to Carlyle's mother, commented

> "*Pretty fairish* for a prim Quakeress don't you think? Just fancy her speaking all these transcendental flatteries from under a little starched cap and drab-coloured bonnet! I wonder how old she is; and if she is, or has been, or expects ever to be—married? don't *you*? Perhaps the *spirit may move her* to come hither next, and cultivate still more her 'favourable sentiments'. Well, let her! . . . An enthusiastic Quaker once gave Edward Irving a Gig. I wonder if this enthusiastic Quakeress will give Carlyle one —it would be excessively useful here."

Carlyle had told his brother John that, as he had no book to write in the coming year, there would be "a cheerfuller household than of old." On the whole, he was as good as his word. He did not stop worrying about his position, describing himself, when beginning an article in November for Mill's Review, as sitting at his desk "like a galley-slave scourged back by the whip of necessity"; he feels "in general that my only hope is to die." Strong words; but then Carlyle without worry would have been inconceivable to himself, and alarming to Jane. He meant, in this case, simply that he did not care for writing review articles, and felt that at forty-two he should be beyond the need for it. But the winter, judged by Carlyle standards, was peaceful, and both kept tolerably well in health—that is to say, Jane, by confining herself rigidly to two rooms, with the windows tightly closed, succeeded in reaching the better weather with no more than a cough, intermittent stomach trouble, and a headache so frequent that when her maid asked her in the morning if she had her headache, and she was able to answer "No", the girl thought it quite "mysterious".

This maid, rather than any addition to her circle, was the event of 1838 for Jane. Anne Cook had not lived up to her hopeful beginning, and a new girl, Helen Mitchell, took her place. Helen—soon known as Kirkcaldy Helen—was from Fife: "a very curious being" said Carlyle "mixture of shrewdness, accurate observancy, flashes of an insight almost genial, with

utter simplicity and even folly." She had travelled—compared
Cheyne Row aptly with the Boompjes in Rotterdam—read
widely whenever she had the time, was exceptionally good-
natured, and had a typically Scottish form of dry humour. She
was almost as quick as Jane to see the weaknesses of the various
visitors to Chelsea—to say nothing of the inmates—and her
comments in broad Scots and with an unexpected use of
adjectives kept Carlyle in fits of laughter when retailed by Jane,
with suitable improvements, during his evening half hour of
relaxation.

Harriet Martineau came often to see them, praising John
Sterling, who had returned only to leave again for the Continent: "so wise, so cheerful, so benignant"; wishing that Carlyle,
whose views "are deplorably dismal, and very unreasonable"
would learn from him. She was fascinated by Carlyle, nevertheless, and thought him a great man, and she was beginning to
see more in his wife: "Found her looking pretty in a black velvet
high dress and blonde collar. She and I had a nice feminine
gossip for two hours before dinner, about divers domestic doings
of literary people." This kind of talk, she adds, seemed "really
almost to justify the scandal with which literary life is assailed".
Jane—that "very elegant creature"—had evidently carried her
away for the time; and the conversation, if it went on long
enough, was pretty sure to end in a review of other people's
failings or peculiarities—which in Jane's skilful hands was made
to appear, at the time, quite proper and even praiseworthy.

Henry Taylor's affair with Mrs Norton could not pass without comment, but the behaviour of Mill and Mrs Taylor was
the most fruitful topic. Mrs Taylor had taken a house by the
river, at which Mill spent all his weekends—gone were the
Sunday walks with Carlyle. The couple was now, said Jane,
practically shameless, getting on "as charmingly as ever—I saw
them together very lately looking most ecstatically '*Moony*' at
one another, and sublimely superior to the rest of the world!"
Nothing escaped her—not even the fact that James Spedding,
in whom she had little interest, was visiting Henrietta Wilson
frequently—"not that I fancy anything amiss in that quarter".

Harriet Martineau did more, however, than sit and listen to
gossip. Early in the year, the drain on his capital had again
begun to worry Carlyle—*The French Revolution*, though well

received, had not so far brought in much money—and he once more talked of going to the Continent, of becoming a farmer, of lecturing in America. He was dilating in this strain when Harriet Martineau arrived one February day "with an ear-trumpet, muff, and cloak." She at once took the matter in hand. She was beginning to rub Carlyle up the wrong way, was "too happy and too noisy"; and perhaps that is why, after talking only an hour and a half, assisted by Jane, she wore down his objections to another series of lectures, and departed in a whirl of optimism, leaving the exhausted man to scribble in his journal, "I wish this good Harriet would be happy by herself." A few weeks later, she, Henrietta Wilson and Erasmus Darwin had hired a lecture room off Portman Square. Carlyle decided, after consulting Henry Taylor, to give twelve lectures on the History of Literature. Why such a confined subject? Milnes wanted to know. But Carlyle was in no mood for jokes. He read ferociously, and when the lectures began, though "as white as a pocket-handkerchief", made "no gasping and spluttering, as I found him doing last year". The lectures were successful, and Jane reported that

> "on the whole, if he could get sleep at nights, while the lecturing goes forward, and if I might look on without being perpetually reminded by the pain in my head, or some devilry or other, that I am a mere woman . . . we should find this new trade rather agreeable."

At the last lecture, in June, Carlyle had some of his audience in tears, and there was talk of a dinner in his honour. He refused, but was satisfied with the £260 he had made and agreed to a further series the next year on The Revolutions of Modern Europe. But his main thought, as always after a pro-longed mental effort, was to get out of London. He would not stay, he declared, "to have the brain burnt out of me". Hardly a day had passed since his return the previous autumn, he said, "in which I have not stormfully resolved to myself that I would go out of this dusty hubbub." Only Jane, who "likes it far better than I" stood in his way; but for her "I might easily cut and run". But Jane "herself seemingly sinking into weaker and weaker health, points out to me always that I cannot go; that I am tied here, seemingly as if to be tortured to death. So in my wild mood I interpret it." But he knew that Jane was right; that his place was in London. He then sought for some relief. John

Carlyle suggested that the Carlyles winter in Italy near him. "We think of it" said Carlyle. "My unhappy sick wife might be benefitted by it. For me the cry of my soul is, 'For the love of God let me alone' ". Everything and everybody began to turn sour on him—his meeting with a new admirer, the wealthy North Country manufacturer John Marshall; his breakfasts at Milnes' to meet Landor, Rogers, Tom Moore; and even John Sterling, whom at a dinner Carlyle found "argumentative, babblative, and on the whole unpleasant and unprofitable to me."

Clearly there could be no waiting for winter in Italy or anywhere else; and Jane, satisfied that she had for the moment at least prevented any disastrous retreat from London, persuaded him without difficulty to take a month or two looking up old friends and his family in Scotland. Before going, he sat to Samuel Laurence for his portrait, the second by this artist, whom Jane made tea for and encouraged with her "exquisite clitter-clatter". She was writing to John Sterling, persuading him to come to her rather than she to him. "I can listen to you with composure of soul, and talk to you very prettily on my own sofa; but no where else am I good for anything, except to remind people of their latter end."

Jane was in a state that was to become more and more common with her, neither ill nor well, and easily depressed. She disliked Carlyle being away, although she had no wish to follow him out of London. Her conscience reproached her for the wounding things she had said to him during the fights (more numerous than usual) about London as a home. John Sterling added to her depression. He was soon on his way to Italy for his health:

> "I told him, he seemed to me a man who had a diamond given him to keep, which he was in danger of breaking all down into sparks, that everyone might have a breast-pin of it. He looked as Edward Irving used to do. I do not think that, morally, he is at all in a good way—*too much of virtue 'and all that'* on the lips. Woe to him if he fall into the net of any beautiful Italian! People who are so dreadfully *'devoted'* to their wives are so apt, from mere habit, to get devoted to other people's wives as well!"

This to Carlyle, who was staying at Kirkcaldy with the brother of Elizabeth Fergus. To Sterling himself, she wrote

> "I wish we had been going to Italy—since you are. One wishes so

many things!—for instance I wish I could get some sleep without doctors' draughts. But *il faut s'arranger!* God bless you—I say many things with levity, but *that* I say in deep earnest".

As far as hypochondria was concerned, there was already not a pin to choose between Jane and Carlyle. She, like him, was morbidly preoccupied by her sleep, her bowels, her general state of body and mind. But unlike him, she rebounded quickly into a kind of cheerfulness. So now, for all her underlying depression, she preserved a lively front, and often distracted herself better than she expected. She told Carlyle of two "tea-shines" that went off "with éclat"—the first, including the Rennies, Mrs Sterling, Pepoli, Darwin, and her Templand admirer, Robert Barker, now in the Army; the second, as Helen said, rather "insipid", consisting mostly of the Wilson set— many of them elderly—nick-named "the saints" by the Carlyles. Jane could be all things to all people if she chose; and that particular evening she did choose: "I am sure the saints think that all this while my light has been hid under a bushel—that in fact *they* have '*discovered me*'. They kissed me all over, when they went away." Two of them, Frederick Elliot and his wife, had given her the use of their carriage while they were on holiday, and each day she drove out for a couple of hours. Henrietta Wilson had asked her to Ramsgate, where she had taken a house; Cavaignac was often about the place, and Darwin, and the elder Sterlings, until Jane "put the Stimabile in a great fuff—purposely, that I might not have him dangling here in your absence". Old Sterling was not to be kept at bay for very long, however; his carriage was soon at the door again, to take Jane for a drive; and "the Tempest" (as he had for the moment become) was insisting on showing her what the Cockneys "call a 'heath' " at Hampstead. Susan Hunter, now married (and so, completely forgiven) to a Scottish engineer by the name of Stirling, was in London during the summer. They had much to tell each other, for Jane had not written to Susan since her marriage, because she had "always been myself so sick and dispirited—hardly equal to writing to the Mother that bore me".

Her greatest pleasure was Cavaignac, who "shouted" at her stories, and treated her with exactly the right blend of deference and assurance. He "was found sitting yesterday when I came home from my drive, and said, with all the cold-bloodedness imaginable, '*Voulez-vous donner-moi à dîner, madame?*'—an astounding question to a woman whose whole earthly prospects in the way of dinner were bounded there and then to *one fried sole* and *two* pommes de terre! And when this sumptuous repast was placed on the table, with the addition of a spoonful of *improvised* hash; he sat down to it exclaiming *à plusieurs reprises*: '*Mon dieu, comme j'ai faim, moi!*' However as Helen remarked 'It's nae matter what ye gie *him*; for he can aye mak the bread *flee!*' "

She had excellent news for Carlyle. Emerson had sent £50, from the American sales of *The French Revolution*, and promised twice as much to follow. *Sartor*—the "poor beast" Jane called it—was at last coming out as a book. She also sends a reassuring message to Elizabeth Fergus "to be in no sorrow about Pepoli. He is merely lackadaisical".

In September, John Carlyle came back, and as Jane listened to him dilating on the beauties of Italy it became clear to her that he would again unsettle Carlyle's mind unless she took precautions. When he went on to Scotsbrig later in the month, he carried with him, unsuspecting, a letter intended to counter-act every specious argument he could put forward. It was a very affectionate letter to "My *Sweet* love." Jane besought her "precious Good" not to indulge in "*iffing*", but to say, "for instance 'I *will* go back to my wife that is waiting for me in Chelsea . . . and *I* will *not* go to Italy." Rome, she pointed out

"may be the best place for him—but for you it were great nonsense to quit the pool you have waited by so long—just at the moment when the Angel is beginning to trouble the waters. You think, infatuated man that you are, it is the greatest of hardships to have a house and wife tied about your neck, so that you cannot follow every fly-away impulse—but I declare, looking at the matter in pure abstraction, I consider it to have been a real blessing for you, that you have been hindered in this way from bolting out into infinite space—where you may rely on it you would not have the faculty of always *bobbing up* again like Ulysses. And I also regard it as a blessing for *you*, that you had to *work* on the impulse of *hunger*. If you had been born to the future of Byron I question if you would have done any good in the world, or if I should have been able to exist beside you for above six months at longest."

She ended "God bless you dear and put home-tendencies into your head and feet."

Carlyle saw her point: "The Angel, as thou sayest, does stir the waters more ways than one. Surely our better days are coming". He had not yet forgotten their scenes—"my good wife —though very hot-tempered one"—and assured her "Oh, my dear Jeanie, I have more regard for thee, perhaps, than thou wilt ever rightly know." This, though pleasant hearing as far as it went, scarcely went far enough for a loving woman, but Jane let it pass; the great thing was, that he was coming home in October. At this news her spirits, and so her health, shot up into a flourishing state, and she was all cheerfulness when he arrived. Carlyle, too, felt less nervy. It was plain that he need have no serious worry about money for some time. He therefore took life as easy as his nature permitted throughout the winter, reading for his lectures and becoming more and more interested in Cromwell and his times as he did so.

One result of the recent series of lectures had been a free pass for Covent Garden Theatre from the manager, William Charles Macready, the famous Shakespearean actor. Carlyle, feeling himself entitled to a little leisure, used the pass frequently throughout the winter for any good play. Jane joined him with alacrity. They both admired Macready's acting, and when Carlyle met him at the Sterling Club, founded that year by John, they became friendly and Macready called at Chelsea with his wife. Jane's first venture behind the scenes a year earlier, when she "had a fly at Fanny Kemble", had not been an outstanding success; Fanny, she had discovered, was "green-room all over, and with a heart all tossed up into blank verse— blank verse too of the 'fish—be it ev—er so salt—is ne-er—too salt for me' sort!" And she had the mortification of seeing this famous young actress, still in her twenties, "bolt in" on Carlyle "in riding-habit cap and whip (but no shadow of a horse, only a carriage—the whip, I suppose, being to whip the cushions with, for the purpose of keeping her hand in practice)—my inexperienced Scotch Domestic remaining entirely in a nonplus whether she had let in 'A Leddy or a gentleman'." But she took to the Macreadys at once, and they were soon in the heart of the Cheyne Row circle.

Another member of the circle, Leigh Hunt, still came across when asked, and still sent his little notes from time to time, asking Jane, or perhaps both of them, to come to hear him read a play, or whatever it might be. Recently, nothing had been seen of him; he had influenza. Jane became anxious as the weeks passed, for the epidemic had caused many deaths. She was still fancying him ill, or convalescent, when he suddenly appeared to announce his recovery. She impulsively jumped up and kissed him; and this characteristic action inspired the most charming of Hunt's poems.

> Jenny kissed me when we met,
> Jumping from the chair she sat in;
> Time, you thief, who love to get
> Sweets into your list, put that in:
> Say I'm weary, say I'm sad,
> Say that health and wealth have missed me,
> Say I'm growing old, but add,
> Jenny kissed me.

XIX

JOHN FORSTER
1838 – 1839

Not all the visitors to Cheyne Row thought well of Jane. One of her sternest critics called at Chelsea this November. He was Charles Darwin, not long back from his cruise on the Beagle, brought to tea by his brother Erasmus. The tea was scarcely a success: "One must always like Thomas" Charles Darwin told Elizabeth Wedgwood, whom he was to marry; but it was otherwise with Jane. She, said Charles, "sent some civil messages to you, but which from the effects of an hysterical sort of giggle, were not very intelligible. It is high treason, but I cannot think that Jennie is either quite natural or lady-like."

He did not change his opinion when they met again, early the next year, 1839, at a dinner given by Erasmus. Hensleigh Wedgwood, the philologist, was there with his wife, and Jane and Carlyle. "Carlyle was in high force, and talked away most steadily; to my mind Carlyle is the best worth listening to of any man I know". But

> "I find I cannot by any exertion get up the due amount of admiration for Mrs Carlyle; I don't know whether you find it so, but I am not able to understand half the words she speaks, from her Scotch pronunciation. She certainly is very far from natural; or to use the expression Hensleigh so often quotes, she is not an unconscious person."

No more is heard of Charles Darwin at Chelsea. Carlyle by no means returned his admiration, believing Erasmus to have the better intellect of the two, and castigating *The Origin of Species* when it appeared: "Wonderful to me, as indicating the *capricious* stupidity of mankind; never could read a *page* of it, or waste the least thought upon it." Erasmus remained a devoted friend. Perhaps the most interesting aspect of this episode is Charles Darwin's realisation that, in disliking Jane, he was running counter to an accepted view.

For one Charles Darwin, Jane was to have several new friends and admirers this year—perhaps the most significant year of all in this way. The first of these people came into their life through Carlyle's efforts to form what afterwards became the London Library. To his astonishment he discovered, when reading for his third series of lectures, that in some respects he was little better off for books in London than he had been at Craigenputtock. He therefore set on foot an agitation for the institution of a public lending library. By the middle of January he had obtained as guarantors a number of distinguished men—a list of whom he gave in letters to certain influential people, soliciting their help. One of these was John Forster. The Carlyles knew Forster by name; he had for several years been dramatic critic on the *Examiner*, and Macready, whom he knew well, had spoken favourably of him. Now Carlyle called at his chambers in Lincoln's Inn Fields, and was not only promised his support, but found in Forster an admirer and in many ways a kindred spirit. Forster, then 27 years old, had come down from Newcastle ten years earlier to study law, had later joined the staff of the *Examiner* and for the last two years had been writing the *Lives of the Statesmen of the Commonwealth* for Lardner's '*Cyclopaedia*'. They had much to say to each other on this subject, then so much in Carlyle's mind, and Forster was invited out to Chelsea.

He made an immediate impression on both women—for Mrs Welsh had again come down from Templand—who, after the first alarm had worn off, realised that they had met, not only a character, but a good man. Forster was a tremendously emphatic man—another Dr Johnson, one friend said—for ever stamping a foot, pounding a table, or rapping the cane he took everywhere with him. He had a great burly laugh that compelled everyone to laugh with him; a ferocious glare and a shout if anyone dared to thwart him. He was also something of a dandy, lifting a glass on its black silk ribbon to stare at an audacious questioner, twirling his cane with an air, and always immaculately dressed. With women, he had a courtly, old-fashioned air of respect; bowed deeply; raised his hat high; listened with deference, and handed them into their cab with a gesture so grand that they had the illusion of entering a royal coach. He had a warm heart as well as a hot temper, and was for ever helping lame dogs; and the picture that comes nearest to life is of him marching into the office of a periodical with a contribution from some down-at-heels young writer, and slamming the manuscript on the office table with a warning shout that if it wasn't properly read and the poor young devil given his fair chance, they would hear from him. Much of this Jane sensed at that first meeting; and she did not fail to notice that Forster's great laugh boomed out at her bits of stories and pawky judgments, and that he had like herself a turn for irony. He went away, not only a new friend, but one of the soundest friends the Carlyles were ever to find.

Carlyle's list of guarantors for the London Library scheme was an indication of his growing stature in the social as well as the literary world. This spring he went to many dinners and breakfasts. "Why" he asked himself in his journal "do I ever agree to go and dine? Were it revealed to me as tuft-hunting, I would instantly give it up for ever. But it seems to be the only chance of society one has." In this, he is being a little disingenuous even with himself. In fact, he liked it very well; what he disliked was the next day's biliousness. "By this time" he says "we were . . . what is called 'rather rising in society'. Ambition that way my Jane never had; but she took it always as a something of honour done to *me*, and had her various bits of satisfaction in it." What he called "snob ambition" was not quite wanting in him, he admitted: "Certain of the Aristocracy, however, did seem to me still very *noble*." That was his view, and he had every right to feel pleased that he, a peasant, was being courted by them.

Jane did not go so often to these dinners as he; it was fairly common for the wife of a literary man not to be included in invitations; but she took "no manner of offence *not* to participate in my *lionings*." Such gatherings were not, in a typical phrase of hers, "in my line"; she had not his respect for such people; big parties made a wreck of her even more thoroughly than of him; and, most cogent reason of all, her wish was, if not to rule, at least to be the recognised focus of her own more intimate circle. She tried one soirée of her own, persuaded to it by her mother, but embarked on it in a bad humour—she had trouble with Carlyle, who groaned at his house being turned upside down for mere show, as he saw it—and it led to a scene. Mrs Welsh, who liked preparations better than the event itself, busied herself into a mild frenzy, determined that her daughter's soirée should be as memorable as possible. As a final surprise, she bought cakes, confectionery and large coloured candles, set the table, lit the candles, and, when all was done, called Jane to see how attractive the room appeared. But the display only angered Jane, who took much pride in her household economy. She reproached her mother bitterly; the guests would say she was extravagant, and would ruin her husband. She snatched two candles and some cakes from the table and put them away. Mrs Welsh, deeply hurt, began to weep, and Jane repented of her anger, but all pleasure in the evening had gone. Carlyle, who knew nothing of this, probably enjoyed the evening most, although after it had ended he "smoked a peaceable pipe, praying it might be long before we saw the like again."

Carlyle had then only just recovered from a dinner at Bath House, the town house of Lord Ashburton, given by his son William Bingham Baring. This dinner, "one of the most elevated affairs" Carlyle had ever seen, "ruined him for a week", but it was notable for his first meeting with Baring's wife, Lady Harriet. This lady had an eye for the unusual, and a passion for novelty, and a few minutes with Carlyle convinced her that she had discovered a rare treasure. He was not at all awed by her despotic, almost insolent manner, coolly watched her despatching a bore with ruthless efficiency, talked freely and unconventionally, and obviously appreciated her liveliness. She kept him with her more than an hour, and left him gratified:

> "one of the cleverest creatures I have met with, full of mirth and spirit; not very beautiful to look upon . . . a clever devil as Taylor calls her, *belle laide*, full of wit, and the most like a dame of quality of all that I have yet seen."

Soon after the soirée, Mrs Welsh went home. Jane had put herself out to make up for her unkindness, Carlyle had made himself agreeable, and both had agreed to spend some part of the summer at Templand. Jane detested partings, even when it was from someone that she could not live with:

> "I cried all the way home; and then sat down so *dowie* by the fire, indisposed to speak to any son or daughter of Adam. But Helen was determined I should not despond for lack of a little of her Job's comfort; so she broke the silence by an announcement that we were 'out of baith dips and moulds'. 'There' said I, giving her money, and returned to look

into the fire. But she lingered as she went, and at the door she made a stand and gave a great sigh, and then broke forth, 'I declare it's no like the same hoose, sae dull and dismal-like, it's just as if a *corp* had gaen oot! She was so attached!' What could one do in such a case but either jump up and fell her, or burst into new weeping? Having little spirit remaining, I chose the latter alternative."

She was particularly vexed that her mother had just missed visits by two unusual men. One day

"the sound of a whirlwind rushed thro' the street, and there stopt with a prancing of steeds and footman thunder at this door, an equipage, all resplendent with skye-blue and silver, discoverable thro' the blinds, like a piece of the Coronation Procession, from whence emanated Count d'Orsay! ushered in by the small Chorley. Chorley looked 'so much alarmed that he was quite alarming' . . . partly from apprehension of the effect which his man of Genius and his man of Fashion were about to produce on one another."

This "Prince of Dandies", said Jane, "convinces one, shortly, that in the face of all probability he is a devilish clever fellow." Helen was quite overcome: "such a '*most* beautiful man and most beautiful carriage! The Queen's was no show i' the worl' compared wi' that! Everything was so grand and so preceese!' " D'Orsay provided weeks of fun and many letters. Jane, said Carlyle afterwards, "laughed for two days at the contrast of my plaid dressing-gown, bilious, iron countenance, and this Paphian apparition."

Carlyle had met the second visitor before Mrs Welsh left, and had aroused the curiosity of both women. A. F. Rio, a priest who had fought for the French Royalists against Napoleon, had been taken up by Rogers and Milnes, who, like Lady Harriet, liked someone piquant to produce at their breakfasts.

Carlyle asked him to Chelsea. "He is a sort of French John Sterling" Jane said: "if possible even more voluble and transparent; and his Catholicism sits on him just about as lightly as John's Church-of-Englandism sits on him." Jane, knowing that Rio and Cavaignac were at odds, promptly asked them both to dinner. Rio

"seemed amazingly charmed with his prospect. Not so Carlyle, who began, before he was well out at the door, 'Mercy, Jane, are you distracted?' 'What *can* you do with these two men?' &c, &c. I assured him it would go off without bloodshed, and began to think of my *dinner*."

The dinner was not a success;

> "Rio appeared on the scene at half-past three, as if he could not have enough of it. Latrade came as the clock struck four. But Cavaignac—alas! Two of his friends were on terms about blowing each other's brains out, and Cavaignac was gone to bring them to reason; and not till they were brought to reason would he arrive to eat his dinner."

The Macreadys arriving unexpectedly "Mrs Macready asked me how I liked Harriet's Book. I answered 'how do *you* like it?' She made wide eyes at me and drew her little mouth together into a button. We both burst out a-laughing, and that is the way to get fast friends." When Cavaignac finally came, after dinner was finished, "not one reasonable word would he speak the whole night."

Cavaignac, Rio thought, though a most unusual man, "was much less interesting than Carlyle and his wife." He was touched by Carlyle's welcome:

> "as for his wife, the expression of her features is the best imaginable. I was received by her when I went in, as her husband had not come back from his walk. She entertained me with delicious details of how they had lived two alone together for six years in the country. . . . The difference between them, in manners and appearance, and particularly in accent, suggests a difference in class. But when the conversation becomes alive, this man with the rugged face and plebeian accent seems to grow into a giant."

At another Carlyle dinner that year, Rio was faced with the latest and the most remarkable of all the exiles who found their way to Chelsea—Giuseppe Mazzini. Mazzini was then thirty-four years of age, a slim dark man of medium height, with a fine forehead and eyes. His manner was usually grave and sad, and he dressed always in black because of the subjection of Italy to Austria. He had fled to London two years earlier and had spent much of his time in the Reading Room of the British Museum, writing pamphlets to expose the Austrian tyranny. He was then reviewing Carlyle's *The French Revolution* for the *Morning Chronicle*. When he was first brought to Cheyne Row by Mrs Taylor's all but deserted husband, Carlyle was impressed. Two thoughtful men could scarcely have been found who differed so fundamentally, and it says much for Mazzini's goodness, and for Carlyle's perception of it, that they remained intimate as long as they did, and that Carlyle respected him, though not his ideals, to the end of his life.

What attracted Jane to Mazzini, apart from his beauty, was his unlikeness to her. There is no charm like the unconscious charm of a good man, and Jane responded to it at once. She recognised, without respecting, the source of his charm, which lay in his goodness, his simplicity, his freedom from guile or malice, his selfless devotion to the cause of Italy. He was the most delightful of companions, she felt better merely for sitting and talking to him, and that was enough. And as an unsuspecting comic figure he surpassed even the choicest members of her collection. His English, though good, had its curious moments; Jane's letters were soon glittering with "as Mazzini says", and his malapropisms were added to the current language of the house.

Jane's problem was how to find time for all the entertaining, and to avoid disastrous clashes. If she had any spare time, there were drives, theatres, parties. As a result, both she and Carlyle were too busy during the first half of this year to spend much time examining their state of health. Carlyle could scarcely disguise from himself the fact that his financial condition was improving, that the time for worry had passed. He had no need and felt no inclination to write, but two subjects were stirring in his mind, thus preventing him from torturing himself—and Jane—on account of idleness.

This year's lectures, in May, though less striking than before, passed off successfully, in spite of a determined attempt by Carlyle to persuade himself and Jane that he was no lecturer and had failed miserably. He thought the audience stupid when they applauded, but to Jane complacently listening

"it was *he* that was out of *his* wits to fancy himself making a stupid lecture, when the fact is, he really *cannot* be stupid if it were to save his life. The short and the long of it was, he had neglected to take a pill the day before, had neglected to get himself a ride, and was out of spirits at the beginning."

At one of the lectures she noticed the widowed Mrs Irving, and philosophised very properly "when I thought of her lot and all the things that must be passing thro' her heart . . . she seemed to me set there expressly to keep me in mind 'that I was but a woman' "; but she marred this admirable sentiment by the comment that the poor woman was "looking as ugly as sin"; the two remarks providing a fair summary of Jane herself.

There was again no difficulty about arranging another course of lectures for the following year. These, Carlyle promised himself, would be the last, and he sat down almost happily to write "an article on the working-classes"—a subject that the growing Chartist agitation, and the lectures just given, had fixed in his mind. Craik was still about them, but had been scared off for a while. "Creek has been but once since you went away" Jane tells her mother: "Carlyle was in the midst of *Deerbrook* when he came in, and gave such a smack with his teeth as could hardly escape notice, and has produced this amelioration of our lot."

Carlyle had undergone his usual phase of uncertainty about the future—Emerson had again pressed him to lecture in America, where the rewards promised to be considerable—but Jane steered his thoughts towards safer objects, such as a visit to Templand. But even when his agreement to a course of action had been given, Carlyle was a difficult man to move. "Carlyle cannot yet 'tie himself to a day' " she told Helen Welsh, to whom they proposed first going: "no man indeed has such a dislike of being 'tied'." But when they eventually reached Templand, Carlyle was greeted by two pleasant surprises—his mother, invited over by Mrs Welsh, and a horse and gig, a present from John in which he could drive his mother or Jane about the country. After a week or two, he drove his mother back to Scotsbrig and stayed there, talking and smoking contentedly with her. Jane, left at Templand, slept badly, and quarrelled with her mother, all her good resolutions sliding away under the weight of boredom. Time, she complained, "stifled" her at Templand; and she grasped at a chance to go to Ayr. There she consoled herself slightly, despite "a *beautiful* prospect of housetops" from her attic window; a town clock "which chimes every quarter, and rings for a long time at six in the morning, with a sort of passionate solemnity"; and the "brattling and brainging 'of the servants late and early', a universal quoit-playing with all the crockery." She adds: "of course I get little sleep." She bathed once, and, after Mrs Welsh had given her "a gulp of brandy", was the better for it all the afternoon, and only began to feel "like taking a great cold" the next day. There were Burns excursions—already part of the town's stock in trade—but there was little escape from her mother, who, she tells Carlyle, "continues the worst-natured of women—but I let her be doing and 'keep never minding'. Once a day—generally after breakfast she tries a fall with me—and in three words I give her to understand that I will not be snubbed—privately resolving to be sore *up* in the world indeed, before I subject myself to such unreasonable usage again."

Her most satisfactory moment was in the coach from Ayr, when a passenger asked her if she knew any literary people in London. Leigh Hunt? "Yes." "And do you know anything of Thomas Carlyle?" "I am his wife." The traveller's astonishment Jane hugged to herself as comfort until Carlyle should fetch her—which he did fairly soon. They returned to London at the beginning of September, travelling from Preston in the newly opened railway.

XX

GIUSEPPE MAZZINI
1839 – 1840

Jane began the winter badly, suffering from one violent cold after another and day after day of nervous headache that kept her in bed. Helen proved a godsend, as Jane admitted ungraciously:

> "She has no *suggestiveness* or voluntary help in her; but she does my bidding quietly and accurately, and when I am *very* bad, she bends over me in my bed, as if I were a little sick child, and *rubs her cheek on mine!* Once I found it wet with tears. One might think one's maid's tears could do little for a tearing headache; but they *do* comfort a little."

Carlyle, too, had his bad moments. "Ah me!" he complained to his brother John, "I am no man whom it is desirable to be close to—an unhappy mortal. . . . To work is the sole use of living. But we will speculate no longer; above all, we will not complain." Fortunately, he had work to hand, and he had a horse "dear though it be" to ride every day. *Chartism* was finished by November, refused by Carlyle to Mill, who had offered to print it in his last number of the *Westminster*, and was eventually printed in pamphlet form by Fraser. Carlyle's refusal was largely the doing of Jane, who, he said, had "a kind of spite" against Mill "and his wooden set". This wooden set, for Jane, consisted of a single person—Mrs Taylor—described by Cavaignac as the Armida of Mill's distinguished quarterly. Mrs Taylor had committed the unforgivable sin, not of leaving her husband (which did not worry Jane overmuch, for she thought him a dull stick) but of detaching Mill's allegiance from the Cheyne Row circle. She was therefore determined that both parties should be kept at arm's length. Elizabeth Fergus, who had married Pepoli, now lived only fifteen minutes away and this romance excited general interest in the Chelsea circle. Old

Sterling protested that she must be fifty if she was a day—
"What a wreck she is!" Darwin merely remarked "Ah!"
Love, said Jane hopefully, has no arithmetic.

In December, as she was struggling out of one bout of colds
and headaches, Mazzini called. He was still on formal terms
with Jane and, as Carlyle was out, she invited him back to meet
him at dinner: "I was there from half-past four till eleven, and
grew weary: talking does weary me." Mazzini meant that a
monologue wearied him, but when he read *Chartism* he came
to Chelsea gladly enough to dispute the matter with Carlyle.
Carlyle's essential point in *Chartism* was that the remedy for the
deplorable condition of the working classes did not rest with
those classes, whom he considered mere pawns, but with the
leaders of industry and society, the one hope of mankind. To
them he preached moral progress, the only form of progress
worth having, which would automatically open their eyes and
hearts to their duties to other men. To Mazzini, busy organising
revolution by the education of the masses, this pamphlet was
anathema. They strove long and uselessly evening after evening.
When Mazzini's review of *The French Revolution* appeared, the
argument burst out afresh. Mazzini appreciated the "grandeur
of the work" but "I cannot but criticise severely." He had
some doubts about his reception at Chelsea. He called on New
Year's Day, 1840, found that Carlyle had not yet seen the
review, and was given a bottle of eau de cologne by Jane—"I
don't know why," he tells his mother. The significance of the
Scottish holiday had escaped him—but not, perhaps, the
significance of the little gift. He began to notice what in the heat
of argument may have escaped him—that there were two
individuals in the house. He returned a few days later; Carlyle
had read his review, invited him to come often. He did come
often. Occasionally he rebelled—"I lose too much time. He is
good, good, good; his wife is good, we dine without ceremony,
but he insists on introducing me to this, that, and a third
person"—but he still had faith in Carlyle as a man who would
show how order could be brought out of chaos, he was helping
him to assemble his thoughts on Cromwell, and not least he was
becoming aware of the pleasure of talking to Jane about his
hopes and plans for a united, republican Italy. About this time
Cavaignac returned to France under an amnesty, and thereafter

Mazzini found himself more and more in demand at Chelsea. He had not Cavaignac's dominant personality, but he could be as charming in his quieter way, as Jane discovered.

Carlyle, who had laid aside his Cromwell reading to prepare for the final series of lectures, on *Heroes and Hero Worship*, complained incessantly. London was intolerable. His lectures displeased him. His daily rides brought him no nearer health. His friends became a burden: "Welfare, at least the absence of *ill* fare and semi-delirium, is possible for me in solitude only." Yet his one real pleasure in these months—apart from the negative pleasure of indulgence in unhappiness—came from what he most condemned, the dinners and parties. He enjoyed the sparkle and glitter, the "lords and lions", the magnificently dressed women, the deference to his own words, but this pleasure could not apparently be enjoyed without after-misery to himself and others. He moans after one dinner of "a shattered set of nerves and head set whirling for the next eight and forty hours". His life, he says, "is black and hateful to me." He meditates "passionately" flying from "this immeasurable, soul-confusing uproar of a life in London." He even talks of Craigenputtock: "Had not my wife opposed, I should probably have returned thither before now." When the lectures were over, again successfully, and he knew there need be no more, he still made restless grasps at the ever-tempting American lecturing project. He was horrified by a summons to serve on a jury. He complained about the heat: "I get so dyspeptical, melancholic, half-mad in the London summer."

Sometimes the victim of his outbursts was an unsuspecting stranger, such as the "wretched Dud" who unwisely began to differ from his host on the Copyright Bill just when the table had been laid for dinner. "Jane says I treated him inhumanly, as a bulldog might some ill favoured *messin*," but, as Carlyle explains, "my nerves were shattered asunder by a gallop in the wind." There was not even as much explanation for another scene, described by Mazzini, when "a certain poor devil" remarked that the first essential was the happiness of the people. Carlyle fell on him with a hurricane of abuse, and the wretched man left the house "more dead than alive", escorted to the door by Jane, apologising. Carlyle was still pacing up and down the room, running his fingers through his hair, and crying out

"Happiness! Happiness! the fools ought to be chained up!"

Jane bore the brunt of Carlyle's spleen. She was not, perhaps, the best woman for him at such times, herself nervy through headaches, broken sleep and, until the better weather came, a succession of colds (Harriet Martineau claimed that she enjoyed eight influenzas every winter). Yet he avoided even his mother when in this frame of mind; declining to go to Annandale because: "she is old and weak; I am sick, sleepless, driven half mad." He and Jane were therefore penned in the Chelsea house that spring and summer, and had to fight it out or simmer apart. Of the two she was the more forbearing, but there were many times when her quick temper flared, and her tongue, which Carlyle said would take the skin off at a touch, drove him upstairs, hurt and angry. "Work ruined for the day" says one journal entry. "Imprudently expressed complaints in the morning filled all the sky with clouds". There was no peace for anyone until in August he was packed off on a riding tour of Sussex.

During these trying months she consoled herself with the antithesis of Carlyle—Mazzini. They began to go out together; to the play, to see Macready in *Mary Stuart*; to tea with Harriet Martineau; but mainly to the city, or for strolls about Chelsea. Neither possessed a sense of direction, and one summer day, taking a fourpenny steamer to London Bridge, they promptly lost themselves. Eventually they came out at St Paul's, went inside—"filthy and disorderly" Mazzini found it—and climbed up to the Ball. The famous view was spoiled by smoke from the chimneys all around, but they had plenty to talk about by this time. "We remained there three-quarters of an hour alone, with the wind howling most diabolically." Another day, he arrived at Chelsea with toothache, and Jane suggested a walk, which, perhaps following Carlyle, she seems to have regarded as a sovereign remedy. By August, he was writing to his parents that he had walked more in the last eight months than in all the other years of his life. On one of these walks Jane began her complaints of the difficulties of life with Carlyle—the first of a long series, sometimes in the form of mockery, sometimes without even so much disguise. Mazzini counselled patience and Christian resignation. Jane urged him to live in Chelsea, and found rooms for him and his fellow exile and follower, Giovanni

Ruffini. She also found pupils for Ruffini. She was the only person, he told his mother, who had taken any interest in him. And when his mother fell ill, Jane was kind and sympathetic as she knew so well how to be. Mazzini announced after the move that he was "dead for everybody" except the Carlyles.

He and Jane then saw even more of each other, improving one another in their respective languages, talking and working together. She tried to chaff him out of his melancholy—he brooded over the state of Italy and his own ineffectual efforts to rouse the people. She wrote often to his mother, and arranged for Mrs Buller, who was going to Italy, to call on her. Mazzini told his mother that Jane was sending her a token of loving admiration: "I do not know what the present is to be, but yesterday she cut off a lock of my hair."

The present soon arrived—a brooch, with Jane's and Mazzini's hair entwined, and an engraved motto *Ora e Sempre*. This gift aroused the anxiety of Mazzini's father. Who is this Jane Carlyle, he wanted to know, and what was Mazzini doing with women instead of preparing for the republic? Mazzini tried to dispel his fears by posing their absurdity:

> "I dress badly. . . . I smoke from morning till night. . . . I have no small talk, I don't know how to be '*galant*'. . . . I am what the French call '*gauche*' in the fullest sense of the word. I only can suppose that women see that I have a good and affectionate heart."

What kind of woman is this Jane Carlyle, his uneasy father asked again, and why does she write such flattering letters?

> "Mrs Carlyle" replied Mazzini "is still young; she is not beautiful and she is not plain; her eyes are dark, and her hair, as you will have seen, is as dark as mine. She is tall, thin, vivacious, but of very delicate health, suffering terribly from headaches and other ailments".

He begged his father not to misunderstand him when he said that Jane was still young. Her feeling for him is "sisterly devotion . . . though perhaps tenderer and more demonstrative.' He loves Carlyle and Carlyle loves him—there is no question of an estrangement between husband and wife. With this his father had to rest content, but, nearer home, Ruffini was also worrying about the friendship. He wrote to his mother, "I tell him that a man with his fascinating qualities, his gifts of mind and intellect, his winning ways, ought not to indulge in intimate friendships

with women and then expect them not to fall in love with him."
Mazzini, however, had less faith in his own attractions, or
greater faith in Jane's good sense, than his friend, and the
intimacy developed harmlessly. Both, for their own reasons,
needed a confidant and sympathiser, and such are not readily
given up. One effect of this friendship was to make Jane more
tolerant of Carlyle's difficult moments. This was as well, for
Carlyle was missing his usual summer holiday, and the shades
of another book were gathering round him. He did not improve
matters by getting rid of his horse when he returned from
Sussex on the grounds that it cost too much. Jane preserved a
light tone:

> "Carlyle is reading voraciously great folios preparatory to writing a
> new book—for the rest he growls away much in the old style—but one
> gets to feel a certain indifference to his growling—if one did not, it would
> be the worse for one."

This to his mother. To John Forster she adopted the mocking
note that was to run more and more through those parts of her
letters dealing with Carlyle. "This man of mine will absolutely
do nothing but write books and be sick" she declared when
Carlyle refused an invitation " . . . Think of some means of
consoling me." And again: " 'Why do women marry?'—God
knows; unless it be that like the great Wallenstein they do not
find scope enough for their Genius and qualities in an easy life."
She was as yet merely enjoying herself at one of the oldest of
pastimes, but comment on the failings of a husband, however
lightly entered upon, once begun has no end, as she was to
discover.

Forster, in his robust way, was proving a good friend. He took
her to the play, gave her lunch in his fine rooms, flattered her
stertorously, and stimulated her to write some of her brightest
letters. She finally won her way to his heart by her attitude
during the illness and after the death of one of the Macready
children, a particular favourite of his. He had thought of her
as a charming companion, a wit, but rather hard; but he altered
his opinion when he saw her impulsive sympathy with him and
with Macready, who had to appear as usual at the theatre, and
her instant rush to the bereaved parents—"I love them all so
much—and they were so happy when I last saw them!" After
this, Forster could find no fault in her. Actually, his first and

second impressions were both correct. Jane was often hard and unfeeling, although her wit and charm glossed over these qualities. She also showed a warm and most practical sympathy in trouble, but this sympathy usually lasted no longer than the moment in which she felt it. She had little true benevolence, although, like many witty people, she fell easily into sentimentality, and she was capable of mockery and malice against the very people she had helped, as soon as their trouble had passed and her own impulse had exhausted itself.

Of all her friends the Frenchman, Cavaignac, alone recognised without surprise or moral judgment the existence in her of these supposed irreconcilables. All he demanded of her was that she should present herself to him as she felt at the time.

"One evening that I was talking to him rather *'wittily'* (as I thought) he said to me *brusquely*—'Spare me your *cleverness Madame*. Je ne le veux *pas—moi!* it is not *my pleasure* to rank among those for whom you have to *make minced meat* of yourself'!!"

Jane was delighted: "*regal* words truly! as all his words were!— if that man be not an absolute monarch yet before he die, Nature will have missed her intention with him!"

In the autumn of 1840, when Carlyle was out walking after tea, two men called. One was Matthew Allen, whom Jane had met and liked when she visited his model lunatic asylum at Epping, but who had later slipped from grace by describing her as "the remains of a fine woman". He now made amends by introducing Alfred Tennyson. Jane had heard much of Tennyson. She had read his poetry, and Carlyle had met him at the Sterling Club. She knew that he was a great smoker, and invited both men into the garden where they could light their pipes. Carlyle did not come back for more than an hour, so she had plenty of time to study the newcomer, eight years younger than herself. He was a genius, there was no doubt about that; he looked and behaved like one: "a very *handsome* man and a noble-hearted one—with something of the *Gipsy* in his appearance which for me is perfectly charming." It was as well, she thought, that her little cousin Babbie from Liverpool could not see him "for she must have fallen in love with him on the spot, unless she be made absolutely of ice."

Carlyle thought a great deal of Tennyson, and did his best to overlook the fact that he was a poet. For his part, Tennyson could teach the older man much about his gospel of silence. Soon Tennyson became, in Jane's opinion, "the man he likes best"; they smoked together furiously, sometimes talkative, sometimes silent; and they grew into the habit, for the years that Tennyson remained in London, of walking together much at night "discussing everything." Jane had to admire from a distance;

> "Alfred" she explains "is dreadfully embarrassed with women alone— for he entertains at one and the same moment a feeling of almost adoration for them and an ineffable contempt! adoration I suppose for what they *might be*—contempt for what they *are!*"

Another man who sought Carlyle in vain at this time was Crabb Robinson. He had been doing his best to give up the "wild man", but never entirely succeeded because he recognised sincerity in him and suspected greatness. Jane was evidently on her best behaviour, for, after chatting a while, Crabb Robinson went away to write in his diary "a sensible woman." The Aitkens—David and Eliza—looked in on their way back to the Manse at Minto. But the event of 1840, if Mazzini be excepted, was the downfall of Helen, who had long since become like one of the family. Jane told the story to her mother-in-law:

> "My poor little Helen has been gradually getting more and more into the habit of tippling—until some fortnight ago she rushed down into a fit of the most decided drunkenness that I ever happened to witness. Figure the *Head of the Mystic School* and a delicate female like myself up till after three in the morning, trying to get the maddened creature to bed, not daring to leave her at large for fear she should set fire to the house or cut her own throat. Finally we got her *bolted* into the back kitchen, in a corner of which she had established herself all coiled up and *fuffing* like a young tiger about to make a spring—or like *the Bride of Lammermoor* (if you ever read that profane book). Next day she looked black with shame and despair, and the day following, overcome by her tears, and promises, and self-upbraidings I forgave her again, very much to my own surprise. About *half an hour* after this forgiveness had been accorded I called to her to make me some batter—it was long of coming—and I rang the bell—no answer. I went down to the kitchen to see the meaning of all this delay— and the meaning was very clear, my penitent was lying on the floor dead-drunk—spread out like the three legs of Man—with a chair upset beside her, and in the midst of a perfect chaos of dirty dishes and fragments of broken crockery."

After this Helen was "finally" dismissed.

> "I called her up to pay her her wages, and to inquire into her future

prospects—her future prospects! it was enough to break anybody's heart to hear how she talked of them. It was all over for her on this earth, plainly, if I drove her away from me who alone have any influence with her. Beside me she would struggle—away from me, she saw no possibility of resisting what she had come to regard as her Fate. You may guess the sequel—I forgave her a third time—and a last time—I *could* not deny her this one more chance—the creature is so good otherwise. Since then she has abstained from drink, I believe, in every shape—finding abstinence, like old Samuel Johnson, easier than temperance—but how long she may be strong enough to persevere in this rigid course in which lies her only hope—God knows. I am not very sanguine. Meanwhile I feel as if I had adopted a child."

XXI

GERALDINE JEWSBURY
1840 – 1841

One of the most noticeable signs of Carlyle's increasing nerviness during 1840 was his frenzy at any untoward noise. This tendency had been growing in him since his Edinburgh days, twenty years earlier, and threatened to become an obsession.

"Perhaps I am a genius too, as well as my husband?" Jane suggested to her mother-in-law " . . . Some new neighbours, that came a month or two ago, brought with them an accumulation of all the things to be guarded against in a London neighbourhood, viz., a pianoforte, a lap-dog, and a parrot. The two first can be borne with, as they carry on the glory within doors; but the parrot, since the fine weather, has been holding forth in the garden under our open windows. Yesterday it was more than usually obstreperous—so that Carlyle at last fairly sprang to his feet, declaring he could 'neither think nor live.' Now it was absolutely necessary that he should do both. So forthwith, on the inspiration of conjugal sympathy, I wrote a note to the parrot's mistress (name unknown), and in five minutes after Pretty Polly was carried within, and is now screeching from some subterranean depth whence she is hardly audible."

Mazzini could not help laughing at Jane's stories of her husband's hypochondria, but he was more often annoyed by Carlyle's selfishness. He saw that Jane was not only being worried unnecessarily by his obsessions, but that she soon showed every sign of becoming equally neurotic. She bore Carlyle no ill will, however, having relieved her mind to Mazzini and one or two other intimates; and on the eve of his forty-fifth birthday she sat up till four in the morning finishing a waistcoat for him. Mazzini had been sufficiently well educated in Scottish customs by New Year's Day, 1841, to note without surprise, "already, before I was up, came from Mrs Carlyle a letter, a present, and some hot tarts." Soon afterwards "I,

happy as a boy, ran over to Mrs Carlyle, who, from some
Scotch superstition, wished mine to be her first visit, and I was
in time to be her 'first foot' ".

Early in 1841 Jane reported that she had spent her best
winter for four years. She was in better health, as she understood the term, and was surrounded by friends. Carlyle was

"as usual—never healthy, never absolutely ill—protesting against 'things
in general' with the old emphasis—with even increased vehemence just
at present, being in the agonies of getting under way with another book.
He has had it in his head for a good while to write a life of Cromwell and
has been sitting for months back in a mess of great dingy folios, the very
look of which is like to give me lock-jaw."

But Jane spoke too soon. Another jury summons arrived. The
atmosphere in Cheyne Row at once became impossible.
"Intolerable suffering, rage, almost despair (and resolution to
quit London)"—so Carlyle described his feelings. His fury grew
almost to madness on the second day of the trial (the truth
about which, he claimed, was clear to him after the first half
hour) when one of the jurymen—"stupidest-looking fellow I
ever saw"—differed from Carlyle and the other ten and declared
that nothing would make him change his mind. They were all
shut up in a small stone cell to fight the matter out. The ten
were for arguing, but Carlyle, desperation lending him cunning,
saw that the one hope was flattery. He took the man aside, and
in an hour had won him over and was free.

This incident had its humorous side, and Jane later added it
to her store of good tales with Carlyle as the butt. But during
the trial and for weeks after it she was in no mood for fun—
swinging between sympathy with the almost distracted man
and annoyance at his extravagant self-pity. His work was
ruined, he said, his digestion fatally impaired. Craigenputtock
was brought forward again, and the American lecture tour.
Jane kept these bogies at bay until Carlyle had struggled wrath-
fully through a bout of influenza, and had done with the proofs
of *Hero Worship*. The difficulty then was to get him away:

"His portmanteau had been standing on a chair, half packed, for the
last four weeks—with a direction on it—Mr Carlyle *Passenger*—but
passenger in *what*, or *whither*—no man, least of all himself, has the
faintest idea."

Jane at last persuaded him to accept an invitation from

Milnes. Carlyle went off to Fryston at the beginning of April, and was immediately remorseful: "The last look thy face wore today has haunted me all the way hither. . . . O Jeannie, would thou wert happier! Would I could make thee happy!" And a day or two later, still trying to get his bearings in this first experience of an English country house, "Think not hardly of me dear Jeannie. In the mutual misery we often are in, we do not know how dear we are to one another. By the help of Heaven, I shall get a little better, and somewhat of it shall abate."

At Chelsea, the moment he was away, Jane collapsed. She got in a stock of porter, and reported after ten days that it was doing her good. She always had great faith in remedies of one kind or another, but her improvement was due mainly to the peaceful atmosphere of the house, to the visits of her friends, and to her letters, in which she wrote out her ill-feeling:

> "For the first time in my life I could sympathise with Byron's Giaour— and, so soon as I had the house all to myself, I flung myself on the sofa with the feeling
>
> > 'I would not if I might be blest;
> > I want no paradise but *rest*'
>
> I shall have to return to my post again presently—one has to *die* at one's post has one not? The wonderful thing for me is always the prodigiously long while one takes to *die*."

Letters more than passed some of her spare time; and friends occupied a great deal of the rest of it. She had "a spate" of visitors. Mazzini, of course, and Giovanni Ruffini, until he "dined with a Greek the other day and eat *three dozen and a half of snails!* I shall never be able to endure him any more." Then there were regular visits from the elder Sterlings, Forster, Darwin, "Contessa Elizabeth", George Rennie—"three times within the last ten days, which I impute to his having had Influenza"—and Jeffrey. Jeffrey she thought "is decidedly become a little *old* man, and more frivolous and worldly I think than ever"; Mrs Jeffrey, who called for her husband with the carriage was "*younger* than ever I saw her, but *jerking à faire peur*." She and old Mrs Sterling visited the Derwent Coleridges "I *despise* the man and rather fancy his wife." Darwin drove her out regularly, and was always ready with the appropriate word. He said "when he found me sewing a table cover the other day that I 'looked decidedly *virtuous*' " but, she complained, "one gets horribly meagre and *moony* on 'virtue's own reward' ". Darwin, she said, was "the likest thing to a brother I ever had in the world, not even excepting my brother-in-law". The brother-in-law, John Carlyle, for whom her feelings hovered between boredom and respect, affection and dislike, was not at his best. He "staid till after dinner—more demoralized I think than ever—repeating the same words six times over, and absolutely not *hearing* any thing one says to him unless it concerns his own personality." Helen, still abstaining from liquor, remained a godsend—"she is the greatest goose! but so cheery and good a goose!"—and still full of good sayings. Jane, she said, "would never be *fit to be seen* in this world again" after she had blistered herself in an effort to cure a sore throat. And when Jane took her to the National Gallery, Helen's comment on a Virgin and Child was "most *handsome!*" but "most *expensive!*"

The time left for reading was not extensive, and not all that she read pleased her—as, careless of heresy, she told John Sterling:

> "There is a copy of Emerson's Essays come for you here—I wish you good of them! I find him getting affected stilted mystical, and in short a considerable of a bore! A bad imitation of Carlyle's most Carlyleish *translation* of Goethe's most Goetheish passages!"

Sterling had moved to Falmouth in the hope of arresting the trouble in his lungs. Jane wrote him long, gay, affectionate letters, encouraging him to continue his writing and sometimes actually placing his work with Forster. He told one of his Falmouth friends, Caroline Fox, that Jane was the most brilliant letter writer he had ever known. The young Caroline had heard Carlyle lecture, and at Mill's house had heard Jane give "some brilliant female portraiture, but all in caricature". These glimpses, following after the praise of Sterling and Mill, who both insisted that the Carlyles were "a very happy pair", determined Caroline to know more of them.

Another new friend of Sterling was James Anthony Froude, whose eldest brother, Richard Hurrell, had come into prominence through his association with Newman at Oxford. Froude had followed his brother to Oriel, but had not yet taken his degree. He had read *The French Revolution* "but had not known what to make of it" until "Sterling made me understand that it was written by the greatest of living thinkers".

Froude was not one of the many who wrote to Carlyle—the growing army whose ranks had to be thinned by Jane.

> "In my character of *Lion's* wife here I have writing enough to *do*, by constraint, for disgusting even a Duchess of Orleans. Applications from young ladies for autographs, *passionate* invitations to dine, announcements of inexpressible longings to drink tea with me—all that sort of thing which as a provincial girl I should have regarded perhaps as high promotion, but which at this time of day I regard as very silly and tiresome work."

Most of the letters were acknowledged and forgotten; but one, although highly emotional, struck both the Carlyles by its power and evident sincerity. The writer, Geraldine Jewsbury, declared that *Sartor* and the *Miscellanies* had changed her life. She longed to be a writer. Carlyle invited her to call. She had come down from her Manchester home a month before he went off with Milnes, and he thought "our fair pilgrimess . . . one of the most interesting young women I have seen for years; clear delicate sense and courage looking out of her small, sylph-like figure." Such praise was too good to last. The next day he discovered that Geraldine was a devotee of George Sand, and his admiration cooled. He could not be emphatic enough in his hatred for "George Sandism"—the school that taught what he called the "new Phallus worship, with Sue, Balzac and Co for prophets, and Madame Sand for a Virgin."

Geraldine was less disturbed by her failure to retain Carlyle's admiration than she would have believed possible when she set out on her pilgrimage. Like many another, though with an unexpected thoroughness, she came to worship at one shrine, and went away worshipping at another. She was a woman in love with love; she wanted a husband; but she had to love somebody, even if another woman, and when she met Jane she immediately fell in love with her. She could do nothing by halves. She tried to make Jane promise, before she left her, to come to Manchester, holding out as bait a friend, Elizabeth Paulet, charming, literary, wealthy, who lived in a big house in the country nearby. The moment she returned home she began to write long, eager, intimate letters.

Jane was by no means so sure of her regard for Geraldine. She believed herself to be growing out of the way of passions, for women at any rate, and she regarded with some suspicion the ardent little provincial, with her untidy mass of reddish hair, her sharp, high-cheekboned face, and the bright, brown, worshipping eyes. True, such admiration appealed to her vanity though it also made her conscious of her age, (for Geraldine was eleven years younger), but the whole thing was too sudden and too complete. This abandonment to the emotions roused all the dour Scot in Jane. Besides, Geraldine had talked too much, too fast and too emphatically, and now she was writing too often and too obsessedly: "Today I have a prodigiously long letter from Geraldine containing a philosophical dissertation on the passion of *love* as it differs in Men from Women!! She is far too *anatomical* for me". She was in danger of becoming a bore— the last thing that Jane would tolerate. But she reckoned without Geraldine. "So, my dear" Geraldine had written in her "anatomical" letter, "let us look our lot boldly in the face at once; if it has been given to us to love—for it is not every woman who receives that terrible gift—let us submit without vain struggling". Jane struggled a good deal, but her determined adorer was too much for her.

Geraldine was not the only person who pressed Jane for a visit. The role of London lioness had proved too strenuous for Harriet Martineau, who moved to Tynemouth where she was trying to recover from a nervous breakdown. From her, too, came effusive letters; Jane and Carlyle must spend the summer beside her. The suggestion coincided with Carlyle's return in May, little better than when he had gone away. "I am sick with a sickness more than of body" he wrote, "a sickness of mind and my own shame. I ought to know what I am going to work at—all lies there." He could not settle himself to the Cromwell reading—that was the truth of it—and needed a longer holiday. They discussed the matter interminably, but when he again left London at the end of June no more had been decided than that he should go on ahead, stay a day or two with Harriet Martineau, and examine lodgings at Tynemouth.

Forster had been a faithful attendant on Jane in Carlyle's absence, "I have always thought rather well of his judgment" she told John Sterling; "for, from the first he has displayed a most remarkable clearsightedness, with respect to myself— thinking me little short of being as great a genius as my husband." He was, however, unromantic: "He is one of those people who go about, that one likes, in moderation, without feeling them to be worth the pains of a particular study." To Forster himself she praised the "something *sunshiny* about you, that cheers my gloom."

On the day before Carlyle went to Tynemouth, they had both dined with him—and their notes confirming the engagement show even Carlyle quite skittish: "We will stand good for Tuesday with ready heart,—and the sorrow of my life here tells me withal that she is now *off* from Mrs Jameson for the time! So we will come alone." Jane's letters had a particular flavour to suit each correspondent, as her acceptance of Forster's invitation, written in the flurry of packing, shows: "A *Yes* written under the *present circumstances*, in spite, one may say, of the world, the Devil, and the flesh, ought to stand with you for a million protestations of the most undying, most romantic attachment! Yes then!" Carlyle duly got off, and was given the latest news:

> "There is come for you today from Mr Browning something between a poem and Legitimate dramar entitled 'Bells and Pomegranates. No 1 Pippa Passes'. God only knows what such names can mean. Elizabeth was here at the time and we both laid it away as a *grandi mistero*."

This was the first letter from Browning, who, like Thackeray, was to remain outside the Cheyne Row circle. John Carlyle was too much inside it for Jane's liking. He was in London trying to make up his mind what to do. He had been to a phrenologist, she told Carlyle, who pronounced him "*capable* of *any*thing but not capable of turning his capability to account." Day followed day, and still she waited, feeling like "a Ghost that cannot get itself *laid*". Carlyle could not make up his mind where to stay or what house to take. She began, she told Forster, to be ashamed of showing her face in the streets—"I fancy them all saying to themselves 'Christ Almighty what is that woman still doing above ground?' What indeed but waiting for the crowing of the cock!—and no cock will crow!" Eventually, she waited no longer and set off for Templand. The holiday was doomed from the beginning. At Liverpool, she was fêted too long and too often—"I was not the Rose but I had been near the rose— and in that mercantile city . . . they are ready to fall into raptures even over the rosified clay!"—and she was nearly killed in a driving accident.

"A very dashing lady, one of that sort of people born to write a book on 'the rights of women' carried me off in her carriage one day *par vive force*, so to speak—the horses were *dashing* as well as their mistress—they also seemed born to maintain *the rights of horses*—and at the top of a steep Hill called *Mount Pleasant*, they commenced a violent protest, and appealed to posterity—reared, plunged, played the Devil, finally got both coachman and reins among their feet and were rushing down with us into a *grand peutêtre* when mercifully a gentleman dashed forward and seized their heads at the risk of his life."

She adds: "the horse of course was finished but that was no pity!"

She found an oasis for a day or two at Seaforth House where the rapturous Geraldine took her to meet the Paulets, a wealthy Genoese merchant and his young English wife. Carlyle, now in Annandale, had not stopped in Manchester, as begged, to see Geraldine. "Wretch!" wrote Jane, not at all displeased " . . . It it quite true what Darwin says 'Carlyle does not take to *women* the least in the world' ". He had missed an admirer and a very pleasant woman in Mrs Paulet, she told him. Perhaps it was a pity, Carlyle replied, but he was living and thriving "in a *silence* unequalled for many years." He would see no one, even in Annandale, but he had a message for Geraldine: "I wish she could once get it fairly into her head that neither woman nor man, nor any kind of creature in this universe, was born for the exclusive or even for the chief purpose of falling in love, or being fallen in love with".

He ended his letter: "Adieu, dear little creature! sail prosperously. Be not too sick. Come jumping up when I step upon the deck at Annan Pool." There was no possibility that she would be anything but very sick. So much did she dread the crossing that she was tempted to pay the extra fare and to go by coach, and let her maid go alone by the boat. But she could not bring herself either to face Carlyle's annoyance at the waste of money, as he would consider it, or to abandon Helen.

"For a few minutes, just till we got out into the deep sea, I flattered myself I was going to have rather a *sublime* night of it. To give myself the best chance of escaping the old agonies, I had a mattress spread out on deck, and stretched myself there to pass the night in the cool air—with the 'starry vault' as they call it right overhead—the dark waters plashing around—nothing alive beside me except the man at the helm—but all too soon my poetic feeling gave place to one of the most desperate prose— and this night like all others I have passed at sea, was one long *conscious* fainting fit—even the occasional torrents of rain which poured down on me could not revive me out of this horrible state. . . . "

When Annan came into sight, Helen made no attempt to conceal her anger as she looked at her mistress: "I think it will but be picking up a dead dog."

Harriet Martineau had given Jane an excellent report of Carlyle:

"I had seen all manner of other good things in him before; but what he was in good spirits I never had witnessed,—nor imagined. O! he was so light and gay! He had given all his cares to the winds on his voyage, I suppose; for he seemed to have no more troubles than a schoolboy."

But there was nothing light and gay about him by the time he met Jane at Annan. He drove her to Templand in an open gig. Mrs Welsh cried when she saw her, wet to the skin, and at once put her to bed. When night fell, there was no bed for Carlyle except the one that Jane was in. For the first time since they had left Craigenputtock they had to sleep together. They did not sleep, and a cock crowing drove Carlyle frantic. He got up at three in the morning and drove off to his sister at Dumfries, where he slept, leaving Jane to explain his disappearance to her mother. He wrote penitently: "I have done little but think tragically enough about my poor lassie all day: about her, and *all* the history we have had together. Alas! but let us not take the tragic side of it. All tragedy has a moral and a blessing in it withal." He begged her: "let us not meet tragically."

He rented a cottage at Newby, on the Solway Firth, just below Annan, and to this place he, Jane, his mother and Helen went at the end of July. It was, said Carlyle, "the loneliest place surely I could have found anywhere" with "no phenomenon at all but the everlasting roar of the loud winds, and the going and coming of the great Atlantic brine . . . the very image as of a grey objectless eternity." In short: "It is all like a kind of vision of Hades."

The whole holiday seemed like Hades to Jane. The cottage was tiny, dirty, there was nothing to look at, no one to see. She and old Mrs Carlyle took turns in the gig, but that was the only break in what he called "a savage existence". He would see no one, speak to no one outside the cottage, although he had friends and relatives all round about. "It is not to be a Lion" said Jane "but to be a Tiger." She was disgusted, and made no effort to hide it. After a month the cottage was given up. "The adventure", Carlyle said "was full of confused pain, partly degrading, disgraceful; cost me in all, seemingly, some £70. We shall not all go back to Annandale for rustication in a hurry."

Jane poured out her woes to Forster:

> "Oh such a place! Now that I am fairly done with it I look back upon it all as a bad dream! never shall I forget its blood-red, moaning sea—its cracked looking-glasses, its 'industrious fleas', its desolation and hugger-mugger such as hath not entered into the heart of man to conceive! This Templand looks a paradise in comparison—never before did I know how to appreciate material comforts! my heart dilates over the *white* sheets, the soft carpets, the silver spoons in which one can see oneself, and above all over one's own *dear* nice looking Lady-Mother."

The house as usual was filled with relatives from Liverpool, but Jane went her own way cheerfully enough for a few days. When her cousin, Walter, preached at Penpont — where Mr Dobie, Mary Russell's father, was minister—Jane stayed at home: "my abstinence from public worship gives great scandal, but I would rather be scandalized than wearied to death." Harriet Martineau tried to tempt her to Tynemouth.

> "Here is a god-send of a house. If you don't come, and settle, and be happy for 3 months, I won't speak to such thankless people any more, as long as I live—(if I can help it). . . . The next house to mine is to let after Friday week (the 23rd). It has the same beautiful view, and only a *very thin* wall separates your drawingroom from mine! . . . And next door to me! We can knock thro' the wall;—we can nod out of the window;—you can run in at the back door without your bonnet; I shall probably invite myself to tea with you."

Jane resisted the temptation without difficulty. She could spare a weekend, that was all, she said. Darwin, then visiting Tyne-mouth, found, Jane told Carlyle:

> "that she looked much worse than he was prepared for—'misled' he supposes 'by what he had heard of her from T.C. *without believing him*'—for the rest, he appears most dreadfully exhausted 'by the tremendous tour he has made' and hopes soon to have 'the happiness of seeing me in my proper suburban Sphere'."

Darwin could not have wished Jane home sooner than she wished herself. The charm of Templand quickly wore thin. A note from Cavaignac, visiting London, increased her restless-ness. Helen had already returned. "It is a good Thing" she wrote "you Sent me Before you for the Little Time We have

Ben gone the hous apears to me Like a Barren Wilderness. Everything had Such a Bad Smel for the Wether sems to have Ben much the Same very Wet."

Jane arranged with Carlyle to meet her at Dumfries, as "this place is so antipathetical to you." She dreaded the travelling so much that "I often wish myself dead for the very *fear* of being alive." A pleasant surprise was awaiting her when she returned home in the middle of September, dazed with three days of incessant talk by Harriet Martineau. She had gone to bed at once and, she told Mazzini's mother,

> "the first thing which met my eyes on awaking were your flowers. . . . In the evening, my friend gave me the ring with an apology more modest than reasonable for the words inscribed by his mother, as if those words were not more precious than gold to me. . . . 'Love Italy's martyr?'—No need to bid me do so. I cannot do otherwise. Ah! if you knew how I love him! It is no case of *must*, I am happy in doing so. Henceforth I can say in loving him—'Another bids me love him'—and I think there is no hypocrisy dearer to us women than to give to our delights a varnish of duty."

But the last word in 1841 must be given to Carlyle. Sitting in his study, trying vainly to make a beginning with *Cromwell*, he considered his financial position, and was forced to admit that it was promising, in spite of the drain of Newby. His books were all in good repute and were selling well on both sides of the Atlantic. He had, in fact, nothing to worry about. "I begin to see now" he said "that it is not on the money side that we shall be wrecked, but on some other."

XXII

THE DEATH OF MRS WELSH
1841 – 1842

Jane passed the winter with no more than the usual number of colds, and in tolerable spirits—now up, now down, as her manner was. She was busy arranging with Forster to print articles by John Sterling and Mazzini, and often pressed him to dine when, as in this case, she felt too unwell or feared the cold too much to venture to the theatre. "Now answer me in two words will you dine here on Wednesday or Thursday or Friday or Saturday? I give you four days to choose on—and let us enact the legitimate Dramar at home." The letter is dashed off, because "I write with an Italian conspirator staring on me and in fear of being too late for the post."

This picture of Jane—just recovering from a spell in bed, writing to Forster to arrange another entertainment, mocking the promoters of the "legitimate drama", then a catch word at Chelsea, and with one of her exiles attending her in the drawing-room—is typical of her life at the beginning of 1842.

As typical was a renewed outbreak of night noises.

"We are gone to the devil again in the sleeping department" she wrote to her mother from her bed late in February. "That dreadful woman next door, instead of putting away the cock which we so pathetically appealed against, has produced another. . . . The night before last they woke me every quarter of an hour, but I slept some in the intervals for they had not succeeded in rousing *him* above. But last night they had him up at three. He went to bed again and got some sleep after, the 'horrors' not recommencing their efforts till five; but I, listening every minute for a new screech that would send him down a second time and prepare such wretchedness for the day could sleep no more. What is to be done God knows! If this goes on, he will soon be in Bedlam; and I too, for anything I see to the contrary. . . . Carlyle swears he will shoot them, and orders me to borrow Mazzini's gun. . . . If there is to be any shooting, however, I will do it myself."

267

Her chief fear was that the noise would drive Carlyle from the house just when, since the Newby disaster, he was becoming reconciled to London. "How one is vexed with little things in this life!" she complained.

By the time this letter reached Templand Mrs Welsh was on her death bed. She had been unwell for some time, but apparently not seriously. Then, suddenly, came a letter from Dr Russell; she was dangerously ill. Jane caught the first train to Liverpool. It was a wild, blustering, rainy night as she and Carlyle set off to the station: "Never shall I forget her look . . . her beautiful eyes full of sorrowful affection, gloomy pain, and expectation." "I travelled all night in the cruellest suspense" she told Eliza Aitken "and arriving in Liverpool in the morning, was told that my Uncle and Walter were already gone—to her funeral! Oh, Bess is it not a wonder that I kept my senses?"

She collapsed, and "lies there very ill" Carlyle told Forster, " . . . waiting till I come up, and decide whether she shall go further." But when he reached Liverpool, travel was out of the question; she lay like one dead. She would never go to Templand again, she said. She told him to sell everything, "annihilate all vestige of our past time there." Carlyle protested but was overborne, and went off to Templand leaving Jane "very desolate and poorly in all ways."

The return of John Welsh from Templand and the account he gave her of her mother's last days (she had died of an apoplectic stroke), added to the remorse which, more than grief, was prostrating her. There was no escape now from her mother's love. She lay in her darkened room at Liverpool recalling the time after innumerable time when she had rebuffed this love and abused the woman who offered it. She turned over and over in her mind every unselfish act of her mother up to the end.

> "All her last weeks seemed one continued thought about *me*—to ward off anxiety from me while she lived and to soften the shock for me should she die. . . . And when the first stroke came upon her, Margaret Macqueen being by—she uttered no thought for her own future, only in sinking down exclaimed, 'I am dying, Margaret! Oh, my poor Jeannie'."

There was no escape from her thoughts, and no hope. Mazzini wrote at once to console her, but she could not share his faith. "Sad! Sad!" he tells his parents, "Dwelling on all the little things in which she did not fit in with her mother, unable to feel that she is not dead, but knows all and loves more."

She returned to Chelsea in March with her cousin Jeannie who, she told her uncle, "is the dearest little soul I ever tried living beside . . . she sleeps with me, and comforts my nights as well as my days." No one was admitted to the house. Carlyle, still at Templand selling up the house and furniture, became alarmed, and appealed to Forster to call: "My poor wife seems to suffer terribly." Forster had already called in vain. When Jane discovered this, she roused herself:

> "Had I foreseen that *you* would come that day I would not have given orders that no one should be let in; but I felt so helpless on my first arrival—the house looked so dreary—the whole world is dreary—God bless you—do you know why I say this fervently at this moment?—it is because you once gave her a little pleasure—you took her to the play do you remember and she was so pleased with her evening—and so pleased with you. She often mentioned you in her letters after, and spoke of you often when I was last in Scotland as the only man she had met in London 'whom she took to'—I should care for you in thinking of this, even if I had not cared for you before."

He came again, and she began to revive.

She relapsed when Carlyle, who was "not unhappy" at Templand and still reluctant to sell the furniture, suggested that it might be moved to Craigenputtock, and a home set up there, far from the noise and worry of London. Jane sent him a frantic note. How could he hurt her at such a moment with such a suggestion? He at once withdrew it: "You are evidently very ill. I entreat you to take care of yourself. Do not tear yourself in pieces." But he went on re-living in his letters to her the past brought up before him by Templand—memories of Walter Welsh, of Aunt Jeannie, of himself and Jane, of the very death of Mrs Welsh. She begged him to stop tormenting her. She was sick of the world. That, he replied, he could understand:

> "My prayer is, and always has been, that you would rouse up the fine faculties that *are* yours into some course of real work which you felt to be worthy of them and you. Your life would not then be happy, but it would cease to be miserable. It would become noble and clear with a kind of sacredness shining through it. I know well, none better, how difficult it all is, how peculiar and original your lot looks to you, and in many ways *is*. Nobody can find work *easily* if much work do lie in him; all of us are in horrible difficulties that look invincible, but that are not so. The deepest difficulty which also presses on us all is the sick sentimentalism we suck

in with our whole nourishment, and get ingrained into the very blood of us in these miserable ages! . . . It is this that makes me so impatient of George Sand, Mazzini, and all that set of prophets; impatient so far as often to be unjust to what of truth and genuine propriety of aim is in them. Alas! how often have I provokingly argued with you about all that! I actually will endeavour not to do so any more. It is not by arguing that I can ever hope to do you any service on that side; but I will never give up the hope to see you adequately *busy* with your whole mind. . . . Courage, my poor little Jeannie! Ah me! Had I been other, for you too it might have been all easier. But I was not other: I was even *this*."

Jane was unable to follow this advice. She was a practical person in the superficial sense of the word, and she could think only that he would again raise the cry, leave London. Her wish to remain at Cheyne Row became an obsession. He reassured her,

"if *you* like it, do not regard much my dislike of it. I cannot be healthy anywhere under the sun. I am a perceptible degree unhealthier in London than elsewhere; but London, I do feel withal, is the only spot in the earth where I can enjoy something like the blessedness of freedom; and this I ought to be willing to purchase at the expense of dirt, smoke, tumult, and annoyance of various kinds. I must run into the country when the town gets insupportable to me."

He was home again early in May, and found her "feebler than I ever saw her."

Carlyle's return did her good, if only because she was obliged to look after him and could no longer refuse visitors. In fact, after a few weeks the rôles were reversed, and Carlyle shut himself up at the top of the house with his pipes and Cromwell books while

"poor Jane and her cousin sit in the low room which extends through the whole breadth of the house. . . . There they sew, read, see company, and keep it out of my way. Poor Jane is still very sad, takes fits of crying, and is perhaps still more sorrowful when she does not cry. I try to get her invited out as much as possible . . . she seems to get no good of anything but the sympathy of her friends."

Jane did not admit even this consolation: "what are friends? —what is a husband even, compared with one's Mother? Of *her* love one is always so sure! it is the only love that nothing—not even misconduct on our part—can take away from us." She did not think she would ever have the heart to set foot in Scotland again. But if she would not go to Scotland, all who saw her felt that she needed a change of scene. Mrs Buller invited her to Troston in Suffolk, where her youngest son, Reginald, was rector, and Jane accepted. Jeannie was to look after Carlyle, and protect him from visitors. She was by this time a general favourite.

> "Even a certain Miss Wilson, the most dreadfully 'superior woman' I know, smiled on her last night with exceeding graciousness—and begged her to understand her visit to me as including a special call to herself!"

She was greatly heartened by an unexpected thoughtfulness from Carlyle. On her forty-first birthday, he gave her his first present to compensate for the absence of her mother's invariable gift:

> "he who never attends to such *nonsenses* as birthdays, and who dislikes nothing in the world so much as going into a shop . . . he actually risked himself in a jeweller's shop, and bought me a very nice smelling-bottle! I cannot tell you how *wae* his little gift made me, as well as glad; it was the first thing of the kind he ever gave to me in his life. In great matters he is always kind and considerate; but these little attentions, which we women attach so much importance to, he was never in the habit of rendering to anyone; his up-bringing, and the severe turn of mind he has from nature, had alike indisposed him towards them. And now the desire to replace to me the irreplaceable, makes him as good in little things as he used to be in great."

Carlyle, noting the pleasure his present had given, kept up this practice every year, and Jane for her part made a point of sending gifts on her birthday, at Christmas, and often on the anniversary of her mother's death, to Mary Russell for handing on to Mrs Welsh's last servant, Margaret Hiddlestone, and a former servant, Mary Mills, who had remained partly dependent on her. To Mrs Russell, Jane wrote regularly from this time. She was grateful to the Russells for their kindness to her mother, and felt her conscience soothed slightly by maintaining friendly relations.

At Troston the next month, Mrs Buller, she discovered, read George Sand like herself, Mr Buller gave her a good game of chess, and Reginald, though lazy, was kind and amiable. Being now as neurotic as Carlyle about noises, she slept with difficulty. Cocks, asses, dogs, church bells, "the *hooing* and *squealing* of a child" ("some varmint of a creature hired to keep off the crows from the grain")—all conspired to rob her of sleep. She even lay awake one night imagining herself to be contracting a "miasma" from former occupants of her down bed. But although she threatened in almost every letter to come home in sheer despair, the air and the food, the restful atmosphere (in the daytime at least)—and, even more, the centring of all attention on herself, began to do her good. She not only stayed on, but persuaded Carlyle to join her. He showed himself reluctant to agree to any settled course of action and proposed, if he did come, to walk by way of the Cromwellian sites in the district. Jane dealt firmly with this:

> "the steamboat-and-knapsack speculation is all nonsense—and will come to no good—better get yourself transported here first and foremost in the least fatiguing way—and then astonish the world with your white hat and knapsack afterwards as much as you like."

Her spirits, as this letter shows, were improving, and they improved still more when Carlyle came as she requested. He pleased himself until the day before they left for Chelsea, when he was persuaded, almost by force, Jane told Jeannie, to meet a certain Lady Cullum. Charles Buller escaped, to shoot partridges; Carlyle, said Jane, trapped in the drawingroom, looked as if he would shoot "*himself*—or her." They were home by the middle of September.

A month later Jeannie went back to Liverpool. Carlyle, to console Jane, made what sounded, she thought, like a funeral oration on the departed guest, and Helen took nearly an hour to clear away the breakfast so that she might pronounce one lugubrious remark after another, to the tune of "Poor thing! I wonder what sort of night she had? I never saw a sweeter Cretur!"

Hitherto, Jane had had no lack of admirers in men, but women on the whole tended to treat her warily. Jeannie plainly worshipped her brilliant London cousin, and during the long stay at Cheyne Row became her confidante—particularly in the matter of Carlyle's shortcomings. So far Jane had complained seriously to Mazzini alone—with the other regulars, Darwin, Sterling, Forster, her criticism was confined to satirical anecdotes. Mazzini would do no more than counsel patience and appeal to her to seek satisfaction in higher things; but Jeannie, young, cheerful, impressionable, who had lived for months in the house, was wholeheartedly sympathetic. The opportunity was too tempting for Jane to resist. When Jeannie returned to

Liverpool, a correspondence began which flourished for some years and in which Jane relieved her feelings without much reserve. Jeannie had barely settled down at home before complaints of Carlyle followed her: he had "kicked up . . . a considerable of a row" about a missing book, discovered eventually in his study; complained that there was no home-baked cake; accused her of making herself the advocate of whores, because she had championed a woman who had left her husband and fled to France with her lover; broke out in "terrific explosions at breakfast" after sleepless nights; had begun to lose patience with her repeated plaints about her mother; and was looking more and more "thundery" on her "nest of young conspirators".

Bereft of Jeannie, who had been not only a confidante but a buffer—for Carlyle liked her well—Jane was moving through the months in a chastened mood, doing good works. Her "conspirators" had grown on her hands. She found sitters for another Italian exile, Gambardella. She even persuaded Carlyle to sit for him, but this was a disastrous failure; Carlyle, cried the excitable Italian, had been so "capricious" that he would never visit Chelsea again—but, noted Jane, Gambardella would "spill his blood for me, or go to the world's end". He offered to shoot on the spot all the cocks whose crowing was disturbing her sleep. He declared that she was one of the world's two perfect women. Jane at once became curious about the other perfect woman. She was an American, a Mrs Follen; but, added Gambardella consolingly, Jane was not so old. "Good God," exclaimed Jane to Jeannie, "how old *is* Mrs Follen?" She agreed after some persuasion to sit for her portrait, with much more satisfactory results. She then sent him to Liverpool, to paint portraits of the Welshes and their friends, and to Manchester, where he threw Geraldine into a flurry. Geraldine was still writing ardently: "I feel towards you much more like a lover than a female friend!"; retailing her own not very successful affairs of the heart at Manchester—"the dénouement has been neither matrimony nor death"; shouting down Jane's self-accusations of idleness and vanity, and trying to assuage her grief after her mother's death by the strange comfort of "If you were happy I don't think I should care for you half so much". Now she pronounced agitated judgment on Gambardella; she could not love him with passion; she did not even know that he was the kind of man with whom she could have "a *modified arrangement*"—as if, said Jane to Jeannie in disgust, the man had been sent north for the express purpose of allowing Geraldine to fall in love with him.

Cavaignac was in France again, and she had heard nothing from him for months. He had been ill, he had troubles, but "n'avoir pas senti au besoin de vous écrire un mot de sympathie et d' amicale consolation qui l'importat sur tout ce qui me tenait—c'était a ne pas se reconnaître soi-même." Jane's comment on this is, "so long as the *soi-même* continues friend to me I am mighty indifferent about the rest." From Cavaignac came another exile, a half-mad but attractive German like Cavaignac in appearance. Plattnauer—"Plato" to Jane, "Gludder" to Carlyle because he spoke "as if through slush"—was helped by Jane to a tutor's post, and from time to time she dealt out consolation when the work threatened to prove too much for his small stock of sanity. But her main work was helping Mazzini to raise money for the school for Italian organ boys which he had begun when his work in Italy seemed at a standstill. Jeannie—as susceptible as most women to his charm and goodness—had sent off, the moment she reached Liverpool, her subscription to the organ boys' fund. Jane's part in this enterprise was restricted by Carlyle's disapproval—"as if the education of organ boys were something nearly amounting to felony"—and by her own uncertain health, to unspectacular duties. She was soon in humorous despair about his finances; he was generous to the point of madness, and was already, largely on behalf of friends, involved with money-lenders. Her efforts to sell watches and jewellery for these friends were unsuccessful. Even less successful were her efforts to restrain his optimism. He came this autumn of 1842 to tell her, radiantly, that an Italian had discovered how to regulate the flight of balloons. You really mean to invade Italy by balloons? asked Jane, not very seriously. Yes, replied Mazzini in deadly earnest; he felt that such a manner of "starting up a nation" was romantic and imaginative. But Jane said she didn't intend "to impersonate a fallen angel", and would give up her part in the expedition (for Mazzini firmly believed that she intended to help him free Italy). He was hurt and astonished. He had been particularly glad, he explained with flashing eyes, that an invasion by balloon would now be possible, because it would save her from seasickness and bombardment; it would also be peculiarly suitable for her to descend "as it were out of Heaven to redeem a suffering people". At this, Jane had the grace to feel ashamed of herself. Was it not a desecration, a crime, to jest with such a man, she asked Jeannie? He "lives, moves and has his being in *truth*, and take him out of that, he is as credulous and ignorant as a two year old child."

Mazzini, then, was her chief preoccupation throughout the latter part of the year, and well into 1843. But there were other good works, as Jane saw them, from finding a situation for an old Italian woman to finding patience for entertaining at one and the same time George Darley, dramatic critic of the *Athenaeum*, who stuttered badly, William Weir, the Scottish journalist, who was deaf, and Craik who could not be spoken to for fear that such encouragement would go to his head. Craik, who "*did* seem to get a great good of me (perhaps I should say *of us*—but it is more sincere as I have written it)" had she feared "got some new light, or darkness, or, I know not what, which makes him seek my company more from habit than from any pleasure." But his devotion had not, as she thought, begun to cool. Carlyle accused her of "inhumanity"; but though Craik looked wretched often enough, he still preferred her house to any other, including his own. She maintained "my *right* to treat 'poor Creek considerably worse than a dog!'"

Old Mrs Sterling fell ill during the winter, and Jane saw even more than usual of her husband, who came now for consolation as well as distraction. Once at least he found her drawingroom so soothing that despite his anxieties he fell asleep. At other times, as she told John Sterling, he would be needlessly alarming:

> "He will come in sometimes looking the picture of despair and answer to my Question how is she? 'Sinking rapidly; there is nothing for me now, but to prepare myself for the worst'—and when I go, I will find her at her worsted work not worse to appearance than I have seen her a hundred times over. . . . The very *sighs* he gives in looking at her would do *me* a world of mischief."

She had to visit Mrs Sterling, write to John Sterling, keep old Sterling in check, induce the shy Alfred Tennyson to talk—"Ah Babbie what you have lost" she writes after a dinner with the handsome poet—entertain the "*tame Foxes*" (as she described Caroline and her relations), as well as the rest of the dozens now calling at Cheyne Row; deal with Carlyle's admirers, by letter if possible, in person as a last resource; watch over Helen lest she suddenly considered that her resolution not to drink "deserves a dram"; feed and find occupation for John Carlyle, a too-frequent guest, and preserve Carlyle from the worst of people, noises, food and himself—all this, with headaches, colds, biliousness as the background to her life. The life itself was re-lived in her letters, now being sent abroad more widely than ever, and in conversation with her friends. She had many satisfactions to set against her trials—Carlyle's growing fame, so much of it her work, and the devotion of good men. John Sterling summed up their feelings when he said that "if it were merely 'eternal smart' with her, it would be very tiresome, but she is a woman as well as a clever person." Sterling's view of the marriage was also generally held; that there was a certain lack of sympathy, and that, although Carlyle and Jane were basically suited, he was a difficult man to live with, and she was the greater sufferer of the two. That this view was held, did not escape Jane; and, except in her moods of self-depreciation, she was conscious of rectitude. She therefore failed to appreciate the zeal of her aunt Anne, living with her sisters in Edinburgh since the death of old Mrs John Welsh, who judged that Jane's own loss would have softened her infidel heart, and that Christmas was the time to strike. But she struck too zealously; sending, her contemptuous niece complained, "a blockhead of a tract entitled 'Knowledge of Sin' ".

XXIII

THE CIRCLE SPREADS
1843

Carlyle had written nothing on Cromwell. He declared again and again that to write on Cromwell was impossible. But he read on, through "tons of dull books". Matters might have gone hard with him, and even harder with Jane, had he not, at the beginning of 1843, felt impelled to postpone Cromwell and to write on another subject. Jane was not accepting his temperamental flights with the requisite calm; and when he ordered a lamp to be "flung out of *his* way" she wrote that "much else will have to go before Cromwell is finished—perhaps the animate as well as the inanimate". But this threat of a threat was now put aside. Carlyle was still worried about the condition in which the working classes had to live, and the even more shocking fate of the workless. He could not walk along the streets, he told his mother, without seeing "frightful symptoms" of poverty. He could not avoid thought of

> "eleven thousand souls in Paisley alone living on three-half-pence a day, and the governors of the land all busy shooting partridges and passing corn-laws the while! It is a thing no man with a speaking tongue in his head is entitled to be silent about."

The result was *Past and Present*, a continuation in argument of *Chartism*. It was written in two months, and published in April. Two months later Carlyle, tired, and still unable to face Cromwell, went off on a series of visits, and did not return until the autumn.

Before he left, Geraldine had stayed for the first—and it seemed likely the last—time at Chelsea. The invitation, though she was not allowed to know it, had come from Carlyle—a fact which did not predispose Jane in her favour. Late in the previous year Jane had received from Seaforth a bundle of

277

manuscript which she did not open for some little time, partly because of "a sort of *vague apprehension*". It was a draft of part of a novel in letter form, written by Geraldine with Mrs Paulet's help. Jane had promised to continue it, but it was "*so stormy*" that she "backed out". She read the manuscript, she told Jeannie "with a feeling little short of *terror!*" She did not believe there was a woman living—not even George Sand—who could have written some of the most powerful passages, or who would have had the courage to write them if she had had the ability. But

> "there is an indecency or want of reserve (let us call it) in the spiritual department—an exposure of their whole minds naked as before the fall— without so much as a fig-leaf of conformity remaining—which no respectable public could stand—which even the freest spirits among us would call 'coming it too strong'."

She told Geraldine what she thought and was greeted with "a whole *pamphlet*" of objections to her objections. Jane abandoned her to her fate—"if she *will* run about the streets naked it is not I who am her keeper"—but Geraldine later recanted so sensibly that Carlyle said she ought to be asked to Cheyne Row—it might be of great use to her.

> "A proposition of such a *novel* character on *his* part quite took me by surprise and I sat staring at him without making any answer. 'Why' says he 'you seem *doubtful* about it—she is very easy to do with is she not? and you like her company?' 'Oh' said I at last 'as to the *doing with* I have no misgivings about *that* but—' 'but what?' 'Why I am afraid that having her beside me from morning till night would be dreadfully wearing!' 'You had Jeannie beside you from morning to night—what would be the difference?'!! 'Jeannie! Jeannie was not always in a state of emotion! dropping hot tears on my hands, and watching me and fussing me as Geraldine does!'—'Oh as you like! only I think it would be a kindness to *the poor lonely girl*—and that her company might be useful to yourself when you have so little of mine.' "

Jane lay awake half the night trying to make up her mind. Geraldine was enlivening, she was very fond of both Carlyles, the visit might, as Carlyle said, be good for her in many ways, but

> "to say the truth—tho' I am not jealous of my husband (pray read all this unto yourself and burn the letter) tho' I have not only his *habit* of preference for me over all other women (and *habits* are much stronger in him than *passions*) but also his indifference to *all* women *as women* to secure me against jealousy—still young women who have in them, as

Geraldine has, with all her good and great qualities, a born *spirit of intrigue* are perilous sort of inmates for a married pair to invite—they may make mischief in other ways than by *seducing the husband's affections*."

She decided to ask Geraldine "in a sort of way" for two or three weeks. Geraldine leaped at the invitation. She wrote reassuringly; she would be "much *quieter* to *live* with" than as a caller; she had other friends in London and would not be on Jane's arms altogether. "God grant! for 'my arms' are of the weakest" commented Jane to Jeannie, who was being given the history of the affair from day to day.

Naturally, the visit was a failure. After three weeks, and with Geraldine showing no sign of leaving, Jane could scarcely bring herself to speak to her, and was usually unpleasant when she did so. Geraldine could hardly be said to have outstayed her welcome since she had never been given one, but blind worship certainly made her obtuse. She thought that Jane would be best pleased if she made herself agreeable. She may even have thought that a woman of close on forty-two and many years married would no longer take undue pleasure in the company of men, or would at least expect to surrender gracefully to an unmarried woman a dozen years younger than herself. Unfortunately, Geraldine's one idea of making herself agreeable was to throw herself at the head (or more literally at the feet) of the nearest man. Unfortunately, too, the older Jane grew, the more insistent she became on remaining the centre of attraction. What she had lost in looks—and she had never rated them very highly—she reckoned that she had more than gained in breadth of sympathy, general increase of poise and wit, and all that men admired in a friend and hostess.

One complaint followed another. Geraldine was for ever gazing at Carlyle, trying "all sorts of *seductions* on him;" she even "took the strong measure of stretching herself on the hearth rug at his feet and sleeping there"; but all to no purpose —Carlyle "proved absolutely *unseducible*". Her protégé Garnier was another intended victim, Jane persuaded herself. He came into the drawingroom one evening to find all three stretched out asleep—Carlyle on three chairs, Jane on the sofa, Geraldine on the hearth rug. Are you not well, he asked Jane, cossetting yourself in this way? Geraldine leaped out of sleep to a torrent of words in Jane's defence; she had been "to that *confounded*

Chinese exhibition" had tired herself, and so on, until the bewildered Garnier, lifting both hands, protested that he could not follow her. How fast she talked! Was she a relation? Geraldine, observed Jane darkly, pretended to be "vastly amused with the quizzing which he carried on the whole evening—but I believe she had her own private misgivings"—and so, it seems, had Jane.

Even John Carlyle had to be defended from this excitable, designing female. John had for a long time past been getting on Jane's nerves. He had obtained a post in London as medical attendant to a wealthy but weak-minded young man, but had a great deal of time on his hands, most of which he spent in Cheyne Row. He was a restless man, well meaning but persistently unattractive, doing all his kindnesses with a lack of grace that often made them resented; and, final heresy, a man who expressed strong doubts about his sister-in-law's weak health. He threw her a box of her beloved blue pills now and again with a growl, but told her that her real trouble was idleness. Jane quoted with delight old Sterling's description of him as an "accursed *Vegetable* . . . not a man at all but a walking Cabbage!", and although he read to her when she was not well, and helped her with her Italian (he was translating Dante), her general view of him, when any better company was available, was that he "is, has been, and will ever be *for me* an insupportable bore."

All his faults were overlooked in the indignation and hurt vanity of the moment. Geraldine, Jane declared, was

"wheedling John Carlyle at a great rate pretending all the while to have the greatest dislike to him. Every Sunday and on no other day—she makes a *grande toilette*—comes down *in the forenoon* with *a bare neck*—and a black satin gown—or coloured silk!—all wasted I assure you."

She was slightly shaken when John, a few days later, in a moment of "super-human generosity" sent Carlyle a tweed and Jane some fruit and a ham from Fortnum and Mason's: "Geraldine I dare say secretly persuades herself that *her* Sunday's bare neck—and *grande* toilette was the moving spring of his generous proceeding—but that is incredible truly!" Jane, however, made quite sure, and had the satisfaction ten days later of hearing John speak of her friend as "a very *unfortunate* young woman" who, with her present absurd figure, might be

best advised to go into the Catholic Church to keep herself out
of worse mischief.

Geraldine could do nothing right. She took a jesting remark
of Jane's seriously, and replied—"most *free and easy*"—on her
behalf to a letter from Plattnauer, whom she did not know.
Jane, furious, tried to stop her, but the unsuspicious Geraldine
brushed aside all remonstrance. What did it matter if she had
not met Plattnauer? "My dear there is no such word as *impossible*
where your convenience is concerned." Jane did her far from
negligible best to enlighten her friends about Geraldine.
Darwin, Mazzini, Elizabeth Pepoli—they all, she declared, had
a "*sacred horror*" of her. Carlyle thought her "an incurable fool"
and very ill looking.

After five weeks, when Geraldine at last had the sense to go,
Jane confessed that they parted without a quarrel only because
of Geraldine's "good nature or self-possession" (her affection
did not, apparently, occur to Jane as a reason). Now she had
done with her; she was "a vile creature". But again she
reckoned without Geraldine, and without the power of affection; perhaps also without her own vanity. Her conscience was
far from easy—she admitted that she had been "cold, cross,
ironical, disobliging" from the first day—and when Geraldine
wrote as usual from Manchester she replied, though stiffly, and
the friendship began to recover.

Gambardella, returned from Liverpool—"fatter—more hairy
—and more in love with himself than ever"—was pressing Jane
to sit for the portrait she had promised him and Jeannie. He
besieged Cheyne Row, regardless of his vow never to enter the
house again. Jane agreed to come the next day, then felt ill, and,
after cooking a dinner for Thackeray and Fitzgerald—now
occasional visitors—she fainted, and remained for three hours
hovering between unconsciousness and retching (the form her
severe headaches were taking) with Helen "weeping" over her,
and the men, who had been joined by James Spedding and
John Robertson, an associate of Mill on the *Westminster Review*,
"raging and laughing"·in the next room. Gambardella was
at the door early the next morning. Helen told him that her
mistress was too ill to come. He ordered Jane to be there at
twelve with the black veil he had seen her wear over her head.
So great were her powers of recovery when she had an object in

view or a strong will to command her that she rose and sat to him for four hours that day and five hours the next. The portrait was then all but done. The features, Jane said, were hers exactly, but not the expression, which she thought had "the look of a rather *improper female* DOING a sort of St Anthony's ecstasy! and *doing* it not well." This, declared Gambardella, was her habitual look; but at a final sitting he "worked the *ecstasy* pretty well out of it—and it looks *simple* enough." Carlyle thought the portrait far too simple, with the eyes lacking expression and the mouth lacking character, but most of Jane's friends were delighted with it. The one other critic was Elizabeth Pepoli, who could see only "a *young* lady that never knew a day's sorrow or a day's ill health." Darwin thought it a masterpiece—at which Carlyle commented that it was plain he knew nothing at all about Jane. When he heard that Gambardella was making no charge for the portrait, Darwin said the artist must be very much in love with Jeannie, for whom it had been painted. "He must be very much in love with *the subject!*" corrected Carlyle. Gambardella's view—"with a look of ineffable self-complacency"—was that the portrait looked too young. He must put in some wrinkles.

Old Sterling, who had long wanted a portrait of Jane, came "puffing" up to the studio during the final sitting and Gambardella, to Jane's delighted horror, slammed the door in his face. She thought she had seen the last of the old man, but he was soon in need of her again. His wife died in the middle of April and two days later he lost his daughter-in-law, John's wife. He crumpled up, and "at such a moment he was welcome to make any use of me that he pleased." He took her literally. "I have not had five minutes' speech with Mazzini for the last week!" she writes in dismay; and no sooner do they settle down in their usual position "our two pairs of feet on the fender" than Sterling would be heard asking for her. Anthony Sterling, with another Cheyne Row familiar, William Cunningham, walked home with her on the day of Mrs Sterling's death, both talking hard about anything but the subject of which they were all thinking: "as if manhood" commented Jane "could consist in talking about the favour-change in the weather and the effect of St Luke's steeple against the blue sky when their hearts were full of the dead."

GIUSEPPE MAZZINI
from a coloured crayon sketch, 1828

GODEFROI CAVAIGNAC
from a painting by Langlois,
June 18, 1839

JANE WELSH CARLYLE
from a painting by Gambardella,
April 1843

Despite this criticism Jane did not feel the loss greatly. In the early years at Cheyne Row the Sterling family had been a godsend to her, but the passing of time and the widening of her acquaintance had done their usual work. Old Mrs Sterling had therefore lost much of her charm for Jane long before she died, and John Sterling's wife had never possessed it—"*I* never felt any affection for Mrs John" she remarks after the news of her death.

The management of all who called at Chelsea, and some who expected to be called upon in return, was becoming almost a life's work, especially for a woman as frequently unwell as Jane. She rallied quickly, however, and was in her element, not merely entertaining but often enough protecting one friend from another. In these middle months of 1843 when Carlyle was away she had to deal with friends, exiles, disciples, waifs and strays, curiosities, as well as turn the house upside down in preparation for his return. She managed all triumphantly.

Of the friends, plain and simple, Macready also disappeared for a time, going off on an American tour. Jane had a special fondness for him: "Poor dear *William!*" she said " . . . to see a man who is exhibiting himself every night on a stage, blushing like a young girl in a private room is a beautiful phenomenon for me!"

Jeffrey wrote to her "in the patriarchal vein" but behaved otherwise when in London; he perplexed William Cunningham with his "my darlings" and by kissing Jane "*à plusieurs reprises*". Darley was still sitting all of a stammer in the Cheyne Row drawingroom:

> "However, it is to be hoped that he got a little good for having a mouthful of human (or rather, to speak accurately, inhuman) speech with someone. . . . For myself individually, I feel as if I had spent the evening under a harrow."

Milnes was not a regular caller—he had fallen in Jane's favour because of his preference for Lady Harriet Baring—but she met him occasionally at other people's parties. At one boring dinner, Jane found him " 'affable' enough, but evidently overcome with a feeling that weighed on all of us—the feeling of having been dropped into a vacuum." He said, in Jane's hearing, "that 'Lord Ashley was the greatest man alive; he was the only man that Carlyle *praised* in his book.' I dare say he knew I was overhearing him 'the little *Tick*'!"

Milnes was not alone in disgrace. At this same dinner

> "Mrs Austin was an insupportable bore; she has lost all her *sweet* look and what remains is highly questionable; she has surely the air of a retired unfortunate female. . . . She talked a deal about America and her poverty with exquisite bad taste."

Dinners of this kind were exceptions. She was no better able than Carlyle to withstand them, and she was far less sure of obtaining an audience. On every count she preferred her own home, with new friends and old ones to pay homage. Of the new, Arthur Helps—"little Helps"—was one of the more interesting to her; thirty years old, a Cambridge man, and now private secretary to Spring Rice. He too had been at the dull dinner, "but even I could not animate him." It was otherwise at Chelsea. He would drop in to chat amiably, or to sit listening with his quiet, complimentary laugh. Sometimes he brought "his beautiful little atom of a wife" and they drove Jane into town. Newly married as he was, he considered Jane at times hardly done by when Carlyle went off for his holiday:

> "It is odd what notions men seem to have of the scantiness of a woman's resources. . . . When I answered that question from Arthur Helps yesterday in the negative—'Why should I feel lonely? I have plenty to do—and can see human beings whenever I choose to look out at the window'—he looked at me as if I had uttered some magnanimity worthy to have place in a *Legitimate Drama* and said 'Well—really—you *are* a model of a wife!' "

Jane was not in any event left for long to enjoy her grass-widow-hood undisturbed. Darwin, one of the most regular of all the Cheyne Row circle, took, on the surface, an opposite view to Helps. When he was drinking tea with her one evening, the lamp was brought in, and he said "it was surely far too much light for a *single* woman." But when he called and found her under one of her headaches, or in a temporary depression, he would say "she looked as though she needed to go to Gunter's and have an ice" and would drive her there, and sit beside her while she ate her ice, and tell her in the dry way she liked so well about Maurice's latest pamphlet or some other scrap of news or gossip that he knew would make her laugh. Or he would take her for a drive into the country about Parson's Green or some such district just outside London, and quiz her about her prodigies of housecleaning and mending:

" 'wondered if Carlyle would give me admiration enough for all my needlework &c &c, feared *not*—but he would have a vague sense of comfort from it'—and uttered many other sarcastic things by way of going off in good Darwin style."

Forster was ill part of the spring and summer. Jane, visiting him, thought it deplorable to see "all that prodigious 'Brummigam enthusiasm' and foaming vitality bottled up in a sick arm chair." But he bounced up into life again soon after Carlyle's departure, and breezed into Cheyne Row "with 'great Gods' enough to blow up a steam vessel" and an invitation to dinner. John Sterling pleased her by sending a novel of Tieck which contained, he said intriguingly, a woman after her own heart:

> "Thank you *passionately* for giving me *Vittoria Accoramboni*—and thank you even more for knowing beforehand that I should like her. Your presentiment that this was 'a woman after my own heart' so pleases *my own heart!*—proves that I am not *universally* 'a woman misunderstood!' But you said nothing of the *man after my own heart*. . . . My very *beau-idéal* of manhood is that Paul Giordano—could I hear of the like of him existing anywhere in these degenerate days, I would—even at this late stage of the business—send him—my picture! and an offer of my heart and hand for the next world—since they are already disposed of in this. Ah what a man that must be who can strangle his young beautiful wife with his own hands, and—bating one moment of conventional horror—inspire not the slightest feeling of aversion or distrust! When a man strangles his wife nowadays he does it brutally—in drink, or in passion, or in revenge; to transact such a work coolly, nobly, on the loftiest principles—to *strangle with dignity* because the woman 'was unworthy of him'—that indeed is a triumph of *character* which places this Bracciano above all the Heroes of ancient or modern times! which makes me almost weep that I was not born two centuries earlier that I might have been—his mistress—*not his wife!*"

Jane begged Carlyle to read the book. He was then in the first stage of his holiday, staying near Cardiff at the house of an admirer, Mr Redwood. He thought the book "a dreadful piece of work" before he had finished it, then changed his mind sufficiently to call it "a grand thing; but Bristol diamond, not a little of it."

Sterling saved Jane during the summer from the importunities of Terrot, minister at Haddington in Jane's childhood, now Bishop of Edinburgh. At their first meeting in London

> "We had an immense deal of Edin^r-logical disputation on 'What was life'!—on what was the *use* of *religion*, what was the *cause* of *marriage*—what

was the chief end of man—on all which questions it seemed to me that I had the better of him at his own weapons (tho' in London one's *logic* is allowed to get rather rusty) and also that *I*—and not he the Bishop—was on the orthodox side!"

Jane remarked "that *here* one was allowed to be anything one liked except a fool or a bore" but the Bishop did not take her hint; he soon became exceedingly tiresome. Helen's description of him as "really a wee *noughty* body as ever she had set een upon", though it made Jane laugh, was no compensation for so much of his company. Her veneer of politeness wore thin;

"He writes to tell me that he 'did not like his reception ... From what he heard of my preferences and saw of my society he was inclined to suppose that what I objected to in *him* must be the want of that *first great requisite earnestness*'! But he begged to assure me &c, &c,—in short that he had as much earnestness 'as he could bear'!! A letter from a man calling himself Bishop to a woman whom *he* calls infidel—and pleading guilty to her of want of earnestness! Bah! I wish I could snort like Cavaignac."

She did not reply, and Terrot, now forever Cutikins because of his gaitered bandy legs, came to know the reason why.

"I declare when Helen told me he was below I almost *sprung the rattle*. I had not answered his letter—had made up my mind not to answer it at all—a man puts one in quite a false position who demands explanation of one's *coldness*—coldness belongs to the great sphere of Silence—all speech about it can only make bad worse. . . . I *said* that I had not answered his letter because it seemed to me *that* was the best way of counteracting *the indiscretion of his having written it*—that . . . *warmth of affection* could not be brought about by *force of logic*."

This was not the end of him. He came again, and, watching Jane diplomatically salute the baby of their "jewel of a post-man" he

"looked at me as if he could have eaten me raw and remarked with a concentrated spleen — 'Well I *must* say never did I see any human being so improved in *amiability* as *you* are! Every *body* and every *thing* seems to be honoured with a particular affection from you!' 'Every *thing*' thought I 'except *you!*' "

Then came John Sterling who took in the situation at a glance and "exploded" him by saying to Jane

" 'Well my good friend if you cannot keep your engagement with me I must go by myself—I am too late already!' The *cool assurance* of this speech was inimitable for I had no engagement in the world with him!—but Terrot suspecting nothing sprang to *his* feet and was off in a minute with apologies for having *detained* me!"

Another of her curiosities was dismissed in record time. This was the famous Kitty Kirkpatrick of Carlyle's early London days who called to see him, but found only Jane in the midst of her house-cleaning. Jane's view of her visitor was short and to the point: "Oh my dear she is anything but good-looking!"

The third curiosity was the Irish priest Theobald Mathew, then famous for his crusade against intemperance. Jane confesses to Carlyle of "a little piece of *Hero-Worship* that I have been after." She persuaded Robertson to take her to Mile End, where Mathew was speaking to "thousands of people all hushed into awful silence; with *not a single exception*." She pushed her way through the throng, scrambled up and "flung myself *horizontally* on to the scaffolding at Father Mathew's feet!" She watched him administer the pledge.

"Did I take the pledge then? No—I *would* tho', if I had not feared it would have been put in the newspapers! No—not *that*—but . . . having bethought me of a pretty memorandum-book in my reticule—I drew him aside and put it into his hand and bade him keep it for my sake, and asked him to give me one of his medals to keep for his!—and all this in tears and the utmost agitation! Had you any idea that your wife was still such a fool! I am sure *I* had not."

She was still busy with her exiles.

"Poor Garnier walked in at five and staid till after nine—and if you had seen the difference in him at his entrance and his exit you would have said that I had worked a miracle! . . . I gave him tea and took him a walk and lent him some music and soothed the troubled soul of him, and when he went away he said the only civil thing to me he ever said in life. 'I am obliged to you, Mrs Carlyle—you have made me pass one evening pleasantly—and I came very miserable.'"

Plattnauer brought his pupil to see Jane, but more often came alone. His patience "seems near the end of its tether, and he proposes emancipating himself shortly 'before he loses his faculties altogether.'" His outward likeness to the absent Cavaignac had begun to extend itself:

"there is an *earnestness* a something of *noble* of *self-sacrificing* in him now which gives him about the same amount of resemblance to Cavaignac *spiritually* which I used to find in him *externally*—it is not very *striking*—but still something to be glad of."

Cavaignac had hoped to visit London again this summer but could not, but he wrote "*je voudrais bien vous voir, voir Madame, bonne et noble ame s'il en fût!*" Jane commented: "And Madame is almost as content as if he had come!" His letter ended

> "Adieu, chère dame, je déclare que de vous on peut dire *bien!* toute mortelle que vous soyez, je me suis dit plus d'une fois, depuis que je vous ai quitté: par le ciel, il n'y a pas sur cette terre trois femmes comme celle-là! Adieu tous deux—Madame une lettre!"

Such words, says Jane, "from any other man might be mere *words*—and I should not care rigmaree for them—but from *him!* Ah c'est autre chose! *he* never praises except as it were *on compulsion*."

During the summer Mazzini left Chelsea, which he did not find central enough, and moved to the house of an Italian family in Bloomsbury. He walked over to Cheyne Row regularly, but Jane missed his daily visits. He was arranging another concert to raise funds for his organ boys' school; had been of late, she said,

> "so over head and ears in what Richard Milnes would call 'beastly little businesses' that I get next to no good of him—I never saw a mortal man who so completely made himself into 'minced meat' for the universe!"—

—a comment that tells as much of Jane as of Mazzini. He took no care of himself, fell ill, and she frets—"I have not seen him for a week. It always puts me into such a bad humour going there—to see the *mess* in which these wretched Tancionis keep him; and the silly way in which he submits to be made their *prey* as it were."

When he recovered and came to Chelsea regularly, he was in a fever of another kind, and the welcome he received proved very different from the one both he and Jane had imagined. Jane tells the story to Carlyle, who was with his mother at Scotsbrig:

> "Well! the Italian 'movement' has begun—and also I suppose *ended*—Mazzini has been in a state of violent excitement all these weeks . . . nothing hindered him from going off to head the movement—except that—unexpectedly enough—the *movement* did not *invite* him—nay took pains to 'keep him in a certain ignorance'—and his favourite conspirator abroad the movement sent into Sicily 'to act there *alone!*'—Plainly indicating that it meditated *some arrangement of Italy* such as they two would not approve—something, what shall I say—*constitutional*. He came

one day and told me quite seriously that a week more would determine him whether to go singly and try to enter the country in secret, or—to persuade a frigate now here, which he deemed persuadable, *to revolt openly and take him there by force.* 'And with one frigate' said I 'you mean to overthrow the Austrian empire—amidst the general peace of Europe?'— 'Why not? the *beginning* only is wanted.' I could not help telling him that 'a Harrow or Eton schoolboy who uttered such nonsense and proceeded to give it a practical shape would be whipt and expelled the community as a mischievous blockhead.' He was very angry of course—but it was impossible to see anybody behaving so like '*a mad*' without telling him one's mind. *He* a conspirator chief!—I should make an infinitely better one myself. . . . Our dialogues become 'warm'!"

She had on her hands not only the exiles but one or two of the waifs who were for ever appealing for help. She was now working hard—too hard for the comfort of some of her friends— to place Amelie Bölte, "a fine *manly* little creature with a deal of excellent sense—and not without plenty of German enthusiasm for all so humdrum as she looks." Thackeray seemed an obvious choice, but he thought otherwise:

"My Dear Mrs Carlyle—For God's sake stop Mme Bölte. I have governidges calling at all hours with High Dutch accents and reams of testimonials. . . . And I don't want a Gerwoman; and all our plans are uncertain. Farewell."

Jane went on trying, and won Amelie Bölte's devotion: "You are a dear angel" she wrote "to trouble yourself with all your calamities of Eve about the poor German Sceptic."

Her other waifs at this time were Elizabeth and Juliet Mudie, daughters of a London Scot who had died in poverty. Carlyle had to endure the girls in his house—"flary, staring, and conceited, stolid-looking girls, thinking themselves handsome" —so that they might be saved from "the maternal element" until work was found. They were the cause of a rapprochement with Geraldine, who took such pains to find places for them that Jane began to wonder whether she had not misjudged her;

"she *has* some sort of strange, passionate—incomprehensible *attraction* towards me that leads her thro' what is even more repugnant to natural feeling than 'fire and water'—thro' *the miry puddle*—of teazing and *begging*—to do me pleasure."

Then there were the young men who came to Cheyne Row for a glimpse and, if lucky, a word with Carlyle, but who at times had to console themselves with half an hour's chat with his wife. Jane would sum up the visitor to Carlyle—partly for his amusement, partly so that he might know whether to encourage or avoid. She did so now:

> "Robertson brought here last night to tea a youth from Aberdeen of the name of Masson—a news-paper Editor poor thing and only twenty!— he is one of your most ardent admirers and imitators. . . . He is a better 'speciment' of Aberdeen than I ever saw before—an innocent intelligent modest affectionate-looking creature—I quite took to him. When he went away, which he seemed to do very unwillingly, I said that he must come and see us when he returned to London and I hoped to make up then for his present disappointment by introducing him to you—to which he answered with a cordial grasp of my hand 'Eh! what a real shame in ye to say *that*'! He told me 'if I would come to Aberdeen they would get up a mob for me in the fishmarket Place and give me a grand hurrah—and a paragraph, *of course!*' " She adds, for good measure: ". . . when Helen was handing me over some of the books she said 'take care, that ane's the Master's *Sartor Resart* and a capital thing it is—just *noble* in *my* opinion' !!"

The second disciple of this summer was Francis Espinasse, a young Edinburgh man whose father was a friend of Jeffrey. Now, trying for a post in the British Museum, he called at Cheyne Row, and found a "little lady, plain and rather sallow, but with beautiful dark eyes, and the most expressive of countenances" with a Scotch accent "as marked as I afterwards found her husband's to be." Jane thought him "a painful youth —whose 'conversation' does not promise to be a treat."

A third youthful visitor was the nephew of the Miss Scot of Haddington whose unexpected call at Craigenputtock had caused Jane such delight. He, as a schoolboy, had watched her sit long by her father's grave when she and Carlyle were wintering in Edinburgh nearly ten years earlier. Now, she says,

> "How you will *like* me when you see me heaven knows. *Realised ideals* are always dreadfully precarious. Nor do I remember the least in the world what sort of a sketch of myself I gave you in '41. Most likely it was wide of the mark—would depend more on *how I had slept* the previous night than on 'the fact of things.' My views of myself are a sort of 'dissolving views' never the same for many minutes together."

This young man came into collision with Carlyle, who appeared in a flowered dressing-gown and a clay pipe a foot long (he was now permitted to smoke up the chimney). The visitor mentioned that he and his mother had been reading a Disraeli novel.

"Then" said Carlyle, "you and your mother are fools." The conversation did not flourish, and he was soon dismissed as "a damned impudent whelp of an Edinburgh Advocate!"

Between visitors, Jane kept abreast of the novels and did her best with some earlier ones. She was, she told Carlyle, "carrying on simultaneously" *Amelia* and *The Vicar of Wakefield*.

> "I find the first a dreadful bore—one prays to Heaven that the poor woman could but once for all get herself *seduced* and so let us have done with her alarms and precautions, on any terms! '*Upon my honour*' I do not see the slightest sense in spending one's whole existence thro'out three volumes in taking care of one's *virtue!*"

For the latter part of the summer, novels, disciples, waifs, friends, exiles, formed an ever-changing background to the sterner work of one of her most thorough "earthquakes". Since the death of her mother, the rent of Craigenputtock had been paid into Carlyle's bank, and she could with a clear conscience suggest a complete renovation of the house. Carlyle had abandoned his last objection to living there, and wanted his writing room turned into a library. Jane fell to with delight:

> "Ever since my husband saved himself in Wales", she told John Sterling "this house has afforded the liveliest image of a sacked city!—has been a house possessed with seven devils!—two carpenters, a painter, a paperhanger, a nondescript apprentice lad and '*a spy*'—the latter hardly taller than your boot—the master's son, placed there to see that every man did his duty. . . . I go about scolding my work-people and cutting out furniture print—and suggesting improved methods of doing things. Even the Apprentice-lad's *singing* I take cognizance of—always in grinding with the pumice-stone this Devil of a boy *will* sing. . . . I said to him at last grimly but with an outward calm—'how happy you must be that you *can* sing at such unmusical work'! 'Oh, thank you Mam' says he quite unconscious that I was in a bad humour 'I's quite happy—*so far as I knows*—(beautiful illustration of Carlyle's doctrine of unconsciousness!) but I's always a-singing anyhow—it sounds pleasant at work, doesn't it, Mam?' 'Oh *very* pleasant' said I! 'but if you *would* sing a song from beginning to end it would be still pleasanter for *me*'. 'Thank you Mam—I will try'! But he does not succeed. . . . Sometimes I am seized with a passion for rural life—and then with *my own* hands I construct a gypsy-tent in the garden out of clothes lines—long poles—and an old brown crumb cloth! . . . But at night? I cannot sleep in my tent and as your father said 'God Almighty, Mrs Carlyle if you sleep in that stew of new paint *you will awake dead*'!"

Old Sterling begged his "Angel of Consolation and Mercy"

to go away with him for a holiday, and in August, tired by the 'earthquake' and anxious to see John Sterling, now in Ventnor, Jane agreed to go to the Isle of Wight. But in five days she was back again, having got no further than Ryde. She did not sleep a wink in the hotel, moved to rooms, and was "bitten infamously" by bugs. Old Sterling proved mean as well as boring, and was for ever roaring "This is torture, by Jove! My God, this is agony!" about a pain in his thigh. A letter from Geraldine saying that she could place the second Mudie sister (one was already in Manchester) gave an excuse for an immediate return home "sleepless, bug-bitten, bedusted and bedevilled." Mazzini calling to ask after her

> "was astonished to find *myself*—still more astonished at the extent to which I had managed to *ruin* myself in so short a time—I looked, he said '*strange*—upon *my* honour!—most like—if he might be allowed to say it— to Lady Macbeth in the sleeping scene!' "

She recovered quickly. The redecorated house looked even better than she had hoped, and she had not stopped short at the redecorating.

> "should you find that I have exceeded by a *few pounds* your modest allowance for painting and papering, you will find that I have *not* been *thoughtless* nevertheless when I show you a document from Mr Morgan . . . equivalent to a lease of the house for five years 'with the reciprocity all on one side'—binding him and leaving us free—'such a thing', old Sterling said . . . 'as no woman but myself would have had the impudence to ask, nor any lawyer in his senses the folly to grant'. . . . This was one of those remarkable instances of fascination which I exercise over gentlemen of a 'certain age'. Before I had spoken six words to him it was plain to the meanest capacity that he had fallen over head and ears in love with me— and if he put off time in writing me the promise I required it was plainly only because he could not bear the idea of my going away again!. . . . For respectability's sake, I said in taking leave that 'my husband was out of town or he would have come himself.' 'Better as it is' said the old gentleman 'do you think I would have written to your *husband's* dictation as I have done to *yours?*' "

Helen worked hard, and although Jane had to hide all liquor, and from time to time gave her notice, she merely asked "in a tone of the most authoritative remonstrance 'What would become of you I should just like to know—fancy you ill and me not there to take proper care of you! I think *that* would be a farce!' " So she stayed on, but in the late summer she fell into serious disgrace:

"She said to me one morning *in putting down my breakfast*—'*My!*—I was just standing this morning, looking up at the corner of my bed ye ken, and there what should I see but two *bogues!*—I hope there's nae mair.'— '*You hope?*' said I immediately kindling into a fine phrenzy; 'how could you live an *instant* without making sure? A pretty thing it will be if you have let your bed get full of bugs again!' The Shadow of an accusation of remissness was enough of course to make her quite *positive*. 'How was *she* ever to have thought of bogues, formerly? *What a thing to think about!*—but *since* she had been just *most particular!* To be sure these two must have come off these Mudies' shawls!' I left her protesting and appealing to posterity and ran off myself to see into the business."

After a struggle, Jane killed off all the bugs, and washed, aired and repainted the bed.

"I have small apprehension of bugs anywhere else" she assures Carlyle—"in *your* bed I had *ocular conviction* that there were none—when it was in pieces—in my *own* I have inferential conviction for they would have been sure to bite *me* the very *first* Adam and Eve of them."

The bugs destroyed, she sat back, telling him "it will be such a pleasure to receive you and give you tea in your new library!" She was longing "to hear of your Paulet-day and of the *transports* of Geraldine"—for he had at last paid his calls. To her annoyance John Carlyle returned before his brother, "plunging in to send all the books afloat, and litter the floors with first and second and third and fourth scrawls of verfehlt letters." Then at last, in October, came Carlyle, "very bilious".

For three days, writes Jane to Susan Stirling

"the man was in 'a certain' admiration over the improved state of things especially over his new-papered—new-carpeted—new-everythinged Library—but on the fourth day the young Lady of next house took one of her fits of *practising*—whereupon he started up and declared in a peremptory manner to the Universe that 'he neither would nor could write, or think, or *live* any longer, alongside of *that accursed thing*'! In pursuance of which resolution the carpenter (that last man on earth I was wishing to see in a hurry again) was summoned to hold deep consultation on all the possibilities and impossibilities of the case—and the practical result thereof was a new household earthquake, little inferior in awfulness to that which I had just got so thankfully to the end of! Up went all the carpets which my own hands had nailed down for twelve months at least—in rushed the troop of incarnate demons—bricklayers, joiners, whitewashers &c whose noise and dirt and dawdling had lately driven me to despair—down went a partition in one room up went a new chimney in another."

After some weeks, the house was again made clean and orderly "but when my husband proceeded to occupy his new study he found that Devil a bit could he write in *it* any more than beside the piano—'it was all so strange to him'! The fact is the thing he has got to write—his long projected life of Cromwell—is no joke—and no sort of *room* can make it easy. And so he has been ever since shifting about in the saddest way from one room to another like a sort of domestic wandering Jew! He has now a fair chance however at getting a settlement effected *in the original library*—the young Lady next door having promised to abstain religiously from playing till two-o'clock. . . . Alas! one can make fun of all this on paper but in practice it is anything but fun I can assure you—there is no help for it however—a man cannot hold his genius as a sinecure."

In the same letter Jane finished the story of the Mudies.

"The last sent is back already—having *preferred* to return and starve here—or do worse—to conducting herself in a reasonable way where she was. She was lazy, heedless, and dirty to a degree—and when her mistress tried to remonstrate with her she *lay down on the floor and kicked and screamed!* So she was dismissed and when my kind Geraldine Jewsbury had found a home for her till she should get her one more trial in a place—the young Lady informed her that her Mother wished her to return 'if we pleased'—and that she expected to be companion to a Captain's widow—we fear it was rather to a Captain's self."

Geraldine, who had been given her share of the house-cleaning and altering story, felt "horribly uneasy" for Jane, "for though you laugh and make witty speeches, I know the state you are in". But the final comment was left to Helen "the strangest mixture of Philosopher and perfect idiot." "Well" she said, "when one's doing *this* one's doing nothing else anyhow."

XXIV

LADY HARRIET BARING
1843 – 1844

In May, 1843, Jane first met Lady Harriet Baring. By this time Carlyle was a regular caller at Bath House when the Barings were in town, and had begun a correspondence with Lady Harriet. He had been asked for the first time to their country house at Addiscombe some ten miles south of London, in the summer of 1842, when Jane was at Troston, but in spite of her encouragement he declined the invitation. This refusal pleased Jane, who did not take kindly to the thought of Lady Harriet. Her feeling was given a little substance before she left Troston because Charles Buller twice broke his promise to visit his parents there, each time because he preferred to go to the Barings—"as if," remarked Jane, "he had not flirted with *her* the whole season thro'!"

Carlyle could scarcely have behaved with greater acuteness had he consciously tried to arouse interest. Lady Harriet was not accustomed to having her invitations declined. She summoned him to Bath House. She had never met his like before—his uncompromising attitude, plain speech, and refusal to be patronised, while making clear that he was sensible of the honour done to him. In her circle, large and varied though it was, he proved by far the finest talker—original, pungent, humorous, all qualities highly rated by her. To Carlyle, Lady Harriet's despotic manner was a delight even when he defied it; he had already taken his stand on the side of a benevolent autocracy, and in her he saw an autocrat born and bred, ruling her circle without ceremony, but with a sense of her responsibilities. She was a Great Lady in every sense, he felt, by virtue of her birth (daughter of the Earl of Sandwich), her brains, and her manner. He liked her way of calling her men friends by their surnames, and he appreciated her wit, and her caustic, keen, masculine approach to people and things. She could be hurtful, brutal, no one more so—"I don't mind being knocked down" said a victim of her tongue "but I can't stand being danced upon afterwards"—but she could also be kind; and this too was an amalgam which Carlyle understood and approved. All she needed was an interest in life, an opportunity to use her gifts otherwise than in the mere give and take of social inter-course. So, at least, Carlyle believed; and he saw in himself the man who might lead her into useful, honourable paths. He began practically by persuading her to learn German, so that she might absorb in the original the wisdom of Goethe and of his other gods. Lady Harriet agreed; she was somewhat amused, but it was at least a new experience to be taken so seriously.

Jane regarded the friendship with mixed feelings. As the great man she believed him to be, it was right and proper that Carlyle should be received with respect everywhere. But it was one thing for him to be the centre of an admiring circle; quite another for him, the most independent of men, to become, as she began to imagine, the bond-servant of one grand lady. People were beginning already to talk about his frequent visits, always without her, to Bath House and Addiscombe; this was not easy to bear with equanimity; and he, at first, made matters worse by his eulogies.

This was the position when Helen, clearing away the break-fast one May morning in 1843, began to philosophise on the decline in conjugal affection—love nowadays, she said, was just "*momentary and away*". John Sterling would soon marry again she felt sure, the milkman had remarried seven months after his wife's death, and the woman next door had got over the death of her lover with indecent speed. She could imagine only one possible exception: "I *do* think that Mr Carlyle *will be* a very *desultory widow!* he is so *easily put about*—and seems to take no pleasure in *new females*"! So Jane reported to Jeannie in Liver-pool, adding almost too casually

"there is one *new female* in whom he takes a vast of pleasure, Lady Harriet Baring. I have always omitted to tell you how marvellously that liaison has gone on. Geraldine seemed horribly *jealous* about it—nay almost '*scandalized*'—while she was here—for my part I am singularly inaccessible to jealousy, and am pleased rather that he has found *one* agreeable house to which he likes to go and goes regularly—one evening in the week at least—and then *he* visits them at their 'farm' on Sundays and there are flights of charming little notes always coming to create a pleasing titillation of the philosophic spirit!"

Not all her friends were content to gossip:

"Mrs Buller in her graceful quizzical way insisted I should 'see a little into the thing with my own eyes,' and promised to give me notice the first time she knew beforehand of the Intellectual Circe's coming to her house—and accordingly Mr Buller came last Monday to ask me to meet her that evening at tea at seven o'clock—she is in *delicate health* you may remember and not up to parties or late hours—I said at once yes".

Jane was reassured:

"I liked her on the whole—she is immensely *large*—might easily have been one of the *ugliest* women living—but *is* almost *beautiful*—simply thro' the intelligence and cordiality of her expression—I saw nothing of the impertinence and hauteur which people impute to her—only a certain *brusquerie* of manner which seemed to me to proceed from exuberant spirits and absence of all affectation. She is unquestionably very clever—just the *wittiest* woman I have seen—but with many aristocratic prejudices—which I wonder *Carlyle* should have got over so completely as he seems to have done—in a word I take her to be a very lovable spoilt Child of Fortune—that a little *whipping*, judiciously administered would have made into a first rate woman—we staid till eleven—and as there were no other strangers, I had ample opportunity of estimating the amount of her seductions. What *she* thought of *me* I should rather like to know—she took prodigious looks at me from time to time. In the *last* note to Carlyle inviting him to Addiscombe for next Sunday she says—'I meditate paying my respects to Mrs Carlyle—so soon as I am again making visits—she is a *reality* whom you have hitherto *quite suppressed.*' "

Her alarm revived when she heard a few weeks later that Mazzini had been summoned to Bath House. This was really too much; Carlyle, at a stretch, might be said to belong to the country, but Mazzini was clearly her property. She had 'discovered' him, she felt; and her attitude towards him—towards all her 'exiles' and most of her men friends, for that matter—resembled that of an indulgent mistress to a pet dog. She would not recognise that they—and Mazzini particularly—had any serious existence beyond their relationship with her. At any sign, as now, that this was not so, she immediately became sarcastic and spiteful.

"Mazzini's visit to Lady Baring (as he calls her) went off wonderfully well" she told Carlyle. "I am afraid my dear this Lady Baring of yours and his and John Mill's and everybody's is an arch coquette—she seems to have played her cards with Mazzini really too well. She talked to him with the highest commendations of George Sand—expressed the utmost longing to read the new edition of 'Lelia'—nay she made him 'a mysterious signal with her eyes having first looked two or three times towards John Mill and her husband'—clearly intimating that she had something to tell him about Nice which they were not to hear—and when she could not make him understand she 'shook her head impatiently'—' which from a *woman*, especially in your England, was—what shall I say—*confidential* upon *my* honour.' I think it was."

Mazzini's own account was milder: "Lady Baring is a woman of spirit, and highly cultured, very tolerant of other people's opinions."

The weeks after Carlyle's return in October were dreary; not only was the house again in confusion, and Carlyle difficult to deal with, but their friends were almost all out of town. Jane saw a little girl playing her hoop in the middle of Piccadillys which she thought fittingly illustrated "the desert state of things". Geraldine sympathised—not so much about the friend, as about Carlyle: "You have the length of two lives to live in one, which is more than one bargains for."

Jane was not without visitors of a kind, for American tourists had begun to make their way to Cheyne Row. She found one of them—"a tall, lean, red-herring-looking man"—writing a letter at Carlyle's desk, and doing the honours of the house to her friends. He had come, he said, "to congratulate Mr Carlyle on his increasing reputation". He refused to be put out by Jane's chilliness.

"Does Mr Carlyle enjoy good health *Mrs Carlyle?* '*No!*' Oh, he doesn't! What does he complain of *Mrs Carlyle?* '*Of everything!*' Perhaps he studies too hard—does he study too hard *Mrs Carlyle?* 'Who knows?' How many hours a day *does* he study *Mrs Carlyle?* 'My husband does not work by the clock.' And so on—his impertinent questions receiving the most churlish answers—but which seemed to patter off the rhinoceros-hide of him as tho' they had been sugar-plums." "But really" she admitted "these Yankees form a considerable item in the ennuis of our mortal life. I counted lately *fourteen* of them in one fortnight! of whom Dr Russel was the only one that you did not feel tempted to take the poker to."

Another party of Americans squeezed her hand so vigorously that she "almost screamed, 'for all my rings are utilitarian and have seals.' " This was told to Caroline Fox, who was fascinated by her skill in anecdote and in "dotting off" a character in a few words. "Carlyle" remarked Jane "has to take a journey always after writing a book, and then gets so weary with knocking about that he has to write another book to recover from it."

She summed up the winter months in a terse postscript: "Carlyle is over head and ears in Cromwell—is lost to humanity for the time being". The atmosphere in the house became tense. "I am very miserable at present," Carlyle tells John Sterling in December " . . . I see almost nobody." He appealed to Sterling, who was extending his house at Ventnor, to "build me some small Prophet's chamber" with "some dumb old woman to light a fire for me daily." Jane had her usual bout of influenza, and more headaches than usual, which left her feeling "all beaten into impalpable pulp" as the winter crawled into spring, with Carlyle "fidgeting and flurrying about all the while like a hen in the distraction of laying its first egg, and writing down every word as with his heart's blood."

He had helpers—Mazzini, Espinasse, Mill (making his final appearances as a member of the Cheyne Row circle), and Forster as a tower of strength—but they could not prevent him from disgustedly burning all he had written by the end of the year. Their main use was to save Jane from utter distractedness. Her letters—sure indication of her health and spirits—dwindled, and even Forster received only an occasional note, as this, after Carlyle's Welsh admirer had sent game for Christmas:

> "knowing our feelings about the Bird called Pheasant, you can estimate the *'tremendous sacrifice'* of sending you this one—from Wales. I am enchanted with my flowers this morning—as pleased as a *child* with my glorious *die die!*"

But for the most part her history was "to do the amiable to company, and take all the principal *bores* off Carlyle and go about indoors as if nothing ailed me—for" she reminds Jeannie " . . . Carlyle has long since appropriated the chief right to raise an outcry." Geraldine from Manchester gave her in reply to complaints what she may have regarded as doubtful comfort:

> "He is much too grand for everyday life. A sphinx does not fit in comfortably to our parlour-life arrangements, but seen from a proper point of view it is a supernaturally grand thing! You must feel proud of belonging to him, after all, and he deserves to have you! Mortal praise can go no higher!"

She was not without her adventures; and if they were not

lively enough to retell, she would refashion them, preserving
the substance but adding the imaginative word or two that
turned a dull story into a good one.

> "I received by post a little while since a letter in a handwriting not
> new to me, but I could not tell in the first minute whose it was. I read the
> first words 'Oh those bright sweet eyes!' I stop amazed 'as in presence of
> the Infinite.' *What* man has gone out of his wits? In *what* year of grace
> was I? *What* was it at all? I looked for a signature, there was none! I
> turned to the beginning again and read a few words more: 'There is no
> escaping their bewitching influence!' 'Idiot' said I, 'whoever you be'—
> having now got up a due matronly rage! I read on however. 'It is
> impossible those sweet eyes should be unaccompanied with a benevolent
> heart; could you not intercede with the possessor of them to do me a
> kindness? The time of *young Ladies* is in general so uselessly employed that
> I should think you would really be benefiting(!) Miss Swanwick in
> persuading her to—translate for me those *French Laws on Pawnbroking*'.
> Now the riddle was satisfactorily solved. The 'bright sweet eyes' were
> none of *mine*, but Miss Swanwick's; and the writer of the letter was
> Robertson, who, you may remember, I told you raved about those same
> eyes to a weariness. My virtuous married-woman indignation blushes
> had been entirely thrown away!"

A Christmas party for the Macready children became a riot
of fun. After seven weeks of coughs and colds Jane rose deathlike from her bed, as so often, and, braving Carlyle's gloomy
verdict that her face was green and her eyes bloodshot, went
off to watch Macready's friends exert themselves to make up
for his absence in America. Dickens played the conjuror with
Forster as his assistant, the perspiration "pouring down",
followed by dancing, with "the gigantic Thackeray" capering
about, and Dickens doing everything but go on his knees to
make her waltz with him. Forster did not ask, but seized her
round the waist and whirled her into the dance. Jane protested,
not too strongly, that he would dash her brains out. "Your
brains!" cried Forster, "who cares about their brains *here? let
them go!*"

Her once elegant cousin James Baillie, the six foot two life-
guardsman, moved into the picture for a moment. He had come
down in the world, and was now trying to borrow a pound or
two from the woman he had flirted with years ago. And when
he had spent that, he asked her to pawn something to help his
illegitimate child.

Mazzini, anxious to please her "Scotch superstitions", walked miles through the snow on the morning of New Year's Day to be her "first foot" once again, "looking pitiable" with big drops of sleet hanging from his moustache. Jane was not so grateful as she should have been. "What on earth could tempt you to come out on a day like this?" was her greeting.

Her existence was brightened in the early part of the year by the behaviour of the woman Anthony Sterling had married. Mrs Sterling, after a mental breakdown, declared that her husband was in love with Jane, whose name she would not allow to be mentioned in her house. She suffered much from jealousy, and was helped little by her husband. The poor woman's state is retailed at length by Jane with a self-satisfaction—she was, it is true, in her forty-fourth year and beginning to look even older—that shines out of every sentence. Anthony, she told Helen Welsh, still visited her "by *stealth*—without carriage or servants—like a man going to rob a hen-roost!" She would really have to complain to Carlyle if he did not change his tactics. Craik was trying to discipline himself—had reduced his visits to about once every two months—but

> "if I fling him one civil word he looks as if he would fall down and kiss my great toe! and answers in the plaintive tone of a love-lorn shepherd in the Poetry of the Middle Ages—I begin to be *wae* for 'poor Creek'!"

She also had cause to feel *wae* for two of her exiles. Garnier reappeared suddenly after a long absence. He looked "blown up", his hair was uncombed, his clothes dirty, his shirt wide open at the neck, and his manner fearful. He had discovered "*a nest of murderers*" he said, and had informed the authorities, who had grossly insulted him by disbelieving his word. Was he, who had fought twenty-five duels to preserve his honour (the one particle of truth in his story) to be insulted by the English? The blood of the entire nation should wash out the insult. In future he would be the deadly enemy of every Englishman.

> " 'Well' said I trying to seem unconcerned tho' my eyes were intently watching his least *movement*—'I am not an *Englishman*, but a *Scotch-woman*, so you need not look so furious at *me!*' 'I have *done for* Mazzini however' said he—'and that is so far good!!!' then suddenly turning on me the most benevolent eyes in the world he said with a quite *paternal* tenderness 'you look *better* than when I saw you last! a *little* better, but always pale!' No wonder that I was pale just then!"

After half an hour of "the *bloodiest* talk" he strode to the door and crushed her hand so that she screamed and fell half fainting over his arm. He looked at her red and swollen hand for a moment with "a devilish satisfaction" then said kindly "I am sorry—but it was *necessary*" and walked out of the house.

"Heaven preserve me from any more such *necessaries!*" cried Jane to Jeannie—for the moment her most regular correspondent. She had a few minutes of normality with Mazzini, who came in, fortunately, to show her that he was not *"done for"*. While they were discussing what they could do for Garnier, old Sterling made his daily call, and, seeing them together, fell into a fit of jealousy, uttered *"an impertinence"* and was sent away, threatening, as usual, never to return. The next day she went out with Mazzini to escape Robertson and Plattnauer, who were settled grimly in the drawingroom, determined to sit each other out, and on returning found them gone, and in their place Helps asleep on the sofa.

Jeffrey called soon afterwards when Plattnauer was again there, and, after his manner, kissed Jane many times

> "not '*on the brow*' or any of those delicate spots, but *plump on my lips!*—calling me 'my darling Jeannie!—my sweet Child! my dear Love'!!!! and then when we had got over *the brunt* of the business he ceased not a moment from kissing my hands, stroking my hair, patting my face—and saying the tenderest things in the tenderest tones!"

Plattnauer snatched up a newspaper convulsively, blushed deeply, then "reeled" across the floor and said goodbye "with a look significative of much". He staggered over to Elizabeth Pepoli, who tried to comfort him by telling him that Jeffrey was seventy. This he did not believe—Jeffrey was too handsome, he asserted, to be so old. Besides, he said, what of Count Krasinski (yet another addition to Jane's circle of foreigners)?—he was "preposterously fond of Mrs Carlyle". "Oh all *the men are that*!!" was Elizabeth's reassurance. "Slightly splenetic don't you think?" commented Jane when Plattnauer repeated the conversation.

There was always news of a kind when Jane felt sufficiently far from downright illness to put her hand to a pen. But she was worried. Although Carlyle had little time to spare for her from *Cromwell*, although he refused himself to most of his friends, his visits to Addiscombe and Bath House continued. She was worried and she was puzzled. Carlyle had never been interested in women. What had Lady Harriet to give him that she had not? Her preoccupation with this topic, her wretched health, and Carlyle's ill-temper over the difficulties of *Cromwell* made her an indifferent hostess to anyone who overstayed his welcome. In May, Carlyle was writing "my progress in 'Cromwell' is frightful". Frightful too was the strain of living with him in this torn and agonizing mood. And at this moment Amelie Bölte arrived. "When a person asks one to seek her a *lodging knowing* that one possesses a spare bed . . . it is equivalent to saying 'will *you* take me in?' " Jane took her in for two days. At the end of a week the guest was still there, sitting for "hours together, especially when I am *doing* company, staring at me with her horn-eyes, and speaking never a word, till I feel somehow as if I were fallen under the power of a bad dream!" Two weeks later, her stay was "assuming an air of *permanency* which made my blood run cold, and not only *mine* but everyone's that frequents the house—for you know her way of sitting gazing at one's visitors without ever speaking a word." Could not Jane marry her to Plattnauer, Anthony Sterling demanded, so that the two Germans could stare at one another? Jane made superhuman efforts to get her guest placed, and at last, helped by Mrs Buller, settled her as governess in the house of Sir James Graham, the Home Secretary.

It was this man who, innocently enough, completed Jane's discomfiture. In the early summer Mazzini discovered that his letters were being opened by order of Graham on the grounds that he was plotting against a friendly country. Mazzini's many friends rallied to his defence, and Carlyle, even though he had begun to lose sympathy with him, wrote what Jane called "a glorious letter" to *The Times*, protesting against the insult to this "man of genius and virtue, a man of sterling veracity, humanity, and nobleness of mind; one of those rare men, numerable, unfortunately, but as units in this world, who are worthy to be called martyr souls." Jane was aflame with indignation, and not with indignation alone. Her friendship with Mazzini was almost as popular a topic in some London circles as Carlyle's with Lady Harriet: "Mrs Carlyle, too, is in a great way at all her letters having been overhauled", wrote Milnes. Jane had for years written freely to Mazzini, and was now pouring out her fears about Carlyle's growing desertion to

Bath House and Addiscombe. The Home Secretary and Baring were in the same government; they both knew much of her; it was impossible to say where the thing might end. In fact, nothing was said; but Jane, her nerves in tatters, accepted a long standing invitation and fled to Liverpool.

Geraldine received the news rapturously:

"My dear child, are you quite sure that you are coming? I fear something will happen to the railway, or the house, or 'Oliver Cromwell', and when there is anything good before me at a distance of a few days I always get afraid that I shall die before it comes close to me. Now do make haste! I am in a fever already."

She offered strange reassurance:

"provided I get my fair share of you, I will promise not to torment you, which is promising a great deal, for I am as jealous as a Turk, and don't, besides, care half a straw for seeing my friends except *tête-a-tête*, when I feel strongly disposed to assassinate everybody who does not keep out of reach!" But she warned her " . . . I don't want to worry you, but if you don't stay to the utmost moment with me it will take more magnanimity than I possess to forgive you, and so I feel as jealous as a tiger, and not at all friendly or amiable."

Jane had no sooner set foot in the train than she began to regret leaving Carlyle and Chelsea. She was even more ill than usual, "seasick *without the sea!*" As soon as she entered the house in Maryland Street, memories of her last visit there overwhelmed her and she had hysterics—"a very ugly thing I can tell you—must be just the next thing to being hanged". When she recovered, and began to look about her, all was not as it should be:

"I am afraid my Babbie has been *deteriorating* in these latter times—she looks most painfully indolent, and *young-ladyish*—I have got into no free communication with her yet—alone with me she is the same gentle sweet Babbie as ever—but *impenetrable*. I shall find out what is at the bottom of all this by and by. . . . The one that pleases me least of all is Alick—his Toryism is perfectly insupportable."

After a day or two:

"The manner of being in this house is really—'what shall I say?—strange—upon *my* honour'! the preparation, and deliberation, and unwearying earnestness with which they all dress themselves *three times a day* is a continual miracle for me, combined as it is with total want of earnestness about every thing else in Heaven or earth! . . . .As for Babbie, she is sunk into the merest *young lady* of them all! Her indolence is

absolutely transcendental! . . . How grateful I ought to be to you Dear
for having rescued *me* out of the young-Lady-sphere!"

She did not care for the atmosphere of the house—"everyone
coming down to breakfast half asleep and continuing half
asleep till they go to bed again." She did not care for the
visitors, including "that unleavened lump of dough Miss
Hunter" and the "hideous spectacle" of one Walter MacGregor
and his "wooden little wife".

Her uncle, specially dear to her as the one direct link with
her mother, dealt the final blow.

> "Sir James Graham" he declared, when the conversation again moved
> to the Mazzini letters "had *said* he only opened *one* of Mazzini's letters;
> that if Mazzini said he opened more he was a d--d lying rascal--and
> every body knew whether to believe the word of a gentleman like Sir
> James or of a beggarly refugee—turned out of his own country for
> *misconduct*."

Jane was almost beside herself:

> "Fancy *me* swallowing all that without answer! To be sure the only
> alternative was to hold my peace altogether or produce a collision that
> must have ended in my calling a coach!"

Nothing would have pleased her better than to have called a
coach. She could not sleep, she was a bundle of nerves, and she
was heavy with a cold. These people—the stiff Tory uncle and
cousin, the young-ladyish Jeannie, even the saintly Helen— in
their dull, heavy house and with their dull and heavy visitors,
made Jane long, as she always longed when away from it, for
the liveliness of Chelsea, even for the intolerant grumbling of
Carlyle. He was a living man, looking to the future, using his
brains—he was a great man—he could laugh—and the company he and she kept were living people, with ideas, humour, a
sense of proportion. There she was alive, here dead. For good
or evil she belonged to Carlyle and to all that Chelsea symbol-
ised for her. She longed passionately to be back. Her fears of
Lady Harriet, her anger at Carlyle's selfishness, their many
disputes, her threats—all were now seen to be of no account.
Her letters were bright with affection. He was again her
"Dearest, most punctual Good" when his letters arrived day
after day.

> "It is curious how much more uncomfortable I feel without you, when

> it is *I* who am gone away from *you* and not, as it used to be, *you* gone away
> from *me*. I am always wondering since I came here how I can ever in my
> angriest moods talk about leaving you for good and all—for to be sure if
> I were to leave you today *on that principle* I should need absolutely to go
> back tomorrow *to see how you were taking it!*"

But there was no going back at the moment. She was engaged
to Geraldine and the Paulets; and whatever she might think
and say of the Liverpool Welshes, they were the only relations
in whom she felt interest, they were genuinely fond of her and
had done her many kindnesses. She stayed on, filling the time
as best she could with excursions. On one excursion, to the
further shore of the Mersey, the party of women was escorted
by Gambardella, again painting in Liverpool. He kept Jane
amused, organising a donkey ride, singing Italian songs, and
drinking Carlyle's health.

> "Even *you* would have been conquered by the creature's efforts to
> amuse—and endless consideration for *my* comfort. Just think of his taking
> off a beautiful light-coloured coat and making it into a cushion for me to
> sit on—because the sand was damp. He is far best in the open air—being
> in fact a sort of savage."

She rewarded the "creature" with more commissions, so that
Gambardella is soon found painting portraits of the Gladstone
family—Liverpool merchants who had retired to the estate of
Capenoch across the river from Thornhill.

Early in July she moved to Seaforth House, arriving in true
Jane fashion with a "streaming cold and sore throat". The
welcome cheered her—"Geraldine's joy over me was quite
enlivening, and Mrs Paulet's sunshiny looks and cordial harum-
scarum speech"—she was shown to a room with a great fire
roaring in the grate, and the bed aired with a warming pan,
and Mrs Paulet ordered Geraldine to come away and leave
Jane to herself. In the morning, Geraldine brought Jane a cup
of tea "with a demure air which was quite edifying—plainly
Mrs Paulet had been lecturing her into it."

A few hours later, before this particular letter was sent off,
Geraldine was still behaving herself—she "is good just now
upon *my* honour". She had cause to be good, for Jane had done
her a service a few months earlier, placing her novel *Zoe* with
Chapman and Hall in spite of Carlyle's prophecies of failure.
Jane now thought it "the *cleverest* Englishwoman's book I ever

remember to have read". Geraldine, then, was in favour again, and so was the entire Paulet household as Jane's cold disappeared. "*Morally* speaking" she said, Mrs Paulet was an excellent hostess. The cooking at Seaforth House could be improved, but she would gladly eat indifferent food, as long as it was not actually poisoned, when she could have such pleasant company with it. Mrs Paulet's sister was there when Jane arrived, and a Mrs Darbyshire came soon afterwards:

> "She seems a sensible *Gentlewoman* enough—a Unitarian *without the Doctrines*. But I could not very well comprehend at first why she had been brought—till at last Mrs Paulet gave me to understand that she was there to *use up* Miss Newton—so that Geraldine and herself and I might have the coast clear to speculate '*to all lengths*'! 'Not' she said 'that my sister is an illiberal person—tho' she believes in Jesus Christ, *and all that sort of thing*, she is quite easy to live with!' "

This atmosphere of peace and goodwill was too good to last. Geraldine began to show signs of running a temperament; a severe bilious attack, reports Jane, "having not only taken the *wit* out of her but the good nature, for a wonder! to see Geraldine *cross* is a sight for sore eyes!" But the biliousness "turned out to have been all rage at *me* for 'giving such a *stab* to her feelings as she had never suffered the like of from man or woman'." The "stab" was Jane's suggestion that the proposed visit to Geraldine at Manchester now seemed unnecessary as they were together at Seaforth.

> "She answered me pettishly that 'if I *wished* to *sacrifice* her to Mrs Paulet and the Welshes—in God's name to do so!'—and went off in a nice little *tiff* . . . her vagaries exceeded my reminiscences of Mrs Jordan in *The Jealous Wife!* Nothing but outbursts of impertinence and hysterics from morning till night—which finished off with a grand *scene* in my room after I had gone up to bed. . . . Such mad *lover-like* jealousy on the part of one woman towards another it had never entered into my heart to conceive. By a wonderful effort of patience on my part—made more on Mrs Paulet's account who was quite vexed—than from the *flattering* consideration that *I* was the object of this incomprehensible passion, the affair was brought to a happy conclusion. I got her to laugh over her own absurdity, promised to go by Manchester if she would behave herself like a reasonable creature—and with her hair all dishevelled and her face all bewept she thereupon sat down at my feet and—smoked a cigarette!! with all the placidity in life! She keeps a regular supply of these little things—and smokes them before all the world. In fact I am not at all sure that she is not *going mad!*"

Jane disliked and feared excessive emotion. She could deal with an outbreak of anger because she understood and felt it herself, but passionate love was beyond her. Geraldine therefore had to be punished; and although she had soon "returned to her usual devotion", the recollection of what she herself called her "Tiger-jealousy" would not, said Jane,

> "be easily effaced from my mind, or any one's who *assisted* at them. I set the whole company into fits of laughter, the other day, by publicly saying to her after she had been flirting with a certain Mr Telo that 'I wondered she should expect me to behave decently to her after she had for a whole evening been making love before my very face to *another man!*' "

This major incident apart—and even this, when the outbreak was over, was both funny and flattering—life at Seaforth was pleasant. Carlyle wrote regularly, and Jane replied as often. She escaped "the *rosbeefs* and dreadfully prosaical demonstrations" that would have greeted the celebration at Maryland Street of her forty-third birthday. Carlyle sent a jewel box, and a letter:

> "one is right glad to see the brave little Goody with the mind's and the heart's eye on such an occasion, and wishes and prays all good in this world and in all worlds to one's poor Goody—a brave woman, and, on the whole, a 'Necessary Evil' to a man."

Mrs Paulet told only her husband that they were celebrating Jane's birthday, and drank to her happiness. "She has a beautiful tact that woman! I really love her considerably! It is a thousand pities to see her wasted on such a place as Liverpool." By the time she reluctantly went back to Maryland Street she had

> "sworn everlasting friendship with Mrs Paulet. We suit each other perfectly—neither of us has been rash in coming to this conclusion—and now that we *have* come to it, I feel confident that we shall be each other's dearest *friend* as long as we both live."

She had promised to visit Mrs Darbyshire

> "who is fallen deeply in love with me—and I with her to *a moderate extent*. She reminds me somewhat of poor Mrs Sterling, only much more cultivated and less given to *talk*."

She was given an "ecstatic" welcome back by the Welshes, and, feeling in better health herself, found less to criticise. But:

"there is a prodigious quantity of human faculty expended on the business of *eating* in this place; it looks very strange to me after London where the people *eat* certainly, but without any appearance of thinking about it."

She met Harriet Martineau's brother at a musical soirée:

"Most of the company were Unitarians; the men with faces like a meat-axe; the women most palpably *without bustles*—a more unloveable set of human beings I never looked on. However, I had a long, rather agreeable talk with James Martineau, the only 'Bae-ing I could love' of the whole nightmare-looking fraternity."

She made another conquest in her hostess, who, at another visit, sang to her and gave her some songs she had composed: "a charming woman—only that she has too great a gift of *fluency*".

Jane was not to leave the north without another scene with Geraldine, who came to Maryland Street

"to carry me off in a sort of *triumph*. . . . My Uncle's sorrow at parting with me, showed plainly enough that he as well as myself had great doubts of our ever meeting again—and Babbie had taken to crying in the morning—and gone on with it the whole day—and the other good little souls were all grave and silent—and into the midst of all this came Geraldine all flippancy and fuss bringing with her Mrs Paulet, Julia Newton and even Mr Paulet, *to witness the partings*."

Jane asked Mrs Paulet to take the party away. She agreed and, seeing that Jane now had no wish to go to Manchester, promised to make all right with Geraldine: "And my uncle was *so* pleased and the *children* all dancing for joy—and the servants laughing when they had to carry up my trunks again."

She came home towards the end of July, and reaction immediately set in. Carlyle was still sunk in *Cromwell*, but had found time to call often at Bath House. Jane was still trying, without success, to accustom herself to this phenomenon—that Carlyle, so ruthless when his work was threatened, should think his time better spent with Lady Harriet than in his study.

She was not alone in finding him irrational. One of the few visitors he had admitted that month was W. B. Hodgson the educationalist. They smoked a couple of pipes in the garden. In between puffs Carlyle "talked much and strongly about silence." Hodgson, who liked his discussions to correspond with reality, went away disillusioned. "He is an unsatisfactory man."

Darwin had written, hoping that she would come back before "the poor man died outright for want of having someone to grumble to!" Darwin had postponed a journey from London because Jane was returning—"and yet" she remarked "to have seen him walk in with his nonchalant air, one would have said he could have dispensed with a sight of me till the end of the world." But the most immediately disturbing news concerned Mazzini, who also called to greet her on her first morning at home:

> "*Lady Harriet* has been making new advances to him—which for a Tory woman of *her* distinction connected with the enemy as she is, does infinite 'credit to her head and *hort*.' He was engaged to her last night and she had brought divers persons in authority to meet him and Carlyle was there *of course*. But Mazzini will not be caught by that syren—the insensible man that he is! He did not come!!! It must be strange for the Lady Harriet to have found *one* man that can resist her fascinations and refuse her invitations."

But a few days later, "in a most dejected state" she told Jeannie:

> "Carlyle is to dine with Lady Harriet again today—and this time poor Mazzini *must* go—I begin to have a real *admiration* for that woman—her *fascination* of Carlyle proves her to be the most masterly coquette of Modern Times!"

She was worrying unnecessarily about Mazzini; he was merely one of the unusual types that Lady Harriet liked occasionally to gather round her to demonstrate her independence of convention. But before Jane's dejection could clear she had other troubles to meet. John Sterling was dying at Ventnor, and had written his farewell: "Your wife" he said, "knows my mind towards her, and will believe it." Nothing could be done but grieve for the premature end to such promise, and for the impetuous charm and affection that had given her such happiness in the early London days. Later, he had been little more than a gay correspondent, calling forth even gayer letters from her; as a man he had slipped in favour—he "wanted backbone" she said.

Nearer at hand the living called for help. On her return from Liverpool, she had found a strange letter from Plattnauer. She wrote to him several times without answer. Thoroughly alarmed, she made old Mr Buller drive her to Plattnauer's lodgings. He had left an address, which read to Jane as "one of

those dreadful *vegetable, fraternal, universal-religion* establish-
ments". No wonder, she thought, that Plattnauer had dared
not confess "to *me*" that he had joined such a place. But she was
sure he was too manly to be humbugged for long, and too
honest to live in such a humbug when he saw it as such. She set
herself to wait with as much patience as she could muster. Then
she heard a rumour that Plattnauer had become insane. She
went at once to Carlyle and told him that something must be
done. Carlyle said he would go to the "establishment" the next
week if she could get no one else to go "or *do not like to go
yourself*(!)" Jane put on her bonnet and called on Craik, who
"desired no better even than to be *suffered* to do me service."
He was back that night with his news. Plattnauer had reproached "The Pater"—the head of the establishment—and
his "children" for not living up to their principles. There was a
quarrel, and Plattnauer began to break everything within reach,
and to hit every disciple he could catch. The police were
summoned, he was taken to prison, was discovered in his cell
the next morning raging mad, and was moved to the asylum at
Wandsworth. There he had been ever since, unable or unwilling to give his name or that of any friend.

After a wretched night, Jane set off for Darwin, who drove her
to the asylum. A few days later she was allowed to see Plattnauer:

> "in a minute we were walking arm in arm thro' the garden as if we had
> met after our long separation under the most natural circumstances in
> the world. During all the half hour that I staid with him he was perfectly
> rational and composed (more so I am afraid than myself for I was 'too
> happy for anything')—recognising his actual position with a mixture of
> stoicism and humour—which rendered it rather *absurd* than *horrible*—
> nothing could be more manly and dignified than his whole way of taking
> the thing—even to his last action—insisting *dressed as he was*—in attending
> me to the carriage in which he *knew* Darwin was waiting for me, and
> apologizing to him in the most courteous manner for having detained me
> so long. You may fancy Darwin's astonishment!"

Soon afterwards, the doctor from the asylum paid an unexpected
call at Chelsea. Jane rushed upstairs to him "as white as milk".
Had Plattnauer escaped, committed suicide? No, he was cured,
but a friend was needed to take him out and be responsible for
him. Would she send someone? She would go the next morning,
she said. But where will he go then? the doctor asked.

> "I looked imploringly at Carlyle who, good as he always is on *great*

occasions, said directly 'Oh he must come *here* for a while till he sees what is to be done next.' And so it was settled and I had no difficulty in bringing *himself* to consent to the arrangement!"

Jane spent the whole of the next day at the asylum "and a *happier* day I hardly ever passed". She brought Plattnauer home at night, Carlyle was kind to him, and she was so busy fitting him out with clothes, and keeping him calm—for he remained highly excitable—that Carlyle's departure for his first visit to The Grange, Lord Ashburton's country house in Hampshire, passed off with little comment. All she had to say was:

> "Lady Harriet like the Queen must have her Court about her wherever she goes or stays, she has summoned Carlyle down to The Grange for a week at the least—and *he never* by any chance refuses a wish of *hers*—the clever woman that she is!"

Mrs Buller was fearful that Plattnauer would kill her, but, says Jane, "no madman will ever hurt a hair of *my* head. I have too much affinity with them." Carlyle did not worry: "he paid me the compliment of supposing that I had presence of mind and clearness enough to manage perfectly well without any protection—and I am quite of his opinion." As soon as Carlyle was away, she called in the painter, paperhanger, carpet beater and sweep to prepare the house for the winter, but had no sooner got everybody to work than she fell into "the crossest possible humour"—a reaction to the death of Sterling, the weeks of worry and excitement about Plattnauer, and the belated realisation that the Grange visit was an omen of trouble to come. Plattnauer depended on her for everything, and showed a fanatical and often embarrassing devotion. He took violent dislikes to her visitors, threatening to dash out the brains of Alexander Bain, a friend of Mill, with a poker, "and so put an end to his eternal clack." More convenient, he was "savage" with Bishop Terrot who had suddenly reappeared in London. But, says Jane, Terrot "will not trouble us again I think while he is here."

But she remained low; the house was upside down, the doorbell was always ringing, Plattnauer went on talking, her head ached, her digestion was at sixes and sevens, and Carlyle was with Lady Harriet. Even Mazzini and Darwin appeared "mortally stupid". Henry Taylor—a rare visitor now—looked in and **said the right** thing.

> "I put on my bonnet, and went with him to the boat; and he complimented me on going out without gloves or shawl. I was the first woman he had ever found in this world who could go out of her house without at least a quarter of an hour's preparation!"

But this small satisfaction soon passed. Of the women, Mrs Buller alone pleased. Before she left for a holiday in Italy Mazzini "so turned her head with his passionate pleadings for Italy that nothing would serve her but to take his bust *with his name on it in large letters* to his Mother." As it was "*death* for anyone in Italy to have a book of Mazzini's or a picture of him in their possession", Jane dissuaded her, and they spent an affectionate farewell evening—"indeed indeed you do her injustice when you think her heartless or that she does not *love me excessively*."

Jane's self-confidence, like that of most vain people, was only skin-deep and it was now badly shaken. Never before had she been so anxious to prove herself loved; and the proofs were presented to Carlyle as if the marks of ill health and pain on her face—the pallor, the lines, and the dark shadows under her eyes—drove her to insist again and again that the perceptive loved and admired her through this unflattering mask. She was not above satisfaction in causing a little jealousy, especially when herself suffering from it.

> "The Lewises were all there again—hang them! Lady Lewis looked very much astonished at the caresses Mrs Buller was making me all the evening—holding one of her arms about my neck and kissing me ever so often. I am sure Lady Lewis was thinking by her vinegar expression that her Sister liked *me* a good deal better than *her*."

She could not forget that this was the first time that Carlyle had stayed with the Barings longer than a day. "Give my love to *Mr* Baring" she wrote. Carlyle, anxious to keep the whole matter on a light footing, explained that "your lover Baring" owed his features to his American mother. But he showed less tact elsewhere. "We are not a brilliant party here; nay, if it were not for the Lady Harriet and myself, we should be almost definable as a dull, commonplace one." He returned, short of sleep and of temper, to wrestle with *Cromwell*, which Jane began to wish

> "at the bottom of *Something* where I might hear less about it. It *is* at the bottom of rubbish enough, I am sure, to judge from the tremendous

ransacking of old folios and illegible manuscripts which Carlyle is always going on with—but still he manages to bring it up, in season and out of season, till I begin to be weary of him (the Protector) great man though he was."

Plattnauer's brother-in-law, Count Reichenbach, had come over from Germany to take charge of him—but a visit from Mrs Paulet gave Jane a new interest. Mazzini, instead of "staring at her with his great black eyes", became unusually talkative.

"Oh such a pretty discussion Mrs Paulet and Mazzini had on the subject of *love*—I taking part in it according to ability. What a pity she did not stay longer. By the way what on earth do you think was old Sterling's criticism on her—'She is pretty, and witty, and good-humoured and charming—and yet—one cannot fall in love with her and I think the reason of this is—that her face is too *exclusively intellectual!!!*'"

Before Sterling arrived at this answer, he had, he told Jane, stayed awake all night wondering why he did not fall in love with Mrs Paulet. Perhaps, suggested Jane, it might simply be because he was seventy-four years old.

She offered Geraldine consolation for missing London and Mazzini. Count Reichenbach wanted to see Manchester before he left England and Anthony Sterling was accompanying him:

"I am sending you two men; this time with no view to *your* matrimonial interests, both being already provided with wives better or worse; but chiefly with a view to *their* intellectual interests. . . . He is a curious man this Anthony Sterling—worth some *making out*—externally he is hard and angular—but I who thro' the late distresses in his family have had opportunity of getting to know him intimately am persuaded that at the bottom of all his disagreeableness there lies a good and a clever man—his coldness and sharpness of manner being merely the very natural *reaction* produced in him by his abhorrence, from youth upwards, of his own Father's humbug and *fine sentimentalities*. I said to him yesterday that I would . . . give you a hint to *put on* as much of *propriety* with him as you could conveniently stand. 'Why on earth should you do *that*'? said he— 'because', I told him, 'sent by *me* she will naturally fall into the mistake of fancying you one of *my* sort of people, with whom it is unnecessary to make-believe *respectability* and *conventionalism*—and so good Heavens she would talk to you in a way to make the hair of your head stand on end!'— 'Now *don't* write pray'! said he very earnestly—'pray leave her to her own inspiration—I am less easy to shock than you seem to think'—humph!— *I* have seen him occasionally dreadfully shocked with *me* anyhow—and in that case—I advise *you* to steer clear of the topics of *Religion* and *Love* with him—on all other topics you may be as witty and unique as you please."

This was the end of Jane for the season. In November she

told Mrs Russell that she had had no influenza "as yet". A few days later she was in bed; and a month later she was still ill—so missing the honour of being the only woman to hear Dickens read *The Chimes* to a "select few" in Forster's rooms. Carlyle and his wife were "indispensable", said Dickens, who was coming specially from Italy for the occasion, but even this compliment could not bring Jane from her bed.

XXV

ADDISCOMBE AND BAY HOUSE
1844 – 1846

For four months Jane did not leave the house. She had one cold after another, violent headaches, and a perpetual cough. She was not helped by Carlyle or by his brother, who was now in lodgings at Brompton but still spent much time at Chelsea. John, she complained, advised her to get out a little when the cold had gone, but did nothing to make it go. Carlyle was so "deep in the Hell of his *Cromwell*" that he had not "the smallest idea how ill I am."

"We are a grim pair" she concludes, living in an atmosphere "far too sulphury and brimstoneish." But neither *Cromwell* nor her own condition explained fully why she was so depressed and Carlyle so irritable in the early months of 1845. Lady Harriet had for some time been pressing Jane to visit her at Addiscombe, and Carlyle finally promised on Jane's behalf in the middle of February:

> "Sunday, yes my Beneficent, it shall be then: the dark man shall again see the daughter of the Sun for a little while; and be illuminated, as if he were not dark! Which he justly reckons among the highest privileges he has at present. Poor creature! My wife will follow, on Monday or on Tuesday, according to your will."

But Jane did not follow; she refused to leave the house, denying that Carlyle had any right to commit her—particularly when she was unwell. Carlyle had to explain away her absence as best he could, and the weeks following his return were so unpleasant that Jane declared herself downright ill, she was "so sick" and the world so "disgusting."

There were occasional breaks in the gloom even before she again took a breath of fresh air outside Cheyne Row. Her friends were always calling when she was well enough to see them. In January and in April, experiences of five years earlier were repeated. Tennyson came, this time with Moxon, to find that Carlyle had gone to a dinner:

"The only chance of my getting any right good of him was to make him forget my womanness—so I did just as Carlyle would have done, had he been there: got out *pipes* and *tobacco*—and *brandy and water*—with a deluge of *tea* over and above. The effect of these accessories was miraculous—he *professed* to be *ashamed* of polluting my room, 'felt,' he said, 'as if he were stealing cups and sacred vessels in the Temple'—but he smoked on all the same—for *three* mortal hours!—talking like an angel—only exactly as if he were talking with a clever man—which—being a thing I am not used to—men always *adapting* their conversation to what they *take to be* a woman's taste—strained me to a terrible pitch of intellectuality."

In April, D'Orsay made his second call:

"all in black and brown . . . that man understood his trade . . . he had the fine sense to perceive how much better his dress of today sets off his slightly enlarged figure and slightly worn complexion than the humming-bird colours of five years back would have done. . . . Lord Jeffrey came unexpected while the Count was here. What a difference! the Prince of Critics and the Prince of Dandies. How *washed out* the beautiful dandiacal face looked beside that little clever old man's! The large blue dandiacal eyes you would have said had never contemplated anything more interesting than the reflection of the handsome personage they pertained to in a looking-glass—while the dark penetrating ones of the other had been taking note of most things in God's universe, even seeing a good way into millstones."

This judgment shows that Jane, rather late in the day, had perceived something of the wisdom in their old friend. Later that month, she and Carlyle had "a sort of Irish *rigg* . . . consisting of three stranger Irishmen—real hot and live Irishmen." One, Charles Gavan Duffy, then editor of the Dublin *Nation*,

"quite took my husband's fancy and mine also to a certain extent. He is a writer of national songs and came here to 'eat his terms.' With the coarsest of human faces, decidedly as like a horse's as a man's, he is one of the people that I should get to think *beautiful*, there is so much of the *power* both of intellect and passion in his physiognomy."

But she gained most entertainment during the wearier weeks from Geraldine's novel and Geraldine's love affairs. The one led to the other. *Zoe* seemed as if it might have a *succès de scandale*—though, as Jane remarked, her least moral friends were shocked by the book, while her more straightlaced ones either liked or tolerated it. Even Henrietta Wilson thought it very clever and amusing although of course "you did not expect *me* to approve of it." But the oddest thing, said Jane, was that Geraldine appeared to be "in the fair way of getting a husband by it!!!" Robertson "in a fit of distraction" wrote her a letter of criticism, a correspondence followed, and Geraldine, who could scarcely write to a man without hope of a kind rising in her, began to take "a fit" to him. Before many letters had passed, Geraldine had read sufficient into a warm remark to enable her to accept Robertson as a suitor forthwith. He went up to Manchester. A storm immediately broke. Geraldine's brother Frank, for whom she kept house, flew into a passion, and wrote long letters to Jane, begging her to make Geraldine break off the match; he was "ready to die", he declared, if such a criminal act were to take place. Geraldine wrote letter after letter, seeking Jane's advice; Robertson wrote; and Mrs Paulet, to whose house they had both been driven, wrote also—they were mad, she feared, and Seaforth House had been turned into a Bedlam. Four letters arrived one day, three the next morning, "and heaven knows what the evening post may bring" cried the delighted Jane, her illnesses forgotten. Frank Jewsbury appealed to her for comfort—"comfort *thee* thou poor Manchester dud!" Robertson declared that he must go back to her for comfort— "Oh poor me who have so many times comforted him when no one else could!" Geraldine, who "went off in great style as a Heroine of the first magnitude" but had been writing "of late days less like a Heroine than a bladder with the wind let out of it" now asked, "*can* I break off; for I am *frightened* out of all *love*." Jane sat in Cheyne Row reading her swollen Manchester correspondence and dealing out advice. She "poured a few drops of vitriol" on Frank which "brought him to his senses with a suddenness"; and on Geraldine, which "brought *her* to her senses," and she summoned Robertson back from Manchester, saw him twice, and "brought *him* pretty well to his senses."

Geraldine might be man-mad, but she was also a philosopher. She had told Jane, of an earlier passion:

> "I have indulged in a matrimonial scheme, but the gentleman is so dreadfully in love with himself that I have not patience, energy, hope, or inclination enough to persevere. Indeed, these things are not much in my way; it was only the eligibility that put it into my head."

Now she turned almost with a sigh of relief to her second string, whom Jane christened "The Egyptian." This was Charles Lambert, a French Mohammedan in the service of the Pasha of Egypt. He had startled the people of Manchester by walking about in Oriental costume, a novelty enhanced by his black eye-shade—for he had lost one eye. To Geraldine he looked purely romantic, and she sat, literally, at his feet on the hearthrug, listening to his exposition of the St Simonian faith. As a peace offering, she sent him down to Chelsea with something to keep her friend's feet warm—one of Jane's lesser troubles was an imperfect circulation. Geraldine soon went off to Paris and Brussels for a holiday with Lambert and her brother. Jane was "disgusted", but when Geraldine came to Chelsea before going home:

> "I received her very coldly but there is no quarrelling with that creature! Before she had been in five minutes she sat down on the floor at my feet and untied my shoe-strings—'What are you doing?' I asked—'Why my dear I am merely going to rub your feet—you look starved—I am sure your feet have not got well rubbed since I did it myself last year!!' and all the two days she did not leave off rubbing my feet whether I would or no for a quarter of an hour together. I never saw her look so well—she actually looked like a *woman*—not as formerly like a little boy in petticoats. Whether it be her love affair that has developed some new thing in her I cannot say; but there was now and then a gleam on her face that was *attractive*—I could now fancy a *man* marrying her!"

By the beginning of summer, *Cromwell* was within reasonable sight of an end, and Jane was walking and even dining out again. One dinner, at the Wedgwoods, was memorable for a tussle between Carlyle and Mazzini. Carlyle

> "could see nothing in Beethoven's sonatas 'it told nothing'. It was like a great quantity of stones tumbled down from a building, and 'it might as well have been left in the quarry.' He insisted on Mazzini telling him what he gained by hearing music, and when Mazzini said inspiration and elevation, Carlyle said something not respectful of Beethoven and Mazzini ended with *Dieu vous pardonne.*"

A month later, in June, Lady Harriet paid her first visit to Cheyne Row. Jane was vexed beyond words when Craik sat immovable through the entire visit, and even more when a cousin, son of Robert Welsh, "a sort of cross between a man and a greyhound", an argumentative and priggish young Scot, began "dashing in with the rudest questionings and contradictions." If there was one point on which Jane was anxious that there should be no mistake in the mind of Lady Harriet, it was that in the matter of breeding there was nothing to choose between them. The Edinburgh cousin did little to encourage the impression, but Jane underrated her visitor who, though managing by nature, was far too sensible to attempt patronage. Lady Harriet—"like a heathen goddess" Jane told Carlyle— held the view of John Carlyle, that Jane cossetted herself, that she should be more active, go out more. For a beginning, she invited her to the opera. On the appointed day, Carlyle had his now customary ride in the Park—he had acquired another horse—and on his return began to change his clothes. Jane watched him struggle into evening dress. He was coming to the opera. "Nobody" she commented "knows what he can do till he tries! or rather till a Lady Harriet tries!"

Taglioni was dancing in *La Sylphide*—one of the first ballets in which pointe work was used. The Carlyles, whose view of the arts was unashamedly Philistine, did not pretend to appreciate what they saw, but Jane used it, as was her way, as a motif which is subsequently found running through her letters of this time, until a new image took its place.

> "I saw a very curious sight the other night, the only one I have been to for a long while—viz: some thousands of the grandest and most cultivated people in England all gazing in ecstasy, and applauding to death, over a woman, not even pretty, balancing herself on the extreme point of one great toe, and stretching the other foot high in the air—much *higher* than decency ever dreamt of! It was *Taglioni* our chief dancer at the Opera, and this is her chief feat repeated over and over to weariness— at least to *my* weariness—but Duchesses were flinging *bouquets* at her feet— and not a man (except Carlyle) who did not seem disposed to fling *himself*. I counted twenty-five bouquets!—but what of that? The Empress of all the Russias once in a fit of enthusiasm flung her diamond bracelet at the feet of this same Taglioni—'Virtue its own reward' (in this world)? *Dancing* is and *singing*, and some other things still more frivolous—but for *virtue?*—'It may be strongly doubted' (as Edinburgh people say to every- thing one tells them). Monday is my birthday—how fast they come, these birthdays of mine! and how little are they marked by any good done—*I* cannot even balance myself on the point of my great toe!—but *that* perhaps is not so much to be regretted!"

This *"debut* in fashionable life" left Jane with a racking head- ache that lasted for days. Then came news from France that Godefroi Cavaignac had died. He was forty-four, like herself, and had been ill for some time, but this did nothing to lessen the shock. She fell into a "frightful depression," she felt she was going mad, could gain no comfort from the knowledge that her trouble was aggravated by the physical changes through which she was passing, and was driven at last after "a dreadful fit of crying" to confess her state and her fears to Carlyle. He was shocked, and insisted that she go away at once to the country. She thought of Haddington, where the Donaldsons were anxious to see her; she did not feel able to go to Scotsbrig—it was too much connected in her mind with Templand; but before she had decided on any place, Lady Harriet had insisted and Carlyle had agreed that she should have an immediate change at Addiscombe for a day or two. Carlyle took her there, and, to save money, they walked from the nearest railway station, two or three miles away. Jane, observed Carlyle, "grew very tired and disheartened" but he felt proud of her later when she joined the company on the lawn "with such a look of lovely innocency, modesty, ingenuousness, gracefully suppressed timidity, and radiancy of nature, cleverness, intelligence, and dignity, towards the great ladies and great gentlemen". Jane did not see herself or her visit in this light: "Fancy it!—in such a state of mind—having to get up fine clothes and fine 'wits'! having to proceed with my *first season* of *fashionable life* while I was feeling it the dreadfullest problem to *live* at all!" She spent four days there, sleeping an hour and forty minutes during the whole stay:

> "The house was full of fine people among whom there was only one (Lord Ashburton) who did not feel it his duty to make 'incessant wits'. These said 'wits', in my sleepless state of nerves, grew to look like a shower of fire sparks falling falling for ever and ever about my ears till I had not a grain of common sense remaining."

Carlyle returned to Addiscombe on the Sunday—"as usual (he has established a small permanent wardrobe there!)"— bringing a letter from Jeannie suggesting that they take a holiday together. Charlotte Williams Wynn, whom she had met at Addiscombe, had already invited her to Wales, but Jane refused both invitations. She proposed instead a week at Liverpool before Jeannie set off, and another week or so at Seaforth House. Until this was settled she stayed at home trying to recover from her outing to Addiscombe—"my husband always *writing*, I always *ailing*, which is perhaps the most laborious business of the two"—and scarcely bearing out in her manner Carlyle's assurance to Lady Harriet: "My wife returned in much satisfaction with Addiscombe and her visit."

Jane had recently collected for a few awkward hours a lost child, at which Carlyle looked "rather aghast". The child was claimed, to the relief of all (for Jane's impulses usually recoiled on her), and she, having lost Plattnauer and having narrowly escaped having on her hands that "shabbiest of done up Dandies", James Baillie, felt the need of some safer pet. When she went off to Liverpool towards the end of July, she left a leech in Carlyle's care.

Still mindful of the previous year's nightmare journey, she travelled by coach, and, short of having the coach to herself, shared it much as she would have wished, with four men. One of them, a German, wrapped his coat round her feet; another, a colonel, was soon telling her of his part in the wars; a third "had one eye boiled—the other parboiled—*no* leg—and his mind *boiled*—to jelly! and yet he got to Liverpool just as well as the rest of us!"; and the fourth, an English dandy with a "Heaven-blue waistcoat slept the whole way exactly in the attitude of 'James' waiting for the Sylphide to come and kiss him; but he might sleep long enough, I fancy, before any 'bit of fascination' would take that trouble."

A "cat-opera" every night, and cocks crowing every dawn made sorry work of her sleep; but despite this, an east wind, and 'the eternal smell of roast meat in this house" she felt less deathlike than in London.

"Elizabeth Pepoli would impute the improvement to '*the greater variety of food*'—oh Heavens!—and above all the the excellent *porter*. I, who though my Sylphide's wings have long fallen off, can still manage by *stilts* and other means to keep myself above such depths of prose as *that* comes to, find '*the solution*' elsewhere—namely in '*the great comfort*' which it is somehow to be made sensible from time to time that if oneself is miserable others are 'perhaps more to be pitied that they are *not* miserable.' . . . 'I for one solitary individual' would rather remain in Hell—the Hell I make for myself with my restless *digging*—than accept this drowsy placidity. Yes I begin to feel again that I am not *la dernière de femmes*— which has been oftener than anything else my reading of myself in these latter times—a natural enough reaction against the exorbitant self-conceit which put me at fourteen on setting up for a woman of Genius."

She sends her compliments to the leech, and reminds Helen

to give it water. "The leech" Carlyle reassures her in one of his lighter moods (*Cromwell* was now nearly done) . . . "complains of nothing, lying all glued together at the top of the glass (the little villain) and leading a very quiet life of it." He was going regularly to "Baringdom" but was not getting a great deal from it.

Jane had an occasional good story for him:

> "Maggie, of all people in the world, told me a small specimen of *french sentiment* which she had read somewhere—worth repeating even to *you*—who have not all the sympathy with french sentiment that could be wished. An injured husband rushed in upon his wife and her lover, in an illfated moment, and was proceeding as in duty bound to kill the lover—whereupon the wife threw herself frantically between them and passionately remonstrated 'would you kill the Father of your Children?'"

But after a few days the house and people began to get on her nerves and she was "ready to have even Geraldine."

Geraldine "with all her ecstasies" soon followed when she went to Seaforth House at the beginning of August. Before her arrival, Jane had heard more of the Robertson affair. One "unmentionable" story made her laugh; it was unfit for a letter, but she thought she might retail it to Carlyle "*from under the table.*" She adds "no wonder poor Geraldine bolted!" She recovered rapidly. The "gypsy" existence they led seemed to suit her; she was very happy and comfortable and remarks accurately "I fancy that being very much *made of* agrees with my constitution."

Geraldine was by now a confirmed cigarette smoker, and Jane, who had begun to follow her example the previous year, again took up the soothing habit. Geraldine was on her best behaviour:

> "is very amusing and good humoured, *does* all the 'wits' of the party: and Mrs Paulet and I look to the *Pure Reason* and *Practical Endeavour*. I fancy you would find our talk '*amusing*' . . . if you could *assist* at it in a *cloak of darkness*—for one of the penalties of being 'the wisest man and profoundest thinker of the age' is the royal one of never hearing the plain 'unornamented' truth spoken—everyone striving to be wise and profound *invita natura* in presence of such a one and make himself as much as possible into his own likeness. And this is the reason that Arthur Helps and so many others talk very nicely to *me* and *bore you* to distraction. With *me* they are not afraid to stand on the little 'broad basis' of their own *individuality*, such as it is—with *you* they are always balancing themselves like Taglioni, on the point of their moral or intellectual great toe!"

Jane occasionally tried "to *get up a sentiment* more or less, towards *Nature*" and her walks produced a story or two. She met a child of seven driving cattle "and—smoking a pipe! I asked him when he learnt to smoke, and he answered that *he did not remember!*" All was passed on gaily to Carlyle, together with a compliment in a sermon by James Martineau. Carlyle was a little flattered, but quoted the Dumfries deacon "Oh, gentlemen, remember that I am but a man." He, like her, was writing regularly and with much affection—no trace left of the acrimonious tone so often heard at Chelsea during the years of *Cromwell*. For the moment, all was well. Jane was the admitted queen of the gathering; Geraldine plied her with cigarettes, rubbed her feet for hours at a time, and adored her incessantly, the Paulets ordered the household for her convenience, the other guests hung on her every word. She flourished. She was also in full cry after James Martineau. "I never saw a man whom I felt such an inclination to lead into some sort of wickedness—it would do him 'so much good'!" He appeared "so very near kicking his foot thro' the whole Unitarian concern" that Jane could not take her hand from the whip. Martineau began to dig his own pit.

> " 'Mrs Carlyle is the most concrete woman that I have seen for a long while.' 'Oh' said Geraldine 'she puts all her wisdom into practice and so never gets into scrapes.' 'Yes' said Martineau in a tone 'significant of much'—'to keep out of doctrines is the only way to keep out of scrapes'. Was not that a creditable speech in a Unitarian?"

This decided her: "I told him today quite frankly that he had better cut Unitarianism and come over to us. He asked who I meant by 'us', and I said Carlyle." Only Carlyle halted the pursuit. He did not want disciples: "let him hang on there till the rope of itself gives way with him." He returned compliment for compliment. Forster had been to Cheyne Row, "passionately solicited and thankfully received your address." He and Dickens were getting up a play; "and it is an immense feature of it to Fuz that you are to be there."

Maggie Welsh came over to Seaforth for a day or two, and was matched by Mrs Paulet with another girl: "It is a great talent that of Mrs Paulet's of making two negatives into an affirmative." Jane herself met an old admirer, Storey of Roseneath: "If you had only seen the man! His transports were 'rather exquisite'. I do not remember to have seen anybody so outrageously glad to see me in all my life before."

The sensation of the visit was reserved for Geraldine, who had so far "behaved like an angel". She was sitting next to Jane as usual at dinner one day when the letters arrived. There were three for Jane; from Carlyle, Robertson, and Lambert.

"while I was innocently reading *your* Letter thinking only of *that* I was startled by Mrs Paulet exclaiming 'Miss Jewsbury what have you in the name of God?' She had turned first pale as milk and then all over crimson —while her eyes were fixed on the Egyptian's letter as if reading it thro' clairvoyance! 'Who can that be from' said I. 'I can tell you' gasped Geraldine 'it is from the *Egyptian*—and why he should have written to *you* instead of *me* is a mystery I cannot pretend to fathom.' 'And can you tell me who *that* is from' said I handing her Robertson's note which had no signature as usual—and I could not for the moment tell whose handwriting it was, only that I *ought* to have known. 'Yes it is from *Robertson*.' The whole of us . . . burst into laughter—such a *complication!* Next day *she* also had a letter from her Egyptian but it was *short* 'because he had spent all his time in writing to Mrs Carlyle.' "

This led to a scene the next day, when Geraldine

" 'had a devil' and as usual selected *me* for the object of her fury—'*because*' —as she tells me when it is over—'she *loves* me better than all the rest of the world put together!' . . . So long as she merely cried and sulked in rooms by herself *looking daggers* at me whenever I appeared I took no notice—but when she set herself down beside Mrs Paulet and me in the evening—and fell to speaking *at me* the most inconceivable rudenesses—I rose up abruptly and said in a good hearty rage 'Geraldine, until you can behave like a *gentlewoman*—if not like a woman of commonsense, I cannot possibly remain in the same room with you'—and walked off to the Library. Mrs Paulet also left her. And in half an hour's time she came to me drenched in tears, and making the humblest apologies. I had '*hurt her feelings*' in the morning—she would not say *how*—if I were told ever so particularly *I* 'could not *understand it*—nor Mrs Paulet either—it was a something in my *manner* that grated on her soul'!! . . . This morning she has been making new apologies such as *I* really could not bring myself to make except to God Almighty—and covering me with kisses and tears. Decidedly she is more 'powerful' in the Christian virtue of humility than I am! But all that does not give me back the sleep I lost thro' having had to get in a rage."

What Geraldine had to endure is not touched on; Jane, she said, "pours oil into your wounds, but it is oil of vitriol". She was no match for her friend, and soon afterwards rushed back to Manchester:

> "I fancy to compose her mind—that she may be able to write a sufficiently penetrating letter to the Egyptian. As Mrs Paulet says: 'Well I would sooner die at once than go on living as Geraldine does on *faute de mieux!*' "

The upset with Geraldine was followed by a little trouble with Carlyle. Jane could not endure delay of any kind in letters from him, nor indecision in the letters when they arrived. She passed off a Sunday hitch with a joke—

> "The Seaforth minister does not allow the postbag to be opened till after Church time—'that people's thoughts may not wander to their letters during service.' I should fancy one's thoughts likely to wander much more after a letter *in the bag* than *out of it*."

But when Carlyle finished *Cromwell* at the end of August, and did not at once tell her his plans she burst out at him impatiently. She apologised twenty-four hours later, before he had time to write, but complained.

> "Husbands are so obtuse! They do not '*understand*' one's movements of impatience—want always to be 'treated with the respect due to genius', exact common sense of their poor wives rather than 'the finer sensibilities of the heart', and so the marriage state 'by working late and early, has come to what ye see'—if not precisely to 'immortal smash' as yet, at least to within a hair's breadth of it!"

He elected to visit Seaforth on his way to Annandale; he joined her there early in September after travelling up with a party of men "talking dull antiquarian pedantries and platitudes all day; I as third party silent, till at length, near sunset, bursting out upon them . . . to their terror and astonishment and almost to my own." Perhaps this was why, according to Jane, he "remained a week in a highly reactionary state."

> "It is a curious place" he told to Lady Harriet, "with many features of real loveability—a very musical creature the lady, and the man as newsy as a French cricket; and Zoe with her scraggy yet not ungraceful ways, with a certain lean sincerity of laughter in her."

Jane went south as Carlyle went north, and was back at Chelsea in the middle of September, to find a book from Duffy, sent from Ireland with "sincere respects and regards"—"To be *respected* by Young Ireland at *two seeings* is a compliment I feel duly touched by!" The leech was

> "alive and '*so* happy!' Helen radiant with virtue's own reward!—the

economical department in a very backward state, but *not confused*; for it is as clear as day that not a single bill has been paid since I left."

She at once began an "earthquake", taking advantage of Carlyle's absence to turn the house upside down. A few people knew that she had returned, and called regularly—Forster, Helps, Craik, Mazzini, old Sterling. Browning spent an evening; John Carlyle, translating his *Dante*, was there only too often until Jane drove him back to his lodgings by a liberal use of paint. Sterling, who was beginning to break up, came every day: "he is not *laughable* any more—'I am very glad to see you so well as this' said I. 'And *I*—am very, *very* glad to see you *at all*,' he said."

Mazzini was having trouble with his women admirers.

"He had received many invitations to the house of a Jew-Merchant of Italian extraction, where there are several daughters—'what shall I say? —horribly ugly—that is; *repugnant* for me entirely!' One of them is 'nevertheless very strong in music' and seeing that he admired her playing she had 'in her head confounded the playing with the player'. The last of the only two times he had availed himself of their attentions, as they sat at supper, with *Browning* and some others—'the youngest of the horrible family' proposed to him in sotto voce, that they two should drink 'a goblet of wine' together, each to the person that each loved most in the world. 'I find your toast unegoist' said he, 'and I accept it with pleasure'. 'But' said she 'when we have drank we will then tell each other *to whom?*' 'Excuse me' said he 'we will if you please drink without conditions.' Whereupon they drank 'and then this girl—what shall I say?—*bold*— upon *my* honour proposed to tell *me* to whom she had drank and trust to my telling *her* after.' 'As you like'! 'Well then it was to *you*!' 'Really?' said I, *surprised* I must confess. 'Yes,' said she *pointing aloft* 'True as God exists.' '*Well*'*!* said I, 'I find it strange!' 'Now then' said she, 'to whom did *you* drink?' 'Ah!' said I, 'that is another question;' and on this, that girl became ghastly pale, so that her sister called out *Nina!* what is the matter with you? and now, thanks God, she has sailed to Aberdeen.' Did you ever hear anything so distracted?"

A few days later, he confessed to

"two other declarations of love!! . . . 'What! more of them?' 'Ah yes! *unhappily!* they begin to —what shall I say—rain on me like *sauterelles*'*!* One was from a young Lady in Genoa who sent him a bracelet of her hair (the only feature he has seen of her)—and begged 'to be united to him—in *plotting*'*!* . . . 'And the other?' 'Ah!—from a woman here—*married* thanks God—tho' to a man fifty years more old—French—and *sings*—the other *played*—decidedly my love of music has consequences!' "

Forster rushed in and out, excited, important, reminding Jane of Mrs Gamp on the station platform explaining that

> "this resolute gent a-coming along here as is apperrantly going to take the railways by storm—him with the tight legs, and his weskit very much buttoned, and his mouth very much shut, and his coat a-flying open, and his heels a-giving it to the platform, is a crikit and beeographer and our principal tragegian."

Her view of the theatricals was moderate

> " 'how did the Creatures get thro' it?' *Too well* and *not well enough!* . . . Forster as Kitely and Dickens Captain Bobadil were much on a par—but Forster preserved his identity even thro' his loftiest flights of *Macreadyism*, while poor little Dickens all painted in black and red, and affecting the voice of a man of six feet, would have been unrecognisable for the Mother that bore him!"

She was more interested in an encounter she had there:

> "Passing thro' a long dim passage I came on a tall man leant to the wall with his head touching the ceiling like a *Caryatid*—to all appearance *asleep*, or resolutely *trying* it under most unfavourable circumstances! '*Alfred* Tennyson' I exclaimed in joyful surprise. 'Well!' said he, taking the hand I held out to him and *forgetting* to let it go again. 'I did not know you were in town' said I. 'I should like to know—who you are!' said he— 'I *know* that I *know* you but cannot tell your name!' And I had actually to name myself to him. Then he *woke up* in good earnest, and said he had been meaning and was still meaning to come to Chelsea. 'But Carlyle is in Scotland,' I told him with due humility. 'So I heard from Spedding already, but I asked Spedding would he go with me to see Mrs Carlyle and he said he would.' "

Jane was still disbelieving, but the very next evening

> "Alfred Tennyson—*alone!!!* Actually, by a superhuman effort of volition he had *put himself* into a cab—nay *brought himself* away from a dinner party, and was there to smoke and talk with *me!*—by myself *me!* But no such blessedness was in store for him. . . . He staid till eleven, Craik *sitting him out* as he sat out Lady Harriet and would sit out the Virgin Mary and *Monsieur son Fils* should he find them here."

The house was still topsy-turvy when Milnes called, and, going on to Bath House, mentioned the state of confusion Jane was in. The next day came a note from Lady Harriet, followed by her brougham. Jane—"guy ticht aboot the *head*; I *think* I had on *my new bonnet*"—went off on her first visit to Bath House. She found Lady Harriet "very gracious and agreeable." They talked over the theatricals: "It seems that a great many of the

aristocracy assisted at that Tom-foolery. . . . I thought it rather
'a rum-looking' gathering"—discussed the books they were
reading, and enjoyed a little gossip about Tennyson.

> "Lady Harriet told me that he wants to marry; 'must have a woman
> to live beside—would *prefer a Lady*, but—cannot *afford* one—and so must
> marry a maid-servant.' Mrs Henry Taylor said she was about to write
> him on behalf of their housemaid, who was quite a superior character in
> her way."

Lady Harriet pressed Jane to spend the winter by the sea—at
Bay House:

> "On the whole our interview went off quite successfully; and I dare
> say in spite of Mrs Buller's predictions we shall get on very well together—
> altho' I can see that the Lady has a genius for *ruling*—whilst I have a
> genius for—*not being ruled!*"

This, to Carlyle; to Jeannie she was more candid:

> "More than *gracious! incomprehensible* upon *my* honour! She insisted that
> I had promised to 'give her *my whole winter* at Alverstoke!'—and yet I
> have an unconquerable persuasion that she does not and never can
> like me!"

Carlyle, trying in vain to find rest at Scotsbrig—"cocks, pigs,
calves, dogs, clogs of women's feet, creaking of door hinges,
masons breaking whinstone, and carts loading stones" were his
main bogeys—approved the visit.

> "The Lady Harriet has a genius for ruling. Well! I don't know but
> she may; and, on the whole, did you ever see any lady that had *not* some
> slight touch of a genius that way, my Goodikin? I know a lady—but I
> will say nothing, lest I bring mischief about my ears."

But he was alarmed about the suggestion to winter at Alverstoke:
"If you promised Lady Harriet to 'stay the whole Winter', there
will be no possibility of keeping such a promise!"

He had no wish, when it came to the point, to be long away
from his home—the only place where his comfort was considered to the exclusion of all else. He chiefly enjoyed his talks
with Lady Harriet at Bath House, where he was free to come
and go as he pleased, where he had the illusion of doing good,
and from which he returned with a mental exhilaration and
confidence by no means illusory. For all his professed realism,
he was essentially a romantic; no doubt much of his pleasure in
the relationship with Lady Harriet came from the parallel he

could draw between it and the Elizabethan poet-courtier with
his Gloriana. Hence the salutations with which his letters to her
are sprinkled—"My Beneficent!" "Adieu my Sovereign Lady!"
"Oh my Queen!"—and his obeisances—"Yours to Command"
"Your Noble Ladyship's obedient servant." This contact with a
brilliant mind so unlike his own, yet which he could meet on
equal terms, restored a confidence so often weakened by
unavailing hours in the library at Cheyne Row, and he came
home the better able to think clearly and work well. But days
or even weeks at The Grange or Bay House in the midst of a
large company were another matter. There, he had little
chance of the talks he appreciated so much; Lady Harriet was
then the hostess, her time given to all her guests—and given, he
felt, unworthily; for although his vanity was touched by his
position as lion of the gathering, he could not disguise his sense
that such parties were merely killing time, and that their hostess
was the most adept at this pastime. If Jane became intimate
with Lady Harriet, a prospect opened out of endless weeks of
such futility, and of fewer quiet talks at Bath House. Moreover,
his wife and Lady Harriet were, he feared, too similar in
temperament, in ability, in ambition, to spend much time
together without friction—"the whole winter", for example.
Jane reassured him:

> " 'If I promised to spend the whole Winter with Lady Harriet!' Bah!
> When did you know me to do anything so green—so *pea-green* as *that*? *She
> told me* I had promised it formerly; that was all. . . . I have already taken.
> in a bit of my ground *very* wisely, in stipulating that when I *did* next visit
> her I should have some little closet 'all to myself' to sleep in."

Before she and Carlyle went to Bay House—"a large
fantastical looking *New* Building on the shore of the Sea"—in
the middle of November, she had arranged that they should
have separate rooms; there was, otherwise, no hope of sleep for
either of them. At the last moment, the Paulets came down to
London unexpectedly—Mr Paulet was to have an eye operation
—and Jane felt unable to leave Chelsea and them at such a
time. Mrs Paulet, as her daughter Julia told Jane, "always
seems to think you are some kind of an angel married to some
kind of a god," and Jane was by no means willing to allow such
a reputation to fall for the sake of Lady Harriet. At the eleventh
hour "in rushed Mrs Paulet fresh and rosy like a lump of coral"

to say that the operation was postponed until the new year, and that they were on their way home at once. The Bay House plans were resumed. No definite answer had been given to the "whole winter" proposal but, says Jane, "I fancy Carlyle's need to be ugly and stupid and disagreeable without restraint (never to speak of my own) will send us back to London in a month or two." In fact they were back at the end of December, Jane the better in health for her weeks of sea air and good food: "not so much *dressing* as *you* have to transact in Maryland Street—rational hours—and no strain on one's wits—for Lady Harriet *does* all the wit herself".

Of Lady Harriet, she had at first little but good to say; she was

> "kind as possible and has not done said or looked a single thing since I have lived beside her to justify the character for haughtiness and caprice which she bears in Society—in fact a woman more perfectly regardless of *rank* I never happened to see. . . . In fact she is a *grand* woman every inch of her—and *not* 'a coquette' the least in the world—if all the men go out of their sober senses beside her how can she help *that?*"

But she remained cautious:

> "I am sure I shall never feel *warm affection* for her nor inspire her with warm affection—her intercourse will remain *an honour for me*, never be a heartfelt delight—as it might be if she were as loving as she is charming."

Of her hostess' manner of life she was critical. Both she and Carlyle were thoroughly tired of what she called "*strenuous Idleness*" and he "*Do-nothingism*"—"the prospect of such a thing *for life* was absolutely equal to death." Jane, sending her usual end of the year letter and gifts to Mrs Russell, explained

> "Six weeks have I been doing absolutely nothing but playing at battledore and shuttlecock—chess—talking nonsense—and getting rid of a certain fraction of this mortal life as *cleverly* and uselessly as possible. . . . This Lady Harriet Baring whom we have just been staying with is the very cleverest woman—out of sight—that I ever saw in my life . . . yet so perverted has she been by the training and life long humouring incident to her high position that I question if in her *whole life* she have done as much for her fellow creatures as *my mother* in *one year*. . . . The sight of such a woman should make one very content with one's own trials even when they feel to be rather hard!"

Carlyle had been "as cross as the Devil" since their return, for the curious reason, she thought, that *Cromwell* had sold out and a new edition was needed. This involved the addition of many letters and gave him a great deal of work, lasting well into 1846. It also brought him more money, an even greater increase in reputation—he was now one of the most talked-of men of letters in Europe—and preserved him from the idleness he dreaded. However, he grumbled—as much out of habit as anything else.

The Paulets came up to London again, the operation was a success, and "Julia has *come out* poor child! with a proviso that she is to *go in* again on her return home". Old Sterling was always calling, as dependent on her as ever. Garnier, sane again, came in from time to time to see Jane and "to take Carlyle to bathe him and give him a swim" but Carlyle "had fortunately gone to ride." Gambardella had installed a telescope in his studio and carried Jane off to see a comet. But she was preoccupied by Lady Harriet, who had suggested a winter in Rome the following year and, when she returned to London, sent a carriage to Cheyne Row to fetch Jane to Bath House for an evening every week or so. Finally, in the spring, seeing that, after a tolerable winter, Jane's health was again beginning to fail, she insisted on a month at Addiscombe.

Jane did not know what to make of all this. Lady Harriet was most considerate; her manner, when she chose, was fascinating; and Jane's own feelings fluctuated wildly:

> "for my part I *love* her now as much as I *admired* her in the beginning. She is the only woman of *genius* I have found amongst all our pretenders to it—I only wish I had got to know her twenty years ago when I was better capable of enjoying the advantages of such an acquaintance."

She thought she might enjoy the Addiscombe visit if her hostess kept to her plan that they should stay there alone, to be joined by Baring, Carlyle and Charles Buller at weekends: "but I cannot fancy Lady Harriet anywhere leading *a life of privacy;* however she may propose it to herself". She was frankly puzzled:

> "She is 'a bit of fascination' (as the Countrymen said of '*Taggl*ioni') a very large bit. I profess never to this hour to have arrived at a complete understanding of her—but *that* I fancy is just a part of her fascination—the insoluble psychological puzzle which she is and bids fair to remain for me!"

Before she could get away to Addiscombe, Jane had reached the edge of a nervous breakdown. Sleep left her, she took drugs, again began to fancy herself going mad. Quiet and rest were essential, and at first Addiscombe promised both. Lady Harriet held to her intention of inviting no one but Jane, and old Mrs Carlyle at Scotsbrig was told:

> "I have been here for a week with Lady Harriet Baring whom you have doubtless heard Carlyle speak of with enthusiasm. A very clever woman, and very lovable besides—whom it is very pleasant to live with—if she likes you—and if she does not like you, she would blow you up with gunpowder rather than be bored with your company. So that one clearly understands one's footing beside her."

But Jane was a sick woman, and could by no means be described as stimulating company, especially for a woman who preferred the company of men. After a couple of weeks Lady Harriet began to tire of the tête-a-tête and for the last ten days of Jane's stay the house was filled with people. She returned to Chelsea "with the mind of me all churned into froth." She grew more and more melancholic:

> "*Ach Gott!* if I had not such an eternal hundredweight of leaden thoughts on my heart I might live *pleasantly* as other people do, but once for all, life is *not pleasant* for me and the best I see in it is that it does not last very long."

This depression was emphasised by her reputation as a wit which dogged her wherever she went:

> "I called at the Macreadys the other day—in a humour that a person under sentence of death need hardly have envied. For days and weeks a cheerful feeling had not been in my mind—but of course one does not make calls to show oneself as *a spectacle of wae*. I talked talked—about the feats of Carlyle's horse &c—and they laughed till their tears ran down. *I* could not *laugh*—but no matter—perhaps my own gravity made the things I was saying only more amusing by contrast. By and by Mrs Macready who is in the family-way began to talk of the dreadful 'depression of spirits' she occasionally laboured under. 'Ah said I, everyone I suppose has their own fits of depression to bear up against if the truth were told.' 'Do you say so?' said Miss Macready. 'Oh no surely! some people are never out of spirits—yourself for example, I really believe you do not know what it is to be ever sad for a minute!!! one never sees you that you do not keep one in fits of laughter!' "

Lady Harriet sent her an Indian scarf, and the gift sent Jane into a rhapsody.

> "She would not put an *affectionate* sentence in her letters for the world but she will put *violets*—leaves of the *flowers one likes*—sometimes sends me

envelopes by post containing nothing else!! What a contrast I often think betwixt that woman and Geraldine! the opposite poles of woman-nature!"

Geraldine had been in disgrace for months—ever since Jane succumbed unwillingly to the fascination of Lady Harriet. Her crime was a "blaze of enthusiasm" for Charlotte Cushman, the American actress who had caused a sensation in London by act-ing Romeo to her sister Susan's Juliet. Geraldine's letters, Jane complained, were "filled with lyrics about this woman." Jane, who would have no rival, and to whom Geraldine's devotion did not appear essential at the moment, finally wrote her "such a screed of my mind as she never got before—and which will probably terminate our correspondence—at least till the finale of her friendship for Miss Cushman."

Towards the end of June the weather turned hot, which Jane was no better able to stand than the winter. She felt that she must get away at once. Carlyle, on "desperately bilious days" revived his dream of living in Scotland "in seclusion for his few remaining years"—he was now fifty—and although Jane did not take this too seriously she felt herself "no longer in a *home* but in a *tent* to be struck any day that the commanding officer is sufficiently bilious." The more they talked, the more she became convinced that he would settle nothing until he knew Lady Harriet's wishes. As this thought fastened on her mind, all her admiration for Lady Harriet faded away, all her fear and distrust returned. She accused Carlyle of putting another woman's whims before her own health, insisted that the in-timacy with the Barings must cease, and, early in July, without a friendly word, fled to Seaforth House.

XXVI

THE GRANGE
1846 – 1847

Jane's anger with Carlyle did not outlast more than an hour or two of absence. He once more became blameless and necessary. The fault lay clearly in Lady Harriet, who, not content with a husband and a brilliant retinue, was absorbing Carlyle's time and attention, snatching them from a wife who had particular need of them. So she brooded in her bed at Seaforth House. She felt unequal to a letter when she first arrived, but sent off a marked newspaper in the Carlyle fashion. This only reached Carlyle with the letter she wrote to him the following day. The delay agitated him.

"I hope it is only displeasure or embarrassed estrangement from me, and not any accident or illness of your own, that robs me of a note this morning. I will not torment myself with that new uneasiness. But you did expressly promise to announce your arrival straightway. This is not good: but perhaps an unfriendly or miserable letter would have been worse, so I will be as patient as I can. Certainly we never parted before in such a manner; and all for—literally nothing. . . . Yesterday I suppose you fancied me happy at Addiscombe. Alas! I was in no humour for anything of that laughing nature. . . . Adieu, dearest—for that is, and if madness prevail not may for ever be, your authentic title."

The next day he read both letter and newspaper, and all was well. But his agitation was as nothing to the frantic outburst of Jane a few days later, on the morning of her forty-fifth birthday, when no letter from Carlyle could be found. It arrived two hours after the usual time—two hours, said Jane, of "suffocating misery". She walked back from the post office, where she had gone to fetch the letter,

"with such a tumult of wretchedness in my heart as you who know me can conceive. And then I shut myself in my own room to fancy everything that was most tormenting—were you finally so out of patience with me

335

that you had resolved to write to me no more at all?—had you gone to Addiscombe and found no leisure *there* to remember my existence? Were you taken ill so ill that you *could* not write? That last idea made me mad to get off to the railway, and back to London—oh mercy what a two hours I had of it!"

Carlyle in his birthday letter had assured Jane that "thou art dearer to me than any earthly creature".

"I wonder" Jane added in her reply "what *love-letter* was ever received with such thankfulness! Oh my dear I am not fit for living in the world with this organisation—I am as much broken to pieces by that little accident as if I had come thro' an attack of Cholera or Typhus fever. I cannot even steady my hand to *write* decently. But I felt an irresistible need of thanking you, by return of post . . . oh why can I not believe it once for all—that with all my faults and follies I *am* 'dearer to you than any earthly creature'."

Seaforth House, as this letter indicates, had done her little good. She was eating but not sleeping, and her thoughts remained morbid. For the first time she began to criticise Mrs Paulet, reading a lack of consideration into her concern, and lack of method into her deliberate suspension of household order on her guest's behalf. She went for an excursion or two, talked brilliantly at dinner, allowed herself to be petted by Mrs Paulet and Geraldine, read the manuscript of Geraldine's new novel, but spent most of her time in her room, coughing, retching, blinded by headache, brooding.

Before leaving London she had dashed off a few lines to Mazzini. Her life was empty, impossible, she could see no point in living, she was going away and did not know when she would be back. Mazzini could only repeat what he had told her again and again:

"none can help you but yourself. It is only you who can, by a calm, dispassionate, fair re-examination of the past, send back to nothingness the ghosts and phantoms you have been conjuring up. It is only you who can teach yourself that, whatever the *present* may be, you must front it with dignity, with a clear perception of all your duties, with a due reverence to your immortal soul, with a religious faith in times yet to come. . . . I am carrying a burden even heavier than you, and have undergone even bitterer deceptions than you have. . . . Your life proves an empty thing, you say! Empty! Do not blaspheme. Have you never done any good? Have you never loved? Think of your mother and do good."

This could not satisfy her. She wrote again, and again he appealed to her to have faith:

"Don't you think, after all, that this is nothing but an ephemeral trial; and that He will shelter you at the journey's end under the wide wing of his paternal love? You had, have, though invisible to the eyes of the body, your mother, your father too. Can't you commune with them? I know that a single moment of true fervent love for them will do more for you than all my talking!"

The Christian consolation was lost on Jane, the emphasis on death reinforced only too strongly the trend of her thoughts. She was still convinced that her reason was going, and she longed for death. Carlyle tried to dispel her "haggard thoughts" —death was indisputable, but so was life, and life "is our present concern." He begged her "Compose thy poor Soul; and *know well* that to the wise no sorrow is in vain, no sorrow is not precious." This, like the consolation offered by Mazzini, passed over her head; she was in no state to believe anything but her own obsessions. Of more moment were Carlyle's efforts to show that he was trying to carry out her wishes. He had been to Bath House:

"To the lady I have, of course, told nothing, except that you are very unwell. But she seems to have discerned pretty clearly for herself that our intercourse is to be carried on under different conditions henceforth, or probably to cease altogether before long: to which arrangement she gives signs of being ready to conform with fully more indifference than I expected. . . . An opening is left for my meeting them about Carlisle or Edinburgh on their Scotch tour; but it seems to be with little expectation on either side that it will take effect."

A few days later:

"I took leave of the Barings last night. All is handsome and clear there, and nothing is wrong; except *your* and my ill-genius may still force it to be so a little. To the lady I 'said' simply nothing; and her altered manner, I suppose, might proceed altogether from the evident chagrin and depression of mine. Was that unnatural in me? In fact, I myself was heartily weary of a relation grown so sad, and in my mind almost repented that it had ever been. But you may take it as a certainty, if you like, that there is no unkindness or injustice harboured to you there. . . . My relation to her is but a very *small* element in her position, but a just and laudable one, and I wish to retain that if I can and give it up if I cannot. *Voilà tout!* Oh, Goody dear! be wise, and all is well."

This reassurance did something to soothe her; and when he,

having sent off the second edition of *Cromwell*, spent a few days
with her on his way to Annandale and to Duffy and his friends
in Ireland he found her somewhat better, as he in his own way
told Lady Harriet:

> "It is one of the most perfect Castles of Indolence this; a spacious
> square mansion, with verandahs, with quiet lawns, and trees or at least
> bushes all round; rocked by the softest western breezes under grey warm
> skies, and the perpetual humming lullaby of seas and woods, all day and
> all night. . . . Last Wednesday this day week, late, past midnight, while
> you were at Lansdown House, all radiant to see and beautiful there, I,
> very ugly at Chelsea, amid my packages and lonesome wrecks, wrote you
> a note: but that also you never heard of; I put it straightway in the fire,
> and went to sleep in silence. O daughter of Adam most beautiful; O son
> of Adam, in several respects, most unbeautiful! But the essential thing is
> to tell you that my wife is considerably better, and still in the way of
> improving; that she means to continue here for certain weeks yet, and
> then proceed to East Lothian (Haddington) before she return. We have
> talked of you: do not suppose that she does other, or ever did other, than
> respect and even love you, tho' with some degree of terror, baseless I do
> believe. Adieu dear Lady mine, *mine* yet, and yet forever no!"

Jane did not find him easy going: "For a week" she told
Forster, "I had my hands full! That man is worse to provide for
than a whole family of small children!"

Much of this was merely her way—long since grown a
habit—of complaining humorously of Carlyle's foibles. Unfortunately, he had to tell her before he left that the Barings
were after all expecting to meet him at Carlisle, and to make a
short excursion with him before going into the Highlands. This
threw her into a passion; again she upbraided him, would not
listen to anything he had to say, and refused to consider joining
the party. He left her early in August a good deal worse than he
found her. "I do not remember" he wrote on arrival at Scotsbrig "a more miserable set of hours for most part than those
since I left you. . . . Oh, my dearest, how little I *can* make thee
know of me!"

He tried again to reassure her. The weather had been bad,
and the Barings might still decide not to come:

> "How incredible is it to my poor little Jeannie, and yet how certain
> in fact, that an intimation to that effect would be among the *gladdest* I
> could get in a small way during these days! I will write to the lady
> tomorrow that I am here according to engagement, but of invitation to
> her I cannot have much."

He wrote to Lady Harriet:

> "My poor Jane is fallen rather worse again; she is still at Seaforth;
> has an uncle and then 'Zoe' to visit before leaving that region: she is, as
> you may fancy, the weightiest item of my cares at present." He added:
> "if I do not hear from you again . . . I mean to be in Carlisle waylaying
> you."

He still did not hear from Jane, and grew uneasy:

> "Write to me as briefly as vou like—but write. There can be no
> propriety in punishing me by such feelings as *these* are. It is like seething
> a kid in its mother's milk. If I cared less about you, the punishment would
> be less. It is not fair or right. . . . Oh, if you could look into my heart of
> hearts, I do not think you could be angry with me, or sorry for yourself
> either!"

On the day he set off for Carlisle to meet the Barings—eight
days after leaving Seaforth House—he still had heard nothing.
He began to grow angry:

> "It is not right, my poor dear Jeannie! it is not just nor according to
> *fact;* and it deeply distresses and disturbs me. . . . This, however, I will
> say and repeat: 'The annals of insanity contain nothing madder than
> "jealousy" directed against such a journey as I have before me today.' . . .
> Oh, my Jeannie! my own true Jeannie! bravest little life-companion,
> hitherto, into what courses are we tending? God assist us both, and keep
> us free of frightful Niagaras and temptations of Satan. I am, indeed, very
> miserable. My mother asks: 'No word from Jane yet?' And, in spite of
> her astonishment, I am obliged to answer: '*None*'."

The outing, to Moffat, was a failure. The weather was bad,
the accommodation worse—"noisy cabins" and "confused
whisky inns"—Lady Harriet was in bad humour, Carlyle
worried, irritable and "half distracted"; only Baring kept
cheerful throughout. Before returning to Scotsbrig, Carlyle
persuaded Lady Harriet to write to Jane: "The only check to
our felicity" she said "has been the missing you." She was sorry
to hear of Jane's continued ill health, but reproached her: "You
are very, very foolish to go on without some trial, at least, of
advice and remedies." She invited her to Bay House in November, where "we shall improve and take still further care of you."
This note, commented Jane contemptuously, did not seem to
want an answer.

At Scotsbrig, Carlyle found that he had just missed a letter,
which had remained there almost the entire five days he had

been away. Another had followed it, and a third came soon afterwards. She had not written earlier, Jane explained, because "I *could* not write any letter that you would not have found worse than none—and—so you got none!" After he had gone, everything, even the unpleasantness of their parting, had given way to "the only thing like a purpose that would stay one instant in my mind"—to get away from Seaforth House.

> "That great echoing, disorganised place had got to look to me a perfect madhouse; and Betsy, with her fixed idea of my 'liver-complaint', and incessant tactless remarks on my 'wild looks' . . . had become more like a tormenting demon for me than the kind friend I had been used to think her."

After some days, she managed to go without hurt feelings on either side to Geraldine at Manchester "with that sort of blind, instinctive seeking for relief which makes sick people turn off one side upon the other."

Geraldine abandoned all ecstasies, was quiet, kind, and full of suggestions that would occupy her guest's mind and time. Her house Jane was surprised to find orderly, quiet, clean; and her plans—to show Jane something of the business life of Manchester—provided exactly the distractions needed. Jane saw Whitworth the machine inventor, Bamford the weaver-poet, factories, printing mills, foundries, until, she said, she was likely to be "as well qualified to write *little books* on the 'Manufacturing Districts' as either Camilla Toulmin or Arthur Helps". These examples of practical life, and the friendliness of the manufacturing people took her thoughts away from herself. She swore "eternal friendship" with Stauros Dilberoglue, "*What* is it?—A man!—a young Greek . . . a sort of young merchant that one might expect to meet in the *Wanderjahre*, but hardly in Manchester." He is "an admirer of yours," she told Carlyle, "but still more, I am afraid, of Emerson's".

She came for two days but stayed a full fortnight and she parted reluctantly from Geraldine, whose delicacy and wise and sympathetic treatment "brought back something like colour into my face and something like calm into my heart—but how long I shall be able to keep either the one or the other when left to my own management God knows, or perhaps another than God knows best." The idea of a visit to Haddington was given up—she could not bear the thought of a place with so many memories. She spent a few duty days at Liverpool, then hurried home, early in September. At first, all was well; she found fresh satisfaction in her house and friends as always after she had been away. Helen had been "most diligent" in her absence, and had left her little to do but "top-dressing". The pianos on each side of Number 5 had been "calmed down and reduced to reason". Mazzini, Elizabeth Pepoli, Robertson, Forster, old Sterling and Anthony had all called, and were exceedingly glad to see her back. The old man, Helen reported, had been for ever calling "in dreadful impatience" to know when she was returning. With Anthony, Jane was on her best behaviour. She agreed to visit the Sterlings' house, but refused in the most exemplary manner to be shown his pictures, to eat, or, indeed, to visit any other room than old Sterling's bedroom. The old man "held my hands and kissed them incessantly, and cried and laughed alternately—the laughing was the dreadfullest part of it—it was so insane".

In October, Carlyle returned from Scotsbrig where he had lain "totally inert" since the disastrous trip to Moffat, "like a dead dry bone bleaching in the silent sunshine." He had been much relieved to hear of Jane's recovery at Manchester: "we will hope all that black business has now got safe into the past, and will not tear up our poor forlorn existence in so sad a way again." But though rested and relieved in mind, he was in no mood to endure one of the now rare London visits of Harriet Martineau, whom he found "broken into utter wearisomeness, a mind reduced to these three elements: Imbecility, Dogmatism, and Unlimited Hope. I never in my life was more heartily bored with any creature."

Jane was, on the whole, well pleased with herself and her Chelsea world, and her ruffled vanity was being satisfactorily smoothed down. Helen's devotion, humour and usefulness were not the least of the blessings she began to count: "she has been growing, like wine, and a few other things, always the better by keeping." She had become so much her companion, so much a part of the household, that it became difficult to remember London days without her. Then Helen's brother appeared suddenly, and wanted to take her back to Dublin with him. He was making money by the manufacture of

"*coach fringes:* thanks to the immense consumption of that article on the railways! He is now by his own showing a regular *gentleman*—so far as money goes!—and has 'two hundred girls in his pay.' He looks—to *me*— a foolish, flustering sort of incredible creature." He had been "seized with a sudden fit of Brotherly love and offers to take her to be '*mistress of his house*' engaging that should he marry at any time he will 'settle a handsome provision on her'."

Helen accepted the offer out of hand—"to be made a lady of all on a sudden, does not fall in one's way every day!"—and Jane, in spite of misgivings, felt that she ought to encourage her to go. She wrote at once to her friends for a maid. Susan Stirling thought she knew of a girl. Jane gives her news of Craik, now forty-eight:

> "He is much changed poor Craik—his red hair turned quite white and allowed to float over his coat-collar like a German student; and his nose very red indeed! but he is the same good soul at heart as ever, bearing up manfully against a weight of domestic trouble that would break the majority of backs, and always ready to lend a helping hand to any one that cannot bear up as well as himself. He is often a living reproach to me."

In the midst of the domestic crisis, at the end of October, Jane, after "packing my clothes and *hiding* my silver spoons" went off with Carlyle to the Barings at The Grange. This was her first visit—and in no respect a welcome one. "The Place is like, not *one*, but a conglomeration of Greek Temples set down in a magnificent wooded Park some five miles in length. The inside is magnificent to death." She was not in her element:

> "We are here professedly on a visit to the Ashburtons—*virtually*, at least so far as Carlyle is concerned, on a visit to Lady Harriet. . . . In all *my* life I never drew my breath in such a racket! . . . It is the ruling Principle of the Host and Hostess to keep the house always full. *We* shall remain till the end of next week and by that time I shall have had enough of it I fancy . . . as you can easily conceive, I feel myself in *a false position*."

She went back to Chelsea after ten days, a good deal the worse for her stay, but having half promised to visit Bay House in the new year—Lady Harriet being determined to make her healthy in spite of herself. A girl had been found in Edinburgh— not by Susan but by Betty Braid. The new girl, Isabella, was a devoted member of the Free Church, and Jane, desperate for help, promised that she could go to church "at least once a day. . . . My Aunt Anne seems to have stuffed her very full of 'free grace' and I should not wonder if she had more of that than of 'works'—but she looks like a person who would fall into no sort of *vice* anyhow."

In a day or two Jane's fears hardened; Isabella, quickly named Pessima, had: "a terror about her work not apparently because *we* should be disappointed if she proved inadequate but because *herself* would be disappointed in the easiness of the place." At this point Jane caught a chill and took to her bed. Helen Welsh was sent for, but Isabella became more sulky and slovenly

"and on the first washing day she burst out on me with a sort of *hysterical* insolence, declared she 'had never been told by anybody that she was to wash'—that 'no woman living could do my work'—and when I told her the answer to *that* was, that it had been *done* by 'one woman' for eleven years without the slightest complaint, she said, almost screamed 'oh yes there are women that *like to make slaves of themselves*, and her you had was of that sort but *I* will never slave myself for anybody's pleasure!' "

Jane told her to go at the end of the month, but after a fortnight

"she sent me word in my bed that if I did not let her go—next day (Sunday!) she '*would take fits* and be *laid up in my house a whole year* as happened to her once before in a place where the work was too hard'. Carlyle told her to go in the Devil's name—and a little more of his mind he told her, which was a satisfaction to me to have said in *his emphatic way* since I was unable to rebuke her myself! . . . When my Dr came the next day he said it was 'well he had not been here at the time, as he would certainly have *dashed her brains out!!*' . . . he could tell by her looks the first day she opened the door to him that she had then or had quite lately had *the green sickness.*"

To Lady Harriet, Carlyle said

"I do not write . . . I cannot. . . . Some Fate seems to prohibit me . . . the sordid smoke of my confusions, why should it blear your bright eyes? You know well, I suppose, that it is not my *blame*—alas, no, not my *blame!* My wife has had a cold, been close confined to her room, mostly to her bed, for three weeks past."

He did not see how Jane could come to Alverstoke, but "I will hope." Since the departure of Helen "the white-bearded Ape" whom Lady Harriet had seen, "we have had nothing but a similitude of servants. . . . And a young cousin is here, a thin well-meaning *Liverpool fine lady.*"

The "similitude", after Isabella, consisted of an "old half-dead *cook*". Jane, living in her bedroom and the library, and resigned to spending the rest of the winter between the two rooms, interviewed a number of women, and at last settled with

> "a cheery little *button* of a creature with a sort of cockney resemblance to Helen . . . 'she had *only one Lover* who came to see her and *one female friend*' (happy little woman!) both highly respectable and not too troublesome."

Carlyle gave her a pleasant surprise at Christmas by defying his dislike, his almost terror, of shops to buy her a cloak:

> "he was much consoled by my assurance that *it could be worn*. He had bought it 'by *gas light*' he said and 'felt quite desperate about it when he saw it in the morning.' But it is a wonderful cloak for *him* to have bought —warm, and not *very* ugly—and a good shape—only entirely unsuitable to the rest of my habiliments! being a *brownish colour* with *orange spots* and a brown velvet collar!!"

The new girl, another Anne, came on the last day of the year. She showed herself willing, and Jane began to recover slightly. But only slightly; and Carlyle had to tell Lady Harriet early in January, 1847, that she could not come to Bay House as he had hoped. She was still very feeble and never went down stairs. "Of you," he added "I think as of the beautifullest creature in all this world; divided from me by great gulphs forever more." Lady Harriet did not relish refusals. She was still determined to rescue Jane from herself, and she was even more determined to enjoy the company of Carlyle. She obtained her way with some skill, telling Carlyle that he could not come to Bay House without Jane, as there would be no other people in the house except at weekends. This at one stroke made Jane feel "too *proud* to stand in the way", and assured her that she would not be bothered, as at The Grange, with hordes of visitors. At the end of January she left her sickroom and, to her astonishment, "worn out by *the violence of my emotions*", slept soundly in the train on her way to Bay House. She also had to admit that she was received "with a certain recognition of my *weak* state— hardly to have been hoped from her".

Before many days had passed, she had to admit still more. Lady Harriet pressed her to stay on; Carlyle, she said, could go back to London if he wished, but "*he might really spare me a while*

THE NEW LADY ASHBURTON AND HER DAUGHTER
from a painting by Landseer, 1861

LADY HARRIET BARING
from an engraving by Francis Holl

LORD ASHBURTON
from a painting by Landseer, 1861

for my good". She abandoned the study of German, which Carlyle had been teaching her, and, perhaps most gratifying of all, she was paying "marked attentions" to a new pet—"the Parrot does not mind interrupting *him* when he is speaking—does not fear to *speak thro' him* (as the phrase is) and her Ladyship *listens to the parrot*—even when Carlyle is saying the most sensible things!" This was reassuring and also put ideas into the head of Jane, who hitherto had respected Carlyle's right to dominate the conversation. Lady Harriet's personality was too strong for a sick woman to resist:

> "By Heaven she is *the very cleverest* woman I ever saw or heard of. *She can do what she wills with her own*—I am perfectly certain there is not a created being alive whom she could not gain within twenty-four hours after she set her mind to it. Just witness myself—how she plies *me* round her little finger whenever she sees that I am taking a reactionary turn."

Her view changed when she felt unwell:

> "So long as you can keep on foot, and play your part as an agreeable—at lowest a *not boring* member of society you are treated with courtesy . . . but fall ill—have to take to bed—and you are lost! The Lady never comes near you—the housemaids do not find it *in their department* to look after sick visitors—you are like an unfortunate toppled over in the treadmill—in danger of perishing there while the general business—or rather I should say *amusement* of the house rushes on over your body!"

But on the whole she had to admire her hostess and her treatment of Carlyle: "I cannot make out what Lady Harriet is after —but to look at her one would say she was systematically *playing my cards for me*."

After rather more than a month—most of which had been free from a flood of guests—Jane went back to Chelsea better in health than she had left it. She still did not understand Lady Harriet although her feelings against her had been lulled. But she felt weary and dispirited and borne down by an obsession that was scarcely to be avoided until she had passed through her long period of physical and mental disturbance. This obsession was the common one in women at this time of their lives—that they are useless to their husband, that their marriage has been a mistake. She had no long history of satisfactory sexual life to give her confidence when most needed. On the contrary, for years past her behaviour and her erratic health had been that of a frustrated woman. Such women blame themselves at heart, whatever they may say, and there is no reason to suppose Jane an exception. Carlyle's apparent determination to continue his friendship with Lady Harriet in the face of her disapproval and his own assurances seemed additional, incontrovertible proof that she had failed him. The contrast between Lady Harriet and herself was now too marked to be ignored, and underlined her own limitations. Lady Harriet, she told herself, had the vitality and charm and wit that Carlyle demanded and which she lacked. Every time she looked in a mirror, she could find reason why no man, not even Carlyle, could be interested in a woman so prematurely aged—her skin sallow and lined, her eyes disfigured by heavy shadows. She did Carlyle less than justice, but justice did not flourish in her state of mind. She felt old and tired, she was always ailing, and she brooded on the causes.

She did more than brood, she began to speak to others than the one or two—Mazzini, Jeannie and Geraldine in particular —in whom she had so far confided. Even Caroline Fox, no more than an acquaintance, was given a long history of her past when she called at Chelsea in May. By this time, Jane in self protection had persuaded herself that she had not really wanted to marry Carlyle. They were made for independence, she said, and would probably never have wished to live together, but their intimacy was not considered discreet in Haddington, so they had to marry. She had said much the same thing to Jeannie:

> "in virtue of his being *the least unlikable* man in the place, I let him dance attendance on my young person, till I came to *need* him—all the same as my slippers to go to a ball in, or my bonnet to go out to walk. When I finally agreed to marry him, I *cried* excessively and felt excessively shocked—but if I had then said *no* he would have left me—and how could I dispense with what was equivalent to my slippers or bonnet?"

At the end of the month Geraldine was to come for her second stay at Chelsea. Mazzini "first stared, then said 'Well! after then I come for ten minutes only!' and then, looking into the fire, gave a long, clear whistle!" But this was poor comfort, for Geraldine was not the danger but Eliza Ashurst, who had "sworn eternal friendship" with Geraldine in Manchester earlier that year and was not to be mentioned in Jane's hearing.

Jane professed, and no doubt believed, that Geraldine "will right herself at last." But the Ashursts had now laid a finger on a more precious possession. Mazzini, Jane reported bitterly, was

"not so solitary as he used to be—having got up to the ears in a *good* twadly family of the name of Ashurst—who have plenty of money—and help 'his *things*' and *toady* him till I think it has rather gone to his head. A Miss Eliza Ashurst—who does strange things—made his acquaintance first—by going to his house to drink tea with him all alone, &c, &c!! and when she had got him to *her* house she introduced him into innumerable other houses of her kindred—and the women of them paint his picture—and send him flowers—and *work* for his bazaar—and make verses about him—and Heaven knows what all—while the men give *capital* towards his *Institutions* and adopt 'the new ideas' at his bidding— Miss Ashurst would *marry him* out and out with all the joy in life—but *that* is not in Mazzini's way."

Her reception of Geraldine—"to stay *ten days* she says—but she will stay longer than that I wager"—was therefore chilly, and the most minor offences of the last visit—"Geraldine *would empty the slops!*"—were held against her. But Jane was not proof against adoration. Besides, they were not often left to themselves. As the author of *Zoe*, Geraldine was almost a notoriety. She and Jane breakfasted with Rogers, dined at the Macreadys' with Jenny Lind as one of the guests of honour, attended a ball, and went to a special Sunday breakfast given by Milnes in their honour. Geraldine's joy knew no bounds. They were the only women at the breakfast. She had eight men at table, men on either side of her, men facing her, men everywhere. Jane was not so happy:

"the situation would just have suited Lady Harriet, but me it was too *strong* for—obliged to make conversation with all these men brought to meet us—and obliged at the same time to keep an ear open to what Geraldine was saying to her next neighbour lest she should get on dangerous ground."

But "the chief apprehension which haunted me" was that she should be "mixed up in the minds of these men with *the Chapel scene* and certain other questionabilities in Zoe."

John Carlyle, who had improved, Jane thought, since getting to work on his Dante translation, gave her a rest by showing Geraldine most of the sights. Indeed

"for a few days it looked almost as if he were trying to work himself up

347

into a matrimonial sentiment for her—but she did not play her cards well—she made him take her to too many Plays &c—and John dislikes paying out shillings on all hands—she was becoming rather expensive, and his incipient sentiment was too weakly for bearing up against constant demands on his purse. On the whole I rather imagine no man will ever be found so constituted as to fall in love with Geraldine and think of her as a Wife—which is a pity—as her heart seems to be set on being married to any sort of a male biped who could maintain her—at all risks!"

This "racket" made Jane ill once more; she complained of "a large tumour on her throat" (possibly an enlargement of the thyroid gland), of the heat, of going about "as poor Darley said"—he had died the previous year—"like a serpent trying to stand on its tail." Yet she was still ready to join her friends, to laugh and talk and listen. Nothing, it seemed, short of death could for long keep down the zest for life which again and again lifted her above prostration, sickness, headache, sleeplessness. "Little does one know in this world what will *finish* them or what will *set them up* again. I question if a long course of mercury would have acted so beneficially on my liver as this party." So she had written some years earlier; and the vitality of spirit that put her—"half dead"—into a party dress then, sustained her still. There were visits from Jeffrey, still gay and affectionate, from Irving's old chief, Dr Chalmers, and, by way of John Marshall, from the young Duke of Saxe Weimar, whom she missed by ten minutes, after assuring Marshall at Carlyle's request: "Of course he will be ready to receive his Highness's visit—I may add out of my own head that I will endeavour to *cross* him as little as possible in the morning that you may find him in his gentlest mood."

There were the more regular distractions, such as the weekly visits of Plattnauer, back again, as mad, Jane found, but as devoted as ever. Anne was proving invaluable: "I miss the *enthusiasm*—the *birr* that was in Helen—*the-ready-to-fly-at-every-thing-ness*, but on the other hand things go on equably—without *flare-ups*." She and her butcher-lover were "a *rational* pair, and not likely to marry till he gets a business of his own—and meanwhile it rather pleases me to know of a little *decent* lovemaking going on in the house." Jane's "regulars" were about her as usual, but the moment she was left alone her thoughts returned to Carlyle, Lady Harriet, and her own poor state of health,

Carlyle was complaining less than usual; he was in fair health, he was riding regularly, he was an honoured guest in almost every house he chose to enter, his books were bringing in far more money than he would ever spend, and although he had no book on his mind he was not entirely idle. His tour in Ireland and his concern for the working class in England and Scotland, were in a fair way to producing a new *Chartism*. But he hesitated; were books, pamphlets, of any real use? He thought of setting up a newspaper, he told Lady Harriet. Or why should he not go into Parliament "and then *speak* pamphlets, hot and hot, right from the heart, and burn up the *World-Humbug!*" The Parliament idea was killed by Jane; had he thought, she asked, that Parliament often sat late? No more was heard from Carlyle on this subject, but he had much to read and think about, and remained tolerably calm. Ann's excellent cookery played some part in this, Jane asserted; but Carlyle was also genuinely concerned about her and trying to accommodate himself to her state of health. Nevertheless, said Jane in June, "there is no talk yet of summer schemes—nor will be while Carlyle's *aristocratic* friends are all in town—I see very little of *the* Lady—as usual when she is in her town-house—with plenty of other people to keep her from wearying."

Her forty-sixth birthday was spent by her in tears: "*his* gifts" she says of Carlyle "always distress me more than a scold"; the gifts from Liverpool "brought all sorts of reminiscences of *home* and of Templand along with it"; and

> "a *hat-box* from poor Bölte completed the overthrow of my sensibilities. . . People wonder always why I let myself be bored with that woman, but with all her want of tact in the everyday intercourse of life she manifests a *sentiment* on occasions so delicate and deep that I should be a brute not to be touched by it."

She was, as Carlyle said, "very unwell". She was taking opium for her cough, but this relieved the cough only to disturb her nights. She had nightmares; dreaming in one of them that she was lying on her mother's tombstone carving her own epitaph. Her list of ailments was alarming: "I cannot eat or sleep—can hardly sit upright—and am in a continual high fever—obliged to keep wet cloths on my head all day long."

"In these astonishing circumstances," she said, "Carlyle

declares I absolutely *must* go away—and best to Haddington."
This suggestion merely precipitated "what Darwin calls 'The
5 Cheyne-Row-spring-fever' "—"frantic speculations about
where to go." The decision this time was rather odd. Jane and
Carlyle set out together late in July for Matlock on, as she put
it, "*The Pursuit of the Picturesque under Difficulties.*"

XXVII

W. E. FORSTER AND R. W. EMERSON
1847 – 1848

This was the first time, said Jane, "that we ever figured as declared Tourists. And I fancy we should have broken down in the first blush of the business, but for a special interposition of Providence in the shape of a spirited young Quaker who came to the rescue at Matlock."

The young Quaker was William Edward Forster, a Bradford wool-stapler, and related to the Fox family by whose means he had met John Sterling and, through Sterling, Carlyle. He was a Radical and an enthusiastic reader of Carlyle. Now, hearing that they were in Derbyshire, he rode over and placed himself at their service.

Rarely had the Carlyles been so glad to see anybody as they were to see this tall young man bound—for he never just walked —into their hotel and hail them with a certain assured reverence. Jane was feeling ill, rather worse than she had felt in London, and spent most of the day in her bedroom; the hotel food was disagreeing with Carlyle; both were utterly bored with the hotel life and people; Carlyle had shown no sign of being able or even willing to arrange the necessary excursions; and the tour was plainly foundering before it had rightly begun.

Into this state of suspended animation Forster blew like a fresh breeze. Difficulties vanished. He would arrange everything, would show them the best parts of Derbyshire in a few days, and, if they would honour him, take them over to his new home at Rawdon, where they could have more excursions or perfect quiet just as they pleased and for as long as they pleased.

Jane, who liked the look and sound of the young man, accepted the offer out of hand. She recovered so quickly that the first tour was made that very day—a drive and picnic in Dove-dale. The next day Forster took them to Haddon Hall and Buxton, and by the evening everyone was feeling well satisfied. Jane, reported Forster, was "like a girl in her delight in new scenes and situations, and the master uncommonly good-humoured and accommodating." His frank but far from un-critical admiration was not displeasing to Carlyle, who had no use for sycophancy; and Jane, who had a weakness for tall, plain-speaking men, was basking under his attentions. He was a trifle absent-minded, which did not lessen his charm, he was careless in his dress, which she forgave, and he had a most un-Quakerlike humour which sent her into fits of laughter. She heard all about him. He was twenty-nine, unmarried, well-to-do, it was his habit to leap up the steps of the Bradford Wool Exchange, he had a fine new house on the hill above the River Aire. She began to feel young again.

Their contentment was not disturbed by the "rich scene" that evening. At dinner in their Buxton hotel, Carlyle and Jane, sitting on one side of Forster, faced "a tall, starched gentle-manly Irish Parson". The state of Ireland came into the con-versation, and Carlyle began to argue with the parson, then to declaim. "How they did stare," Forster reported, "All other speech was hushed; some looked aghast, others admiring." Carlyle was finally persuaded out of the room, leaving the parson shattered and the entire company lost in amazement. Carlyle would not divulge his name, in spite of Forster's proposal to Jane "to save our expenses by showing him at so much a head."

This kind of thing endeared Forster to Jane, and did him no harm with Carlyle; and as he was discovering that "they have both of them so much real heart and genial kindness about them that I shall form a decided friendship with them," they all left in good spirits the next morning for the Peak and Castleton. Here the harmony of the party suffered a setback. Forster, noting that "it's little notion of a Sunday they have" success-fully "deluded them into a Methody meeting-house, for which I did catch it afterwards. It was a sad failure, a local preacher full of fluent cant." Carlyle was furious; the Methodist belief, if they had any, he declared, was in "a heaven of lubber-land, a paradise of Burton ale and greasy cakes." Forster found that

Carlyle "constantly utters shocks to all one's ideas and principles . . . but it is no use arguing with him as he takes no notice."

This incident brought back much of Jane's nerviness. She was in no state to stand "explosions", and she scarcely slept that night. Plans for further tours were given up, and Forster drove his "distinguished company" through Sheffield to Rawdon. "I suppose" he said "they will soon find it unbearably dull and take themselves off." But he was mistaken. Carlyle, whom he supplied with a horse, a good library, plenty of cigars and well-cooked food, was content to ride and laze about. As for Jane: "I never enjoyed a visit so much before; and so far as I can dive into the secret of my contentment, it lies in the fact of there being no *women* in the house, except servants!"

This was right enough as far as it went, but Jane did not mention the main cause of her satisfaction, Forster himself. It was not only that she liked him—"he's the sort of person that would have suited me very well," she said of him later—but that his admiration could not have come at a better moment. She had many good friends in London—men more devoted to her than W. E. Forster, and for whom she felt more affection—but their feeling for her could always be attributed in her mind to their earlier knowledge of her, when she was livelier, better to look at, in every way more attractive. She could not decide how large a part loyalty now played in their affection. But with this young man no such possibility arose. He liked her for what she was at that moment, a sick woman of forty-four, and looking even older when her face was not animated. She had not lost her charm, that was clear—some such assurance she had craved and Forster supplied it. She began to sleep well, eat well, look well. And even when she was "pitched head over heels" out of the gig, she remarked merely, "I have felt rather better for the tumble."

This accident increased Forster's admiration. The horse galloped, but Jane "behaved with wonderful presence of mind." She and Forster drove about, played chess, talked interminably, and after ten days he was writing "Carlyle and his wife are still with me, and seem to take to Rawdon kindly." Carlyle was at that moment "busy sleeping." Jane was in better health, and "a most pleasant companion she is. I have formed quite a friendship with her, and I trust with him too."

Milnes came over for a day:

"a pleasant companionable little man, well-fed and fattening; with some
small remnant of poetry in his eyes and nowhere else, delighting in
paradoxes, but good-humoured ones; defending all manner of people and
principles in order to provoke Carlyle . . . reminding me of a naughty boy
rubbing a fierce cat's tail backwards, and getting on between furious
growls and fiery sparks."

When the Carlyles finally left in the first week of September,
Forster missed them a great deal:

"His holiness and I have got on remarkably well these last few days,
quite lovingly, and before leaving he actually committed some pretty
speeches to the effect that they had 'reason to be thankful for three
pleasant peaceful weeks.' "

Carlyle was, he found, a "most delightful companion" although
he could well see "what a fearful, fiend-like creature he would
be in his dark moods, when the devil of dyspepsia is upon him,
without the merciful safety-valve of humour". For Jane he had
nothing but praise. He found her "one of those few women to
whom a man could talk all day, or listen all day, with equal
pleasure." With her eyes always open for new pets, difficult ones
if possible, she took with her "a wild, furious, spit-fire of a
kitten, out of which she has been seduously and most vainly
trying to 'love the devil' *à la* Emerson. She begged me for a
name, and so I have suggested 'Quack' as short for Quaker."

After a typical comedy on the railway platform at Leeds,
when Jane sailed away without saying goodbye while Carlyle
vainly ordered the train to stop, she reached Mrs Paulet's
brother at Barnsley. She enjoyed herself there, in spite of "one
of my very worst fainting headaches" after visiting two large
factories and taking a long drive. She had to be carried to bed
"where I lay in what they took for a last agony."

By the second week in September she was home again, clean-
ing, sorting drawers and cupboards, and painting. She returned
to find that old Sterling had died the previous week. The week
before his death

"he had insisted on having himself brought in the carriage to this door,
tho' even then he was *speechless!* Anne said it was the saddest thing she
ever saw—he waved to her to come to him and made signs as if he were
leaving a message for me—pointed repeatedly to his lips and then to the
house and then shook his head with tears running down."

Carlyle, following Jane's example of the previous year, was shown round Manchester before going on to Annandale. Much of what he saw troubled him. She had flourished on her excursions. He could not visit prisons, factories, mills, and come away untouched, seeing the quaint, the fantastic, but rarely the human side of it. She was kind—few more so—when she met trouble singly, in recognisable form; he saw it as now, in the mass: "The mills! oh the fetid, fuzzy, ill-ventilated mills!" He could not forget what he saw, writing to Jane in a way that gave her "the feeling of a letter written out of Hades".

After a day or two setting the latest "earthquake" in motion, she announced her return to John Forster in a characteristic note:

> "Here I am then! . . . I believe besides *you*, there is still a *man*, or perhaps *two* of my acquaintance left. But I feel so mesmerised by the silence and the *dimness* that I have no power to announce my return. Write to me. I am prepared for anything."

Forster called—"very *fat*"—and promised "by all that was sacred" to read with her the manuscript of Geraldine's second novel *The Half-Sisters*, "*trusting in God* that on that night he should find me in good voice." Were there "any *books*—anything *on earth*"—that she wished? He would send them tomorrow. But she went herself to the London Library, now flourishing, and brought back some parts of *Vanity Fair* which she thought "beats Dickens out of the world". Anthony Sterling was still calling, but Mazzini had suddenly grown mysterious; revolution was in the air, he had for some time been expecting to be summoned at an hour's notice, but as no news had come he intended to go to Paris for a month "into the valley of Madame Sand". Would he put himself at the disposal of the Pope? Jane asked. No, he wanted to organise and lead an expedition into Lombardy, which would be "*better than being an individual under the Pope*." In this, Jane told Carlyle, "seemed to me to lie the whole secret of Mazzini's *failed life*". She was watching from her window certain "brick fabrics" being built before a neighbour's house. What could they mean? She told the workmen that she thought they must be mad to build such senseless objects. They agreed, but the building went on, and eventually declared itself a brick porch.

355

John Carlyle reminded Jane "of the grey chicken at Craigen-puttock, that went about for *six weeks* cackling over its first egg. If everybody held such a racket over his *book* as *he* over this *Dante* of his the world would be perfectly uninhabitable." But she was glad enough of him in a day or two, when she developed "some sort of a bilious or nervous fever". He read to her whilst she lay in bed, and called regularly to see how she was. And a servant in the next house silenced the pianos by telling the pianists that Mrs Carlyle was at death's door.

Then Lady Harriet called—"she would not of course venture into a sick room"—and invited her to Addiscombe. Jane accepted at once "as I always do every kindness she offers." But she was not at all pleased when told that Lady Harriet had spoken of her *"unheard-of imprudence"* in diet.

This was a pointer to her treatment at Addiscombe. Lady Harriet had long thought that Jane coddled herself; they drove there in an open carriage, preparing Jane for spartan treatment, and when there, complained Jane, "she made a point of ignoring the fact that anything ailed me. I fancy it must be one of her notions about me that I am hypochondriacal and to be made well by being treated as tho' there was not a doubt of it." She adds: "When I look at my white white face in the glass I wonder how anyone can believe I am *fancying*." As the visit lasted only four days, the effects were not serious either way; Jane thought herself "a little stronger;" but she reported with pleasure a week later that during a call from Lady Harriet "I could not but think from her manner that day that she had bethought her I had been rather roughly handled on my last visit."

By this time Jane was certainly in spirits, though she did not know whether this was due to her "monarch of all I survey" feeling on returning home, or to the after-effects of her stay at Addiscombe, or to the "splendid *soirées*" given by the Hunts who, in one of their sudden bursts of prosperity, came back for a moment into the picture. Most probable of all as reason was the imminent return of Carlyle and a promised visit from Emerson for which, though still weak, she was preparing in spasmodic bursts of energy:

"When Mrs Piper came this morning and found me on *the steps* she looked quite aghast and said 'you *will* lay yourself up again'! 'Not a bit'

I told her 'I feel quite strong today'—'I am afraid Mam' suggested the little woman 'it is not *strength* but *the false excitement* of Mr Carlyle coming home'! Anne remarked 'whatever it was, it was no use stopping Mrs if she had any thing on her mind. She was *an example*'! She 'wondered whether there was another Lady that could stuff chair-cushions and do *anything* that was needed and be a *Lady* too'! So now I think I am *strong* enough in Anne's respect to even *smoke* in her presence."

Her view of Emerson was scarcely more flattering than her opinion of his work.

"He is come then—is here this Yankee-Seraph!" she told Lady Harriet. "We have seen him 'face to face and (over—)soul to (over—) soul'! For two days I have lived on the *manna* of his speech, and now I have escaped to my bedroom, to *bathe my head* in *cold water*, and report progress to *you*. So far all has gone better than you predicted; they do not *hate* one another *yet;* C still calls Emerson 'a most polite and gentle creature! a man of a really quite Seraphic nature! tho' on certain sides of him overlaid with mad rubbish'—and Emerson still (in confidence to me) calls C 'a good Child (!) in spite of all his deification of *the Positive, the Practical*—most astonishing for those who had first made acquaintance with him in his Books'! *Polite* and *gentle*, this Emerson certainly *is;* he avoids, with a laudable tact, all occasions of dispute, and when dragged into it, by the hair of his head, (morally speaking) he *gives*, under the most provoking contradictions, with the softness of a feather-bed. For the rest, I hardly know what to think of him, or whether I like him or not. The man has *two* faces to begin with which are continually changing into one another like '*dissolving views*', the one young, refined, almost beautiful, radiant with—what shall I say?—'*virtue its own reward*'! the other decidedly old, hatchet-like, crotchety, inconclusive – like an incarnation of one of his own *poems!* In his speech he is not dogmatical the least in the world, nor anything like so *fantastical* as his letters give one to suppose, in fact, except for a few phrases consisting chiefly of odd applications of the words '*beauty*' and '*child*' he speaks simply and clearly, but without any eloquence or warmth. What I should say he failed in is what the Yorkshire Wool-cleaner called '*natur*'—he is *genial*, but it seems to be with his head rather than his heart—a sort of theoretic geniality that (as Mazzini would say) 'leaves me *cold*'. He is perhaps the most *elevated* man I ever saw—but it is the elevation of a *reed*—run all to height without taking breadth along with it. . . . I am sure C is *disappointed*, thinks him, if he would 'tell the truth, and shame the Devil' a man of no sort of significance—but he is still under the restraining grace of Hospitality, and of a *certain* regard to consistency: besides he has had no opportunity of unbosoming himself to me on the subject, as we have literally not been *five minutes* alone together since Emerson arrived: He (Emerson) sits up after me at nights and is down before me in the mornings, till I begin to feel as if I had got the measles or some such thing".

She told Espinasse—still at the British Museum—that Emerson

had no ideas, except mad ones, that he had not got from Carlyle. Espinasse answered disarmingly, "but pray, Mrs Carlyle, *who has?*"

What Carlyle thought of his visitor was expressed to Lady Harriet a few days after Emerson had gone to Manchester.

> "I was torn to pieces, talking with him; for his sad Yankee rule seemed to be, that talk should go on incessantly except when sleep interrupted it: a frightful rule. The man, as you have heard, is not above a bargain; nor, if one will be candid, is he fairly much below it. A pure-minded elevated man; *elevated* but without breadth, as a willow is, as a reed is; no fruit at all to be gathered from him. A delicate, but thin pinched triangular face, no jaws nor lips, lean-hooked nose; face of a *cock:* by none such was the Thames ever burnt! A proud man too; a certain sensitive fastidious *stickishness,* which reminded me of a miniature Washington's, very exotic, tho' Anglo-Saxon enough; rather curious to think of. No getting into any intimacy with him, talk as you will. You have my leave to fall in love with him if you can! And so he plays his part: gone to lecture in Lancashire; to return hither he knows not when: it is privately hoped he may go to Rome! I wish him honestly well, do as I am bound respect him honestly; but *Friends,* it is clear, we can never in this world, to any real purpose, be."

Emerson went to Seaforth House and so did Geraldine, to Jane's annoyance: "Every thing seems on the road to perdition! Here has that little Good-for-nothing streamed off to Seaforth, for no more pressing object than to spend a day under the same roof with the Yankee-Seraph!"

Geraldine, not surprisingly, had to admit failure: "I don't fancy he took to me. I am too tumultuous for him". Her new novel, and particularly her wish to dedicate it to Jane and Mrs Paulet, was causing some perturbation at Chelsea.

> "I do think there is much truth in the *young german* idea that Marriage is *a shockingly immoral Institution* as well as what we have long known it for—an extremely disagreeable one. Please countermand the proofs—for every one that comes occasions a *row.*"

So she told John Forster, but as she read further into the book she found herself forced to agree with Carlyle:

> "This is worse than anything in *Zoe* to my judgment; in fact perfectly disgusting for a young Englishwoman to write—and from Chapman's point of view quite 'unfit for circulation in families'. I would not have such stuff *dedicated to me* as she proposed, for any number of guineas. But I am done with counselling her, her tendency towards the unmentionable is too strong for *me* to stay it."

This is a far cry from the raptures of Haddington days about Rousseau, and it is a little difficult to understand why Geraldine's mild defence of women's right to love freely, yet strictly within the bounds of matrimony, gave such offence. Perhaps the actress heroine reminded Jane unpleasantly of Charlotte Cushman; perhaps her attitude was dictated by the reaction expected from her by Forster; but whatever the cause, the cries of disapproval went on:

" *'Great God!'* (as you say). Is not our young friend 'coming it rather strong?' More *actresses!* more 'hysteric seizures' more of 'all that sort of thing' which played the deuce with her last book! But what can you or I help it; since as herself said of herself long ago, she 'has absolutely no *sense* of *decency!'* What I regret more than the *questionability* of these chapters is the total want of commonsense. But perhaps my illness makes me see things worse than they are. At all events I feel it idle for *me* to protest any more."

Although Jane was again confined to the house with a cough and cold, she bore her affliction with more than common resignation because it enabled her to refuse another pressing invitation to Bay House. She and Carlyle had some hard words about the invitation—Jane was by no means minded to go through a second course of spartan treatment—and about the fact that most of these invitations came through him. "We are all in mud here still" Carlyle told Lady Harriet; "but perhaps you will enlighten us a little. I have no means to write more, and indeed was partly bound, but for the accident (good luck to it!) not to write at all." He strove hard to reconcile the irreconcilable, begging Lady Harriet a few days later: "My Queen! Do not write—or rather do (when you have spirits for it) but not to *me*—and *ignoring* this, never having *received* this! heaven help us."

Jane remained adamant; she was not well enough to go; and in the first days of the New Year, 1848, Carlyle set off by himself. The invitation had been for a month, but he did not enjoy himself; he was "weak and wretched", worried with "the idleness, the folly, the cackling and noise".

"In fact", he told Jane "if it were not for my own consolation—for I know thou lovest me in spite of thy harshnesses and mistrusts—I think I need not have written at all. It seemed to me last night . . . that I had been much better in my own bed at Chelsea."

After he had been there barely ten days Jane tells Forster, not without pleasure:

"Carlyle writes that he is coming home immediately (from Alverstoke) if he did not get rid of a cold which *he* had caught there. An interesting family aint we? and my maid barks like a house-puppie—and my kitten when I saw her last was running at the eyes." She asks casually: "by the way was it not from *you* that I took this cold?"

She was far from being neglected at Cheyne Row, as her account of a single day makes clear. Darwin and Anthony Sterling called before she was up. Darwin came again

"and this time I had him up—very *quiet* and kind. Then Miss Williams Wynn came and undaunted by the fact of a *bedroom* stayed with me two hours. . . . She is a good kind woman I think and with plenty of sense when she *dare* come out with it. She tells me the Town is all full of the news that 'Jane Eyre' has been written by Mr Thackeray's *mistress*".

In the evening Anthony Sterling came again, and John Carlyle who "read us Agamemnon during which Anthony *slept*—under shelter of his spectacles." Her cough, she tells Carlyle: "or as Mazzini would say my *cuff* is less frequent and does not tear my chest so badly." Forster was in and out; John Carlyle looked in every evening and read to her "when I can bear it;" and Charlotte Wynn came often and once "kissed me when she went away—*that* was nothing, but, having done it, she *blushed* up to the very roots of her hair, and that was lovely." She was like Mrs Welsh when she blushed, said Jane.

Mazzini had left George Sand "more *enthusiaste* than ever." He had, he said, thought much of Jane while there, and came back to tell her all he had seen, but he said little of what was in his mind, remaining mysterious, excited, scarcely able to be still a moment. Jane was indignant about a rumour that Landor was boasting that he had forged some Cromwell letters for a joke against Carlyle. Her loyalty, not always apparent in recent days, was up in arms—"if he said so in joke it was a bad joke."

One of the main topics in the Carlyle circle was the biography of John Sterling which had just been published by Julius Hare. Anthony Sterling, Jane told Carlyle, felt "that if *you* did not feel yourself bound to place his Brother in a truer light *he* must attempt it himself." Carlyle considered the whole matter in his journal when he returned from Bay House. He had fifteen hundred pounds in the bank and more coming in regularly. He had more than enough:

"For my wife is the best of housewives; noble, too, in reference to the property which is *hers*, which she has never once in the most distant way seemed to know to be hers. Be this noted and remembered; my thrifty little lady—every inch a lady—ah me!"

But:

"For above two years now I have been as good as totally idle, composedly lying fallow. It is frightful to think of! After getting out of 'Cromwell,' my whole being seemed to say, more sulkily, more weariedly than ever before, 'What good is it?' I am wearied and near heartbroken. Nobody on the whole 'believes my report.'"

Nevertheless, the period of silence "unless I will go mad, must end, as I begin to see, before long." He therefore set out four possible tasks, of which a biography of Sterling was one, but did no more about it.

Tennyson was then visiting Chelsea often; Jane sometimes sang him Scottish ballads, they had an occasional comforting discussion of their ailments—for Tennyson was as much a hypochondriac as the Carlyles—and the men had many walks and talks, agreeing sometimes, differing often. On poetry, they were far apart. Tennyson's *Princess* proved to Carlyle "the futility of what they called 'art' "—"gorgeous piece of writing" though it was—for in his view it did nothing, got nowhere, was a mere mass of words. He was even more decided when he sent a copy to Lady Harriet—"very gorgeous, fervid, luxuriant, but indolent, somnolent, almost imbecile". Henry Taylor's *Notes from Life* was "*dull* as the Lake of Haarlem!" But this criticism of other men's books and consideration of his own idleness did not bring Carlyle to the point for some time. As Jane put it later in the year: "He is working very hard just now at finding out—what to work at!"

The impasse over Geraldine's book had been overcome. Forster undertook to make a few deletions, then gave it his approval. Jane at once capitulated: "Since *you* say there is no impropriety now in the book, it is all right and the Dedication may stand as it is."

XXVIII

REVOLUTION
1848 – 1849

On February 24, 1848, the French rose and drove out Louis Philippe. Revolution broke out all over Europe; there was fighting in Berlin, unrest in Italy, in Hungary, in Ireland; and a monster petition was organised by the Chartists in England. Jane's group of exiles began to disintegrate; she was reminded of Cavaignac by the coming of the day he had hoped and worked for so long—the "wise and valorous conduct" of his younger brother, who had been proclaimed President in France, was "the one earthly thing that I have been getting any real satisfaction out of".

Mazzini, whom she still could not take seriously, went off to Paris the moment the Revolution was proclaimed, "to see I suppose if anything could be arranged for a new 'Savoy's Expedition'; the distinct prospect of being permitted to return to Genoa *'in peace'* being *extremely distressing* to him!!" He returned in March, but Jane, tired of mysteries, took

> "the prospect of his final departure with a *calm* that would surprise you. Whether it be that my *feelings* have got extremely chilled by years and suffering—or that *he* has worn them out—perhaps both causes have operated towards making me tolerably unconcerned."

But she was anxious for him when, after seeing nothing of him for some time, she at last received a tiny sheet of tissue paper which had been smuggled through the enemy lines in Italy:

> "I went through the hostile land 'gens inimica mihi' quite safely, and I am where I have little to risk. . . . It would be well if all idle people should be led to think that I am in Genoa or in any other point of the Sardinian States. Try to be physically as well as possible, and morally as strong as possible. Do not forget your friend as your friend will never forget you."

For the rest, of her exiles she seemed to think most of Plattnauer, now in Ireland—"a noble man—and as true as death"—and she was soon to mourn the death of Garnier.

Towards the end of March, Carlyle, perturbed by the tension in London, worried by Jane's health, and pressed by Lady Harriet, urged a visit to Addiscombe. There were more hard words, but he had his way. He came down for an occasional day but spent most of the time at Chelsea, from which he wrote reassuringly:

> "There is *no* revolution nor any like to be for some months or years yet . . . the City of London is as safe and quiet as the farm of Addiscombe . . . empty rumours and 150,000 oaths of special constables is hitherto the sole amount of this adventure for us."

At Addiscombe, Jane veered between well and ill. She began well. She volunteered to show the housekeeper her recipe for marmalade, and her efforts brought out a typical paragraph:

> "I assure you I would rather lead 'a few brave men' against the Austrians than present myself alone in that kitchen—amidst the scowls of *women in pinafores* and suppressed cries of '*à bas la système*'—to give orders and see them obeyed. Mrs Achison however is fairly *got under* now—and the kitchen maid would go thro' boiling sugar for me."

She read Swift, tired of him, discovered *The Romance of the Forest*

> "which I seized on with avidity, remembering the 'tremendous' emotions with which I read it in my night-shift, by the red light of our dying school-room fire nearly half a century ago, when I was supposed to be sleeping the sleep of good children—and over *that* I actually spent the whole evening—it was so interesting to measure my progress—*downwards* I must think—by comparing my present feelings at certain well-remembered passages with the past."

It was, she thought, a good deal better than G. H. Lewes' *Rose, Blanche and Violet*: "Execrable that is—I could not have suspected even the Ape of writing anything so silly."

Her head felt "as usual to be full of melted lead, swaying this way and that. There is no walking off the heaviness *if walkable off* for the pain is incessant." She had not had "one well moment," and she was not only unwell, but ill at ease. She could enjoy herself and keep well away from home only when she was the centre of the house she happened to be in. This was impossible when she was a guest of Lady Harriet. Yet Lady Harriet was a brilliant woman, she had to confess, even when that brilliance was overshadowing her. She felt lost in every way, with some of her friends gone perhaps for good, with uncertainty in the air, and with this sense of strangeness in the new circle into which she was gradually being drawn. At such times of brooding—and they were frequent—Carlyle and her own home appeared more desirable than ever before. When he, as uncomfortable as herself, begged her, "Oh my dear, be sorry for me! I am nearly out of my wits. From three o'clock till now I have been in a tempest of twaddle.... No wonder I am surly at people. The wonder is rather I do not shoot them" (an outburst caused mainly by a visit from G. H. Lewes, anxious to have Carlyle's opinion of his novel) Jane felt pleased and reassured.

> "If better for you in all other respects that I should remain in 'some other part of the country' " she replied, "my return will have at least *one* comfort in it, that I *do* serve to 'stave off' the people from you, especially at *mealtimes!*"

A few days later, at the end of April, she was back at home—just in time to give tea to the indefatigable Geraldine, who had organised another party to Paris, on this occasion to study the Revolution at first hand, in which she was accompanied by the Paulets and W. E. Forster. Carlyle, Geraldine noted, "talked with his fists" at the tea table. There was some talk of another visit to Rawdon and of a tour by Forster and Carlyle in Ireland.

In Paris the party met Emerson, who was back in London the next month lecturing to fashionable and not so fashionable audiences in different halls. Both Carlyles reported on the lectures to Lady Harriet—now Lady Ashburton since the death of her father-in-law the previous month. Carlyle, of a popular lecture, wrote:

> "The High child delivered yesternight his lecture on 'Domestic life', not one of his best, to a large and highly unselect audience, who missed the finer passages, but were fervently alive to whatever touched on progress of the species, the early closing movement, or suchlike. Lady Byron, alone of the Arixtoxy was there. The air grew very hot; the human heart at last began to get weary.... Emerson is coming here tomorrow evening; and Mrs Crowe with the eyes. You too have *eyes*—O Heaven! God Save the Queen—my own Queen."

Froude, with Arthur Clough, saw Carlyle for the first time at one of these lectures, and heard his "loud, kindly, contemptuous laugh" when the lecturer ended.

Jane, busy finding a servant for Mrs Achison, gave her views on a fashionable lecture:

"Nothing brought home from yesterday's lecture except a Persian Proverb—'For the Man who wears *a shoe*, it is all the same as if the whole earth were covered with leather.' And this startling assertion of Emerson's own; 'Men now-a-days are born with *knives* in their heads!'—no wonder one has such head-aches! What little attention I was able to bestow on anything yesterday got spell-bound by the Duchess of Sutherland's gown! As my Helen exclaimed over a *Virgin & Child* in the National Gallery 'my! oh my! how *expensive!*' and the leading *idea* of it so incomprehensible! white lace wandering at its own sweet will all a-down a figured grey silk—and interspersed with the oddest little *plantations* of grey and white ribbon—her beautiful arms were *bare* up to the elbows, for the thin white lace which covered them so far was mere *delusion*—and her cloak and her bonnet who shall dare to describe? She was escorted yesterday by Lyell the Geologist who looked, my Husband said, 'very much *embarrassed* poor fellow!' and sat where she could be seen in detail—in the enclosed space for the lecturer!"

She promised to call at Bath House in a day or two; and on the morning of the appointed day Carlyle sent a note to Lady Ashburton: "I am making ready to *accompany* this afternoon; lest I don't see you again at all."

Jeannie Welsh was down from Liverpool for a short stay—her last as an intimate of Jane—and was taken about, including a dinner at John Forster's. Carlyle, when accepting the invitation for this dinner, explains:

"Cousin's name is a *synonym:* Jane (*Scotico*, Jeannie) Welsh, a cheery bright little girl,—and the only specimen I know or ever saw of the ancient Scottish *golden hair*, once very fashionable, now quite gone out,—hair the colour of a new guinea."

Susan Stirling also came to London for the Emerson lectures. Jane, who had rebounded into liveliness as soon as she returned home, wrote brightly, enclosing a ticket:

"I am in the same turmoil as ever—a great 'breakfast' tomorrow from *three to six*—at Bath House—'*only* about a hundred people'—involving a new bonnet nevertheless and hot walks in search of one . . . how nice it is to find you the identical Susan of long ago—not a day older—in spite of *the cap* and a few hairs turned grey."

Jane was, as she told her cousin Helen,

"very *gay* of late weeks! Nobody unless the paralytic Miss Chorley, I should think, has been going more *resolutely* 'ahead' in 'the gaieties of the season' (*so-called*)—with *my body*—that is to say—for my soul has been at quite other work."

She and Carlyle dined at Mrs Norton's—"a beautiful witty graceful woman"; at the Macreadys, with D'Orsay and Lady Morgan—"naked as robins half way down—aged seventy-five!"; at the Procters'; and went to a music party at Lady Eddisbury's (later the second Lady Stanley)—"the beautiful Mrs Stanley—that was—Darwin's '*moon-face*'". She heard Chopin play twice, and "Chopin has been *here!!* I never heard the piano played before—could not have believed the capabilities that be in it." Even Carlyle found him

> "really a wonderful musician, and what is far better, a truly delicate, interesting and excellent looking character. Sensitive, alas, tremulous as aspen-leaves, and evidently familiar enough with suffering—poor Chopin!"

The gaieties were interrupted, for Carlyle, by a short tour with Emerson to Stonehenge—"the beautifullest, best got up piece of nonsense that was ever seen in the world!" The two men agreed that one of them ought to write a fitting biography of John Sterling. Emerson also introduced Joseph Neuberg, a German then living in Nottingham, and an admirer of Carlyle's work for many years. "We both *took to you*," Jane said when Neuberg, as a compliment, sent her several mementos of his late wife. She had an affinity with the sorrowful, not with those who were "at ease in Zion"—and that, she explained, is why she liked Neuberg, stranger though he was, and could get up no feeling for a man such as Emerson.

Then Emerson went back to America, leaving the Carlyles to their round of pleasure, which consisted, Jane said, of distractions only, carried out as if she were "*in a bad dream*". Inevitably, both she and Carlyle suffered. August came, London began to empty, there were the usual vacillations about a holiday place, and many complaints. "Never till now was I so low" wrote Carlyle, who still could not make up his mind to a book; "utterly dumb this long while, barren, undecided, wretched in mind . . . . Many things close at hand are other than happy for me just now; but that is no excuse".

The long indecision ended, not unexpectedly, at The Grange in September. The Ashburtons had invited many Lords and "one or two official commoners" for this first gathering since they had succeeded to the title, but the Carlyles found little to please them in the other guests. Carlyle relied mainly on Charles Buller, Jane on Lady Sandwich (Lady Ashburton's mother)—"a brisk, talking, friendly, and rather entertaining character; has been very beautiful at one time" said Carlyle—whom Jane soon thought "very agreeable and a good sort of woman to my notion tho' her daughter can hardly endure her." She decided to keep up the acquaintance when she returned to London, although she expected no more than "pleasant superficial intercourse". She hoped more of another acquaintance she had made:

> "The name is romantic enough—Aubrey de Vere—and the man who bears it romantic enough—very handsome—young—*religious*—to the extent even of eating fish on Fridays and fasting in Lent. A Poet—highly accomplished every way—despising '*wits*' (wonderfullest of all) and in short a rare mortal as men go."

Of the two, Jane benefited the more from the stay of nearly six weeks. She had the two new friends, chess with Lady Ashburton, and a houseful of men—for she and Lady Sandwich were the only women guests. Carlyle was bored much of the time. Jane's introduction into the Ashburton circle, the curious half-envious, half-admiring friendship into which she had fallen with Lady Ashburton, and her affection for the good-natured Lord Ashburton, had brought no gain to him. "You are the lamp of my dark path," he had told Lady Ashburton; but he found little light in these long visits with their elaborate social routine, their life of "total idleness". "Why," he protests to his hostess, "will you . . . waste yourself with the frivolities of this generation?" He felt himself to be stagnating he told John: "It is a sumptuous elaborate *representation*, which has to be transacted seemingly for its own sake: no result attained by it, or hardly any, except the representation itself." When they reached home again in the middle of October he confessed that he had never spent "five lonelier idler weeks".

He was relieved, however, to see that Jane and Lady Ashburton had shown signs of accommodating themselves to each other; and Jane was sufficiently amiable when they returned to Chelsea for him to write off straightway to The Grange: "You will write to my wife some day? God bless you evermore, my

Beautiful Lady. 'Beauty and the Beast'—the Beast undeliverable?" A month later he was reporting that Jane had been twice to see Lady Sandwich "to whom she seems to take." He compared himself to an enchanted knight "unable to stir myself, writing with hand and foot glued together, under a load of contemptible miseries." One at least of these miseries was not contemptible; at the end of November Charles Buller died suddenly after an operation. He might well have been a great statesman, he was a very charming man, with his "blithe face", and was, as Carlyle told Lady Ashburton, "the brightest soul in your circle". Jane had never been intimate with him—he was, like Milnes, a Lady Ashburton man first and foremost and had for years been known in London society as "Lord Harriet"— but as usual she was at her best in trouble.

> "It was soon after nine", Carlyle told Lady Ashburton, "when our messenger returned this morning; my wife went off directly after to attend poor Mrs Buller. What in the world will become of that poor bereaved old mother, already at the point of death! her calmness yesterday, Jane said, was almost frightful."

There was again a change of maids. Anne married after the return from The Grange, and went off to Jersey. Helen Mitchell sent an appeal from Kirkcaldy; her Irish adventure had been "*no go*" and she wanted to come back to Chelsea. Jane took her back with misgivings. By the time she wrote to Mrs Russell at the end of the year with her gifts, she was finding Helen "very tiresome". In February 1849 the Carlyles spent a few days at Anthony Sterling's farm near Epsom. Sterling drove them back to Cheyne Row. They knocked and rang for some time without answer. When at last the door opened, Helen stood there

> "like a stage ghost very *ill got* up—blood spurting from her lips, her face whitened with chalk from the kitchen floor, her dark gown *ditto*, and wearing a smile of idiotic self-complacency! I thought Mr C was going to kick his foot through her when she tumbled down at his touch. If she had been his *wife* he certainly would have killed her on the spot, but his maid-of-all work he felt could not be got rid of without his being hanged for her."

As soon as she recovered, Helen

> "rushed out for more drink! She had had *half a pint* of gin in the morning in the afternoon *half a pint* of rum and some ale!! that is what one would call good drinking! Between nine and ten she returned—and lay locked

up all night insensible then she had a fit of *delirium tremens*, then twenty-four hours of weeping and wailing and trying to take me by compassion as she had done so often before—but it would not do.... God knows what is to become of her! I told her yesterday she would be better *dead!* if she were not so old and ugly of course she would go on the streets".

She had not long to wait; Helen went from bad to worse, was sent back to Kirkcaldy, tried to drown herself there, and soon afterwards died.

A new maid, Elizabeth Sprague, was found almost at once, and peace of a kind settled down on the house. Carlyle reassured his mother: "Jane and I go grumbling on as usual, not worse than usual". He could settle to nothing more than an article or two; he scarcely knew where to fix his attention; Ireland, threatened with another famine, most occupied his mind but another book seemed out of the question, and he was not over kind to those who had published recently. Milnes' biography of Keats was

" an attempt to make us eat dead dog by exquisite currying and cooking! Won't eat it. A truly unwise little book. The kind of man that Keats was gets ever more horrible to me. Force of hunger for pleasure of every kind, and want of all other force—that is a combination! . . . at present we try to love and pity, and even worship, such a soul, and find the task rather easy, in our own souls there being enough of similarity. Away with it! there is perhaps no clearer evidence of our universal *immorality* and cowardly untruth".

Macaulay's History was pleasant, easy reading,

"clear, definite, every corner of it; but without concentration, modulation, a formless *flat*, flat, like a Russian *Steppe* . . . in fine *no story* to be told, and nothing but a *Whig Evangelist* to tell it us!"

So he told Lady Ashburton, to whom he was writing even more frequently in an effort to take her mind from the loss of Charles Buller. One of her letters to him Jane thought "sad as death—as sorrowful a letter as *I* could have written." Lady Sandwich was going to her daughter—"but *that*" commented Jane, "will be no comfort." Jane was disappointed, because "Lady Sandwich . . . is the pleasantest person I have here just now to go off and talk with when I am too bad company for myself." She was in fact taking the place of Mrs Sterling, of Mrs Buller, of the mother Jane wished for. Mrs Buller was now asking from Jane what she had been accustomed to give; help,

consolation, sympathy. Jane went often to see her "from a sense
of duty", was kind and patient but could not resist criticising
her "infinite *clatter* . . . like pailfuls of water poured all over me".
By the early summer Mrs Buller was dead.

The last of the Sterling family remained assiduous, the more
so as his wife grew more difficult;

> "he comes to town every week and calls both in coming and going—and
> brings me flowers—the beautifullest hothouse flowers tho' it is winter
> now—and if he could being me health and happiness there is no man
> who would sooner do it. I wonder what strange attraction lies in me for
> all of the blood of Sterling? For Father and Mother and *both* sons I have
> been more than any other woman—not married to them. There is no
> understanding these things."

G. H. Lewes, coming in from time to time with "his charming
little wife" had become quite a favourite of Jane's, who thought
him "the most amusing little fellow in the whole world," the
best mimic, and "full of famous stories"—a sure way to her
regard—"and no spleen, or envy, or *bad* thing in him, so that
you receive him with open arms in spite of his immense ugliness." He was to lecture in the north, and she gave him
introductions; but when he returned after making, Geraldine
asserted, "a prodigious sensation down here, only his mous-
tachios have hurt people's sense of propriety", he quite shocked
Jane. "Poor Lewes looks to be going rapidly to you know
whom!" So to John Forster; to her cousin Jeannie she elabor-
ates: "it is Julia Paulet who has taken his soul captive!! he raves
about her 'dark luxurious eyes' and 'smooth firm flesh'—! his
wife asked 'how did he know? had he been feeling it?' "

> "I used to think these Leweses" Jane went on "a perfect pair of love-
> birds always cuddling together on the same perch—to speak figuratively
> —but the female love-bird appears to have hopped off to some distance
> and to be now taking a somewhat critical view of her little shaggy mate!
> In the most honey-marriages one has only to *wait*".

By the time of this last, she was at Addiscombe, having
cancelled a dinner with Forster:

> "it may seem like throwing you over for *principalities and powers*—but you
> will not think so ill of my social tastes . . . to refuse to go because I wished
> to dine in Chambers, God bless them! one day of the week would sound
> questionable—tho' heaven knows I am in the humour to do it."

However, she went; but not in the best frame of mind, having just been given a taste of the gossip that played about Carlyle and Lady Ashburton. She had felt reasonably well most of the winter, had been to a number of parties, to dinner at Thackeray's and, just before going to Addiscombe, to a dinner given by Dickens. There, she met Mrs Gaskell, who had made a name with her *Mary Barton* and who had already called at Chelsea—"a natural unassuming woman whom they have been doing their best to spoil by making a lioness of her"—and she had an unpleasant exchange with Rogers "who ought to have been buried long ago". He asked

" 'is your husband as much infatuated as ever with Lady Ashburton?'— 'Oh of course'—I said *laughing*, 'why shouldn't he?'—'Now—do *you* like her—tell me honestly is she kind to *you*—as kind as she is to your husband?' 'Why you know it is impossible for *me* to know *how* kind she is to *my* husband; but I *can* say she is extremely kind to *me* and I should be stupid and ungrateful if I did *not* like her.' 'Humph! (disappointedly) Well! it is very good of you to like her when she takes away all your husband's company from you—he is always there isn't he?' 'Oh good gracious no! (still laughing *admirably*) he writes and reads a great deal in his own study.'—'But he spends all his evenings with her I am told?'— 'No—not all—for example you see he is *here* this evening.' 'Yes,' he said in a tone of vexation 'I *see* he is here *this* evening—and *hear* him too—for he has done nothing but talk across the room since he came in.' Very devilish old man! but he got no satisfaction to his devilishness out of *me*."

Rogers complained bitterly of this particular party: "everybody talked so much and so loud that one could not hear a word said." "That is" explained Jane, "*he* had not the talk all to himself—in other words *Mr Carlyle was there*—the greatest affliction that can befall Rogers at a dinner party." But Rogers was not alone in the gossip, as Jane well knew; she was no favourite with many women who, eyeing her retinue at Cheyne Row, would talk with delight of her inability to keep her own husband there. There was only one answer to this chatter; hence Jane's acceptance of the invitation to Addiscombe and of all subsequent invitations from Lady Ashburton; but she could not keep bitterness out of her letters and much of her talk. It says a good deal for her and for her hostess that the week at Addiscombe—for the first half of which the two women were alone—passed off as well as any of the preceding visits.

Jane had already noted that Lady Ashburton had "crushed down out of sight into the bottom of her heart, or perhaps *out of it* altogether" all her "wild grief" over Charles Buller. Carlyle, she was sure,

> "will never succeed in making her 'more *earnest*', dear, gayhearted, high spirited woman that she is! God bless her for her seeming determination *not* to be '*earnest*' for *his* pleasure, or anyone else's, but to be just what God has made her, the enemy of *cant* and lover of all mirthful things."

Here appears one consolation which Jane sedulously set against the lost battle of "wits" in the company of Lady Ashburton.

> "It is a great faculty that of being able to throw off grief—I would not somehow care to have it and yet I see well enough how much better people, who have it, both enjoy their life and contribute to the enjoyment of 'others' ".

She was thinking of her grief for Cavaignac which had been roughly handled a few weeks earlier. Robertson called; he wished to bring a Frenchman, Louis Blanc, to see them. Jane, in the midst of one of her headaches perhaps, had shown little interest, and Robertson, piqued, cried:

> " 'I am sure you will like him—he was talking to me today many things that would have interested even *you*—it was in *his* arms he tells me, that Godefroi Cavaignac died!'—I started as if he had shot me—the thing took me so by surprise—and I could not answer one word—this man was coming on Friday night! I felt as if he would transmit to me even thus late Godefroi Cavaignac's last breath! And Robertson was watching the effect of his words! I cared not—why should I? I had my boa gloves reticule &c in my lap, I flung them all violently on the floor—why, I don't know—I could not help it! Robertson went on to say that he Louis Blanc talked of Godefroi as of a Divinity that General Cavaignac was very inferior to *him* in Blanc's opinion—and then seeing that I was not even going to make an effort to converse on this topic he stooped and gathered up my things saying with a significant look—'*That*, I *suppose*, is not the place where these articles are meant to remain, Mrs Carlyle.' I took them out of his hands and left the room—I could have killed him."
>
> "I believe" Jane told Jeannie, who shared her weakness for the romantic attitude, "Robertson said that about Godefroi, in the devilish intention of watching its effect on me—I *know* he has been heard to speculate on my intimacy with him. Well! let him draw his inferences—it is no disgrace to *any* woman to be accused of having loved Godefroi Cavaignac—the only reproach to be made me is that I did not love him as well as he deserved. But now he is dead I will not *deny him* before all the Robertsons alive."

Geraldine, to whom all this and more was repeated, and whose view of Robertson had deteriorated, burst into indignation:

"Bah! that such creatures have a right to decide on a woman's good name; it is enough to make one trample it under one's feet as a thing utterly worthless when held by their permission. . . . I'll be hanged if I don't ease my mind in the next book I write!"

Mazzini was also a great deal in Jane's mind, and in Carlyle's too:

"If he *could* stand there in Rome, in sight of all Italy, and practically defy the whole world for a while, and fight till Rome was ashes and ruin, and end by blowing himself and his assailants up in the last strong post, and so yielding only with life, he might rouse the whole Italian nation into such a rage as it has not known for many centuries. . . . Perhaps that is really what he was worth in this world."

Jane had heard again from Mazzini. She also, a month or more before Carlyle expressed the same thought, half-wished that Mazzini would blow himself, Rome, the French and all to atoms, to rouse Italy. But more often she thought simply of

"poor dear Mazzini—all my affection for him has waked up since I knew him in jeopardy and so gallantly fulfilling his destiny—and not mine only—the public sympathy is fast going over to his side. . . . I have had an *Italia del populo* sent me daily since Mazzini started it in Rome—and you may fancy how anxiously I expect it every morning."

Then, early in July, "poor Rome forced to capitulate after all!"—and all was uncertainty, Mazzini's fate unknown.

Before the fall of Rome there had been another tumultuous visit from Geraldine to Cheyne Row, the first meeting with Froude, and a few more days at Addiscombe. Geraldine was rather preoccupied at this time with the Chevalier Neukomm, a German organist of repute, who was visiting her in Manchester, and whose portrait now had a place of honour in her bedroom. Jane was told about him, and Geraldine saw a good deal of the Chelsea circle and of John Carlyle, at the moment in high favour with Jane. She had "terrible bouts" of headache, and "John is excessively kind to me on these occasions; has sat on his knees at my bedside for hours together holding me down and being sorry for me, which is just all that can be done in the way of alleviation."

Geraldine's short visit closed under a cloud. Lewes had followed up his success as lecturer in Manchester by returning to play Shylock at the Theatre Royal and to stage his own play, *The Noble Heart*. Charlotte Cushman had been talking freely of

Lewes' inadequacy as man and actor, and Jane defended him.

> "Miss Cushman," she told Forster, "I have heard a man I *implicitly* believe—Macready—call 'not only a woman who *lied*, but a woman who *spoke no truth*.' Why should we now believe in Miss Cushman *for the first time*—when a fellow creature's good name is concerned? There has been no doubt *something wrong*—but how much or how little we don't know—and we have *our own ways* to mind which we *can* measure the extent of."

This moral utterance barely covered Jane's rancour—a rancour which broke out again when Geraldine, giving her own impressions of the affair, took the actress' part. She left in a huff; and Jane reported to Forster, almost too indifferently: "Oh by the way—Geraldine has cut me ever since the Lewes business!—and I—resign myself."

Froude called in the next month. His recently published *The Nemesis of Faith*—described by Caroline Fox as "a wild protest against all authority, Divine and human"—had caused, again in her words, "an ugly stir". It was publicly burned in Oxford, and Froude threw up his fellowship. "The young man" said Carlyle "should burn his own smoke and not trouble other people's nostrils with it."

> "Nevertheless" said Froude "he was willing to see what I was like. James Spedding took me down to Cheyne Row one evening in the middle of June. We found him sitting after dinner, with his pipe, in the small flagged court between the house and the garden. . . . He was then fifty-four years old; tall (about five feet eleven), thin, but at that time upright, with no signs of the later stoop. His body was angular, his face beardless, such as it is represented in Woolner's medallion, which is by far the best likeness of him in the days of his strength. His head was extremely long, with the chin thrust forward; the neck was thin; the mouth firmly closed, the under lip slightly projecting; the hair grizzled and thick and bushy. His eyes, which grew lighter with age, were then of a deep violet, with fire burning at the bottom of them, which flashed out at the least excitement. The face was altogether most striking, most impressive every way. And I did not admire him the less because he treated me—I cannot say unkindly, but shortly and sternly. I saw then what I saw ever after—that no one need look for conventional politeness from Carlyle—he would hear the exact truth from him, and nothing else."

Carlyle took them into the diningroom, where Jane gave them tea.

> "Her features were not regular" said Froude, "but I thought I had never seen a more interesting-looking woman. Her hair was raven black, her eyes dark, soft, sad, with dangerous light in them. Carlyle's talk was

rich, full, and scornful; hers delicately mocking. She was fond of Spedding, and kept up a quick, sparkling conversation with him, telling stories at her husband's expense, at which he laughed himself as heartily as we did."

Although Geraldine had missed Froude by a week or two, she was soon to see him, for he took a post as tutor to a Unitarian family in Manchester. She found him "a very nice natural young man, though rather like 'a lost sheep' at present." Ominous words; but Froude was already engaged to a sister of Charles Kingsley's wife; and Geraldine, who was nothing if not generous, admired his choice. This engagement brought about another link with the Carlyles; Kingsley's father was rector of Chelsea, and Kingsley himself had a great admiration for Carlyle's work.

Geraldine also missed her friend of the previous year's Paris tour, W. E. Forster. Forster—Edward now—came to Cheyne Row at the end of May and was better company than ever—so much so, that Jane practically accepted on the spot an invitation to Rawdon that summer. He also spoke of joining Carlyle in Ireland—for Carlyle, still finding himself sterile, had almost decided on another tour: "much that I had lying in me to say might perhaps get nearer to some way of utterance if I were looking face to face upon the ruin and wretchedness that is prevalent there." Some weeks later, Forster's flattering attentions were still lingering in Jane's mind when Caroline Fox called. Her hostess was rather melancholy but brightened up when Forster was mentioned. She was very fond of him, she said, and grateful.

At the beginning of July, Carlyle set out for Ireland. Jane saw him off, watched the ship sail away until his white hat could no longer be seen, and returned home to cry. Then she discovered that he had left his plaid behind, and went to Bath House and on to Addiscombe much depressed:

"But 'no sympathy there thank God'! '*Wits*' enough if that could have helped me. 'You would have the sense to wrap yourself in a sail if you were cold' or 'depend upon it you would seize on the rugs of all the other passengers' beds. At all events you had promised to stay with *them* in Scotland and that would quite set you up if you *had* taken cold!' Clearly I must 'come out of that' if I were going to do any good—and I did—to appearance—but all day I was fancying you shivering—like myself."

There were more complaints—cold food, a cold room, a cold picnic in a hayfield—but her three days at Addiscombe proved in retrospect the most pleasant she had ever spent there. For this she had two people to thank—Aubrey de Vere, who sent her a twenty-four-page letter, and the devotion of one of the guests, Blanche Stanley, the second daughter of Lord Eddisbury. She developed a passion for Jane, and "confided to me all the secrets of her heart". This conquest, in Lady Ashburton's own house, and the sight of the twenty-four-page letter sent Jane's morale bounding, and she was for once no more than amused by the "tearing spirits" everyone was showing.

Back in London, the devotion continued:

"No such 'everlasting friendship' has been sworn to me these thirty years as this of Blanche's! She flings herself on my neck, begs me to call her Blanche, says with tears in her eyes 'Oh! does not every one love you?' protests that she 'would like to stay with me for ever'—and in fact embarrasses me considerably with a sort of thing I have been quite out of these many years."

Jane made the best of the embarrassment:

"While we were at tea (and these girls too had each *four* cups! with cakes and bread and butter in proportion) up drove Lady Ashburton which was great fun for all parties. She was in '*tearing* spirits' and so were *we* by that time—and the racket that followed for the next hour and a half was what Forster might have called '*stupendous!* great God!' She said my picture (Laurence's) was the horridest thing she had ever seen—'like —but so disagreeably like—exactly reminding one of a poor old starved *rabbit!*' "

Jane had now made her plans. Invitations had poured in—from the Neubergs in Nottingham, from Forster at Rawdon, the Newtons at Barnsley, her cousins at Liverpool, Geraldine (reconciled) at Manchester, the Donaldsons in Haddington, the Russells at Thornhill, her aunts in Edinburgh, the Ferguses in Kirkcaldy. She felt in better health—her headaches apart—than for many a year, and she decided to make as comprehensive a round of visits as possible, and, at last, to go into Scotland again, which she had not seen for eight years. First on the list were the Neubergs. John Carlyle had preceded her there, and sent favourable accounts. Neuberg wrote, "*so* delighted" by her acceptance, reports Jane, that "I hardly like to venture to him 'without an escort of dragoons!' " He had written to Carlyle also, but this letter, she said, "had no poetry of expression." The letter to her was " 'what shall I say? passionate, upon *my* honour!!' "

Her last week was "beset with visitors"—"*every* evening there was an *improvised* tea-party." Then, at the beginning of the second week in July, she "cut out of it all" and went off to Nottingham.

377

XXIX

RETURN TO HADDINGTON
1849

Jane had intended to stay one day with the Neubergs, but she stayed four. Neuberg, five years younger than herself, was courteous, kind and intelligent, and he and his sister Rosella laid themselves out to give their distinguished visitor a royal time. The house was ordered to suit her wishes, she could do exactly what she desired at any moment, her lightest word was law, her stories were laughed at, and above all she was not left with time on her hands. This treatment suited her well, and she sailed through the daily tours without a headache. Even lack of sleep seemed to worry her little, for these were newe pople, their devotion was fresh and unstinted. Neuberg's German earnestness, from which she might have shrunk, was not too obvious.

> "Every moment here" she writes to John "is taken up in seeing sights and being made much of—you who have so lately gone thro' the thing yourself can understand 'how I am situate' (as Mr C's phrase is). Here is a letter from him—which I wish you all much good of—that sort of letter all about every thing and for the public good is nothing to *me*."

She had already decided John's future; "I am enchanted with Miss Neuberg and intend that you should marry her—she is extremely fond of you—and really there is no objection that I can see."

In the evenings she played chess with Neuberg—she was by now a player of some merit—made music and talked. Neuberg told her of his wish to retire from business and to devote himself to literature. He spoke of going back to Bonn unless one of his ideals for many years could be realised, and Carlyle would allow him to act as his literary secretary. To Jane, foreseeing pleasant company in Neuberg and remembering the mass of papers in the Cheyne Row library, the offer was attractive.

She promised to speak about it.

By the fourth day she was even more determined that the Neubergs should come to London and that John should marry the sister and settle himself and them. There was no question of leaving Nottingham alone, they would come as far as possible with her on her way to Barnsley. So she left "with the dear Neubergs whom I am deeply in love with" she tells John

"—the man on my *own* account and the little sister on *yours* (*I am* quite serious and determined—you *must* marry her—she will make you an excellent wife—would like it extremely—and *I* would like to have her for a sister-in-law)."

She was still complaining about Carlyle's letters: "making *me* his human *notebook* for the moment".

The party went by train to Rowsley, and after inspecting Haddon Hall they came back to their "beautiful little Inn" for "a rough tea". Before going to bed Jane and Neuberg sat on the garden seat smoking cigarettes and "*dreaming* beautifully without having gone to sleep." They slept at the inn: "or to speak accurately so far as *myself* was concerned—*lay in bed there broad awake* till six in the morning," and walked before breakfast, with Jane "apparently better for having practically not slept since leaving London".

At Matlock they parted—"Tell me *what you will do* about Rosella Neuberg" demanded Jane of John—"she *cried* when I came away and I *know* that *half* the tears were for you." At Barnsley Mrs Newton was waiting to drive her home for tea and dinner before she resumed her journey. John Carlyle (who was making good use of all the Carlyles' friends) had preceded her here also, and with effect. Mrs Newton told Jane: "that if she were going to fall in love with any man besides her husband it *would* be with *you*".

In the evening she was "*squalling* towards Leeds" where "Edward will pick me up." But Forster—"with his usual infectious impetuosity"—was better than his word. At Normanton a man jumped into her carriage—"rather impertinent I thought"—just before the train started, sat down, and said "Well, how are you?" It was Forster, come to spare her a lonely journey. His gig was at Apperley Bridge, as well as another guest. However, this "tiresome man" went off the next morning to the water-cure at Benrydden, and Jane sat back happily to enjoy another bout of adulation, of the drives and chess and confidential talks which had been her fare at Rawdon two years earlier. But Forster had acquired another idol. The Paulets arrived the next day—Jane's forty-eighth birthday—Paulet went off to the water-cure, and Forster was left with two women to entertain. Mrs Paulet "young and pretty and happy looking" proved as difficult for him to resist as her daughter had proved for Lewes. Jane wrote disillusionedly that there was not the life at Rawdon that there had been at Nottingham:

> "Contrary to all previous experience I am likely to be *too* 'well let alone here'. William Edward is no longer the devoted *Squire of Dames* he was but the Squire of *one* Dame and that *one* is not *me!* . . . The gig cannot carry *three*—so I *walk* 'mostly by mysell' ".

Her position was complicated by a fear, so she said, that Mrs Paulet would consider as a personal affront every minute spent by Jane in her own room. Being no respecter of persons when roused, Jane confided this fear, for which there was at least one other good explanation, to Neuberg, an acquaintance of five days' standing.

The deadlock was broken for a moment by the arrival of Marioni, Mazzini's emissary, who had brought Mazzini's note to Jane some months earlier, and who was now to represent the Italian Republic at a meeting in Bradford to protest against the taking of Rome by the French. The meeting, reported Jane, went off successfully, though "the Bradford *gentlemen* on the platform were like Bess Stodart's legs 'no great things'!" Marioni gone, the position at Rawdon reverted to the impossible, and in despair Jane went off to the water-cure. Here she was "packed" for courtesy, being swathed in a wet sheet, blankets and a feather bed, and left for an hour "to go mad in my leisure!" But she found a good deal of compensation in her after-treatment:

> "I . . . am now laid out" she told Carlyle, "on a remarkable Sofa, in the Dr's private room, where I am going to be *exceptionally* regaled with coffee—I have made them give me this paper on my knees and Dr Nicol is holding the ink bottle".

She had met a man—she was the kind of woman who was always meeting such men—who remembered her from long ago. This particular man had a "vivid recollection of my '*white veil* at Haddington' (having lived exactly at the bottom of our entry!—his Father keeping a china-shop)". She wondered whether she should revisit Haddington. Meanwhile, she was thoroughly enjoying herself queening the water-cure establishment: "It is perfect nonsense trying to write in this position which they are forcing me to keep—and with Dr Macleod standing with a handful of letters for the post only waiting for mine."

Eventually she decided to go to Haddington—her first visit since that day sixteen years earlier when she had sat long by her father's grave—but to arrive there in darkness so that she should not be recognised. This entailed a night and morning at the junction of Morpeth, and Forster redeemed himself slightly by accompanying her—"out of purest charity" she said. She explained that "I looked so *horribly helpless* that he could not reconcile it to his conscience to leave me *a chance* at losing myself." He played his part well; ordered a fire and a brandy for her at her inn, the Phoenix, walked with her by the river after "a modest dinner" of chops and cherry tart, then back for tea, chess and "speculative talk" till midnight. The next morning being "bright as diamonds" they walked about the town and the hills near it, and,

> "rendered unusually communicative by our isolated position, I informed William Edward that my maternal grandmother was 'descended from a gang of gipsies'—was in fact grand-niece to Matthew Baillie who 'suffered at Lanark'—that is to say was hanged there. A genealogical fact, Forster said, which made me at last intelligible for him 'a cross between John Knox and a gipsy, how that explained all!' "

Then dinner at the inn, after which she went off to Haddington and he began his journey to meet Carlyle and Duffy in Ireland.

For the next twenty-four hours Jane surrendered herself to the past. At Haddington she took a room at the George and sat by a window looking up the street towards her old home: "It was the same street the same houses; but so silent, dead, petrified!" The main-line railway, passing well outside the town, had gone far to kill it. The coaches were all but finished. All the bustle of the place had disappeared; but its grave-like demeanour suited her mood. She had the feeling of one returned from the grave, recognising in old women flourishing matrons of her day, in buxom wives with tall children girls of her own time, and, being recognised by none, was spoken to "with that compassionate distinctness which one puts on with only foreigners or idiots." The illusion deepened when she asked to see the church, and the sexton pointed out familiar sights on the way—the school, the playground, the bowling green. She went into the churchyard alone after the gate had been unlocked. In the ruined chancel were two new graves:

> "*His* looked old old—was surrounded by nettles—the inscription all over moss except two lines which had been quite recently cleared—by whom? who had been there before me, still caring for his tomb after twenty nine years?"

Would she not like to see the church? she was asked. She went in: "I almost fancied I saw my beautiful mother in her old corner and myself, a bright-looking girl, in the other!" She asked the sexton where he lived:

> " 'Next door to the house that was Dr Welsh's' he answered with a sharp glance at my face—then added gently 'Excuse me Mam for mentioning that, but the minute I set eyes on ye at the George I jaloused it was her we all looked after whenever she went up or down' ".

She asked him to keep her secret, arranged to meet him at the churchyard gate early the next morning, then strolled round for the first time in twenty-three years by her old evening walk. Nothing had changed—"the very puddles made by the last rain I felt to have stepped over before". So far she had walked veiled; she threw it back, and visited her old friend the turner in Hardgate. He told her

> "amongst other interesting things 'Dr Welsh's death was the sorest loss ever came to the place' that myself 'went away into England and—died there!' adding a handsome enough tribute to my memory. 'Yes! Miss Welsh! he remembered her famously, used to think her the tastiest young lady in the whole place—but she was very—not just to call proud—very reserved in her company'. In leaving this man I felt more than ever like my own ghost."

She looked through the barred door of her father's old coach-house, stood at the entrance to Sunny Bank, then went back to the George to write a long letter to Carlyle " 'all about feelings' (as Lady A would say)" which she burned soon after dawn. Long before seven she was outside her house, reached the churchyard an hour too early, "made a dash at the wall" and scrambled over—

> "Godefroi Cavaignac's '*Quoi donc, je ne suis pas mort!*' crossed my mind; but I had none of that feeling—*moi* was *morte* enough I knew whatever face I might put on it—only what one has well learnt one never forgets."

She scraped the moss from the inscription on her father's grave, then looked at other grave-stones. Of the older stones she lingered round two that had drawn tears from her when she was a child—of young Sutherland and little Ann Cameron. She was still there when the sexton arrived. How had she got into the churchyard? She told him. "Lord's sakes then, there is no end to you!"

Before she left, he promised to tell her father's old groom, James Robertson, that she had come back. She wandered into the school and sat down in her old seat; then walked up to Sunny Bank again. This time she went inside and was shown into the drawingroom. The door opened, and Catherine, changed into an old woman, stayed there

> "motionless, speechless, and I couldn't rise off my chair—at least I didn't —but when I saw her eyes staring 'like watch faces' I said 'Oh Miss Catherine don't be frightened at me!'—and then she quite shrieked 'Jeannie! Jeannie! Jeannie Welsh! my Jeannie! my Jeannie!' oh mercy! I shan't forget that scene in a hurry".

At the hotel was Robertson.

> "I threw my arms round his neck—that did I. He stood quite passive and quite pale with great tears rolling down; it was minutes before he spoke, and then he said only low under his breath 'Mrs—Carlyle!' So nice he looked and hardly a day older and really as like 'a gentleman' as some lords—he had dressed himself in his Sunday clothes for the occasion . . . 'And you knew me Jamie at first sight?' I asked. 'Toot! we knew ye afore we seed ye.' 'Then you were told it was me?' 'No—they told us just we was to speak to a lady at the George and I knew it was Mrs Carlyle.' 'But how could you tell dear Jamie?' 'Hoots! who else could it be?' Dear funniest of created Jamies!"

In the train she spoke to an old man whom she remembered by the name of Lea, living on her side of the High Street. "Was it you who got over the churchyard wall this morning?" he asked "I saw a stranger lady climb the wall and I said to myself that's Jeannie Welsh! no other woman would climb the wall instead of going in at the gate." On Longniddry platform was George Cunningham, the boy who never got into trouble and never helped others out of it. She had seen him once at Craik's about twelve years earlier. She talked to him without enthusiasm. She had travelled in the Haddington omnibus with a couple whom old Lea reminded her were the Richardsons. Both had been at school with her, but "they were not people I had ever visited with." At Edinburgh, Jeannie pointed them out, staring at her. They came up, they had not known her until they saw her smile. She made up her mind to call on them when she returned: "I like their hop-step-and-jump over ceremony, their oblivion in the enthusiasm of the moment that we had 'belonged to different circles' (Haddington speaking)".

She went straight on to Walter's manse at Auchtertool, inland from Kirkcaldy. She did not enjoy her stay there. The house was filled with Welshes, she was beginning to feel the effects of her travelling, and even more of her agitation at Haddington. Carlyle, now back at Scotsbrig, had planned to join her at Auchtertool, but she warned him off: "*you* could not get on at Auchtertool—even I cannot hold out much longer"—late meals, "chitter-chatter", " 'dandering individuals' constantly dropping in—dressing and undressing, world without end!"—she found all this "wholly out of place in a Scotch Manse", and, what was more to the point, highly disturbing to her. Even her old uncle fell from grace. If he, she complained, "could only speak *intelligibly* I should get good talk out of *him*—but since he lost his teeth his articulation is so imperfect that it needs one to be used to it to catch one word out of ten".

Carlyle was complaining of his Irish trip: "Ugly spectacle, sad health, sad humour, a thing unjoyful to look back upon". He had to take calomel the moment he reached Scotsbrig. "I do not think" replied Jane, always deadly serious when discussing an ailment, "it ever answers for us nervous people to *subside* all at once; we should be let down by degrees." She introduced a lighter note by sending her "character" by Donovan, a physiognomist then all the rage in London. Anthony Sterling had been anxious to spend half a guinea for her to be "done"—"and I wished to try what *perfect silence* and *unknowingness* could do in putting him (Donovan) out—he had *no* idea of my name, and I *spoke* not at all. Here you have the result." She was "wholly without observing faculty, with large reflectiveness turned inward:". Her comment on this is: "Ah *mes amis; mais peutêtre c'est pas vrai*".

In the middle of August she went to the Ferguses in Kirkcaldy, and was joined by Carlyle who was going on to the Ashburtons' shooting box in the Highlands. They stayed a day or two with Thomas Erskine—"Saint Thomas" to Jane—at Linlathen, but they were "much out of sorts" and had "a miserable enough hugger-mugger time", to use Carlyle's words; tired of travelling, tired of strange food, strange routines, strange houses. And they did not see eye to eye about the Highlands.

In the first days of September, Jane crossed to Edinburgh where her three aunts in Clarence Street were "much gladder to see me and kinder and pleasanter than I expected and poor Betty gave me such welcome!" In spite of her aunts' kindness, she had a few frank words with them about "their bothering me about my soul". Anne reassured her; they would not set themselves to reform her: "it is plain enough that nothing short of God's own grace can do that".

Then back she went to Haddington for a day or two at Sunny Bank, from which she called on all her old friends. Her stay was marred by the Donaldsons' fear of cholera, which "is carrying off many people in Haddington", and by their prophecy, "that every sort of illness must end in *that*". This dread was particularly awkward when, on her last day, Jane felt ill. She managed to reach Edinburgh then went straight to bed.

After a couple of days she was on her way again, to Scotsbrig now, playing a sort of Box and Cox with Carlyle: "Here I am Dear!" she begins her first letter from his mother's, "You *there* and I *here*." A letter was awaiting her from Lady Ashburton, expressing regret that she had not come with Carlyle. Lord Ashburton's health was better, but there were too many guests and not enough servants: "difficulty too about sufficient food— difficulty about Beds—about the people in them suiting each other." Carlyle, Lady Ashburton reported, had been complaining about his stomach and loss of sleep. He took to broth and brown toast, and retired from society until his hostess sent a doctor to him, who "pronounced his Tongue as clean as his own and nothing necessary to be done. Today all is right— Cigars puffing away—the day long."

What Lady Ashburton did not say was that the doctor had been practically driven out of Carlyle's room by a storm of invective ending with "a man might as well pour his sorrows into the long hairy ear of a jackass." Carlyle was enjoying himself miserably; shocked at the waste of time and money, indignant at the lack of comfort—"crammed like herrings in a barrel" and without even a washing tub. He had spent "ten wretched days", and asks Jane "Pity me when thou canst, poor little soul! or laugh at me if thou wilt. Oh! if you could read my heart and whole thought at this moment, there is surely one sad thing you would cease to do henceforth."

> Lucky for him, she replies, that he was not "laid up in *my* houses. As my Aunt Grace told *me* very often during *my* bad day; 'there is mercy mixed up with all our afflictions!—it is a great comfort to think you are in *even* better hands than our own—I mean in Jesus Christ's'—'Oh ay!' said dear Betty—'Christ has care of my Bairn *A*wheres—even on the *railway!* and a great comfort that is for me to think, now that she gangs sae muckle be them' ".

Her few peaceful days at Scotsbrig were overclouded by a severe fright. While they were playing one evening with Jamie's children, old Mrs Carlyle stole up behind Jane and tickled her under the arms. At first Jane laughed with the rest of them, then suddenly the blood left her face, and she fell down as if she were dead. John Carlyle was summoned, and managed to bring her round. It was a heart attack, he said; but before she left Scotsbrig all the family had been warned that no word of the attack was to be mentioned to Carlyle.

By the middle of September she had moved on, accompanied by John, to Liverpool. Thornhill she could not face, it was too close to Templand. She apologised to Mrs Russell:

> "when I left Edinburgh for Ecclefechan, I did not know whether the Railway went thro' Thornhill! had not dared to satisfy myself! and at all the stations after I got into Dumfriesshire I *kept my eyes shut*. This will sound to you like sheer madness—but it was no more than extreme *nervousness*—which I *could not* control."

At Liverpool, she found Helen ill—"there is death in her face"—and summoned Jeannie from Auchtertool. Helen refused to consult John, who was sleeping at Seaforth House: "no bed for him here unless he had chosen to sleep in a little one in *my* room which I told him he was welcome to do if he liked!! but he declined". She too went to Seaforth, but for a very short time—the days of enchantment were long since gone, the memory of Rawdon was still fresh in her mind, and Mrs Paulet had ominously become "she"—"a few hours will be enough of *that*—she looks to be more than ever in a state of *'mild delirium'* ".

From Liverpool she moved to Manchester "to make amends to Geraldine for the vexation caused about me by that foolish Harriet Martineau". A scapegoat had been found, and Jane could with an easy mind accept the petting that Geraldine was so anxious to resume and she to receive. She read the latest chapters of Geraldine's new book *Marian Withers*. It was a dull version of *Mary Barton*, but Jane hailed it with relief.

> "It is *good* so far—no 'George Sandism' in it at all—indeed Geraldine is in the fair way to become one of the most moral 'women of England'. Seriously she has made an immense progress in common sense and common decency within the last year—and I begin to feel almost (as Mazzini would say) 'enthusiast of her'!"

For all Geraldine's kindness, Jane was soon "desperate" to get home. "Ah my Dear!" she wrote to Carlyle the day after she arrived back in London, late in September, "this has been bad work!" It had become "more and more clear to me that something is gone *deadly* wrong in my interior." Before Carlyle, who had now taken her place at Scotsbrig, followed her to No. 5, she had despairing thoughts of "resigning from Society", taking a cottage in Scotland with Margaret Hiddlestone or somebody as like Margaret as possible to look after her, "and so have outward *quiet* at least for the close of my useless existence"—but she realised that such a project "was only a genteel version of poor Mrs Gummidge's wish to 'go into *the House* and make nobody uncomfortable any more.' "

Carlyle was still trying to recover from his holiday in the shooting box:

> "Inexpressibly wearied is my poor body and poor soul. Ah me! People ought not to be angry at me. People ought to let me alone. Perhaps they would if they rightly understood what I was doing and suffering in this Life Pilgrimage at times; but they cannot, the good friendly souls! Ah me! or, rather: Courage! courage!"

He was shaken out of his woes for a moment by Jane's letter.

> "There remains at all times" he told her "and in all conceivable situations, short of Tophet itself, a set of quite infinite prizes for us to strive after—namely, of duties to do; and not until after they are done

can we talk of retiring to the 'House'. Oh no! Give that up, I entreat you; for it is mere want of sleep and other unreality, I tell you." .

He adds his now familiar words of encouragement:

"I reasonably calculate, not *un*reasonably according to all the light I have, that our life may be much more comfortable together than it has been for some years past. In me, if I can help it, there shall not be anything wanting for an issue so desirable, so indispensable in fact. If you will open your own eyes and shut your evil demon's imaginings and dreamings, I firmly believe all will soon be well. God grant it. Amen, amen! I love thee always, little as thou wilt believe it."

Her depression persisted, she could only sleep "by a large consumption of morphia", and her letters to Carlyle remained wild and hopeless. He appealed again:

"Oh my best little Jeannie!—for on the whole there is none of them all worth naming beside thee when thy better genius is not banished—try to sleep, to compose thy poor little heart and nerves, to love me as of old, at least not to hate me. My heart is very weary, wayworn too with fifty-three rough years behind me: but it *is* bound to thee, poor soul! as I can never bind it to any other. Help me to lead well what of life may still remain, and I will be for ever grateful".

But his return soon afterwards did nothing to lighten the gloom. He looked back with horror to his three months' absence: "Physically and spiritually don't remember ever to have suffered more." He was bilious, sleepless, and still uncertain what to do—"I seem to be farther from *speech* on any subject than ever"—and the mass of papers in his room threatened to overwhelm him. "No lonelier soul, I do believe," he groaned in his library, "lies under the sky at this moment than myself."

Both took weeks to recover from their holidays. Jane only managed it by the help of her morphia and when at last she felt better and some sleep came to her—and when Carlyle had at last begun reading again upstairs—the house was found to be overrun with mice and the curtains infested with bugs. And by the time this was dealt with, she caught the first of her colds and prepared to give up the winter as lost.

XXX

NERO
1849 – 1852

At the beginning of December, Jane's spirits improved and she began to drop a number of mysterious hints to Carlyle about a possible increase in the Cheyne Row household. At last, when Carlyle had been sufficiently prepared for almost anything short of another madman, she became a little plainer: "My dear, it's borne in upon my mind that I'm to have a dog!" And forthwith, late one evening, a railway guard delivered a dog to the house. He had brought him down from Manchester, a present from Stauros Dilberoglue. Jane had met the young Greek in London soon after her return, had told him of the death of her cat (drowned for "unexampled dishonesty" during her absence), and had spoken lightly of the pleasure that a well-behaved dog would give her. Dilberoglue had taken her at her word. A dog would soon be on the way, he said. Now, here it was, a small white terrier. He made the second animal in the house; for Jane had already admitted a stray black cat. Not since she had taken in the lost child had she faced such a critical moment.

She tells Betty Braid at the end of the year how the matter had progressed:

"I have got a little dog, that is almost as engaging as *Shandy*—tho' no *new* dog can ever *replace* dear little Shandy in my affections. . . . He is about the size of Shandy but has long white silky hair hanging all about him—and over his eyes which are very large and black—I was afraid Mr Carlyle would have found him a plague and ordered him about his business—and so he would if the dog had been noisy—but he is as good as dumb—*never* barks unless I make him do it in play—and then when Mr C comes in in bad humour the little beast never troubles its head but dances round him on its hind legs—till he comes *to* and feels quite grateful for his confidence in his good-will. So he gives it *raisins*, of which it is very

389

fond, one by one, and blows tobacco smoke in its face which it does not like so well—and calls it 'you little villain' in a tone of great kindness."

Nero, as the dog was called, considerably lightened the atmosphere in the house. Carlyle grew fond of him, and took him for his late night walks. Jane unashamedly adored him. He followed her about the house, slept on her bed, shopped with her, played with her. Her health improved, she threw off her winter cold, and told everybody about her acquisition. For weeks after her return she had seen practically no one, was too listless even to summon her friends to Chelsea. Now she wrote in her gayest style to Forster:

"I died ten days ago and was buried at Kensal green—at least *you* have no certainty to the contrary—what *is* the contrary? Do you mean to fulfil that promise of coming in the evening?"

The news was reserved for the postscript

"Oh Lord! I forgot to tell you—I have got a little dog!—and Mr C has accepted it with an amiability!—to be sure when he comes down gloomy in the mornings, or comes in wearied from his walk the infatuated little beast dances round him on its hind legs as *I* ought to do and can't, and he feels flattered and surprised by such unwonted capers to his honour and glory."

Letters flew out from Cheyne Row, radiant with Nero's charms:

"it sleeps at the foot of my bed without even stirring or audibly breathing all night long and never dreams of getting up till I get up myself—it follows me like **my** shadow and lies in my lap—and at meals when animals are apt to be so troublesome it makes no sort of demonstration beyond standing on its hind legs."

He was almost too attractive she found:

"*yesterday*, oh Heavens, I made my first experience of the strange-suddenly-struck-solitary, altogether ruined feeling of having lost one's dog! and also of the frenzied feeling of recognising him from a distance, in the arms of a dog stealer! but mercifully it was near home that he was snatched up —I missed him just opposite the Cooper's—and the lads who are all in my pay for odd jobs—rushed out to look for him and stopt the man who had him till I came up and put my hand firmly inside his collar—not the *man's* but the *dog's*—he said he had *found* the dog who was *losing himself*— and was *bringing* him after me!! and I would surely 'give him a trifle for his *trouble*'!! and I was cowardly enough to give him *twopence* to rid Nero and myself of his dangerous proximity."

Carlyle asked her, while Nero was still missing, how much she would give the dog-stealers: "I answered passionately with a flood of tears 'my whole half-year's allowance'! So you may fancy the fine way I am in."

"Mrs Carlyle," Geraldine wrote to Neuberg, "sends wonderful accounts of her *dog*. I am glad she has anything to interest her, and *dogs* are a *safe* investment of her sympathies." Neuberg had moved to Hampstead, and was now acting for a time as Carlyle's literary secretary before returning to Germany. The result of his help was seen almost at once; a number of articles on social questions of the day were soon ready for printing—the *Latter-Day Pamphlets* as they were called.

> "After much counsel," Carlyle told Lady Ashburton, "it seems now to be actually settled that these Pamphlets are to go forth; the first of them at the beginning of Feby., I suppose: terrible stuff, alas, alas! About bad, bad; sure to shock and enrage great quantities of people, for I really cannot manage to dress my talk at present, and besides there *is* no dressing of it on such a set of topics!"

The first pamphlet was sent to him at The Grange where he stayed for a few days at the end of January with Lady Ashburton and three other men, including Milnes. Carlyle, who was enjoying himself, was nicknamed Boreas by his hostess; and the absent Jane, Agrippina.

Nero and the black cat would stand together outside the diningroom door, scratching to be let in, and, when admitted, came "waltzing in" just like Harlequin and Columbine, remarked Jane, and the cat was Columbine from that moment.

> "Dear Master," wrote Nero, "I take the liberty to write to you myself, my Mistress being out of the way of writing to you she says, that you may know Columbine and I are quite well and play about as usual. There was no dinner yesterday to speak of; I had for my share only a piece of biscuit that might have been round the world, and if Columbine got anything at all *I* didn't see it."

and a little later:

> "My mistress brought my chain and said to 'come along with me while it shined, and I could finish after.' But she kept me so long in the London Library and other places that I had to miss the post. An old Gentleman in the omnibus . . . said '*Sharp*, isn't he?' and my mistress was so good as to say, 'oh yes!' And then the old Gentleman said again '*I* knew it! easy to see *that!*' And he put his hand in his hind pocket and took out a whole biscuit—a *sweet* one—and gave it me in bits—I was quite sorry to part from him, he was such a good judge of Dogs."

Jane was at the Library on most fine days during the next months; and at home, lying on the sofa with Nero on her lap, she read herself abreast of the novels. She read *David Copperfield* —"no feeling but remorse for wasting mortal time on such arrant nonsense"; *The Caxtons; Pendennis;* "waded" through *Alton Locke.*

> "It will surely be gratifying to you" she tells Carlyle, "the sight of your own name in almost every second page! But for *that* I am ashamed to say I should have broken down in it a great way this side of the end!"

She wondered what would become of Kingsley: "go mad, perhaps".

She had been told by Elizabeth Pepoli that a young girl, Dinah Mulock, who "has read 'absolutely no books' and seen 'nothing whatever of Society' " had written a successful novel. Could Forster get it for her? He sent her *The Ogilvies,* and received "1000 thanks (as Lady Ashburton writes it)".

> "It is long" she told him "since I fell in with a novel of this sort—all about love and nothing else whatever. It quite reminds one of one's own love's young dream. I like it, and like the poor girl who can still believe— or even 'believe that she believes' all that. God help her! she will sing to another tune if she go on living and writing for twenty years."

So Jane on the first Mulock book, little dreaming that the authoress was in the course of time to succeed where all others had failed, in taking the faithful Craik from her. She also read the chapters of Geraldine's new book as they were written— read them aloud, whenever possible, to Neuberg, who found time from his work for Carlyle to sit with her, listen, and play chess. Neuberg had been revealing unsuspected imperfections. For one thing, she generally beat him at chess; for another: "What is it," she asks John Carlyle, "that makes that man so heavy? He is clever and well-informed and well-bred and kind and has some humour and yet—when he goes away every time I yawn and yawn and feel so dished!"

She was interested by the latest Brontë book, *Shirley.* She had read *Wuthering Heights* when it appeared, to Carlyle, without any practical results, but *Jane Eyre* intrigued her: "curious how this woman says things that I have said exactly in my own words—which are often absurd and wild enough." So much so, that "I get the credit with certain *critics in style* of writing these

Jane Eyre books myself—and I was curious to see whether the new one was up to my reputation!'" There was another good reason why she wanted to read the new book; Anthony Sterling had told her that Shirley "was so ridiculously like myself that the author must have drawn it from me feature by feature." She spent two days with the book, and, as far as Shirley was concerned, had "reason to be satisfied! especially with the *age* of my likeness." But that was about her only satisfaction,

> "Now that this Authoress has left off 'Corsing and schvering' (as my German master used to call it) one finds her neither very lively nor very original. Still I should like very much to know her name—*can* you tell it me?—as if she have not *kept company* with *me* in this life, we must have been much together in some previous state of existence—I perceive in her book so many things I have said myself printed without alteration of a word."

Another novel, *Armand Carrel*, was even less successful; Lord Ashburton read it to his wife and Jane one April evening at Addiscombe, where Jane had gone for a few days to recover from the winter: "it sent us all off to bed in the midst" she reported. Lady Ashburton was "looking beautiful and in tearing spirits"; she also, Jane thought, bore a strange likeness to Maria Manning, who had just been hanged for murder. Jane was becoming increasingly absorbed in the crimes which were occupying much space in the newspapers, her letters of this time often refer to the Mannings, and she cuts out their pictures and sends them to Jeannie. A trial of another kind much talked about showed, she writes to John Forster, "the dangers of calling anyone 'My Dear' before the Nursemaid!" Forster had been ill, unknown to the Carlyles, and there was a slight misunderstanding. Carlyle, "too occupied with the Dead just now to have time for the living", had once more exaggerated the hostility he imagined to be ranged against him—this time, because of the *Latter-Day Pamphlets*. "Forster" he said, "soon fell away, I could perceive, into terror and surprise;—as indeed everybody did." Forster was, in fact, wondering why the Carlyles did not look him up. Jane reassures him:

> " 'With my soul on the pen'—as Mazzini says—I declare that if we ever look *not to care for you* it is a pure *deceptio visus*. My Husband may be a little—too little *demonstrative* in a general way but at all rates he is very *steadfast* in his friendships, and as for me I am a little model of Constancy

and all the Virtues!—including the rare gift of knowing the value of my blessings *before I have lost them*."

Her visit to Addiscombe had been her second in a month; the first, in March, gave her a cold—"that house being *incapable* of getting itself heated in cold weather"—which sent her to bed the moment she reached home. When she had enough strength to leave her bedroom, she returned to Addiscombe to try to rid herself of the effects of the cold she had caught there. She enjoyed her second stay well enough, but was put out by a pimple on her nose—with the Ashburtons, of all people, she was anxious to look her best. She was relieved to hear Anthony Sterling's "Damn your nose! for a sensible woman you have really the *oddest* ideas! as if anyone *really attached* to you could love you an atom less if you were all covered over with small-pox!" Most reassuring, Jane felt; "I should not like however to *try* human love with permanent smallpox."

Carlyle, who joined her for half her week's stay, was pre-occupied by his pamphlets during the days at Chelsea, and in the evenings when they both came home was, according to Jane, "generally at Bath House or elsewhere." Nero, then, was undisputed hero, letters were written to him when she was away, his deeds and misdeeds more or less faithfully chronicled when she returned. He had lost himself again, had jumped out of the window, was a nuisance, a darling, was indispensable, she did not know how she had lived more than forty-eight years without him.

As Carlyle came to the end of his pamphlets, in June, he began to entertain and to be entertained. At Thackeray's they met Charlotte Brontë, still supposedly incognito: "a less figure than Geraldine and extremely unimpressive to *look at*." Geraldine was up in London again, and very friendly—too friendly, thought the proprietorial Jane—with a new heroine, Fanny Lewald, the German George Sand, whom they had met at a Milnes breakfast, graced also, to Geraldine's excitement, by Thackeray. Carlyle finally astonished Jane by a wish to go to a great Ball at Bath House. She protested, but he was determined: "if I chose to be so peevish and ungracious as to stay away there was no help for me." He waved aside all objections. She had no dress; he would buy one. She shrank from "being bare" at her age; he retorted angrily that "true propriety consisted in con-forming to other people's fashions, and that Eve he supposed had as much sense of decency as I had and *she* wore no clothes at all." They went, and Jane enjoyed the blazing diamonds, the young beauties, the rooms hung with artificial roses, the kind eyes of the Duke of Wellington, and even Lady Ashburton receiving her guests with her "Grand-Lady airs". What Carlyle thought of the ball appears sufficiently in his letter of thanks:

"You gave us a glorious Ball; and were, and are, a glorious Queen. It is something to have seen such a one, and been seen by her,—tho' only as if from precipice to precipice, with horrid chasms, and roaring cataracts, and black rivers of Acheron flowing between, forever! It is the will of Fate; bountiful enough, and sad enough. Thank you always."

After the ball there was another weekend at Addiscombe with, said Jane disgustedly, "a party of *boys* and *girls*". Why was she asked to help with these flirting young things, she wanted to know? She felt more like wringing their necks.

This was the end of what Jane described to Mrs Russell on the day after her forty-ninth birthday as:

"a dreadful racket here this season—worse I think than in any London season I ever lived thro'—it has seemed to me sometimes as if the town must burst into spontaneous combustion. All the people of my acquaintance who come to London occasionally have come this year at one time ... and I feel like a Landlady after an Election week."

Not a day, scarcely an hour of repose has she had for weeks, she complains to Helen Welsh; people coming in and out all the time, and "the house has got to look like a Hotel with this only difference that no charges are made." Then came the sudden death of Peel

"like a black cloud over this scene of so-called 'gaieties' for a few days but only for a few days. Nothing leaves a long impression here. People dare not let themselves think or feel in this centre of frivolity and folly; they would go mad if they did, and universally commit suicide: for to 'tak a thocht and mend' is far from their intention."

Lady Ashburton called at Chelsea in tears, and begged Carlyle to come to Addiscombe for a week to console her: "as one asks the Clergyman when one is in affliction" commented Jane sourly.

Two of her exiles returned within these months. There was a rap at the door one evening, a familiar rap which Jane could not quite place. Plattnauer walked in, and she screamed in terror, but he was tolerably sane—had merely given up his post in Ireland through boredom. Jane, fearful that lack of money in London would eventually send him back to the asylum, at last persuaded him to go back. The other return, in August, was more dramatic. A friend of Fanny Lewald, Maurice Hartmann, was listening to a monologue on the failings of German democracy when

> "suddenly Mrs Carlyle started: a voice in the hall had reached her ear, stirring her like an electric shock. Her eyes sparkled, and opening the door she grasped the hands of the visitor in such a transport of joy that it seemed almost like an embrace."

Carlyle stopped talking, strode across the room, and shook hands. Jane, with tears in her eyes, was stroking the beard of the newcomer, exclaiming on its whiteness—for Mazzini, formerly with black moustache only, now had a grey beard. He told them how he had escaped from Italy, and Jane was fascinated by his audacity—his taking shelter in a madhouse at Marseilles because "they would not seek him amongst *mads*, decidedly"; and his lodging for two months at Geneva in the house of the magistrate who was trying to arrest him—for, explained Mazzini, his own house was surely the last place in which the magistrate would look for him. Jane found him "the same affectionate simple-hearted high-souled creature—but immensely more agreeable—talks now as one who has the habit of being listened to"—a revealing remark.

A few days after Mazzini arrived, Carlyle, having read all his proofs, went off to South Wales and then to Scotsbrig. Jane, who had had more than enough of travelling the previous year, stayed at home to stage another "earthquake". She was quite content that Carlyle should go, the house could not otherwise be cleaned, she was more peaceful without him, and she had plenty of friends. She insisted only that he wrote to her regularly; and if his letter did not arrive when expected she at once became frantic with anxiety. One of his letters—he wrote as a rule every other day—arrived by the midday instead of the early morning post, and by twelve she "had fallen so *low* for want of it that I might have had no news for a week!" She felt so "fluttery" for the rest of the day that she had to lie on the sofa whilst the ever-obliging Geraldine, now over the first violence of her adulation for Fanny Lewald, read a novel to her and rubbed her feet. Jane laughed at these scares when they were over, but could do nothing about them:

> "It is sad and wrong to be so dependent for the life of my life on any human being as I am on you; but I cannot by any force of logic cure myself of the habit at this date, when it has become a second nature—if I have to lead another life in any of the planets I shall take precious good care not to hang myself round any man's neck either as a locket or a millstone!"

Another morning she dashes off a letter:

> "Oh my Dear why haven't you sent me the least scrap this morning; tho' it were but to say that all these cocks have been made into one huge *cockyleekie*, or that you have learnt to sleep *thro' them*."

Carlyle was having trouble with night noises, and was feeling sorry for himself. Jane sympathises: "You as well as I are 'too vivid'." She was in the thick of trouble herself—trouble of another kind, but almost as familiar; with workmen and with her maid. Elizabeth's conduct since Carlyle left had been "more like insanity than anything else." The secret, Jane discovered, was that the girl had found what she imagined to be a better place "and wishes to have the train all ready for firing". She fired the train soon afterwards, leaving Jane in the midst of whitewashing, carpet beating and chimney sweeping with only a young daily help. She was soon on the track of another servant

> "I have had the offer of *two* 'likely to suit' one recommended by Mrs Newton—the other by Miss Darby—have decided for the latter, after sitting with my elbows on the table and my head in my hands for something like half an hour praying your 'immortal gods' to give me sound judgement—and now I fancy I should have taken the Yorkshire woman —but God bless me! one doesn't *marry* one's servant—one can *divorce* her in a month if one like, or in a minute paying a month's wages! so what need to take the matter so gravely."

Elizabeth had added insult to injury by moving a few doors up the street, passing number five daily, and calling to the butcher's boy in Jane's hearing, "better than ever I was, *my love*"! "A thoroughly bad character", observed the incensed Jane. Emma duly arrived from Essex; "her manners are *distinguished!* so self-possessed and soft-voiced, and *calm*, as only English people *can* be!" She was, Jane found,

> "very like Lancaster Jane" (the girl who had spoken so ecstatically of Jane after she had been dismissed) ". . . with a dash of Anne and of

Phoebe Baillie! She is not what is called 'a *thorough* servant', but that will be no objection to signify, as I am not 'a thorough *Lady*' which Grace Macdonald defined to be one 'who had not entered her own kitchen for seven years'."

The household began to simmer down, and Nero came from the corner into which he had been driven during the "earthquake."

Geraldine had gone back to Manchester "very unwillingly" —she had practically to be ordered home. Jane found her too exhausting; she was again sleeping only after taking morphia, and she looked on many of her visitors with a more than usually critical eye. Amelie Bolte, who had been writing her "love letters" ever since she had obtained the governess-ship, was now found to be "undependable". Mazzini was "so busy so busy!" that she saw practically nothing of him. He was working hard for the Society of the Friends of Italy; had been to Paris and back; and had just organised another concert to raise funds to help patriots still escaping from Italy. The concert, like most of Mazzini's undertakings, was erratic:

> "at the hour of commencement not a performer had arrived, nor for half an hour after! then all the gas suddenly went out! then a very fat—what shall I say?—*drunk* woman fell on Mazzini's neck and almost stifled him 'upon *my* honour.' Then the Principal Singer did not come at all and had to be brought *par vive force*, 'in a state of *horrible* drunkenness' and was only sobered by Mazzini's taking his hand and 'appealing to his— Patriotism!' Then Mario and Grisi arrived for the last act *without their music!* and the Music Shops all shut!"

Charlotte Wynn remained kind but unexciting; the Pepolis went off suddenly to Bologna; Craik "*insisted*" on playing chess, lost "*three* games in no time", and went away "heavy and displeased"; Anthony Sterling came in and out, restless and unsatisfactory. The rest of the Cheyne Row circle were out of town. Jane was feeling unsettled about Garnier. She had heard months earlier that he had been killed in the fighting at Baden —"a respectable happy death compared with what he had to anticipate here in London"—had told Plattnauer, who replied "poor Garnier, and so he is *dead!* but I should not be surprised to see more of him." Now, she heard "Garnier is *not* dead! worse—in a madhouse at Baden. Plattnauer is always a true prophet." Plattnauer's brother-in-law, Count Reichenbach, who had been in London, and who, like Garnier, was always spoiling for a fight and sad when there was no war, did not cheer her; he came to take leave "as mournful-looking as he came." Fanny Lewald also paid a farewell visit; she

> "eat a 'shop' (chop) with me yesterday on her own invitation. Tonight she sails for Paris and the arms of Stahr—there awaiting this 'bit of fascination'—how strangely people are fascinated in this world!"

In the midst of this melancholy came an invitation to The Grange for October. Jane tried to get a decisive word from Carlyle, but he would not be committed. He was nursing his wounds at Scotsbrig. He had seen Landor, who had "something of old Sterling" about him, had given way to "angry growlings" at the "fussiness and *fikery*" of Redwood, his host in Wales, where he had endured, he said, "the inanity of worse than solitude" and, after looking in at Liverpool, had relapsed into "silent misery" at Scotsbrig. He was not silent with Jane: "To whom can we complain, if not to one another, after all?" He acknowledged, when he heard about the misdoings of Elizabeth:

> "Oh! my dear little Jeannie, what a quantity of ugly feats you have always taken upon you in this respect; how you have lain between me and these annoyances, and wrapt me like a cloak against them! I know this well, whether I speak of it or not."

Later, at Scotsbrig and at Dumfries with his sister Jean, when further from the comforts of home and the provider of them, he fell wholly into self-pity: "I am a very unthankful, ill-conditioned, bilious, wayward, and heartworn son of Adam, I do suspect." But whatever his suspicions, he wrote on:

> "no minute can I be left alone to let my sad thoughts settle into sad composure, but every minute I must talk, talk. God help me! To be dead altogether! But fie!! fie! This is very weak, and I am but a spoony to write so. Tomorrow I will write to you more deliberately. I had no idea I was so sick of heart and had made such progress towards age and steady dispiritment. Alas! alas! I ought to be wrapped in cotton wool, and laid in a locked drawer at present. I can stand nothing."

He deplored his "grim" ways with friends; he really liked them better than they would ever dream from his manner. Nevertheless, he thought of leaving them for good, and he resurrected yet again his idyllic vision of Craigenputtock: "Sometimes it has struck me, could not I *continue* this *Sabbatic* period in a room at Craigenputtock, perhaps? Alas! alas!" He summed up Scotsbrig:

"my dear old mother, much broken since I had last seen her, was a perpetual source of sad and, as it were, sacred emotions to me. Sorrowful mostly and disgusting, and even degrading, were my other emotions. God help me! Much physical suffering. Morality sunk down with me almost to zero so far as consciousness went. Surely there should be a hospital for poor creatures in such a condition as mine. But let us not speak."

He had by that time made up his mind not to make up his mind. Miserable he might be, but he was by no means sure that a houseful at The Grange would not make him even more so.

Jane went off to The Grange by herself, but unhappily. Carlyle's reluctance to commit himself seemed to her, illogically enough, not so much a sign of his independence of the Ashburtons, as yet another illustration of her own uselessness to him. She told herself that she had failed to give him children, she was now unable to be a true wife to him, and she disappointed him even as a companion.

"My company I know is generally worse than none—and you cannot suffer more from the fact than I do from the consciousness of it. God knows how gladly I would be sweet-tempered and cheerful-hearted and all that sort of thing for your single sake if my temper were not soured and my heart saddened beyond my own power to mend them."

Carlyle tried to comfort her: "Oh! if you could but cease being conscious of what your company is to me! The consciousness is *all* the malady in that." He was off to the Speddings and the Marshalls, where "poultry, children, and flunkeys" kept him from sleep, where the "worship of the picturesque in all its branches" fretted him and where only a meeting with the newly-married Tennyson gave satisfaction. He liked Tennyson's wife; and his liking was in no way lessened when she replied to one of his more than usually extravagant tirades, "That is not sane, Mr Carlyle." He told Jane, "She has wit, she has sense."

He came home in the first days of October. The news of his arrival was given to Jane by Mrs Henry Taylor in the midst of a crowd:

"and the shouts of laughter and cutting 'wits' with which my startled look and exclamation 'oh gracious!' were visited when the news was told me as we sat down to dinner were enough to terrify one from 'showing feeling' for twelve months to come."

She was furious:

"Mrs Henry Taylor shan't *snub* me however—I am quite as clever as her any day of the year, and am bound to *her* by no ties human or divine. And so I showed her so plainly that I was displeased with her impertinent jesting at my expense that she made me an apology in the course of the evening."

When she was alone in her room that night her anger turned to tears: "it is the *first* time in all the twenty years I have lived beside you that you ever arrived at home and I away." She could not leave the subject alone: "I am not consoled but 'aggravated' by reflecting that in point of fact you will prefer finding 'perfect solitude' in your own house." But wanted or not, she refused to stay another three weeks, as Lady Ashburton wished: "*Who* cares one doit for me here that I should stay here, when you who still care a little for me—more anyhow than any other person living does—are again at home?" She is coming home in a few days:

"unless you are savage enough to *wish* not to see my face till the 20th and honest enough to tell me so; or unless you prefer to accept the invitation which Lady A is again writing to you to come here after you are rested."

Carlyle rose to the occasion; he had missed the welcome that had always awaited him until now, and which he had too often taken for granted; he missed Jane; and for the first time he said what she had waited twenty years or more to hear. He looked forward to his next return home:

"I shall know better than ever I did what the comfort to me is, of being received by you when I arrive worn out, and you welcome me with your old smiles and the light of a human fire and a human home."

He praised Nero who "had barked enthusiastic reception" and had shown himself, contrary to Carlyle's belief, "capable of a profound sentiment of affection." Columbine expressed no emotion whatever, but he had been glad to see even her. This was Jane's language, and she loved him for it. He showed all and more of the pleasure expected in the spring-cleaned house:

"Oh Goody! incomparable artist Goody! It is really a series of glad surprises; and the noble grate upstairs! all good and best. My bonnie little artistikin. Really it is clever and wise to a degree, and I admit it is pity that you were not here to show it me yourself. But I shall find it all out too. Thank you, thank you a thousand times!"

Finally, he agreed to come to The Grange but only, as Jane advised, when the guests were more to his liking.

In much improved spirits, although she still disliked the racket in which she had to spend a great part of her time, she writes to Carlyle of the people expected—including Thackeray, Brookfield and Kinglake. Neither of the Carlyles had met Kinglake, but they, and Carlyle particularly, had seen a fair amount of Brookfield—one of the Trinity College set at Cambridge with Milnes, Tennyson, Hallam, Venables, and the two men who were coming with him. Brookfield, who had taken orders some years ago, was now Inspector of Schools. He and his wife were already known for their dinners, where interesting people were sure to be found and good talk heard.

Jane also gave the list of expected guests to Charlotte Wynn, who commented to Mrs Brookfield: "How that woman does contrive to skim the cream off for her parties; one wonders what she does with relations and duty people which usually so entirely swamp a country house." Jane's letter was written before she had heard from Carlyle that he would join her, and Charlotte Wynn goes on:

> "Mrs C is evidently a little overturned by the different life she is now leading, which is very funny, as I did not fancy she could be influenced in the slightest degree by it . . . she has far more *esprit* in her own home than she is likely to find at Lady Ashburton's."

Jane was diverted by the effect of Thackeray's arrival on Henry Taylor, "who had 'had the gang all to himself' so long." She watched the two men with some pleasure; they

> "*fraternised* finally *not* like the carriage horses and 'railway steam-engine' as might have been supposed but like *men* and *Brothers!* I lie by and observe them with *a certain interest;* it is 'as good as a play.' "

Then Carlyle came. He was bilious, he told John after a week, and could not sleep: "the late hours, the flatter and the glitter do not suit me at all." Jane, however, was much better. Jane added a postscript: "*my* view of the matter is that he finds his present quarters extremely agreeable—and is 'pretty well' in health—and for me—he knows little about how I am or how I like it." For all this, she was glad to have him there. Her return was delayed a day or two by the illness of her hostess. Jane's offer to stay was accepted gratefully:

> "tho' *why* were difficult to tell, for—she would not have me sit with her above an hour in the day while in bed, and when out of it, the third day,

she had absolutely nothing to say to me! I don't know whether she is always so when alone with women—but the longer we know one another and the more we are intimate to outward appearance the less have we to say to one another *alone*."

Her own health was rather improved, she writes to Mrs Russell, and she was glad to be home.

"one brilliant person at a time, and a little of him, is a charming thing; but a whole houseful of brilliant people, shining all day and every day, makes one almost of George Sand's opinion, that good honest stupidity is the best thing to associate with."

Both the Carlyles had been interested in Kinglake, who called at Chelsea one night in November when Darwin was there.

"I like Kinglake," Carlyle told Lady Ashburton, "even him, as compared with the grinning inanity of most men's 'conversation' to me: a hard man, but always means something by what he says; a feline element in him too, I fear; but even a genuine *felis* is something!"

As for himself: "I feel myself sometimes, with almost a kind of terror, the most utterly lonely man I ever read of." A few days later he is still "very low" and "to nearly all mortals I am silent from choice; to the infinitesimal remainder, to whom my poor heart might long to speak, I seem to be compelled to silence."

This meant simply that he was again without a definite subject to work on, that he was bilious, and that all was not well in the house. The outward cause, he explained in a letter of the same month, November:

"Poor Jane is full of troubles again, about 'help' as the Yankees phrase it. Our new maid, a promising good creature, of Irish breed, proves entirely broken in health—unable to eat a morsel of food; and so, after a fortnight, all we can do with or for the poor soul, is to get her a place in the Middlesex Hospital: thither she is now wending; and her mistress is out on the great Deep, trying to catch another girl, who again will last but for a short span."

He added—for Lady Ashburton thought as he did:

"I really think, since one cannot get rational little niggers (the Hindoo breed, I should prefer) or other permanent domestic really helpful to one, it would be well to have done with this mockery of 'service' ".

The more fundamental trouble, as he saw it, is hinted in a journal entry:

"It is man's part to deal with Destiny, who is *known* to be inexorable. It is the woman's more to deal with the man, whom, even in impossible cases, she always thinks capable of being moved by human means; in this respect a harder, at least a less dignified, lot for her."

Nero was a blessing to both of them:

"I generally go out for an hour's walking before bed-time," Carlyle told his mother, "the little snaffle of a *messin* called Nero commonly goes with me, runs snuffling into every hole, or pirrs about at my side like a little glassy rat, and returns home the joyfullest and dirtiest little dog one need wish to see."

He was again stolen during the next few months, and Jane wails:

"I wish I had never *set up* a dog. I did not think there was so much superfluous sensibility left in me—that I should lose my sleep for the dog's absence out of my bed."

She lay, wondering what had happened to him: "What his life is today I am afraid to conjecture." She had no rest until he was found.

The winter was mild, and she got through it with less pain and with fewer colds than usual. The house was rarely empty of visitors and early in the New Year, 1851, Carlyle began to write his *Life of John Sterling*, which was done in three months, and left him in the Spring feeling more contented than usual. Jane was still having a struggle with maids—her latest was deaf—but the main break in her routine was the whirlwind appearance on New Year's Day of Theresa Revis (the child of Arthur Buller's mistress) who had been adopted and brought up by old Mrs Buller, and whom Thackeray wrote into Blanche Amory in *Pendennis:* "the looks, the manners, the wiles, the *Larmes* 'and all that sort of thing' are a perfect likeness."

The Carlyles were alarmed lest the girl were to be with them for good, since no one seemed anxious to have her—she "has just been playing the Sultana in India for a year" explained Jane to her uncle—but after a day or two she produced

"a most devoted Lover. *She* 'does not love *him* a bit' she told me—'had been hesitating some time betwixt accepting him, or going on the stage, or drowning herself.' I told her, her decision was good, as marrying did not preclude either 'going on the stage' at a subsequent period or 'drowning herself.' Whereas had she decided on *the drowning*, there could have been no more of it."

The main point was, that the Carlyles were delivered from her:

"you can have no notion how the whole routine of this quiet house was tumbled heels over head. It had been for these three days and three nights *not* Jonah in the Whale's belly—but the Whale in Jonah's belly! that little creature seemed to have absorbed the whole establishment into *her*self."

Jane's view of marriage was expressed again, this time to Jeannie, who had told her that she intended to marry Andrew Crystal:

"Oh Babbie! how I wish it had not been your *idea* to pitch your tent in this 'valley of the shadow of Marriage'—it is a very *relaxing air* I am sure and peculiarly unsuitable to *your* constitution. But certainly *I* am not the best authorized person to tell people how they should manage their lives under that head of Method—having made such a mess of my own life— God help me!"

She also wrote in a somewhat similar sense to the youngest Carlyle girl, Jenny Hanning, whose husband was proposing to emigrate to America.

The Great Exhibition had been opened in Hyde Park, and she invited Helen Welsh down to see it, and to hear Thackeray lecturing on the English Humorists. She had little good to say of the Exhibition—"a beautiful sight" but the exhibits contained "nothing really worth looking at" and the fatigue of seeing them was "indescribable". Carlyle was disgusted. He had walked in Kensington Gardens, he told Lady Ashburton, but: "Oh Heaven, avoiding carefully that monstrous Beehive of the Wind-dust-ry of all Nations, and the gaping blockheads that simmer round it".

They had news this April of three people well known to them:

"John Mill, did you see in the Times, is wedded to his widow Taylor; a fact in Biography: poor good Mill! He has not announced it to anybody; somebody showed it to Jane in the Times. We hear likewise that Rd Milnes is going to be—*à la bonne heure:* I believe it may be really good. Finally Mrs Alfred Tennyson has not prospered, poor soul: they say she is herself doing well. Heigho!"

So Carlyle wrote to Lady Ashburton, in Devonshire, and away from the gossip.

Helen Welsh, undismayed by the Carlyles' sombre reports of the Exhibition, came down, and Jane was telling Mrs Russell just before her fiftieth birthday:

"I never went to so many fine parties and bothered so much about *dresses* etc., and seemed so much like just *coming out!* as this Summer! Not that I have like the eagle renewed my age (*does* the eagle renew its age?) or got any influx of health and gaiety of heart; but the longer one lives in London one gets of course to know more people and to be more invited about—and Mr C having no longer such a dislike to great parties as he once had, I fall naturally into the current of London life—and a very *fast* one it is!"

The usual spate of holiday plans was being discussed and they went, eventually, to Malvern towards the end of July. A Dr Gully had invited them many times to "come, lodge in my house; only come and I will cure you!" Such an appeal was irresistible. Both Jane and Carlyle steadfastly ignored the effect of mind on body. They never once got to grips with the main cause of their hypochondria—their own relationship. Perhaps there was no cure for either of them, but certainly it did not consist, as both fondly imagined, in change of scene or, as now, in Dr Gully's water-cure.

They took the waters nevertheless, and left Malvern a month later rather worse than they came, separating soon afterwards, Carlyle bound for Scotsbrig and Jane for Manchester. There was a typical misunderstanding; Jane, over-quick to detect a slur, left in bitterness because Carlyle had gone "through the form of kissing at parting with a lighted cigar in your mouth(!)" Carlyle protested vigorously at "the frightful, hateful whirl of such a scene." He reproached her: "You unkind woman, unfortunate with the best intentions, to send me off in that humour with such a *viaticum* through the manufacturing districts!" His explanation was simply that he had come close to her, not to say goodbye, but "to whisper to you that I had given the maid half a crown, nothing more or other, as I am a living sinner." He went off to Scotsbrig "full of gloom and heaviness, and totally out of health, bodily and spiritual," and rested there until the time came to join Jane for a promised visit to the Stanleys (formerly the Eddisburys) in Cheshire.

Jane recovered quickly. In Carlyle's words to Lady Ashburton, she was: "apparently very well, and tolerably amused with what Manchester offers, which a crowd of devoted servants are very ready to get up for her always in that quarter." Jane put the matter more gratefully: Geraldine "manages to surround me with 'all things most pleasant in life' ". Nero was

"the happiest of dogs goes all the journeys by railway—
smuggled with the utmost ease—and has run many hundreds of
miles after the little Lancashire birds." Mrs Gaskell called with
her husband, invited them to dinner and took them for a
"beautiful drive." She is, says Jane, "a very kind cheery woman
in her own house but there is an atmosphere of moral dulness
about her, as about all Socinian women." She added: "I am
thinking whether it would not be expedient however to ask *her*
to give *you* a bed when you come—she would be 'proud and
happy' I guess—and you do not wish to sleep at Geraldine's."
She was fascinated by the Dilberoglues; she read Carlyle's
latest letter, she said:

> "with great contentment during a Greek repast—reminding one of *the
> Arabian Nights*. All sorts of dried fruits and delicate cakes interspersed with
> cold roast ducks(!) delicious coffee and tea etc—presided over by the
> loveliest large-eyed Greek girl that Imagination ever conceived, and an
> old Greek Lady that seemed the Ideal of a Scotch Covenanter's Wife!—
> I never spent a more exotic evening."

She saw more factories, and had a good tale to tell of Espinasse,
who

> "has—renounced his allegiance to you! When his Father was in London
> lately, he (the Father anything but an admirer of yours) was greatly
> charmed to hear his Son declare that he had 'quite changed his views
> about Carlyle—and was no longer blind to his many and great faults'.
> Whereupon the Espinasse Father in a transport of gratitude to Heaven
> for a *saved* 'insipid offspring' pulled out—a five-pound note! and made
> Espinasse a present of it. Espinasse, thanking his Father, then went on to
> say that 'he no longer liked *Mrs* Carlyle either—that he believed her an
> excellent woman once—but she had grown more and more into Carlyle's
> likeness, until there was no enduring her!' The Father however did not
> again open his purse!"

Jane was repeating the history of her stay with Geraldine five
years earlier—the history of her life, for that matter; she
flourished in activity and under active, open love and admiration. All went well until, towards the end of her visit, she
dreamt:

> "that I had gone home to Haddington to see my Mother—and found a
> good fire and tea all set out, with a sort of purple-coloured cups (which I
> have not remembered these twenty years) but she did not come—and I
> sat waiting and waiting till it slowly came over me that she was dead, and
> I awoke myself with a cry—to find my head splitting and my throat
> refusing to swallow."

Carlyle was ready to leave Scotsbrig, and Jane told Mrs Gaskell "Mr C shall be *delivered* at your door tonight about ten." Her dream had been the beginning of a cold, and she was "stuffed" with it when they left the following day for Alderley Park. Carlyle begged her to limit the stay to a single day—preparations were going forward there for the marriage of Blanche and Lord Airlie, and he was terrified at the thought of becoming involved in the ceremony. He was unpopular with some of the Stanley family, as appears in a letter to Lady Stanley this year from her mother-in-law:

> "We have got C's Life of Sterling and it makes one *hate* and *fear* C more than ever—I wish that Lord Airlie may not participate in your and B's regard for him. He is not fit for a young woman's society, such a daring, mocking infidel."

But he also had his defenders, and Jane was a great favourite with the Stanley girls—the Bright Young Things—and they stayed on. Jane was

> "supremely wretched; tho' the Place is lovely and there was a fine rattling houseful of people—and the Stanleys . . . as kind as possible—alas too kind! for Lady S *would* show me all the 'beautiful views and that sort of thing' out of doors—and Blanche *would* spend half the night in my bedroom!"

The trousseau was

> "about as wonderful a piece of nonsense as the *Exhibition of all Nations*. Good Heavens! how is any one woman to use up all those gowns and cloaks and fine clothes of every denomination? And the profusion of coronets! every stocking, every pockethandkerchief, every thing had a coronet on it! Lady S is nearly out of her wits with joy at having at last got *one* daughter made a Countess and off her hands! Poor Blanche doesn't seem to know, amidst the excitement and rapture of *the trousseau*, whether she loves *the man* or not—she *hopes* well enough at least for practical purposes."

They were home again near the end of September, but Carlyle left almost at once for Paris, where the Ashburtons were staying. His method of replying to Lady Ashburton's invitation was all his own:

> "How strange" he says, ". . . that human creatures should be important to one another! But, in all ways, whether of water or not, (Dr E says 19/20 of humans is water, the rest mostly lime, magnesia &c) we are fearfully and wonderfully made. And some of us are very well made too;

and are inexpressibly beautiful and good, and were made in Heaven, the essence of them I do believe!"

He went off with the Brownings, also bound for Paris.

Whatever Jane may have thought of this trip, she appeared pleased enough to be home again where she could nurse her cold. "Really," she told Carlyle, "Nero makes a capital little nurse! never left me for an instant, except for *inevitable purposes*, and these he transacted with a despatch!"

Awaiting her was some work after her own heart—finding employment and a home for more exiles. These were Saffi and Quadri, comrades of Mazzini, who had escaped from Italy and were almost destitute. Mazzini first brought Saffi along late one evening

> "a very gentlemanly, grave, sincere looking young man—with an unfortunate habit of tumbling over the fire irons. He does this, Mazzini says, wherever he goes—not once, but three or four times at one visit—last night he restrained himself on account of my weak nerves and did it only twice!"

She found rooms for them nearby, lent them furniture, and arranged for Saffi to give Italian lessons to the Sterling and Wedgwood children; and, as she told John Carlyle after his brother had come back from Paris: "so now to use Mazzini's expression '*he is saved*.' " Carlyle, she added "is extremely fond of Saffi—I have not seen him *take* so much to any one this long while"—as appears in his description to Lady Ashburton: "I have seen no sadder milder-minded more priestlike young man than this Head of the Revolutionists, who has now got 20 shillings a week to rejoice over."

The Paris trip had been a failure. Carlyle "got nothing by the business but confusion, pain, disappointment; total (or almost total) want of sleep." After a few days of it he cut his losses and returned home abruptly "glad beyond all things, and almost incredulous of the fact, to find myself in my own bed again." Jane was ready for trouble, and, in such a mood, trouble came. The Ashburtons also came back earlier than they had planned —"a fact" she said, "which threw some light on his return home sooner than was expected." Lady Ashburton had knitted her a scarf—an act which brought from Carlyle:

> "a thousand thanks, O noble woman. You are good and royal; and to

me, when I think of everything, the most miraculous being (or nearly so) that has been created in these epochs."

Jane took a less generous view of the gift. Lady Ashburton had also knitted a smaller scarf for Carlyle, and, says Jane: "I believe the dear woman would never have done all that knitting for *me* unless as a handsome preparation for doing the comforter for Mr C." She was not at home when Lady Ashburton called with the scarf and with an invitation to The Grange. She refused the invitation on the grounds of having only just settled in her own home again, but offered to call at Bath House during the three days Lady Ashburton was to be there. This, Lady Ashburton told Carlyle when he called there, was not possible—she had no spare time. Jane flared up. During these three days, Carlyle was at Bath House three times; why should she not be received there? And why, she demanded of him, was he there so often? They had words. He:

> " 'could not see what the devil business I had to find anything strange in that or to suppose that any slight was put on *me*'—'on the contrary she had spoken of the *impossibility* of receiving me—*in the most goodnatured* manner!!' "

So she reported to Jeannie at Liverpool.

> "It is not of course any caprice *she* can show to me that annoys me— I have long given up the generous attempts at loving her—but it is to see *him* always starting up to defend every thing she does and says and no matter whether it be capricious behaviour towards his *wife*—so long as she flatters himself with delicate attentions."

The problem appeared insoluble unless Carlyle agreed to give up his visits to Bath House. This, feeling innocent of harm, he would not do. There was an impasse, and he wrote gloomily to Lady Ashburton: "We are in a very dark state here; nearly altogether silent, given up to our own thoughts, such as they may be in this decadent state of the year and of the world." Lady Ashburton, he added, was "the only one glow of radiancy that still looks of Heaven to me, on a ground which is black and waste as the realms of Phlegethon and Styx." Exaggerated language, but he was uneasy. To feel justified in his friendship for Lady Ashburton, he had to think of her as a serious person, but she did not always help him. He sometimes felt about her as Milnes had felt years earlier, when he spoke of her "charming sense when tête-a-tête, her odious frivolity when a third person enters." Carlyle had by no means given up hope of turning that sense to account in the world. Meanwhile, he continued to visit Bath House, and, when the Ashburtons were away, to write:

> "I am cultivating solitude and silence. . . . Of you I think often, or indeed *always;* but only as a *ghost* might, and in terms which neither God nor man, if they could be well seen into, need find much to punish!"

A few days after this letter, in November, Lady Ashburton invited them again to The Grange—this time, for the following month. Jane, understandably, received the invitation ungraciously:

> "put" she said "on the touching footing of requiring my assistance—to help her 'in amusing Mama.' Heaven knows what is to be said from *me* individually. If I refuse this time she will quarrel with me outright—that is her way—and as quarrelling with her would involve also quarrelling with Mr C, it is not a thing to be done lightly."

This to John Carlyle, who was not included in the Ashburton circle, but might be trusted to confide her dilemma to his brother. She decided, however, without a word to Carlyle.

> "Jane surprised me last night," Carlyle wrote to Lady Ashburton, "by saying she *had* written to you, accepting for us both! I was obliged to *deny*, on the spur of the moment, that I wished to go, or could go, which indeed is not far from the very truth, so fatally am I situated just now! For reasons that my noble Lady understands too well; and in her beautiful soul, does all justice to, and knows what to think of. Oh my Lady!"

He would have to consider the matter for himself. "Anyway I am right glad Jane is going." His meditations were brought to an end a few days later by a letter from Lady Ashburton.

> "Principessa! it shall be as you desire: how else? In all things you are beautiful and good; and much is managed by you which nobody else could manage! You will write to Jane when you want her; to me when you want me."

Eventually, Jane set off by herself at the beginning of December, leaving Carlyle to follow at his leisure. She sent him a bright little note on his fifty-fifth birthday:

> "Thro' 24 years the *first* Birthday which has found you without your— 'What shall I say?'—*Shadow!* remembered all the same, and good luck to it all the more—I have left order that Nero shall have a tumbler of Brandy negus."

Although she caught a cold before she had been twenty-four hours at The Grange, the time passed more endurably than she had imagined. She did not stint complaints to correspondents, but as usual when in Lady Ashburton's company she found much to admire—her hostess' quickness and aptness of speech was too much like her own to be otherwise than applauded, however wryly.

> "I gave my 'noble Hosts' " she told Carlyle, ". . . your '*respects*', as desired—and I must say they were received by Lady A just as I should have received them in her place—with a great burst of ironical laughter— 'If *I* were simple enough' she said—'to be taken in by *that dodge, she* wasn't—that Mr C knew very well he had gone a great way beyond '*respects*' with her—expecially since that visit to Paris' ".

This was Jane to the life, and reassuring into the bargain.

The guest who most struck her attention was Macaulay— this was her first proper sight of him. "I used to think," she told Mrs Russell, "my Husband the most copious talker, when he liked, that was anywhere to be fallen in with—but Macaulay beats him hollow!—in *quantity*." Before the Carlyles went home, early in January, 1852, Lady Ashburton had made a determined effort to remove all traces of suspicion in Jane's mind. For a time she succeeded; and the grateful Carlyle told her soon after reaching home: "I know not what you did to her that Monday morning; but she has looked much *happier* ever since, and is at her ease beside me."

XXXI

FREDERICK THE GREAT
1851 – 1853

Towards the end of 1851 Carlyle told Lady Ashburton that, after thinking about it for several years, he had at last begun to read Preuss' *History of Frederick the Great*. "Frederick" he said, "the more I know of him, pleases me the better; a man and King whose love of *reality* was instinctive and supreme." He had long considered writing a book about him. He would have preferred an English hero, but the hostility (not without cause) of Panizzi, Librarian of the British Museum, had made research there actually more difficult for him than in Germany.

He was still reading Preuss in February of the next year: "I do not even grow to love him better," he explained to Lady Ashburton of Frederick: "a really mediocre intellect, a hard withered soul: great only in his invincible courage, in his evident unconscious loyalty to truth and fact: the last and only *King* I know of in Europe since Cromwell." His many doubts about the wisdom of attempting the work disappeared for a time as he looked round at Europe's "batch of Temporary Kings" of which the saddest, he thought, was Disraeli, "a Pinchbeck-Hebrew, almost professedly a Son of Belial." He was utterly disgusted. "I think" he assured Lady Ashburton,

> "if I had ever believed in suffrage, free parliaments, force of public opinion, and all that melancholy rubbish of which men's heads are now full, I should have rent my garments . . . and gone about in sackcloth and ashes for a sign!"

The world, he felt, needed another Hero, a Frederick, to lead it back to sanity. It was his duty to write this book, shrink though he did from the labour. Jane warned him, vainly, that he should leave such a subject alone. From this moment he was dedicated to Frederick, but with many misgivings. He was conscious of a falling away. The Hero of *The French Revolution* had been God himself; of *Cromwell*, a soldier of God; but of *Frederick* no more than a very earthbound Hero, parts of whose mind he shuddered to penetrate.

He first approached the task without realising what it would demand of him, and Jane was no more than vaguely uneasy. On the whole she appeared lighter-hearted this winter and spring than of late years, her rancour against Carlyle quite forgotten, and he was ecstatic in this thanks to Lady Ashburton, to whom he attributed the change:

> "Had I never seen you in such circumstances, even in *such*, I should never have known how beautiful and constantly royal you are, how like a queen you vanquish contradictions under your feet, and are a daughter of the Harmonies, you, meet you amid what dissonances one will. Blessings on you, I have seen one royal woman; this too is something in one's life, as life now goes."

Jane had caught a fresh cold when they returned home the previous month—a change of any kind in winter had but one result with her—but she threw it off, and was soon "daily" Carlyle reported to Lady Ashburton, "out with her 'imaginary truffle dog' as you defined the glorious Nero to be." Nero had shown "unspeakable joy" at her return, Jane told Mrs Russell in her end of year letter. She sent the money as usual for her mother's dependents, and would have sent the *Life of Sterling* for Mrs Russell herself, but the second edition was not yet ready. "None of Mr C's books have sold with such rapidity as this one—if he would write *a novel* we should become as rich as— Dickens!"

She was seeing as much as possible of Mazzini, for he was again hinting at a return to Italy. He was tireless at raising funds, and Lady Ashburton was given at second hand the story of his latest soirée. Jane went to it with some of his "disciples." It was, said Carlyle,

> " 'perfectly successful' after its kind: a very harmless meeting; properly a kind of *Lecture*, with fringings of coffee (voluntary coffee): Lecture which M. read in the most artless manner, 'with the candles *between* him and the little slips of paper', and as practical as a grocer's bill, since to be seen (by me not to be read) in the public papers, and listened to without commentary, except of feet and hands, by a believing auditory of the youthful middle-classes near a thousand strong."

In May, Carlyle felt off colour, and the house relapsed into gloom. When he was better, Jane wrote a humorously reproachful postscript to a letter to his mother:

> "I am surprised that so good and sensible a woman as yourself should have brought up her son so badly that he should not know what patience and self-denial mean—merely observing 'Thou'st gey ill to deal wi'.' Gey ill indeed, and always the longer the worse."

In the beginning of July, Carlyle signed a thirty-one-year lease for the Cheyne Row house—"*that* should serve our time I think!" observed Jane—so ending the long drawn out struggle about a permanent home in London. Then began a process of "getting it made habitable", as Carlyle put it.

> "Did you ever," Jane asks Neuberg, "have a house pretty well *gutted* and try to *live in it* while *gutting?* If not, you can form no adequate idea of the 'hubbub wild and dire dismay' in which we have for already one fortnight lived, moved, and NOT had our being."

She was of course delighted. Carlyle had handed the whole transaction over to her; within reason, she was to have the house made as she wanted it. She leaped at the chance, regretting only that he did not go away at once and leave her a clear field. But Carlyle—waiting probably to be at home on her fifty-first birthday—was still "hanging on by the eyelids" in one tiny room, reading his Frederick books, whilst confusion reigned about him, with ceilings coming down, partitions going up, and the thermometer at eighty degrees in the shade. Jane did her best for the obstinate man: "I have taken back the little girl I had during my servant's illness to specially go after Mr C with a watering can to keep his floors continually wet and dustless as he requires them!" A week after her birthday, she got him away—first to Thomas Erskine at Linlathen, then to Scotsbrig, where he began translating in preparation for *Frederick.* Jane, he tells Lady Ashburton,

> "who is architect, and general manager, rectificator, and commander-in-chief (and really quite expert at the art, 'with an eye equal to a carpenter's square' and other appropriate virtues and gifts), continues there constantly all this while except one little journey into Dorchester; hardly defending now two little rooms from the general influence of chaos; and appears almost to like it, there is such action and reaction and victorious excitement going on. As for me, I do not in the least like it."

This was in the middle of August; Carlyle had "bathed in the

German Ocean (unable to swim across to you)"—the Ash-burtons were abroad—and, on the way to Scotsbrig, "passed thro' some shadows of you about Beattock and elsewhere (as is perhaps too much my wont in all roads and localities)."

He was right; Jane did like the struggle at Cheyne Row; as she said, she had no time to think and plenty to do:

> "in superintending all these men I . . . am infinitely more satisfied than I was in talking '*wits*' in my white silk gown with white feathers in my head and *soirées* at Bath House 'and all that sort of thing' ".

She even took in her stride a further change of servants and she found time for her friends in the midst of the tumult. She went off to Mrs Macready:

> "who is dying and wishes much to see me once more—*that* will hardly be much of a *relief*—still I wish to go—she was always a dear kind friend to me and an affection which stands the test of conscious dying deserves every satisfaction that one can give it."

Forster too was ill, in Dickens' house, and, like Mrs Macready, very glad to see her bright face and smile.

As for Mazzini; he

> "was here on Sunday morning and made my hair stand on end with his projects. If he don't be shot, or in an Austrian Fortress *within the month!* it will be more by good luck than good guiding. I rely on the promise 'God is kind to women fools and drunk people'."

She had taken him to the Brownings, and was not over pleased:

> "such a fuss the Brownings made over Mazzini this day! My private opinion of Browning is, in spite of Mr C's favour for him, that he is 'nothing' or very little more 'but a fluff of feathers!' *She* is *true* and *good* and the most *womanly* creature."

But Elizabeth Barrett Browning did not stay in favour many months. Jane met the Brownings again at a tea given by Forster after he had recovered. They took her in their carriage—"an ugly dull thing"—to her omnibus at Piccadilly. "I like Browning less and less—and even *she* does not grow on me."

Carlyle asked after Nero; had she forgotten him?

> "Poor Darling, it is no forgetfulness of him that has kept me silent on his subject—but rather that he is part and parcel of *myself*; when I say I am well, it means also Nero is well! *Nero c'est moi! moi c'est Nero!*"

He had been jealous of the cat, "and I 'felt it my duty' to box his ears. He stood a moment as if taking his resolution, then rushed up the kitchen stairs and, as it afterwards appeared, out of the House!! for in ten minutes or so a woman came to the door with Master Nero in her arms!... He would take no notice of *me* after for several hours! And yet he had never read 'George Sand Novels' that dog, or any sort of *novels!*"

She even managed to entertain in the upset house, reporting "a tea-party 'quite promiscuously' in *my end of the parlour* on Saturday evening!" The next day, after dining with Mrs Fraser, she came home in the evening "and very soon after Darwin drove up—'sick to death of the whole thing'—I am to dine with *him* today at four." This was followed by the excitement of a balloon ascent by her cousin John Welsh which Darwin took her to see. But having seen it, Jane could not rest easy: John was to return "at whatever hour" to tell her that he had landed safely: "if he don't come I shall just have to sit up all night to no purpose—sleeping with that boy up 'in the clouds' is out of the question." She tells Carlyle the result in her breathless fashion:

> "Had little sleep last night—thro' expecting that boy down from the skies—at one in the morning a telegraph dispatch came from him (*at the public expense*). But the awful double knock at one in the morning, and the hollow-voiced man in green who presented the letter, and the evasion of Nero who full of sleep thought it was Mr Piper come for *him* and went off with the Telegraph Man without my noticing—and only returned after I had come downstairs and unbarred the door for the second time and whistled some ten minutes in the street! all that was not a good preparation for a night's rest."

Later, but still at one end of the livingroom, she had a tea-party consisting of Alexander Herzen, Saffi, Darwin, Brookfield and the Reichenbachs, with whom she had become very friendly: "There were six of us and we spoke four languages."

She and Carlyle were having a friendly battle about a visit to Germany. He wanted to get material for his book, and had talked earlier in the year of them going together. This, Jane saw, was now impracticable; she could not leave the house for long until the autumn. She urged him to go with Neuberg, who was already back in Germany. Carlyle, doing his best to be unselfish, held out for a while.

> "Jane urges me to go 'myself' but that is only generosity and female

human heroism; I know well she ought to go with me, and she cannot in these weeks be well spared at Chelsea, were all else right and ready. Today I have a letter from her full of spirits, but arguing that she cannot be spared till the work is further on."

So he told his "beautiful Lady, and friend sent me by the Heavens!" He even thought of withdrawing from the venture altogether: "Shall we cower into some nearest hole and leave Germany to the winds?" Jane, to whom this was proposed, treated it as it deserved: "As to 'cowering into some *hole*'! you are 'the last man in all England' that can do that sort of thing with advantage so there is no use speculating about **it**."

Still he hesitated. He was not enjoying his holiday. Everyone was kind at Linlathen: "The only evil is that they will keep me in talk. Alas! how much happier I should be not talking or talked to!" He appealed to her again: "You surely deserve this one little pleasure; there are so few you can get from me in this world." But she still held out: "When it comes to putting everything in order again it will be a much greater pleasure than going to Germany I can tell you." He tried again; would she come to Scotsbrig, where he now was? His mother "would like right weel to have a crack wi' her ance mair." No, she could not leave the house; Scotsbrig next year, she hoped. But what ailed him? she asked; his letters were growing more and more unhappy. He reassured her: "It is the nature of the beast; and he lives in a continual element of black, broken by lightnings, and cannot help it, poor devil!" He was merely reluctant to make the decision to go, loathed all that lay before, even *Frederick*, and was not sleeping well. At the end of August he pulled himself together: "Last night I slept much better, and, indeed, except utter dispiritment and indolent confusion, there is nothing essential that ails me." He went for a final evening walk along "the loneliest road in all Britain." He re-read Jane's letters:

> "On the whole, I was very sore of heart, and pitied my poor Jeannie heartily for all she suffers; some of it that I can mend and will; some that I cannot so well, and can only try. God bless thee ever dear Jeannie! that is my heart's prayer, go where I may, do or suffer what I may."

With this now almost automatic benediction he set off, only to find, at Leith, that he had either left his passport behind or had lost it. He wrote a frantic letter to Jane who, she declared, "had to gallop about in street-cabs *by the hour* like a madwoman, and lost two whole nights' sleep in consequence." The passport was sent off, and with it a note: "I am in a little better humour now after a walk to Darwin's—where I saw 'a man more miserable than myself'—for Darwin is in the slow agonies of *removing*." She ended with "Nero's blind love." But she was soon writing indignantly again—to Germany—refuting Carlyle's accusation that she had not written a letter to await his arrival there. "I do wrong things by the dozen, but to *not* write when expressly desired *to*, and where there was *business* in question, *that* is a sort of wrong thing not the least in my line!"

Lady Ashburton had invited her to Addiscombe for the first weekend in September, and for once Jane accepted gratefully, having alternated for some days between the sofa at home and a bed a door or two away in which she had been "devoured by *bugs*." She was pleasantly distracted by the news that John Carlyle intended to marry—not Rosella Neuberg, but a friend of fifteen years standing, a widow with three boys. They ought to do well together, she thought," but you put so little *emphasis* into your love-making—that it won't surprise me if this one too gets out of patience and slips away from you!" At the end of the month she was writing:

> "*Quelle vie!* Not yours but mine! You I hear from some who saw you 'never looked so well nor were in such good spirits'—Naturally!—if a man don't look well and be in good spirits *before* his marriage what is to be expected *after?* But I who am not going to be married, I don't 'look well' at all, and my spirits, and *nerves* too are at the lowest."

The decorators were still all over the house, and she had moved to lodgings "in spite of my sad nights among the 'small beings' (as Mazzini calls them)". The latest maid, Fanny, was being helpful "though not without a dash of Irish confusion."
She treated John to a breath of scandal.

> "Do you know William Fraser is lying ill—dying it is thought—in the Middlesex Hospital? And his '*Wife*' (so called) 'gone into the Workhouse'. Mrs Fraser whom I dined with yesterday talks of him with more indifference than one would like to talk of a dead cat. She seemed excessively vexed that *you* had not awaited his death to marry *her*."

But this was as nothing to the behaviour of Doctor Weber.

> "He came to see me at Lady A's desire and—saw me—and he looked

down into the bottom of my eyes as if he meant to take my whole soul captive—but my soul had something else to do than be so taken—and he has since called *five times!!* without seeing me—three times I was really *out* and twice too dirty to be *at home*. And he is 'Physician to the Austrian Embassy and in extensive practice'! Why then come so often to Chelsea—Perhaps he knows I am a friend of Mazzini's—and 'all Austrians are born spies' Reichenbach says."

Carlyle in Germany was complaining of miseries at night, "but he cannot *conceal* that he is really pretty well." She wondered "what he would have made of *my* sleeping accommodations during the last three months." Nevertheless, he returned "half dead" after a tour that he described as "done as in some shirt of Nessus; misery and dyspeptic degradation, inflammation, and insomnia tracking every step of me"—only to be met at the door of the house by Jane's warning cry, "take care of the paint." His "bilious misery" reached such a pitch that she thought the best thing they could do would be to go into the garden and blow each other's brains out. "We did nothing so sensible however but went instead to The Grange"—but the retreat from paint to "eight o'clock dinner and the excitements of high life" proved scarcely less disastrous. After a fortnight she fled home again, leaving him to follow when she had the house in order. "Let us be patient" he told his mother, "'canny as eggs,' and the better day will come at last." He "collapsed" when he left the "bright environment" of Lady Ashburton.

> "I love you for your noble cheerfulness of heart" he said, "for your frank courage and ready and gracious sense—in fact I love you for several things. I have seen nobody . . . all evening we read, mainly in silence; all day, solitary . . . I am 'annihilating rubbish' ".

He and Jane had been reading *Henry Esmond*, just published:

> "my wife first, with great admiration 'for the fine delineations of women'; I next, with aversion and contempt mainly for his feline phantasms of 'women', and many reflections on his singular fineness of sense and singular want of do."

This was in the middle of November, and his condition remained indifferent: "Here are we", he wrote in his journal, "fairly *fronting* our destiny at least, which I own is sufficiently Medusa-like to these sick, solitary eyes." He was convinced he had "a diseased liver", and for some time he suffered what he described as "silent weak rage, remorse even, which is not common with me." When he looked back on the past few years he felt "a solitude of soul coupled with a helplessness, which are frightful to look upon."

The year closed quietly but dismally, "now" Jane told Mrs Russell

> "that we have got that weary Duke's funeral over—for a while it made our neighbourhood perfectly intolerable. I never saw streets so jammed with human beings in all my life. I saw the *lying in state*, at the cost of being crushed for *four hours*—and it was much like scenes I have seen in the Lyceum Theatre only not so well *got up* as Vestris would have had it. I also saw the procession from Bath House—and that too displeased me."

For all this, she "fell to crying and couldn't stop till it was all over."

On Christmas Day, Brookfield called at Chelsea. He was on his way to Henry Taylor, but he found Jane so easy to talk to, and so well worth listening to, that he stayed on. Eventually, thinking about her Christmas dinner, she asked where he proposed to eat. At home, he said, but showed no eagerness to leave. He was persuaded without difficulty to stay on. They had soup, haunch of mutton, woodcocks, and Christmas pudding with brandy sauce, port, sherry, madeira, and ale from the Cricketers' up the road. Carlyle affected despair when he saw the small joint, turning it over and over on the dish. Would Brookfield carve it? Brookfield declined, but agreed that the butcher had cut up this particular sheep in a peculiar manner. "It's not the butcher's fault" said Jane. "It was to have been only a leg, but when you agreed to stay the loin was added." Brookfield did not leave till ten, and was back again a few days later, asking them, to Carlyle's amusement, "to use their influence with each other" to persuade each other to come to a dinner he was giving. They went, to this and to others, and he began to call frequently at Cheyne Row. He talked to Carlyle about Tennyson's marriage, describing marriage as "dipping into a pitcher of snakes for the chance of an eel and that Tennyson had found an eel." Carlyle fumed a good deal at this: "Eels" he said "had a faculty by natural transformation for becoming snakes." Brookfield spoke admiringly of Carlyle to Lady Ashburton, who he thought was the only person in the world who dared put a ring through his nose. She replied that she had few friends, but she had "my dear old Prophet Carlyle, and has one any right to more than one such friend in a lifetime?"

Soon after the beginning of the new year, 1853, the winter pause was broken by an old enemy. A few days earlier Carlyle told his mother that Jane

> "is stronger than in past years. She reads now with *specs* in the candle-light, as well as I; uses her mother's specs I perceive, and indeed looks very well in them, going handsomely into the condition of an elderly dame."

What Jane would have thought of the "elderly dame" may be imagined, but the general sense of his analysis was right enough —she was in better health than for some time past. Then cocks began to crow. Carlyle's sleep forsook him. When he was not disturbed by the crowing of a cock, he was lying waiting in sullen rage for the cock to crow. He would stamp on the floor, thump on his bed in a passion of anger, and pace the room, smoking furiously—so waking Jane, when she slept, her bed-room being immediately beneath his. Soon she was awake before him, listening for his angry shout and bangs to begin. Sleep almost disappeared, tempers were frayed, hot words passed, Carlyle rushed off to The Grange. But this was "worse than useless . . . a long nightmare; *folly* and *indigestion* the order of the day." Why did he go there? he asked; lonely he was, lonely must remain.

He came away with one satisfaction from his week; he had snubbed D'Azeglio, representative of the King of Sardinia. Mazzini had again slipped off to Italy, taking leave of her, Jane told Caroline Fox, "as one who never expected to see her again; he kissed her and said 'Be strong and good until I return.' " He had since been in the thick of the abortive Milan insurrection. Carlyle appealed to Lady Ashburton to "think of the insurrection at Milan; and pity poor mad Mazzini and Co., in spite of the big ugly bullying *Times*." He assured Lord Ashburton: "The Austrians will not get Mazzini in the *coffins* at Milan. Jane and our Postman (M's late landlord) ascertain that from the Great Deep of Philo-Italian Sansculottism here." Mazzini's adventures were not to the liking of Carlyle, but he was a friend of Jane and a good man; and when D'Azeglio spoke slightingly of him: "Monsieur" he said, "vous ne le connaissez pas du tout, du tout!" He then turned his back, sat down, and began to read a newspaper.

This little triumph did nothing to save Carlyle from the cocks, who were still crowing or about to crow. Nor did it save him from his long indecision about *Frederick.* He was resolved to write the book, as he had been resolved to write *The French Revolution* and *Cromwell*, but, more than with them, the prospect of this new and almost endless labour so appalled him that he could not believe even in his own resolution. "An unfortunate subject," he told himself—a sentiment which Jane echoed at every possible opportunity until she realised that she was wasting her breath.

The cocks persisted.

> "It seems" said Jane "as if the universe were growing into one poultry yard! There is also a *Parrot*, named *Sara*, at next door. All that has waked up Mr C into the old phrenzy to be off—'*into silence*'!—but the three or four hundred pounds laid out last year give pause. And besides as the old Servant said to his Master, when threatened with *parting* 'where the deevil wud ye gang to?' I also feel often enough a desperate need of being off 'into silence'—but a *silence* more deep and impregnable than is anywhere to be found in the land of the living."

There was more trouble, and Jane and Carlyle did not always keep to the point—every failing was examined—so that Carlyle is found writing wearily to Lady Ashburton: "Heaven I suppose will not refuse to let me think of you, whatever else is forbidden!'

One of them, it became clear, must go away for a time. Carlyle wanted to concentrate on *Frederick*, but was worried about his mother, now over eighty and failing. Jane offered to go to Scotsbrig; she was curious to see John's wife—he was now married and living at Moffat—and she hoped to visit Haddington once more while the Donaldsons still lived. She left at the beginning of July, taking Nero openly this time:

> "Did you hear what my male fellow passenger said when I appealed to him about Nero? 'I assure you Sir he will lie quite quiet—will not give you the slightest trouble.' '*I sincerely hope he will not!*' From that specimen you may fancy how courteous he was likely to be. It was by the strongest protest I succeeded in keeping one-fourth of a window down which— there being four of us—I maintained was my right. He put them *both* up, the brute, without asking by your leave—and would have kept them so all the way."

She was not asked for Nero's ticket "and I rather grudged the four shillings."

She found her uncle looking very frail, and Helen "more skeleton-like and more misshapen than ever," but Geraldine, who at once rushed over to see her, was unchanged—talkative, dashing, unorthodox, smoking like a chimney, but gentle with Jane when she needed soothing. Helen came with her to Moffat for a day or two, but this did not save Jane from the distinction of being kept awake her first night by a hyena, as she triumphantly informed Carlyle: "*you* complain of a single *cock!*" Nor did Helen's presence prevent Jane from observing that her new sister-in-law was far from faultless. "She looks to me," she said ominously, "like a woman who had been all her life made the *first* person with those she lived beside and to feel herself in a *false position* when she doubts her *superiority* being recognised." As the days passed, the shortcomings of Mrs John and of John himself became clearer.

> "This" she tells Carlyle dismally after a week of Moffat, "is St Swithin's day and 'it rains hale water' as Helen used to say. But I should go if it rained brimstone. I don't think I ever felt more discouraged in all my life; and that is much to say! Do not suppose however that I am troubling 'others' with my inward dismay—I am sure neither John nor his wife have an idea how little satisfaction my visit has yielded me—or how little purpose I have of ever taxing their *hospitality* again."

Not enough was being made of her—that was the trouble—and a good deal too much was being made of John. He was going over to Scotsbrig daily to see his mother, and, said the disgusted Jane,

> "he talks talks about his own insight and his unheard of exertions on her behalf, in a way to confuse one's senses. His wife is always talking to him of his making himself a perfect martyr to filial affection, and he accepts the merit with a fatuity!"

She arrived at Scotsbrig on her fifty-second birthday. Old Mrs Carlyle, bedridden for months, insisted on getting up and dressing in her best clothes to welcome her, and Jamie and his wife Isabella made her welcome and as comfortable as possible. But the strain of living in a house where old Mrs Carlyle fluctuated almost hourly between life and death was soon aggravated by the arrival of other members of the family. Alick and his wife had emigrated many years since, followed by Robert

Hanning and Jenny, but Mary Austin from her farm, The Gill, near Annan, and Jean Aitken from Dumfries came to stay, and, with John over every day, the atmosphere became difficult.

Carlyle was complaining almost daily of his lot. Letter after letter followed Jane about, from Liverpool to Moffat, from Moffat to Scotsbrig. He could not sleep, life was impossible, the place was an absolute bedlam—cocks crowing, parrots screeching, fireworks banging and shooting from a nearby pleasure-ground, "vile yellow Italians" grinding their organs, and the July heat quite insufferable. But the cocks were still his *bête noire*. "The cocks" he declared "must either withdraw or die." If no one would help him: "I would cheerfully shoot them, and pay the price if discovered, but I have no gun, should be unsafe for hitting, and indeed seldom see the wretched animals." He complained, then repented, then complained again. "What could I do?" he asked, "fly for shelter to my mammy, like a poor infant with its finger cut? complain in my distress to the one heart that used to be open to me?" This was the crucial point—he was not understood—and to this thought he returned whenever Jane's reply lacked the requisite sympathy.

> "Oh Jeannie," he cried, "you know nothing about me just now. With all the clearness of vision you have, your lynx-eyes do not reach into the inner region of me, and know not what is in my heart, what, on the whole, was always, and will always be there. I wish you did; I wish you did."

In despair, he called in a local builder; was there any way of preserving him from the noises that were like to drive him insane? Yes, said the man, a sound-proof room. He could build such a place in the roof. Carlyle wrote off post-haste to Jane— what did she think? She approved; since so much money had already been put into improvements, they might as well take the final step of making themselves "*independent* of Ronca and all contingencies".

This worry by letter, day after day, reinforcing the strained atmosphere at Scotsbrig, made Jane long for home, where she was plainly needed. After a week, she wrote:

> "With John hovering about 'not like one crow but a whole flight of crows', and Jean rubbing everything up the wrong way of the hair, my position is not so tenable as it would have been alone with your Mother and Jamie and Isabella."

Her views of John's doctoring had been strengthened by what she saw at Scotsbrig. She spoke her mind. John, who had not been unaware of her feelings at Moffat, said she would be better away, and she went at once, leaving all the rest "vexed to the heart". She had not energy left for a holiday—"what a botch has been made of my travels"—and returned to Liverpool. There, she stayed a week, tormented by incessant toothache. So broken was she, that she attended church without a murmur. Even Nero felt subdued: "When I came in from *Church* today, tho' it had been the first hour he had been separated from me since we left home together, he could hardly raise a jump." She was back in London on the first day of August, was up all night with raging toothache, went off to the dentist before Carlyle awoke, and had two teeth drawn, only to find that one had been taken out in error. Back she went to have a third tooth drawn. The reaction brought on a bilious attack, and she felt good for nothing for weeks afterwards.

Carlyle was in such a state of frustration when she returned that the sound-proof room was at once put in hand. The house was again invaded by workmen, became "a mere dust-cloud", and all the decorations of the previous summer were ruined at a blow:

> "For the last week however" she tells John Carlyle a month later "Irish labourers have ceased to tumble down thro' the up-stairs ceilings, bringing cart loads of dust and broken laths and plaster along with them —*five* times this accident occurred!!—the last time within a yard of my head as I was stooping over a drawer—had he dislocated my neck as might easily have happened one of us would have been permanently provided with 'a silent apartment' enough without further botheration."

London was empty; Darwin and Forster away; and Mazzini no sooner safely back than yearning to be off again

> "in hopes of kicking up another shine almost immediately. He told me when I last saw him he might go off again within ten days. I am out of all patience at his reckless folly—if one did not hear every day of new arrests and executions one might let him scheme and talk hoping it might all end in smoke—but it ends in blood—and that is horrible—1,300 arrests in the Papal states within a week!"

Reichenbach had gone to America and had taken a farm near Philadelphia. He wrote often to Jane: "asks *me* questions about draining and 'engines for making drain-tiles' but he looks forward I think with secret desire to *a war* in which he may take part and get himself handsomely killed." She was almost thankful for the return of Plattnauer, less mad than in the previous year.

In the midst of this uproar within and stagnation without came news that John Welsh had died suddenly. Fanny seized this moment to run off with one of the Irish labourers, and Jane gave up the fight for a time, and went with Carlyle to live at Addiscombe which was empty—"the noble owners" Carlyle explained, being glad if they would occupy a room or two of this "beautifullest cottage in the world". He "liked it much, and kept busy reading, writing, riding; she not so much, having none of these resources, and except to put *me* right, no interest at all." So little indeed, that he found it necessary to beg Lady Ashburton: "Write—to Jane—if she has written. Your better genius and mine will prompt you to do so."

An uneasy truce prevailed on the return from Addiscombe in November, and Carlyle had a good story to tell of Thomas Spedding, who called in one evening. Spedding years ago had wound up his career as barrister in London by addressing the judge: "Such, my Lord, are the grounds on which I am instructed to support this case; I cannot say I think them very strong ones." This to Lady Ashburton, who was now pressing for their company over Christmas at The Grange; an invitation which Jane felt bound to accept, having occupied Addiscombe in her absence. So, at least, Carlyle informed his mother; but Jane had another and more pressing reason for wishing to be out of her house. "Alas! and the silent apartment had turned out the noisiest apartment in the house! and the *cocks* still crowed and the *macaw* still shrieked! and Mr C still stormed!"

Lady Ashburton suggested that Carlyle brought his work with him—he could have a room set aside. He was delighted, and had in the same letter a good word to say of Froude. But Jane, he warned Lady Ashburton, was poorly and sleepless: "you will be as soft to her as you can." To his mother, he confessed that "In spite of all these tumblings and agitations, I really feel almost better than I have done in late years; certainly not worse." He could not say as much for Jane who is 'not at all strong, sleeps very ill, etc. . . . But she is very tough, and a bit of good stuff too. I often wonder how she holds out, and braves many things with so thin a skin."

She thought hard at The Grange about the problem of noises in Cheyne Row. No structural alterations, it appeared, could give them complete silence; Ronca's fowls could be heard even in the soundproof room. The answer clearly was to turn Ronca out of the next door house by renting it themselves, and Jane was despatched to do it.

"I thought it a most wildgoose enterprise I was sent on" she told Mary Russell a little ingenuously, "and when Lady Ashburton, and the others asked him why he sent poor me instead of going himself, and he coolly answered—'Oh *I* should only spoil the thing—*she* is sure to manage it' it provoked me the more—I was so sure I could not manage it. But he was quite right. Before the week was out I had done better than take a house we did not need—for I had got the people bound down legally 'under a penalty of £10 and of immediate notice to quit, never to keep or allow to be kept, fowls or macaw or any other nuisance on these premises,' in consideration of £5 given to them by Mr Carlyle. . . . You may fancy what I had suffered, thro' the effect of these nuisances on Mr C, when I tell you that, on having this agreement put in my hand by their house agent I—burst into tears!—and should have kissed the man if he had not been so *ugly!*"

She had no sooner "put down" Ronca for good, and was still enjoying her triumph at Chelsea when she heard of the sudden death of Helen Welsh, a few weeks after her father. They had never been intimate—Jane had long had reservations about the entire Maryland Street household—but Helen's death was the end of the Liverpool era. Jeannie was married and in Glasgow, Maggie and Mary with Walter at Auchtertool, Johnnie did not interest her, and Alick, still in Liverpool, she could not endure for more than half an hour at a time.

At The Grange, Carlyle was as usual dominating the entire company, when, just before Christmas, he heard that his mother was dying. "What to do I knew not" he wrote in his journal. "At length shaking aside my sick languor and wretched uncertainty I perceived plainly that I ought *not* to be there—but I ought to go to Scotsbrig at all risks straightway." He spoke to his hostess, was given leave to go at once, and arrived in time to see and be known by his mother. She died on Christmas Day, and her last words were to him, and typical of her. "I'm muckle obleeged t'ye."

He returned just before the New Year, worked grimly on *Frederick*, saw as few people as he was able, spoke little. "My

soul," he wrote, "is exceedingly sorrowful, all hung with *black*."
He was living on memories and on resolves to make himself
worthy of his mother. "But alas all is yet *frozen* within me."
Jane was gentle with him: "You must feel," she wrote as soon
as she heard the news, "that you have always been a good son
to her, that you have always appreciated her as she deserved,
and that she knew this, and loved you to the last moment." As
she consoled him, she thought of herself and her mother.
Carlyle at least had his mother's last look and had been given
her last words: "but the words that awaited *me* were, 'your
Mother is *dead!*' And I deserved it should so end."

XXXII

TROUBLE
1853 – 1856

Jane spent most of the winter and spring of 1853-4 reading and nursing her colds, with Carlyle upstairs in his sound-proof room. Now that he knew Ronca's fowls and parrot had gone, he discovered that the room was more silent than he had suspected. He was working, he told Lady Ashburton, in a garret: "light—no noise but east wind—downstairs all bells, organs, dogs, fishermen, *Times* articles and other noises." He was not contented. Nothing that he wrote for *Frederick* satisfied him, and he despaired when he surveyed the hundreds of books and manuscripts to be mastered before the work could take shape. He thought a great deal of his mother and of death. The world seemed full of death. Jeffrey had gone already, followed by his friend and biographer, Lord Cockburn, and by John Wilson. Carlyle wondered whether his vast project—its vastness becoming ever more apparent—could be finished within his own lifetime. He was saddened still further by the unthinking enthusiasm shown everywhere for the Crimean War on which England was just embarking—"I have hardly seen a madder business." But he kept his despair as much as he could to the journal so fully employed at this time; there were few outbursts; and Jane had the negative satisfaction of calm, even though it were a sad, despairing calm. And Carlyle kept to the house; the visits to Bath House seemed at an end.

For her, ailing often, but with a good maid at last (yet another Anne) many books and always Nero, the time slipped by, until she was crying out on the eve of her fifty-third birthday:

"Isn't it frightful, dear Mrs Russell, what a rate the years fly at! . . . The days look often long and weary enough in passing, but when all '*bunched up*' (as my maid expresses it) into a year, it is no time at all to look back on."

Forster called, and Darwin when well enough, but visitors were few, and a visit from a country cousin — daughter of Robert Hunter of Moffat, but now married and living in Tynron— was an event to be treasured:

> "I have seen my cousin Mrs Pringle, and like her very much; there is a mixture of cultivation and rusticity about her, which is very refreshing here, where every thing is *cultivated to death*. At first glance I confess her *fine clothes* rather appalled me. . . . The child I never wish to see again! It is an '*enfant terrible*'. How such a sensible woman allows her child to be so tiresome is almost as incomprehensible to me as how she comes to wear such a cloak!"

Her one substantial outing of these months—a dinner at the Procters—also provided a meeting with one who had long since faded from her mind:

> "I saw '*the Noble Lady*' that night—and a strange tragic sight she was- sitting all alone in a low-ceilinged, confined room at the top of Procter's house—a French bed in a corner—some relics of the grand Bedford! Square-Drawingroom—(small pictures and the like) scattered about— herself stately, artistic as ever—not a line of her figure, not a fold of her dress changed since we knew her first, 20 years ago and more! She made me sit on a low chair opposite her (she had sent for me to come up), and began to speak of Edward Irving and long ago as if it were last year—last month! There was something quite overpowering in the whole thing— the pagan grandeur of the old woman—retired from the world, *awaiting death*, as erect and unyielding as ever, contrasted so strangely with the mean bedroom at the top of the house and the uproar of *company* going on below—and the past which she seemed to live and move in felt to gather round me too, till I fairly laid my head on her lap and burst into tears! . . . You may fancy the humour in which I went back to the *party* which was then at a white heat of excitement—about nothing!"

With a sudden change of tone, she passes on in the same letter gossip about the Ruskins:

> "Mrs Ruskin has been taken to Scotland by *her* parents—and Ruskin is gone to Switzerland with *his*—and the separation is understood to be permanent. There is even a rumour that *Mrs* Ruskin is to sue for a divorce—I know nothing about it—except that I have always pitied Mrs Ruskin while people generally blame her—for love of dress and company and flirtation—she was too young and pretty to be so left to her own devices as she was by her husband who seemed to wish nothing more of her but the credit of having a pretty well-dressed wife."

All this to John Carlyle, who was moving to London with his wife and family. Soon after they reached London, and just before the birth of his first child, he and his wife were involved in a railway accident. The shock led to the death of mother and child. Jane was something less than sympathetic:

"That was a horrid business" she told Mrs Russell, "it looked such a *waste* of a Woman and Child. Of course she was to die—yet humanly viewed one could not help believing if she had staid at home and taken the ordinary cares of herself that her situation required, she might have borne a living child and done well. But her constant excursions on railways and sightseeing and house-hunting seemed to us often even before the *accident* which brought on her mortal illness, a sheer tempting of providence."

Of the bereaved John she remarked: "he has not seemed to know what he was doing—and is now in an apathetic state that I do not feel much interest in. My Husband positively looks more heart-sore than *he* does." This last remark was made to her cousin John, whose mother, widow of George Welsh of Boreland, had moved near London for the winter. Jane thought well of the boy—the hero of the balloon ascent—"a good and clever lad".

The event of the year for her was yet another and most important move to London. Geraldine, she explained to Mary Russell,

"the most *intimate* friend I have in the world—and who has lived generally at Manchester since we first knew each other, has decided to come and live near me for good. Her Brother married eighteen months ago—and has realized a Baby, and a Wife's Mother in the house besides—so Geraldine felt it getting too hot for her there. It will be a real gain to have a woman I like, as near as the street in which I have decided on an apartment for her."

Carlyle kept away from Addiscombe as well as from Bath House, spending only one weekend in the country, when he made a pilgrimage from Addiscombe to the new Crystal Palace: "a monstrous mountain of glass building." Apart from this excursion he worked on in his "garret" with the faithful Neuberg while Jane and Geraldine talked and smoked and read downstairs. His intention, he said, was "to stay at home, and if I can do no work, be at least very miserable for doing none."

Cholera had come back, and Jane found it "very sad to walk out here for many weeks—in a single half-mile of street I often met as many as six funerals." She worried herself about the war.

"I am haunted day and night with the thought of all the women of England, Scotland and Ireland who must be in agonies of suspense about their nearest and dearest. Thank God I have no Husband or Father or Son in that horrible war. I have some few acquaintances however and one intimate friend—Colonel Sterling—and I read the list of killed and wounded always with a sick dread of finding his name."

In October, Plattnauer came in to tell of the death of Charlotte Wynn's brother, and she spent the evening in tears.

In the latter part of the year, when Carlyle relaxed some of the seclusion he had found necessary after his mother's death, visitors came more freely. Among them was Duffy, now a Member of Parliament. He took Jane and Geraldine to lunch at the House of Commons, "where Mrs Carlyle" he said, "met some old friends, and her lively fancy played about the subject so habitually afterwards that Carlyle was incited to take a little interest in it." Duffy found her appearance "peculiarly inter-esting. Her face was colourless but most expressive, answering promptly to every emotion; her eyes were frank and pleasant, and her smile, which was gracious, passed easily into banter or mockery."

Thackeray came in one evening:

'was very gentle and friendly-looking" Carlyle told Lady Ashburton, "ingenious too here and there; but extremely difficult to talk with, some-how—his talk lying all in flashes, little detached pools, you nowhere got upon a well or a vein."

Brookfield looked in from time to time, and enjoyed Jane's stories, which he often repeated and wrote down. And another occasional visitor was old Lady Sandwich. "She and Jane pull well together", Carlyle noted to Lady Ashburton.

Lord Ashburton had for some while been pressing Carlyle to follow his example and grow a beard. Lady Ashburton, from Scotland, now added her persuasions. He would consider it, Carlyle said. A few days later, he was admitting to Lord Ashburton:

"Really the Beard-movement does proceed, I perceive. Leigh Hunt, I heard not long since, had produced a copious beard, white or nearly so; he complained that there were two drawbacks, (1) the little boys laughed at him; (2) the beard abolished an uncommonly sweet smile he was understood to have. That latter evil will not apply to me. Nor do I think practically the little boys will much interfere. Moustaches are already very abundant; and one young gent (of the *gent* species) carries a beard in these streets, black, immure, sticking out from the chin of him like a kitchen kettle."

But he did nothing, or Jane would allow him to do nothing, until, early in October, "Lord Ashburton, *himself beaver*, came in one morning fresh from the Highlands and, pleading former promise, took away razor." Lord Ashburton was a handsome man with a fine flowing beard, a kind man and courteous, with a winning manner which neither Carlyle nor Jane could resist. The beard began to grow. There were the usual outcries from the man who was growing it, and the wife who had to watch it grow. After three weeks, "it is as if I had got a dirty gorse common on my chin". Another week, and he is still gloomy; the beard, he tells Lady Ashburton, is making him uglier. Even after three months, at the beginning of 1855, he was, he told the same correspondent, "seldom out of doors till the Sun is down; striding along like a gaunt spectre in the dark"—like an "escaped maniac", Jane thought. More months still were to pass before both of them were reconciled to the change.

In the autumn of 1854 Jane heard of another death that saddened her—of old Mary Mills at Thornhill, to whom she had been sending regular gifts ever since the death of Mrs Welsh. Now, she said, there is "one heart fewer in the world who loved my Mother." But she agreed that "Mary would have been very pleased could she have *seen her own funeral!*" The news of the losses before Sebastopol distressed both—"this thrice stupid, hideous blotch" of a war, Carlyle called it—and both became more unwell than usual. John Carlyle, still undecided about what to do, was staying with them, "to confuse us further," as his brother put it. Jane did not stir outside the house in December, cancelled an arrangement to go to The Grange, and, as Carlyle was staying at home, would not go the next month. Her second refusal, Carlyle admitted to Lady Ashburton, "took me by surprise", but he thought her wise— "she is still weak."

She had a little excitement at the end of the old year with a manuscript sent to her by Reichenbach:

"Oh Mr Neuberg! for the love of God, and man—and woman—glance over these pages of MS and tell me; *are they publishable* and *where?* I am sure, tho' an idiot in *politics*, that I cannot be mistaken in finding *this article* full of sense—for haven't I heard Mr Carlyle say the same things over and over again? At all events, sense or nonsense, it is sent to me—with a touching faith in my goodnature (*my* goodnature!!) to be 'got into a conservative newspaper'—or printed in some shape or other. In fact there never was an intensely silent man seized with such a phrenzy to get a hearing!"

Then she mislaid the manuscript and her feelings became less amiable:

"On my knees—with my hair all dishevelled—clasped hands—and eyes fixed anxiously on your serene countenance—I ask; *have* you got back the accursed thing and *have* you sent it to Ireland? and *have* you told Ireland if he—even *he* couldn't stand it—to send it back to you; and if he *could* stand it, to send you the *paper* in which it appeared."

Friends, she concludes, "are—the Devil!"

She had not been wasting her time during these winter weeks of illness; she had something on her mind; and early in February, when Carlyle returned from a smoke in the frosty garden he found many pages of her writing neatly laid on his desk upstairs. The papers were headed "Budget of a *Femme Incomprise*".

"I don't choose to speak again on the money question! The 'replies' from the Noble Lord are unfair and unkind and little to the purpose. When you tell me '*I pester your life out about money*'—that '*your soul is sick with hearing about it*'—that '*I had better make the money I have serve*'—'*at all rates, hang it, let you alone of it*'—all that I call perfectly unfair, the reverse of kind, and tending to nothing but disagreement. If I were greedy or extravagant or a bad manager, you would be justified in 'staving me off' with loud words; but you cannot say that of me (whatever else)—cannot think it of me. At least, I am sure that I never 'asked for more' to myself from you or anyone, not even from my own mother, in all my life, and that through six and twenty years I have kept house for you at more or less cost according to given circumstances, but always on less than it costs the generality of people living in the same style."

She explains in great detail, and with wit, that their cost of living has gone up by exactly £29 11s. 8d., and she asks for this sum to be paid to her in quarterly instalments. She ends:

"Mercy! to think there are women—your friend Lady A for example ('Rumeurs!' Sensation)—I say for example—who spend not merely the additamental pounds I must make such pother about, but four times my whole income in the ball of one night—and none the worse for it nor anyone the better. It is—what shall I say?—'curious' upon *my* honour. But just in the same manner Mrs Freeman might say: 'To think there are women—Mrs Carlyle for example—who spend £3 14s. 6d. on one

435

dressing-gown, and I with just two loaves and eighteen pence from the parish, to live on by the week.' There is no bottom to such reflections. The only thing one is perfectly sure of is 'it will come all to the same ultimately,' and I can't say I'll regret the loss of myself, for one. I add no more, but remain, dear Sir, your obedient humble servant,

JANE WELSH CARLYLE.

Carlyle gave in at once, writing at the foot of the last page before handing her back the document: "Excellent, my dear clever Goody, thriftiest, wittiest, and cleverest of women. I will set thee up again to a certainty, and thy £30 more shall be granted, thy bits of debts paid, and thy will be done." This put Jane in high humour, and she promptly wrote off to Forster:

"Since you will ask us to dine with you on Monday, it is a clear case of your being disengaged on Monday, and at leisure. *Ergo*, you *can*, if you *like*, come and dine with us here. And won't you like? There's a good man!"

She was determined to show that she too could be generous. One day soon after Carlyle had given her the money she asked for, he was working upstairs as usual when he heard Nero's paw scratching the door. He let him in, and found tied round his neck a picture of a horse and a cheque from Jane. He would not take the money—he still thought it an extravagance to buy a horse—and eventually Neuberg lent him one during the summer.

But the "Budget" was symptomatic of more important things. Carlyle had begun to go to Bath House again. When, evening after evening, Jane heard him leave his work, walk downstairs and out of the door, she could not contain her suspicion and hatred. She had, round the corner in Oakley Street, Geraldine, and, also near, Elizabeth Pepoli, back from Bologna. They were with her almost every day, and she unburdened herself to them. They sympathised and were hot against Carlyle. Geraldine, said Jane, was "my Elektra". Geraldine played the role only too well. Her indignation was unrestrained. Her beloved Jane was being slighted—that was how she saw the matter—and she inflamed her friend's sense of injury. Jane persisted in reproaching Carlyle, but he would not listen—in his eyes, he was doing no wrong. Then, half hysterical with anger, she began to cross him publicly. Hitherto she had confined herself to satirical stories about him at which he had laughed with the rest. Now she interrupted him, talked across him at table, seized every opportunity to assert herself. This change of front was noticed everywhere. At a Rogers breakfast, in the last year of the old man's life, she began talking the moment she could stop Carlyle, to the fury of both men: "As soon as that man's tongue stops" old Rogers snapped, "that woman's begins."

Nor did she stop there; she opposed every suggestion of Carlyle's if there was any possible alternative. They could not agree about a summer cottage, and she made an abortive attempt to go to Scotland—abandoned it when she discovered that the third-class railway carriages were open to the sky—and reluctantly accompanied Carlyle with his books and papers to Addiscombe, which had again been lent to them by the Ashburtons. There were more reproaches and sharp words, she could not sleep, and, after a couple of days, at the beginning of September, she returned to Chelsea first thing in the morning without a word.

> "My poor little Jeannie is away" wrote Carlyle that night. "You may fancy, or rather, perhaps, in your spleen you will not fancy, what a dreary wae sight it was to me this morning when I sallied out, stupid and sad, and found your door open, the *one* cup downstairs, tea-pot washed out."

He ended: "I calculate you will come, and take the reins in hand for another stage. My poor little Protectress!"

He calculated rightly; Jane would not, could not keep away. She alone knew his wants, she insisted, and except in the first heat of anger she had every intention of seeing that they were attended to. So she went back from time to time to make sure that he was as comfortable as he would allow himself to be made. For the rest, she remained in Chelsea, brooding. She still wrote often to him and expected regular replies, but her letters had lost much of their affectionateness.

He welcomed the solitude of Addiscombe, where he stayed for more than three weeks. He was sad but contentedly sad. *Frederick* seemed "as good as 'impossible' etc., etc—that is still my private opinion about it;—nevertheless, I do not mean to give in." He had by this time been thinking of the work for at least four years, and had worked on it for two, but not a line had yet been written that satisfied him.

At Chelsea the next month, Jane had a call from a Haddington man, David Davidson. He was only fifteen when she had left the town to marry Carlyle, but he remembered watching her and, better still, he remembered being bled when a small child by her father. He was tall, good-looking, and was both poet and soldier. This was a recommendation to Jane, but still more so were his stories of Haddington and praises of her mother and father. She invited him to dine at Cheyne Row with Tennyson, and listened eagerly to all he had to say of their native place. These meetings did her harm. She was living more and more in the world of the past, and, like most unsatisfied middle-aged women, she found the past a two-edged sword. Davidson's visits plunged her into rose-coloured dreams. Lying on her sofa at Chelsea she thought of herself in Haddington—a Haddington where all were kind and she was queen of all, young, fresh, brilliant, adored. Nero, on her lap, became the faithful loving Shandy frisking devotedly at her heels in the Haddington streets. Her father and mother ruled with love, grudging her nothing, hanging proudly on every clever word. The more she surrendered to the dangerous charm of these images, the more intolerable her present lot appeared. Carlyle could not spare time for her; his work must come first—to this she was accustomed, she was even agreeable. But after all these years, after all her sacrifices, all her self-discipline, for him to spare time, evening after evening, for Bath House—this black thought became an *idée fixe*. Confidences to Geraldine gave only illusory relief, and added self-reproach to her burden. She could not sleep. She tried to relieve herself in another way. Carlyle kept a journal; she would keep one too.

She began it towards the end of October:

"'The only sort of journal I would keep should have to do with what Mr Carlyle calls 'the fact of things'. It is very bleak and barren, this fact of things, as I now see it—very; and what good is to result from writing of it in a paper book is more than I can tell. But I have taken a notion *to*."

At that point Carlyle came back from a visit to Bath House:

"That eternal Bath House. I wonder how many thousand miles Mr C has walked between there and here, putting it altogether; setting up always another milestone and another betwixt himself and me. Oh good gracious! when I first noticed that heavy yellow house without knowing, or caring to know, who it belonged to, how far I was from dreaming that through years and years I should carry every stone's weight of it on my heart."

438

She pulled herself up: "About *feelings* already! Well I will not proceed, though the thoughts I had in my bed about all that were tragical enough to fill a page of thrilling interest for myself."

Three days later she had company, but when they had gone: "My heart is very sore tonight but I have promised myself not to make this journal a '*miserere*' so I will take a dose of morphia and do the impossible to sleep."

At the beginning of November: "Alone this evening. Lady A in town again—and Mr C of course at Bath House.

> "When I think of what I is
> And what I used to was
> I gin to think I've sold myself
> For very little cas."

She struggled to keep "my heart from throbbing up into my head and maddening it." All her fear of madness returned: "my most constant and pressing anxiety is to keep out of Bedlam!" The next day, she cries: "What a sick day this has been with me. Oh my Mother! nobody sees what I am suffering now."

An invitation came from Lady Ashburton to spend Christmas at The Grange. Bitter words passed, but Carlyle replied that he would brave even a large literary party to see the hostess. Jane wrote in her journal:

> " 'S'exagérer ses droits, oublier ceux des autres, cela peut être fort commode; mais cela n'est pas toujours profitable et on a lieu souvent de s'en repentir. Il vaudrait mieux souvent avoir des vices qu'un caractère difficile. Pour que les femmes perdent les familles, il faut qu'elles aillent jusqu'a l'inconduite, jusqu'au désordre. Pour les y pousser, il suffit souvent qu'un homme gâte toutes ses bonnes qualités et les leurs par des procédés injustes, de la dureté et du dédain.' It is not always however that unjust treatment, harshness and disdain in her Husband drives a woman jusqu'au désordre, but it drives her to something and something not to his advantage any more than to hers."

Soon afterwards she went to the Tax Commissioners to appeal against their assessment of Carlyle's income:

> "It was with feeling like the ghost of a dead dog that I rose and dressed and drank my coffee and then started for Kensington. Mr C said 'the voice of honour *seemed* to call on him to go himself.' But either it did not call loud enough or he would not listen to that charmer."

Her sense of humour flickered up during the appeal, at which she persuaded the commissioners to reduce the assessment, but when Carlyle walked off to Bath House in the evening she relapsed into unhappiness and bad temper, and went up the road to her Elektra.

Anthony Sterling, on leave from the Crimea, called early in December, his beard, exclaimed the approving Carlyle, "as big as a moderate corn-sheaf". He (until they fell out) Darwin and Forster, in particular, kept Jane's self-respect alive, but a day or two later the visit to The Grange had to be faced:

> "Oh dear! I wish this Grange business were well over," she writes in her journal. . . . "To have to care for my dress at this time of day, more than I ever did when young pretty and happy (God bless me, to think that I was once all that!) on penalty of being regarded as a blot on the Grange gold and azure is really too bad. *Ach Gott!* If we had been left in the sphere of life we belong to, how much better it would have been for us in many ways".

She went off in bad humour, determined to show her hostess, and Carlyle, that she was as worthy and as capable of holding the attention of the company as they. She could have made no greater error—her gifts were best seen in more intimate surroundings—but she was in no condition to consult her common sense. Mrs Brookfield, who had found her most entertaining in her own home describing the struggles with Carlyle about country cottages and other matters, could not say the same of her in this large and varied gathering:

> "Mrs C's instinct was always to take the lead. At The Grange this was not easy, for the grandeur and brilliance of our hostess, who, according to Mrs Twisleton, scattered 'pearls and diamonds whenever she spoke', made her the first attraction and interest to all around her. In conversation, clever and amusing as she often was, Mrs C had the fatal propensity of telling her stories at extraordinary length. With her Scotch accent and her perseverance in finishing off every detail, those who were merely friendly acquaintances and not devotees sometimes longed for an abridgement, and perhaps also to have their own turn in the conversation."

She is described by Mrs Brookfield as "very slight, neat, erect in figure, animated in expression, with very good eyes and teeth, but with no pretension to beauty." Nothing is said of her ravaged face, but portraits of this time show what pain and sleeplessness and worry had made of her. She had nothing, outwardly at least, to complain about in the general treatment

THOMAS CARLYLE
from a photograph by Tait, July 28, 1854

JANE WELSH CARLYLE
from a photograph by Tait,
July 1, 1856

GEORGE RENNIE
from a painting when Governor of
the Falkland Islands

she received at The Grange this Christmas. She used to stay in her room in the mornings, while Carlyle went for a walk with the now customary crowd of admirers. When Jane did appear "she was always especially taken care of by Lady A, and she expected and was conceded a certain prominence among the many other visitors of more or less distinction." But this, it seemed, did not please her. Attention, as much as neglect, can be hurtful; and whether it was so or not in this case, Jane chose to interpret it unfavourably. She was looking for slights and on Christmas Day she found one. Lady Ashburton had consulted Mrs Brookfield about a suitable gift for Jane to be put on the big Christmas tree that was always a feature of The Grange festivities. They decided on a silk dress. When Jane unwrapped the parcel she flew into a passion. She was being insulted, she vowed, by this plain indication that her taste in dress was unsuitable and her wardrobe insufficient. She refused to accept the gift, shut herself in her room, and would not join the guests until Lady Ashburton had sought her out and assured her "with tears in her eyes" that she had meant no offence.

This capitulation soothed Jane for the time, and the visit was allowed to peter out in comedy. One of the guests of honour that year was Tennyson, whose *Maud* had been so much talked about since its publication in the summer that he won his first invitation to The Grange. All the women were agreed that he was remarkably handsome, and he endeared himself to all by coming down to breakfast late, looking troubled and holding up his watch. "My watch has stopped" he said, "what am I to do?" There was general concern until a guest rose, took the watch from Tennyson, asked for the key, wound up the watch and returned it without a word. This was the behaviour expected from a poet. Henry Taylor looked sourly on the favour shown to the newcomer, by Lady Ashburton in particular. He attacked her. "Twenty years ago I was the last new man and where am I now?" Lady Ashburton, defending herself, said one would expect a difference in the treatment of new and old friends. How long, asked Tennyson, did it take to be an old friend? With Lady Ashburton, replied Henry Taylor, five years was usually enough to reduce friendship "to the decencies of dry affection." Lady Ashburton protested, and appealed to Venables to uphold her, but before Venables could speak,

Tennyson had interrupted, "why, Venables, you told me yourself that when you first came Lady Ashburton was very kind to you, but that now . . ." The flustered Venables began to explain away his remark, but Taylor overrode him with a "well, Tennyson, all I can say is that my advice to you is to rise with your winnings and be off."

This little passage pleased Jane until she saw with vexation that Carlyle was clearly unconcerned. Favourites, sensations of the year, came and went, but old "prophet Carlyle" stayed on, his voice booming over all, his advice sought, his opinions revered. Tennyson was still his ideal smoking companion, and the two men escaped whenever possible to the conservatory to nod and puff and grunt approvingly over their pipes—and in nothing were they more united at this particular moment than in avoidance of a certain Goldwin Smith, another guest, who had recently reviewed both of them unfavourably. But good companions though they were, Carlyle could not bring himself, even for Tennyson, to endure a poetry reading. This brought about a dilemma. Tennyson was asked to read *Maud*—he was a good reader, and preferred this poem above all others—and one morning all assembled to hear him. All, that is, except Carlyle, who paced the hall, waiting for a disciple or two to join him in his walk. Someone, clearly, had to forgo *Maud*. There was an awkward silence, broken only by Carlyle's footsteps. Then Goldwin Smith went out to join him, followed hastily by Brookfield, fearful of a collision if the men were left together. Of Brookfield, tactful, kind, humorous, Jane thought well, and spent some of her remaining days at The Grange trying to open his eyes to what she considered the less intelligent tenets of the faith he preached.

At home again in January 1856, Jane as usual immediately caught a cold. It turned to influenza. She was in bed for days, in the house for weeks, and when she got about again she had, she thought, no strength, no feeling; she had exhausted it all. Carlyle, who had borne the brunt of it, and who described himself after The Grange visit as "much broken by this long course of gaieties," worked upstairs on *Frederick*: "I dare not write to you, dare not speak to you, scarcely think of you," he told Lady Ashburton. "I see nobody, I sit here, in grim task work." He refused all invitations to Addiscombe: "You are indeed the best and beautifullest, bountiful as the summer and the sun." But "no, I cannot come—must not if I am wise." He went out little, but at one dinner at Lord Stanhope's:

> "well do I remember the first time I ever saw that little man; the first time I saw *you*, and long before I could make any long acquaintance in your house: the very voice of the man, bad as it is, has had a meaning to me ever since."

In his self-imposed solitude, he missed Lady Ashburton's enlivening company, and said so in his own way: "Oh best and beautifullest of Heaven's creatures, I kiss the hem of your garment."

Towards the end of March, Jane was venturing out. Geraldine organised many little excursions—to picture galleries, to Hampstead, to the Crimean Enquiry Committee, even to a confirmation service—but the result was usually "came home half dead and lay on the sofa." Geraldine told her friends that she thought Jane was dying. Jane wrote

> "I am very feeble and ailing at present—and my ailment is of a sort that I understand neither the ways nor outlooks of—so that the positive suffering is complicated with dark apprehensions. Alas alas and there is nobody I care to tell about it—not one—poor ex-spoilt child that I am! To keep up the appearance of being alive is just as much as I can manage."

Jane's friends did not all survive the test of this time without blemish. Charlotte Wynn was

> " 'very much detached' as that lady generally is now—hithering and thithering among the *Stump-orators* of every denomination, threatening to deteriorate into a mere dingle-doosie."

This attitude, though Jane does not mention it, was due to her talks with Brookfield at The Grange a few months earlier. He had written, rather disturbed, to Charlotte Wynn, who replied:

> "She is so restless and uncomfortable in her own convictions that she wishes to persuade others to roam with her, and tries to believe that they are *willing* to do so. No one cares to answer her sweeping declamation against Christianity and the Church, and so she thinks one agrees with her and in consequence every proof of a distinct adherence to certain doctrines annoys her. . . . She has certainly had experience sufficient of the utter ruin that follows the trade of a popular Preacher . . . to induce her to preserve her friends from entering on that career, but in your case I am quite convinced that it was merely annoyance that one to whom she looks up should openly profess a belief which is denied to her . . . I am

well aware that any effect upon her must be made at the cost of being scalped yourself, but a thorough bit of self-sacrifice would, I know, not be unpleasant to you."

She has already had "a regular explanation" with Jane.

Plattnauer was still coming in often and still in favour. Once, in April, "I was too poorly for walking with him, so we talked *intimately* over the fire." The same day Neuberg came to tea, but he was not wearing so well as Plattnauer:

> "Mr C fled off to Bath House and *walked him out*. I would advise no man to creep into another's favour by making himself 'generally useful'—he is sure to get kicked out of it when the other has got blasé on his subserviency. . . . Neither should any man or woman get up a *quasi*-liking for another on the ground of his subserviency 'obligingness' and that sort of thing—for when the other has gained the end of his subserviency a certain favour or at least toleration—he tires of being obliging and sets up for himself and complains perhaps, like the Colonel, that he is 'made a convenience of!' "

The Colonel was Anthony Sterling, another who had fallen by the wayside—"shot rubbish" was Jane's comment when she heard that he had been saying "If only she would leave me in peace!"

As Geraldine's efforts were not proving successful, Jane tried going out by herself, but with no better result:

> "I feel weaklier every day" she wrote in her journal in April, "and 'my soul is also sore vexed'. 'Oh how long?' I put myself in an omnibus, being unable to walk, and was carried to Islington and back again. What a good shilling's worth of exercise! The Angel at Islington! It was *there* I was set down on my first arrival in London. . . . 'The past is past and gone is gone!' "

But she would not let the past go; and now it rose for a moment into the present and revived her. She had half persuaded herself that her trouble was purely physical. Ill she was, certainly, but sick in mind too; and how much her mind preyed on her body was now to be shown. Carlyle told her one day that a man had stepped out of a carriage in Piccadilly to speak to him: "an iron-grey man with a bitter smile; who do you think?" She guessed at once; George Rennie. He had been Governor of the Falkland Islands for the last eight years, and his return was a complete surprise. The next day he called, and,

> "flinging my accustomed indifference and the 'three thousand punctualities' to the winds I sprang into the arms of George Rennie and kissed

him a great many times. Oh what a happy meeting! For he was as glad to see me as I was to see him. Oh it has done me so much good this meeting! My bright, whole hearted impulsive youth seemed conjured back by his hearty embrace. For certain my late deadly weakness was conjured away. A *spell on my nerves* it had been which dissolved in the unwonted feeling of gladness. I am a different woman this evening. I am well! I am in an atmosphere of *home* and *long ago!* George spoke to me of Shandy while he caressed Nero!"

She added, "I shouldn't wonder if I were too excited to sleep." But, as she noted in her journal the next day: "I slept all the better for my little bit of happiness—and I really am strengthened body and soul. I have walked more today than any day these two months." Her improvement remained. The following day her journal entry was more in her old style—"all the world has been down at Chelsea today hearing Charles Kingsley preach. Much good may it do them!"—as was the entry the day after:

"Mrs George Rennie came to *insist* on our dining with them. . . . I had been fretting over the need of a *new dress* for the Bath House affair—but now I went after it with alacrity. George should see that the smart girl of his Province wasn't become a *dowdy* among London women of 'a certain age.' "

She began to dine out again, to go to tea parties and to call at Bath House once, where she found Lady Ashburton "perfectly civil, for a wonder." As she put the matter: "Last week I was all for dying; this week, all for Ball dresses." She even developed a new passion—this time, for a wealthy Welshwoman, six feet two in height, beautiful, and with

"a charm of perfect naturalness about her that is irresistible. When she went out of the room I felt quite *lost*—like to cry! I said to Geraldine when she returned from seeing her off 'What an adorable woman!' Geraldine burst out laughing and said her (Madame de Winton's) remark on me had been 'I could adore that woman!' "

She asked her new friend to Cheyne Row in May, when Carlyle had permitted himself a day at Addiscombe, and her renewed spirits survived an embarrassing mistake by the visitor—a mistake which Carlyle passed on, with much amusement, to Lady Ashburton. The visitor

"looking up saw your picture (it now hangs downstairs, on one side of the mantlepiece, I on the other). Hon. Lady said 'There is a beautiful woman; who is that?' They told her; she then said 'And he yonder, **is** that her husband?' They smiled. 'Rather hers than mine' added this good judge of mankind and womankind."

Then came the Rennie dinner, and the Bath House soirée to celebrate the end of the Crimean War. The dinner was:

"like *everything looked forward to with pleasure*, an entire failure! The Past stood aloof looking mournfully down on me ... the recollection which I could not rid myself of that the gentlemanly 'iron-grey' man who as Landlord offered me 'roast duck' and other 'delicacies of the season' had been my lover—my *fiancé*—once on a time, served only to make me *shy* and in consequence stupid. And it was a *relief* when Ruskin called for us, to go to a great soirée at Bath House. *There* I found my tongue and used it 'not wisely but too well'."

The next day she is noting in her journal "a general debility and despair", an intolerable lethargy which she imagines might well be "a premonitory symptom of apoplexy"—from which her mother had died. Her depression was so heavy again that she could not enjoy the confidences of the young poet William Allingham. He

"staid a long while telling me all about himself. . . . When I was young and charming, men asked me about *myself* and listened with interest real or pretended to whatever I pleased to tell them. Now they compensate to themselves for the want of charm in my company by using me up as a listener to *their* egotism. A woman who will *accept* and exploit that role may still exercise an influence—of a sort. And if she cannot do without influence with men she had better accept it. For myself I think the game isn't worth the candle. At least that is my profound belief tonight after my dose of Mr Allingham's early difficulties with an unpoetical Father and an ill-tempered Step-mother and an unsympathetic public."

Another man who followed on his heels was George Cooke—"a man between thirty and forty—tall, strong, silent, sincere—has been a sailor, a soldier, a New Zealand settler, 'a Man about Town' and a Stock Broker!!" He talked pleasantly, she admitted, "but then it was only his second visit and *he* had still to make his place good. He staid two hours and a half! not busy it would seem!"

Of Ruskin, who had also called, she said nothing beyond repeating the divorce gossip; but Carlyle thought well of him.

"Ruskin" he told Lord Ashburton, "I have found in all things to mean well, and aim high with the very highest; but he strikes me always as infinitely too hopeful of men and things, in fact as having soared aloft out of all contact with rugged *facts;* which class of objects accordingly he contemplates, as with outspread wings, very much at his ease, far up in the azure aether. It is certain, however, he does teach various working young men to *draw*, and has a boundless zeal to continue teaching more and more."

Carlyle had just been looking into the fourth volume of *Modern Painters*, and found it

> "full of the finest 'eloquence'; Swiss descriptions etc. the like of which I have hardly ever seen; but tending nowhither, so far as I could surmise. It is one of the strangest books, for gift and want of gift, I have ever met with. The man himself I find exceedingly amiable, in spite of all that is said. But he flies out like a soda-water bottle, gets into the *eyes* of various people (being incautiously *drawn*) and these of course complain dreadfully."

There was a four-day break at Addiscombe with Carlyle in June, but it did Jane no good. "The place in full bloom and her Ladyship affable. Why? What is in the wind now? As usual at that beautiful place I couldn't sleep." On her return, Rennie called, but not satisfactorily: they talked about prayer, Palmer the poisoner and the prospects of war with America—"Nice topics for dear friends meeting after a dozen years."

There was some improvement when he came again a few days later—one of Jane's busiest days, in the course of which she entertained twelve people—"if that isn't society enough for one day!" She sailed through it with an ease that would have astonished her a month or two earlier. "Today" she writes in her journal towards the end of June, "is the first time I have felt *natural* with George Rennie—the presence of Geraldine helped to give me possession of my present self. He looked at me once as if he were thinking I *talked* rather well."

She visited Mrs Montagu again

> "who is 'breaking up' they say—but her figure is erect and her bearing indomitable as ever—'the noble lady' to the last! Browning came when I was there and dropt on one knee and kissed her hand with a fervour! And I have heard Browning speak slightingly of Mrs Montagu. To my mind Browning is a considerable of a 'fluff of feathers' in spite of his cleverness, which is undeniable. He kissed *my* hand too with a fervour—and I wouldn't give sixpence for his regard for me."

This is the authentic Jane, kind and ruthless in a blow. Then came the heat, and her last journal entry:

> "Spent the forenoon reading in Battersea Fields. In the evening alone

as usual—a very sick and sad day with me like many that have gone before and many that will come after if I live to the age that the Prophetess foretold for me, seventy-two."

Her thoughts for the past year had been so much in Scotland —in Haddington especially—that she determined to go there. Carlyle thought of Annandale, but hesitated to leave *Frederick*. The matter was resolved by Lady Ashburton. She was going to her place in the Highlands; she was again unwell, and had hired the "Queen's saloon" on the railway to make the journey easier. There was plenty of room for them; they must come with her, to Edinburgh at least, to Inverness if possible. And so, after a struggle, it was settled.

XXXIII

THE DEATH OF LADY ASHBURTON
1856 – 1857

The party left London on a blazing day early in July. The journey was not a success. Lady Ashburton, explains Carlyle,

"sat, or lay, in the saloon. A common six-seat carriage, immediately contiguous, was accessible from it. In this the Lady had insisted we should ride, with her doctor and her maid; a mere partition, with a door, dividing us from her. The Lady was very good, cheerful though much unwell; bore all her difficulties and disappointments with an admirable equanimity and magnanimity: but it was physically almost the uncomfortablest journey I ever made. At Peterborough, the *ne-plus-ultra* was found to have its axletree on fire; at every station afterwards buckets were copiously dashed and poured (the magnanimous Lady saying never a syllable to it); and at Newcastle-on-Tyne, they flung the humbug *ne-plus* away altogether, and our whole party into common carriages. Apart from the burning axle, we had suffered much from dust and even from foul air, so that at last I got the door open, and sat with my head stretched out backwards, into the wind. This had alarmed my poor wife, lest I should tumble out altogether; and she angrily forbade it, dear loving woman, and I complied, not at first knowing why she was angry."

Jane made no obvious complaint, it seems, once the disastrous journey was begun—she was too glad to be going to Scotland again to cavil at the manner of getting there—but she made up her mind that the experiment should not be repeated. Carlyle took her across the Forth to Auchtertool, stayed a day, and then went down to his sister Mary's farm, The Gill—Scotsbrig had been filled by John and his three step-sons, who were no favourites of the Carlyles. His view of the journey from London changed as he became soothed by the peace of the farm and countryside. "Certainly" he writes to Lady Ashburton, "you did a good thing that day in tearing me up from Chelsea, and whirling me off, with burning axle, in a whirlwind of dust, into these dumb regions." He found it necessary to apologise for

Jane: "How beautifully you did it, too; I really never saw a better behaviour under baddish usage; but you do belong to the clouds, in a sense you, though some others of us do not." She was pressing him to join them at their place at Loch Luichart: "And will I come to the Highlands?" he replied "Bright Lady, believe me, if it stood with me, the answer were not difficult. But it stands with so many persons." To one of these people, Jane herself, he wrote in a different strain. He would be quite content, he told her, to stay where he was until the return to London. The visit to the Ashburtons he would avoid if he could. "That is the whole truth", he assured her.

Jane was too busy revelling in Scotland to worry overmuch: "if ever a woman was thankful to see her own land and her own people again, after long and weary exile, it is *I*". There were no complaints about Auchtertool this time:

> "I am never done thanking heaven for the freshness and cleanness and quietness into which I have plumped down—and for my astonishingly comfortable bed and the astonishing kindness and good humour that wraps me about like an eiderdown quilt!"

She adds, her memories playing her false in this sentimental mood: "It is next thing to being at Templand." She even went down to bathe at Kirkcaldy—the first time she had been in the water for years—and when she left her cousins early in August it was with reluctance and a promise to return.

At Edinburgh, she stayed with her aunts in their new house at Morningside. They, too, were "so unexpectedly *tender* and glad over me" that she forbore to make her usual acid remarks on the morning prayers, the grace before meals, and the general "Free Church" air of the house. She found Betty Braid's only son dying slowly of paralysis—and she promised to come back after she had visited Haddington. Even in the midst of grief, Betty had some quaint things to say which Jane passed on to Carlyle:

> "speaking of the Photograph I had sent her, the one with the bonnet and the dog—and which together with yours she had got handsomely framed and keeps in a pocket *handkerchief in a drawer!*—'it has a look o' ye—but I dinna ken what that white thing is aboot the face?'—'That is the white roses of my bonnet Betty.' 'A weel! a weel! *May be sae!* but as ye wur kindly sending me yer pictur, Dear, I wud hae liket better ye had goten't dune wi' yer *bare pow!*' I promised her one with the bare pow."

At Haddington station, the Donaldson carriage was waiting for her, but empty—the only one of the sisters able to go outside Sunny Bank had died since Jane's last visit. Inside the house "the two dear old women clasped and kissed and wept over me both together. . . . And what a house! so quiet and clean, and so perfectly the same as I knew it thirty years ago!"

She went "home", as she now called it, in a spirit of devotion, looking only for the good things and finding them. Her old friends, proud of this return of the wife of a famous man to her own people, made a great deal of her. This, Jane could rarely resist, and she had no wish to resist it now. She renewed a friendship with two schoolboy lovers—John Ferme and William Dods—now men of moment in the town, and married to women well known to her ; Mrs Ferme, when Helena Howden, had lived in the doctor's house. Jane came down to Aberlady, Haddington's little seaside resort, to watch the Ferme children bathing. She begged everyone to write to her, to visit her, to keep her in their minds so that in this way she might remain a living part of the town. She was overcome by her welcome: "I often burst out crying with pure thankfulness to them all." They pressed gifts on her—a shawl, a veil, a ring, china, and, even more prized, plants for her garden, and " '*whatever*' will you say or sing?" she asked Carlyle—"two live—ca-ca-naries!! They were born in our own house—the darlings!" Her return to Edinburgh in the middle of August was mourned by all, and old Mr Lea "who has otherwise lost his wits . . . said angrily to Miss Brown 'Are you going to let *that Lassie* go away by hersell? send *the Man* with her'! (The man, meaning *his keeper!*)"

In Edinburgh this time her aunts' "religiosity" proved too much for her patience. One of his letters, she tells Carlyle, arriving as breakfast was served, caused them all to fall

"quite unconsciously into *Sin!* Sin against '*T'olly Goast*'! I was reading my letter, and had taken a sip or two of tea and bitten into my soda-scone, and the others had done the same, when Grace suddenly shrieked out like '*a mad*', 'Mercy! we have forgotten the *Blessing!*' I started on my chair, and (to such a pitch of compliance with '*Coostom in Part*' have I already reached!) dropped *instinctively* the morsel *out of my mouth into my hand*(!!) till I should see what steps were to be taken, for making our peace with Christ. But the case was judged past remedy—and the breakfast allowed to proceed *unblessed!*" Why, she complained to Betty, did her aunts live "in such a *fuss* of religion"? "My Dear!" explained

Betty, "they were idle—plenty to leeve on and nocht to do for't—*they micht hae ta'en to waur!* So we *maun just thole them* an' no compleen."

The first substantial blot on the holiday appeared at the end of the month. She went to hear the celebrated preacher, Dr Guthrie—"most 'artfully simple', thrice 'opulent in imagery', mirroring next to nothing of real" said Carlyle to Lady Ashburton—and caught cold coming out of the packed church. She was made worse by the Forth crossing the next day, and began her second stay in Auchtertool by going to bed. Nor was this all; the house was filled; Jeannie and her husband came over from Glasgow to see her, and Alick's wife came from Liverpool with her two small children. "In the dead watches of the night," said the disillusioned Jane, "there will arise a sound of 'infants weeping in the porch'—and on the whole it is not now like Paradise here as it was in my first two weeks." After a few days, in an effort to cure her cold by the sea, she went down to the Ferguses at Kirkcaldy; sleeping, she remarks characteristically, "in what Miss Jessie calls 'a sweet little room'—the *littleness* I perceive plainly but not the *sweetness*."

Carlyle was still deep in cream and butter at the Gill—how, Jane asked Anne at Cheyne Row, would they ever be able to please him again with London food? Anne and Nero, in a joint reply, took the question seriously. "As for the Master, I don't know what to say but that you must not look on the black side of things. All I can say is that we can but do our best to please him." Now Carlyle prepared to leave his land of milk and honey. He had been assuring Lady Ashburton in every letter that he wanted to go to Loch Luichart, hoped to go, was doing his best to go. Now he broke the news to Jane that he was going. She was not pleased. He spent an unhappy day or two with her in Kirkcaldy on his way to the Highlands. Her letters to him after this, though almost as numerous as in earlier years, are cooler, and she began to sign herself "yours faithfully". He complained of his hardships but she would not listen. In vain he repeated that no fire was allowed in the drawingroom, that he was cold, that he slept so poorly as to be forced to lie on the bed before dinner, a hat over his eyes and every woollen thing he could find piled over him, and that his hostess "is in worse humour than usual; is capable of being driven to extremities by your setting up a peat from its flat posture." All this she dismissed:

> "In spite of all objections 'for the occasion got up' I dare say you are pretty comfortable. Why not? When *you* go to any house, one knows it is because you *choose* to go, and when you stay it is because you *choose* to stay. *You* don't, as weakly amiable people do, *sacrifice* yourself for the pleasure of 'others'. So pray do not think it necessary to be *wishing yourself at home* and 'all that sort of thing' on paper."

She also found fault with his handwriting and the shortness of his letters; they appear, she said,

> "as if you were writing in a house on fire! and bent on making *a little* look *as much as possible!* I have measured the distance between your lines in the letter just come, and it is precisely *one inch!* In the first letter it must have been an inch and half! I call that a foolish waste of writing paper!"

Finally, she refused flatly to join Lady Ashburton on the return journey to London:

> "Lady Ashburton is very kind to offer to take me back—pray make her my thanks for the offer. But tho' a very little *Herring* I have a born liking to '*hang by* my own head' and when it is a question simply of paying my own way or having it paid for me—I prefer 'lashing down' my four or five sovereigns *on the table all at once!*—if there were any *companionship* in the matter it would be different."

He protested; her letter "is wholly grounded on misknowledge, or in deep ignorance of the circumstances." But she had already written to Lady Ashburton:

> "two lines in great haste and *excitement* to beg you to *make* Mr C go back to London with *you*, and not let him do anything so absurd as come eighty miles out of the way to pick up me, who can get myself home fully better without him than with him."

She hoped to see Lady Ashburton—who was going to Nice for her health—before she set off. She adds: "I think Mr C writes in good spirits and as if he had got good of the Highland expedition."

By this time, late in September, she had travelled down to Scotsbrig, having as little as possible to do with John's three stepsons, and had gone on at last to the Russells at Thornhill. There, in the doctor's house in the main street, she began to recover health once more. They put her to bed for a day or two, Dr Russell forbade her to take morphia, Mrs Russell sat on the bed by the hour to "make of me", and even old Mr Dobie came in regularly to cheer her with stories of the countryside now grown so dear. Then she was taken out in the carriage with Fingland—long known to her—on the box. They drove in the warm autumn sunshine past places bound up with her youth and early womanhood—over the Penpont bridge to Penfillan, up Drumlanrig Street to Morton Mains, and, when she was strong enough, by the river to Templand where she stood for some time at the door in "*a perfect agony of desolation*". From her bedroom in the doctor's house she could see across the wide street the little-used prison; Douglas, the barber, who kept a toyshop and was now experimenting with the new photography; the tailor, Robert Shankland, who had read and approved *Sartor*—places which seemed not to have changed since she first saw them almost fifty years earlier. She strolled down the street to the shops so often visited by her mother and herself—to Sandy Wallace the weaver, John Thompson the draper, and the ever-fascinating room of the watchmaker, William Scott. Neither she nor her mother had been forgotten—memories are long in Scottish villages—and for these few moments she had the illusion of immortality, her mother being no longer in Crawford churchyard but in the hearts of these kind people.

She left reluctantly for London at the end of the month, and within a few days was complaining to Mary Russell:

> "Oh my Dear! my Dear! my Dear! To keep myself from going stark mad, I *must* give myself something *pleasant* to do, *for this one hour!* And nothing so pleasant suggests itself as just writing to *you*, to tell you how miserable and aggravated I am!"

She explains. She had had, after all, the dubious benefit of Carlyle's company on the way home, and

> "I arrived here with a furious faceache, Mr C having insisted on my sitting in a *violent* draught all the journey. *That* kept me perfectly sleepless all night in spite of my extreme fatigue—and so I began to be ill *at once* and have gone on *crescendo*—in the same ratio that my worries have increased."

Everything is wrong. Chelsea is "enveloped in dark yellow fog," Carlyle is "remarkably bilious", she is "half dead", there are bugs in his bed, Anne is bitterly reproached, and the three years of faithful service are forgotten in an instant: "I never liked her *as a woman*—from the first week I perceived her to be what she has since on all occasions proved herself—cunning, untrue, and intensely selfish." Anne gave notice. The house had to be ransacked for bugs. No one helped. "In cases of this sort" Jane cries, "Geraldine with the best intentions is no help. She is *unpractical*—like all women of Genius!" Then Jane caught a chill, could not sleep, and suffered "a fearful pain" in her left side. She screamed for half an hour without end. "Who shall I send for, what shall I do?" asked the troubled Carlyle. "Nobody, nobody, only put me in hot water." Anne, shocked by so much suffering, withdrew her notice. Jane was sure she would die, but by the latter part of November she was well enough to go to a farewell party to Mrs Brookfield, who was following Lady Ashburton to The Riviera.

She was much better, she told Mrs Russell, her cough gone, her sleep improving, only weakness still troubling her. But her state was most accurately reflected in her letters, and particularly in her references to Geraldine, who was once more in disgrace. She had fallen in love again—this time, with Walter Mantell, a friend of George Cooke's. He was a fine-looking, bearded man, with an open but rather curt manner which, backed by his romantic appearance and adventurous history— for he had been scientist, explorer, administrator in New Zealand—quite carried away Geraldine's heart. But she had committed two sins; she kept this man to herself, and she talked about him when she should have talked about Jane. On the other hand, she "comes for 'orders' in the mornings and sits with me in my bedroom an hour or two every night." But, though too useful to be cast off, she could be criticized with some freedom.

"You can't think," Jane tells Mrs Russell, "what difficulty I have had to keep Geraldine from firing off Letters at you every two or three days, with the most alarming accounts of my bodily state. It is her besetting weakness by nature—and her trade of Novelist has aggravated it—the *desire of feeling and producing violent emotions* ... my hard, practical Anne who never utters a sympathising word, but *does* everything I need, punctually, has been a far more agreeable nurse for me than poor Geraldine, who if I asked for a glass of water would spill the half of it by the way, and in compensation would *drop tears on my hand*, and assure me that I was 'sure to die!'—and then fall to kissing me *wildly* (when I was perhaps in an interval of retching perfectly *hating* to be kissed) and bursting out into passionate sobs! (which of course did not prevent her from going out into company half an hour after, and being the life of it!)"

Geraldine was not wholly mistaken. Jane was less strong than even she believed; she caught cold after cold, grew weaker and weaker, and not until April 1857 was she able to leave the house. For the greater part of the late winter and early spring months she did not leave her bedroom. She had to refuse an invitation from Mrs Tennyson to the Isle of Wight:

"You *are* a darling woman to have gone and written to me on the 'voluntary principle' such a kind little note! *You* to have been at the trouble to know that *I* was ill! *You* to express regret at *my* illness. I feel both surprised and gratified, as if I were an *obsolete* word that some great Poet (Alfred Tennyson for example) had taken a notion to look up in the Dictionary. . . . Wouldn't I like to go and visit you if that man would leave his eternal *Frederick* and come along! nay wouldn't I like to go on my own small basis if only I had the *nerve* for it, which I have not yet! *He* goes nowhere, sees nobody, only for two hours a day he rides like the wild German hunter on a horse he has bought, and which seems to like that sort of thing. Such a horse! he (not the horse) never wearies in the intervals of *Frederick* of celebrating the creature's 'good sense, courage and sensibility!' 'Not once' he says 'has the creature shown the slightest disagreement from *him* in *any question of Intellect*' (more than can be said of most living Bipeds!)"

This was at the beginning of the year, just before she took to her bed again; and from this time for the next few months she was too unwell to see visitors, and her letters dwindled, although she always found time to write to Haddington and Thornhill; indeed, the less able she felt to take part in the life of London, the more her thoughts returned to Scotland. She now never omits to send Christmas gifts to the children of Helena Ferme:

"I often think" she says, "of that visit to Aberleddy; and those children stark naked, and dripping wet; the drops on them sparkling in the sunshine like diamond beads as they held up their little mouths to be kissed; and such a beautiful sea for a background! There never was a prettier sight before or since! At least, not since Venus issued from the sea and was kissed by *The Seasons!!* . . . The canaries have gained all hearts in this house (but one!). Even Mr Carlyle takes to them; tho' truth to say, I rather expected he would wring their necks! . . . I have not been well enough to go down to breakfast for upwards of eight weeks but the other morning, the doors being all open, I was thunderstruck to hear my young friends chirruping at the very top of their lungs! When Mr C came into my room soon after, I apologized for the disturbance, and spoke of removing the cage. 'Oh let them alone there!' said he 'the little wretches have been all this time *as merry as maltsters!* But their incessant distracted chirling rather amuses me!' The *one* heart they have failed to gain is my Dog's! He is in fact madly *jealous* of them, and has been so all along! If I so much as approach the cage in his presence to do them any little service or ask them how they feel themselves, Nero runs to me, tears at my skirt, whimpers, gur-r-rs, and rises in the end to a loud, spiteful single bark! The creature has been so exclusively devoted to me for years and years, that I am indulgent even for his egotism, and so I refrain from *making of* the birds, speaking endearingly (!) to them and all that, *before his face* but I *do it all the more in his absence.*"

She writes lovingly to Mary Russell when her father dies, and tries to cheer her with an anecdote:

"I must tell you an instance of Anne's *gentility:* It was in shaving a *bath-brick* that she cut her finger. Today when she opened the door to the Lady Alice Hill (a lovely girl whom Anne *respects* very much as the Daughter of a real live Marchioness) Lady Alice, who is the most bewitching little monkey in the world said 'Oh Anne, what ails your hand?' (the finger was wrapped in a bit of scarlet cloth!!) 'I have cut it my Lady.' 'How did you cut it?' 'Well I did it in cutting up a—*fowl!!*' She told me this substitution herself. 'You know Mam' said she in telling of Lady Alice's kind enquiries 'I couldn't go and say to a *real* young Lady that I did it cutting a *bath-brick! that* sounded so *common!* I thought a *fowl* was more the thing!!' "

At Easter she sent another picture book to the Fermes:

"I don't know if you are old enough to remember hearing of Mrs Jordan the great comic actress? I once saw her, when I was six years old. At all events you are old enough to have heard of King William! Well, the man who drew these clever little pictures is a grandson of these two people, and takes I suppose his comic talent from the actress-grand-mother. . . . I fell very ill again . . . and have been all these months confined to two rooms, coughing, and not sleeping, and very weak and dull. So, since my return from Scotland in the beginning of October, up to nearly the present time, I have had only a fortnight (about Xmas) free from colds! The weather is now very favourable for the like of me, and I have been out a few times. But instead of walking *twelve miles* at a stretch, as was my practice, I now think much of twelve yards! My cough is nearly quite gone however, and I have no other ailment but weakness. In such a long confinement, I found *consuming my own smoke* about as much as I was *up* to. *That* I must certainly have managed to do; for Mr Carlyle has paid me so many compliments on my 'patience'! and compliment is not in Mr C's line."

She also made time to write at length to a schoolteacher and would-be poet in Carlisle, Mary Smith, whom she had tried unsuccessfully three years earlier to place in London as "assistant to a literary lady." She tells the story (one of her favourites for many years) of her first bread baking at Craigenputtock, when, at three in the morning, she was still in the kitchen,

> "my whole body aching with weariness, my heart aching with a sense of forlornness and degradation 'that I who had been so petted at home, whose comfort had been studied by everybody in the house—who had never been required to do anything but *cultivate my mind*—should have to pass all those hours of the night in watching *a loaf of bread!* which mightn't turn out bread after all!' "

This handful of letters, which she would normally have written in a day or two, were now the work of half a year. In March, Carlyle was telling Lady Ashburton—still on the Riviera—that Jane had not been able to breakfast with him for five months. She had been "a model of patience" all the winter. He was better than usual. He rode regularly on his horse, named appropriately Fritz, and he had a secretary, Frederick Martin or "Peesweep"—the second such in Cheyne Row. Martin proved useful to Jane that winter as "a lightning conductor"—"the poor little fellow" admitted Carlyle, "keeps a good deal off you!" But he did not last long. Carlyle had to send him off, he explains to Lady Ashburton, because "he took to whistling through his nose."

There was illness in Nice also, serious illness, and Carlyle was doubly worried. He rides to the heights of Norwood, and thinks how easily he could gallop to Addiscombe "if there were anything now there for me". He tells Lady Ashburton of the few visitors he allows himself—though in the spring many people call to see Jane—such as the "blustery questionable" Kingsley, who "did nothing but spoil poor Froude, who is good for something to me." But for the most part he is anxiously waiting for report of her. Lord Ashburton was keeping him posted, but the reports varied. She was better, then she was worse. Then came the news that she was suffering from dropsy. She had been given mercury, she said, and felt like "an electrified cat". In April, the severe treatments were said to be over, and she was living on milk. Carlyle redoubled his appeals—give up all this travelling, he begged, and settle down at The Grange. But it was too late. She reached Paris, her state was said to be more favourable, she was even making arrangements for a house by the sea in Sussex for the autumn; then, one evening early in May, Milnes called hurriedly at Chelsea—Lady Ashburton had died suddenly in Paris. Her death, said Carlyle, was "a great and irreparable sorrow to me, yet with some beautiful consolations in it too. . . . Her work—call it her grand and noble endurance of want of work—is all done!" He told John "I have indeed lost such a friend as I never had, nor am again in the least likelihood to have, in this *stranger* world; a magnanimous and beautiful soul."

While Lady Ashburton lived Jane pitied her:

> "I know several women whose death would be a greater sorrow to me; but there is something dreadfully painful to think of, in the contrast between her transcendent worldly advantages of *all sorts* and the dark stern fate hanging over her—that no human skill, no resources of wealth and position, no devotion of worshippers may perhaps be able to avert!"

So she was writing in February. A month later, when the news was no better:

> "Poor woman! this sick life must be a sorer trial to her than to any of us—she has been so used to have everything bend to her will—her life looked to me always like a *Triumph!* . . . She will hardly admit anyone to see her now—and those she chooses to see are almost solely *clever men!!*"

When the news of Lady Ashburton's death came, she made no pretence of sorrow:

> "I was shocked, and dispirited, and feeling *silence* best. *But* you could *not* guess the *outward* disturbance consequent on this event! the letters and calls of inquiry and condolence that have been eating up my days for the last two weeks! distressingly and irritatingly".

Many impertinent pseudo-condolers were calling at the house, "to see how we, especially *Mr Carlyle*, were taking her loss!" And she remarks on the funeral

> "last Tuesday Mr C went to the Grange to be present at her funeral. It was conducted with a kind of royal state, and all the men, who used to compose a *sort* of *Court* for her, were there; in *tears!* I never heard of a gloomier funeral."

When, soon afterwards, she was invited to Addiscombe for a few days to recuperate, she commented "I am getting accustomed to missing her; and her Mother, who is here, and Lord A himself do all they can to make one comfortable in the house."

But the week here and there were not what she wanted. She

felt ill, restless, and pined to be out of London. In April, Carlyle had finished the first two volumes of *Frederick* and suggested that they both go to Germany and that he write the next two there— a project which, as he had taken a good five years to produce two volumes, made Jane *"like to scream!"* The plan fell through, Carlyle decided to stay in London, Anne (who had again given notice and again withdrawn it) would look after him, and Jane could be off. But where? She was "dithering" for weeks, until an invitation arrived from the Donaldsons. That, and the offer of Craik and his daughters, travelling to Edinburgh by a night "excursion" train, to escort her, was all she needed, and by the first week in July she was away. She was still following murder trials. What does Dr. Russell think of Miss Madeleine Smith, she wanted to know. "I feel quite ashamed of her being a Scotchwoman." She was shocked to hear that Glasgow merchants were raising a fund "to testify their *sympathy*" for "this cockatrice". The fund had already reached nine thousand pounds. One man had given a thousand, reported Jane disgustedly. "He had better marry her and get poisoned."

XXXIV

SCOTLAND AGAIN
1857 – 1859

There were sixteen people in her compartment of the "excursion" and all but one small window tightly closed the whole night. Her white face haunted Georgina Craik for months afterwards: "you looked as if you were slowly expiring by inches." She arrived at Sunny Bank tired and cynical.

"If you could fancy me in some part of the house and out of sight" she wrote to Carlyle, "my absence would make little difference considering how little I see of you – and how preoccupied you are when I do see you."

Even Nero had seemed too troublesome to take: "oh be kind to Nero and slightly attentive to the canaries," she begs.

Her day rarely varied: breakfast soon after eight—tea, eggs, brown bread and honeycomb; drives—"I recognize places that I had *seen in my dreams!*"; a rest before three o'clock dinner—"always strawberries and cream *ad libitum!*"; a walk to the churchyard "or some place that I care for" before tea at six; then she talked, or read to the sisters, until her supper of arrowroot milk at half-past nine. Just before supper she made a point of slipping down the road "to speak a few words of encouragement to my poor unlawful cousin in her sick bed." This natural daughter of Jane's uncle William, Jackie Welsh, was busy "proving the authenticity of her relationship by appearance of consumption" but Jane believed she was dying of remedies. "I think she would recover if she could overcome the effects of the frightful quantity of mercury Mr Howden had given her. My Heavens what my Father would have said to him!" What she needed was company: "The poor Thing got quite cheerful and *laughed* several times while I staid with her; tho' 'she hadn't spoken a word all day'." Once she walked to

Grant's Braes, only to find the old house pulled down and a new one there

> "and it was as if my heart had knocked up against *it!* A sort of (moral) *blow* in the breast is what I feel always at these sudden revelations of the new uncared-for thing usurping the place of the thing one knew as well as oneself."

She began to recover slowly. Every night she went to bed as hoarse as a crow, she said, after reading *"excessively aloud"* to the almost stone-deaf old women—"and *I like that!*" In her fifty-sixth-birthday letter she showed signs of returning vitality. She found the chapel

> "transformed into quite a little blossom of Puseyite taste! Painted glass windows! Magnificent organ! *Airs* from the opera of *Acis and Galatea!!*—the most snow white and ethereal of *surplices!* and David Roughead (he of the 'fertile imagination') *chaunting* his responses behind us, and singing 'a deep bass', and tossing off his *Ā-mĕns!* in a *jaunty* style that gave me a strong desire to box his ears."

She had also bought a hedgehog "from a wee Boy". She thought of taking it home to eat the cockroaches.

She visited a good deal after the first few days:

> "I went to see 'old Mrs Todrick' last night whom I had not seen since I left Haddington. . . . One thing I find this dear stupid little place infinitely superior to London in—and that is its old women! Age does not masquerade and make a fool of itself here."

She saw the Howdens in her old home. The place looked beautiful to her—"the young girl-wife who lives there is very lovely and writes poetry—God help her"—she was given a basket of pears from the old tree—but she was offended by a full-length portrait of old Thomas Howden over the mantelpiece "vulgarising everything by its groom-like presence". She had not forgotten his description of her when a young woman as "an impudent baggage".

She had hard work leaving the town.

> "At the least allusion to my departure, my dear old friends fall to *fluttering on their chairs*, like birds frightened in their nests—and utter such plaintive almost sobbing protests, that I haven't the heart to pursue the subject."

Finally, after three weeks, she left for Edinburgh and Auchtertool, promising to return before going back to London.

On the way to the ferry across the Forth she met an old acquaintance:

"After having settled myself in the Omnibus and looked out a little at the lovely Braid Hills, my eyes unconsciously *fixed* on the broad plaid-waistcoated *belly* of the Gentleman opposite me, and next to whom Grace had taken her seat. What a big man, I thought—and glanced from his belly to his face; it was rather handsome—at least very goodhumoured and gentlemanly—or rather *gentleman-farmerly*—and with its light brown hair and whiskers, looked younger than the ample belly—which was not however a *pot-belly*—only a broad stout one. Suddenly Grace having looked at his face also, commenced a hearty shaking of hands with him, and said, 'there is Jeanie—Mrs Carlyle—don't you know her?' He held out his hand with a smile and a *blush* in which I recognized Robert MacTurk! I was very uncomfortable to have been staring at his belly for five minutes and then to find in him an old lover."

She stayed a fortnight at Auchtertool.

"Oh Heaven! or rather, oh, the other Place! 'I am degenerating from a woman into a dog, and feel an inclination to bark; *bow! wow! wow!*' Ever since I came here I have been passing out of one silent rage into another, at *the Things in general* of this House! Viewed from the Invalid point of view, they are enough really to make one not only bark but bite."

She could not sleep, the food disagreed with her, the hours were too late, she lived on blue pills and castor oil. Jeannie brought her baby over from Glasgow. Jane never forgave desertion; marriage (being in her present view a mistake) was no excuse; Jeannie was out of favour, and the birth of her child earlier in the year had been greeted by the comment: "I hope she will now at least turn to dressing *it* instead of herself." Now, Jane waited only until "the insipid offspring with two nurses arrive on the scene." She made some play with the nurses—"Jeannie is coming over with her Baby and *two* Nurses (!!) a *wet* and a *dry*, tomorrow week. Neither she nor the rest would forgive me if I took myself off before this Royal Progress"—but this did not save her from anger when "Jeannie and her suite" arrived.

"The baby is about three finger lengths long—the *two* nurses nearly six feet each!—*five* packing cases came before them by the Carrier! and as many portmanteaus and carpet-bags in the carriage *with* them!—'Did you ever?' 'No—I never!' I have kept my temper with all this nonsense wonderfully—to outward appearance at least—but it is only the speedy prospect of getting far away from it that has enabled me to keep from bursting out into swearing."

As for Jeannie herself "such an affected, bedizzened caricature of a *Fine Lady* I never came across. I could hardly keep my hands off her. My Mother always predicted what she would grow to." All in all, she found Auchtertool "a scene of waste, and fuss, and frivolity, and vanity, and vexation of spirit"— which may have meant no more than that she was unequal to cheerfulness even when its purpose was to cheer her; and that, after Jeannie's arrival with the baby, she was no longer the centre of interest. Her bitterness was increased by the reminders, in Geraldine's letters or in her lack of them (Geraldine erred either way), of yet another falling away, as she saw it. Geraldine was "too much taken up with Mr Mantell". In Edinburgh came another shock to her vanity. She made haste to call on her old Mathematics tutor at Miss Hall's school. He would remember and applaud his fascinating pupil. But he had grown deaf and showed himself uninterested to the point of boredom. Then a woman she had not seen for twenty years came to see her: " 'You were ill I heard,' she said, 'Ah yes—it is easy to see you have suffered!—*an entire wreck*, like myself'—then, looking round on my three aunts—'Indeed, like all of us'!!"

Her self esteem revived somewhat after meetings with two men. She wrote delightedly to Carlyle: "I observe the only people who recognise one readily are the men who were in love with one. John Stodart looks always as if he not only knew me at any distance, but was meeting me *by appointment!*" Her pleasure in the other man, Davidson, held an undercurrent of criticism that betokened the beginning of the end:

"I sat out with Major Davidson yesterday, two hours and more . . . and got such capital good talk out of him! I do think he is a real kind-hearted, serious-minded man . . . not without a tinge of insanity in him perhaps!"

Carlyle was behaving himself in almost exemplary fashion. He plied her with letters, which pleased her greatly, even though she "turned quite *sick* at the sight" of some, fearful that there might be "some word in the letter that I would rather hadn't been there or that the *tone* of the letter might show you were ill or uncomfortable." Carlyle took warning by this confession of extreme sensibility; he had begun with a mild and complimentary growl or two:

"All I complain of is gloom, and I do not know how I should get well rid of that at present even if *I had you* to throw some portion of it upon! Tea is the gloomiest of all my meals. No Goody there! I am thankful even to Nero for reminding me of you."

He had headaches, felt feverish, could not sleep for heat and noises. Then he pulled himself together. He told her to write fully:

"I am glad you make your bits of complaints freely to me; if not to me, to whom else now alive on the earth? Oh! never distrust me, as the devil sometimes tempts your poor heart to do. I know you for an honest soul, far too sharp-tempered, but *true* to the bone; and if I ever am or was unkind to you, God knows it was very far against my purpose. Do not distrust me. Tell me everything, and do not mind how weak you are before me. I know your strength and your weakness pretty well by this time. Poor little Goody! Shan't I be glad to see you back again? Yes; for a considerable number of reasons."

This, despite the plain speaking, was good to hear, and Jane, whose heart was never far from him however she might try to harden it, looked even on the abhorred *Frederick* with a kindly eye. Carlyle had sent up the proofs of the first two volumes and she returned good for good:

"Oh my Dear! What a magnificent Book *this* is going to be! The best of all your Books! *I* say so, who *never flatter*, as you are too well aware; and who am 'the only person I know that is always in the right!' . . . Really one may say of these two first Books at least, what Helen said of the letters of her sister who died—you remember—?'so *splendidly* put together one would have thought that *hand* couldn't have written them!'"

When she reached Haddington again towards the end of August, she read the proofs to the Donaldson sisters.

"And Miss Donaldson said, 'I see more than ever in this, my Dear, what I have always seen in Mr Carlyle's Books; and what I think distinguishes him from all the writers of the present day; a great love of Truth;—and *what is more* (observe the fine discrimination!) *a perfect detestation of Lies!*'"

Her bitterness against Geraldine increased.

"*You*, indeed she represented as well, and in the best humour and spirits—*dwelling on it*, as if she wished to '*make me sensible*' how much happier you were for having me out of your way! Her letter rasped me all over like a file."

To Jane, now as desperate to be home as she had been to leave it, and ever more conscious of her position as kingpin of the home, this was dangerous heresy.

465

"I think she is growing into what is called an 'ill-natured old Maid'—only that, so long as Mr Mantell is to the fore, she has no idea of old-Maid-hood! In her last she gives me to understand that Anne would much prefer me to stay away! In fact all along she has been impressing on me in sly terms, that my absence was felt to be good company at Cheyne Row—and that if I ever came back it would be at the risk of spoiling everybody's good humour! Nevertheless, I may be looked for on Wednesday night."

She duly arrived, attended by William Dods who was also travelling down to London. She had not been home a month before she was down with another cold.

"He has a mania about 'fresh air', this man" she tells Mrs Russell "and is never happy unless all the doors and windows are open. From *open violence* of draughts I can partly defend myself; wearing a Cloak and bonnet the same as if I were out of doors! &c—but when he surreptitiously opens a window at my back (the back of my seat) when I am out of the room, and the curtains are drawn over it, I often receive my first notice of the fact in the form of a sore throat. As he never takes cold himself, he can't be made to understand how sitting between two open cross windows, at midnight, in an east wind, should not be excessively bracing and healthy for me!"

She remained more or less unwell throughout the winter, having by the end of March 1858 gone outside the door twice only, for a quarter of an hour. She read a great deal, and had one pleasant surprise early in the year, when *Scenes of Clerical Life* arrived with the author's compliments.

"I read it—at least the first volume" she told the unknown author "during one of the most (physically) wretched nights of my life—sitting up in bed unable to get a wink of sleep for fever and sore throat—and it helped me through that dreary night as well—better than the most sympathetic helpful friend watching by my bedside could have done!"

Her picture of the writer was "a man of middle age, with a wife, from whom he has got those beautiful *feminine* touches in his book—a good many children, and a dog that he has as much fondness for as I have for my little Nero!"

She was unusually sad this winter, for she had lost Mazzini and she had lost a great deal of the company of Forster. Forster was now a happily married man. He was as friendly as ever, and his wife—the widow of Colburn the publisher—liked Jane rather more than might have been expected, but there were no more "larks", no more escorts to the theatre, no more invitations to dine in Chambers. Times had changed, her circle was diminishing, her power of attraction, it seemed, was growing less. Mazzini was quite dead to her. He had gone back to Italy the previous year, and on his return to England lived outside London. There had been no definite break, but he did not call when he came to London—discouraged by Carlyle's growing disapproval—and Jane had, after a struggle, resigned him to the Ashursts. This blow at her self esteem—for so she saw it—kept her low and irritable. She occupied herself by differing with Anne and Geraldine, by dwelling minutely and wearisomely on the state of her health, and by writing highly critical accounts of one friend to another.

She complained unceasingly about everything including the artist who was painting their sittingroom "to be 'amazingly interesting to Posterity a hundred years hence' ". In her view "the dog is the only member of the family who has reason to be pleased with his likeness as yet."

Even Nero did not escape. When she came back from her holiday

> "He knew me quite well but took me very coolly indeed. Anne said he had 'just been sleeping'. Let us hope he was in a state of indigestion, in which dogs are not capable of being amiable any more than their Masters!"

Carlyle, she confessed, "seems to have got on better without me than my vanity led me to expect". To banish this intolerable thought there was always Geraldine, the scapegoat. She is alone in the house, she tells Mrs Russell in January

> "as utterly *alone* as I ever felt at Craigenputtock with Mr C gone over into Annandale! The difference is; that Mr C is gone, not to Annandale, but to *The Grange;* and that my servant, instead of being too uncouth to talk with, is too ill-tempered. The very dog had a bilious attack overnight, and has lain all day in a stupor!"

Geraldine, her prop and stay,

> "is all but as good as gone out of my life!!! . . . Latterly she has quite ceased to write to me!!!! She has been making 'a considerable of a fool' of herself; to speak plainly—and has got estranged from me utterly *for the time being;* partly because her head has been pack-full of nonsense, and partly because I made no secret of that opinion."

She then gave Mrs Russell the full story, as she saw it.

> "Geraldine has one besetting weakness—she is never happy unless she

has a *grand passion* on hand—and as unmarried men take fright at her impulsive demonstrative ways, her *grand passions* for these *thirty years* have been all expended on *married* men—who *felt themselves safe*. . . . But when I was in Scotland—with *you*—she made an intimacy with a Mr Mantell . . . unhappily *not* married. . . . For a long time it was an intimacy 'with the reciprocity all on one side.' But she went on writing him letters inviting him to her house, flattering him, consoling him (he is a proud shy man) doing him all sorts of kindnesses; till he declared to his friends 'he couldn't help liking Miss Jewsbury, she was so extraordinarily kind to him'!! He relied I suppose on his being ten or twelve years younger than herself for security in accepting her kindness. I could not see her committing herself as she did, and hear all her acquaintances chattering about her 'assiduities' for Mr Mantell, without testifying my displeasure; and in proportion as she attached herself to *him* she drew away from *me*, got pettish, suspicious, and mysterious. So it has gone on, till now Mr Mantell's bosom friend speaks indignantly of 'the mischief he is getting by Geraldine's flatteries' and of 'the impropriety of her fuss about him, when he (the friend) seeing her going ahead in her enthusiasm had himself told her Mantell was engaged.' And everybody speaks! and nothing comes of it! nor *will* come of it, I could swear!"

When Geraldine came back to London (on the very day Jane wrote the last letter) and saw her friend, she was horrified: she found her

"so changed in appearance, so frail and worn that she cannot hold onto life much longer, so that all question of rights and wrongs between us has been (for me at least) set on one side. . . . She will not see a doctor but it is because she knows *full well* none could do her any permanent good."

This to Mantell, whose opinion of Jane from what he had heard from Geraldine was low. But Geraldine begged him "please don't speak scornfully or bitterly about her. You see her like an ugly bad *photograph* and we all know how that is—that there *is* better than it shows."

Jane was by no means so charitable as her friend, though not averse to making use of her. "With Geraldine at hand" she wrote to Carlyle "I don't suffer the same practical inconvenience—I can send *her* on *any* message and ask her to do *anything*." A week or two after she tells Mrs Russell:

"Geraldine comes every day for longer or shorter time—but she is no use to me in this matter or any other—she is so unsettled—'carried' as *we* call it. I *won't* hear a word about Mr Mantell out of her head—and there is nothing else she has care to talk about or think about."

Geraldine, forbidden to speak of what most concerned her,

reported sadly to Mantell that the main cause of the estrangement was Jane's "extreme indifference, not to say dislike to hearing of anybody I care about and the extreme rudeness she has shown them on every opportunity." She again defends Jane:

"She is not what you fancy her or she could never have held together and kept up her influence over her friends all these years. She has good *granite* underlying her alluvial deposit and she has the faculty of calling out the *best* qualities of those she deals with. She takes no excuse, makes no allowance, and with pitiless clear-sightedness walks into any sort of sham or pretence, any 'charming illusion with beautiful blue' which may be set up. So I would say to you go to see her. . . . You would like her better if you knew more."

Mantell, however, was not at all anxious to know Jane: he was, in fact, in love with the beautiful Calliope Dilberoglue, and most of his interest and his time, when permitted, was given to her. For the rest, Geraldine was a good, though embarrassing, friend as long as he could persuade her to remain a friend.

Geraldine was concerned in the departure—following many false alarms—of Anne, after more than five years. Jane told Geraldine that she would give Anne her notice on 29th February. "Geraldine has a way when amused of raising her voice to a scream; and she screamed out 'you cannot give her warning on the 29th my Dear, for it isn't Leap Year!' " Anne, sweeping in the next room, heard Geraldine, and promptly gave in her own notice. Jane then engaged a "Miss Cameron", daughter of a lieutenant. Miss Cameron, Jane found, was an "Irish impostor" a liar and a thief, and after seventeen days she left late one night and did not return. Carlyle was highly indignant: "My poor little sick partner. I declare it is heart-breaking for her sake, *disgusting*, otherwise, to a high degree, and *dirtier* for the mind than even brushing of boots oneself would be for the body." After some trouble Jane heard of a girl of sixteen, Charlotte: "Of course she '*slept-in*'; little girls always do! I who had slept none at all, naturally, had to get up and awake her". But in spite of this unpromising beginning, Charlotte prospered, and the household settled down again.

The ban on mention of Mantell—and indeed of any friend not approved by Jane—continued, and the estrangement went on.

"I know her tactics so well" Geraldine told Mantell "for those *outside* it will be: 'G. has gone off to new friends and is absorbed by them. She is giving in to dissipation and has *left me*'. For *me* the silence means, 'You will be glad to return to me *but you shall not*.' "

She again protested her innocence:

"if ever a human being *can* be faithful and entire of heart in their relation to another *I* have been, I am still to her. . . . She is now trying, as I have seen her do in other cases, to *make* herself as indifferent and harsh as possible to *put* me out of her life and to exaggerate all my faults and differences of character."

Jane could not go to The Grange with Carlyle in January 1858, and she wrote caustically of his wish to stay at home:

"In vain I urged on him that as he had left me often before ill, to go to that same place, his declining to go now would give the idea that either I was 'waited on for death' or that I was grown strangely exacting. The truth came out at last; 'he had no will to go, and *was very glad of the pretext*'!"

However, she went on, "a note from Lord A showing plainly *he* did not believe in my illness—at least as a reason for *his* (Mr C's) not coming—and some other reasons have decided him to go." She was still too unwell in the spring to accompany him to Addiscombe, but both of them were concerned about Lord Ashburton.

"It is not so much *sorrow* that troubles him, as *bewilderment*." Jane explained. "He looks like a child who had lost its nurse in a wood. I expect some scheming woman will marry him up—not because he is likely to care for anybody, but because he does not know what to do with himself, and would be glad that someone took the trouble of him off his hands."

Carlyle warned his friend as lightly as he was able. Jane went further. She had every cause to like Lord Ashburton, and she did like him, but he was not, like Mrs Russell and Dr Welsh, sacrosanct in her eyes. Now, with her sense of self-pity indulged to the uttermost, it seemed more than ever necessary to dissect the weaknesses of others.

"Curious!" she says of a letter Carlyle had forwarded, "that man seems in a general way so sweet-natured; and yet the only sentiment I ever see him express in a *real human* way is *anger!* Several times, for moments, I have seen him really, *humanly* angry (tho' *shriekily* and *hysterically* enough), but all the rest of his sentiments (his grief included) seem no more really *his* than the sentiments of Macbeth and William Macready's—indeed not so much! He plays the part of *his own Life* like a *thirdrate* Actor who can't identify himself for a moment with the feelings he has got to express—unless you make him *angry!*"

When at last—in May—she felt herself well enough to accept an invitation to Addiscombe, she was obliged to confess how well she was looked after, but even so there was a sting in the tail: "Lord Ashburton's kindness and womanly-attentions were quite touching—he used to be just like one of the *visitors* in his wife's time."

No one escaped:

> "Thackeray's daughters were here yesterday, and speaking of their grandmother's sleeplessness. . . . 'We told her about *you*' said the eldest Miss Thackeray 'we thought it would be *such a comfort* to her to hear of somebody in the same way as herself—and you can't think how pleased she was'!! *Naive* at least!"

As for the cousins from Auchtertool, Maggie and Mary, who spent a fortnight with her after wintering in the Isle of Wight, words failed her.

She was, in fact, nearly impossible as friend, companion or wife during these dreary months, her critical sense sharpened almost to the point of mania by her wretched health. Nothing and nobody could please her, and she was, not surprisingly, left more to herself than she expected or liked. She had many callers, but her friends were not increasing. And she saw no more of Carlyle and got no closer to him than she had when Lady Ashburton was alive. *Frederick* took almost all his time and thought and energy. He, busy with his proofs, had been made well aware of her condition, and wrote often to John, seeking advice for treatment of a pain of which she complained below the heart and in the back. He was moody, though rather less so than usual, with the prospect of the first instalment of *Frederick* off his hands, but he was no more successful in pleasing than anyone else. When he went to The Gill in June, after seeing the proofs off, he was followed by reproaches:

> "to see *you* constantly discontented, and as much so with *me* apparently as with all other *things*, when I have neither the strength nor the spirits to bear up against your discontent nor the obtuseness to be indifferent to it—that has done me more harm than you have the least notion of. You have not the least notion what a killing thought it is, to have put into one's heart, gnawing there day and night, that one *ought* to be *dead* since one *can* no longer make the same exertions as formerly!—that one was

taken only 'for better'—not by any means 'for worse'! and in fact, that the only feasible and dignified thing that remains for one to do is to just *die* and be done with it!"

He parried the charge with some skill:

"I was indeed discontented with myself, with hot, fetid London, generally with all persons and things—and my stomach had struck work withal; but not discontented with poor you ever at all. Nay, to tell you the truth, your anger at me (grounded on that false basis) was itself sometimes a kind of comfort to me. I thought, 'Well, she has strength enough to be cross and ill-natured at me; she is not all softness and affection and weakness'."

He urged her to go to a doctor.

"What could any Dr do" she replied scornfully, "but tell me to take care of myself? My constitution is completely worn out—my nerves, my spirits worn out! Can all the Drs on earth renew nerves and spirits?—you are indeed sanguine if you imagine any 'air' any Dr, any anything can ever make *me* into a healthy or even approximately healthy woman again! You will have to just put up with me as I am; even as I put up with myself as I am—for the rest of my appointed time."

She brushed aside one suggested explanation after another. Mrs Forster had not made her worse, though she "gabbles like a mill-clapper when she has any ideas; the Dickenses and Bullers have given her plenty at present!" No, she was really ill, and he must accept the fact.

He was penitent:

"I lay awake all last night, and never had I such a series of hours filled altogether with you. . . . Alas! and I had to say to myself, this is something like what she has suffered 700 times within the last two years. My poor, heavy-laden, brave, uncomplaining Jeannie! Oh, forgive me, forgive me for much that I have thoughtlessly done and omitted, far, far, at all times, from the poor purpose of my mind."

Then one of her letters was delayed for a day, he began to think of rushing back to London, and when the letter came his apologies were redoubled. "Oh my little woman! what a suffering thou hast had, and how nobly borne! with a simplicity, a silence, courage, and patient heroism which are only now too evident to me." He again tried to soothe her. "We have had a sore life pilgrimage together . . . but . . . if it please God, there are yet good years ahead of us, better and quieter."

For the greater part of their married life Carlyle had been

writing in this strain, praising her heroism, promising amendment, prophesying a better future. Now, this kind of letter did more harm than good, for it encouraged her to reply with a long list of her ailments—written with such detailed care that they give something of the appearance of cherished devils. She had been ill—recognizably ill—for nearly two years. No one had ever been able to discover exactly what ailed her, nor was anyone to be more successful in the future. She was in danger of becoming a confirmed invalid, a chronic malcontent, and her face—ashen, shrunk and lined like that of an old woman—told the same tale. "I can't say" remarked Charlotte to Jane "that *you* look *particularly brilliant*". This was passed on to Carlyle, as was the story of an unexpected visit, just before her fifty-seventh birthday, that pointed the change in her appearance:

"When we opened the door behold David at the bottom of the steps and Bess preparing to knock. 'Is this Mrs Carlyle's?' she asked *of myself* while I was gazing dumbfoundered! 'My goodness!' cried I—at the sound of my voice she knew me—just think! *not* till then! tho' at my own door! And certainly the recognition was the furthest from complimentary I ever met. She absolutely staggered—screaming out '*God* preserve me!—Jane!—*That* you!'—Pleasant!—David coming up the steps brought a little calm into the business—and the call got itself transacted better or worse. They were on their way home from Italy. Both *seemed* rather more human than last time—especially David—whose face had taken on an expression of 'Peace on Earth, and goodwill unto men.' Bess had lost a tooth or two, was rather thinner—and her eyes hollower—otherwise much the same. They invited me very kindly to Minto—and *he* seemed really in earnest."

This characteristic description of the Aitkens belies the evidence of the sad, worn face in portraits of these years. Even more so does her picture of another visitor a few days later:

"Botkin (what a name!), your Russian translator, has called. . . . He burst into the room with wild expressions of his 'admiration for Mr Carlyle.' I begged him to be seated, and he declared 'Mr Carlyle was the man for Russia.' I tried again and again to 'enchain' a rational conversation, but nothing could I get out of him but rhapsodies about you in the frightfullest English that I ever heard out of a human head! . . . even the young Russian Ladies now read *Hero Worship*, and 'unnerstants it thor-lie.' He was all in a perspiration when he went away—and so was I!"

She wrote in the light of a change; she was going at the

beginning of August to Bay House at the invitation of Lord Ashburton's sisters. When she left London

> "a *fast* Lady of my friends told me she had 'never set eyes on a more *seedy* looking *party*'! And various men, who came, *kissed* me at parting; a clear indication of their conviction that they should never see me again!"

At Bay House, as at Haddington the previous summer, she began to grow stronger. At the end of the month she went back to London, but only to pass through on her way to Dumfriesshire. She enquired after her pets; a sparrow "whom I did design to train to flying and 'eventually' to *flying away*" had died, but the sickly canary had recovered under the care of an old cook now coming in to help Charlotte, "in whose '*bosom* it spends several hours every day'—I should think not too happy hours!" She was escorted to the station by little Charlotte, Nero, George Cooke, who had been assiduous during her illness, and Henry Larkin, bringing a bouquet from his garden. This neighbour had been helping Carlyle for some months, and, like Neuberg, had already proved a boon in lightening the labour on *Frederick*. As Jane was carried northward, Carlyle was at sea bound for Germany, to gather material for what he hoped would be the final section of the work.

At Carlisle, her cousin Janet Pringle was waiting for her. In the morning, while she was still in bed,

> "a white child-looking figure glided in thro' the door opening into Mrs Pringle's bedroom, and sat down on her knees at my bedside in night clothes and fell to kissing me! She is a very curious woman this Mrs Pringle . . . she will serve me to study for all the time I stay."

She had plenty of time for study during the next fortnight at Mrs Pringle's house, Lann Hall, in Tynron—"the very loveliest glen I ever saw, endeared to me by old associations". Near Tynron her grandfather John had met and married Elizabeth Hunter of Pingarie, and near Pingarie was her grandfather Walter's farm of Strathmilligan, where she had spent summer after summer as a child. The result of her reappearance "has been a perfect explosion of lunches to my honour and glory all over Glen Shinel and Glencairn". She found it

> "so much *heartier* a sort of hospitality than one finds in the south! It makes one feel younger by twenty years! I catch myself *laughing* sometimes with a *voice* that startles *myself* as not being like my own but my Mother's, who was always so much gayer than I."

She visited Craigenputtock "with the most ghastly sensations" but all else went well until she moved on for a week with the Russells at Thornhill. Then she had "an attack of something extremely like—cholera!" However, it was not cholera: "I declare it was almost worth while to fall ill here, just for the satisfaction of seeing once more a *real* live Doctor!" She recovered quickly, called in at The Gill on her way home, collected a bee-hive for the Cheyne Row garden, and was met by Carlyle in London at the end of September. The house was as clean as a new pin, a black kitten—"oh unexpected joy!"— had been added to the household, and Charlotte became "quite a jewel of a servant" by adding to her many virtues a fine devotion. "I think Scotland" she told Jane "must be such a fresh, airy place! I should like to go there! You did *smell so beautiful* when you came in at the door last night!"

But she was still weak, still liable to colds that kept her house-bound for weeks, and still involved in trouble with Carlyle, whose good resolutions slipped from him when he was within reach of her bitter tongue. The first two volumes of *Frederick* had been a success, but he took no comfort from this: "no better to me than the barking of dogs"—though he had "to believe that there are rational beings in England who read one's poor books." But "no luck for me till I have done the final two volumes. . . . Health unfavourable, horse exercise defective. . . . Much is 'defective', much is against me. . . . Ah me, would I were through it!"

A similar prayer was being made at the same time by Jane to Jean Aitken: "I wish to heaven this book were off his hands—in *any* way. He has never taken heartily to the subject—ought never to have *tried* to make a silk purse out of a sow's ear." She had been trying to comfort her sister-in-law, who had lost a child, by telling her about Betty Braid and her paralysed son "Garg" who could now move only his head. Betty wrote to Jane "My Der, its sore trouble but we mon just hav pashiens". "I wonder" said Jane "how many of who's sermons it would take to make up such a lesson as is in these few poor ill spelt words!"

Carlyle was not the best company for a nervy, hot-tempered woman; yet her complaint was that she did not get enough of his company. To this there was no answer. A few days after she had come home, she wrote to Cooke, who had begun to take Forster's place in her correspondence:

"I am here again—the more's the pity! Once for all this London atmosphere weighs on me, I find, like a hundredweight of lead! No health no spirits one brings from 'the country' can bear up against it! Come and console me! at least come and try '*to*'! . . . Mr C is home from his battle-fields and as busy and private as before. So my evenings are now sacred to reading on his part and mortally ennuying to myself on mine."

Cooke was her strongest support through the winter—

"The fact is" she explains with some pleasure to Mrs Russell "I have been belated in my letters and everything this week—by having had to give from *two to three hours every day* to a man who has unexpectedly lost his Mother. He has *five Sisters* here and female friends world without end —is in fact of all men I know the most *popular*—and such is relationship and friendship in London, that he has fled away from everybody to *me*, who wasn't aware before that *I* was his particular friend the least in the world! But I have always had the same sort of attraction for *miserable* people and for *mad* people that *amber* has for *straws!*"

Mrs Cameron, later to be famed for her photographs, including a study of Carlyle, begged them to come to her daughter's wedding. Carlyle replied

"my wife is unable to go out at all; and for me I am buried to the eyes in such a welter of Chaotic litter as is horrible to think of—in which I work all day, and all days; riding abroad a little in the dusk, like a distracted ghost, to try if I can keep alive till the thing get done, and gloomily returning to my dungeon. . . . Pity me; and ask me not to be corporeally present, but only spiritually!"

A regular visitor at Chelsea was Froude, now working on his *History;* primarily a disciple of Carlyle, but already influenced by his talks with Jane. Like other disciples of Carlyle who were also devoted to Jane, Froude had a difficult path to tread:

"If any of us were to spend the evening there, we generally found her alone; then he would come in, take possession of the conversation and deliver himself in a stream of splendid monologue, wise, tender, scornful, humorous, as the inclination took him—but never bitter, never malignant, always genial, the fiercest denunciations ending in a burst of laughter at his own exaggerations. Though I knew things were not altogether well, and her drawn, suffering face haunted me afterwards like a sort of ghost, I felt for myself that in him there could be nothing really wrong, and that he was as good as he was great."

In the early part of the new year, 1859, Jane gives Betty

Braid a fair report of her winter: "except for bodily languor and weariness, I really have now little to complain of." She had seen Rennie again:

> "Oh you can't fancy what an old worn-looking man he is grown. He has a grand house, and his cousin Jane whom he married (instead of *me*) seems to make him a devoted Wife; but his life is not a happy one, I think."

She read many books, including George Eliot's second book, *Adam Bede*, which pleased her as much as the first. She wrote another "ardent" letter to the still anonymous author, thanking "him" for making her feel "in charity with the whole human race" and filled with "gentle thoughts and happy remembrances"

In the spring her spirits again failed, her appetite disappeared and she called in the local doctor, Dr Barnes, who pleased her because he discussed her ailments seriously and at length. She called him in, she explained to Mrs Russell, because

> "in the first place my head was getting *light* which threatened to disable me from giving directions about myself—in the second place there was need of somebody with authority who *knew* to explain to Mr C that if care were not taken, I should die of sheer weakness! a thing which makes no show to inexperienced eyes—especially to eyes blinded with incessant contemplation of *Frederick the Great!*"

The doctor told Carlyle that there was no cause for alarm, but that he was surprised by Jane's excitability and by her excessive weakness. He said enough to move Carlyle to action. "In that wild blast of winter which was our month of May" he told Lord Ashburton, "my poor wife had a dreadful attack of illness—we decided to go North." He too, though not ill—he was scarcely ever ill in his life—was greatly cast down. As he put it to Lord Ashburton, "I have led the life of a solitary galley-slave chained to his oar, with his own sad consent." And after "months of uselessness and wretchedness' he found himself "dark, inert, and stupid to a painful degree, when progress depends almost altogether on vivacity of nerves." He had no more of vivacity then than Jane had of strength, and by June it became clear that they must both go away. He rented the upper floor of a farmhouse on the Fife coast and set off by sea with Charlotte, Fritz and Nero, while Jane came by railway, pausing a few days at Haddington.

477

XXXV

THE NEW LADY ASHBURTON
1859 – 1860

Jane's exit from London—like her comment on it—was as typical as anything she had ever done. She was seen off at the station by Geraldine and Cooke. Before leaving, she persuaded Cooke to urge Mantell to visit them in Fife. And as soon as she reached the farm at Humbie, near Aberdour, she wrote to him:

> "I was very glad of your letter—not only because it was a letter from you, but a sign that you had forgiven me—or, still better,—that you had never been offended! I assure you, an hour or two later, when left alone and quiet in the railway carriage, I wondered as much as you could do, what Demon inspired the tasteless jest with which I bade you goodbye! in presence too of the most gossiping and romancing of all our mutual acquaintances!"

She had thus killed one bird with two stones; Mantell was to be drawn away from Geraldine's side, and Cooke was warned against any attempted siege in Jane's absence.

She was not rewarded for her zeal by a pleasant holiday. She spent four days resting at Haddington before moving up to Humbie, but all she could say after some weeks was that everyone except herself was flourishing; Charlotte was blooming and Carlyle "if not essentially in better health is in what is almost as good—that make-the-best-of-every thing state which men get into when carrying out their own idea—and *only then!*" Even Nero "*bathes* with his master from a sense of duty; and is gradually shaking off the selfish torpor that had seized upon him in London—he *snores* less, thinks of other things besides his food, and shows some of his old fondness for *me*." But as for herself—"there is everything here needed for happiness, but just *one* thing—the faculty of *being* happy! And *that* unfortunately I had never much of in my best days—and in the days that

478

are, it is lost to me altogether!" Carlyle tried to persuade her to ride Fritz, but she was too weak. He got a donkey for her to ride, but "that was only half successful." She walked occasionally with him in Humbie wood, but without pleasure.

He—"hoping still to recover myself by force"—was riding hard, walking late in the woods, and bathing regularly in company with the much revived Nero, who, like his mistress, had breathed so little fresh air and attempted so little exercise in the past year or two that he was in poor condition. Not only Jane's long illness but the coming of Fritz had borne hardly on him, for he had lost many of the walks with his master. Carlyle now did his best to repair the damage:

> "Twice or thrice I flung him into the sea there, which he didn't at all like; and in consequence of which he even ceased to follow me at bathing time, the very strongest measure he could take—or *pretend* to take . . . but the third or fourth morning, on striking out to swim a few yards, I heard gradually a kind of swashing behind me; looking back, it was Nero . . . ready to swim with me to Edinburgh or to the world's end if I liked!"

Jane looked on all this revivalist activity with a sour eye. Carlyle, she said tartly, was behaving "more like a man of sixteen than of sixty-four". He gave it up. This, he said, was "the last time I tried the boy method."

In an effort to improve her health they moved a few miles inland, to Auchtertool House, near the Manse. Here there was a complete reversal of fortunes; Carlyle became bilious—"rode and bathed himself" into it at Humbie, Jane declared—and she began to pick up some of her lost strength and cheerfulness. For the first fortnight, she said, looking after Carlyle in his "bilious crisis" was

> "more like being keeper in a madhouse, than being 'in the country' for 'quiet and change'. Things are a little subsided *now* however and in spite of the wear and tear on my nerves, I am certainly less languid and weak than during all my stay in the farmhouse."

She gave a number of reasons for her improvement—change of air, "kind little cousins" within reach, and so on—but did not mention one fact that sent her spirits up with a bound. Mantell had actually visited them, and Jane flattered herself that his objections to her had been pretty thoroughly removed.

> "I liked Mr Mantell much when I saw him away out of the valley

of the shadow of Geraldine—so did Mr C like him—'far too clever and *substantial* a man to be thrown away on a *flimsy tatter* of a creature like Geraldine Jewsbury' was his remark."

John Carlyle also met and liked him. "To *the last*" Geraldine told Mantell, "Mrs Carlyle, who detests him as though he were a *sister-in-law*, says, 'what happiness for Mr Mantell!' "

In the middle of September Carlyle went down to Annandale, and Jane to Edinburgh and Haddington. She had caught a slight chill coming over the Forth.

> "Pity there should be 'always a something'! But for this apprehension of an overhanging illness and these horrid 'cold shivers', I should have enjoyed my last visit to Sunny Bank so much. . . . Even when I left this morning, I did not despair of seeing them again!"

Then, after a night at York, she was home again at the end of the month, preparing for Carlyle's arrival a few days later. She was better in every way for her weeks away but she had an unpleasant shock the night before Carlyle returned. Charlotte came home with the dog in her arms.

> "A butcher's cart driving furiously round a sharp corner had passed over poor little Nero's throat! and *not* killed him on the spot! But he looked killed enough at the first. When I tried to '*stand him* on the ground' (as the servants here say), he flopped over on his side quite stiff and apparently unconscious! You may figure my sensations! . . . by little and little he recovered the use of himself—but it was ten days before he was able to raise *a bark*—his first attempt was like the *scream* of an infant!"

Then came a note from Mantell, and she revived:

> "Pray *do* come! We should be sorry to *not* shake hands with you again. And for me, as one individual; I feel as if I couldn't like you enough and be sorry enough at your going, in amends for the almost *detestation* I had conceived against you, from hearing you spoken of in season and out of season as a good deal higher than the angels! I have such a horror of *angels—moi!*"

He was going back to New Zealand; he had been unsuccessful with Calliope Dilberoglue, who was marrying one of her countrymen; but he had been only too successful with Geraldine who besought him—in vain—to take her back with him.

He was soon writing again; could he come and make his farewells?

> "When your note was brought in" Jane replied, "I was in the act of telling Miss Pardoe authoress of *The City of the Sultan* (good god!) a

woman who makes calls with a head bobbing all over with waterlillies! . . . the shocking catastrophe at London Bridge!—and Politeness of course exacted that I should not read your note till the Waterlillies had sailed out in a high state of excitement! I wonder if you are only *saying* you will come; to avoid a leave-taking? Men are so cowardly in giving themselves pain—and there is always a certain pain in saying a long farewell even to persons indifferent to one! Geraldine could doubtless tell you *why*—*I can't;* being like the old Edin^r Lady, 'No Philosopher but just a plain human *cretur*.' I only know it is a fact."

Mantell came again; the generous Geraldine applauded:

"I am very glad you like *her*. She is one of those who cannot be judged, but must be accepted. She is a *heroine*, and right or wrong makes a prescription for herself. If she is cruel sometimes and hard, at others she is more noble and generous than ninety-nine just persons who need no repentance, and as to her *fascination* I appeal to *yourself!*"

Since the rise of photography, Jane had a new pastime— pasting prints on to a screen. Susan Stirling was added, among others, this autumn:

"You dear nice woman! there you are! a bright cheering apparition to surprise one on a foggy October morning. . . . It (the photograph) made our breakfast this morning 'pass off' like the better sort of breakfasts in Deerbrook—in which people seemed to have come into the world chiefly to eat breakfast in every possible variety of temper! Blessed be the inventor of photography! I set him above even the inventor of chloroform! . . . I have often gone into my own room in the devil's own humour —ready to swear at 'things in general' and some things in particular— and my eyes resting by chance on one of my photographs of long-ago places or people, a crowd of sad gentle thoughts has rushed into my heart and driven the devil out. . . . And that bright kind indomitable face of yours will not be the least efficacious face there for exorcising my devil when I have him!"

Ruskin had long been a Carlyle enthusiast. Of *Past and Present* he wrote "I find everything that has to be said on any matter is all in that, and other people may for ever hold their Peace (I'll hold mine—if I can get a little to hold)". At this time, just back in London, he writes to Jane about "the badness of German painting", and says

"I think I shall have to give up painting—writing—talking—everything but reading—and I read little now but Mr Carlyle. Fiction sickens me because it is fiction—I weary of it. Truth depresses me—because it is true."

He called often and was made welcome by both, Jane having long since abandoned her championship of his wife.

Cooke was still the most regular caller, and Jane was no longer dependent on Darwin for her drives—Carlyle had hired a carriage for her. She visited a good deal, glad at times to be out of the house when he was trying "to vanquish by sheer force the immense masses of incondite or semi-condite rubbish which had accumulated on *Frederick*, that is, to let the printer straightway drive me through it." *Frederick* was not to be finished so easily, but for months he would not admit it. Not until February, 1860, "after dreadful tugging at the straps", did he take Jane's "serious advices" to abandon the attempt at a short cut— "advices which I could not but admit to be true as well as painful and humiliating."

A chill in December had prevented Jane from spending Christmas at The Grange, but she recovered quickly enough to spend a few days there early in the new year. This was the most important visit she had ever made to The Grange, for she met there for the first time the new Lady Ashburton. Lord Ashburton had married Louisa Stewart Mackenzie in the autumn of 1858, but as the newly-married pair went abroad at once, there had been no opportunity for Jane to meet her. Carlyle, for all his congratulations on this "grand and unexpected news", was dubious. "I have had the honour to see that admirable Lady more than once" he told Lord Ashburton, "nor has rumour been silent about her many qualities." This was perhaps the nearest approach to tact that he ever reached; he had not, in fact, formed a favourable impression of the new Lady Ashburton; and he noted in his journal a dismayed "Ah me! Ah me!" The fact that the new Lady came of a fine old Scottish family made Jane try to suspend judgment, and if she had any doubts they soon disappeared.

> "I frankly confess that 'French Cookery' agrees with *me* remarkably well! and that I can drink Champagne to dinner every day, not only without hurt, but with benefit to my health. Then it is cheering to get out of the 'valley of the shadow' of *Frederick the Great* for even eight days! ... And so I was unusually well at The Grange; and came home in better case than I left it! and much pleased with the new Lady, who was kindness's self! A really amiable, lovable woman she seems to be; much more intent on making her visitors at their ease and happy, than on shewing off *herself*, and attracting admiration."

This to Mary Austin at The Gill. To Mrs Russell she permits herself a flicker of the old Eve:

"Even I who had set my mind against liking her, could not resist the pains she took to make me. By the way—I don't wonder you thought Lord A not too happy when you took that sentimental letter I sent you for *his!* The letter was from *Lady A* who then signed *his* name! Oh no! He shows no sign of regret! His devotion to the new Lady is perfect. And really he never was so 'made of' before!—I can't wonder that he likes it!"

It was a dying flicker. She had been attracted more than she knew. The new Lady was affectionate, unselfish, kind—that was plain—but how much so, Jane did not yet realise.

She came home in "sickening apprehension" about Nero:

"It was the first time for eleven years that his welcoming bark had failed me! Was he really dead, then? No! Strange to say, he was actually a little better and had run up the kitchen stairs to welcome me as usual; but there he had been arrested by a paroxysm of coughing, and the more he tried to shew his joy the more he could not do it! Mr C keeps insisting on 'a little prussic acid' for him! At the same time he was overheard saying to him in the garden one day, 'Poor little fellow! I declare I am heartily sorry for you! If I *could* make you young again, upon my soul I *would!*' "

Nero had never recovered from his accident. He could not breathe properly, he was in pain. On the last day of January, Carlyle went for his usual walk late at night. Nero, who had never allowed him to go alone, insisted on trying to follow. Carlyle, turning, saw him dropping behind, unable at last to do more than drag himself along. The next morning Jane went out and Nero "weak and full of pain" tried to accompany her. She would not let him come with her, but when she returned with the doctor he came panting to welcome her: "and the reward I gave him—the only reward I could or ought to give him, to such a pass had things come—was ten minutes after to give him up to be poisoned."

Three weeks later she is writing:

"If I am less ill than usual this winter, I am more than usually sorrowful. For I have lost my dear little companion of eleven years' standing. . . , Only to *me*, whom he belonged to and whom he preferred to all living, does my dear wee dog remain a constantly recurring blank, and a thought of strange sadness! What *is* become of that little beautiful, graceful *Life*, so full of love and loyalty and sense of duty, up to the last moment that it animated the body of that little dog? Is *it* to be extinguished, abolished, annihilated in an instant; while the brutalized, two-legged, so-called *human* creature who dies in a ditch, after having outraged all duties, and caused nothing but pain and disgust to all concerned with him, is to live forever? It is impossible for me to believe that! . . . One thing is sure, anyhow; my little dog is buried at the top of our garden—and I grieve for him as if he had been my little human child."

Mantell, with whom she corresponded occasionally, had lost his dog:

"You may be thankful however that this grief befell you far from the *coeurs sensibles* of London! for the sympathy and condolences they would have lavished on you here, would have roused in you an instinct of murder!—'Poor dear Nero! of course you will have him *stuffed?*—No?— Why not? he was *so* pretty and curious!—just a dog for being stuffed!— and then you could have him always in the room with you in a glass case! He would *still* be quite a companion!!' 'Don't have another Dog dear Mrs Carlyle—have a *cat!* Cats live longer, and one doesn't mind when *they* die!' 'Well, I am *so* sorry about Nero! but you mustn't be so concerned about it; *I* am looking out for a *worthy successor* to him, and you shall have *a dog quite as pretty* in a day or two!'—that is a specimen of what was said to *me* in my *real* sorrow. Yes! and *six dogs* were offered me in succession!—two of them brought to the house!—and I wouldn't so much as look at them! How *could* I? Ach! such experiences throw one into the fashion of Miss Squeers, who 'hated the world and wished that every body was dead!' "

A surprise from the Dods at Haddington in the middle of February broke into her grief:

"Oh you dear nice People! I am so glad! so obliged to you! I don't know *when* I was so pleased at anything; or so surprised at anything; or so grateful for anything! No Valentine delivered in Chelsea yesterday, and there were *many*—to judge from the lateness of our Postman—caused more enthusiasm, I'll be bound to say, than just this Valentine of *mine!* (Of course you *meant* it for a *Valentine?*). . . . you have come and comforted me a bit, when I was sorrowful! As for the portraits *per se*, they are very like—but very far from flattering. My Recollections can touch them up a little however—so as to make them 'all right' to my own heart at least."

She added a postscript: "I *do* wonder often and sadly how my poor old friends at Sunny Bank are standing this cruel weather", and she had no sooner written it than she heard of the death of old Miss Donaldson. The one remaining Donaldson sister died two months later, and Jane grieved for the loss, not only of her Sunny Bank friends, but of Haddington—for she knew that she would never have the heart to go there again. Then two of her lovers of long ago died suddenly: Robert MacTurk and George Rennie. "My oldest friend," she wrote to Mrs Forster, "is at the point of death. I shall go immediately after breakfast tomorrow and stay to help his wife *if she will let me*. . . . I am so stunned I don't know what I am writing." A few days later she told Rennie's aunt:

"George—*your* George Rennie and *my* George Rennie—is dead—died yesterday morning. . . . By a strange fatality it was I who watched by him thro' his last night on earth—I, his first love, who received his last breath and closed his eyes! Was it not a strange sad thing—after so many separations—so many tossings up and down this weary earth! . . . Never was there a man—as I told him . . . who did himself more injustice. I believe he had the warmest truest heart, but it was encased in pride and distrust of others' affection for him, making it of no use to them or himself."

Carlyle had given up his attempt to "force" *Frederick* and was grinding painfully through the third volume; but the reaction from his months of pressure, the unpalatable self-reproach of this admission that he could no longer work so hard or so well, and the thought of the overloaded years that stretched before him—all this made him savage with himself and others. He had little time for pity, and none for comprehension of Jane's feelings. All he saw was that, though still weak, she was less ill than in previous winters, that she complained less and was out more. But if Jane complained less to him, it was mainly because she was complaining more to others. The carriage provided by him on certain days of the week merely extended the range of her tongue. Not Carlyle alone, but a composite of Carlyle and *Frederick* began to obsess her as an impossible double burden to be placed on the shoulders of a sick woman. Scarcely a letter is without its sarcastic reference to "the valley of the shadow of *Frederick*". And in her visits almost anyone was fair game— Thackeray's eldest daughter, for instance, with whom Jane was never intimate, and of whom she had spoken so scathingly barely a year earlier. Even the new Lady Ashburton, so recent an acquaintance, was not spared:

"That unlaid and apparently *unlayable* ghost of '*Frederick*' has broken all bounds latterly; reminding me rather poignantly of old Dr Ritchie, the Edin^r Professor of Divinity's description of a certain Personage; 'with *the trumpet of Discord in his mouth*, and *the Torch of Dissension* in his hand (Pray picture him to yourself) he goeth about as *a roaring Lion* seeking whom to devour! and when he hath set Son against Father and Husband against Wife, he returns to his Den, *with a horrible grin on his countenance*, rejoicing in the mischief he hath wrought'!! Whereby I merely mean to say—in plain English—**Mr C** has been getting on dreadfully ill with that unlucky book—and his health and spirits, and especially his temper, have suffered in consequence, to a degree that has been making me not only very sorrowful but very anxious. Indeed I never before in all my life have seen him so—what shall I say? '*put out*'*!* (that is the strongest cockney term for mental upset, from whatever cause! A woman here, who had just seen a poor little Boy's head split in two by a wheel of one of Pickford's Vans, and waited till the mother was brought, answered my question; 'Oh what *did* become of her?' with, 'Oh, well Mam; as you may think, she was sadly *put out*'*!!*) Now, besides the worry of seeing *him* and *feeling* him in this state, I have been '*suffering Martyrs*' (as a French friend of mine used to express it) from rheumatic pains in my own head; and all this together has produced a solution of continuity in my small Life, torn up, as it were, a furrow thro' it—which alters nothing of what was a few weeks since but alters my own firm hold of it all—so that I need to take a new grasp, over the interruption. *Do* you understand what I mean? I should think not! When one lives much alone, one feels so many things one never puts into thoughts, not to say, words! No wonder one gets to express oneself obscurely and fancifully."

She adds, in a different tone:

"When *will* that Baby take a notion of coming to light? I declare I never cared so much for any prospective Baby, in all my life before! I actually *dreamt* about it the other night! dreamt that I was at The Grange, and heard it crying, and felt it my duty to go and feed it (!!) and went wandering about in the dark and could never find it! And still the crying became more and more plaintive till—it awoke me! Awoke me to the vexatious discovery that our poor cat had been shut out from her week-old-kittens."

In April, Carlyle was persuaded to go to the Sandwiches at Hinchinbrook for a few days. Jane was unwell but, says Carlyle, "she will not hear of my staying; and indeed has specially invited a *Bore* on Saturday to keep me away!" At Hinchin-brook, and away from *Frederick* and from Jane, he began to see his imperfections more clearly: "He was the unhappy animal but did not mean ill." He asked her to be patient with him. But when he returned after a few days, he was more difficult than ever, biliousness having added itself to his other worries. The atmosphere in the house grew heavy with hostility, and Jane took an unprecedented step—she refused to read the manuscript of *Frederick*.

XXXVI

THE VALLEY OF THE SHADOW OF *FREDERICK*
1860 – 1863

In June, 1860, when Jane was still battling with discord in Cheyne Row, with shock from the death of friends, and with desolation from the loss of the nearest to a child she was ever to enjoy, a daughter, Mary, was born to Lady Ashburton. This event lifted Jane out of herself:

"Oh my Lady! I should *so* like to see Her! Lord Ashburton's own wee bairn! I am going on Monday to Brighton for a week, and that would be long to wait. Will you give orders that, if She be awake when I call tomorrow, they will show her to me for a minute? Of course she will be quite *red* still! But I am as sure as you are, that she will grow up very beautiful and very good; and be the light of her Father's eyes and the joy of his heart. And no little Brother who may come will ever be able to displace her from the first place in your hearts."

"When I got Lord A's announcement," Jane went on, "I ran with it to Mr C, and what do you think were his next words after the 'Well! thank God it is all safely over'! his next words were 'Is your note *from the Lady herself?*'!!—'My gracious!' I cried, 'how *can* you be so absurd as to imagine her *up to* writing notes the instant after her confinement?'—'Well my Dear'! said he, 'I don't pretend to know *what* people are up to in these cases. The Lady seems to have all along been up to more than most women who *have nothing of the sort the matter with them*, and how could *I* know that she would *break down at the last*'!!!! What a wonderful thing a Man of Genius is to be sure!"

Lady Ashburton was doubtful whether Jane could see the baby so soon:

"I have no sort of communication with the outer world, but through my Nurse—to whom in comparison Pharaoh's task Masters were beneficent angels—she stops notes—visitors—*Everything*—I sent 3 *orders* that day that you were to be shown up to see my wee Brown Beauty—not one was given!"

"But I *did* see Her, my dear Lady!" Jane announced triumphantly a week later, "*did* see your 'little brown Beauty' before I went to Brighton;

and carried away the most bewitching impression of Her! Every facility was given me; the *men* seemed to have constituted themselves *nurses* for the time! the Porter, Groom was each as proud of Her as ever nurse was of her charge, and vied with each other in zeal to show her to me!—'only I was to walk softly, and not let my voice be heard by her Ladyship in the next room; it was the Dr's orders, when he left, that her Ladyship was to be kept *very* quiet.' And it was charming to meet the enquiring, pleased looks of these men on my return from the Nursery, bearing out their words 'she *is* an uncommon fine Child Mam?' The Porter added '*did* you ever see such a head of hair? why it is as long as *that!*' (measuring two inches on his own finger)! Oh yes! I saw her all over, lying like a pearl in an oyster shell in her pink and white basket! and not only saw her but *touched* her—with the tip of my finger! and I drew a finger thro' her long dark soft hair—and finally, my enthusiasm having reached a pitch, I went on my knees and kissed her cheek, lightly as if it had been a butterfly's wing that might have the colours rubbed off with a touch! The dear wee Bairn!—It puckered all its bit face together into the queerest, funniest yawn! as much as to say; 'Please don't! now— *do* go away!' and I went away vowing inwardly a life-long interest in her and a loyal affection to Her—the first human child that has ever, so to speak, come home to my business and my bosom! and awakened what is called *the maternal instinct* in me—me whose lines have always been cast in Babyless Places!"

She added: "I have enough to tell about Brighton! how *cocks* crew! and it all ended in 'immortal smash'. Oh dear oh dear! I am like poor Martha in the Scriptures 'troubled about many things' ". She did not exaggerate. Buoyed up by excitement over the child and the revelation that her heart could still be so moved, she persuaded Carlyle—still tortured and torturing with *Frederick*—to lodgings she had taken by the sea, but the crowing of cocks, and other night and early morning noises, real and imagined, drove him, after three days, distractedly back to Chelsea. Jane followed, herself no better, to find that two Haddington families had called in her absence, the Dods and the Fermes. The Dods she saw, but the Fermes had already gone home. She sent a book to Helena Ferme for her children:

"Oh my Dear! how provoked I was to find your and your husband's names on my return from Brighton! I hadn't been a day out of London since New Year time and I was gone only a week! . . . But I can trust to its not being out of sight out of mind with you and him. In spite of all the cross things you say of yourself, I have always thought you had a warmer heart than many *sweeter*-spoken people!—so I expect you to keep me in kind remembrance tho' you failed to see me here, and tho' I have no definite prospect of ever seeing you at Haddington again! Now that dear old Sunny Bank is fallen empty and silent—forevermore empty and silent for *me* at least—I shudder at the idea of ever setting eyes on Haddington again! While even *one* of *them* lived, I had still a feeling of homeness there! But now . . . "

Carlyle had begun to fear "that I should never get my sad book on Friedrich finished, that it would finish me instead." Unable to sleep easily for this new thought, he "sat smoking 'up the chimney', huddled in rugs, dressing gown and cape, with candle on the hob", or lay awake "still as a stone", fear rushing through him that his work was in vain, was merely killing him; then he rode out in the early mornings and returned unrefreshed to his "work and sadness". But he did not always lie as still as a stone, nor did he always sit silently by his chimney. His state, Jane agreed, was

> "very dismal for him to whom waking betwixt lying down and getting up is a novelty. For me, my own wakings up some twenty or thirty times every night of my life for years and years back are nothing compared with hearing him jump out of bed overhead once or sometimes twice during a night."

Soon, she complained, "that sound overhead used to set my heart a-thumping to such a degree that I couldn't get another wink of sleep—and I was on the brink of a nervous fever." Late in July neither could bear the strain any longer, and Carlyle went off to Thurso Castle, in the far north of Scotland, to join Sir George Sinclair. This man pleased Jane at a dinner she had given for him and Edward Twisleton, whose American wife she had become very fond of. Sir George, she said, had been most amusing. "But not here could he amuse" wrote the disillusioned Carlyle from Thurso. However, having gone so far, he stayed on for several weeks.

Jane's "nervous fever" abated quickly when she was left alone except for sympathetic callers such as the Forsters, Cooke, Lady Ashburton, and Thomas Woolner the sculptor, who had met and liked her at The Grange, and was soon a correspondent and champion. By the middle of August, the doctor did not object to her going away "provided I don't go to Mr C!"—the doctor too having been taken into her confidence. Carlyle suggested The Gill, but this did not please her:

> "decidedly, mooning about all by myself at The Gill, and lapping milk which doesn't agree with me, and being stared at by The Gill children as

their 'aunt!' is not the happy change for which I would go far, much as I like Mary Austin and like to speak with her *for a few hours*."

She made up her mind at the last moment to go to the Stanleys at Alderley Park, and then on to the Russells, who had moved to Holm Hill, a house by the Nith, just outside Thornhill.

She reached Alderley Park without mishap, but without telling Carlyle that she had left London, and leaving at Cheyne Row only the "Treasure", the seventy-one year old Jane, whom she employed occasionally. She spent a pleasant week with Lady Stanley and her Bright Young Things. Then, as she was preparing to move up to Holm Hill, a letter from Carlyle was sent on to her from London, announcing that he was about to leave Thurso and "sail South". He meant, to Leith on his way to Annandale, but to Jane "South" meant London, and she rushed home, abandoning the rest of her holiday, to prepare the house for him. She left no doubt in the mind of anyone how badly she was being treated. "Poor Mrs Carlyle," Lady Stanley tells her husband, "who was going to Scotland Tuesday has heard from the Philosopher that he returns to Chelsea like a cannon ball and so she goes to meet him. She is very amusing and tells no end of stories."

Back at Chelsea in a flaming temper, Jane almost lost her reason when she discovered that Carlyle had no intention of returning until the end of September. She wrote one bitter letter after another; he replied, sorrowing, but reproachful too. She could get no satisfaction from him, and began to ease her mind in another way. Everyone should know. She told everyone. Lady Ashburton would sympathize:

"Oh Lady fair and dear! My mischances of late have been so outrageous, that I think of working them up into a Farce, to be called *the Unlucky Woman*. But I haven't quite made up my mind whether to do *that*, or let myself go to an *access* of misanthropy! Meanwhile, under the possibility that some day I may lay my misfortunes at your feet— dramatized; I shall abstain from troubling you with a literal account of them here, except in so far as is necessary to explain my delay in answering your letter. In the first place, that letter was detained from day to day thro' *four* days at Holm Hill; in the fond hope, *excited by its own appearance*, that I would arrive to claim it! For alas, I had never reached Holm Hill— never got further north than Alderley! My week there was hardly expired when I had 'felt it my duty' to stream back to Cheyne Row to prepare for my Husband; who, all in writing (as Sir George Sinclair says) 'immortal pages for Unborn Generations' had written an uncommonly stupid, confusedly expressed page for his own *born* Wife! leading her to suppose that he would sail from Thurso straight to London by the next steamer. And what *could* she do, the poor wretch of a wife, under the circumstances —his bedcurtains at the Cleaners!—all the keys locked up *unlabelled* in *the piano!*—the house in charge of an old '*Treasure*', who had turned out as *Treasures* generally do—a most 'beggarly account of empty boxes'! under such circumstances what *could* she do, but just what she did—rush wildly home! '*a huge error*' on her part! Mr C has since loftily declared; '*a miserable infatuation*'! '*a sheer chimera of the female Brain*'! But all these epithets applied to my proceeding don't alter the fact; that I have been cheated out of my holiday by his having failed to make his meaning intelligible!"

The exchanges with Carlyle were still proceeding briskly but with little satisfaction to either party; until Carlyle, exasperated, accused Jane, to her fury, of having her own reasons for wishing to return to London.

"Heaven and Earth!" she exclaimed to Maude Stanley "I appeal to Lady Stanley—to the bright young Beings—even to the white dogs—to all living who saw me at that crisis if this *Solution* be not enough to drive even *me* 'into a convent'? But—I have had my revenge!—I have written him with a very bad pen—as bad as this one—12 pages of *reasons* for doing as I did and for believing that, '*under the circumstances*, I could do no otherwise'!"

Her sarcastic letters to Carlyle tailed off into a list of ailments; headache, sickness, sore throat, influenza—she had them all in the next few weeks. She was in a change of servants. Little Charlotte had been sent off—she was too untidy, Jane had discovered; the old Treasure had been dismissed—found to be a liar; and two new girls (for Jane now decided to increase her establishment)—had not yet come. Little Charlotte came back when Jane first took to her bed: "I don't know what I should have done without her, to cook for me, and show me some human kindness", but although she pleaded to be allowed to stay, Jane resisted her: "she really *loves* both of us passionately— only that passionate loves, not applied to practical uses, are good for so little in this matter-of-fact world!" Geraldine "has been obliging and attentive, but oh Heaven! what a fuss she does make with everything she does! And how wonderfully little sense she has!"

Carlyle, bowing at last before the deluge of reproaches and complaints that followed him about, had again promised amendment: "I will be quiet as a dream. . . . Be still; be quiet. I swear to do thee no mischief at all." When he was home again and, as he phrased it, had got his "smithy fire kindled again, and there is sound of the hammer once more audible" he made some effort to keep the blows as quiet as possible. Jane's letters again became lively:

> " '*Good gracious alive!*' dear Mr Mantell—(allow me to use that favourite ejaculation of London House-maids; it expresses so concisely my emotion at this instant of time!) Oh good gracious alive!—I was taking it quietly, the letter due to you, was fancying at least a week between me and the Australian Mail; and 'did design' to make you a handsome return for your two letters and the little drawing—and behold, here I have just received a note from Geraldine dated 'The Waiting Room' of some Railway; excusing herself for not having come to bid me goodbye on the plea that 'being the *last hour* for the New Zealand mail' she had had to leave everything to write to you, as you 'were disappointed last month' . . . First, thanks for your letters—when I read the last to Mr C he said 'that's all well, write to him and give him my kind remembrances and *encourage him* (!) to do the poor fellows all the good he can; and to be—*patient with fools!!*'—a singular advice from Mr C don't you think?—that last! George Cooke is in raptures! Geraldine ditto. They are 'so glad that you are using your talents'—and I am 'so glad' that you *have* talents to use!"

Mantell was not so sure: "I have indeed been 'patient with fools' but am getting impatient of the only one I see much of—myself."

In the first days of the new year, 1861, Jane and Carlyle were again at The Grange, but he, unable to rest unless he was at work on *Frederick*, and still feeling strange and sad under the new conditions there, insisted on coming back after four days. She was taking more and more to the new Lady, whose affectionate and demonstrative nature was so congenial to her, and to little Mary, and Carlyle noticed her disappointment when they returned home. He apologised to Lady Ashburton; he was ashamed of his "sad fiasco of a visit". He wished Jane had stayed on: "the poor soul has done nothing but pine ever since." This was an appeal not to be disregarded, and the two women were soon seeing much of each other:

> "It was such a relief on arriving at Marochetti's yesterday; out of temper and out of breath, to find that you had not come, and—gone. *That* was what I expected; to be told, that her Ladyship had been gone a quarter of an hour! All the World and its wife took a notion of driving down to Chelsea yesterday, and doing the civil thing by Mrs Carlyle; and

the result was that, altho' I tied on my bonnet *in the street* and *ran* all the way, I didn't reach Marochetti's till a quarter after four. He came to the door himself, and told me you would still come, with a calm certitude of belief which quite imposed on me, and persuaded me into an easy chair from which he displaced his Cat. 'Do me the favour to sit down here *at once;* because if you don't there is to be feared, my Cat will again take possession of this chair!' The chair commanded the best view of your Busts. The one in clay struck me as *much* improved since I had seen it; I could have recognised *it* anywhere, tho' it certainly bears no trace of that power of flattery which the Baron has given such evidence of in his other female heads—as for the marble one, I can't understand how it has *happened!* or what it *would be at!* Perhaps the *tinting* had something to do with the sickly, Madame Tussaud wax-work impression it made on one. Anyhow, the lower part of the face, especially, seemed to me utterly without expression or likeness—and I had the audacity to tell Marochetti so! He did not smite me, but agreed that 'there was still much to be done —the likeness could not be judged of while it was still so unfinished.' Perhaps it will come right then after all!—the brow and upper part of the face is fine, even now. 'The truth is' he said to me with a little air of telling me a secret, 'that Lady Ashburton is *veree* difficult to *make!* She is a beautiful woman—amazingly beautiful, and her eyes—! there is in them such goodness and *a something wild* that is very beautiful, and difficult *to make!*' He appealed to me if I didn't think so. As to your being so *difficult to make* I couldn't say, not having ever tried; but I said I knew what he meant about your eyes, and that there was the same expression in your Baby's!!! a grave statement of a fact on my part which was received by him with an explosion of mirth quite beyond what he had seemed capable of, and cries of 'Oh!'—'Oh!'—'Oh!'—'So young a *Babee* Madame! Such young Babee cannot yet have beauty!' Why not I should like to know! The Baron may be a dextrous Sculptor, but clearly he is no Poet!—and has neither sense, nor feeling, nor knowledge about Babees!''

Mantell was still writing. Maori chiefs were coming to Wellington for a day or two, and

"in that day or two we are going to do our little utmost to make life a burden to them. Addresses of all sorts—a public dinner—a converzione (as I see they spell it), and the usual driving first piles and laying first stones."

After this there was a gap before his next letter:

"I *knew*" replied Jane "that you would write to us in the fulness of time, and in the meantime would remember us. . . . But, how did I know? . . . I have the *second sight—moi!* inherited along with some acres of peat bog from my great ancestor John Welsh the Covenanter; who foretold *the Plague,* 'in three weeks', on a City that rejected his preaching (Orleans); and the Plague came, and justified him,—to a *day! My* second sight is less positive; is, in fact, the second sight of a *Woman*—somewhat misty, somewhat introverted, exercising itself mostly on *all about feelings;* still it is perfectly up to discerning what any one I know and *am at the pains to think about* is feeling, or will feel towards one in certain given circumstances; and this, just as well when the person is at a distance—say, at Wellington, New Zealand (far enough for practical illustration) as alongside of me— say, in Humbie green lanes. Accordingly I remained *calm* (!) and assured in my foresight of the letter now come; the while that the *authorities* (they are plural; 'male and female created He them') were *fluttering* and croaking round me, like—not *two* crows—but like a whole flight of crows! because you didn't write to 'the Carlyles'! . . . Then there was questioning, as if said letter were also *their* property! 'What sort of letter was it?' 'was I *pleased* with it?(!)' 'Was it in good fashion?' 'You had called it, to *her*, "a little note" '; wrote the female authority (from Manchester)—'but *she hoped* it was a nice one! *What was in it?*' (!!!) The charm of questions asked *by letter* is, that there isn't the slightest call to answer them! and in any case I possess a *cruelty of silence*, (my Husband says) that he never saw matched in any other woman!"

Jane seemed unable to prevent herself, even in her moment of satisfaction, from little stabs at Geraldine. She asks him about his occupations, amusements, companionships, but

"for the rest; your '*Soul, her Sorrows and her Aspirations*',—your Heart, her (?—or *his?*—C'est égal) good and bad '*fashions*', *all that* I make no point of your telling *me;* because Geraldine claims it as *her* especial perquisite, and besides, I shall hear it all at second hand!"

For once, she over-reached herself; Mantell was neither so blind nor so fond as Geraldine, and from this time the correspondence declined.

Another acquaintanceship perished at her hands about the same time, but consciously. Davidson in Edinburgh was unable to leave well alone.

"I pressed upon her" says he "as earnestly and affectionately as I could the importance of making sure work for eternity. I told her that in my dressing-room were hung portraits of many dear old friends who had entered into their rest; and that the only ones that represented living friends were those of her husband and herself. And I added that, as I looked at hers, I was often filled with anxious thoughts as to what assurance I should have, if she were taken before me, that we should meet again in the happy land."

Too great a price could be paid even for reminiscences of Haddington. "That letter" he ends "closed our earthly correspondence."

As Carlyle assured the Ashburtons, Jane was decidedly in better health this year than in the two previous ones. Despite colds, despite more servant trouble, she was out and about—to the Thackerays, the Forsters, the Dickenses whenever Carlyle could be torn from *Frederick*, to Lady Sandwich, Lady Ashburton, and to Mrs Twisleton, whenever they were in town. She still had her little court—Froude, Cooke, Woolner, Masson, Neuberg, Espinasse—although only Darwin, Cooke and Woolner came primarily to see her. And with them she was not always a comfortable companion; witty as ever when stirred, but with too many jokes about Carlyle which came too close to the bone. Even the sympathetic and chivalrous Froude was worried: "it struck me, even then, that the wit, however brilliant, was rather untender". Elizabeth Pepoli was still about, though less intimate. Geraldine was for ever dropping in, to smoke furiously, shout with amusement or horror, always with her shattering "My Dear!" to preface some tasty piece of news. Ruskin, too, was coming to see them frequently, and Jane went off this spring with Carlyle to hear his lecture "on *Tree Twigs!* And perhaps that will do me good." So she told William Dods. For she was too conscious of the dead and the dispersed; of her own lack of life and often even of wish to live. "I never felt so dull and weary in my whole life as just at the present time."

This feeling was intensified by a visit she paid to Mrs Oliphant, who was writing a biography of Edward Irving and sought help from Carlyle. Mrs Oliphant's obvious admiration did not come amiss; particularly as Geraldine's sympathy had been called on too often; Jane, she reported to Mantell, "is *pretty well* and is capable of making rather extensive purchases from *Elise* . . . and when a woman is up to feeling an interest in such vanities, she is not thinking of making her will!"

As the summer came round, Jane began to think longingly of Scotland. Haddington was closed to her, but she had not yet seen the Russells in their new home. Carlyle could not be stirred—he had made up his mind not to visit Scotland until *Frederick* was done—but she began to make plans, only to abandon them because of more changes in the kitchen. She went instead to Ramsgate with Geraldine, but one week was enough: "the letter that came from him every morning was like the letter of a *Babe in The Wood!* who would be found buried with dead leaves by the Robins if I didn't look to it!" Soon after her return, towards the end of August, she tells Mrs Russell

"again a glimmer of hope arose. Lady Sandwich had taken a villa on the edge of Windsor Forest, for a month, and invited us to go with her there. Mr C is very fond of that old Lady, partly for her *own* sake, and partly for the late Lady Ashburton's (her daughter). . . . So on the whole, after much pressing, he consented to go. And the idea came to me, if *he* were all right *there*, mightn't *I* slip away meanwhile to *you!* Before however it had been communicated, he said to me one day: 'What a poor, shivering, nervous wretch I am grown! I declare if you weren't to be there to take care of me, and keep all disturbance off me, nothing would induce me to go to that place of Lady Sandwich's. . . . Humph! very flattering! but very inconvenient! And one can't console oneself at my age for a present disappointment with looking forward to next year—one is no longer so sure of one's next year!"

The invitation was accepted. The house was short of curtains, Lady Sandwich said; would they object?

"Mr C *is* particular as to *curtains*" Jane replied, " 'but now you aren't to *worrit* yourself Mam' (as my new housemaid is always urging on *me*) for if particular as to *curtains,*—he isn't at all particular as to *the sort* of curtains; and when I read your question to him the answer was, 'Pooh! I can make myself curtains in two minutes! tell Lady Sandwich.' 'How' I asked, thinking the secret worth any housewife's knowing: 'Why—easily—with *a clothes horse and my plaid!* It was an expedient that suggested itself to me on my first visit to Germany, and *I went all over Germany on the strength of it!*' Whoever has it in his head to write Mr C's Biography might gather many curious and valuable particulars, I am sure, from *German Chambermaids!*"

Almost at the last moment Fritz was bitten by another horse, and, declared Carlyle, "wasn't fit to appear in Lady Sandwich's stables nor indeed *to appear at all!*" "I suppose," Jane added, "if the Cat were to fall upon, and scratch *my* face—as might easily happen just now when she has kittens—*I* shouldn't be taken either! but be sent *out to grass!*"

The visit was not a success, and the proposed month in September shrank to little more than a week. The failure was explained by Jane in her own way to her doctor's daughter:

"it was the very first day of being here that Mr C saw fit to spread his pocket-handkerchief on the grass just after a heavy shower and sit down on it! for an hour or more in spite of all my remonstrances!! The lumbago following in the course of nature, there hasn't been a day that I felt sure of staying over the next, and of not being snatched away like Proserpine —as I was from *The Grange* last winter! For what avail the '*beauties of*

Nature' the '*Ease with dignity*' of a great House—even the Hero Worship accorded one—against the lumbago? Nothing it would seem! less than nothing! Lumbago my Dear, it is good that you should know in time, admits of but one consolation—of but one happiness! viz: '*perfect liberty to be as ugly and stupid and disagreeable as ever one likes!*' And that consolation, that happiness, that liberty reserves itself for the domestic hearth!—as you will find when you are married I daresay. And so, all the ten days we have been here, it has been a straining on Mr C's part to tear his way through the social amenities back to Chelsea!—while I have spent all the time I might have been enjoying myself in expecting to be snatched away!"

At home again, she relapsed into her lethargy of earlier years. Colds, influenza, headaches followed each other through the months, leaving her weak and depressed. She was roused for a moment by Cooke, who came early on new year's day, 1862, to be her "first foot" and who left a gift for her. "What an adorable little proceeding on your part! . . . And how early you must have risen . . . dressed, perhaps, by candle-light! good God! *all that* for *me!* Well! I *am* grateful." She was grateful; but as she lay in bed looking over Cooke's letter and gift, she was also sad. She remembered those other many "first foots" in happier days. They seemed far away. Mazzini was gone as if he had never existed. Her little effort to bring him back—a gift of the portrait of the Cheyne Row sitting room—had made clear that he was not for them again. She had even been obliged to send it through a mutual friend—Emilie Hawkes, one of the Ashurst sisters.

"I am very thankful for the little interior," he had replied to Emilie. "Mrs Carlyle is herself. Carlyle, except for the pipe and dressing gown, I would not have recognized. I have now been too long away from Carlyle for me to begin anew. Our paths are too widely apart, and the attempt would prove a fruitless one."

And then the one small consolation:

"But I do feel the same deep esteem and affection for Mrs Carlyle, and any little thing I might do for her would be a pleasure to me."

Just before Christmas she had been offered another dog, this time by the Stanleys, but she again refused: "the little grave at the top of the garden, the little portrait of him in my brooch—would be desecrated for me by a successor." And there was another reason: "I believe Mr C *couldn't* be brought to tolerate a new dog! He *suffered* so much thro' that other in various ways!

the worst way of all being *grief* at his death! and at thought of him since!!!"

She was living too much on memories. Every present pleasure was overcast by the memory of a greater; every friend, by the memory of two who had died or gone away. Her memories were almost always unshared, and so turned sad and sour. Carlyle was too much absorbed in *Frederick*, and, had he not been, was too impatient of her brooding, as he thought it, to go far with her in such a pursuit. For all his many words of sorrow and pessimism, he still looked forward into life; she in almost all things looked back. They had shared their lives, and would have had their lives no other way, but they had not always shared common experiences, and more and more rarely since coming to London had they shared sympathies. Thus she had to look back alone, with the desolating sense of a survivor. This sense was aggravated at the beginning of the year by another quarrel with Geraldine. Mantell had not replied to her last letter, and for some time she suspected Geraldine. She then discovered that Geraldine had actually begged him to write to her. She fell into a passion, and all Geraldine's sins were invoked—her rôle as Elektra (now seen in a very different light) and the other unauthorised friendships she had made in London.

> "The final *break*" Geraldine told Mantell "was so sudden, so entirely unlooked for, that I might say of it as the maids say when they break a precious piece of china: 'Ma'am, I was holding it quite carefully when it *flew out of my hand*'." But, she said, "I can only feel that if I were in her position domestic and physical, that *I* should be less reasonable and more disagreeable."

Jane's one steadfast interest outside the house—in Lady Ashburton and her daughter—was constantly frustrated by ill health, and not hers alone. "I think we *ought* to try to meet oftener" Lady Ashburton wrote towards the end of the year. "Life is too short, and love too rare for us never to meet." But it was not easy; Lord Ashburton was not strong; he had again been ill, and could not have guests. And when he recovered sufficiently for The Grange to be thrown open again, in January, Carlyle had to go there alone, as Jane felt too unwell to leave her room. One of the memories in which Carlyle indulged—one in which Jane could not share—made this visit sad for him too.

JANE WELSH CARLYLE
from a photograph by Tait, 1862

THOMAS CARLYLE
from a photograph, 1876

JANE WELSH CARLYLE
from a photograph by Tait, 1857

"I have been round my old walks" he told Lady Sandwich, "a *Shadow* very sad and very beautiful escorting me throughout: the 'Hall of the Past' it has all grown to me; and will so remain. One of my pilgrimages was to the *Church of Northington;* I walked silently round that Building; visited the inside,—and read a little Tablet, '4th May, 1857,' which will be memorable to me all the days of my life. *Weak* sorrow does not beseem one, dear Lady, as *you* well know; but there is no forgetting possible in certain cases;—and if I mention that one to *you*, it is sacred and silent from all other mortals."

In the same month, the doctor's daughter asked the Carlyles to her wedding:

"Oh, you agonising little girl! How *could* you come down upon me in that slap-dash way—demand of poor weak *shivery* me a positive *Yes* or *No* as if with a loaded pistol at my head?!! How *can* I tell what I shall be up to on the 18th? After such a three months of illness and relapse how can I ever guess? . . . As for Mr C . . . he expressed himself as *terrified*—as was to be expected—at the idea of *his* being included in anything *joyful!*"

She did attend the wedding, but found it too showy. Carlyle, in his attic study, was not concerned one way or the other, but both he and Jane became alarmed by the news of Lord Ashburton, who had again been taken ill soon after Carlyle came back from The Grange in the first days of February. Not until May was he able to write to Carlyle, who replied warmly:

"it is one of my *two hopes*, pretty much all I feel to have in the world at present; first, that I shall see you at The Grange one day soon as I *saw you last*, or gradually coming round to that pitch; and *second* (which runs into the *first*, and is somehow almost one with it), that I may then leave my sad work behind me, and be out of this imprisonment, which has really been like a living burial to me for long years past."

He had read Mrs Oliphant's biography of Irving:

"Darling woman" wrote Jane who had taken a great fancy to her, "I never heard him praise a *woman's* book, hardly any man's, as cordially as he praises this of yours! You are 'worth whole cartloads of Mulocks, and Brontës, and THINGS of that sort'. 'You are full of geniality and genius even'! 'Nothing has so taken him by the heart for years as this biography'! You are really 'a fine, clear, loyal, sympathetic female being'."

Carlyle had published a third volume of *Frederick*, but this was little comfort either to himself or to Jane, because it was now clear that at least two more volumes would be needed to finish the work. He was thus, in Jane's eyes at least, no further forward than he had been a year ago.

Before her anxiety about Lord Ashburton had been completely allayed, and soon after the death of a favourite of hers, John Sterling's daughter, Jane was mourning three more friends—Elizabeth Pepoli, Mrs Twisleton, and Lady Sandwich. She was wild to be out of London.

> "Nothing could keep me here for an hour but Mr C's determination to stay;—since at the top of the house *he* is safe enough from tiresome interruptions, simply refusing to see anybody! which, alas! makes it all the more needful for *me* to be civil. . . . If I go on in *this* way however I shall *die*."

Lady Ashburton took pity on her, and invited her to Folkestone, where Lord Ashburton was recuperating. There she stayed a week in June and was joined by Carlyle for a second week, but she was so fearful of outstaying her welcome that she went home sooner than necessary. Both she and Carlyle took to another guest, Miss Davenport Bromley, whom they at once christened "the flight of Skylarks".

Home again, she still was too weak to walk in the streets although she drove out once or twice a week, and she panted to be away to Scotland. She pestered Carlyle to make up his mind, until he said "Then go to Mrs Russell—pack yourself up and be off as soon as you like." So she reported to Mrs Russell. By the middle of August she was at Holm Hill.

> "Mrs Russell has never ceased to regret the tumble-down old House in Thornhill!!! where 'there was always something going on'!! 'Looking out on the trees and the river' here makes her so melancholy, she says, that she feels sometimes as if she should lose her senses! The wished-for, as usual, come too late!"

She was charmed by the beautiful house and she was touched by the Russells' consideration: "Mrs Russell put me into the ground-floor room; and I *know* why,—because the upstairs windows *must*, some of them, look towards Templand. Oh how kind they are." At first, "I merely sit bewildered in presence of my own Past!" She and Mrs Russell had their photograph taken by the hairdresser "for fun, and if I had dreamt of coming out so well I would have dressed myself better and turned the best side of my face." Fingland had been put by the doctor into a chemist's shop of his own at the end of the old doctor's house, and a new coachman drove her about the country when she had settled down. She began dining about Nithsdale: at Capenoch

—"a superb place the Gladstones have made it!"; with the Misses Whigham of Burnfoot—"perfectly beautiful scenery"; with Mrs Veitch of Eliock; at Bellevue; at Keir Manse. "So you see" she boasted to Carlyle, "I am 'uncommon popular the day' ". When she felt stronger, she revisited the old family homes. For Morton Mains she could not "get up any sentiment" —it was "so completely *ducalized*". Penfillan "is more pathetic for me by far", and she went up the avenue and "surveyed the remaining wing of the *old* house." She dined early with the Hunters at Milton, her grandfather John's old home, so that she could drive up the glen to "take a look at dear old Strath-milligan". She retraced her rides with grandfather Walter by the river to Sanquhar: "these old roads where I have been both as child and young lady give me a feeling half charming, half terrible! The people all gone or so changed! and the scenery so strangely *the same!*" She could not repeat the ordeal of Temp-land but for the first time she drove over the hills to her mother's grave at Crawford. She spent a day or two at The Gill towards the end of the month, then back by Holm Hill to her aunts at Edinburgh. But fêted and flattered though she was, the caustic chronicler of the world's imperfections remained un-sleeping even in moments of triumph. In the same breath as she applauds the "really nice people" at Capenoch and the "high-art style of dinner—even to the two separate kinds of ice" served in her honour, she comments unwinkingly on the portrait, facing her on the dining room wall, of her host's ancestor— "a harder, cunninger old *Baker* I never saw."

So far, although she had slept no better away from London than in it, change and excitement had produced an impression of improvement. In Edinburgh she relapsed quickly into depression: "Oh my Déar my Dear!" she wrote to Mrs Russell "My head is full of wool! Shall I ever forget those green hills and that lonely churchyard and your dear gentle face! Oh, how I wish I had a sleep!"

From Edinburgh, she moved for a short stay to Auchtertool, but "I feel here as if I were '*playing*' with nice, pretty-behaved *children!*" She was soon back in London, "sick at *stomach* or at *heart*—(I can't tell which)" and decided to accept Miss Brom-ley's invitation to Dover. Carlyle told her not to leave him so long by himself again, and this sent her off cheerfully. Brookfield was there and Charlotte Wynn, and Jane came home with a sufficient store of energy to amaze Charlotte Cushman, who thought her "clever, witty, calm, cool, unsmiling, unsparing."

Yet another visit remained before she settled in for the winter —but this a welcome one, to The Grange. Lord Ashburton, still convalescent, was to winter in Nice with his wife, and the Carlyles came to wish them godspeed. Jane deplored the shortness of their stay, but made good use of it, and her references to Carlyle lost their bitterness. He was in good humour, having just finished the fourth volume of *Frederick*:

> "The Bishop of Oxford was there two days, and He and Mr C argued extensively; Mr C being on the religious side and the Bishop on—the other side! But 'if he is a Humbug (Mr C said) and of *that* there can be no doubt; at least it must be owned he is a very amiable Humbug!' . . . We staid just the one week Mr C had agreed to stay—and he was very impatient to be 'home to one's work' all the while. The little mouthful of *human* Life did him good however; in spite of the terrific growling he carried on *in my room*."

She was, her letters made plain, contented:

> "Every time, I come away from there with increased affection for the Lady, and in a sort of amazement at her excessive kindness to me. That she is naturally a very kind woman, and also a very demonstrative woman, is not enough to account for the sort of passion she puts into her expressions of fondness and unwearied attention to me! I always wonder will it last?—but it has lasted a good while now; and I begin to feel ashamed of myself for not accepting it all with absolute faith."

Having changed servants yet again, Jane settled down lightheartedly. "I write you cheerful scraps" Ruskin told her "because it makes me cheerful to think of you—but it was very cool of Mr Carlyle to say I was leading a life 'with a touch of sadness' in it. I'm entirely miserable—that's all." The "touch of sadness" had been deduced from Ruskin's confession to Jane "Yes—it is quite true that I not only don't know that people care for me—but never can believe it somehow. I know I shouldn't care for myself if I were anybody else." Carlyle was back at work on his fifth and he hoped last volume, and, like Jane, was in better spirits than usual. Aunt Anne had told Jane that the maidservant "*converted*" by her sister Grace was "still *praying* earnestly" for Carlyle. "She has been at it a long while now" commented Jane, "and must be tired of writing to my Aunts to ask whether they had heard 'if anything had happened'!!!"

Then came bad news. Lord Ashburton had been taken ill on the way to Nice, and lay in Paris unlikely to recover. Jane offered to help Lady Ashburton to nurse him—

"it looks like throwing myself into the sea to try whether I can swim"— but "this morning I had a few hurried lines from her—No—I was not to come 'it could do her no good and would knock me up'; for the rest, she was 'past all human help', she said 'and past all sympathy'."

She sent the note to Mrs Russell "to observe how she has dashed her pen thro' the words *past all sympathy*—so like her! kind, unselfish soul that she is! Even in the agony of her grief and dread she had bethought her, *that* expression might seem unkind to one who was offering her sympathy". Jane was thankful that she had not been taken at her word—"given in a moment when my sympathy overcame my discretion". Throughout November and December the news fluctuated, and they had little time to think of themselves or their troubles. A few days before Christmas, Lord Ashburton's condition was again critical, and Carlyle sent off a message which appeared to leave no room for hope: "God go with you, guileless, brave and valiant man, who have accompanied me in my Pilgrimage so far, and been friendly to me like a brother; whom I shall soon follow. Farewell!" But as Jane truly said of Carlyle "he has so much more *hope* in him about everything than I have! Who would believe that to hear how he talks!" After Christmas, Lord Ashburton began to recover, and the Carlyles were free to engross themselves once again in their own concerns. The illness brought to Jane's notice one of the oldest of her women friends, who had been reminded of her by Dr Christison of Edinburgh, Lord Ashburton's physician in Paris. "In two days it will be 46 years since I became acquainted with you" began one of the many Christmas letters for Jane. The "quiet passion" she had inspired nearly half a century earlier still lived on, the writer assured her, though the passion was "somewhat ideal."

Jane soon fell into another wrangle with her servants which "made me deadly sick at stomach and struck the pain into my back". There was a fresh change, and in March, 1863, she was trying to persuade Carlyle to accept Milnes' invitation to them both to spend Easter at Fryston with Thackeray and

Spedding—but "it is no go! I was a fool to hope that anything so pleasant could get carried out, and the ghost of that old Prussian despot still unlaid." Nevertheless, she was in better health than for some time past, and she even went, though with many fears, to a couple of dinners, one at the Forsters where Dickens was the only other guest.

Her affection for Lady Ashburton had grown warmer during the illness of Lord Ashburton, and when, later in the month, a ticket came from Paris to view the Royal Wedding procession from Bath House she replied:

> "My dear, dearest Lady Ashburton, a thousand thanks for the card, and the lines! which arrived with the oddest, most perplexing appearance of the ink being still *wet!* (I actually touched them with my fingers to feel if they *were* wet!) Yes! the card was a godsend as a sign of your remembrance—that it was also an admission to what I had heard people longingly aspiring to as a new seventh Heaven did not so much signify, for I have still a good deal of the *Great Original Oyster in me!* Could not get up a sentiment or even a sensation about that 'procession'! Was not meaning to go near it—and have not gone! even with that card for the new seventh Heaven in my pocket! If you and Lord Ashburton had been at Bath House, it would have been a very different matter! *Then,* I should have let nothing hinder me—not even the idea of a *crowd,* which has more terror for me than the idea of an Earthquake! I should have been delighted to add this one more sight from those windows to those I had already seen from them (The Duke of Wellington's Funeral the last!). But that scaffolding, prepared in your own absence, and own troubles, for the amusement of 'others'; and the *empty,* sorrow-struck House, looking out over it, made me like to cry, every time I have driven past. And while so many people were ready to do the most impudent things to obtain a seat there, I have felt that if I were sitting up there, in the present state of the dear old house, I should be able to do nothing but cry. *That* was not a feeling to 'go out for to see' a show with! so I am at home, writing this note to you instead! Oh Darling! *your* face, with all the anxiety and trouble taken out of it, and Lord Ashburton's dear face with its sweet patient smile, would be a sight for me, worth all the Royal Processions that were ever got up! When will you come back? Oh when will you come back? 'I am to be patient, Dr Christison says, and set an example of patience—and it will be all well!' I try—but I cannot help its asking itself every now and then in my heart; '*when?* oh when *will* it be all well?' "

The other curiosity of the time, Bishop Colenso—"such a talk about him too!"—was brought to tea by Froude, who was rather shocked by his reception.

> "Oh! my dear Mr Froude! I surely couldn't have looked so bored as

that. I couldn't because I wasn't. I own to feeling rather antipathetic to the anomalous bishop. A man arrived at the years of discretion wearing an absurd little black silk apron, disturbs my artistic feelings to begin with. Then consider whom I am descended from, the woman who when King James offered to make her husband a bishop if she would persuade him to return to his country and be a peaceable subject, held up her apron and answered '*I would rather kepp his head in there!*' "

Lady Ashburton paid a flying visit to London—a visit that brought a happy eager letter from Jane:

"I wonder if you are returned to Paris? I wonder if you are better? I wonder if the wee darling *knew* you? Oh I wonder so many things! It wouldn't surprise me to find that you hadn't been able to let the little 'lump of delight' out of your arms, after having again got her into them; and so, that she had accompanied you back to Paris! Oh what a pleasure it will be to think of you all under one roof again, and a roof of your own! The Grange!—oh to be going to see you—to be with you all at The Grange again—after all these troubles and terrors! I think you scarcely *take in* the deep glad interest with which your return is looked forward to. 'People are so illnatured'! Ay, that they are!—illnatured and disloyal—most of them! but People are *human!* are capable of being touched by noble patience and warm-hearted devotion. *I* know not the man or woman who speaks of Lord Ashburton and you, in these *sad times*, otherwise than sympathizingly and reverently. Even women, whom envy and jealousy made spiteful towards you before, have quite changed their tone, and speak of you now as fellow-women not as rivals!"

Lady Ashburton's brother-in-law had just died, and she had to comfort her sister, Mrs Anstruther, in London and nurse her husband in Paris.

"What that woman goes thro' in the way of fatigue to body and soul is quite astounding!" said Jane to Mary Russell. "I said so to Monckton Milnes and he answered coolly, 'Oh! Well! you know she is *Scotch!* these Scottish women have enormous strength! nothing can knock them up!' '*For example!*' I said, pointing to myself, who . . . haven't the strength of half a sparrow."

When Carlyle was riding one day this spring, Fritz fell, cut his knee badly, and had to be sold. Jane reports, with many exclamation marks, that Grace, in Edinburgh, said the servant was "still *praying diligently* for Mr C, and that perhaps it was due to *her prayers* that Mr C was not hurt on that occasion." Lady Ashburton also wanted to know whether lack of exercise was affecting Carlyle's health and work. Jane reassured her:

"Mr C is *really* thriving (for the time being) on his horselessness! Finds it 'an unspeakable deliverance' he says 'to be no longer strapped to the back of that miserable quadruped, as he had been for the last eight years, but at liberty to walk out into the streets and speak to human beings!' So he has taken no steps toward replacing '*Fritz*', nor will, so long as the novelty of *walking* pleases him. 'It will be time enough to return to his *dreary isolation*', he says, when his health seems to require horse-exercise again. So you see—most generous of created women! Poor Fritz was sold to a neighbouring apothecary for *nine pounds!!!* Mr C rode him *once* before he was sold 'just *to soothe the poor quadruped's feelings,* by showing him he was forgiven'! I wonder what *Biped* he would have done as much for?"

Lady Ashburton was not reassured; she knew Carlyle's need of exercise and his love of riding, and she intended, if Jane approved, to give him a horse. She still wrote sadly about gossip that was worrying her. Jane sprang to her defence, determined to show that she at least preferred her to her predecessor:

"Oh my Darling! my Darling! I know the effect that a letter from *you* has now always on *me;* it makes me long to take you in my arms and hush you to sleep, as if you were a tired wee child, and kiss off all the tears from your eyes! But the last letter excites beside *this* longing, another not less vehement longing which is, to shake some others within an inch of their life! Good Heavens! I cannot understand what these others are made of, or *who* made them; that *knowing—seeing* how you are situated, and how you bear, and strive and love, and are more like an angel than a grand Lady, they still cannot put away their jealousy and envy of you. Yes! It must be so! that they envy you your *very troubles;* because you take them in a way to make you doubly dear to *Him*, and to all who have hearts to be warmed by your untiring devotedness! Don't think of them! they are so small! Think just of what you are to *Him*, your Husband; you are his Consolation, his Hope, his Life! without you he *could* not have lived thro' all this! would not have cared to live! and it may well comfort you, under worse than the coldness of these others, to feel that you are *all in all* to that man; who in nobleness, and unselfishness and gentleness of heart is not surpassed, I firmly believe, in God's earth! And think, if you like, of the brotherly sympathy and affection that is cherished for you by some who do not open their hearts to such sentiments lightly and who are *not 'small'*. I have seen my Husband's eyes fill with tears in speaking about you! and I have heard Mr Venables *warm* to enthusiasm in your praise! Oh you do not know how we all care for you! You must come home, to read it in our faces."

When is she coming?

" 'The end of June'? that is the first set time I have ever heard spoken of. Miss Bromley told me last night, it was hoped you might come then. I wish she could have staid with you longer—she is such a pleasant companion, and she loves you so much! And how lonely she seems here, in that large house; with the Pictures 'all to be sent to Christie's'! Mr C and I went and dined *entirely alone* with her yesterday! And the thing was wonderfully successful!—Mr C, of course, did most of the talking himself! but *that* is no hardship to *him* if he be well listened to, and Miss Bromley listens to perfection! 'She says little herself' he remarked on the way home 'but she gives *the clearest evidence* of understanding and taking interest in everything one (he) says to her! A real *bonnie* woman too! and with a fine, elegant, quite superior, modest dignity about her', and it is *you* we got her from—so that I always delight in her, as I do in *my flowers*, with a mental reference to *you*."

As for the offer of the horse:

"I must leave it to Mr C to speak for himself about that horse when he shall be told about it; for, indeed, I have more thanks to render you, already, on my own account, than power of putting them into words! I often wonder that I should not feel oppressed by your kindness, almost irritated by it; so being that I am without ability to repay it, or even adequately to express my sense of it! Often wonder *what it is in you*, that makes it possible for me to be *always your debtor* without fuming or wincing in the position! It is not enough to esteem or even love a person; something more, that I cannot define, is needed to make *gratitude* a pleasant, even a *bearable* feeling for me!

Oh my Heavens No! He didn't sell poor Fritz for *the money!* the money was but *nine pounds!!* But he thought him too young for being invalided at grass—said to turn him out for the rest of his life would be 'like turning an old servant *into the Workhouse*.' So he sold him for anything he liked to offer to a respectable man in the next street who meant to *ride* him, not punish him into *drawing*. The poor brute looks so well in his new service, was brought to our door this morning to report himself."

A few days later, " 'a young gent' ", wrote Carlyle to Lady Ashburton "said there was a *parcel* for me if I would please to step down." He stepped down, to find the parcel outside his front door "a beautiful bay-chestnut horse". It was, he said, "the finest little fellow in the world; full of taking ways." To Jane, however, he compared the horse unfavourably with Fritz; the new one, he complained "shows no desire to please him whatever." What became clear soon enough was that the horse could not save him—or Jane—from the effects of *Frederick*.

This summer, a woman called:

"very tall, dressed in deep black, and when she turned round, she showed me a pale, beautiful face that was perfectly strange to me! But *I* was no stranger to *her* seemingly; for she glided swiftly up to me like a Dream and took my head softly between her hands and kissed my brow again and again, saying in a low dreamlike voice 'Oh you Dear! you Dear! you Dear! Don't you know me?' I looked into her eyes, in supreme bewilderment. At last light dawned on me, and I said one word—'*Bessy?*' '*Yes!* it is Bessy!' And then the kissing wasn't all on one side you may fancy!"

Bessy Barnet, their first London servant, whom Jane had believed to be dead, was married to Dr Blakiston of St Leonard's. She was worried by Jane's appearance—"I looked so ill, she was sure I had some disease!" "None that I could specify" Jane replied "except the disease of old age, general weakness and discomfort." Bessy feared that Jane had cancer—she looked like it—and if this were not so, she still feared that Jane would catch smallpox, then so prevalent, " 'and if I took it and died before she had seen me again, she thought she would never have an hour's happiness in the world again!' Oh Bessy! Bessy! just the same old woman—an imagination morbid almost to insanity!"

She was shocked by Jane's pallor and frailty, and would not be satisfied until she had the promise of a weekend by the sea. Jane liked the place, the house, the people; Blakiston's prescriptions suited her, and Bessy waited on her devotedly. Her only anxiety was Carlyle. "Pray don't sit up till two" she begged him, "nor *take in* a sixth cup of tea—nor commit any indiscretions in your management of yourself." She came back in good spirits only to have a bilious attack that left her "weak as a dishclout". The doctor was called in, but had no sooner put her on her feet, just before her sixty-second birthday, than she began to suffer pain in her left arm, which became more and more difficult to move freely. Of this, as of many of her troubles, Carlyle noticed little; he was too much absorbed by his own sufferings over *Frederick*, was too well accustomed to her ailments and her wasted face, and too easily persuaded to take at its face value her light way of despatching unpleasant subjects. This she did, whenever possible, in self-preservation, and because she had trained herself to respect his work, even the hated *Frederick*, and to give it first place. Sometimes, when her endurance failed and she felt that she must get away or die, she would confess her fears, Carlyle would be shocked by his lack of consideration, insist that she go at once, write her worried, loving letters, forget himself and his work. But for the most part she wrote out her uneasiness in letters, and said little directly to him except by way of joke or sarcasm, releasing all her anger on his irritability. Of this she had much to say, and her bitterness must sometimes have seemed too savage to fit the crime, for

Carlyle was not perceptive enough to discern the true source of her reproaches. They had seen little of one another intimately for some years, and it had become a point of honour with both to respect that one invariable half hour they spent together every evening when he returned from his ride. She waited for him, lying on the sofa in the sitting room, with his glass of brandy and water and his pipe ready by the fire. She was always dressed in her best, the room was warm and shining with cleanliness, and she gave him the kind of welcome he liked—a neat pin-pointing of a visitor, an anecdote about the maids, some pungent comment on an unsatisfactory book, or, as now, some witticism about her inability to use her arm freely. He would sit on the hearthrug in his old dressing gown, his back against the side of the fireplace, puffing smoke up the chimney, sipping his brandy; and when she had given him the piquant opening he expected, he would talk, usually of his work. She said little to this because she did not expect to live to see the work in print. This half hour or twenty minutes together was, Carlyle said later, the one bright point in his day during the writing of *Frederick*—a task now some ten years old. He suspected nothing, she concealed all—the time was sacrosanct. Apart from this, he seldom saw her alone except at the meals free from visitors. But some relief she must have, and at last in desperation she called on Geraldine, who was shocked by her appearance. "She looks *terribly ill* and weak. *He* is always in the depths of *Frederick*".

In the first days of August, the sitting room was brightened during these evening meetings by a new dressing gown—a thanksgiving present from Lord Ashburton, well enough at last to return to England. His return brought up the question of a holiday. Jane wished to get away—she was as anxious now to leave London as Carlyle had been in earlier years—but his concentration on *Frederick* put her to shame. He had a tent in the garden during the hot weather and worked there, and had apparently no thought of leaving London until the tempter John appeared. Then it seemed likely that Jane would be left to her own devices.

"You have seen children building card-houses" she writes to Lady Ashburton, "as eagerly as if it were houses to live in? and you have seen, at some push against the table, the *Houses* become a shower of cards?

With just such an absurd suddenness and completeness did your letter yesterday morning sweep down the schemes of travel, which Mr C and his Doctor-Brother had been building up, and hithering and thithering amongst for the two preceding days—to say nothing of my own separate schemes (the fullest liberty to dispose of myself, in Mr C's projected absence, having been accorded me, in the offer of 'a draft to any amount you choose to specify'!). We were sitting at breakfast, which, to judge from the look of the table, consisted mainly of pocket maps and Bradshaws, with a supply of which my Brother-in-law *always* surrounds himself; and for the twentieth time Dr C had just urged on Mr C that, 'say what he liked, to sail to *Jersey* would be the most feasible thing, *or to—Denmark!*' and Mr C had just detailed the superior advantages of 'taking a look at Orkney and Shetland'—or 'perhaps better, after all, sail to Plymouth, and go by land to Froude's; tho' it *would* be a nicer thing a cruise round—the Western Isles'!!! the only point of agreement between them being that they should start for *somewhere* tomorrow;—when your letter was brought in, which, when I had read it in silence, I handed to Mr C, who, having read the first page, said quite simply, 'Oh! that is all right! we are going to The Grange Sir'. 'And you won't *sail* anywhere?' 'Certainly not! I tell you we are going to The Grange'! I could hardly help laughing, as the Dr swept together, in an indignant manner, his aids to locomotion!"

Carlyle had already half-promised himself and Jane to the Lothians in Norfolk. Was he now going? asked Jane; and tells Lady Ashburton what followed.

" 'Certainly not! how am I to leave my work again on the tenth?'—'Then what am I to say to Lady Lothian? You *promised*, you know! and I must answer her letter today'. 'Say?—Oh!—just say everything that is most courteous!! only making it perfectly clear that we are not coming'!! A pretty difficult problem, that combination!"

She ends:

"Oh dear! how glad I am to be going to the Grange again after all. At *one time* I felt to *hate* the dear old place in spite of the good days I had spent at it, and all the kindness I had received there! You know when that time was!"

They spent three weeks at The Grange in August and early September—"three weeks of beautiful green solitude" Carlyle declared; but Jane, who had longed so much to be with her friends again, was utterly wretched: "being in constant pain, day and night, and not able to comb my own hair or do anything in which a *left* arm is needed as well as a right one!" Lord Ashburton was still far from well, and his doctor was often at The Grange. Jane was driven to consult him.

"He told me before I had spoken a dozen words that it wasn't rheumatism I had got, but neuralgia (if any good Christian would explain to me the difference between these two things I should feel edified and grateful!) It had been produced, he said, by extreme weakness, and that I must be stronger before any impression could be made on it."

Within a week of returning home, in the middle of September, she was telling Lady Ashburton:

"Decidedly Quain is very clever—very prompt and dexterous! also—he writes remarkably pretty and ingenious notes! The one he sent me about *the Books* was as good as a Poem! When I was calling for Lady William Russell yesterday, who is too poorly to move to Walmer Castle as she had intended, she talked of Dr Quain as 'the most rising' medical man in London. She was always, she said, hearing of cases 'where he had at once hit the nail on the head when other Drs were puzzling to find it'. It always does one good to visit Lady William! she has such an unsurpassable gift of flattery! However *Cinderella*ish may be my opinion of myself in entering her room, I always come away thinking myself 'one and somewhat'! Yesterday, for example, I found a Colonel Percy with her whom she 'begged to introduce to Mrs Carlyle—the wife of Mr Carlyle the *distinguished Philosopher* and herself a very distinguished woman *altho' she was not aware of it'! What more delicate compliment could be devised? the 'altho' she was not aware of it* at once investing me with an *admirable modesty* to my own eyes! and anticipating any doubts I might feel as to the fact! She must have made a first-rate Ambassadress in her time!"

XXXVII

ACCIDENT
1863-1864

Nine days after she had written this letter, Jane went to tea with a distant cousin who was Matron at the General Post Office. After tea, she walked across to St Martins le Grand to take an omnibus home. An excavation in the road prevented the omnibus from drawing up to the kerb. As it approached, she stepped into the road to board it; but before she could do so, a cab appeared suddenly from behind the omnibus, and drove through the gap between it and Jane, flicking her skirt as it dashed past. She pulled up short, tried to get back to the pavement, slipped on the muddy road, and swayed towards her left side. She made a spasmodic effort to protect her useless arm and shoulder, but could not right herself. She fell heavily, unable to put out hand or arm to break the fall. She lay there in dreadful pain, unable to move. A crowd gathered quickly, a policeman came up, and she was put into a cab and driven home.

When the cab arrived, she sent the maid for Larkin. "Do get me up to my own room" she begged, "before Mr Carlyle knows anything about it. He'll drive me mad if he comes in now." But Carlyle had heard the cab, and when Jane did not soon appear he rang for the maid. The girl was confused and evasive. He rushed downstairs. When he saw Jane, her face convulsed with pain, he looked "terribly shocked". He and Larkin carried her upstairs to her bed. The doctor was summoned. He found no bones broken, but the sinews of the left thigh had been torn. Such at first appeared to be the full extent of her injury. For three days and nights she suffered "such agony as I had never known before"; then, although movement was difficult, the pain lessened. She was touched by the instant rallying of all to her help: "My Servants have been most kind and unwearied in their attentions—my friends more like Sisters or Mothers than commonplace *friends*. Oh I shall have such wonderful kindnesses to tell you of when I can write freely!" The Ashburtons, in spite of their own trouble (for Lord Ashburton's health was declining), were assiduous in their inquiries and offers of delicacies. Lady Ashburton was afraid that the accident had occurred when Jane was on an errand for her, visiting Elise the dressmaker about a maid. Lord Ashburton asked Carlyle if this was so. Carlyle reassured him, and Jane also insisted on writing:

> "In the first place; thanks *from the heart* for the kind letter you wrote about me to Mr C! The sympathy shown me on this 'melancholy occasion' has been of much the same benefit to me as the *quinine* Dr Quain advised for my neuralgia; it has not lessened the positive pain, but it has made me stronger to bear it! I am—*we* are—sincerely glad to hear the capital account of you, given in Mrs Anstruther's letter of this morning. I have news of Baby too this morning, from Mrs Mackenzie, which removes one's anxieties on *her* dear little account! So I am in good spirits this morning; having nobody to feel anxious about! and my own pains being *rather bearable!* In proof thereof I send you a printed document which arrived for Mr C last evening. And if it only amuse you half as much as it seemed to amuse *him!* Especially the writer's solemn prayer for Mr C's *death* gave him (Mr C) the highest gratification! The Thing is rather too inflated for *my* taste, but Mr C declared 'no—there is a great deal of a very high sort of Talent in it—and a profound sincerity'! It is to be hoped, *not* of a practical sort! for if *that* 'profound sincerity' felt a need of putting itself into action Mr C's assassination would be inevitable!"

Carlyle summed up the position after ten days: "sleep has never yet reached 4 hours, oftenest about 3, all broken into patches. She is very quiet, clear of head, as 'patient' as the Dr could prescribe." This to Lady Ashburton; to her husband the next day:

> "The first *pain*, as I said, is quite gone; but the Dr seems to intimate that the one remedy is time and rest; and that it will take *time*. If she were able to move at all, even to get freely out of bed and in, it would be a great relief—out of bed she manages to get without much difficulty by means of the sound leg and arm; but the getting in is always something of a problem. But she is the shiftiest creature in the world; full of contrivances, ingenious adjustments; has her wits thoroughly awake, her temper patient as against the inexorable and unalterable; and shows a really wonderful gift, already in this new case as in others, of 'doing all things decently and in order'. I am sorriest for her want of sleep; she never yet gets beyond the stinted '3 hours, all in fractions' and at present she cannot read, or rise to mend her fire, and will not have anybody to sit with her, absolutely *not*."

What he meant was, that he was not allowed to attend to her in the bedroom. Jane wished to save him—he was even more miserable away from *Frederick* than he was with it, and his helplessness in the face of pain was proverbial. His visits were limited to a few minutes three or four times a day. "She speaks little to me" he tells his brother John "and does not accept me as a sick nurse, which, truly, I had never any talent to be."

Larkin called every day, and she directed him and a carpenter to fix cords and appliances about the bed so that with her usable hand she could pull the bell, lift and move herself, and, to use Carlyle's words, made herself "*mistress* of the mischance". Her sick room, he thought, "*looked* pleasanter than many a drawing-room". "I might have known too" he says some years later "better than I did, that it had a dark side . . . but I merely thought, 'How lucky beyond all my calculations!' " He applauded, in particular, the device arranged by her for extracting, without effort on her part, a glassful and no more of champagne from the bottle, and her gay triumph after a demonstration. This was what he understood and expected from her—the sort of gaiety that, opposed to his moroseness, had first attracted him forty years earlier. When she was silent (unless he was speaking), when she looked and behaved as though she were ill or unhappy—as distinct from her outbursts of temper—he became uneasy; he felt that he was dealing with a stranger. But Jane spared him most of the time. He was treated like a child, the ugliness hidden for as long as possible. Thus, although he had seen her growing weaker, older, more and more ill, he had not perceived what he saw; he accepted the illusion put before him, of the still lively mind, the quick retort, the gay or sarcastic laugh. What he did not see was that this liveliness had worn her body out before its time. So now he laughed with her about her ingenuity, retired to his work comforted, and praised her bright resourcefulness in letters to his friends. He was further reassured some six weeks after the accident when one evening as he was "sitting solitary over my dreary Prussian books, as usual, in the drawing-room" the double doors leading into her bedroom opened suddenly and Jane appeared in a gaily coloured dressing gown, leaning on a stick and followed by the maid with more candlesticks to brighten the room. The doctor had encouraged her to get up, and she had been practising, with the maid's help, to hobble along so that she might surprise Carlyle. Surprise him she did— he never forgot that evening.

For some weeks, until well on in November, Jane kept on her feet, and was silent about her pain and her fears. She even began to entertain a little. The last of the visitors were the Froudes, who had now settled close to Cheyne Row, and who came in often for the evening—"almost the only pleasant evening company we now used to have; intelligent, cheerful, kindly, courteous, sincere" says Carlyle. This particular evening was as cheerful as any; Jane sat on the sofa talking to Mrs Froude much of the time, and Carlyle, who had plenty to say to Froude, noticed nothing amiss. When the Froudes had gone, Jane went to bed as usual. She did not sleep, and by the next morning she was almost distracted by pain. Carlyle could be sheltered no longer, she could no longer hide her despair and anguish. She was tortured day and night. The doctor, Barnes, came day after day, Quain was called in, Blakiston hurried up from St Leonard's, others were consulted; they could neither cure nor diagnose the pain—neuralgia was the only name they could agree upon—"by which" said Carlyle "they mean they know not in the least what." He watched her sufferings, horrified:

"such a deluge of intolerable pain, indescribable, unaidable pain, as I had never seen or dreamt of, and which drowned six or eight months of my poor darling's life as in the blackness of very death. . . . There seemed to be pain in every muscle, misery in every nerve, no sleep by night or day, no rest from struggle and desperate suffering. Nobody ever known to me could more nobly and silently endure pain; but here for the first time I saw her vanquished, driven hopeless, as it were looking into a wild chaotic universe of boundless woe—on the horizon, only death or worse. Oh, I have seen such expressions in those dear and beautiful eyes as exceeded all tragedy! (one night in particular, when she rushed desperately out to me, without speech; got laid and wrapped by me on the sofa, and gazed silently on all the old familiar objects and me). Her pain she would seldom speak of, but, when she did, it was in terms as if there were no language for it; 'any honest pain, mere pain, if it were of cutting my flesh with knives, or sawing my bones, I could hail that as a luxury in comparison!' "

She was terrified of losing her reason, and begged Carlyle to promise that she should not be put into an asylum. She was convinced that she would die, and reminded him of his promise many years earlier that she should be buried by her father, and that some of her money should be given to poor Haddington people she had known. In her worst moments she besought Quain to poison her and put an end to her torture.

Sometimes it seemed to Carlyle also that she must die, but he put the thought from him, comforting himself by the fact that she could still take food. He worked on at *Frederick*—it was the prime cause of her sorrows, he believed, and his duty was to end it as soon as possible. This done, he believed that she had strength enough to revive. He worked, if anything, all the harder because it was now clear that there must be a sixth volume, and he was still writing the fifth.

Maggie Welsh was sent for from Auchtertool to nurse her. Carlyle kept the Ashburtons informed. Early in December, he says that for a fortnight she has had "no sleep, no food, nothing but torture and agitation. I do not recollect to have seen the poor soul so beaten before." A fortnight later, he confessed that the last four weeks had been terrible. Jane seemed to have rheumatic fever. The doctors could do nothing: "I never saw a being in such a continuous agony!" By the first days of the new year, 1864, he could still give no good news: "She has no sleep, can get none, 'one sound sleep in 7 weeks', that has been her allowance. They are trying opiates again." Jane had made him promise to write: " 'one word of acknowledgement' whispered she passionately, 'for all these continual kindnesses: I am surrounded, wrapped up and supported on all hands by gifts and actings of hers!' "

A month later, Geraldine, who had practically lived in Cheyne Row since the accident, wrote to Mantell:

"poor Mrs Carlyle is *very* ill and nobody knows what is the matter with her. The doctors declare that it is all on the nerves, but both I and her cousin who is nursing her fear that she injured herself in her *fall* and that there is a cause for all the pain and terrible restlessness. She suffers dreadfully and her restlessness is worse than pain."

Another month passed, and Geraldine could give Mantell only slightly better news:

"her health has improved but the deep black depression of spirits increases, she does not sleep and she cannot be roused to interest or pleasure in anything. Mr Carlyle is killing himself over *Frederick*. He has aged very much since his wife's illness."

Everyone who saw Jane was horrified. Woolner had come at her bidding on New Year's Day, kissed her hand and went away with "a great sob", sure that this was a last farewell. Larkin did not believe she would ever recover. Her aunt, Mrs George Welsh, gave Caroline Fox "piteous" accounts of her sufferings and broken nerves. Mrs Oliphant found her looking like "a weird shadow". Ruskin begged for "the *merest* line" to tell him how she was. The doctors were baffled, and even tried the favourite cure of Harriet Martineau, "Animal Magnetism". Finally, they decided that the one hope was a change of air. Jane, living now in a deadly, hopeless depression, had come to hate her room, hate the whole house. Blakiston offered rooms in his house at St Leonard's, and a move there was decided in the first week of March. A special railway "invalid-carriage" was ordered, which looked ominously like a hearse, and she could not restrain a cry of terror when she was slid feet first through the window. She was put in by Larkin. "This time" she had told him "I have insisted on Carlyle's keeping out of the way till I am safe in the carriage. I don't think you'll find me very heavy." He was appalled to find her "like a child of twelve" to lift. Carlyle had to watch from his window until Jane and Maggie were in the carriage. Having seen Jane in her bed at St Leonard's, he caught the last train back to London. He still worked on at *Frederick*, but wrote to her every day. He came down with the Forsters for a weekend at the end of March, but saw little of her. Blakiston spoke confidently of a recovery. She said neither one thing nor the other, her mood remained "of fixed quiet sorrow".

Blakiston had diagnosed a derangement in the womb, but he was no more successful than the other doctors in relieving the pain once the first benefit of the change had worn off. Carlyle, believing Jane to be stronger, had broken the news of two deaths, hitherto kept from her—of Thackeray on Christmas Day, and of Lord Ashburton a week before the visit to St Leonard's. She at once wrote to Lady Ashburton.

"Oh my Darling! my Darling! I have only been told now. The Dr ordered it should be kept from me till this morning. Oh God comfort you! if ever there was a man ready to pass from this sorrowful earth to be an angel in Heaven it was he! My spirit flies to your dear side, while my poor body is chained here with a cruel malady that *I* believe will prove fatal;

tho' the Drs hold out hopes still. Oh God! it is among the few things for which I pray to be spared in life a little longer, this that I might prove to *you* my love and gratitude. Oh do not forget me and may your kindness to me help to warm your own sad heart."

To Carlyle, almost as soon as he had returned home, she scribbled despairing notes.

"Oh my own Darling! God have pity on us! Ever since the day after you left—whatever flattering accounts may have been sent you—the *truth* is I have been wretched—perfectly wretched day and night with that horrible malady. Dr B *knows nothing* about it more than the other Drs. So God help me—for on earth is no help! Lady A writes that Lord A left you two thousand pounds. . . . 'The wished for come too late!' *Money* can do nothing for us now!"

Money had come too late, she said—and also, it seemed, another blessing. She had been given undeniable proof that after all these years Carlyle still cared for her. Since the renewal of her illness in November he had become an old man, bent, worn, beset with anxiety for her, but he had shown her what she had wanted so long to know. She could not bear to be parted from him:

"Oh my Husband! I am suffering torments! each day I suffer more horribly. Oh, I would like you beside me!—I am terribly *alone*. But I don't want to interrupt your work. I will wait till we are in our own hired house and then if I am no better you must come for *a day*."

The idea of moving to a house of their own was not hers, she said, but the Blakistons': "I have rather wondered at the short time their benevolence has held out—but it is natural as not even the honour of a *cure* is to be gained for all their pains!"

To Lady Ashburton, Carlyle reported: "Poor Jane, in her own sad mind, is hardly at all better; and indeed her evident miseries (only broken off at intervals) cut me to the quick; but it was clear to me that she had made considerable progress." She was still lamenting: "Oh, my Dear my Dear, shall I ever make fun for you again? Or is our life together indeed past and gone? I want *so* much to *live*—to be to you more than I have ever been—but I fear, I fear!"

At the beginning of May a house was rented, and Carlyle brought *Frederick* with him. John Carlyle came down too. Jane said he would be welcome for a day, but, remarks Carlyle, John "I could perceive, was silently intending to pass the summer with us . . . and occasionally was of some benefit, though occasionally also not." Jane was dressed and waiting for him when he reached the house, and insisted on presiding over the dinner table. It was plain to everyone that she was too ill to be there, but she sat the meal out. She never came to dinner again. She was a painful sight, all light gone from her, beaten down by pain. She was still convinced that she would die, and often would have been glad to die. But she went unsmiling and without hope through all the motions of convalescence—the drives, the special food, the medicines, the exposure to sunshine, everything that they and Blakiston and Barnes, who came from London to see her, recommended.

At the end of the month Carlyle told Lady Ashburton that he believed Jane was improving. The weather was lovely, and she was driving out twice a day; but she could not walk, though she had tried hard, "is utterly weak (as if *broken on the wheel* for six months long!)", and was still greatly depressed. Lady Ashburton was sending them every day a hamper of butter and cream from Addiscombe, and special bread for Carlyle. She pressed them to come to Addiscombe as soon as Jane was well enough to be moved. Carlyle, thanking her early in June, reported an improvement after a renewal of sleeplessness "though we are not permitted to say it, so despondent is she always, poor little soul."

Jane spent as much time as possible in the carriage. Carlyle always joined her for the last drive of the day, when *Frederick* was put aside. She was silent most of the time, but she forced herself to comment occasionally on some curious street name, some feature of the district through which they were driving, to give the illusion of interest. When they came back—they drove for an hour or more—Carlyle went off for a three-hour ride on his horse. Jane was always waiting for him on his return, often in the darkness, to preside over his tea, but without a word, for she was by that time too tired and dispirited even to attempt speech. The meal over, she at once went to bed.

Later in June she relapsed.

"The poor wife" Carlyle told Lady Ashburton "has fallen into utter sleeplessness again (as have others of us that could be named in consequence of her) . . . she has got quite wretched in noisy Marina, is in horror even at the sea; and we must all, evidently, march again. . . . I

> myself have no resource except back to Chelsea, where I know of sleep, but she remembers only horrors of the 5 last months." ·

All plans were thrown into chaos by this new attack of pain and insomnia. Addiscombe, Jane decided, was out of the question ("she is too weak and miserable to have company—sees no one" Carlyle told Lady Ashburton). A return to Cheyne Row seemed inevitable. Miss Bromley offered to have her room repapered, so that she should not have to look again at the wallpaper associated for ever with hour after hour of misery. She never wished to see the house again, Jane replied. Then John suggested that she should go to Holm Hill by easy stages as soon as she felt able; and there take the long drives she liked, through country dear to her. This suggestion pleased, and Jane began to lengthen her drives round St Leonard's, to test her ability to make long excursions in the Nith valley.

A few days later, in the beginning of July, sleep deserted her entirely. For twelve nights in succession she did not sleep at all. Desperate, and convinced that she was going to die, she hurried back to London escorted by John, passed the night with the Forsters, and the night following—her sixty-third birthday— took the train to Scotland. She and John quarrelled incessantly, she said, and he was "*dreadfully* ill-tempered", but "on the whole it was a *Birthday* of good omen. My horrible ailment kept off as by enchantment." By the middle of the next morning she was at The Gill: "oh my dear I am quite as amazed as you to find myself here, so promiscuous!" The Austins were very kind, found a carriage for her to drive in, gave her plenty of milk, and she slept almost the whole of her first night there—her first good sleep for ten months.

The next day the carriage collapsed while she was driving, she was a good deal shaken, and most of her pain and sleeplessness returned. Life at the farm could no longer be endured, and she went on to Holm Hill. She travelled alone, refusing John's offer to go with her:

> "He has been very hard cruel and *mean*. Fancy him telling me in my agony yesterday that if I had ever *done* anything in my life this would not have been—that no *poor* woman with *work* to mind had ever such an ailment as this of mine since the world began!"

For a time she despaired still:

"I am cared for here as I have never been since I lost my Mother's nursing—and everything is good for me—the *quiet* airy bedroom—the new milk—the beautiful drives—and when all this fails to bring me human sleep or *endurable* nervousness, can you wonder that I am in the lowest spirits about myself."

But the inducements to recovery were many: the lovely house, the unhurried life, the drives through peaceful country, the good air and food, the brightness of her little maid who, bringing her morning milk, would say, smiling "I think ye'r gaun to get better noo!"—and slowly sleep came back and pain dwindled, and, more important, a shade of hope came into her mind. There were many fluctuations, but some headway was plain. In the middle of August she reported that she had laughed for the first time. Mrs Russell, telling a story of a man found in bed with one of the servants in a friend's house, cried "only think what a terrible thing! And a great *big* man" and her husband remarked drily "my Dear, would it have been any better if it had been a *little* man?" Jane burst out laughing, and she felt for a time that she would recover—not only health but sanity. "I fear horribly for—not my life—but my reason". And a month later

"if *the misery* would but fall into abeyance again! . . . I can bear all the rest—my neuralgic pains, my lameness &c. with patience; but *that* seems to be connected with the nerves of my brain! I go wild under it. To keep up the pretence of *rationality* is the most I am up to."

When she did sleep, she dreamed. Once, Carlyle told Lady Ashburton,

"she had met *Him* in her dream; 'his face was all transfigured, grown pellucid; he said to her, yours will be so too, when *you get out of your sickness!*' which I could see she interpreted in a bad sense for herself."

Again she dreamed that she was "*running!* and that I cleared some steps upstairs at a bound! . . . and I awoke with the joy of the thing!" Carlyle helped her, in his own way, by showing his need of her: "People do not help me much. Oh darling, when will you come back and protect me?" A few days later: "I am out of sorts; no work hardly; and run about as miserable as my worst enemy could wish; and my poor little friend of friends, she has fallen wounded to the ground and I am alone—alone!" The next day he was contrite:

"your poor nervous system ruined, not by those late months only, but by long years of more or less the like! Oh, you have had a hard life! I, too, not a soft one: but yours beside me! Alas! alas!"

Best of all were the practical indications that she was missed:

"Poor little soul! You are the helm, intellect of the house. Nobody else has the least skill in steering. My poor scissors, for example, you would find them in perhaps five minutes. Nobody else I think will in five months."

He felt like weeping a day later. "I am but low-spirited, you see. Want of *potatoes*, I am ashamed to say, is the source of everything." He was still out of sorts the next week.

"Oh, how I wish I had you here again, ill or not ill. We will try to bear the yoke together, and the sight of your face will do my sick heart good. . . . Your account would have made me quite glad again, had not my spirits been otherwise below par. Want of potatoes, want of regular bodily health, nay—it must be admitted—I am myself too irregular with no Goody near me. If I were but regular! There will be nothing for it but that you come home and regulate."

Forster wrote to her in the middle of August; the first letter, except for Carlyle's, that she had received,

"which makes me feel sometimes as if I were officially dead. Curious that Geraldine, above all, who makes more protestations of undying love to me than all my other friends put together, does not see what '*a bad effect*' such inconstancy would have in a Novel!"

When, as now, Jane drew closer to Carlyle, she wished she could unsay her many disloyalties. Instead she did the next worst thing and took out her uneasy conscience on her confidante. Geraldine could do nothing right. When letters did come from her, they failed to please, Jane refusing to see that her friend was trying to cheer her by writing brightly:

"every one of them *disagreeable*, about her parties and her new clothes &c.! I should have delayed answering 'into the vague'—had there not been enclosed in the letter to *me* a note to Mrs Russell—full of passionate anxiety to have news of me (which could have been got any day at Cheyne Row)! and imploring Mrs Russell to write and tell her how I was —quite Geraldinish, the whole thing!"

Jane, as these letters indicate, was recovering, slowly and with many backward steps. She told Mrs Forster that she did not see how she could ever bring herself to go back to Chelsea, but the suggestion of various changes to be made cleverly took her mind off the horror. She was soon discussing what colour the walls should be; and she finally settled that her bedroom, dressing-room, and the drawingroom should be repapered "nearly white". This done, and her bed shifted to another part of the room, she had only to sum up courage to return:

> "It looks to my excited imagination, that Bed I was born in—like a sort of instrument of red-hot torture; after all those nights that I lay meditating on self-destruction, as my only escape from insanity! Oh, the terriblest part of my sufferings has not been what was *seen!* has not been what *could* be put into human language!"

Towards the end of September she made up her mind to return; she felt strong enough for the journey, she did not feel able to trouble the Russells longer, and even though she dreaded re-entering her bedroom, she longed to be home again. A day or two before she left for London, her sleep again failed and much of her pain and all of her despair returned:

> "I had looked forward to going back to you so much improved as to be, if not yet of any use and comfort to you, at least no trouble to you and no burden on your spirits! And *now* God knows how it will be! . . . Oh Dear! *you* cannot help me tho' you would! Nobody can help me! Only God— and can I wonder if God take no heed of me when I have all my life taken so little heed of Him?"

This letter gave Carlyle some satisfaction.

> "Oh, my poor suffering little Jeannie!" he replied ". . . And yet, dearest, there is something in your note which is welcomer to me than anything I have yet had—a sound of *piety*, of devout humiliation and gentle hope and submission to the Highest, which affects me much and has been a great comfort to me. Yes, poor darling! This was wanted. Proud stoicism you never failed in, nor do I want you to abate of it. But there is something beyond of which I believe you to have had too little. It softens the angry heart and is far from weakening it—nay, is the final strength of it, the fountain and nourishment of all real strength. Come home to your own poor nest again. . . . We have had a great deal of hard travelling together, we will not break down yet, please God."

Two days later, on the first of October, she came home.

XXXVIII

LIVING MIRACLE
1864–1866

She was welcomed ecstatically. She arrived late and Carlyle

"was momentarily expecting a Telegram to say I was dead. So he rushed out in his dressing-gown, and kissed me, and *wept* over me as I was in the act of getting down out of the cab! (much to the edification of the neighbours at their windows, I have no doubt) and then the maids appeared behind him, looking *timidly*, with flushed faces, and tears in *their* eyes! And the little one (the cook) threw *her* arms round my neck and fell to kissing me in the open street; and the big one (the Housemaid) I had to kiss, that she might not be made *jealous*, the first thing!"

The same feeling was shown to her by all, even the most unexpected. George Cooke was "the last man on earth one would have expected to make one 'a *scene*'. But . . . he took me in his arms, and kissed me two or three times, and then he sank into a chair and—burst into tears!" Then a card was sent up, from Milnes.

" 'Oh yes! *He* might come up.' Nobody could have predicted *sentiment* out of Lord Houghton! but, good gracious! it was the same thing over again. He clasped me in his arms! and kissed me, and dropt on a chair,— not *crying*—but quite pale, and gasping, without being able to say a word!"

Forster pounded upstairs, more deliberately now, for he was grown portly, but as emphatic as ever, and gave her great smacking kisses of joy. Woolner "was especially *trying!* for he dropt on his knees beside my sofa, and kissed me over and over with a most stupendous beard! and a face wet with tears!" The sittingroom, where she lay on a sofa, was for days filled with callers:

"The Countess of Airlie was kneeling beside my sofa yesterday embracing my feet, and kissing my hands! A German girl said the other day, 'I think Mrs Carlyle a many many peoples love you very dear!' It is true, and what I have done to deserve all that love I haven't the remotest conception."

Geraldine stormed in, tempestuous and tearful, the first day, and besieged the house thereafter. When Jane could get out, she went to her dressmaker "to get the velvet bonnet she made me last year stript of its finery! White lace and red roses don't become a woman who has been looking both death and insanity in the face for a year!"

The triumphant reception had its effect, and she again rose from the dead.

"Oh my Darling" she cried to Mary Russell "if I might continue just as well as I am *now!* But that is not to be hoped! Anyway I shall always feel as if I owed my life chiefly to your Husband and you, who procured me such *rest* as I could have had nowhere else in the world."

Gifts showered in. Carlyle said she must choose her own brougham, which she did soon after her return. She was given a little dog, Tiny, which she accepted. The Rector's wife sent her fresh milk every day so that she should not miss the country milk of Thornhill. From Addiscombe came hampers three times a week of new-laid eggs, butter, cream, apples, vegetables, and, from Lady Ashburton direct, a grey for the brougham. Lady Ashburton, though unwell herself, came to London with her sister-in-law to see Jane.

"Come at last! Oh dearest of created *Ladies* 'past present and to come!' I wonder if you have any adequate conception how your coming has been watched and waited for, by the person now addressing you, and that person's better half? From day to day, since this day week, expectation and disappointment alternating! Every day the one or the other of us has ridden or driven up to Bath House, to examine the windows and the gate; sometimes even to cross-question Hannah, who had never more positive information to give than that you 'might arrive any day'. 'Every day'—till yesterday; just the day when one's perquisition would have had happy results! for yesterday I had to stay at home to nurse 'a chill'— and Mr C was made too late out, by an *inburst* of Mrs Cameron and Mr Watts (the Artist) the former hardly to be restrained from forcing her way into Mr C's bedroom while he was changing his trousers!! I told *her* as Baillie told *me*, when I was pursuing Mr Heath 'to the Back' with your message; 'It is a dangerous affair, rather, that you are there entering on, Mam!' So when your note arrived this morning it was *news* that it told! Oh my Darling! my Darling! how I love you! how glad I am—nay it is but just towards *him* to say how glad *we* are, at the prospect of having you here tomorrow night! *Will* you really come? Bless you for even *intending* it!

But at all events you will arrange for my seeing you, one way or another, with the least possible delay? and Mr C is *really impatient* to see you, also. If you heard how eloquently he was talking of your 'exquisite kindness and *loveableness*, and *beautiful transparency of soul*', on the way home that evening, and on several occasions since, you would know whether he has the 'eyes to see and the heart to understand' which a certain young Lady would have persuaded you he had *not!* Oh my Darling! my Darling! who that comes near to you, and is cared for by you can help loving you with a whole heartful of love! I am almost frightened at myself when I feel how dear, how indispensable you are become to me! I had fancied myself too calmed down with years and—other things, ever to have bother with my *heart* any more! Yes! I was henceforth to take just such tepid pleasures of friendship as the Gods provided me; leaving aside all strong feelings that can tend to pain and anxiety. If you were to tire of me now!—if you were to die before me—! if you were anyhow taken away out of my Life —! why; I should fall into as great trouble as I ever was in when young and excitable about a 'lost love'."

That week, Lady Ashburton was with her for three evenings, staying till near midnight, visitors were in and out much of the time, and Jane marvelled at "the impunity with which I do and suffer things that used to ruin me for days at St Leonard's". She had worked out a routine, driving every day for two or three hours, to shop (at the brougham window), pay calls "on the new principle of calling out the person visited to sit in the carriage with me!" and, if the need seized her, "I know where to drive for a sight of *sheep* (very dirty ones!) and green fields." She dined at four, received callers till six, and, after tea, one or two of her more intimate friends would come in for the evening. Carlyle was working upstairs on the last volume of *Frederick;* but the end was in sight and he was more peaceable. Jane was contented; not well—that she would never be—but much made of, sleeping tolerably, her pain intermittent only. She was able to walk slowly with the aid of a stick; best of all, she had had no return of "the *special misery*"—her mind was clear, cheerful, as alert as ever it had been. Hopeful she was not; she did not believe that she had long to live; but she felt thankful, after her experiences of the past year, that she might be allowed to end her life in sanity.

One sure sign of her return to normal was her discovery that Lady Ashburton—and so herself—was being misled. When she found that the grey—for which Lady Ashburton's coachman said he had paid "an enormous price"—was too soft to draw the brougham, and when, the moment Lady Ashburton left London, the hampers dwindled to two eggs, a pound of butter and a gill of cream once a week, she made no bones about complaining: "how a great Lady is imposed upon at all hands!"

She also began to go into the household accounts. They shocked her—three pounds of butter at 1s. 8d. used every week in the kitchen, half a pound of tea at 4s. finished in four days, all the napkins gone, sheets in rags, the china disappeared or cracked. She questioned the two girls who had greeted her so rapturously little more than a month earlier. She decided to get rid of the housemaid and to keep the cook, Mary. She then "got a *moral shock* which would, I think, have *killed* me at St Leonard's."

She tells the whole story to Mrs Russell:

"Mary—the one who attended me at St Leonard's—tho' the slowest and stupidest of servants—had so impressed me with the idea of her trustworthiness, and her devotion to *me*, that I could accuse *her* of nothing but stupidity and culpable weakness in allowing the other girl, seven years her junior, to *rule* even in the *Larder!* Accordingly I engaged an elderly woman to be Cook and Housekeeper and Mary was to be the Housemaid and wait on *me* as usual. Helen (the Housemaid) meanwhile took no steps about seeking a place, and when I urged her to do so— declared she couldn't conceive *why* I wanted to part with her. When I told her she was too destructive for my means, she answered excitedly: 'Well! when I am gone out of the House, and can't bear the blame of *everything* any longer, you will *then* find out who it is that makes away with the tea, and the butter, and all the things!' As there was nobody *else* to bear the blame but Mary, and as I trusted her implicitly, I thought no better of the girl for this attempt to clear herself at the expense of nobody knew who! especially as she would not explain when questioned. When I told slow innocent Mary she looked quite amazed and said 'I don't think Helen knows what she is saying sometimes. She is very strange!' Well, Mary asked leave to go and see her family in Cambridgeshire before the new servant came home, and got it, tho' very inconvenient to me. When she took leave of me the night before starting she said in her half-articulate way: 'I shall be always wondering how you are, till I get back.' She was to be away near a week. Mrs Southam, who sat up at night with me last . winter, my Charlotte's mother, came part of the day to help Helen. She is a silent woman, never meddling; so I was surprised when she said to me while lighting my bedroom fire the day my cold was so bad 'Helen tells me, Mam, you are parting with her'—'Full time' said I 'she is a perfect goose'—'You know best Mam' returned the woman; 'but I always like ill to see the innocent suffering for the guilty!' 'What *do* you mean?' I asked; 'who is the Innocent and who is the guilty?' 'Well, Mam,' said the woman, 'it is known to all the neighbours round here—you will be told some day—and if I don't tell you now, you will blame me for having let you be so deceived. Mary is the worst of girls. She had an illegitimate child in your house on the 29th of last July. It was her *second* Child—and all the things you have been missing have been spent on her man and her friends. There has been constant company kept in your kitchen since there was no fear of *your* seeing it, and whenever Helen threatened to tell you she frightened her into silence by threats of poisoning *her* and cutting her own throat'!!"

That was the story.

"Now, my dear," protested Jane, "if you had seen the creature Mary you would just as soon have suspected the Virgin Mary of such things! But I have investigated, and find it all true—for two years I have been cheated and made a fool of, and laughed at for my softness, by this half idiotic looking woman and while she was *crying*, up in my room, moaning out, 'What would become of her if I died?' and witnessing in me as sad a spectacle of human agony as could have been anywhere seen, she was giving suppers to men and women downstairs, laughing and *swearing* and—oh I can't go on. It is too disgusting! I shall only say that while she was in labour in the small room at the end of the diningroom, Mr Carlyle was taking tea in the diningroom with Miss Jewsbury talking to him!!! Just a thin small door between! the child was not born till two in the morning when Mr C was still reading in the *Drawingroom*. By that time Helen had fetched two women—one of whom took the child home to be nursed—need one ask where all my fine napkins went, when it is known that the Creature had not prepared a rag of clothing for the Child!"

She engaged a Mrs Warren as cook and housekeeper, who took over the ordering of food, which Jane had kept in her hands ever since her marriage. A new housemaid was engaged, and an uneasy peace once more settled on the kitchen, for Fanny, the maid, soon showed herself "plaintive, even peevish". The "moral shock" seems to have stimulated Jane for all her protestations, and she moved through the winter without serious trouble.

Early in January, 1865, Carlyle finished the last volume of *Frederick*. On Jane's face when he walked out to post the manuscript "there was a silent, faint, and pathetic smile"—so he remembered a year or two later. An ironic smile, too, for none knew better than Jane that Carlyle was an even more difficult man without a book than with one. So it proved now. The last year had taught him nothing. He saw Jane driving about in the brougham, hobbling along with her stick, making jokes about her crooked back, he heard her laughing and chatting with the callers, and he assumed that all was well. He quickly became accustomed to her fragile appearance. His anxiety, which lived on the obvious, settled to rest, as Jane did not tell him, and he did not ask, how she was sleeping or how much pain she still suffered. When *Frederick* was finished, he made no effort to control his reaction, although the state was now very familiar to him. "For long months after this," he says, "I sank into new depths of stupefaction and dull misery of body and mind; nay, once or twice into momentary spurts of impatience even with her." He mentions two incidents that particularly troubled his conscience later: his surliness during one of his rare excursions in the brougham—"always so glad to get me with her, and so seldom could"—and his refusal to come in and meet Elise when she stopped at her shop. But even in repentance he is overkind to himself. He spoiled some of their last months together, not only by these isolated exhibitions of bad manners, but by a general boorishness and selfish pessimism that made dreary what could so easily have been cheerful. His behaviour did not pass unnoticed among the Chelsea circle. Woolner spoke indignantly about his surliness. Geraldine told Mantell:

> "He is just now what in a mere mortal would be called 'cross', *very* cross; but, as he is a hero and demigod, I suppose the proper formula would be that he sees keenly and feels acutely the unsatisfactory nature of all human and domestic sayings and doings, and he expresses his sentiments very forcibly."

By the middle of February, Jane was glad to be off with him to Lady Ashburton's new house at Seaton in south Devon. Just before they left Cheyne Row, news came that Betty Braid's son was dead.

> "Oh, Betty, Darling!" wrote Jane at once, "I wish I were near you! If I had my arm about your neck, and your hand in mine, I think I might say things that would comfort you a *little*, and make you feel that, so long as *I* am in life, you are not without a child to love you. Indeed, indeed, it is the sort of love one has for an own Mother that *I* have for *you* my dearest Betty!"

She said she would try to see her in the summer "that you might see the *child* remaining to you, which would be a comfort to you, would it not?" Carlyle had already decided to go off on his own.

Jane liked Devon so well that she tried to persuade Carlyle to buy a "Devonshire Craigenputtock" going cheaply.

> "The speculation was wrecked by my answering to Mr C's fear that I should 'die of the solitude in six months', 'Oh no! for I will keep constant company.' George II's '*Non! J'aurai des maîtresses!*' couldn't have given a greater shock!"

After a month of idleness, he became restive, and Jane came home reluctantly. A few weeks later he went off to Scotland, leaving her to superintend an alteration of the diningroom, which he now decided to use as his study. He was nearly seventy, and the many stairs to the top of the house had bothered him of late. This kind of work was to Jane's taste, despite the complaints she sprinkled freely among her friends, but she was again in pain. The neuralgia had shifted from her left to her right arm, crippling it, and giving her little peace. She wrote with difficulty to Lady Ashburton, who was being troubled with rheumatism:

> "My Darling! my Darling! My *heart* is full of things to say to you; and I cannot get them said for my *arm!* Oh that arm! It keeps me miserable and incapable day after day, week after week! And the worst of it is, the pain of it has got to such a pitch that I cannot *sleep* ten minutes together! That morning after Mr C went away, I sat down and *cried!* I felt so little *up to* taking care of myself by myself! I have not however suffered from *Solitude* whatever else! People feel it their duty to look me up when left alone. Especially George Cooke, who came and took Mr C to the Railway, and got him 'a carriage all to himself', and saw to his luggage; and to whom Mr C, at parting, 'consigned his Wife—for protection'!! begging him 'to go and see her as often as he possibly could' a request which George Cooke seemed to consider, like Lady Augusta's marriage, 'exceedingly ridiculous, and perfectly unnecessary!' If it weren't for my arm, I should rather *like* my position. But *you* know how a constant raging toothache in one's arm spoils the fine weather, and the kind people and everything for one. Tho' I suppose we suffer with a difference, the difference between rheumatism and neuralgia, whatever *that* may be!"

She tried to write with her left hand, itself stiff, but Geraldine had often to write for her. There were some letters however that Geraldine could not be allowed to write. Jane dismissed a novel just published by Mrs Paulet, and was cool about Mrs Paulet herself, who had broken the long silence with a call—W. E. Forster was not yet forgotten. "Geraldine, too, came" complained Jane, "and I was not left alone till half-past ten". She also wrote sarcastically to Carlyle about a remark by Froude, praising "*your* gentleness and tenderness of late". She commented "if he had only *heard* you a few hours after that walk with him in which you had made such a lamb-like impression!"

She warns him that she too may fly from Chelsea if the pain— "as if a dog were gnawing and tearing at it"—in her arm continues. There was another change in the household.

> "I am going to be delivered from the tender mercies of Fanny," she writes to Lady Ashburton, "and have a hereditary servant from Dumfriesshire in her stead. A young woman whose Great Grandfather served my Great Grandfather, her Grandfather my Grandfather, her Mother my Mother, her Uncle my Aunt!"

This was Jessie, daughter of Mrs Welsh's Margaret Hiddlestone of Thornhill.

Carlyle was still in sober mood. Jane's left-handed notes did not entirely please him:

> "Thanks for the struggle you have made to get me a word of authentic tidings sent. I can read perfectly your poor little left-hand lessons, and wonder at the progress you have made. Don't be impious, however. Your poor right hand will be restored to you, please God; and we may depend upon it, neither the coming nor the going in such cases goes by the rule of caprice."

Her pain grew worse, sleep again fled, and she tried a change, staying with the Macmillans, the publisher and his family, at Streatham for a few days. But her pain was no better, she slept even less than at home, and in desperation she rushed up to Holm Hill. She arrived there in the middle of June. Carlyle came up for a day as soon as she had settled in. They spent much of the day in the garden. She told some of the anecdotes he loved to hear, including her description of Sir William Gomm's comment after reading *Frederick:* "what a sparkle that was! her little slap on the table, and arch look, when telling us of him and it!" She talked a great deal of the alterations to the diningroom, and of how pleasant it would be for him when he came home. He thought her "lively, sprightly even". She was, had he known, feeling anything but sprightly; Holm Hill was failing to work its magic.

> "The pain continues almost unbearable, and keeps me awake, tumbling about like a wild thing night after night thro' one weary week after

another; so that it is a perpetual miracle to myself that I am able to get up in the morning and keep on foot like other people thro' the day."

This to Mrs Warren, already a confidante. She took the opportunity of making clear the position of Geraldine in the house when she was away: "I have considerable faith in *your* practical judgement but little or none in Miss Jewsbury's. Her talent is of quite another sort."

She had also been frank with Lady Ashburton, who was talking of giving up the holiday abroad recommended by Quain:

"Oh Darling! Darling! I feel as if suddenly struck deaf and dumb! My heart full of things wanting to get said to you, and my right hand gone to the dogs! so that it cannot write to my Husband even, nor cut my food, nor do anything more than an infant can! And tho' I strive frantically to use my left hand instead, the progress I make is contemptible, and the difficulty is heartbreaking and soulconfusing! I wanted above all to have said a great deal on the subject of your change of Plans. Dr Quain seemed so grieved and alarmed at the first mention of it, that for certain he is sincerely convinced of the absolute necessity of your going. When I told Mr Carlyle, when he came to see me last Thursday; he said 'I wonder if my writing to remonstrate with Her would have the least effect'? And I said 'oh *do* try'! Your letter reached me *here*. I could not quite make out from it whether you had got the note I dictated to Geraldine Jewsbury. I came to Scotland hurriedly because Dr Quain and Dr Blakiston advised it, and because I had stupidly taken advantage of Mr C's absence to get some necessary painting done in the house, and because I had a wild instinct to *rush away from my pain!*—at least from the scene of it! Now I have been here a week without the slightest alleviation and long for home, and would just rush back if it were not for the mad look of the thing! Please tell me on what you have decided. And *when* and for *how long* you are to be in London? I never meant to stay long in this country on the present occasion. Should have greatly preferred being with you at Melchet. And I *must* see you before you go abroad—*if* you go. God be with you wherever you go or stay. I can write no more—my left hand protests against its work, by taking the cramp."

Carlyle urged her to visit The Gill, but when she reached Dumfries she collapsed. She lay on a sofa in the station waiting room. They had three hours together. "She was so pleasant, beautifully cheerful, and quiet, I enjoyed my three hours without misgiving. Fool! fool! . . . I had not the least conception of her utter feebleness." Thus Carlyle a year or more after the meeting. He blamed *Frederick:* "I was stupefied into blindness!" Blind he was indeed; writing encouragingly after they parted:

"there was in you such a geniality and light play of spirit, when you got into talk, as was quite surprising to me, and had a fine beauty in it, though very sorrowful. Courage! By-and-by we shall see the end of this long lane, as we have done of others, and all will be better than it now is."

Jane, still trying to find relief from the pain by change, moved to an old friend of her mother's, Mrs Ewart of Nith Bank, for a fortnight. She slept a little, but her arm remained wretchedly painful. She decided that she could not face the journey to Edinburgh to see Betty, still less another projected journey to Linlathen to stay with Erskine.

> "I suppose you *could not* have come here" Erskine wrote to her, "and yet it is with some sorrow that I accept this arrangement, as I scarcely expect to have another sight of your dear face on this earth. One might ask what good would have come of it if I had. I can only answer that ever since I have known that face it has been a cordial to me to see it."

Carlyle came up for another day while she was at Nith Bank. She was waiting for him at the station with the carriage, and made what he calls a "cautious charming preparation of me" for a dinner which the Ewarts had insisted on giving in his honour. They called in at Thornhill to see Jessie Hiddlestone, drove through the Drumlanrig woods, and, says Carlyle, "in spite of my habitual dispiritment and helpless gloom all that summer, I too was cheered for the time." Even the dinner "was saved by her; with a quiet little touch here and there, she actually turned it into something of artistic, and it was pleasant to everybody."

She went back to Holm Hill for a week, but was anxious to be home so that she might have a last sight of Lady Ashburton, who had been persuaded into her health journey on the Continent. Four days after her sixty-fourth birthday, she wrote:

> "My dear Darling Lady Ashburton! If you keep the day you named to me; you will be starting on Friday. So I have left myself hardly more than time to reach you with a parting blessing! I would have given a good deal to get one look of you and one kiss of you before you put the Sea between us. But it has proved impossible for me to get back to Chelsea before the 24th without causing more annoyance and inconvenience than I am all worth! Mr C is gone on a short visit to Mr Spedding at Keswick and comes here on Saturday to see me before I go. He looked anything but improved by his beloved '*Solitude*' when I saw him last—and instead of Solitude he used the term 'Stagnation'!! I got him to take a blue pill and he writes that it had done wonders for him! He is going to cruise round the Western Isles and go on shore at Thurso! For me, I narrowly escaped

an attack of jaundice since I came! the constant day and night shooting pains in my arm had induced it and I had to take *eight* blue pills, *moi!* on *eight* successive nights!!! I am now slightly improved, arm and all, but the small gain does not repay the long journey. . . . Oh what a good and beautiful thing it would be for you and for me too, to be *free of pain*—for a while! God keep you dearest, kindest of Friends! I love you. We love you more than any other living woman!—and that's truth!"

She left Thornhill towards the end of July, taking Jessie Hiddlestone with her, travelled with Carlyle from Dumfries to Annan, and was back in London in time to catch Lady Ashburton at Bath House "looking lovely in a spruce little half-mourning bonnet". She begged her to call, she tells Carlyle,

"and Lady A did come last night. Came at half after eleven! and staid till near one! Mrs Anstruther was left sitting in the carriage and sent up to say 'it was on the stroke of twelve'. And then with Lady A's permission, I invited her up—and if it hadn't been for her I don't think Lady A would have gone till daylight! She said in going—'My regards—my—*what* shall I send to *Him*? (you)'—'Oh' I said, 'send him a kiss!' 'That is just what I should like,' she said, 'but would he not think it forward'— 'Oh dear! not at all!' I said. So you are to consider yourself *kissed*."

Carlyle was distressed by the flight of his "poor witch-hunted Goody". His own fortunes had varied. "My three days at Keswick," he said, "are as a small polished flagstone, which I am not sorry to have intercalated in the rough floor of boulders which my sojourn otherwise has been in these parts." Less satisfactory were the visits which followed: "The horrors of the railway station called Waverley" he told Jane, ". . . are a thing to remember all one's life—perhaps the liveliest emblem of Tartarus this earth affords." After this, Scotsbrig showed its best face: "Silence, sleep procurable; and, indeed, a kind of feeling that I am a little better really since getting home."

Jane, too, was feeling much better, the change now beginning to have its effect. She slept soundly through more than one night, her pain began to ease, and the use of the arm slowly to return. By the beginning of August she was rebounding, as was her way, into good spirits, and she writes more in her old style of a visit to Palace Gate at the request of Forster, who was "stretched among pillows on the sofa of his Library, bemoaning himself in his usual obstreperous way. . . . He himself said he 'was dying—not a doubt of it!' But he was far too impatient and unreasonable for being arrived at that stage." She felt so much better that she almost regretted having committed herself to some weeks at Folkestone with Miss Bromley. But when she had been by the sea for a few days she was thankful she had come.

> "She is adorably kind to me, that 'fine Lady!' and in such an unconscious way! always looking and talking as if it were *I* that was kind to *her*, and *she* the one benefited by our intimacy! And then she has something in her face, and movements, and ways that always reminds me of my Mother—at *her age*."

She was enjoying herself so well that she grumbled at Carlyle's haste to be home "as if the furies were chasing him." The first raptures of Scotsbrig had worn thin. "Nothing could exceed my private weariness, sadness, misery, and depression," he felt. He was mistaken; but that did not prevent him from being exceptionally pleased with his home when he came back at the end of August. He approved of the changes, and took to Jessie, unconscious of Jane's sardonic asides—for the girl, though pretty and with appealing ways, was, she had already discovered, "a *vixen*".

In October, she reported that he "has been off his sleep again listening for 'railway whistles' which have been just audible—nothing more—for years." Her own sleep remained good when she was allowed to sleep: "for the bad nights I have had lately were not my own fault but produced by listening to Mr C jumping up to smoke to thump at his bed and so on." A worse danger than railway whistles appeared suddenly, and threatened to wreck the promised peace of autumn and winter. Jane passed on the story to Lady Ashburton.

> "If you were here beside me, with your beautiful sympathetic eyes, I should have a rare lot of little troubles to tell you; all converging into one great trouble, a protracted fit of sleeplessness! How long I shall be able to hold out under the fatigue of these terribly restless nights, I can't guess; and I know I am *running down* towards 'immortal smash'! Imagine the situation! You have heard, I think, of our troubles in long past years from neighbouring *Cocks!* How I had to rush about to one and other Householder, going down on my knees, and tearing my hair (figuratively speaking); to obtain the silence of these feathered Demons, that broke Mr C's Sleep, with their least croupy crow; when you might have fired a *pistol* at his ear without waking him! Thro' efforts that I still shudder at the recollection of, the neighbouring gardens were quite cleared of Cocks; and Mr C forgetting all the woe *they* had wrought him has been free, latterly, to devote his exclusive attention to—*Railway whistles!!* Bearing this in mind, be so good as to imagine my sensations, one morning

about a month ago, on being startled awake, before daylight, with the loud crowing of a full-grown *Cock*, from under my very bed (as it seemed in the bewilderment of the first moments)!—I sprang to the floor with my heart in my mouth, ran to my dressing closet window and looked out! but it was too dark to see anything; only the crowing, which continued like mad, sounded *just underneath!* I went back to bed, and lay with my heart thumping, till it was light enough to *see;* and then I reconnoitred the ground; and just below Mr C's bedroom window and my own, behold! an ill-conditioned *Hen-House* had been erected overnight, and I counted nine hens and a Splendid Cock in quest of the early worm!!! If I had ever *fainted* in my Life, I must have fainted at that sight! I no longer felt in myself strength or spirit to enter upon the old hand to hand battle with Cocks and Hens! I could have taken a good cry, in prospect of Mr C's nervous terrors and rage when he should have discovered his little feathered neighbours! and me with such a sharp pain always at the bottom of my back, taking away the very breath of me at thought of presenting myself before the people at No 6, with 'complaints of *nuisance* &c.'! For a whole week I carried the bad secret in my own breast! Thanks to the prepossession of *Railway Whistles*, Mr C never heard the *crowing* under his nose! But night after night I expected to hear his foot descend on the floor overhead, with the old frantic stamp—'preluding *much*'! (as himself might say). Sleep, difficult for me in the best of circumstances, was in these circumstances simply impossible! and at the week's end I had to take to bed with a sick headache. Now; nothing clears the brain so much as a good spell of sick headache, I find! Accordingly I came out of this bout with a plan of operations in regard to the poultry, and a modest determination to 'carry it out'. The result of which appeared next day in Golden Silence on the part of the Cock; and in raptures on the part of Mr C who had discovered his Enemy the very day that he was delivered from him, when he 'was just going off to Tyndall to beg him to supply him privately with some strychnine'!! A fine course *that* would have been! But now there was no poisoning needed! and so he clasped me in his arms, and assured me over and over that I was his 'Guardian Angel!' Humph! It is no sinecure!"

As the tone of this letter reveals, life, for all the cocks and railway whistles, was running more smoothly for the Carlyles. Froude says of Carlyle

"during the winter I saw much of him. He was, for *him*, in good spirits, lighter-hearted than I had ever known him. He would even admit occasionally that he was moderately well in health. Even on the public side of things he fancied that there were symptoms of a possibility of a better day coming."

Jane, despite her talk of colds and wakefulness, had not passed such a healthy or such a busy winter for years, as she confessed at the end of it.

"This winter" she told Mrs Dods "I have not been a day confined to the house . . . and I have been to such a many dinner parties! Mr C said this morning 'really my Dear, I think it is time you drew bridle in this Career of Dissipation you have entered on!' But it helps me to—sleep!"

In fact she soared through the months in what Jackie Welsh called her "frail ordinar", driving out every day, paying many calls, attending dinners, receiving more company than had been seen at Cheyne Row for a long time.

Her one substantial grief was the continued absence of Lady Ashburton, who had been detained in Switzerland by a minor accident.

"So it is all certain! you will not come home to brighten the darkness of our winter! Very dark it looks to me in prospect! almost as if you had *died;* so little definiteness there is in my hopes of seeing you and kissing your dear face again! If you had only named as probable a time for your return! If your return were not postponed quite far away into *the vague*. Oh I do hate *the vague!* It has a natural affinity, in my imagination, to all sorts of mischances and miseries! We dined at the Froudes the other day, and met, amongst others the Milmans and the Brookfields, and it seemed as if the only topic under Heaven they could find, one of them after another, to talk to me about was the probable length of your absence and the reasons for it. I grew so cross, and so like to *cry!* All this questioning in a spirit of idle curiosity so jarred my own heart-soreness! What I should have liked would have been to vanish out of the midst of them in a clap of thunder, leaving a strong odour of brimstone! Ah, you needn't keep away to put an end to their talking! they will talk about you wherever you are, as long as you are in every way so superior to themselves! But I do like to talk about you to Miss Bromley. *She* has a Sister's love for you, and her love is worth having. If it were not that you have laid so many obligations on me, that it feels absurd to specify any *one* in particular, I might thank you with all my heart for that friend—the only one that comes near yourself in my regard of all living women! Oh my Darling my Darling! How good and kind you have been to me from first to last! And *I* can do *nothing* for *you* but love you, with all my soul and all my strength! *as I do!*"

Except for Lady Ashburton, all of Jane's now usual set were in town this winter—Miss Bromley, the Stanleys, the Airlies, the Lothians and Lady William Russell, as well as a sturdy remnant of The Grange parties—Houghton, the Brookfields, Twisleton, Woolner, John Tyndall, chief among them. Tennyson was seen occasionally, up from the Isle of Wight, Poet Laureate for the last fifteen years, and now as much an accepted public figure as Carlyle. There was coming and going between Cheyne Row and Palace Gate, for Jane's relationship with the Forsters had long since settled into a steady friendship. There were jolly teas and dinners with Dickens. George Cooke was often at the house, stout now and moving heavily, but as fond as ever. Of a different type of man, Ruskin, Jane also saw a good deal. He went straight to the heart of Jessie by giving her a sovereign on Christmas Day—a custom of his—but he was already a favourite with her master and mistress. Carlyle had for long spoken of him as the most promising man of the time (a few months earlier an unfavourable review of *Sesame and Lilies* had provoked him to fury, and when *Ethics of the Dust* was published he wrote of it in what for him were glowing terms); his concern during her long illness endeared him to Jane. The Froudes were always looking in, as was Geraldine, Mrs Oliphant was a welcome caller, and ghosts of the past also raised themselves this winter. Craik—the long-faithful Craik—and still one of her soundest friends, had married in the previous year Dinah Mulock, author of that first novel "all about love" which had so fascinated Jane years earlier. In Swan and Edgar's, Jane had discovered one day, by the intonation of the man who served her, a native not only of Dumfriesshire but of the next farm to Craigenputtock, and member of a family well known to her. Young Corson was now calling on Jessie, to make the circle of coincidence complete. From Haddington appeared suddenly in London an old school friend, Agnes Veitch of Hawthorn Bank. From America came the Reichenbachs, and even Mazzini, away from London for many years now, was brought at second hand into her life again through a friendship she had formed with Emilie Hawkes and her second husband, Carlo Venturi, an admirer of Mazzini and himself a brave and romantic Italian.

All these people, representing between them almost the whole span of her life and almost every kind of preference she had shown in the course of it, gave her through this winter the sense of a rebirth of the popularity which ill health had denied her for so long. She was once more queen, and not only because her husband was king. Her New Year letter of 1866 to Betty at Edinburgh was warm, bright, uncomplaining:

"The wonder to me is, that for all the sufferings I have gone thro', of one sort or another, I am still in the upper light, with my heart unchanged in its old affections—especially its affection for *you*, my 'Haddington Betty!'"

She ended "I beg to be your 'First-Foot' in the shape of a post-office order for a sovereign. Ah my Dear, if I could but give you a kiss along with it!"

To Mrs Russell at the year's end she enclosed her usual money order for Margaret Hiddlestone, and for other poor Thornhill people whom her mother had known. She sent her New Year greetings to the doctor. "I would be his 'first foot' if I had a 'wishing carpet' ".

She tells Betty that both she and Carlyle may be seeing her soon in Edinburgh. Carlyle had accepted, after much humming and ha-ing, an invitation from the students of Edinburgh University to be installed as their Rector in succession to Gladstone. This honour gave Jane great satisfaction. The prophet had been recognised least of all in his and her own country. The Rectorship would wipe out all humiliations, failures, setbacks, and would publicly set the seal on the rightness of her choice, so much doubted when she had made it nearly forty years ago. Carlyle's pleasure was less whole-hearted. He disliked displays, and thought of the speech gave him real terror—he had not spoken publicly since his last series of lectures, twenty-six years earlier. But he successfully kept the speech out of his mind until the early spring—the Installation was fixed for April 2; "what luck it couldn't be the *first!*" remarked Jane. They noticed with amusement how lost Scottish friends hastened to make themselves known, to invite them, to congratulate:

"It made me laugh, Dear", she told her Aunt Grace, "that Edinburgh notion, that because Mr C had been made Rector of the University, an office purely honorary, we should immediately proceed to tear ourselves up by the roots, and transplant ourselves *there!* After *thirty years of London*, and with such society as we have in London, to bundle ourselves off to Edinburgh to live out the poor remnant of our lives in a new and perfectly uncongenial sphere, with no consolations that I know of but your three selves—and dear old Betty! *Ach!* . . . No! my Dear we shall certainly not go 'to live in Edinburgh'."

Three more spectres from the past came to life with the invitations. Two, David and Eliza Aitken, were sent back, pleasantly, to their resting place: "It was indeed a most agreeable surprise, to receive such a friendly letter from you and Eliza! The more shame to—which of us that it should have surprised as well as pleased?"

The third, always a favourite with Jane, was given good measure for his offer:

> "Dear 'Henry Inglis'! *That* is the name I knew you by, and have remembered you by, for the third part of a Century! *that*, and no other! Mr Masson asked me some days ago; 'Wasn't Mr Inglis a friend of mine?'—'Mr Inglis'? I repeated after reflection; and in the truthfulest ignorance, '*No!* I don't know any Mr Inglis!' 'Are you *sure*'? said Masson; '*Your Husband* knows him very well! He staid at his house when he was in Edin^r last summer.' 'Oh! *Henry* Inglis you mean? I exclaimed enthusiastically! Oh yes! *of course* I know *Henry* Inglis! Why; he baptized my Horse! —broke a cigar over his nose, and named him Harry—after *himself*'! Mr Masson looked as grave as tho' I had suggested that *his* next own Baby should be baptized after that fashion! 'A *rather* strange one,' he remarked!"

As for coming to Edinburgh:

> "I am not so strong as when galloping 'Harry' on the moors! In fact I am *now*, what is pleasantly called 'a *Living Miracle!*' That is a woman who ought in the course of nature to have been dead and buried; but has come alive again, for *some* purpose;—*what?* one does not *see!* But surely it could not have been for the *purpose* of killing myself after all, by outrageous fatigues and agitations, wilfully encountered—to hear my own Husband *speak!!* . . . For Mr C; I don't think *he* has taken a single detail of his visit to Edin^r into his head yet! any more than a single *head* of his *address!* When I ask him anything, he merely says; 'for God's sake my Dear, leave all that dreadful business lying over till the time comes'!"

Many people had invited him to stay in Edinburgh, "but the man he will go to, I will confide to you privately, will not be the man he likes best, but the man who lives furthest away from— *'railway whistles'!*"

At the end of March he was due to leave. Jane kept to her decision not to go:

> "the frost and snow of the last day or two have chilled my spirit of enterprise into one lump of ice! and now I have no hesitation about staying at home; as the suitablest place for Living Miracles!"

Also, as he was on her advice to speak extempore, he might break down, and

> "if anything should happen to you, I find on any sudden alarm there is a sharp twinge comes into my back, which is like to cut my breath, and seems to stop the heart almost. I should take some fit in the crowded house; it will never do."

Carlyle agreed reluctantly, but without giving much thought to the symptoms she described. In these last few weeks he was worried and irritable, having been forced to recognise that the ordeal was close at hand. He could not sleep and prevented her from sleeping but she kept cheerful, bantering and encouraging him by turns as he liked her to do. She did not tell him that the pain at her heart recurred from time to time; but after one of these attacks she told Mrs Warren that, when she died, two candles which would be found wrapped in a cupboard in the spare room were to be taken out and lighted.

On March 29 Carlyle left home, accompanied by John Tyndall. "I was in the saddest sickly mood" he said "full of gloom and misery, but striving to hide it; she too looked pale and ill, but seemed intent only on forgetting nothing that could further me." She gave him a flask of brandy to take before the address, as she had given him brandy before the London lectures long ago. They kissed twice, and Carlyle left her standing with her back to the parlour door, looking after him as he walked away.

The next day she heard of the sudden death of Venturi after a heart attack. She was greatly depressed. One death followed another: the suicide of a daughter of Betty Smail, her old serving woman at Craigenputtock ("what does Dr Carlyle make of such a case as that?" she asked bitterly. "No idleness, nor luxury, nor novel-reading to make it all plain!"); the tragic end of a promising young son of Dr Blakiston; her own doctor, Barnes, dying with horrifying abruptness; Craik "struck down whilst opening his mouth to reprove a pupil"; Hamilton Veitch, her Haddington schoolfellow and admirer, dead in India; Jackie Welsh, who had for years given her all the Haddington news, a victim of consumption. The same disease had killed her cousin John Welsh, the daring balloonist, and was killing her cousin Robert Welsh as it had killed his five sisters. The Welsh family was being wiped out. Soon she would be the only Welsh still living, and she had no hope of carrying on the name for long.

Maggie Welsh had come for the weekend, and had to be entertained, but Jane had already begun to work herself into a fever.

"While drinking a glass of wine and eating a biscuit at five in the morning, it came into my mind what is *he* doing, I wonder, at this moment? and then, instead of picturing you sitting smoking, up the stranger chimney, or anything else that was likely to *be*, I found myself always dropping off into details of a regular *execution!* Now they will be telling him it is time! now they will be pinioning his arms! and saying last words! Oh mercy! was I dreaming or waking? was I mad or sane? Upon my word I hardly know *now!* . . . Why on earth did you ever get into this galley?"

The moment she had news of the address, she wrote off in the highest spirits to Lady Ashburton:

"Dearest, Sweetest, Beautifulest! Oh my Darling! How long you stay away; and Life so short! The night before Mr C started for Edin^r to deliver that dreadful '*Address*', we were talking over people we knew, going from London to hear it: and Mr C said plaintively; 'Had Lady Ashburton been in this country, as she ought to have been, *she* would have been for going to hear me, and we might have done *nice things* together!' What *did* he mean? 'Nice things?'! When you come home you must make friendship with Professor Tyndall. He is a Jewel, that man! Mr C wrote to me of him from Edin^r; 'no adoring son ever watched more carefully and tenderly over a decrepit old Father than Tyndall has done over *me!* I shall never forget him!' And myself he kept *in* my skin with a constant supply of Telegrams and letters. You should have seen the arrival of the Telegram to tell me it was all well over! For several *days* I had been '*suffering Martyrs*' (as a french friend of mine used to express it):—from no over anxiety about the *success of the Speech* when spoken, but from a wild idea that it might never get spoken at all! that what with previous sleeplessness and wild hubbub, and close air of the overcrowded room, and the whole unsuitability of the thing he might *probably*, instead, *drop down dead!* I *knew* it was a *morbid* idea, due partly to the shock I had received from the sudden death of a friend's Husband (Major Venturi) but, if it was my idea, what difference, in point of feeling did it make whether it was *morbid* or *healthy?* So you may conceive how my heart leapt into my throat at the sound of the Telegraph double knock. Mr C was still speaking at four o'clock and at three minutes after six I had the Telegram!

> 'From John Tyndall to Mrs Carlyle
> 5 Cheyne Row, Chelsea—
> A perfect Triumph'.

I read it to myself, then read it aloud to my Cousin staying with me, and both the maids, who all waited gaping for the contents, and forthwith fell to clapping their hands and ejaculating like a Greek Chorus. 'Eh the Maister! Hear to *that!* Hurrah', cried the Scotch Housemaid; '*I* told you Mam! *I* knew how it would be'! cried the Cook; 'He, he, he, tee, tee, tee, *how nice*'! cried the Cousin, hopping round me. And then the chorus combined in a cry for—*brandy!*—'Where's the Brandy?' 'Run for the brandy', 'Don't you see the mistress is *going off!*' '*Where to?*' I asked in the midst of my outburst of weeping; all my Life I have so hated to be thought *hysterical*, but I swallowed the Brandy."

She continued the story to Carlyle the next night:

"the sudden solution of the nervous tension with which I had been holding in my anxieties for days, nay weeks past, threw me into as pretty a little fit of hysterics as you ever saw. I went to Forster's nevertheless with my Telegram in my hand and 'John Tyndall' in the core of my heart! And it was pleasant to see with what hearty good will all there, Dickens, Wilkie Collins, as well as Fuz, received the news; and we drank your health with great glee."

Maggie Welsh came over to the Forsters' in the evening to share in the rejoicings, and Forster did not forget old Silvester, Jane's coachman, sending him out a glass of brandy to drink his master's health. "I suppose I shall now calm down" ended Jane "and get sleep again—by degrees. I am *smashed* for the present." By the next morning she was anything but calm.

"Well! I do think you might have sent me a *Scotsman* this morning; or ordered one to be sent! I was up and dressed at 7, and it seemed such an interminable time till a quarter after nine when the Postman came— bringing only a note about—Cheltenham, from Geraldine! The letter I had from Tyndall yesterday might have satisfied any ordinary man or woman, you would have said. But I don't pretend to be an ordinary man-or-woman. I am perfectly extraordinary; especially in the power I possess of fretting and worrying myself into one fever after another, without any cause to speak of! What do you suppose I am worrying about *now*, because of the 'Scotsman' having *not* come? That there may be in it something about your having *fallen ill—which you wished me not to see!*"

Then, in the middle of the morning, came the newspapers and a letter from Carlyle. He had changed his plans. He had intended to come straight home, but the remarkable reception he had been given—"Do me this, see me that! above all, dine, dine!" was his description of his life in Edinburgh—had exhausted him and made him unwilling to return to London at once. There too, perhaps, he would be "killed with kindness, all the world coming tumbling on him." Annandale was near, he owed his family a visit, himself a few days of quiet in the country. He made for Scotsbrig. "Oh Dear" replied Jane "I wish you had been coming straight back—for it would be so quiet for you here *just now*. There isn't a soul left in London but Lady William." But by the time Carlyle received her letter he was lying in the fields of Scotsbrig. "Seldom" he said at the end of a week "have I been better in the last six months." Jane, still "*smashed*", went off to Mrs Oliphant, now at Windsor, for a couple of days in an effort to get a night's rest—for sleep had deserted her since the excitement began. Mrs Oliphant left her at the railway station "in an agony of apprehension lest something should happen to her on the brief journey, so utterly spent was she, like a dying woman, but always indomitable, suffering no one to accompany her."

She went back to prepare for Carlyle, but again she was disappointed; he sprained his ankle, and had to stay where he was. She rode over this bad news easily enough, buoyed up still by her excitement and her sense of triumph. Never had she felt prouder of Carlyle. She was delighted with everything and everybody—a favourable cartoon on the page of honour in *Punch*, the joy of their greengrocer, the kindness of everyone, in letters and in talk. "The best part of this *success*" she told him "is the general feeling of *personal goodwill*". Tyndall came back, and she went off to the Royal Institution to get "the minutest details". She was utterly exhausted but happy. "I haven't" she said "been so fond of everybody and so pleased with the world since I was a girl." She plied him with news, scandal, sarcasm, good report—a typical medley from the unchanging Jane. She had just heard that two elderly society women were seriously ill—"*Dying* one's hair with a cancer in one's breast! If *that* isn't a kind of spartanism, *what* is it?" She passed on the latest gossip about Mill; his sisters now spoke of him "as '*a poor Eccentric*'— calling him always 'our *poor* Brother John'!" She had seen Lady Gifford's pet monkey—"a weezened little Devil that Huxley would take to his heart!" She castigates importunate letter writers, but tries to help them. She is an indefatigable hostess—

"I had a nice little tea party. . . . Miss Bromley, Saffi and Madame Saffi, Geraldine, Mr Twisleton and George Cooke. Mr Twisleton 'was meant' to *take to* Miss Bromley, but, instead, he took—very decidedly too —to the bright little Patriot Wife!"

Carlyle's ankle had taken some days to mend; not until April 18 was he able to tell Jane that he would be home on the following Monday, the 23rd. She was still busy, answering letters of congratulation, writing to her friends, consoling Emilie Venturi, visiting and being visited. To clear off more of the entertaining before Carlyle arrived, she arranged for a large tea party on the Saturday evening—the Froudes, Mrs Oliphant and some friends of hers, Principal Tulloch and his wife (just back from Carlyle's triumph in Edinburgh) and their two daughters, the Spottiswoodes, Charlotte Wynn and Geraldine.

On Wednesday the 18th—the day that Carlyle had last written—Jane had one of her attacks; she had a "moral shock" and was "very sick". She felt too ill to write to him. He, alarmed, wrote on the Friday

> "I had said, it is nothing, this silence of hers; but about 1 a.m., soon after going to bed, my first operation was a kind of dream; an actual introduction to the sight of you in bitterly bad circumstances, and I started broad awake with the thought, 'This was her silence, then, poor soul!' Send better news, and don't reduce me to dream. Adieu, dearest. Send better news, clearer any way."

She did not live to open this letter. She recovered from the attack, wrote on the Thursday to explain why she had not been able to send a letter the day before, and wrote again on the Saturday morning. She had seen a portrait of Frederick, which might interest him, had knocked down the price from 7s. 6d. to 6s. but thought it only worth 5s. She would get it as a present for him if he wished. But

> "it seems 'just a consuming of Time' to write today, when you are coming the day after tomorrow. But 'if there were nothing else in it' (*your* phrase) such a piece of liberality, as letting one have letters on Sunday if called for, should be honoured, at least by availing oneself of it! All *long* stories, however, may be postponed till next week. Indeed, I have neither long stories nor short ones to tell this morning. Tomorrow, after the Teaparty, I may have more to say; provided I survive it! Tho', how I am to entertain, 'on my own *base*', eleven people, in a hot night, '*without refreshments*' (to speak of) is more than I '*see my way*' thro'! Even as to *cups!*—there is only *ten* cups of company-china, and *eleven* are coming, myself making 12! 'After all', said Jessie, 'You had *once eight* at tea! *three* mair won't kill us'! I'm not so sure of *that*!"

After writing this, she drove to the Forsters at Palace Gate for lunch, posting the letter on the way. She was in high spirits, glad that Carlyle would be home in two days, disappointed that a letter had not come from him that morning, but hoping to find one on her return. She left the Forsters soon after three o'clock in the brougham, with the dog, Tiny, on her lap as usual. Silvester drove through Queen's Gate, and Jane got out and walked a little in Kensington Gardens, the dog running at her heels. She entered the carriage again at the south end of the

Serpentine Bridge, and Silvester drove on until near Victoria Gate. Jane then told him to stop; she put the dog out for a run; and they went on slowly, Tiny running in the road beside the brougham. After a few minutes a brougham coming in the opposite direction knocked the dog over. For a moment it lay on its back in the road, yelping, then crawled on to the path. Jane pulled the check-string, and was out of the carriage and by the side of Tiny almost before Silvester could stop. The other brougham had also stopped, and a woman got out of it and came over to speak to Jane. Some other women came up to look at the dog. He was not badly hurt; the wheel of the brougham had bruised one paw. Jane carried him back to the brougham, took him on her lap, and Silvester drove on. He heard a squeak from Tiny, as if Jane were feeling him for injuries. He asked if the dog were hurt; there was no answer, but he thought that the sound of passing carriages had drowned the words. He drove on slowly, past Hyde Park Corner, up the road to the Serpentine, past the Serpentine, past the scene of the accident, and came round again to Hyde Park Corner. There he looked back, and could see Jane's hands lying on her lap, one palm upwards the other downwards. He was a little surprised to hear no orders, but drove again up the Serpentine road. He then looked round again. Jane's hands had not moved. He became alarmed, turned round and made for the nearest gate. There, he asked a lady if she would look into the brougham. She did so, called a man to look, and then told Silvester to drive at once to St George's Hospital, only a few yards away. The time was then a quarter past four. Jane was leaning back in one corner of the carriage, rugs over her knees, Tiny in her lap. Her eyes were closed as though she slept. She was dead.

Silvester drove back to Chelsea after his mistress had been taken into the hospital, and was soon back again with Jessie, carrying the letter from Carlyle which had come as expected, Blunt the Rector of Chelsea, Froude, Geraldine and Forster. Jane lay on the bed as if asleep, the dog at her feet. She was brought home at midnight, and her mother's two candles were set at the head of her bed. They burned all that night and all Sunday night.

The news reached Carlyle by telegram on Saturday night. The next day he received Jane's last letter, and on the Monday he was home. Forster had used his influence to prevent an inquest or post mortem, which he said would kill Carlyle. Tyndall called, and Carlyle talked to him for hours, of his life with Jane, of her encouragement when he was unknown and without hope, and of how, in their London years, she had protected him "from the rude collisions of the world". The next day he drove to Hyde Park, following the route taken by the brougham, and made Silvester show him exactly what had happened and where, on the Saturday afternoon. When he got home, there was a message from Reichenbach; might he have Tiny, who was wretched for his mistress? "Let him have it" said Carlyle. "I never wish to set eyes on it again."

On Wednesday he took Jane to Haddington. John Carlyle and Forster travelled with him but did not speak to him. Twisleton was also in the train. Jane's body lay all that night in the house of William Dods. The moon was full, and by its light Carlyle walked to the doctor's house and looked up at the tall windows of the room where he had first seen Jane forty-five years earlier. The next day she was buried in her father's grave.

Not for six days more could he bring himself to break the news to Lady Ashburton.

> "Victory (late, but bright and complete to her)" he said "crowned her whole noble life and her. For her life from the time we met was and continued all mine; and she had fought and toiled for me, valiantly at all moments up to that last, how loyally, lovingly and bravely, and through what sore paths and difficulties, is now known only to God and one living person."

And for that one person:

> "Sudden, like a bolt from the skies all shining bright, the stroke fell; and has shattered my whole existence into immeasurable ruin."

Carlyle died fifteen years later.

Appendix

Little has been said in this book about the sex relations of the Carlyles. This is not because we consider the matter unimportant, but because the truth must remain a matter of opinion. Readers interested in the controversy are recommended to consult *Conversations with Carlyle; Mr Froude and Carlyle; My Relations with Carlyle; The Nemesis of Froude; The Truth about Carlyle; The Imputation Considered Medically;* the Introduction to *New Letters and Memorials;* and *Froude and Carlyle.* Also a summing-up in *Jane Welsh and Jane Carlyle.*

Briefly, the controversy arose between those who declared that Carlyle was impotent, and those who, denying this, claimed that, on the contrary, his wife's state of health prevented him for a great part of his married life from enjoying the sexual relations he had a right to expect.

Before expressing our own view, we must comment on one piece of evidence, and add what little new evidence we have discovered. The statement by the daughters of Jean Aitken, that they had been told by their mother that Jane was pregnant when she joined Carlyle in London, is mistaken. It is absolutely clear from Jane's letters of this time that she could not have been pregnant; and there is no suggestion in her letters that she was pregnant at any other time. The mistake almost certainly arose from the fact that Jenny (as distinct from Jeannie) the wife of Alexander Carlyle was pregnant at Craigenputtock at this time.

Through the kindness of Mr H. D. Drysdale, we have seen two letters to Sir James Crichton-Browne which have some bearing on this question. One, dated November 5, 1909, is from Charles G. Fall of Boston, U.S.A. It says: "Mr Thos. Appleton, Longfellow's brother-in-law, told me some years ago that he had been dining, a day or two before, with Sir Lyon Playfair, who was on a visit to Boston; and Sir Lyon told him he had, at one time, been consulted by Mrs Carlyle for her nerves and had found her a virgin. She told him that Carlyle once tried to have connection with her, but was so clumsy about it that she laughed at him and he hadn't tried it since."

The second letter is from Professor Walter Raleigh, who had been sent a copy of *The Imputation Considered Medically.* He says: "I confess that on first hearing the story I said to myself 'That explains Carlyle's writings.' I have always thought them over-violent, in parts hysterically over-violent, and I associate the highest degree of physical virility with great self-containedness and quiet of expression. I should not call either Ruskin or Carlyle virile *writers.* So while I agree with almost all you say, and lament that the question was ever dragged into public discussion, I can't feel that the proof is perfect either way. It is not a thing people would take trouble to *prove*, if they had been told by the persons concerned."

With this view we are in agreement; but the fact that strikes us chiefly about the controversy is that those who took part in it were unduly concerned to prove one extreme or the other—that Carlyle was impotent, or that his wife was incapable of giving him sexual satisfaction. We feel that the truth is most probably to be found in the simple fact that the parties were sexually ill-matched. We think it likely, in view of the evidence in the letters, that there were sexual relations of a kind at least until the move to London, but we think it unlikely that they were continued long, or at all, after the move. This state of affairs is by no means uncommon, and by no means leads necessarily to disaster. Where, as with the Carlyles, there is much mutual affection and a good deal in common, the marriage must be reckoned satisfactory, and the importance of the sexual disparity should not be over-rated. A strain there is; and signs of such a strain are to be seen often in Jane and less often, as would be expected, in her husband. This strain made their marriage more wearing to both than it would otherwise have been; but in our view it does not account mainly for the friction between them, which should be sought rather in diverse temperaments and upbringing.

Bibliography

MANUSCRIPTS

Letters to and from Jane Welsh, Jane Welsh Carlyle and Thomas Carlyle.
Journals of Jane Welsh Carlyle and Thomas Carlyle.
Reminiscences of Thomas Carlyle. *National Library of Scotland*

Letters from Jane Welsh, Jane Welsh Carlyle and Thomas Carlyle. Letters
to Thomas Carlyle. *University of Edinburgh Library*

Letters to and from Jane Welsh Carlyle, Thomas Carlyle and Edward
Irving. *British Museum*

Letters from Jane Welsh Carlyle and Thomas Carlyle. Letters to John
Forster. *Victoria and Albert Museum*

Letters from Jane Welsh Carlyle and Geraldine Jewsbury.
Alexander Turnbull Library

Letters from Jane Welsh Carlyle. *John Rylands Library*
Letters from Jane Welsh Carlyle and Thomas Carlyle. *Carlyle House, Chelsea*
Letters from Jane Welsh Carlyle and Thomas Carlyle.
New York Public Library

Letters from Jane Welsh Carlyle and Thomas Carlyle
Yale University Library

Letters from Jane Welsh Carlyle and Thomas Carlyle.
The Marquess of Northampton, D.S.O.

Letters from Jane Welsh Carlyle. *Mrs H. H. Horsburgh*
Letters from Jane Welsh Carlyle. *Mrs E. E. Morgan*
Letters from Jane Welsh Carlyle. *Mrs N. Rutherford*
Letters from Jane Welsh Carlyle and Thomas Carlyle. *Mrs J. A. Carlyle*
Letters from Edward Irving *Presbyterian Historical Society of England*

PRINTED LETTERS
(Isolated letters not included)

Letters and Memorials of Jane Welsh Carlyle. Prepared for publication by
Thomas Carlyle, edited by James Anthony Froude, 3 vols, 1883.
Early Letters of Jane Welsh Carlyle. Edited by David G. Ritchie, 1889.
New Letters and Memorials of Jane Welsh Carlyle. Annotated by Thomas
Carlyle and edited by Alexander Carlyle, 2 vols, 1903.

551

Bibliography

'New Letters of Jane Welsh Carlyle'. Edited by Alexander Carlyle. *Nineteenth Century Magazine*, January, 1914.

'More New Letters of Jane Welsh Carlyle'. Edited by Alexander Carlyle. *Nineteenth Century Magazine*, August, 1914.

'Mrs Carlyle and her little Charlotte . . . Unpublished Letters of Jane Welsh Carlyle. *Strand Magazine*, March–April 1915.

Jane Welsh Carlyle: Letters to Her Family, 1839–1863. Edited by Leonard Huxley, 1924.

'Letters from Jane Welsh Carlyle'. Edited by Leonard Huxley. *Cornhill Magazine*, October and November, 1926.

Letters of Jane Welsh Carlyle to Joseph Neuberg, 1848–1862. Edited by Townsend Scudder, 1931.

Jane Welsh Carlyle. A new Selection of her Letters. Arranged by Trudy Bliss, 1950.

The Love Letters of Thomas Carlyle and Jane Welsh. Edited by Alexander Carlyle, 2 vols, 1909.

Letters of Thomas Carlyle addressed to Mrs Basil Montagu and B. W. Procter. Edited by Anne Benson Procter, 1881.

The Correspondence of Thomas Carlyle and Ralph Waldo Emerson, 1834–1872. Edited by Charles Eliot Norton, 2 vols, 1883.

Early Letters of Thomas Carlyle. Vol. 1, 1814–1821. Vol 2, 1821–1826. Edited by Charles Eliot Norton, 2 vols, 1886.

Correspondence between Goethe and Carlyle. Edited by Charles Eliot Norton, 1887.

Letters of Thomas Carlyle, 1826–1836. Edited by Charles Eliot Norton, 2 vols, 1888.

Letters written by Thomas Carlyle to Varnhagen von Ense in the years 1837–1857. Edited by Richard Preuss, 1892.

'Letters to Leigh Hunt from Thomas Carlyle', *Cornhill Magazine*, 1892.

'Unpublished Letters of Thomas Carlyle', *Scribner's Magazine*, April, 1893.

Letters of Thomas Carlyle to his Youngest Sister. Edited by Charles Townsend Copeland, 1899.

New Letters of Thomas Carlyle. Edited by Alexander Carlyle, 2 vols, 1904.

Unpublished Letters of Carlyle. Edited by Frederick Harrison, 1907.

'Letters from Thomas Carlyle to Gustave d'Eichthal. *New Quarterly Review*, April, 1909.

'Letters from Thomas Carlyle to Miss Wilson'. *Nineteenth Century Magazine*, May, 1921.

'Thomas Carlyle and Thomas Spedding'. Letters edited by Alexander Carlyle. *Cornhill Magazine*, June, 1921.

Letters of Thomas Carlyle to John Stuart Mill, John Sterling and Robert Browning. Edited by Alexander Carlyle, 1923.

New Letters of Thomas Carlyle. Edited by William A. Speck, 1926.

Letters Addressed to J. Llewellyn Davies (A Victorian Post Bag). Edited by John L. Davies, 1926.

WORKS OF THOMAS CARLYLE USED IN THIS BOOK

Reminiscences of Thomas Carlyle. Edited by James Anthony Froude, 2 vols, 1881.
Reminiscences of Thomas Carlyle. Edited by Charles Eliot Norton, 2 vols, 1887.
Sartor Resartus, 1833.
The Life of John Sterling, 1851.

OTHER WORKS OF THOMAS CARLYLE DISCUSSED IN THE TEXT

Life of Schiller, 1823.
Wilhelm Meister, 1824.
German Romance, 1827.
Wotton Reinfried, 1827.
Signs of the Times, 1829.
The French Revolution, 1837.
Lectures in German Literature, 1837.
Lectures on History of Literature, 1838.
Lectures on European Revolutions, 1839.
Chartism, 1839.
Miscellanies, 1839.
Heroes and Hero-Worship, 1841.
Past and Present, 1843.
Letters and Speeches of Cromwell, 1845.
Latter-Day Pamphlets, 1850.
Frederick The Great, 1858–1865.
Last Words of Thomas Carlyle, 1892.

BOOKS RECOMMENDED

Thomas Carlyle: A History of the First Forty Years of His Life, 1795–1835. By James Anthony Froude, 2 vols, 1882.
Thomas Carlyle: A History of His Life in London, 1834–1881. By James Anthony Froude, 2 vols, 1884.
Life of Thomas Carlyle. By David A. Wilson, 6 vols, 1923–34.

BOOKS AND ARTICLES CONSULTED

Life of Jane Welsh Carlyle. By Mrs Alexander Ireland, 1891.
Jane Welsh Carlyle. By Emma Adler, 1907.
Jane Welsh and Jane Carlyle. By Elizabeth A. Drew, 1928.
Jane Welsh Carlyle. By Townsend Scudder, 1939.
Thomas Carlyle. His life—his books—his theories. By Alfred H. Guernsey, 1879.
Thomas Carlyle. By Moncure D. Conway, 1881.
Thomas Carlyle. By H. J. Nicholl, 1881.

Bibliography

Thomas Carlyle. By William H. Wylie, 1881.

Memoirs of the Life and Writings of Thomas Carlyle. By Richard H. Shepherd, 1881.

Carlyle. Personally and in his Writings. By David Masson, 1885.

Some Personal Reminiscences of Carlyle. By Andrew J. Symington, 1886.

Life of Thomas Carlyle. By Richard Garnett, 1887.

The Story of Thomas Carlyle. By A. S. Arnold, 1888.

Thomas Carlyle. The Story of his life and writings. By R. and M. Cochrane, 1896.

Thomas Carlyle. By John Nichol, 1892.

Thomas Carlyle. By Hector C. Macpherson, 1896.

The Making of Carlyle. By Matthew R. S. Craig, 1908.

Carlyle by Louis Cazamian, 1913. Translated by E. K. Brown, 1932.

Guide to Carlyle. By Augustus Ralli, 1920.

Thomas Carlyle (in Nineteenth-Century Studies). By Basil Willey, 1949.

The Two Carlyles. By Osbert H. Burdett, 1930.

Mr Froude and Carlyle. By David A. Wilson, 1897.

My Relations with Carlyle. By James Anthony Froude. Edited by Ashley A. Froude and Margaret Froude, 1903.

The Nemesis of Froude. By Sir James Crichton-Browne and Alexander Carlyle, 1908.

The Truth About Carlyle. By David A. Wilson, 1903.

'Froude and Carlyle. The Imputation Considered Medically'. By Sir James Crichton-Browne. *British Medical Journal*, 27 June, 1903.

The Carlyle Myth Refuted. By Alexander Carlyle, 1930.

Froude and Carlyle. By Waldo H. Dunn, 1930.

'A Remembrance of *Sunny Bank*'. *Chambers Journal*, 26 February, 1881.

'Some Reminiscences of Jane Welsh Carlyle'. *Temple Bar Magazine*, October 1883.

'Carlyle and Mrs Carlyle'. A Ten Years' Reminiscence. By Henry Larkin, *British Quarterly Review*, July 1881.

'Mrs Carlyle and Her Housemaid'. By Reginald Blunt, *Cornhill Magazine*, October 1901.

'The Carlyles and Crawford'. By D. MacMillan, *Glasgow Herald*, 9 July, 1905.

'A Story From Real Life'. By Jane Welsh Carlyle, *Cornhill Magazine*, March 1920.

'Mrs Carlyle and her "Carina"'. By Reginald Blunt, *London Mercury*, Nov. 1921.

'The Carlyles' Married Life'. By Emily Garrett Bell, *Cornhill Magazine*, July 1924.

'Thomas Carlyle'. By Mrs Oliphant, *Macmillan's Magazine*, April 1881.

'Impressions of Thomas Carlyle in 1848'. By Ralph Waldo Emerson, *Scribner's Magazine*, May 1881.

'Reminiscences of Carlyle and Leigh Hunt'. By Walter C. Smith, *Good Words*, February 1882.

'Carlyle in Society and at Home'. By G. S. Venables, *Fortnightly Review*, May 1883.

'Carlyle's Life in London'. By G. S. Venables, *Fortnightly Review*, November 1884.

'Carlyle and Neuberg'. By Dr Sadler, *Macmillan's Magazine*, August 1884.

The Late Mr Carlyle's Papers. By Sir James F. Stephen, 1886.

'Recollections of Carlyle'. By Charles Eliot Norton, *New Princeton Review*, July 1886.

'Carlyle and Kirkcaldy'. By David S. Meldrum, *Scots Magazine*, November 1891.

'Reminiscences of Carlyle'. By G. Strachey, *New Review*, July 1893.

Two Note Books of Thomas Carlyle. Edited by C. E. Norton, 1898.

'Carlyle's First Love'. By J. Cuthbert Hadden, *Glasgow Herald*, 6 February 1906.

Carlyle's First Love, Margaret Gorden, Lady Bannerman. By Raymond C. Archibald, 1910.

Carlyle and the Open Secret of His Life. By Henry Larkin, 1886.

ALLINGHAM. *William Allingham. A Diary*. Edited by H. Allingham and D. Radford, 1907.

Letters to William Allingham. Edited by H. Allingham and E. Baumer Williams, 1911.

AUSTIN. *Three Generations of Englishwomen*. Memoirs and correspondence of Mrs John Taylor, Mrs S. Austin, etc. By Janet A. Ross, 1888.

BLANC. *Louis Blanc*. By Charles Edmond, 1882.

Louis Blanc. By J. Vidalenc, 1948.

Letters on England. By J. J. L. Blanc, translated by James Hutton, 2 vols, 1866.

BLUNT. *The Carlyles' Chelsea Home*. By Reginald Blunt, 1895.

Memoirs of Gerald Blunt of Chelsea, 1911.

BROOKFIELD. *Mrs Brookfield and Her Circle*. By C. H. E. and F. M. Brookfield, 1905.

Random Reminiscences. By C. H. E. Brookfield, 1902.

BROWNING. *Life and Letters of Robert Browning*. By Alexandra Orr, 1891.

Letters of Robert Browning and Elizabeth Barrett, 1899.

Letters of Robert Browning. Edited by Thurman L. Hood, 1933.

Robert Browning and Alfred Domett. Edited by Frederick G. Kenyon, 1906.

CAMERON. *Julia Margaret Cameron*. By Herbert Gernsheim, 1949.

CAVAIGNAC.
Portraits Republicains. Armand Carrel—Godefroy Cavaignac. By J. Ambert, 1870.

CHEYNE ROW. *Illustrated Memorial Volume of the Carlyle House Purchase Fund Committee*, 1897.

Carlyle's House. Illustrated Descriptive Catalogue, 6th edition, 1914.

CHALMERS. *Thomas Chalmers, the man, his times and work*. By A.J.S.[ymington] 1878.

Thomas Chalmers. By Margaret O. Oliphant, 1893.
A Selection from the Correspondence of Thomas Chalmers. Edited by William Hanna, 1853.

CHORLEY. *Autobiography of Henry F. Chorley*. Ed. H. J. Hewett, 1906.

CLOUGH. *A. H. Clough*. By James I. Osborne, 1919.

CONWAY. *Memories and Experiences of Moncure D. Conway*. 2 vols, 1904.

CRABB ROBINSON. *Diary, Reminiscences and Correspondence of Henry Crabb Robinson*. Edited by T. Sadler, 3 vols, 1869.

Henry Crabb Robinson on Books and Their Writers. Edited by Edith J. Morley, 3 vols, 1938.

The Life and Times of Henry Crabb Robinson. By Edith J. Morley, 1939.

Henry Crabb Robinson in Germany. By Edith J. Morley, 1929.
'Carlyle in the Diary, Reminiscences and Correspondence of Henry Crabb Robinson'. By Edith J. Morley, *London Mercury*, April 1922.

CUNNINGHAM. *The Life of Allan Cunningham*. By David Hogg, 1875.

CUSHMAN. *Charlotte Cushman: her letters and memories of her life*. Edited by E. Stebbings, 1879.
Charlotte Cushman. By Clare C. Clement, 1883.

DARWIN. *A Century of Family Letters*. Edited by H. E. Litchfield, 2 vols, 1904.
Life and Letters of Charles Darwin. By Francis Darwin, 3 vols, 1887.

DAVIDSON. *Memories of a Long Life*. By David Davidson, 1890.

DE QUINCEY. *De Quincey Memorials*. By A. H. Japp. 3 vols, 1891

True and Noble Women. By A. H. Japp.

'Nights and Days with De Quincey'. By James Hogg, *Harper's New Monthly Magazine*, January 1890.

Thomas de Quincey. By Horace A. Eaton, 1936.

DE VERE. *Recollections:* by Aubrey de Vere, 1897.

Aubrey de Vere: a memoir by Wilfred Ward, 1904.

DICKENS. *The Life of Charles Dickens*. By John Forster, 1872.

The Letters of Charles Dickens. Edited by A. Waugh and W. Dexter, 3 vols, 1937.

DOBELL. *Life and Letters of Sydney Dobell*. Edited by E. J.[olly], 2 vols, 1878.

D'ORSAY. *Blessington-D'Orsay*. By Michael Sadleir, 1933.

DUFFY. *Conversations With Carlyle*. By Sir Charles Gavan Duffy, 1892.

My Life in Two Hemispheres. By Sir Charles Gavan Duffy, 2 vols, 1898.

EASTLAKE. *Journals and Correspondence of Lady Eastlake*. Edited by C. E. Smith, 2 vols, 1895.

ELIOT. *George Eliot's Life as related in her letters and journals.* Arranged and edited by J. W. Cross, 3 vols, 1885.

George Eliot's Family Life and Letters. By A. Paterson, 1928.

EMERSON. *The Letters of Ralph Waldo Emerson.* Edited by Ralph L. Rusk, 6 vols, 1939.

The Journals of Emerson. Edited by E. W. Emerson and W. E. Forbes, 1909–1910.

English Traits. By Ralph Waldo Emerson, 1856.

R. W. Emerson; recollections of his visits to England. By Alexander Ireland, 1882.

The Life of Emerson. By Van Wyck Brooks, 1932.

ERSKINE. *Letters of Thomas Erskine of Linlathen.* Edited by William Hanna, 2 vols, 1877.

ESPINASSE. *Literary Recollections and Sketches.* By Francis Espinasse, 1893.

FERGUSSON. 'John Ferguson', *Fortnightly Review*, April 1914.

FITZGERALD. *Letters and Literary Remains of Edward Fitzgerald.* Edited by W. Aldis Wright, 7 vols, 1902.

The Life of Edward Fitzgerald. By Alfred M. Terhune, 1947.

FORSTER. *John Forster by one of his friends*, Percy Hetherington Fitzgerald, 1903.
The Life of the Rt. Hon. William Edward Forster. By Sir Thomas Wemyss Reid, 2 vols, 1888.

FOX. *Memories of old Friends; being extracts from the journals and letters of Caroline Fox from 1835 to 1871.* Edited by H. N. Pym, 2nd Edition, 2 vols, 1882.

FROUDE. *The Life of Froude.* By H. W. Paul, 1905.

Froude: A Study of his life and character. By Marshall Kelly, 1907.

FULLER. *Memoirs of Margaret Fuller Ossoli.* By J. F. Clarke and R. W. Emerson, 1852.

Margaret Fuller (Marchesa Ossili). By Julia Ward Howe, 1883.

GASKELL. *Mrs. Gaskell and Her Friends.* By E. S. Haldane, 1930.

Letters addressed to Mrs Gaskell by Celebrated Contemporaries. Edited by R. D. Waller, 1935.

GILCHRIST. *Anne Gilchrist: Her Life and Writings.* By H. H. Gilchrist, 1887.

GOLDWIN SMITH. *Reminiscences of Goldwin Smith*, 1911.

GOULD. *Biographic Clinics*, Vol 2. The origin of the ill health of George Eliot, Jane Welsh Carlyle, etc, by Gerald M. Gould, 1903.

HADDINGTON. *A Short History of Haddington.* By W. Forbes Gray and James H. Jamieson, 1944.

'Reminiscences of Haddington'. By J. Martine, *Haddingtonshire Courier.*

East Lothian Biographies, 1941.

Sketches of East Lothian. By David Croal, 5th edition, 1947.

HAMILTON. *Memoir of Sir William Hamilton.* By John Veitch, 1869.

HARE. *The Story of My Life.* By Augustus Cuthbert Hare, 6 vols, 1896–1900.

HARTMANN. *Bilder und Busten.* By Moritz Hartmann, 1860.

HELPS. *The Correspondence of Sir Arthur Helps*, 1917.

HORNE. *A New Spirit of the Age.* By Richard Hengist Horne, 1844.

HUNT. *The Life of Leigh Hunt.* By W. C. Monkhouse, 1887.

Leigh Hunt. By Edmund Blunden, 1930.

The Correspondence of Leigh Hunt. Edited by his eldest son, 2 vols, 1862.

Some Letters from my Leigh Hunt Portfolio. Edited by Luther A. Brewer, 1929.

The Autobiography of Leigh Hunt. 3 vols, 1850.

Pre-Raphaelitism and the Pre-Raphaelite Brotherhood. By W. Holman Hunt, 2 vols, 1905.

IRVING. *The Life of Edward Irving.* By Mrs M. O. Oliphant, 3rd edition, 2 vols, 1864.

Observations on Mrs Oliphant's Life of Edward Irving. By David Ker, 1863.

The Spirit of the Age. By William Hazlitt, 1825.

Edward Irving. By Washington Wilks, 1854.

Edward Irving (in *The Catholic Apostolic Church*). By one of its members, 1856.

The History of a Man. By G.G[ilfillan], 1856.

Edward Irving (in *Scottish Divines*). By Robert Herbert Storey, 1883.

Regent Square. Eighty Years of a London Congregation. By John Hair, Revised edition, 1899.

Edward Irving and His Circle. By Andrew L. Drummond, 1937.

'Edward Irving'. By Thomas Carlyle, *Fraser's Magazine*, January 1835.

JAMES. *Literary Remains of Henry James.* By W. James, 1885.

JAMESON. *A Commonplace Book of Thoughts.* By Anna Jameson, 1854.

JEFFREY. *Life of Lord Jeffrey.* By Lord Cockburn, 2 vols, 1852.

Lord Jeffrey and Craigcook. By James Taylor, 1892.

The Letters of Francis Jeffrey to Ugo Foscolo, 1934.

Francis Jeffrey of the 'Edinburgh Review'. By James A. Grieg, 1948.

JEWSBURY. *Geraldine Jewsbury.* By Susanne Howe, 1935.

Selections from the letters of G. E. Jewsbury to Jane Welsh Carlyle. Edited by Mrs Alexander Ireland, 1892.

JOWETT. *Life and Letters of Benjamin Jowett.* By E. Abbott and L. Campbell, 1897.

KINGSLEY. *Charles Kingsley, his letters and Memories of his life.* By his wife, 1877.

Charles Kingsley and his ideas. By Guy Kendall, 1946.

Charles Kingsley. By Una C. Pope-Hennessy, 1948.

LAMB. *Life of Charles Lamb.* By E. V. Lucas, 5th edition, 2 vols., 1921.

Letters of Charles Lamb. Edited by E. V. Lucas, 3 vols., 1935.

LANDOR. *W. S. Landor.* By H. C. Minchin, 1934.

LEWALD. *England und Schottland. Reisetagebuch.* By Fanny Lewald, 2 vols, 1851.

LEWES. *George Lewes and George Eliot.* A review of records by Anna T. Kitchel. 1933.

LOCKHART.   *The Life and Letters of John Gibson Lockhart*. By Andrew Lang, 2 vols, 1897.

LUCAS.   *The Life of Frederick Lucas*. By Edward Lucas, 2 vols, 1886.

MACCALL.   'Letters of William Maccall and Jane Welsh Carlyle'. In *Pall Mall Gazette*, 26 November and 19 December 1884.

MACMILLAN.   *Life and Letters of Alexander Macmillan*. By Charles L. Graves, 1910.

Letters of Alexander Macmillan. Edited by George A. Macmillan, 1908.

Memoir of Daniel Macmillan. By T. Hughes, 1882.

MACREADY.   *Macready's Reminiscences*. Edited by Sir Frederick Pollock, 2 vols, 1875.

Macready as I knew him. By Lady Pollock, 1884.

W. Childs Macready. By William Archer, 1890.

MARTINEAU.   *Autobiography of Harriet Martineau*. 3 vols, 1877.

Harriet Martineau. By Theodora Bosanquet, 1927.

MASSON.   *Edinburgh Sketches and Memories*. By David Masson, 1892.

Memories of London in the Forties. By David Masson, 1908.

MAURICE.   *The Life of Frederick Denison Maurice*. By F. Maurice, 2 vols, 1884.

MAZZINI.   *Epistolario di Giuseppe Mazzini*. Edizione Nazionale degli Scritti di Giuseppe Mazzini.

Life and Writings of Joseph Mazzini. 6 vols, 1864–1870.

Letters and Recollections of Mazzini. By Harriet E. H. King, 1912.

Mazzini's Letters to an English Family (the Ashursts) 1844–1872. Edited by E. F. Richards, 3 vols, 1920–1922.

Mazzini's Letters. Translated by Alice de Rosen Jervine, 1930.

The Letters of Giuseppe Mazzini to Sarah Margaret Fuller, 1942.

Joseph Mazzini: his life and writings and political principles. With an introduction by W. L. Garrison, 1872.

European Republicans. Recollections of Mazzini and his friends by W. J. Linton, 1893.

The Birth of Modern Italy. By Jessie White Mario, 1909.

The Life of Mazzini. By Bolton King, 1912.

Italian Nationalism and English Letters. By Harry W. Rudman, 1940.

MILL.   *The Autobiography of John Stuart Mill*, 1873.

The Letters of John Stuart Mill. Edited by Hugh S. R. Eliot, 2 vols, 1910.

John Stuart Mill and Harriet Taylor. Edited by F. A. Hayek, 1951.

The Metaphysics of J. S. Mill. By W. L. Courtney, 1879.

John Stuart Mill. A criticism; with personal recollections. By A. Bain, 1882.

'J. S. Mill'. By Samuel Wellington, *Westminster Review*, 1905.

MILNES.   *Monographs, personal and social*. By Richard Monckton Milnes, 1873.

The Life, Letters and Friendships of R. Monckton Milnes, first Lord Houghton. By Sir T. Wemyss Reid, 2 vols, 1890.

Monckton Milnes. The Years of Promise. By James Pope-Hennessy, 1950.

Bibliography

MITFORD.   *Memories*. By Algernon Bertram Freeman Mitford, 1915.
Recollections of a Literary Life. By Mary Russell Mitford, 1852.

MOLESWORTH.   *Life of the Rt Hon. Sir William Molesworth*. By Millicent G. Fawcett, 1901.

MURRAY.   *A Publisher and His Friends; Memoir and Correspondence of John Murray*. By Samuel Smiles, 1911.
Autobiographical Notes by Thomas Murray. Edited by John A. Fairley, 1911.

NAPIER.   *Selections from the Correspondence of Macvey Napier*. Edited by his son, 1879.

NORTH.   *Christopher North; a Memoir of John Wilson*. By Mrs Mary Gordon, 1862.

'Christopher North'. By Alexander Carlyle, *Nineteenth Century Magazine*, January 1920.

NORTON.   *Letters of Charles Eliot Norton*, 2 vols, 1913.

OLIPHANT.   *The Autobiography and Letters of Mrs Margaret O. Oliphant*, 1899.

PANIZZI.   *The Life of Sir A. Panizzi*. By L. Fagan, 1880.

POLLOCK.   *Personal Remembrances of Sir Frederick Pollock*, 1887.

PROCTER.   *Autobiographical Fragment*. Edited by C.[oventry] P.[atmore], 1877.

Barry Cornwall. A biography of B. W. Procter. By Richard W. Armour, 1935.

The Literary Recollections of Barry Cornwall. Edited by R. W. Armour, 1936.

RICHARDSON.   *Recollections of an Octogenarian*. By John Richardson, 1881.

RIO.   *Epilogue a l'art Chretien*. By A. F. Rio, 1870.

ROGERS.   *Rogers and His Contemporaries*. By Peter William Clayden, 1889.

RUSKIN.   *John Ruskin, a biographical outline*. By William Gershom Collingwood, 1889.

Letters of John Ruskin, 1892.

SCOTT.   *Autobiographical Notes of William Bell Scott*, 1892.

SINCLAIR.   *Memoirs of Sir George Sinclair*, 1870.

SIMPSON.   *The Gypsies as illustrated by John Bunyan, Mrs Carlyle and others*. By James Simpson, 1883.

SMILES.   *The Autobiography of Samuel Smiles*. Edited by Thomas Mackay, 1905

SMITH.   *The Autobiography of Mary Smith*. 2 vols, 1892.
Sydney Smith. By T. W. Reed.

SPENCER.   *The Autobiography of Herbert Spencer*. 2 vols, 1904.
The Life and Letters of Herbert Spencer. By David Duncan, 1908.

STANLEY.   *The Ladies of Alderley*. Edited by Nancy F. Mitford, 1938.
The Stanleys of Alderley, their letters between the years 1851–1865. Edited by Nancy F. Mitford, 1939.

STERLING.   *Memoir of John Sterling* (with *Essays and Tales*) Ed., Julius Charles Hare, 1848.

STIRLING.   *The Life of J. Hutchinson Stirling*. By Amelia H. Stirling, 1910.

STOREY.   *Memoir of the life of Robert Storey*. By R. H. Storey, 1862.

Memoir of Robert Herbert Storey. By his daughters, 1909.

Autobiography of Robert Storey of Roseneath.

STRACHEY.   'Some Recollections of a Long Life'. By Lady Strachey, *Nation*, 12 July, 1924.

TAYLOR.   *Autobiography of Sir Henry Taylor*. 2 vols, 1885.

Correspondence of Sir Henry Taylor. Edited by Edward Dowden, 1888.

Guests and Memories. By Una Ashworth Taylor, 1924.

TENNYSON.   *Alfred Lord Tennyson: a Memoir*. By his son, Hallam, Lord Tennyson, 2 vols, 1897.

Alfred Tennyson. By his grandson, Charles Tennyson, 1949.

THACKERAY.   *Some Memoirs*. By Lady Ritchie, 1904.

Letters of Anne Thackeray Ritchie. Edited by Hester Ritchie, 1924.

The Letters and Private Papers of W. M. Thackeray. Edited by Gordon N. Ray, 4 vols, 1949.

THORNHILL.   *Thornhill and its Worthies*. By J. L. Waugh, 3rd edition, 1923.

TRENCH.   *Richard Chevenix Trench, Archbishop. Letters and Memorials*. 2 vols, 1888.

TYNDALL.   *New Fragments*. By John Tyndall, 1892.

TWISLETON.   *Letters of the Hon. Mrs Edward Twisleton*, 1852–1862. Edited by Ellen Twisleton Vaughan, 1928.

WELSH.   *Life of John Welsh*. By Edward Young.

History of the Life and Sufferings of John Welsh, sometime Minister of the Gospel at Ayr, 1850.

'The Welsh Family'. By J. C. Aitken. *Dumfries and Galloway Courier and Herald*, 9 January, 1889.

'Mrs Carlyle's Claim to Descent from John Knox'. By Sir P. J. Hamilton Grierson. *Dumfriesshire and Galloway Antiq. Soc.* Trans. 3rd Series, viii, 1923.

WOOLNER.   *Thomas Woolner. His Life in Letters*. By Amy Woolner, 1917.

WYNN.   *Memorials of Charlotte Williams Wynn*. Edited by her sister, 1878.

Extracts from the letters and diaries of Charlotte Williams Wynn, 1871.

Original Letters used in the Text

ALPHABETICAL KEY TO CORRESPONDENTS

D.A.   David Aitken
E.A.   Eliza Aitken (*née* Stodart)
J.A.   Jean Aitken (*née* Carlyle)
F.A.   Fanny Allen
M.A.   Matthew Allen
Lady A.   Lady Ashburton
  (*née* Mackenzie)
Lord A.   Lord Ashburton
S.A.   Sarah Austin
Mary A.   Mary Austin (*née* Carlyle)

H.B.   Lady Harriet Baring
  (afterwards Ashburton)
Dr. B.   Dr Barnes
I.E.B.   Isabella Emily Barnes
  (afterwards Simmonds)
J.B.   John Blackwood
A.B.   Amelie Bölte
B.B.   Betty Braid
Jane B.   Jane Brookfield
W.H.B.   W. H. Brookfield

A.C.   Alexander Carlyle
J.W.C.   Jane Welsh Carlyle
Mrs C.   Mrs James Carlyle
Jamie C.   Jamie Carlyle
Jean C.   Jean Carlyle
J.C.   John Carlyle
T.C.   Thomas Carlyle
S.J.C.   Sir John Carr
Julia C.   Julia Cameron
Georgina C.   Georgina Craik
G.C.   George Cooke

C.D.   Charles Darwin
D.D.   David Davidson
G.D.   Grace Dinning (*née* Rennie)
M.D.   Mary Dods
W.D.   William Dods
C.G.D.   Charles Gavan Duffy

G.E.   George Eliot
R.W.E.   R. W. Emerson
T.E.   Thomas Erskine

John F.   John Fergusson
H.F.   Helena Ferme
J.F.   John Forster
Mrs J.F.   Mrs John Forster
Mrs W.F.   Mrs William Forster
W.E.F.   W. E. Forster
C.F.   Caroline Fox
B.F.   Barclay Fox
Mrs C.F.   Mrs Charles Fox
J.A.F.   J. A. Froude

A.G.   Andrew Galloway
E.C.G.   Elizabeth Cleghorn Gaskell
G.   Goethe
M.G.   Margaret Gordon
W.G.   William Graham

J.H.   Jenny Hanning (*née* Carlyle)
E.H.   Emilie Hawkes
  (*née* Ashurst, afterwards Venturi)
H.   Professor Henshaw
L.H.   Leigh Hunt
S.H.   Susan Hunter

H.I.   Henry Inglis
E.I.   Edward Irving

A.J.   Anna Jameson
F.J.   Francis Jeffrey
G.J.   Geraldine Jewsbury
Frank J.   Frank Jewsbury

D.L.   David Laing
A.L.   Anne Longden

W.M.   Walter Mantell
J.M.   John Marshall
H.M.   Harriet Martineau
C.M.   Charles Mathew
S.M.   Signora Mazzini
G.M.   Giuseppe Mazzini
E.M.   Eliza Miles
J.S.M.   John Stuart Mill
R.M.M.   Richard Monckton Milnes
T.R.M.   T. R. Mitchell

Mrs M. Mrs Basil Montagu

M.N. McVey Napier
J.N. Joseph Neuberg

M.O. Margaret Oliphant

J.P. Julia Paulet
B.W.P. B. W. Procter (Barry Cornwall)

J.R. John Ruskin
M.R. Mary Russell

Lady S. Lady Sandwich
M.S. Mary Scot
R.S. Robert Scot
Mary S. Mary Smith
C.S. Charlotte Southam
Maude S. Maude Stanley
Lady St. Lady Stanley
D.L.S. Dowager Lady Stanley
J.S. John Sterling
S.S. Susan Stirling (*née* Hunter)

E.S. Eliza Stodart
E.M.S. Elizabeth M. Stodart

H.T. Henry Taylor
U.T. Una Taylor
Mrs T. Mrs Alfred Tennyson
W.M.T. W. M. Thackeray

Mrs Wn. Mrs Warren
E.W. Emma Wedgwood
Mrs G.W. Mrs George Welsh (aunt)
Mrs W. Mrs Grace Welsh (mother)
G.W. Grace Welsh (aunt)
H.W. Helen Welsh (cousin)
J.W. Jane Welsh
B.W. Jeannie (Babbie) Welsh (cousin)
Mrs J.W. Mrs John Welsh (grandmother)
John W. John Welsh (uncle)
J. Welsh John Welsh (cousin)
Mrs M.W. Mary Welsh (aunt)
C.W.W. Charlotte Williams Wynn

Reference to Quotations

References are not repeated when a quotation is taken from the same letter as the quotation preceding it.

Chapter 1

Chapter 4

Chapter 6

Chapter 7

Chapter 8

Chapter 9

Chapter 11

Chapter 12

Page	*First words of quotation*	
	Anti-gigmanism	T.C. to J.C. 2.7.32
	I like	F.J. to J.W.C. 22.7.32
172	and really	J.W.C. to E.S. 21.12.32
	everyone	J.W.C. to J.C. 10.2.33
173	talking	T.C. to Mrs C. 27.1.33
	does not attain	*Ibid.;* T.C. *Notebook.* 1.2.33; to J.C. 10.2.33
	hollow jargon	T.C. to J.S.M. Jan. 1833
	inane chatter	T.C. *Notebook.* 31.3.33
	She bears up	T.C. to J.C. 29.3.33
	As if	J.W.C. to E.S. Early March 1833
174	was a tall	T.C. note to J.W.C. to Susan Hunter. 28.6.35
	several things	J.W.C. to S.H. 28.6.35
	wind me up	*Ibid.* July 1835
	I do not know	*Ibid.* April 1833
	distinguished	*Ibid.* 28.6.35
175	The talent	T.C. to J.C. 10.2.33
	one thing	*Ibid.* 8.1.33
	of solitude	*Ibid.* 10.2.33
	boiling uproar	T.C. to Mrs C. 13.2.33
	amid	T.C. to J.C. 29.3.33
	Such a dreary	T.C. to Leigh Hunt 1.5.33
	there is	J.S.M. to T.C. 9.3.33
	a mixture	T.C. to Mrs C. 26.3.33
176	we were	J.W.C. to E.S. 24.5.33
	agony	T.C. *Rem.*
	O Eliza	J.W.C. to E.S. 24.5.33
177	It has even	*Ibid.* 28.7.33
	one of the people	Oliphant *Autobiography*
	I do not	J.S.M. to T.C. 2.8.33
	the most	T.C. to J.C. 27.8.33; to Mrs C. late Aug. 1833
178	thankful	J.W.C. to Henry Inglis. 23.11.33
	extraordinary	*English Traits*
	That is	*Wilson*
	I should	J.S.M. to T.C. 5.10.33
	the most	T.C. to J.C. 21.1.34
	little Janekin	T.C. to J.W.C. 7.9.33
179	detestable	J.W.C. to E.S. 9.11.33
	a broken-down	J.W.C. to H.I. 23.11.33
	It is so	J.W.C. to E.S. 9.11.33
	I understand	T.C. to Jamie C. Sept. 1833
	It is not	F.J. to J.W.C. 4.12.33
180	or if that	F.J. to T.C. 8.12.33
	I do not	T.C. to S.A. 21.1.34
	Smoked	T.C. to John W. 3.3.34
	and I am	F.J. to T.C. 14.1.34
181	a polite	T.C. to J.C. 24.1.34
	very wholesome	T.C. to Mrs C. 28.1.34
	vivacities	F.J. to T.C. 4.2.34
	a man	J.S.M. to T.C. 25.11.33
	Let us	T.C. *Rem.*
	the cup	T.C. to Jean Aitken (*née* Carlyle). 25.2.34
	our heads	T.C. to J.C. 25.2.34
182	he leaves	J.W.C. to J.C. 25.2.34
	tie all	T.C. to J.W.C. 21, 30.5.34
183	O Good	J.W.C. to T.C. 26.5.34
	it is a kind	T.C. *Notebook.* 21.2.34, 25.3.34
	one has	J.W.C. to T.C. 26.5.34

Chapter 17

Chapter 18

Reference to Quotations

Chapter 25

Chapter 27

Chapter 29

Chapter 30

Page	First words of quotation	
406	Come, lodge	T.C. note to J.W.C. to T.C. 5.9.51
	through	J.W.C. to T.C. 5.9.51
	the frightful	T.C. to J.W.C. 4.9.51
	full of gloom	T.C. note to J.W.C. to T.C. 5.9.51
	apparently	T.C. to H.B. 11.9.51
	manages	J.W.C. to T.C. 5.9.51
407	the happiest	*Ibid.* 12.9.51
	a very	*Ibid.* 7.9.51
	has renounced	*Ibid.* 12.9.51
408	Mr C	J.W.C. to E. C. Gaskell. 14.9.51
	stuffed	J.W.C. to H.W. 24.9.51
	We have got	Dowager Lady Stanley to Lady Stanley. 2.11.51
	supremely	J.W.C. to H.W. 24.9.51
	How strange	T.C. to H.B. 13.9.51
409	Really	J.W.C. to T.C. Early Oct. 1851
	so now	J.W.C. to J.C. Nov. 1851
	I have seen	T.C. to H.B. 27.10.51
	got nothing	T.C. *Notebook.* Mid Oct. 1851
	a fact	J.W.C. to B.W. 15.10.51
	a thousand	T.C. to H.B. 13.9.51
410	I believe	J.W.C. to B.W. 15.10.51
	We are	T.C. to H.B. 27.11.51
	charming	Milnes *Monographs*
411	I am cultivating	T.C. to H.B. 14.11.51
	put	J.W.C. to J.C. Nov. 1851
	Jane	T.C. to H.B. 17.11.51
	Principessa!	*Ibid.* 22.11.51
	Thro'	J.W.C. to T.C. 4.12.51
412	I gave	*Ibid.* Dec. 1851
	I used	J.W.C. to M.R. 30.12.51
	I know not	T.C. to H.B. 10.1.52

Chapter 31

413	Frederick	T.C. to H.B. 14.11.51; *Notebook.* Jan. 1852
	I do not	*Ibid.* 16.2.52
	batch	*Ibid.* 28.2.52
414	Had I never	*Ibid.* 5.3.52
	daily	*Ibid.* 10, 17.1.52
	unspeakable	J.W.C. to M.R. 6.1.52, 21.2.52
	disciples	T.C. to H.B. 16.2.52
415	I am surprised	J.W.C. to Mrs C. 5.6.52
	that	J.W.C. to J.N. 16.7.52
	I have taken	J.W.C. to Frank Jewsbury. 15.7.52
	who is	T.C. to H.B. 12.8.52
416	in superintending	J.W.C. to J.C. 27.7.52
	who is dying	*Ibid.* July 1852
	was here	J.W.C. to T.C. 10.8.52
	such	*Ibid.* 27.7.52
	an ugly	*Ibid.* 2.9.52
	Poor Darling	*Ibid.* 6.8.52
	a tea-party	*Ibid.* 23.8.52
417	at whatever	*Ibid.* 26.8.52
	Had little	*Ibid.* 27.8.52
	Jane	T.C. to H.B. 12.8.52
418	Shall we	T.C. to J.W.C. 1.8.52
	As to	J.W.C. to T.C. 3.8.52

Chapter 32

Chapter 33

Chapter 37

Index

Aberdeen, 290.
Aberdour, 478.
Aberlady, 4, 451, 456.
Achison, Mrs, 363, 365.
Adam Bede, 477.
Addiscombe Farm, 295, 296, 297, 302, 304, 316, 321, 322, 332, 333, 335, 356, 363, 370, 373, 375, 376, 393–5, 419, 427, 432, 437, 442, 445, 447, 458, 459, 470, 471, 519, 520, 525.
Airlie, Lord, 408, 537.
Aitken, David, 136, 224, 254, 473, 539.
Aitken, James (husband of Jean Carlyle), 179.
Aitken, James (admirer of Jane Welsh), 44.
Aitken, Samuel, 31, 66.
Alderley Park, Cheshire, 408, 490.
Allen, Matthew, 34, 155, 157, 170, 253.
Allingham, William, 446
Alton Locke, 392.
Amelia, 291.
Anderson, Charles, 111.
Anderson, Miss, of Sanquhar, 143.
Angus, Robby, 44.
Annan, 19, 21–4, 34, 102, 132, 155, 167, 175, 185, 215, 263, 264, 425, 534.
Annandale, 19, 23, 34, 52, 61, 62, 87, 88, 90, 94, 96, 100, 103, 108, 164, 193, 204, 206–8, 213, 216, 223, 224, 229, 250, 263, 265, 326, 338, 355, 448, 467, 480, 490, 543.
Anstruther, Mrs, 474, 505, 513, 525, 534.
Apperley Bridge, 379.
Armand Carrel, 393.
Arthur Coningsby, 197.
Ashburton, Lady (née Mackenzie), 482, 483, 485, 487–90, 492, 493, 495, 498, 500, 502–7, 509, 510, 513, 516–21, 525–7, 529–35, 537, 542, 547.
Ashburton (the first Lord), 241, 312, 321.
Ashley, Lord, 283.
Ashurst, Eliza, 346, 347, 467.

Ashurst family, the, 347.
Athelstaneford, 36.
Athenaeum, The, 275.
Auchtertool House, 479.
Auchtertool, the Manse of, 384, 386, 428, 449, 450, 452, 462, 463, 471, 479, 501, 516.
Austin, Sarah, 152, 156, 169, 171, 180, 183, 189, 191, 203, 284.
Ayr, 245, 246.

Badams, John, 83, 148, 149, 151, 152, 157, 163, 181.
Baillie (a Bath House maidservant), 525.
Baillie family (of Biggar), 3.
Baillie, James, 85, 86, 87, 102, 103, 105, 300, 322.
Baillie, Matthew, 3, 381.
Baillie, Phoebe, 86, 398.
Bain, Alexander, 312.
Baird, James, 44.
Bamford, Samuel, 340.
Baring, Lady Harriet (afterwards Lady Ashburton), 241, 242, 283, 295, 296, 303, 305, 309, 310, 312, 313, 316, 319–22, 326, 328, 329–35, 337–9, 342–9, 356–9, 361, 363–9, 371, 372, 376, 382, 385, 391–5, 400–3, 405, 406, 408–12, 414–16, 418–23, 427, 428, 430, 433–5, 437, 439–43, 445, 447–50, 452, 453, 455, 458, 459, 471, 495, 499.
Baring, Mary, 486, 487, 492, 493, 498, 505, 513.
Baring, William Bingham (afterwards Lord Ashburton), 241, 298, 304, 313, 332, 337–9, 342, 366, 367, 385, 393, 394, 400, 408, 409, 411, 416, 422, 433, 434, 437, 446, 450, 459, 470, 471, 474, 477, 482, 483, 495, 498, 499, 500, 502–6, 509, 510, 513, 516–18.
Barker, Robert, 148, 249, 234.
Barnes, Dr, 477, 483, 515–19, 541.
Barnes, Isabella Emily, 496, 499.
Barnet, Bessy (afterwards Blakiston), 83, 181, 186, 187, 507, 508, 518.

599

W. E. Forster and begins to enjoy herself, 351; stays at Rawdon, 353-4; visits Addiscombe and complains, 356; welcomes Carlyle home, 356-7; on Emerson, 357; and Geraldine's new novel, 358-9; consoled by friends in Carlyle's latest absence, 360; to Addiscombe again, 363-4; a gay season, 365-6; to The Grange, 366-7; return and final fall of Helen, 368-9; friendship with Lady Sandwich, 369; likes G. H. Lewes, 370, and Mrs Gaskell, 371; taunted by Rogers about Carlyle and Lady Harriet, 371; visit from Froude, 374; to Addiscombe when Carlyle leaves for Ireland, 375-6; the devotion of Blanche Stanley, 376; to the Neubergs at Nottingham, 377-9, then to Rawdon where she has a shock, 379-80; consoles herself at the water cure, 380; revisits Haddington, 381; to her cousins at Auchtertool, 384, the Ferguses at Kirkcaldy, her aunts at Edinburgh and Carlyle's mother at Scotsbrig, 385; a heart attack, 386; returns home fearful of her health, 387-8; the coming of Nero, 389; on the latest novels, 392-3; two visits to Addiscombe, 393-4; meets Charlotte Brontë, 394; the Bath House Ball, 394-5; another hectic season, 395; return of Plattnauer, 395, and Mazzini, 396; dependence on Carlyle's letters, 396-7; another new maid, 397; remains unwell and criticizes her friends, 398; an unhappy visit to The Grange, 400-1, until Carlyle joins her, 402-3; episode of Theresa Revis, 404-5; regrets Babbie's engagement, 405; on the Great Exhibition, 405; to the water cure at Malvern, 406; a misunderstanding with Carlyle, 406; another pleasant stay with Geraldine, 406-7; to Alderley Park with comments on a trousseau, 408; more help for exiles, 409, and more trouble with Carlyle about Lady Harriet, 410; to The Grange again, 411, where Lady Harriet intervenes, 412; warns Carlyle against *Frederick the Great*, 413; on Mazzini soirée, 414; superintends alterations at Chelsea, 415; consoles Mrs Macready and Forster and takes Mazzini to see the Brownings, 416; more entertaining

at Cheyne Row, 417; refuses to go with Carlyle to Germany, 417; on funeral of Duke of Wellington, 421; charms W. H. Brookfield, 421; more cocks disturb sleep, 422-3; to Liverpool, 423-4, Moffat, 424, and Scotsbrig, 424-6; an unhappy return, 426; the sound-proof room, 426-7; to The Grange, 428, then back to overcome the cocks, 428; sympathy with Carlyle on death of his mother, 429; entertains a country cousin and revisits Mrs Montagu, 431; on the death of John Carlyle's wife, 432; pleased with Geraldine's removal to London, 432; fears about Crimean War, 432-3; described by Duffy, 433; her views of Carlyle's beard, 434; presents him with "Budget of a *Femme Incomprise*", 435-6; hysterical anger when he renews his visits to Lady Harriet, 436; leaves him at Addiscombe without warning, 437; meets David Davidson, 437-8; begins a Journal, 438; fears of madness, 439; her behaviour at The Grange, 440-1; described by Mrs Brookfield, 440; health very poor, 442; return of Rennie, 444; meets and likes George Cooke, 446; carried off to Scotland in Lady Harriet's "Queen's Saloon", 448; an indifferent journey, 449; her joy in Scotland, 450; made much of in Haddington, 451; caustic comment on her aunts, 451-2; catches cold after hearing Dr Guthrie, 452; angered by Carlyle's decision to join Ashburtons in the Highlands, 452; writes critical letters, 453; to Scotsbrig and Thornhill, 453; drives about Nithsdale, 454; again feels ill in London, 454; quarrels with maid and criticises Geraldine, 455; too unwell to see many visitors or write many letters, 456; on the death of Lady Harriet, 459; travels by night excursion to Scotland, 460; a dreadful journey, 461; recovery in Haddington, 462; meets old admirer on way to Auchtertool, 463; dislikes place and people, especially Jeannie and child, 463-4; still bitter against Geraldine (in midst of passion for Walter Mantell), 464, but Carlyle's plain speaking does good, 465; catches chill soon after return home and is again unwell through the winter,

268–9; disagreement with Jane about future, 269; his advice, 269–70; his first present to her, 271; to Troston and Cromwell sites, 272; more complaints, 273; difficulty with *Cromwell*, writes *Past and Present*, 277; an unfortunate visit by Geraldine, 279; on the Gambardella portrait, 282; dismisses Robert Scot 290–1; returns after long summer holiday, "very bilious" to re-decorated house and rages about next door piano, 293; difficulty in settling down, 294; begins corres-pondence with Lady Harriet and calls regularly at Bath House, 295; development of friendship, 295–6; *Cromwell* causes tension in house, 299, 303; writes regularly to Jane when separated, 308; first visit to The Grange, 312–3; more "sul-phury" atmosphere at Chelsea because of *Cromwell*, 316; takes Jane to Addiscombe, 321; lightening of tension when book nearly finished, 324, but they differ again at Seaforth, 326; his relations with Lady Harriet, 329–30; to Bay House with Jane, tired of "Do-nothingism", 330–1; delays holiday plans because of Lady Harriet, 334; agitated when Jane rushes away, 335; efforts to reassure her, 337; a difficult week at Seaforth and an unhappy parting, 338; uneasiness when she does not write, 338–9; peace on return home, 341; a Christmas surprise, 344; thoughts of Parliament, 349; to Matlock with Jane, 350; glad to see W. E. Forster, 351; in a "scene" at Buxton, 352; on Methodists, 352; described by Forster, 354; distressed by factories in Manchester, 355; on Emerson, 358; trouble with Jane about Lady Harriet's invitation, 359; goes alone to Bay House but regrets it, 359; despair at inability to write, criticisms of those who do, 361; insists on Addiscombe visit during Chartist troubles, 363; on an Emerson lecture, 364; on Chopin, 366; tires of life at The Grange and reproaches Lady Harriet, 367; on death of Charles Buller and final fall of Kirkcaldy Helen, 368; more criticism of contemporaries, 369; on Mazzini in Rome, 373; described after first visit from Froude, 374; tour of Ireland, 375; his letters

don't always please, 378–9; com-plaints on return, 284–5; indigna-tion about conditions at Ashburton Highlands shooting box, 385–6; reproached by Jane, 386, but continues complaints, 387; more promises of better future, 387–8; further despair of his state, 388; on Nero, 389–90, 404; and *Latter-Day Pamphlets*, 391; visits to Bath House increase, 394; on Lady Harriet's Ball, 394–5; to South Wales and Scotsbrig, his letters prized, 396; cocks once more interrupt sleep, 397; his Welsh host does not please, 399, nor does life at Scotsbrig, 399–400; tries to con-vince Jane of his need of her, 400–1; dislikes late hours at The Grange, 402; on Kinglake, himself, Jane's servant troubles, 403, and the Great Exhibition, 405; to Dr Gully's water cure with Jane—an unfor-tunate leave-taking, 406; to the Ashburtons at Paris, 408; "con-fusion, pain, disappointment", 409, but this does not save him from more trouble with Jane, 410; gratitude to Lady Harriet for soothing Jane's feelings, 412; begins reading for *Frederick*, 413; on a Mazzini soirée, 414; signs long lease for No 5, 415; to Linlathen and Scotsbrig, 415–6; indecision about tour of Germany, 417–8; depression, 418; loses passport, 419; returns "half dead", 420; to The Grange, then "collapse" at home, 420–1; on marriage, 421; Lady Harriet's comment, 422; on Jane, 422; more cocks, 422; defends Mazzini, 422–3; more trouble about Lady Harriet, 423; complaints of cocks, parrots, fireworks, Italians and the heat, 425; a sound-proof room is built, 426, but at first is unsatisfactory, 427; takes work to The Grange, 427–8; hurries to his mother's death bed, 428; mourns her and deplores Crimean War, 429; on the Crystal Palace, 432; grows a beard, 433–4; accepts Jane's "Budget", 435–6; resumes visits to Bath House, 436; is publicly crossed by Jane, 436–7; is left abruptly by her at Addis-combe, 437; on the "impossible" *Frederick*, 437; hard words about a Lady Harriet invitation, 439; with Tennyson at The Grange, 442; self-imposed solitude, 442–3; on a

47, 49, 52–4, 60–6, 74–6, 84, 89, 91–4, 100–2, 104–9, 111, 112, 114, 116–9, 126, 129, 132, 135, 137–9, 147, 149, 153, 154, 170–2, 174, 176–8, 182, 184, 185, 203, 205, 206, 208, 215, 220, 222, 224, 225, 234, 239–42, 245, 264, 265, 267–71, 291, 331, 337, 360, 407, 429, 434, 438, 439, 464, 474, 521, 531, 535, 546.

Welsh, Helen (maternal cousin), 155, 177, 178, 245, 301, 305, 343, 365, 386, 395, 405, 424, 428.

Welsh, Jackie (natural paternal cousin), 461, 537, 541.

WELSH, JANE BAILLIE, born July 14, 1801, in Haddington, 3; a fascinating child, 4; educated as a boy, 6; is tutored by Edward Irving, 8; reads early in classics, 10; a pupil of James Brown after Irving's departure, 11; at Mrs Hemming's school, 11; distinguishes herself in Brown's school, 11–12; loses her heart to the soldiers, 12–13; a tomboy, 13–14; holidays in Nithsdale, 14; Craigenputtock willed to her, 15; difficulty with her mother, 16; writes novel and tragedy, 17; begins to attract the opposite sex, 17; sent to Miss Hall's finishing school in Edinburgh, 18; meets Irving again and captivates him, 27; return to Haddington, 28; last ride with father, 29; her grief at his death, 30; renewed interest in men, 31; meets Thomas Carlyle, 37, is interested, 37–8, but has doubts, 39; is introduced by him to the German romantics, 40–1; they begin to correspond, 41; her views of Rousseau and of her admirers, 44; rebukes Carlyle for an uninvited visit, 45; her fears for Irving, 47, 57; becomes Carlyle's pupil, 48; writes verses, 49; visit to Highlands, 52–3; a new friend, Benjamin Bell, 53; confesses to Carlyle's good influence 54–5; works hard and urges him to do likewise, 55; agrees to write joint novel, 56; annoyed by Irving's attempts to sublimate his feelings for her, 58–9; is idealised by Carlyle as heroine of the novel, 59–60; arranges his visit to Haddington, 60; on his rivals—Dr Fyffe, 61, 65, Benjamin Bell, 62, 66, and George Rennie, 62; brief meetings with Carlyle in Edinburgh before being carried off by mother, 63; trouble

with Nithsdale relatives, 64; reproves Carlyle's ardour but fears to lose him, 69; flattered by Irving's visit before marriage, 71, and delighted by his invitation to London, 72; more trouble with mother about Carlyle, 74; arranges for her to read his letters, 76; still interested in other men, 76, but is becoming increasingly dependent on Carlyle, 77; her fury with Irving for postponing invitation, 78; orders hat for "my intended husband", 79; eager for news of Carlyle in London, 81; jealousy of his new friends, 83; but gains admirers in Dugald Gilchrist, 84, and James Baillie, 85; refuses Irving's renewed invitation, 86–7; makes fun of Carlyle's Craigenputtock plan, 88–9; but cannot do without him, 90, and comes to understanding at Haddington, 91; gives her mother the Haddington house and life rent of Craigenputtock, 94; begins to correspond with Mrs Montagu, 95; is unexpectedly driven by her to a confession about Irving, 96; is forgiven, 99; refuses Carlyle's offer to break engagement, 99; visits his family, 101; more trouble with her mother, 102; long struggle with Carlyle about a home, 104, ended by mother renting 21, Comley Bank, 108; her defence of Carlyle to her family, 110; marries him at Templand, Oct. 17, 1826, 111. (Then see Carlyle, Jane Welsh.)

Welsh, Jeannie (Babbie) afterwards Chrystal (maternal cousin), 155, 253, 269, 270, 272–5, 278, 279, 282, 296, 302, 304, 305, 309, 310, 321, 329, 346, 365, 370, 372, 386, 393, 405, 410, 428, 452, 463, 464.

Welsh, Jeannie (maternal aunt), 3, 14, 101, 109–11, 118–20, 123, 269.

Welsh, Dr John (father), 2–6, 8–12, 14–18, 28–32, 50, 55, 64, 116, 126, 138, 176, 228, 337, 381–3, 438, 461, 470, 474, 521, 547.

Welsh, John (paternal grandfather), 1, 14, 15, 64, 70, 501.

Welsh, John (minister of Ayr), 1, 493, 505.

Welsh, John (paternal cousin, son of George), 417, 432, 541.

Welsh, John (maternal uncle), 3, 14, 66, 123, 148, 155, 157, 168, 223, 268, 269, 305, 309, 339, 384, 404, 424, 427.